THE LIFE OF
James Cardinal Gibbons

THE LIFE OF
James Cardinal Gibbons
Archbishop of Baltimore
1834-1921

By

JOHN TRACY ELLIS

PROFESSOR OF AMERICAN CHURCH HISTORY
IN THE
CATHOLIC UNIVERSITY OF AMERICA

VOLUME II

CHRISTIAN CLASSICS, INC.
WESTMINSTER, MARYLAND
1987

Nihil obstat:
  JOHN K. CARTWRIGHT
  Censor deputatus
Imprimatur:
  ✠ PATRICK A. O'BOYLE
  Archbishop of Washington
  September 16, 1951

FIRST PUBLISHED, 1952
REPLICA EDITION, 1987

Contents

Illustrations

THE LIFE OF
James Cardinal Gibbons

CHAPTER XVI

Americanism

By THE time that Cardinal Gibbons paid his visit to Europe in the summer of 1895, all the major controversies which had disturbed the internal peace of the Catholic Church in the United States had been settled save one. During the course of the earlier conflicts the contrary points of view which had divided the American hierarchy had gradually grown sharper, and they were never more clearly revealed. than in the complicated issue which separated the bishops as the century drew to a close. In many ways the seeds of dissension which arose over the problem known as Americanism had been sown in the previous controversies.

As we have already seen, questions like the Catholic University of America, the secret societies, the Knights of Labor, the case of Henry George and Dr. McGlynn, and the school plan of Archbishop Ireland had made it plain that among the leaders of the American Church there were two fairly discernible schools of thought. The one, to which men like Gibbons, Ireland, and Keane generally adhered, was inclined to interpret the Church's attitude toward these matters in a broad and somewhat tolerant manner, in the dual hope that this approach would better serve the end of assimilating the thousands of foreign-born Catholics to the spirit and institutions of their American home, and at the same time deprive enemies of the argument frequently used that the Church was un-American. The other group, numbering bishops like Corrigan, Katzer, and McQuaid, took a more strictly legalistic view, were fearful of the germ of philosophical liberalism which they thought they detected in the ranks of the opposition, and were less inclined to show a spirit of accommodation to American ways. Although this delineation generally held true, a too rigid classification of the prelates of this period along

1

strictly party lines would be misleading, for there were times when the ranks broke and men were found aligned with those to whom they were ordinarily in opposition. For example, the movement of Cahenslyism which rallied so many of the conservative German bishops had no more unflinching enemy than McQuaid, while the resistance to an Italian delegate which gathered in most of the democratically minded bishops found the progressive John Ireland in the opposite camp. As a matter of fact, both groups were perfectly sincere in their point of view, and in neither wing of the hierarchy was there a bishop who was not entirely orthodox in doctrine and fundamentally a loyal American citizen.

In the quarrel over Americanism, as in most controversies of this kind, the differences of opinion and of temperament on the part of the principals at times excited tempers, entered the realm of personalities, and led to reckless statements which engendered hurt feelings on both sides. While in no way minimizing the serious differences which divided the American prelates in these years, it can be said that in all probability there would never have occurred what has rightly been called "a phantom heresy,"[1] had the bishops of the United States been left to work out their differences among themselves. But in this case the trouble was exasperated to an acute degree by the storm which it raised among European Catholics generally, but especially between two conflicting groups of Catholics in France. The Catholic leaders of Europe had long before this time manifested a lively interest in American Catholicism and its problems. The startling growth and impressive strength of the Church in this country naturally attracted attention abroad, and prompted the Catholics of the old world to inquire concerning the reasons for this progress. At a time when the German Church had only recently emerged from Bismarck's *Kulturkampf,* when the anticlerical government of Italy was making it increasingly difficult for the Church to carry on its mission in that country, and when France was in the throes of one of its worst crises between Church and State, the young and robust Church of the United States seemed to democratically minded European Catholics to offer a pattern

---

[1] Félix Klein, *Souvenirs.* Volume IV. *Une hérésie fantome. l'Américanisme* (Paris, 1949).

AMERICANISM 3

upon which their own branches of the Universal Church might model themselves with profit.

The enthusiasm for things American was particularly high among the Catholic republicans of France. But to another party among the Catholics of that country, the royalists, the free and independent status of the American Church in its relations to the State yielded promise of little more than the ultimate separation of Church and State in France, a goal toward which they rightly believed the government of the hated republic was inexorably moving. If the Catholic republicans of France were elated at the success of Gibbons in bringing about more democratic attitudes as, for example, in the case of the Knights of Labor, and if they were inspired by the appearance among them from time to time of Ireland with his unstinted praise of democratic institutions, the Catholic royalists remained unconvinced.[2] To the conservative minds of the latter the republic — whether it were in France or in the United States — represented an offspring of the French Revolution, and in that tradition they could see nothing that was beneficial for Catholicism. It was in that kind of a setting, there-fore, that leading Catholics in Germany, Italy, and elsewhere in Europe closely scrutinized the developments in the American Church in the last years of the century, but it was particularly in France that the debate on American issues became most vehe-ment and ended in an explosion.[3]

Unfortunately, the discussion which took place in European journals at this time on the subject of Americanism was fre-quently conducted by men who knew little of the Church in the United States, except what they had read in various travelogues and had heard from those who had made brief visits to this country. In the sequel the true Americanism, represented in the love and loyalty which American Catholics had for their country and its democratic institutions, was lost to view, and into the

---

[2] On June 18, 1892, Ireland delivered an enthusiastic address before a large audience in Paris on the advantages to the Church from American democracy. It was entitled "America in France." Cf. Ireland, *The Church and Modern Society*, I, 361–395.

[3] Convenient summaries of the Church's position in Europe in relation to the various secular governments at this time can be found in Raymond Corrigan, S.J., *The Church and the Nineteenth Century* (Milwaukee, 1938), pp. 207–237, and Carlton J. H. Hayes, *A Generation of Materialism, 1871–1900* (New York, 1941), pp. 123–164.

debate there entered, at a date which is not easy to determine exactly, a theological connotation for the term to which American Catholics themselves were complete strangers.[4] Any American Catholic of the time would have subscribed heartily to the Americanism which embodied the love he had for his country. But no American Catholic consciously turned the sentiment which he would define as legitimate patriotism into a sort of American Gallicanism that put his allegiance to his country ahead of his fidelity to the Church of Christ.

True, there had emerged in the United States special characteristics which distinguished the Catholicism of this land in the same way that one would find particular customs and manners characterizing the Catholicism of other countries. In other words, the environmental influences of the great Republic of the West had left their stamp upon the Church here in such things as the independent status it enjoyed and cherished in relation to the State, the fact that its wonderful system of churches and schools was supported by the free-will offerings of the faithful, the fact that the energetic period of expansion through which it had come had not to date given much place to the arts of contemplation, and the further fact that in the United States, more than in other countries, the predominant Protestant majority occasioned more frequent fraternization between men of different religious beliefs. Although all these factors were true, the thought that any of these points of difference with the Church of Europe had lessened the loyalty which American Catholics felt for the Holy See and its doctrines would have been regarded as ridiculous.

Of the kind of Americanism understood by love of country there was never in the history of the Catholic Church of the United States a more conspicuous example than Cardinal Gibbons. He never lost an opportunity of putting before audiences both at home and abroad the values he attached to the American way of life. We have already had occasion to mention this characteristic of the cardinal in discussing his famous speech on Church and State in his titular church in Rome in March, 1887, a theme which he touched upon before an entirely different audience when he appeared at the centennial of the Constitution in

---

[4] For the definitions of the various meanings of Americanism and further background to the controversy cf. Thomas T. McAvoy, C.S.C., "Americanism and Frontier Catholicism," *Review of Politics,* V (July, 1943), 275–301, and "Americanism, Fact and Fiction," *Catholic Historical Review,* XXXI (July, 1945), 133–153.

Philadelphia in September of the same year. Whether addressing himself to Catholics or non-Catholics, it was ever the same if the chance presented itself to say something fine about his country. For example, when the Australian hierarchy held a plenary council early in 1886 and sent a letter of greeting to the American hierarchy Gibbons replied to Cardinal Moran, Archbishop of Sydney, in the name of his colleagues. He said he believed they might refer with "pardonable pride" to the progress which the Catholic faith had made in English-speaking lands, and in seeking the cause for the prosperous state of Catholicism in Australia and the United States he said:

> For this advancement of the cause of religion in both countries we are in no small measure indebted, under God, to the religious freedom which constitutes so noble a feature of our respective governments. They hold over us the aegis of their protection without intruding into the Sanctuary; and by leaving inviolate our spiritual prerogatives, enable us to fulfill our sublime mission without fettering our Apostolic liberty.[5]

In like manner the Cardinal of Baltimore never failed to uphold the hand of the President and other civil rulers by public support whenever he felt the cause they represented fell within his province as a churchman and citizen. When President Cleveland issued his proclamation in 1888 setting aside November 29 of that year as a day of national thanksgiving, Gibbons quickly responded and had published in the *Catholic Mirror* of November 24 a circular in which he called on his priests to recite at the close of the Mass on Thanksgiving Day the prayer for public authorities. For, he said, "The faithful of the archdiocese having in common with our fellow-citizens, deep cause for gratitude to the Giver of every good and perfect gift, will, we feel confident, be equally desirous of evincing their spirit of thanksgiving." The cardinal's circular drew a complimentary reference in the New York *Herald* of November 22, in which they maintained that Gibbons was the first Catholic prelate to direct observance of Thanksgiving Day. The circular likewise gave pleasure to a convert doctor who wrote to say:

> Please permit me to say that as a *physician* & former *Protestant*, how *well* I know this will effect the pulse of the American people.

---

[5] 80-W-15, Gibbons to Moran, Baltimore, May 25, 1886, copy.

And pardon me also for saying that if our *American* Catholic prelates, would display like sympathy and tact in dealing with national observances, & questions of the day, those *outside* the Church would be led to look much *less severely* upon Her.[6]

But if the cardinal's patriotic gesture won him admiration from most quarters, it did nothing to enhance his esteem in the mind of one of his suffragans, Benjamin J. Keiley, Bishop of Savannah, who told Monsignor O'Connell that Gibbons had "out heroded Herod" by his Thanksgiving circular in wanting Catholics to recognize "the damnably Puritanical substitute for Christmas." Keiley concluded, "Maybe the poor man doesn't know any better."[7] Fortunately, the cardinal understood the proprieties of the occasion much better than the Bishop of Savannah, and his attitude was far more representative of the American Catholic sentiment toward Thanksgiving Day than that of his suffragan.

The reputation which Gibbons enjoyed for outstanding Americanism among many, both within and without his own Church, was often turned to good advantage in the services he rendered in helping to bring about a better understanding between Americans of different religious beliefs. In the summer of 1889 complaints had been lodged with the Bureau of Catholic Indian Missions in Washington by some western bishops concerning the conduct of agents of the federal government toward the Catholic Indian schools. Archbishop Ireland was one of those who had written a complaint which he asked George L. Willard, vice-director of the bureau, to present to President Benjamin Harrison. Willard preferred that Cardinal Gibbons should approach the President, for it was his belief that a short letter from Gib-

---

[6] 85-I-8, George A. Sterling to Gibbons, Sag Harbor, New York, November 23, 1888.

[7] ADR, Keiley to O'Connell, Atlanta, November 30, 1888. A vindication of Gibbons' attitude toward Thanksgiving Day came years later when the national holiday was made the occasion for a food collection for the countries ravaged by World War II. In a radio broadcast to the American Catholics, Pope Pius XII said, "The highest authority of the State has summoned you — and what an ennobling and refreshing summons it is to hear in the world today — to pause in the midst of your varied occupations to render thanks to Almighty God. . . ." (New York *Times,* November 24, 1947). Two years later the same Pontiff, in receiving a group of American congressmen in audience on November 28, 1949, referred to the American holiday again when he said, "Our heart is touched and comforted by this recurring evidence — and would that it were universal — of one of the very first charges linked to the Mission of responsible statesmanship." *Catholic Review* (Baltimore), December 2, 1949.

bons would be more effective than the protests of all the other prelates. He told the cardinal that in the mind of the President, his cabinet, and Americans generally he was the representative and mouthpiece of the Catholic Church in this country. "I may also add," said Willard, "they know you to be a sterling American of the right stamp. They know that, in a manly way, you will protect all Catholic interests in the United States."[8]

Willard's was a judgment which was, indeed, widely shared, and the manner in which Gibbons handled the matter with Harrison illustrated, in part at least, how he had gained his high reputation with public officials. The cardinal endorsed the letter of Ireland in forwarding it to the President, adding that he had the greatest confidence, as he put it, "that you have at heart the cause of Indian civilization and will welcome and give consideration to suggestions from all those who are actually engaged in the work." He mentioned that a number of western bishops felt the present case should be brought to the President's attention, and in conclusion he said, "They, as well as myself, think you have need only to *know the facts* and will act with justice to all."[9] It would be difficult for any fair-minded man not to be won by consideration and tact of this kind.

The leadership which Cardinal Gibbons had exercised in American Catholic questions during the 1880's had gained for him by the last decade of the century a reputation with democratically minded Europeans much like that which he enjoyed among his fellow countrymen of similar views. Progressive men in Europe were inclined to turn to the Archbishop of Baltimore as the chief authority and inspiration for much of what they admired in the American Church. Among those who looked to Gibbons for inspiration of this kind was J. E. C. Bodley, a free-lance English writer who was a close friend of Cardinal Manning's. Bodley visited Baltimore and sought information from the cardinal for an article on the American Church which he later published in the *Nineteenth Century* for November, 1889.[10] The article paid the highest praise to Gibbons for his memorial on the Knights of Labor and for his view that the Church should be "absolutely

---

[8] 86-J-10, Willard to Gibbons, Washington, August 23, 1889.

[9] LC, Benjamin Harrison Papers, Gibbons to Harrison, Baltimore, August 27, 1889.

[10] 86-J-11, Bodley to Gibbons, London, August 24, 1889; 86-R-10, Bodley to Gibbons, London, October 23, 1889.

free from State control.["11"] The author told of taking a walk in Baltimore with Gibbons, remarked the number of Protestants in the city, and concluded, "Yet, as the Cardinal passes along, nearly every hat is doffed to the simple citizen who has made a greater impression on European policy than any American of his generation."[12] According to Bodley, the article was so well received that he informed Gibbons the *Edinburgh Review* had asked him to write one on the same subject for that journal. In this case, however, he would not be quite so free since his contribution would be unsigned and the editors maintained the policy of accepting responsibility for what was said in their columns.[13]

In April, 1890, the article appeared in the *Edinburgh Review*. While here, too, there was high praise of Gibbons and Ireland, the ending which the editors tacked on to Bodley's manuscript could not help but give offense to Catholics and lead to misunderstanding. After several quotations from the two American archbishops it was stated, "Such is the language of the leaders of the Roman Catholic democracy of America. It presents a singular contrast to the orthodoxy of the Vatican." With further disparaging references to Catholic doctrines as superstitions, the passage expressed amazement that so large a portion of the American people should accept a spiritual government which was repugnant to their national character and political institutions.[14] Regardless of the fact that Bodley disclaimed responsibility for the concluding sentences,[15] a painful impression was made on Catholic readers and Bishop Herbert Vaughan, editor of the *Dublin Review*, for one was determined to answer it. As he told Gibbons, "That he attributes to you a spirit of alienation, not to say worse, from Rome is regrettable."[16] It is not difficult to understand, of course, how an article of this kind appearing in one of the leading journals of the British Isles could easily give an entirely false notion of the type of Americanism for which men like Gibbons and Ireland stood.

---

[11] "Roman Catholicism in America," XXVI (November, 1889), 814.
[12] *Ibid.,* p. 813.
[13] 87-B-2, Bodley to Gibbons, London, January 11, 1890.
[14] "The Catholic Democracy of America," CLXXI (April, 1890), 509.
[15] 87-J-4, Bodley to Gibbons, London, April 19, 1890.
[16] 87-M-10, Vaughan to Gibbons, Salford, May 23, 1890. Vaughan wanted Gibbons to write an answer, but there is no indication in the *Dublin Review* of this time that he did so.

A short time later the Abbé Magnien of Baltimore paid a visit to his native France. He found great satisfaction in hearing Gibbons' name mentioned so often by French priests with respect and admiration, in contrast to the sadness with which they referred to their own bishops who were doubtless good men, said Magnien, but taken all in all so indifferent to the state of things. Reflecting his conversations with the French clergy, he told the cardinal, "Our situation in the United States is far preferable & when I say what it is, there is not one priest who does not wish that it should be the same in France, but that will never be, at least so I fear."[17] Bodley, too, was in Paris that autumn and on several occasions he informed Gibbons how badly the French needed churchmen of the stamp of the Cardinal of Baltimore and Cardinal Manning. It was at the time when Cardinal Lavigerie, Archbishop of Algiers, had caused a sensation by his famous toast to the republic on November 12 at a dinner for a group of French naval officers in his see city. Lavigerie had expressed the obligation of French Catholics to adhere sincerely to the republican form of government. He was immediately attacked with great vehemence by the royalists among the French clergy and, according to Bodley's report to Gibbons, they could not have been more violent "If he had been guilty of the most flagrant heresy or apostacy. . . ."[18]

During this period of tension in France Cardinal Gibbons received repeated evidences of the high regard in which many of the unhappy Catholics of that country viewed the American Church and himself as its principal figure. The Vicomte Alfred de Meaux told him that since his visit to the United States two years before he had sought to share with his compatriots the lessons and hopes which as a Catholic he had received in this country.[19] A naval officer deplored the feud between the Church and State in France and asked Gibbons if he could furnish some literature that would describe how the Church was administered in the United States;[20] and later a writer from Paris told the cardinal

---

[17] 87-S-7, Magnien to Gibbons, Le Puy, August 11, 1890.

[18] 88-D-4, Bodley to Gibbons, Paris, November 21, 1890; cf. also 88-A-3, Bodley to Gibbons, Paris, October 10, 1890.

[19] 89-F-2, de Meaux to Gibbons, Ecotay-près-Montbrison, Loire, December 17, 1891.

[20] 89-P-2, A. Jubault, aide-de-camp to Vice Admiral Ctenchey to Gibbons, Rochefort, February 21, 1892.

that the eyes of the French Catholics were directed to their brothers in America where, in his opinion, the Church owed its pre-eminence to the courage, talent, and virtues of its hierarchy.[21] Gibbons, in turn, occasionally took advantage of this favorable opinion of the Church of the United States and its leaders to present to French readers what he regarded as the proper view on American Church problems, and when the agitation over Cahenslyism was at its height he asked de Meaux to write an article on the subject. As a result there was published in *Le Correspondant* in the spring of 1892 a summary of the movement which ended by de Meaux saying that if the German Catholics in the United States would become good Americans there would be no further trouble.[22]

While it was doubtless gratifying to Gibbons and his friends to know that there was so much admiration among progressive French Catholics for their policies, these Frenchmen were probably not fully aware of a strong opposition on the part of a sizable group of American clergy to the policies which they admired, an opposition which would eventually make itself heard. Although there were no royalists among the clergy of the United States, there were conservative bishops and priests who viewed with increasing concern the emphasis given from time to time by some of their fellow clergy to such themes as the blessings of separation of Church and State and the accommodation of Catholic practices to the spirit of the age. When men feel keenly on matters of this kind they are often inclined to see difficulties where others do not. One such occasion was afforded by Father Walter Elliott, C.S.P., who preached the sermon in St. Paul on December 27, 1889, at the consecration of Bishops John Shanley, James McGolrick, and Joseph B. Cotter. Elliott stressed the view that in the United States the ideas of manhood were not so much loyalty, obedience, and uniformity, but rather worthiness to be free. The aspiration of the American people, said Elliott, was toward progress and intelligence and liberty, the dignity of man, and his capacity to govern himself. "Church and State," said the preacher, "should not be united here, but they must be parallel in

---

[21] ASMS, Daniel Auschitzky to Gibbons, Paris, January 11, 1894.

[22] "La question allemande dans l'église catholique aux Etats-Unis," CLXVII (April 25, 1892), 273–283. Cf. also 89-U-10, de Meaux to Gibbons, Paris, April 25, 1892.

their onward march if they both make for human happiness. . . ."[23]

Although the sentiments expressed by Elliott when fully considered were compatible with perfect orthodoxy on his part and with the views of most American Catholics, some felt distressed by his emphasis upon individual freedom and separation of Church and State. Further reason for concern was given by Elliott when about a year later in his *Life of Father Hecker,* a book which we shall have occasion to speak of more fully hereafter, he gave expression to ideas which one early reader believed would lead to trouble. Bishop Healy of Portland, Maine, told Elliott that a distrust of Hecker's spirit had long been prevalent among a considerable number of the friends of the Paulist founder. As Healy put it:

> If to "old fogies" in the Church anything of F. Hecker is evident it is that his "spirit", his spirit of liberty, liberty of spirit if you please, led him more than once into words and ways that made his devoted friends tremble.[24]

The prompt reaction of Bishop Healy to the Hecker biography was a straw in the wind, and the following spring witnessed a public and more emphatic note in the same general direction. In April, 1891, Monsignor Thomas S. Preston, Vicar-General of the Archdiocese of New York and a convert to the Church in 1849, published an article in which he sought to correct certain impressions which he regarded as false and dangerous. Preston entitled his article "American Catholicity," and its general tone was evident from the first sentence which read, "Under a name often many errors are concealed."[25] The monsignor deprecated such views as that American Catholicism was more consonant with the spirit of the age and less hostile to those who differed from Catholics in faith and morals, that the American form of government was the best possible and most suited to the Catholic religion, and that all religions were good and conducive to the salvation of men, while the Catholic religion was only better and more complete. On the issue of Church and State Preston said, "We yield to no one in devotion to our own country; nevertheless, we cannot hold that the best form of government is that in which the Church is entirely separated from the State and the State

---

23 *Catholic Sentinel* (Portland, Oregon), January 27, 1890.
24 APF, Healy to Elliott, Portland, December 1, 1890.
25 *American Catholic Quarterly Review, XVI* (April, 1891), 396.

from the Church."[26] It was his belief as well that good Catholics were bound by every legitimate means to labor for the restoration of the temporal power of the Pope.[27]

The views of the New York vicar-general were shared by his superior, Archbishop Corrigan, and a year after Preston's article when the Superior General of the Paulists, Augustine F. Hewit, asked the archbishop to write something for the *Catholic World*, he courteously declined until such time as there were actually made in the magazine what he termed "the improvements contemplated." Corrigan enclosed a private memorandum to Hewit in which he said, "When last in Rome, I was directed to repress certain Liberalizing tendencies observed in 'The Catholic World.'" He alluded to views on the right of private property which had appeared in the magazine which he believed were not easy to reconcile with Leo XIII's *Rerum novarum*, and he ended by saying that if the contributors to the *Catholic World* would defend Roman teachings nothing would give him greater pleasure than to help the journal's circulation.[28]

A further indication that so-called tendencies toward a liberal attitude were being watched — and at times reported to the Holy See — came two months later when Cardinal Ledochowski, Prefect of the Congregation of the Propaganda, informed Gibbons that a copy of the New York *Herald* of May 17 had been sent to Rome in which there was carried the story of the funeral of Senator John S. Barbour of Virginia, a non-Catholic, at which Bishop Keane, Rector of the University, had preached a sermon in his prelatial robes. Ledochowski inquired if the fact was true and, if so, under what circumstances it had been allowed to take place.[29] In reply Gibbons defended Keane's action and explained that Barbour went to Mass on Sundays, was not affiliated with any Protestant church, had a fervent Catholic wife, and might,

---

[26] *Ibid.*, p. 401.

[27] *Ibid.*, p. 405.

[28] APF, Corrigan to Hewit, New York, April 22, 1892. Corrigan felt strongly on the dangers of liberalism. In writing Herman J. Heuser, editor of the *American Ecclesiastical Review*, a year before, the archbishop remarked that Monsignor Schroeder of the Catholic University of America had done a great deal to combat it but much more remained to be done. "This is a burning question," said Corrigan, "and if not solved properly and quickly, will do vast harm to souls in this country" (ACHSP, Heuser Papers, Corrigan to Heuser, New York, March 24, 1891).

[29] 89-Y-9, Ledochowski to Gibbons, Rome, June 27, 1892.

in fact, be called a catechumen. Therefore, it was thought well to have the prayers read by Father Cornelius Gillespie, S.J., and a preacher of note give the sermon. The Vice-President of the United States, the cabinet, justices of the Supreme Court, and members of both houses of Congress were in attendance; consequently the cardinal concluded, "It was in my judgment a solemn occasion for the Church to display its beautiful ceremonies and to have heard its holy truths."[30] The inquiry of the Holy See was obviously prompted by the law of the Church which forbade the ministration of priests at non-Catholic religious services, but in the absence of evidence to the contrary it would appear that the Roman officials were satisfied with Gibbons' explanation of the incident.

But what ultimately took on far more importance as a cause of complaint was the Catholic participation in the World's Parliament of Religions held at Chicago in the fall of 1893 in connection with the Columbian Exposition. The role which Cardinal Gibbons played in the events of the international fair was many sided. Almost a year before the opening he was appointed a member of the World's Congress Auxiliary, an organization which represented men from all walks of life who were to promote various conventions of leaders during the fair. He was invited to give suggestions of whatever he might deem expedient with the assurance that his views would receive attentive consideration.[31] Second, the cardinal was made honorary president of the American Catholic Congress held during the fair, although at heart he was not in favor of this particular gathering. It was Archbishop Ireland who gave encouragement to the lay congress, and it was under the force of his persuasion that Gibbons requested a letter of approval for the project from Leo XIII. Ireland met with the committee in Chicago shortly before sailing for Rome in January, 1892, and he assured the cardinal that there would be no trouble in shaping matters to their entire satisfaction, but reminded Gibbons that the demand for the papal letter should come from him since the congress was to be held under his leadership. As he said, "It is most important that the whole project move, ab initio, under your direction & guid-

---

[30] 90-A-8, Gibbons to Ledochowski, Baltimore, July 10, 1892, copy in French in John Ireland's handwriting.
[31] 88-G-4, Benjamin Butterworth to Gibbons, Chicago, January 7, 1891.

ance."[32] Gibbons did as he was requested and he gave full co-operation to William J. Onahan, secretary of the congress, in selecting the speakers and in supervising other details.[33] Yet he harbored an uneasiness about this lay congress which is not alto-gether easy to explain. While Ireland was still in Rome the cardinal told him:

> With regard to the Congress, we must act with caution. Any overt attempt on your or my part to suppress it would raise a hue and cry, and the worst motives would be ascribed to us. The best plan is to enjoin on Onahan and our friends a passive attitude, that little or nothing should be done to advance the Congress till our meeting in October, and then we would try to kill it, or that failing, to determine that this should be the last Congress.[34]

Despite the fact that he was able to tell Ireland that Arch-bishop Riordan had expressed doubts about the wisdom of hold-ing the congress, others among the metropolitans were sufficiently in favor of the gathering to renew at the New York conference in November, 1892, the approval they had given to the project in their St. Louis meeting in 1891;[35] and with this judgment rendered Gibbons fell into line and carried out his part of the arrangements.

In this instance as in others Cardinal Gibbons yielded to the judgment of his colleagues. A possible motive for his reluctance may be found in his reply to Léon Harmel, prominent French Catholic industrialist, who had heard of the plan for a Catholic congress at Chicago and suggested that it be made international. The cardinal confessed that the idea of an international gathering had at one time been mentioned, but since it was, said Gibbons, one "of great magnitude and involving possible difficulties & embarrassments," it was thought wiser to consult the Holy See and be guided by its counsels.[36] In the end the international aspect of the meeting was dropped, the Pope sent Gibbons a blessing

[32] 88-H-5, Ireland to Gibbons, St. Paul, January 8, 1892.

[33] AUND, Onahan Papers, Gibbons to Onahan, Baltimore, January 12, 1892. Cf. also Gibbons to Onahan, Baltimore, January 20 and 23, 1893; July 15, 18, and 22, 1893, and the telegram of August 21, 1893.

[34] AASP, Gibbons to Ireland, Baltimore, February 26, 1892, copy.

[35] 90-Q-3, Minutes of the Meeting of the Archbishops, New York, November 16–19, 1892.

[36] 90-A-5, Gibbons to Harmel, Baltimore, July 5, 1892, copy.

upon the gathering,[37] and the congress was held at Chicago on September 4–8, 1893. It was during this congress that Archbishop Satolli, Apostolic Delegate to the United States, spoke to the delegates on September 5 in Italian and his remarks were translated for the audience by Archbishop Ireland. Satolli had words of high praise for both Church and State in the United States, and in concluding he said:

> Go forward, in one hand bearing the book of christian truth and in the other the constitution of the United States. Christian truth and American liberty will make you free, happy and prosperous. They will put you on the road to progress. May your steps ever persevere on that road.[38]

They were words which must have delighted the hearts of Gibbons and his friends, although within a few years this same prelate would be one of the stoutest enemies of those who were sometimes referred to as "Americanists" within the Church of the United States. Gibbons had opened the meetings in the Memorial Art Palace on the first day and he spoke briefly at the closing session on September 8. He was not feeling well on the final day and for that reason he confined himself to only a few remarks, but he did say, "The voice of the congress has succeeded in dissipating prejudices and in removing many misunderstandings in regard to the teachings and practices of the church of God."[39] It would seem that his earlier misgivings had not been borne out, and from the tenor of his words one would judge that the cardinal was satisfied with the good accomplished by the congress.[40]

---

[37] 91-R-10/1, Leo XIII to Gibbons, Rome, August 7, 1893.

[38] Francis Satolli, *Loyalty to Church and State* (Baltimore, 1895), p. 150.

[39] Chicago *Herald,* September 8, 1893.

[40] Two months later Gibbons reported the American Catholic Congress and the Catholic Educational Exhibit to the Holy See in detail (92-R-3, Gibbons to Rampolla, Baltimore, November 14, 1893, copy in French). For the educational aspect of Catholic participation at Chicago cf. *Catholic Educational Exhibit. World's Columbian Exposition* (Chicago, 1893), compiled by Brother Maurelian, F.S.C. Speaking of the Catholic program, one of the historians of the Chicago fair wrote, "The most imposing of all the denominational Congresses was that held by the Catholic Church." Rossiter Johnson (Ed.), *A History of the World's Columbian Exposition held in Chicago in 1893* (New York, 1897–1898), IV, 331. Some years later M. Joseph Harson, a prominent Catholic merchant of Providence, who had been active in the Catholic congresses of 1889 and 1893, attempted to arouse interest in another such gathering. He spoke with Archbishop Glennon whom he found cool to the idea and Archbishop Ireland was said to be

Cardinal Gibbons figured in two other ceremonies at Chicago during that eventful year. The date for the dedication of the buildings of the fair was set for October 21, 1892, and Gibbons was asked to give a prayer on that occasion. Before the final details were worked out there was some confusion as to the place on the program which the cardinal would occupy in relation to ministers of other faiths. Ireland at first believed that a minister would give the benediction after Gibbons' prayer. He had already asked a number of favors of the committee, and he was in no mood for asking for further changes. Explaining the difficulties that might arise, he told the cardinal:

> What matter. We can defy senseless critics. The occasion is an exhibition of American life — Protestant & Catholic meet, as they do every day. They bear the presence of one another, without compromising their own principles. Satolli & O'Connell will understand & explain the case. Your prayer over you & your friends will step to one side of the platform.[41]

In the end the difficult and delicate point of participating in a religious service with ministers of other religions was minimized by the opening prayer being recited by Bishop Charles H. Fowler of the Methodist Episcopal Church of California and the closing prayer by Gibbons. In his prayer the cardinal thanked God for Christopher Columbus as a providential agent opening the new world to mankind, and he then said:

> But not for this earthly inheritance alone, do we thank Thee, but still more for the precious boon of constitutional freedom which we possess; for, even this favored land of ours, would be to us a dry and barren waste if it were not moistened by the dew of liberty. We humbly implore Thee to continue to bless our Country and her cherished institutions, and we solemnly promise to-day in this vast assembly and in the name of our fellow-citizens to exert all our energies in preserving this legacy unimpaired, and to transmit it as a priceless heirloom to succeeding generations.[42]

"positively opposed." Harson interviewed Cardinal Gibbons who, he said, assured him that he was personally in favor of holding another congress but that he had talked with a number of prelates and, as Harson quoted the cardinal, "their memories of the Chicago Congress were so unfavorable that he did not feel warranted in sanctioning another at this time" (AUND, Edwards Papers, Harson to James F. Edwards, Providence, June 27, 1904).

[41] 90-F-10, Ireland to Gibbons, St. Paul, September 19, 1892.

[42] *Dedicatory and Opening Ceremonies of the World's Columbian Exposition* (Chicago, 1893), p. 186.

Nearly a year later the cardinal performed a similar service for his own state when on September 12, Maryland Day at the fair, he gave the benediction at the ceremonies held in the Maryland building at the invitation of Mayor Ferdinand C. Latrobe of Baltimore.[43]

It was not, however, the appearance of the Cardinal of Baltimore at any of the ceremonies mentioned above that gave rise to adverse comment. It was rather his participation, along with that of Ireland, Keane, and others in the World's Parliament of Religions at Chicago in September, 1893, which later furnished material for criticism. At the time of the dedication of the fair buildings in October, 1892, it had been decided by the directors of the Columbian Exposition to hold a parliament of all the religions of the world as a climax to the series of congresses of the various religious bodies which had been scheduled for the ensuing year. The authorities of the fair approached Bishop Keane and asked him to inquire if the Catholic Church would be willing to participate in such a mixed gathering. Keane outlined the proposal in a lengthy communication for the archbishops which he submitted to them at their New York meeting in November. He made it clear that the parliament would be a forum for exposition, not discussion, of the different religious beliefs. No speaker, said Keane, would be expected to minimize in the least the teachings and practices of his religion and the only restriction imposed would be a charitable regard for the convictions of others which religion itself dictated.

Keane was strongly in favor of acceptance of the invitation. As he said, "I beg leave to venture the opinion that, while the objections against the proposal are obvious, the reasons in favor of it seem paramount." The bishop cited the natural objection that such an affair would encourage religious indifferentism and favor an eclectic or synthetic religion above all denominations. But the Catholic Church, said Keane, was the only really synthetic religion, the only one that could not only stand such a test but must desire that she should be subjected to it by all serious thinkers. He felt this would be an unparalleled opportunity for the Church to show to all the religions of the world that whatever they possessed for man's enlightenment and im-

---

[43] AAB, unclassified, Latrobe to Gibbons, Baltimore, July 13, 1893; Gibbons to Latrobe, Baltimore, July 15, 1893, copy.

provement, the Catholic Church had in superior degree and much besides. Moreover, it was not in the power of the Church to hinder the parliament from taking place. Could the Church, therefore, afford not to be there? He did not think so, but it was not for him to make the decision and consequently he submitted the matter to the judgment of the American archbishops.[44]

The proposal of Bishop Keane was laid before the meeting of the archbishops on November 18, 1892, and according to the minutes, it was resolved, "after a thorough discussion," that Gibbons should instruct Keane in the name of the metropolitans to make arrangements with the proper authorities of the parliament to have twenty Catholic speakers selected by Keane to expound Catholic doctrine during the sessions in Chicago.[45] The arrangements for the Catholic participation were left, therefore, in Keane's hands. This is not the place to tell the history of the World's Parliament of Religions; we are interested only insofar as it concerned the part Gibbons played in it. After he had read the preliminary address of the general committee of the parliament, the cardinal wrote to say that he deemed the movement they were promoting "worthy of all encouragement and praise." He thought the parliament could not help but result in good to the country and if it were conducted with moderation and good will it might result, by the blessing of divine Providence, "in benefits more far reaching than the most sanguine could dare hope for."[46]

During part of the time of the parliament which ran from September 11 to 28, 1893, the cardinal was unwell but he made a special effort to be present at one of the opening sessions since, as he said, he was anxious that the Catholic Church should present its claims to observation, and if possible to the acceptance, of every man who would listen. "But we appeal," said Gibbons, "only to the tribunal of conscience and of intellect."[47] On the fourth day Bishop Keane read a paper which had been written by Gibbons on the subject, "The Needs of Humanity

---

[44] 90-P-6, Keane to the Archbishops of the United States, Washington, November 12, 1892.

[45] 90-Q-3, Minutes of the Meeting of the Archbishops, New York, November 16–19, 1892.

[46] John Henry Barrows, *The World's Parliament of Religions* (Chicago, 1893), I, 14, quoting an undated letter of Gibbons.

[47] *Ibid.*, I, 80–81.

Supplied by the Catholic Religion," in which he summarized the outstanding work done by the Church in purifying the marriage bond, proclaiming the sanctity of human life, and providing remedies for human misery in the persons of orphans, erring women, widows, the sick, and the slaves. Gibbons included an exhortation for all to do what they could in the cause of humanity, reminding his audience that every man had a mission from God to help his fellow man. In conclusion the cardinal said, "Though we differ in faith, thank God there is one platform on which we stand united, and that is the platform of charity and benevolence!"[48]

It was an address which had been carefully worded for the mixed audience and one with which no serious fault could be found. In its preparation the cardinal probably experienced some of the uneasiness, of which he made mention a year and a half before to Archbishop Elder, when that prelate had congratulated him on one of his recent published statements. Gibbons told his friend in Cincinnati at that time:

> I am always anxious about my public utterances. Speak out I must frequently. My position requires it. The interests of the Church demand it. But I am always afraid of erring by excess or defect, & no one knows better than myself that my judgment is not equal to the demands upon it.[49]

There was no excess or defect in what he had said at the Chicago parliament, although faulty versions of his remarks later reached the public prints. The London *Weekly Register* of September 30 was enthusiastic over the Catholic part in the Parliament of Religions. The *Register* quoted approvingly Gibbons' words and then on its own it added, "A new note has been struck by the Catholics of America in their relations with outsiders — there is no doubt of that. And it has been struck with the full approval of the PAPAL DELEGATE, as well as with the personal approval and hearty co-operation of the local authorities of the Church." Others, too, felt that the Catholic participation in the parliament was the harbinger of good things to come. Canon Salvatore di Bartolo of Palermo congratulated the cardinal and told him, "You have wonderfully opened a new era in the history

---

[48] *Ibid.*, I, 485–493. The address was also published in the *Catholic World*, LVIII (October, 1893), 1–9.

[49] AAC, Gibbons to Elder, Baltimore, April 20, 1892.

of the Catholic Church by your presence and discourse at the Congress of Religions";[50] and Father Kenelm Vaughan, the English writer, was another who expressed his pleasure at the share which the American Catholics took in the meetings.[51]

Although the enthusiastic reception accorded to Catholic participation in the Chicago parliament seemed genuine enough to warrant a belief in its success, Cardinal Gibbons felt that the subject called for a detailed report to the Holy See. Knowing the sensitivity of Rome about Catholics sharing in mixed religious gatherings of this kind, the cardinal was at pains to explain to Cardinal Rampolla that the plan for the parliament had not originated with the American Catholics. But when the subject was broached to the bishops they felt it would be well to engage in it, in the hope that it might help to offset the agnosticism and atheism of the day and, moreover, afford a chance of making known the truths of Catholicism to people who were entirely ignorant or even prejudiced against them. He explained the procedure at Chicago, listed the Catholic speakers and their subjects, and stated that from the outset a great number of non-Catholics showed a desire to know more about the truths of the Church, and during the days of the parliament the Catholic bureau of information had distributed around 18,000 books, brochures, and tracts.

In summing up his account, Gibbons told Rampolla that the Catholic Church was officially placed in the first rank at the parliament and its doctrines, morals, and discipline were explained in all their sincerity without the least spirit of compromise or concession. There had been no attempt made at a false union of the churches during the sessions, nor had any such idea been proposed. On the other hand, prejudices were dissipated and, in view of the results, the archbishops of the United States in no way regretted their acceptance of the invitation and the prelates, priests, and religious who came had no regrets about their participation. It was Bishop Keane, said Gibbons, who had suggested the subjects for the papers in such topics as the defense of a personal God, the immortality of the

---

[50] 92-P-3, Bartolo to Gibbons, Palermo, October 27, 1893. Bartolo was the author of *Les critères théologiques* (Paris, 1889), a volume which was the subject of criticism in theological circles and which was put on the *Index* in May, 1891.

[51] 92-P-6, Vaughan to Gibbons, at sea, October 30, 1893.

soul, and the relations of religion to science, art, social problems, and international affairs. The speakers were likewise chosen by Keane from among the prelates of the country, the professors of the Catholic University of America, the rectors of seminaries, members of religious orders, distinguished laymen, and some foreign collaborators, among whom Gibbons mentioned especially the celebrated orientalist of the University of Louvain, Monsignor Charles Joseph de Harlez. Gibbons had only words of praise for Keane who had executed with such success the difficult and delicate charge of organizing the Catholic part of the parliament's program.[52]

About a month later Rampolla acknowledged Gibbons' letter with thanks and said he had brought it to the attention of the Pope who recognized the burden imposed by the parliament on Gibbons and his colleagues, and the fact that the delicate and dangerous aspects of such gatherings were avoided was certainly due to the perspicacity of His Eminence of Baltimore.[53] As far as the letter of the Secretary of State revealed, therefore, the Holy See was satisfied with the American Catholics in the role they had played in the Parliament of Religions. If the Chicago sessions had been accurately reported thereafter, there would probably have been much less question raised concerning the Catholics' part in the program, but unfortunately such was not the case. In March, 1894, for example, an article appeared in the *Review of Reviews* which pictured the opening ceremony of the parliament with Gibbons occupying the center of the stage, but then the author went on to say:

> Cardinal Gibbons contributes a paper in which he declares that he is more drawn to the Catholic Church by her system of organized benevolence than by her unity of faith, or sublime morals, or world-wide catholicity, or apostolical succession. Which remark explains much in the later developments of American Romanism.[54]

Gibbons, of course, had said nothing of the kind, and it was obvious that it would not take many accounts of this character to create an entirely false impression of what had been said and done by American Catholics at the Chicago parliament. As men-

---

[52] 92-P-5, Gibbons to Rampolla, Baltimore, October 28, 1893, copy in French.
[53] 92-T-3, Rampolla to Gibbons, Rome, November 20, 1893.
[54] F. Herbert Stead, "The Story of the World's Parliament of Religions," IX (March, 1894), 307–308.

tioned previously, the Church's reluctance to have its ministers participate in mixed religious gatherings of this kind was grounded in the conviction that such meetings led to religious latitudinarianism and indifference and to the ultimate belief that one church was as good as another.

That there was cause for concern on the part of the friends and associates of Gibbons at this time, on the score of their supposed liberalism, seemed evident to some of them. Keane informed Denis O'Connell in the spring of 1894 that the apostolic delegate, Archbishop Satolli, and the faculty of the university were desirous that Gibbons should go to Rome to dispel what he called "these clouds of whispers & suspicion" in regard to Satolli, the university, and what he termed "the general tendency of so-called 'liberalism' among us." Gibbons, too, was so convinced of the need that he was ready to start in early June but he had been stopped by O'Connell's advice against the trip. Keane said the professors of the university thought that he likewise should visit the Holy See, but he knew Gibbons did not wish him to travel in his company lest it draw comment about the continuance of "the same clique" and their machinations.[55] In the end Keane made the journey in the summer of 1894, whereas the cardinal delayed his visit until the following year.

In all that followed Cardinal Gibbons remained an alert observer, even though he said little for publication. Those who felt the discomfort of suspicion concerning their orthodoxy knew that they had in him a powerful protector, and in the crisis which developed Gibbons repeatedly showed one of his strongest characteristics, namely, an unflinching loyalty to his friends. For example, when the Paulist superior-general sent a copy of a letter of approval of their congregation from Cardinal Ledochowski to the American bishops, Gibbons was quick to congratulate Father Hewit on the commendation from Rome, and he added, "but I congratulate you still more on the fact that the congregation deserves the high character it has received."[56] In the stormy days that lay ahead for the Paulists they would have no more determined defender than the Cardinal of Baltimore. But though his sympathies were on the side of those who in time were to be termed "Americanists," Gibbons' partisanship was never so

[55] ADR, Keane to O'Connell, Washington, April 13, 1894.
[56] APF, Gibbons to Hewit, Baltimore, April 14, 1894.

marked as to cause him to abandon the role of peacemaker. When Archbishops Corrigan and Ryan visited Baltimore in the early summer of 1894 he put forth a special effort to be friendly to Corrigan and he was apparently successful, for shortly after his return home the Archbishop of Philadelphia told Gibbons, "New York seemed most pleased with your reception of him."[57] In fact, Gibbons' endeavor to keep on cordial terms with the Archbishop of New York was even the subject of adverse comment in certain quarters. Later that same summer Thomas O'Gorman, professor of church history in the Catholic University of America, was in Rome and had an audience of Leo XIII, and in informing his colleague, Thomas Bouquillon, of it he remarked that the Pope wondered very much at the indecisive position of Gibbons in relation to Corrigan, and O'Gorman added, "Gibbons has certainly done himself injury in the mind & esteem of the pope by his seeming friendship with N. York."[58] Yet despite the opinion of some of his associates, the cardinal steadfastly pursued his policy and refused to break with Archbishop Corrigan.

The autumn of 1894 in the United States proved to be an exciting time in both ecclesiastical and civil circles, and served to bring out more clearly the American sentiments of some of the hierarchy, with a sharper delineation of their views from their more conservative colleagues. The approaching congressional elections in November stirred the A.P.A. to renewed vilification of American Catholics, and the attacks were so vigorous and mendacious that Bishop Spalding of Peoria decided to answer them. In the *North American Review* for September the bishop insisted that the power which the Pope held over American Catholics was purely spiritual. "Intelligent people among us know," said Spalding, "the Pope would not if he could, could not if he would, hurt America."[59] He frankly acknowledged that the archbishops of the United States had not wanted an apostolic delegate, and he added that if the question had been submitted to the bishops generally they, too, would probably have voted against the delegation. Actually there had never been any interference on the part of the Pope in American civil affairs, but if there had it would have been resented by Catholics more quickly

---

[57] 93-H-4, Ryan to Gibbons, Philadelphia, June 17, 1894.
[58] ACUA, Bouquillon Papers, O'Gorman to Bouquillon, Rome, July 16 [1894].
[59] "Catholicism and APaism," CLIX (September, 1894), 282.

than others. That was why representative Catholics had not wished a delegate in order that there would not be even a pretext for accusing them of being under foreign influences. On the subject of separation of Church and State none, said Spalding, was more thankful for it than the American Catholics.[60] As for the loyalty of Catholics to their country, he believed the historical record of their patriotism was the best evidence. Therefore, he saw no reason for the Catholics of the United States to protest their loyalty to the state. As the bishop expressed it:

> To protest is half to confess, as to exhort is to reproach. . . . Our record for patriotism is without blot or stain, and it is not necessary for us to hold the flag in our hands when we walk the streets, to wave it when we speak, to fan ourselves with it when we are warm, and to wrap it about us when we are cold.[61]

In the same manner Spalding defended the Church against the charge that it was undermining the public schools. He would not, even if he had the power, destroy the public schools but would rather leave nothing undone to develop and perfect them. "If here and there," he wrote, "individuals have made efforts to get public money for parochial schools, the Catholic body is not to be held responsible for their acts."[62] Nor were Catholics, said Spalding, called upon to defend all the deeds and utterances of individual popes. Their faith, according to the writer, never held that the Pope could do no wrong, and if the public law of the twelfth century permitted the Pope to declare forfeit the authority of tyrannical princes, it did not follow that he was permitted to do so now. Catholics, according to Spalding, frankly and sincerely accepted the principles involved in the rule of the people by the people and for the people and they were entirely content to abide the issue.

The article in the *North American Review* was a forthright effort to meet the attacks of the A.P.A., and it attracted considerable attention. But the elections of 1894 held more interest for Catholics than the attacks of the A.P.A. and the effort to offset them. It was during this campaign that Archbishop Ireland engaged actively in behalf of the Republican Party by appearing at its rallies in New York City and prominently identifying him-

---

[60] *Ibid.,* p. 284.

[61] *Ibid.,* p. 285.

[62] *Ibid.,* p. 286.

self with its policies. This invasion of the New York political arena on the part of the Minnesota prelate was deeply resented by Archbishop Corrigan and his friend, Bishop McQuaid of Rochester. In fact, McQuaid was so aroused that he denounced Ireland from his cathedral pulpit on November 25 in a powerful sermon during which he stated that his own efforts to keep the holy office of a bishop clear of entanglements with any political party had caused him to refrain from voting at all for the past twenty-seven years.[63]

A few days after the election Corrigan complained bitterly to Gibbons about the conduct of Ireland and said the Catholics of New York were indignant, and that even Bishop Potter of the Protestant Episcopal Church had inquired of him if it were not contrary to ecclesiastical decorum for a bishop to deliver a *pronunciamento* to those who were not his subjects. "If such a state of things continue," asked Corrigan, "what is to become of Diocesan jurisdiction?" He told the cardinal, "I think Your Eminence ought to know these facts, as we are all concerned in maintaining Episcopal authority."[64] Ryan of Philadelphia was also worried and expressed the hope to Gibbons that the affair would not lead to a newspaper controversy between Rochester and St. Paul.[65] Although the cardinal was in correspondence with Corrigan at the time, there is no evidence that he took note of the archbishop's remarks concerning Ireland.[66] Gibbons was himself an alert observer of party politics but his partisan loyalty was never permitted to become known publicly and, needless to say, he personally never engaged in party politics in the open manner of the Archbishop of St. Paul.

In spite of the fact that Gibbons would say nothing for publication during the press war that ensued between Ireland and McQuaid, his sympathies once again leaned toward Ireland in the attack which McQuaid made on him from his cathedral pulpit. This is one instance where one might have expected the cardinal to exercise a restraining influence on the archbishop, for the latter's conduct in New York certainly presented an unbecoming spectacle before the general public, and ran entirely

---

[63] The McQuaid sermon was published by Zwierlein, *Life and Letters of Bishop McQuaid*, III, 207–210, along with a discussion of the trouble.

[64] 93-M-10, Corrigan to Gibbons, New York, November 15, 1894.

[65] 93-M-11, Ryan to Gibbons, Philadelphia, November 28, 1894.

[66] Cf. AANY, Gibbons to Corrigan, Baltimore, November 14 and 16, 1894.

counter to Gibbons' way of doing things. Ireland received word
of the cardinal's views from Dr. O'Gorman and in thanking him
the archbishop said, "I am so pleased that you have understood
me." He gave Gibbons his reasons for engaging in the controversy,
but it was evident that Ireland was not altogether certain of the
wisdom of his action. He said:

> However, I am coming fast to the conclusion that for peace sake
> it is best, so far as I am concerned, to let the Church jog her
> way, whatever the way be. I think I have definitely entered into
> winter-quarters.
>
> I am writing a long & full letter to Rome, a copy of which I
> well send you.[67]

But before Ireland's letter could reach Rome his friend in
Baltimore had communicated with the Holy See and had told
Cardinal Rampolla of McQuaid's public attack on Ireland in
his cathedral pulpit. In reply Rampolla described the sorrowful
impression the affair had made on Leo XIII, and the Secretary
of State said he had promptly written McQuaid at the Pope's
request deprecating the sermon and saying it was not worthy
of a bishop. He wished, therefore, to thank Gibbons in the name
of the Holy Father for informing the Holy See of what he called
a "deplorable incident."[68] For all of this there was the most
profuse thanks from St. Paul and as 1894 neared its close
Gibbons received a greeting for the new year in which Ireland
fairly exhausted himself in praise of the cardinal. Among other
things he wrote:

> In this desert of ours, so poorly tenanted with men, who see beyond
> narrow frontiers, who put high interests above self, who have the
> courage of convictions, what should have become of us, if God had
> not cared for the See of Baltimore by placing you in it! God
> guard you.[69]

The warm and expansive nature of John Ireland probably meant
this praise at the moment, although less than four months before
in a letter to Denis O'Connell he alluded to the cardinal's anticipated journey to Rome, and he said, "His Eminence is in great

[67] 93-N-3, Ireland to Gibbons, St. Paul, December 7, 1894.

[68] 93-N-6, Rampolla to Gibbons, Rome, December 17, 1894. For McQuaid's
undated reply to the Holy See on his feud with Ireland cf. Zwierlein, *op. cit.*,
III, 216–225.

[69] 93-N-9, Ireland to Gibbons, St. Paul, December 29, 1894.

glee over his approaching trip — 'at the Pope's special invitation!'
Take good care of him, otherwise he will spoil all things.'"[70]

At a time when there were rumors afloat concerning the doctrinal soundness of some of the leading figures in the American
Church, it was understandable that they should feel a certain
anxiety on learning that the Pope had decided to write a letter
to the Church of the United States. As previously mentioned,
O'Gorman had gone to Rome in the summer of 1894 and it turned
out that in the time he spent there he became quite influential in
the counsels which he was permitted to give to Leo XIII. O'Gorman worked over the subjects to be treated in the papal letter,
and after an audience of the Pope he informed Bouquillon that
the material which he had submitted contained all the principal
ideas outlined in the notes which Bouquillon had supplied except
those on the school question. The tone and accent of it all, thought
the church historian, was such as not to offend American sentiment. Leo XIII was quite satisfied with the material and O'Gorman believed that in the end the letter would be favorable to
their interests.[71] Monsignor O'Connell confirmed for Gibbons
the fact of O'Gorman's assistance to the Pope, in quoting the
latter to the effect that the Washington professor had helped him
a great deal and that he would later go over the notes and make
them his own. O'Connell added, "The Pope took a great fancy to
O'Gorman and attaches much weight to his opinions."[72]

If the so-called "Americanists" in the Church of the United
States needed further proof of the fact that their policies were
under fire from some of their coreligionists, they received it when
the seventh German-American Katholikentag assembled in Louisville during the last week of September, 1894. The German Catholics had delegated Father Henry M. Tappert, assistant pastor of
Mother of God Church in Covington, Kentucky, to represent
them at the congress of German Catholics held in Cologne the
previous month, and in Louisville Tappert repeated what he had
stated at the meeting in Germany. Liberalism, according to Tappert, was the great enemy of the day and in referring to the
inroads which it had made among American Catholic leaders
he said:

---

[70] ADR, Ireland to O'Connell, St. Paul, September 8, 1894.
[71] ACUA, Bouquillon Papers, O'Gorman to Bouquillon, Rome, August 23 [1894].
[72] 93-K-7, O'Connell to Gibbons, American College Villa, September 9, 1894.

It holds sway over certain Catholics who have inscribed on their banner: "Union of the Church with the age, with modern ideas, with Americanism." Hence the extolling of modern liberties, not as a requisite for a justified tolerance, but as the ideal of political and ecclesiastical wisdom; hence the cautiousness of preaching Catholic truth, under which truth and Catholicity suffer; hence the more than sparing attitude of this third kind of liberalism towards secret societies; hence the unreasonable breaking away from sane Catholic tradition in the temperance and liquor question; hence, finally, that coquetting with a more or less general, all-embracing christianity to which a far-reaching expression was given at the Chicago religious parliament of unholy memory.

In this summary of the principal grievances of many of the conservative German Catholics against some of their coreligionists, Tappert went on to say that it was from this same source that there arose the fulsome praise of the public schools and what he called "that ridiculous boastfulness about Americanism" which reproached other Catholics for their attachment to the language and customs of their forefathers.[73] Tappert succeeded in expressing practically all the main counts of the German Catholics against the so-called liberals in the hierarchy, and in this indictment there were found as well many of the charges made by conservative American Catholics not of German origin during the controversy over Americanism.

At length Leo XIII's long-awaited letter to the American Church appeared under the title of *Longinqua oceani* on January 6, 1895.[74] We have already spoken of the high praise paid by the Pope in this letter to the American nation, as well as the esteem and affection expressed by him for the young and vigorous branch of the Church in this country.[75] True, the Pontiff warned against the evils of divorce and secret societies, but the only sentence in the letter that was likely to give rise to unfavorable comment from non-Catholics was that in which Leo XIII stated that it would be erroneous to draw the conclusion that in the United States was to be sought what he termed "the most desirable status of the Church, or that it would be universally lawful or expedient for State and Church to be, as in America,

---

[73] ACUA, typed copy from the *Proceedings of the Seventh German-American Katholickentag, held in Louisville, Kentucky, September 24–27, 1894,* pp. 57–59.
[74] Wynne, *The Great Encyclical Letters of Pope Leo XIII,* pp. 320–335.
[75] Cf. I, 469, Note 70, 647–648.

dissevered and divorced."[76] The New York *Sun* of January 29
carried the full text, and on the following day in a friendly
editorial the *Sun* interpreted the remark of the Pope on Church
and State as meaning, they said, "to be received, so far as the
United States are concerned, merely as an *academic* affirmation
of what the author deems an abstract truth. . . ."

The generally sympathetic reception of the encyclical was
reflected by Archbishop Corrigan when he expressed his own
pleasure with it and asked Gibbons if he did not deem it fitting
to write the Pope a collective letter of thanks for the document,
to which he added, "I am glad no exception has been taken by
non-Catholics to the remarks about Union of Church and State,
which they may not understand properly."[77] Gibbons agreed with
Corrigan about the appropriateness of a letter of thanks and it
was his belief that the encyclical would be favorably received
by the American people, except possibly the statement on Church
and State. Distinguishing between the Protestant people in general and their papers, the cardinal continued, "That clause will
of course be assailed by the Protestant Press. They would assail
an inspired Gospel coming from the Pope." He apprehended some
adverse criticism from the secular press on that point, but he
believed the editorial of the New York *Sun* offered the best line
of defense, namely, that an unlimited praise of the American
system on the part of the Pontiff might tempt the French radicals
to say that what was good for the United States was good also
for France.[78] Archbishop Ireland was less impressed with the
papal encyclical than Corrigan and Gibbons. He urged the cardinal to make his acknowledgment of it as diplomatic as possible,
since in his judgment the letter had not made a ripple on the
surface of American thought. "I am sorry," said Ireland, "so

[76] Wynne, *op. cit.*, p. 323.

[77] 93-Q-9, Corrigan to Gibbons, New York, January 29, 1895. Over thirty years
later Professor John H. Latané of the Johns Hopkins University was quoted in
an address at the University of Virginia as recalling a conversation he had held
with Gibbons in which the latter had told him that in an audience of Leo XIII
the cardinal had discussed the Church — State relations in the United States with
the Pontiff. He had explained to the Holy Father that the leading American
Catholics were thoroughly in accord with the spirit of their country's institutions
and, as Latané quoted Gibbons, "it would be the worst possible thing for the
church in this country to undertake to apply here systems that applied in other
lands." John E. Graham, *The Pope and the American Republic* (Brooklyn, [1928]),
p. 9, a pamphlet of the International Catholic Truth Society.

[78] AANY, Gibbons to Corrigan, Baltimore, January 31, 1895.

much was expected, & so little came." He had been engaged by the *North American Review* to write an article on the encyclical for their March number but now he did not want to write it. "That unfortunate allusion to Church & State," said the archbishop, "cannot be explained to Americans."[79]

Two weeks later Ireland had at hand a task which was far more congenial to him than writing on the encyclical. On February 22 he delivered a speech before the Union League Club in Chicago on the subject of "American Citizenship" in which he extolled in ringing phrases the American way of life, much to the satisfaction of his vast audience. He said that when he remarked that the American refusing to vote merited disfranchisement or exile, the applause lasted several minutes and, as he put it, "People were wicked enough to see in those words an allusion to His Lordship of Rochester."[80] Gibbons read the address and wrote his appreciation of it to Ireland. He said that after the archbishop's sermon at the centennial of the hierarchy he considered it the happiest effort of Ireland's life. He wanted Ireland to take steps to have the address published in Europe, and he remarked, "I have been talking about it every day since I got the papers."[81] Ireland replied that testimony from the cardinal was worth to him more than from all others, and he now began to believe that there was some merit in the talk. He continued:

> At any rate the discourse had a wondrous effect in Chicago; it wrought up the people to fever heat. I trust it will have thro the whole country the effect of linking the Catholic Church in the minds of the American people with high American patriotism.[82]

Three months later Cardinal Gibbons attended the golden jubilee of Archbishop Williams in Boston and paid a long deferred visit which he had promised to make to Archbishop Corrigan in New York. Following these appointments he then sailed for

---

[79] 93-R-4, Ireland to Gibbons, St. Paul, February 6, 1895. Gibbons' acknowledgment to Leo XIII was brief and without any particular significance (93-R-11, Gibbons to Leo XIII, Baltimore, February 25, 1895, copy in Latin).

[80] 93-S-2, Ireland to Gibbons, St. Paul, March 4, 1895. The text of Ireland's address at Chicago can be found in his volume, *The Church and Modern Society*, I, 185–214.

[81] AASP, Gibbons to Ireland, Baltimore, March 6, 1895, copy.

[82] 93-S-4, Ireland to Gibbons, St. Paul, March 14, 1895.

Europe on May 18, 1895.[83] The cardinal's time was greatly preoccupied with various important interests which he represented
before the Holy See on this occasion, such as the decree against
the secret societies and the continuing criticism of the Catholic
University of America, but there was one episode which above
all others held prominence in his mind and that proved to be an
exceedingly painful one. Scarcely a week after his arrival in Rome
Monsignor Denis J. O'Connell submitted to Gibbons, as chairman
of the executive committee of the American College, his resignation as rector of that institution.

For ten years O'Connell had served not only as rector but as
liaison man for the American hierarchy with the Holy See. But
as the tension mounted in the American Church over the various
controversies which we have already reviewed, the Roman rector
came to be identified more and more with the party of Gibbons,
Ireland, and Keane. Naturally this identification damaged his
prestige as the representative of the entire body of bishops and
criticism of his policies was heard in certain circles. John Ireland
had gotten wind of some of these rumors a year and a half before, and he warned O'Connell that he had begun to hear mut-
terings about him, which prompted him to say that he feared
their enemies might now turn on him if he were not careful.[84]
Whether or not O'Connell made any effort to heed the warning we
do not know, but at any rate, if he did it was unsuccessful, for on
June 7 he signed his resignation to take effect on October 1. Alleg-
ing reasons of health which caused many enforced absences from
the college at some detriment to the regularity of the institution,
the rector stated that he could not continue to discharge the
labors of his responsibility.[85]

[83] AANY, Gibbons to Corrigan, Baltimore, April 10, 1895. As far back as the
previous November Corrigan had asked if he could see Gibbons before the latter
left for Rome and the cardinal had promised to make the visit (93-M-5, Corrigan
to Gibbons, New York, November 9, 1894; AANY, Gibbons to Corrigan, Baltimore, November 16, 1894).

[84] ADR, Ireland to O'Connell, New York, October 23, 1893.

[85] 93-V-4, O'Connell to Gibbons, Rome, June 7, 1895. The resignation was
accepted by Leo XIII three days later (93-V-7, Rampolla to Gibbons, Rome,
June 10, 1895, copy in O'Connell's handwriting). Something of O'Connell's true
state of mind could be read in his letter a month later to Archbishop Janssens
when he told him he was giving up the rectorship. He said, "Too much contention and I want peace & rest. All the rest is anguish and tribulation of spirit"
(AANO, O'Connell to Janssens, Rome, July 4, 1895).

Actually the reasons for O'Connell's resignation did not pertain to his health. It became apparent in a short time that criticism of his conduct and policies had been lodged with the Congregation of the Propaganda, under which the American College operated, and that this criticism had convinced certain of the officials of the congregation that the rector must go. The news, of course, quickly spread through Rome and Bishop McDonnell of Brooklyn, who was in the Eternal City at the time, reflected the common impression of the moment when he informed Archbishop Corrigan of what had happened and said, "It is to be hoped that the Executive Committee will name as Rector one who will be impartial in controversies or questions that may arise."[86] A month later in the same vein another friend of Corrigan's, Salvatore Brandi, summarized the reasons for the dismissal of O'Connell for the archbishop and likewise ended by expressing the hope that the committee would propose a *terna* of names to the Propaganda composed of men who enjoyed their full confidence, and as he expressed it, "allow no clique to take the upper hand."[87] It was obvious that the opponents of the so-called liberals regarded O'Connell's resignation as a triumph for their interests, and that they believed his partisanship for Gibbons and his friends was the principal reason.

The entire affair was a cruel blow to the Cardinal of Baltimore. For nearly thirty years he had been an intimate friend of O'Connell's, had promoted his interests on every possible occasion, and had sought and followed his advice on important questions more than he did that of any other man. Some years before in sending his annual donation to help defray the expenses of O'Connell's secretary, he had told him, "Your services to me cannot be paid in gold but in the coin of gratitude."[88] The sentiment of 1888 had in no way changed over the intervening years and in the present crisis in O'Connell's life the coin of gratitude was more than paid. Knowing as we do the extraordinary loyalty which Gibbons always showed toward those whom he loved, it is not difficult to imagine the depth of feeling he experienced in the humiliation which had come to his favorite. The cardinal

---

[86] AANY, McDonnell to Corrigan, Rome, June 10, 1895, *Risservatissima.*

[87] APF, Brandi to Corrigan, Rome, July 8, 1895, *confidential,* photostat. These photostats of the Corrigan correspondence were used in the APF; the originals are in the AANY.

[88] ADR, Gibbons to O'Connell, Baltimore, July 10, 1888.

accepted the decision, of course, with the same outward serenity with which he greeted all the commands of the Holy See, but that did not mean that the injury done to the reputation of Monsignor O'Connell had not cost him dearly. The speculation which Bishop McDonnell had expressed immediately after the event as to whether O'Connell would now go to Baltimore or remain in Rome as the representative of Gibbons, was answered when the cardinal continued the deposed rector as vicar of his titular Church of Santa Maria in Trastevere.[89]

Insofar as that was possible Gibbons threw over O'Connell the mantle of his protection, and in the dark years that lay ahead for the monsignor there was no one who remained more constantly on the watch to be helpful than his patron in Baltimore. When O'Connell submitted his final report on the American College which showed it to be in a flourishing condition, Gibbons told him:

> And it is sad to think that this excellent condition of the College was not taken into consideration, as well as your own personal high character & reputation, before your resignation was so peremptorily demanded.

He further remarked that at the meeting where names were proposed for his successor he had had O'Connell's letter of resignation read without giving any chance for defense or explanation, and then revealing the manner in which the affair had touched him personally he concluded, "You are almost hourly in my thoughts."[90] Not only did Gibbons write as consolingly as he

---

[89] AANY, McDonnell to Corrigan, Rome, June 10, 1895. Less than a year after O'Connell's resignation of the rectorship the canons of Santa Maria in Trastevere complained to Gibbons of his long absences from his post as vicar of the basilica, and for that reason proposed the name of Francesco de Paula Cassetta to replace him (94-L-4, I. C. Tani to Gibbons, Rome, April 12, 1896). But Gibbons was not persuaded to make the change, and only when O'Connell left Rome in 1903 to become Rector of the Catholic University of America did the cardinal appoint a new vicar in the person of Monsignor Gaetano De Lai (100-J-2, De Lai to Gibbons, Rome, March 7, 1903).

[90] 94-B-4, Gibbons to O'Connell, Baltimore, October 11, 1895, copy. It was probably only a slight consolation at the time to be told in a birthday greeting from Maurice Francis Egan that as he grew older the realization became stronger with him every day of Gibbons' inestimable value to the American Church. Egan said it seemed that the cardinal's natural gifts and his grace of state combined in causing him to say and to do the right thing at the right time. "The Catholic laymen," said Egan, "who come daily in contact with the people find in you a tower of strength" (93-W-6, Egan to Gibbons, Notre Dame, July 23, 1895). A

could to O'Connell but he also had urged Archbishop Ireland to do likewise. Yet before O'Connell could resume his normal life, allowance would have to be made for time to heal the wound, for Ireland reported that the letter he had written at Gibbons' suggestion had remained unanswered. He said that before that time he used to hear frequently from the former rector but now, as he put it, "there is absolute silence. Why or wherefore — I cannot imagine."[91]

There was no denying the fact that in the forced resignation of Denis O'Connell the party of the so-called Americanists had suffered a defeat. The selection of Father William H. O'Connell of the Archdiocese of Boston to fill the vacant post in Rome, an action which was approved by Leo XIII on October 21, 1895,[92] did, it is true, bring to the rectorship a man who was unidentified with any particular group in the hierarchy, but the elimination of Denis O'Connell contributed in no appreciable way to the making of peace. In fact, it seemed for a time that his dismissal had offered only a foretaste of what was to come. When, for example, Ireland reported confidentially to Gibbons that Thomas O'Gorman had been named second Bishop of Sioux Falls in January, 1896, he remarked that Bishop John Shanley of Jamestown, who was then in Rome, had told him that the whole list of names had met with what he termed "ferocious attacks" as being liberals and semiheretics and O'Gorman especially had been, in Ireland's words, "torn to pieces." Nonetheless, O'Gorman got through, but it prompted the Archbishop of St. Paul to say, "I remain most pessimistic as to Rome's general influence on the movements of the American Church."[93]

In the midst of the uncertainty created by the attitude of some of the officials of the Roman Curia toward the more liberal wing of the American hierarchy, the Church generally in this country was compelled to face another outbreak of the ugly

---

month later in welcoming him home Archbishop Chapelle of Santa Fe told him that he deserved the heartiest welcome from the hierarchy for the distinguished manner in which he had maintained their honor in Europe, and particularly in Rome, where he promoted so efficiently the best interests of religion by his wise and influential counsels (93-Y-3, Chapelle to Gibbons, Santa Fe, August 22, 1895). These were kindly sentiments and, perhaps, they helped to remove the sharp edges of disappointment and grief which the cardinal occasionally experienced.

[91] 94-F-6, Ireland to Gibbons, St. Paul, December 26, 1895.

[92] 94-C-8, Ledochowski to Gibbons, Rome, November 23, 1895.

[93] 94-G-8, Ireland to Gibbons, St. Paul, January 13, 1896.

bigotry of the A.P.A., which served to show up again Gibbons' sterling Americanism. Early in the year 1896 there had begun the preliminaries of what proved to be one of the most exciting presidential campaigns in American history when the youthful William Jennings Bryan was the candidate of the Democrats against William McKinley for the Republicans. It was the last time that the A.P.A. was to figure seriously in national politics, but during the course of the campaign they outdid themselves in abuse of all things Catholic. When it was announced that Satolli, the apostolic delegate, who had recently been named a cardinal, was going to visit St. Louis fallacious accounts were wired to the press from that city which made it seem highly questionable that he would be welcomed even by the Catholic clergy. John J. Kain, Coadjutor Archbishop of St. Louis, distressed as he was by these newspaper stories, stated that the words put in his mouth had never been uttered by him, and he informed Gibbons that some troublesome priest whose identity he suspected, but could not positively prove, had for years been rehashing ecclesiastical affairs in the newspapers and working up scandalous sensations. Kain had begged Satolli not to believe the malicious reports and not to be dissuaded from his intention of coming to St. Louis. As he told the cardinal, "His change of programme would be a veritable victory for the A.P.As. and a surrender to a few truculent priests ever ready to make trouble for those in authority."[94] The A.P.A., of course, eagerly seized on every tale they could find to make Satolli's last months in the United States as uncomfortable as possible, so that with enemies without and a few traitors within there was no relief in Catholic circles to the tension which marked the campaign year.

In fact, the attacks of the A.P.A. grew so virulent and threatening for a time that some candidates for public office showed signs of being persuaded to equivocate on the principles of religious liberty for Catholics in their hope of winning votes. The true Americanism of Cardinal Gibbons was thoroughly aroused at this trend and he decided, quite contrary to his customary policy in political matters, to speak out. He chose to issue his statement on one of the very days that the supreme council of the A.P.A. was meeting in Washington where W. H. J. Traynor, the president, had declared that "The keystone of the A.P.A., in fact, is

[94] 94-H-8, Kain to Gibbons, St. Louis, February 13, 1896.

that a papist, no matter how liberal nominally, is not a consistent citizen of the United States."[95] Gibbons maintained that it was the duty of the leaders of all political parties to express themselves clearly on the principles of religious freedom which underlay the Constitution. Catholics, he said, were devoted to both the major parties, and each individual Catholic was left entirely to his conscience in the matter of his vote. He was proud to say that the Catholic Church had never used or perverted its acknowledged power in the United States by seeking to make politics subserve its own advancement. Moreover, it was the proud boast of Catholics that they had never interfered with the civil and political rights of those who differed from them in religion. But, said Gibbons, "We demand the same rights for ourselves and nothing more, and will be content with nothing less." In language which was very strong for the mild Archbishop of Baltimore he continued:

> Not only is it the duty of all parties distinctly to set their faces against the false and un-American principles thrust forward of late, but much as I would regret the entire identification of any religious body as such with any political party, I am convinced that the members of a religious body whose rights, civil and religious, are attacked, will naturally and unanimously espouse the cause of the party which has the courage openly to avow the principles of the civil and religious liberty according to the constitution. Patience is a virtue, but it is not the only virtue. When pushed too far it may degenerate into pusillanimity.[96]

The statement was generally well received. John D. Crimmins, wealthy Catholic contractor of New York, appreciated what he called the cardinal's "timely words of wisdom," and he said that for some months he had been reading statements from men who seemed authorized to speak for various candidates, to the effect that among the candidates' qualifications for office was the fact that they had never befriended an American Catholic nor did they have any relatives who were ever Catholics.[97] Bishop Keane likewise sent his congratulations and told Gibbons, "On all sides I hear expressions of gratification at your Eminence's

[95] Quoted in Myers, *History of Bigotry in the United States,* pp. 244–245.
[96] Scranton *Tribune,* May 19, 1896.
[97] 94-M-10, Crimmins to Gibbons, New York, May 19, 1896.

pronouncement concerning the A.P.A."[98] But despite the fact that many individual citizens were doubtless grateful for Gibbons' challenge to the politicians to declare openly for religious liberty, it produced no effect upon the Republican platform when it was written at St. Louis on June 16, nor was there any indication of guarantees on this point in the platforms of the minority parties. However, when the Democrats issued their platform at Chicago on July 7 it contained the following plank:

> The Constitution of the United States guarantees to every citizen the rights of civil and religious liberty. The Democratic Party has always been the exponent of political liberty and religious freedom, and it renews its obligations and reaffirms its devotion to these fundamental principles of the Constitution.[99]

On the eve of the election the cardinal again made reference to the political situation in a conciliatory statement in the cathedral on All Saints' Day, in which he testified to his belief that the American people possessed a sense of justice, fair play, and a love for the law both human and divine. He said a foreigner looking on at the violent denunciation of one party by the other, and hearing the terrible predictions in regard to the future if the opponents should win, might think the United States was on the verge of a dreadful revolution. But on the following Wednesday morning he would find that it had been a bloodless revolution and at that time, said the cardinal, "the minority will bow gracefully to the will of the majority." He continued, "The country will survive & the nation will flourish & be perpetuated. Is this not good evidence," asked Gibbons, "that we are subject to the laws. And the people that bow to the civil law are not the kind to reject the divine law."[100] But while the Democratic platform had gone a long way toward meeting the demands of Gibbons in his statement of the previous May, it failed to attract enough votes to carry the election since McKinley emerged the victor, although his plurality was only a little over 600,000 votes out of a total of over 13,500,000 cast.

---

[98] 94-M-13, Keane to Gibbons, Washington, May 23, 1896. From far-off Portland Archbishop Gross sent his congratulations and said the statement was badly needed there as there was an immense number of the A.P.A. in Oregon (94-M-12, Gross to Gibbons, Portland, May 23, 1896).

[99] Kirk H. Porter (Ed.), *National Party Platforms* (New York, 1924), p. 182.

[100] Scranton *Tribune,* November 2, 1896.

In the midst of all the turmoil in the political world during the year 1896 the struggle between the opposing factions within the American Church continued to attract attention. On April 19 Dr. O'Gorman was consecrated as Bishop of Sioux Falls at St. Patrick's Church in Washington and the preacher on that occasion was the Archbishop of St. Paul. Ireland went out of his way to commend the diocesan priesthood and, although he acknowledged that the bishop received help from the religious orders, he said, "He cannot depend upon them for the work of his diocese nor is his care required or allowed in the formation of their priesthood."[101] Despite the protest of Ireland's personal regard for the religious in the sermon, his remarks were generally interpreted as a blow struck at the Jesuits, and John A. Zahm, C.S.C., for one gave it that interpretation when he wrote Gibbons from Rome to say that the reference to the religious had excited no end of comment in the Eternal City, to which he added, "What next? everyone asks."[102]

At the same time Zahm, whose sympathies lay with Gibbons and his friends, called the attention of the cardinal to a recent dispatch cabled by Monsignor Boeglin which had appeared in the New York *Freeman's Journal* on May 2. In this news item reference was made to the possibility of Cardinals Gibbons, Vaughan, and Logue joining in a plea for arbitration of international disputes with a view to supporting Leo XIII's efforts to maintain peace. Boeglin recalled how horrified some had been when Gibbons took the lead with his great pronouncement on the Knights of Labor but remarked what a blessing it had proved to be. And then with a definite slant intended to emphasize American leadership he wrote:

> It would be a new title of glory for the United States if the tocsin of arbitration were to ring out from its towers and the American to become the universal idea. It is long since Leo XIII has foreseen, foretold and proclaimed the influence of the United States on the old continent. Hence his affection for and his confidence in the future of the Starry Banner.

Dispatches of this kind from Boeglin doubtless found an echo in the hearts of thousands of American Catholics and helped to

---

101 *Church News* (Washington), April 25, 1896.
102 94-M-9, Zahm to Gibbons, Rome, May 18, 1896.

offset the unfriendly cables which were furnished to the American press from time to time by the conservative opposition, but they probably contributed nothing to winning over those who resented the strong American tone which Boeglin gave to them.

If the dismissal of Monsignor O'Connell in June, 1895, from the rectorship of the American College cast a temporary gloom over the spirits of the so-called liberals in the Church of the United States, they were destined to suffer genuine dismay a year and some months later when misfortune befell another of their number. In the last days of September, 1896, Cardinal Gibbons as Chancellor of the Catholic University of America received a letter from Cardinal Rampolla in which there was enclosed a communication from Leo XIII to Bishop Keane dismissing him from his post as Rector of the university.[103] The principal reason given was that the rectorship should not be held in perpetuity, and with a view to softening the blow, Keane was promised the rank of archbishop with freedom to remain in the United States or to come to Rome. However, it was apparent that this altogether unexpected decision of the Holy See had behind it the full force of the opposition to Keane and his associates in the hierarchy as well as to the university itself. Once more there was no disguising the fact that the conservatives like Corrigan, McQuaid, and their episcopal friends, the leaders among the German Catholic nationalists, and some of the more active members of the Society of Jesus had scored a new triumph. For the moment those who for some time had been charged with spreading a kind of philosophical liberalism in the American Church, appeared to be in complete rout in the face of the personal disaster which had befallen one of their principal figures.

It became the unpleasant duty of Gibbons to telegraph Keane on September 28 to come to Baltimore in order that he might break the sad news to him. Matters were not made easier for either of them by Rampolla having stated that the Pope did not doubt that Keane would welcome with gratitude the dispositions which the Holy Father had deigned to take in his regard. Al-

---

[103] 94-Q-7, Rampolla to Gibbons, Rome, September 16, 1896, enclosing a letter from Leo XIII to Keane, Rome, September 15, 1896. This episode is fully covered in Ahern, *The Catholic University of America, 1887–1896. The Rectorship of John J. Keane,* p. 162 ff. Father Ahern has completed a biography of Keane which will give more background to the bishop's dismissal. Further aspects of the Keane case can be found in Chapter X of the present work.

though he could hardly be grateful for the action, Keane accepted the decision in a letter to Leo XIII without, as he said, "a moment of hesitation," and availing himself of the freedom of choice granted to him, he stated that he had determined to remain in his own country.[104] At the opening of the new academic year on October 4 the retiring rector announced his departure to the assembled faculty and students, and if the *Irish World* correctly reported the moving scene, the most deeply affected of all those present was the cardinal chancellor.

In his speech on this occasion Gibbons was quoted as saying he trusted that the university would have a long line of distinguished and able rectors but he knew that none would be, as he put it, "more courtly, more able, more thoroughly a man of God than the one we lose to-day."[105] Even allowing for some exaggeration in the account of the reporter, it is certain that the cardinal was deeply shaken by the trial which had come to one of his closest friends and to the institution which he loved so dearly. An announcement was made the same day to the public, and when the news broke there was an immediate reaction which clearly demonstrated the deep resentment felt in most quarters by the action of Rome and the very high regard in which Keane was held throughout the country.[106] Gibbons, of course, was aware of the painful impression created in the country at large and he was the recipient of a number of personal communications expressing indignation and making suggestions to him in Keane's behalf.[107]

Shortly after his farewell to the university, Bishop Keane went to California where he intended to remain in retirement at the home of an old friend, Judge Myles P. O'Connor. But Archbishops Ireland and Riordan persuaded him that he should go to Rome and accept the position offered to him by the Pope and then, as he told Dr. Garrigan, Vice-Rector of the University,

---

[104] Ahern, *op. cit.*, p. 163.

[105] *Irish World* (New York), October 10, 1896, quoted in Ahern, *op. cit.*, p. 165.

[106] For the press reactions to Keane's resignation cf. Ahern, *op. cit.*, pp. 165–173. Bishop McQuaid was gleeful at the news. He told Archbishop Corrigan, "What collapses on every side! Gibbons, Ireland, and Keane ! ! ! They were cock of the walk for a while and dictated to the country and thought to run our dioceses for us. They may change their policy and repent. They can never repair the harm done in the past" (AANY, McQuaid to Corrigan, Rochester, October 3, 1896).

[107] 94-R-9, William E. Starr to Gibbons, Baltimore, October 9, 1896; AAB, unclassified, George Zurcher to Gibbons, Buffalo, October 13, 1896.

"demand an investigation of the charge of heterodoxy made ag'st me by Card. Satolli, — and, thro' me, against so many others."[108] By this time there had taken place the strange *volte-face* of the first delegate to the United States which was mentioned previously in connection with Cahenslyism, and with Satolli now a cardinal in Rome and in high favor of Leo XIII there was ample reason for concern. The motives for Satolli's change of front have never been satisfactorily accounted for but, in any case, it was he, according to Keane, who had questioned the orthodoxy of the former rector and his friends. In all of this, to be sure, Gibbons was implicated at least by association and the prevalence of mendacious stories in the press only added to the distress which the cardinal experienced at the time. In endeavoring to console Archbishop Janssens for a calumnious pamphlet recently published about him, the cardinal remarked that calumnies were something they all had to bear. As he said, "I get my share of them. I am told that a Paris paper 'La Vérité' (save the mark) says that I am favoring Free masons; & the article is copied in a Canadian paper. May the Lord give us strength & patience to do our duty, regardless of poisoned tongues."[109]

In the crisis which had overtaken John Keane the Cardinal of Baltimore defended his friend with the same steadfast loyalty that he had shown in the case of Monsignor O'Connell the year before. He composed a lengthy letter to Cardinal Rampolla, in which he told him of the respectful submission which Keane and the Board of Trustees of the university had given to the Pope's action in regard to the rector. He paid an especially high tribute to the spirit of humility and obedience with which Keane had taken the decision, but he then wrote:

> Nevertheless, Eminence, my respect for the pontifical dignity, my profound veneration for the sacred person of the Holy Father, my love of the Church and the zeal for its dearest interests, make it a duty to make known to you that the decision of the Holy See in regard to Monsignor Keane has been painful to us, especially because of the fact that it has been so sudden and that it was unforeseen.

Then Gibbons proceeded to inform Rampolla of the very general and profound commotion occasioned among the American public at the rector's dismissal, adding that the presidential election

---

[108] ACUA, Garrigan Papers, Keane to Garrigan, San Jose, November 19, 1896.
[109] AANO, Gibbons to Janssens, Baltimore, November 4, 1896.

itself, in spite of the especially absorbing interest it aroused this year, had not been able to turn aside public opinion from Keane. "This truly extraordinary fact," said Gibbons, "proves the interest which the country takes in the affairs of the Catholic Church and also the great place that Monsignor Keane occupies in the esteem and affection of his fellow citizens without distinction." After mentioning Keane's retirement to California without any source of income, the cardinal stated that there had since arisen a series of alarming rumors concerning punitive action by the Holy See against some of the professors of the university. He affirmed his own confidence in the justice and wisdom of the Holy See's policy, but, said Gibbons, if "per impossible" there should be any foundation to these rumors, then he earnestly begged Rampolla in the name of the most sacred interests of souls and of the Church to use all his influence to prevent such a disaster to the university. It was of the utmost importance at the moment to calm spirits and to restore confidence. He had exerted himself to that end and would continue to do so but, as he said, his action was necessarily limited and the prudence and wisdom of the Holy See were now more necessary than ever for the American Church. "I dare, then, to beg Your Eminence," said Gibbons, "to serve our Church by lending it the support of your powerful influence."[110]

Archbishop Ireland was pleased with the draft of the letter sent to him in advance and thought that there should be no change in its language, unless it were to make it stronger. "Satolli is determined," Ireland told Magnien, "to sustain his action toward Bp. Keane, by arraigning others, Card. Gibbons included, & if we lie down as cowards we shall be ruined." The Archbishop of St. Paul adverted to the alarming cables which were then appearing in the American press from European sources about further punishment to be meted out to the liberals, and he said he had written both Rampolla and Satolli, demanding from the latter a denial or a confirmation of these stories.[111]

---

[110] 94-T-7, Gibbons to Rampolla, Baltimore, November 24, 1896, copy in French in Magnien's handwriting. At the meeting of the Board of Trustees on October 21–22 Gibbons had appointed Archbishops Corrigan and Ryan to draft the letter but Ryan told Chapelle he intended to leave the work to the tact of his colleagues (AANO, Ryan to Chapelle, Philadelphia, November 10, 1896). Whether the letter was written originally by Corrigan and then redrafted in Baltimore is not known.

[111] ACUA, Bouquillon Papers, Ireland to Magnien, St. Paul, November 19, 1896.

It was true that the newspapers of those days were filled with sensational cablegrams about various prelates, and some went so far as to report that Gibbons and Ireland would be called to Rome for the purpose of removing them from their sees.[112] Archbishop Elder asked Gibbons if there was not some way to stop what he called "these shameful telegrams from Rome";[113] and when an especially villainous letter from Paris appeared in the New York *Sun* of November 29 Ireland warned the cardinal that many Americans were beginning to believe there was some truth in all the talk of papal disfavor.[114] The situation was brought to the attention of Archbishop Martinelli, the apostolic delegate, who, in turn, wrote to Rampolla about it. The result was that the Secretary of State cabled Martinelli authorizing him to contradict the assertion about the deposition of the bishops and removal of the university professors as a lie.[115] With the publication of the Rampolla cablegram there were set at rest the most absurd features of these published rumors, although it did not succeed, to be sure, in killing all the inaccuracies current at the time.

Through these days of turmoil Cardinal Gibbons was careful to avoid giving carping critics any material for faultfinding with his own public statements, and he was equally anxious that his friends should be on their guard. When he acknowledged the receipt of a copy of Ireland's volume, *The Church and Modern Society,* he said, "I earnestly hope that every sentence is so chastened that malicious souls who are in search of prey will discover nothing to gratify their morbid appetites." He was confident that in-genuous, honest American readers would enjoy the archbishop's lectures, and in referring to the lecture of June, 1892, which Ireland had delivered in Paris in French, it was Gibbons' opinion that this was the one that deserved the most credit since, as he said, "It was a bold — a hazardous undertaking to fight for Republicanism in a foreign tongue before an audience largely unfriendly."[116] Several months later, in again speaking of the book, the cardinal revealed the sympathy he felt for the opinions

---

[112] New York *Tribune*, November 13, 14, and 20, 1896, cited by Ahern, *op. cit.*, p. 179.
[113] 94-T-3, Elder to Gibbons, Cincinnati, November 20, 1896.
[114] 94-U-1, Ireland to Gibbons, St. Paul, December 2, 1896.
[115] 94-U-2, Martinelli to Gibbons, Washington, December 3, 1896.
[116] AASP, Gibbons to Ireland, Baltimore, January 2, 1897, copy.

expressed therein when he told the Archbishop of St. Paul, "If Plutarch gloried in imparting sound political principles to the Emperor Trajan, I must take an honest pride in having made some wise suggestions to the spiritual emperor of the West."[117]

Meanwhile Gibbons had not abandoned his efforts to retrieve the reputations of his friends O'Connell and Keane. In early September, 1896, he had written to Serafino Cardinal Vannutelli, a friend of O'Connell's, asking if he could not do something for the monsignor. Vannutelli replied that Gibbons' desire was in perfect accord with his own sentiments but he had been waiting for the return to Rome of Cardinal Satolli, for it seemed to Vannutelli that it was up to Satolli more than any other person to repair the wrong that had been done since, according to him, the origin of the difficulty went back to the part taken by O'Connell in Satolli's mission to the United States. Without enlarging on this intriguing suggestion, Vannutelli stated that since he had received Gibbons' letter, however, he had decided to wait no longer, although he confessed he did not clearly see his way in view of the difficulties that had to be faced.[118] In a similar fashion Gibbons tried to help John Keane. After Keane had been in Rome for a month without any sign of the honors that had been promised to him, the cardinal wrote a strong letter to Rampolla in which he urged that the Holy See not delay in giving public recognition to the former rector. He reminded Rampolla that Leo XIII's letter promising these honors had been made public, and after Keane's act of perfect obedience he said he

---

[117] *Ibid.*, Gibbons to Ireland, Baltimore, March 4, 1897, copy.

[118] 94-R-8, Vannutelli to Gibbons, Frascati, October 8, 1896. Five months later Rampolla complained to Gibbons that O'Connell was using a false title as "Bishop of Santa Maria in Trastevere," and he said the Pope had asked that Gibbons admonish the monsignor since the latter was dependent on Gibbons (95-K-2, Rampolla to Gibbons, Rome, March 10, 1897). In his reply the cardinal expressed complete ignorance of how O'Connell came to use the title, and he was careful to point out that O'Connell had never been a priest of the Archdiocese of Baltimore. He had appointed him, he said, as vicar of his titular church in 1887, but he was dependent upon him neither in spiritual or temporal matters, to which he added that he would be grateful for Rampolla conveying this information to the Pope (95-L-6, Gibbons to Rampolla, Baltimore, March 26, 1897, copy in French). Meanwhile Gibbons made inquiry and learned that O'Connell had had some stationery made up and the printer had entered the word *vescovo* instead of *vicario* before the name of Santa Maria in Trastevere. All this information was transmitted to Rampolla (95-Q-8, Gibbons to Rampolla, Baltimore, June 23, 1897, copy in Italian) and was duly acknowledged when Rampolla said he would inform Leo XIII of the facts (95-R-2, Rampolla to Gibbons, Rome, July 6, 1897).

feared that further postponement would give substance to the rumors then emanating from Rome that nothing was to be done. Keane ought, therefore, to be nominated as a consultor of the Congregations of the Propaganda and Studies as the Pope had promised, and if there should be a long delay the pontifical authority would suffer in the eyes of the Catholics of the United States and of the American public generally.[119] On the very day that Gibbons wrote his letter action was finally taken in Rome, and Keane was made titular Archbishop of Damascus and given other offices and titles in the Roman Curia which made his status an honorable and dignified one. For the ultimate success of the matter Keane credited the advice of O'Connell and the intervention of the two Cardinals Vannutelli.[120]

The Pope's action in regard to Archbishop Keane was naturally gratifying to his friends in the United States and wide publicity was given to his new honors. But the opposition remained unimpressed, and Father Brandi advised Archbishop Corrigan not to take seriously the news items on the American prelates in Rome. "To believe," wrote Brandi, "that they or anybody else of the same stamp can exercise in Rome, in the present circumstances, an influence over the Holy Father or the Sacred Congregation is an illusion and a grievous error."[121] Three weeks later an entirely contrary view of the situation in Rome was given to Gibbons when Zahm told him Keane and O'Connell were doing very well. "All reports to the contrary," said Zahm, "the future is ours." He said he knew positively that Leo XIII and Rampolla were still with them and that their policy was unchanged.[122] It was, perhaps, an example of how men of opposite opinions could view a situation and in the end see only what they wanted to see.

By the spring of 1897 the spirits of Archbishop Keane had picked up and he was again manifesting some of his customary verve. He told Gibbons that a recent address by Ireland in Wash-

---

[119] 95-B-10, Gibbons to Rampolla, Baltimore, January 15, 1897, copy in French.

[120] 95-B-9, Keane to Gibbons, Rome, January 15, 1897; 95-C-4, Keane to Gibbons, Rome, January 18, 1897. In his second letter Keane thanked the cardinal for his offer of $500, said it would be very much appreciated, and remarked that the fees for his new honors would be "something enormous."

[121] AANY, Brandi to Corrigan, Rome, March 1, 1897. Two months later in speaking of Keane, Brandi told Corrigan, "if the 'Canon' is hardly worked, nobody knows it in Rome. So far, he has not been consulted by any Congregation" (AANY, Brandi to Corrigan, Rome, May 1, 1897).

[122] 95-L-2, Zahm to Gibbons, Rome, March 20, 1897.

ington had made an excellent impression in Rome, and that Rampolla was sufficiently pleased to express the hope that it would be published in full in the French papers. This prompted Keane to say that Ireland should speak out again and again in the months before he came to the Holy See so that it would be made evident to all that it would be a mistake to regard their efforts as a war of races instead of a war to disseminate the ideas of Leo XIII against refractory elements such as those in France. In closing his letter the archbishop said, "How I wish that your Eminence could come here every couple of years to let these people see that what Satolli & Mazzella attack as *'Americanism'* is simon-pure Catholicity & disinterested devotedness to the Holy See."[123] Keane probably made known his desire to Ireland also, but in any case, the Archbishop of St. Paul performed the kind of service which his friend had in mind when on May 13 he delivered an address before the Chamber of Commerce of Cleveland on the subject of "Conscience: The Mainstay of Democracy," in which he emphasized the virtues of the American form of government, but insisted that its strongest support lay in the inculcation of a good conscience in the citizens and their fidelity to religion and the moral law.[124]

Soon thereafter there occurred another event which involved Keane and his friends and their ideas of furthering the Americanizing influence in the Church of the United States. On June 9 Archbishop Francis Janssens of New Orleans died at sea and in the negotiations over the succession Bishop Edward Fitzgerald of Little Rock, a suffragan of the Province of New Orleans, played a leading role. He inquired of Gibbons if Keane would be available and willing to come to New Orleans since a number would like to have him. Fitzgerald was strongly opposed to allowing the French element to predominate because he felt they had proved a serious detriment to the progress of the archdiocese. Keane could speak French and for that reason, as Fitzgerald told the cardinal, "An American who speaks French would give

---

[123] 95-P-3, Keane to Gibbons, Rome, May 9, 1897. When Mazzella's brother died some months later Gibbons sent his condolences to the cardinal and promised to say Mass for the repose of his brother's soul. Mazzella thanked him for his sympathy and remarked, "This fresh mark of the kindly feeling you have always shown me, will be long remembered by me" (95-W-2, Mazzella to Gibbons, Rome, December 7, 1897).

[124] *The Church and Modern Society,* II, 85–100.

more general satisfaction than one whose native language is a foreign tongue — if I may be allowed the Hibernicism."[125] In reply Gibbons stated that the transcendent abilities of Keane were known to the country and he presumed that if nominated the Holy See might induce him to accept. However, the greater part of Gibbons' answer was devoted to Bishop Maes of Covington whose name was also on the priests' *terna* for New Orleans and whom he described as "conservatively progressive"; it was plain that the cardinal favored him.[126] In the meantime Gibbons communicated with Maes and gave it as his judgment that Keane could do more for the Church in Rome than in New Orleans. The Bishop of Covington was grateful for the cardinal's strong recommendation of him for the vacant post, and he took the opportunity to tell him about the splendid work he found Keane doing on his recent visit to Rome. Maes said he had emphasized this to the Pope in his audience and he agreed with Gibbons that he should be left where he was, for in Keane they now had a man enjoying and asserting influence over American interests at the Holy See which, said Maes, "had been denied for years to the entreaties of your Eminence and of the whole American Hierarchy. . . ." Maes would accept New Orleans if appointed, although he was quite happy where he was.[127]

For some months the appointment to New Orleans was delayed but Gibbons did not change his mind when he learned the bishops of the province had named Keane on their *terna*. He told O'Connell he was glad that Keane had been honored with a nomination but he thought it would be a pity to remove him just then from his position in Rome;[128] and in the same vein he wrote to Cardinal Ledochowski, stating that his first choice was Maes and the second Archbishop Chapelle of Santa Fe.[129] Even had Keane been anxious for the appointment, which he was not, it is doubtful if he would have secured it. O'Connell reported that he had heard the Pope would not approve the nomination of the former university rector for New Orleans, and by way of explanation

[125] 95-Q-2, Fitzgerald to Gibbons, New Orleans, June 17, 1897. Fitzgerald enlarged on the evils of the French regime in New Orleans to Ireland who sent the letter on to Gibbons (95-Q-5, Fitzgerald to Ireland, Little Rock, June 20, 1897).

[126] 95-Q-4, Gibbons to Fitzgerald, Baltimore, June 19, 1897, copy.

[127] 95-R-5, Maes to Gibbons, Covington, July 19, 1897.

[128] ADR, Gibbons to O'Connell, Baltimore, July 23, 1897.

[129] 95-S-3, Gibbons to Ledochowski, Baltimore, August 10, 1897, copy in Latin.

he added, "Satolli's opposition is like a passion."[130] After a further delay of some weeks Placide Chapelle, Archbishop of Santa Fe, was named to the vacant see on December 1, an appointment which met with general satisfaction among Gibbons and his friends.[131] Although Chapelle had been born in France, he had come out to the United States as a boy, received his theological education at St. Mary's Seminary in Baltimore, and had for many years been a close associate of men like Gibbons, Keane, and Ireland. They felt, therefore, that American interests would be properly protected in New Orleans during his regime.

Meanwhile what Keane had called the "war of ideas" did not abate. In an article in the *American Ecclesiastical Review* for February, 1897, which was signed in a pseudonym, the writer saw a danger to Catholicism in this country from certain tendencies which he believed were converging in an "American religious liberalism."[132] He regarded what he styled the needless flaunting of the American flag in sanctuaries and schools, and the impatience shown for tried ways of learning true knowledge as an effort to nationalize the Church by robbing its faithful of traditional Catholic instinct and feeling. To his mind there was too much emphasis upon science and a growing disrespect everywhere for authority in matters of both doctrine and discipline. Then without mentioning names he wrote:

> Yet leaders in the Church are found appealing to the masses and the popular prejudices of those who are supposed to need correction and direction. . . . It is this constant appeal to the judgment of the American people which, however flattering to our

[130] 95-U-5, O'Connell to Gibbons, Genazzano, October 21, 1897.

[131] AANO, Keane to Chapelle, Rome, November 17, 1897, and cablegrams of November 24 and 30, 1897; Zahm to Chapelle, Rome, December 3, 1897; Keane to Chapelle, Rome, December 4, 1897; Gibbons to Chapelle, Baltimore, December 4, 1897; Ireland to Chapelle, St. Paul, December 11, 1897. Ireland told him, "I congratulate New Orleans on receiving a bishop who loves La Louisiane Française, & also loves the United States, of which Louisiana is a part." In writing to O'Connell the new Archbishop of New Orleans said he had not previously told him that Keane had sent word that Leo XIII wanted him in New Orleans because he understood the matter was not to be bruited about. He confessed he had repeated it to Gibbons in confidence, only to learn to his astonishment that the cardinal had spoken of it to some friends. "I should however have reflected," said Chapelle, "that on occasions he is somewhat *leaky*" (ADR, Chapelle to O'Connell, Santa Fe, December 31, 1897).

[132] "The Chapter 'De Fide Catholica' in the Third Plenary Council of Baltimore," XVI (February, 1897), 151.

national self-love, is at the same time wholly inconsistent with the divine plan of governing the Church; it is appeals without necessity which in reality weaken the basis of authority.[133]

At any other time views such as these would probably have received slight attention, but at a moment when the atmosphere was charged with suspicion concerning the false Americanism of some churchmen, their appearance in a reputable ecclesiastical journal was calculated to do further damage and to provide material for more speculation in Rome as to what was really going on in the American Church.

A few months later someone in Europe was the cause of bringing the evil of exaggerated and false statements closer to the Cardinal of Baltimore. He received a letter from Lucido Cardinal Parocchi, Secretary of the Congregation of the Holy Office, who said that a book by a certain P. Hoppani entitled *Da Chicago a Parigi* had been denounced to the Holy Office. The author had extolled mixed religious meetings such as the Parliament of Religions held in Chicago in 1893, and he was now working with a French priest, Victor Charbonnel, to stage a similar gathering at the Paris exposition in 1900. In this book Gibbons was quoted as having given to Charbonnel a favorable judgment of Leo XIII on the project of a congress in Paris, a quotation which had likewise appeared in the *Revue de Paris*. Parocchi stated that the Pope had asked him to inform the Archbishop of Baltimore that he had never given such an approval and to request the cardinal to deny it publicly.[134] After the lapse of some weeks Gibbons expressed his pained surprise to Parocchi that he should have been misquoted in this manner, and he informed him that he had authorized the superior of his seminary to deny the gratuitous assertion both in the United States and in a letter to the *Revue de Paris*. It prompted Gibbons to say to the Roman cardinal in reply:

> It is truly sad that men in my position here and elsewhere are constantly exposed to being brought before the public in a false or equivocal position. In the United States public sentiment easily does justice to these sayings and for that reason we are not held to account.[135]

---

[133] *Ibid.*, p. 153.

[134] 95-S-2, Parocchi to Gibbons, Rome, August 8, 1897.

[135] 95-S-11, Gibbons to Parocchi, Baltimore, September 25, 1897, copy in French in Magnien's handwriting.

While he believed that public opinion in this country would know how to interpret reports of this kind, the cardinal felt no such confidence in the kind of reception that would be given to them in Europe, and just a week previous to his reply to Parocchi Archbishop Keane, who was in the United States at the time, informed Denis O'Connell that Gibbons was worried over letters from Rome about the proposed congress of religions in Paris.[136] A month later the cardinal received an adverse review of his recent book, *The Ambassador of Christ,* in the French periodical *Polybiblion,* and in sending him a copy of it Father Gabriel André, S.S., then of the seminary of Dijon, explained that since the publication of the French translation of Elliott's *Life of Father Hecker,* there had sprung up among certain French priests a feeling against what they called Americanism and, said André, because in France "we never know how to keep moderate, those men become at once bitter and passionate in their criticism."[137]

The debate that had arisen in France during 1897 had, indeed, become bitter and passionate. In their anxiety to further democratic ideas and to push the policy of Leo XIII known as the *Ralliement,* by which the Catholics would reconcile themselves to the republican form of government, a number of French Catholics were prepared to put forth extraordinary efforts. In the mind of some of these men Walter Elliott's *Life of Father Hecker* seemed to embody the very ideas which they sought to promote among their coreligionists. Unfortunately, the English version of that work was faulty in that Elliott's expressions concerning some of Hecker's ideas on subjects like the need for a new apologetics to win converts, the relations of Church and State, the question of vows taken by members of religious orders, and the action of the Holy Spirit on individual souls were loosely constructed and could easily lead to misinterpretation. Elliott's intention had not been to write a scientific treatise on Hecker's theology, but instead a summary of his virtues and accomplishments. But in allowing his personal interpretation to govern his

---

[136] ADR, Keane to O'Connell, Saratoga, September 20, 1897.

[137] 95-U-4, André to Gibbons, Dijon, October 21, 1897. Keane told Ireland some months before that he was having a copy of the cardinal's book prepared for presentation to Leo XIII, and he added, "Satolli is talking shamefully about Card. Gibbons's book; says he has not a chapter about the Pope, because he has no love for the Pope! etc. If he attacks him in the press, we must make it hot for him" (AASP, Keane to Ireland, Rome, March 24, 1897, copy).

expression and by an arbitrary selection of facts from Hecker's life, the Elliott biography did not give a careful and accurate account of the Paulist founder's teaching on some points.

Nonetheless, these defects were not taken into consideration abroad and arrangements were made to have a French translation of the biography, done by Mlle. Louise de Guérines, published in Paris in 1897. Elliott gave those interested in the project a broad latitude in their use of his original English text. To the French edition, partly reconstructed and inaccurately translated in some particulars, the Abbé Félix Klein of the Catholic Institute of Paris added a glowing preface, of which the *Tablet* of London was later to say that Klein had out-Heckered Hecker "precisely in those points on which it were possible for a critic bent on fault-finding to attach to his words a meaning of doubtful orthodoxy."[138] But the French life of the founder of the Paulists was an immediate success and within a short time it passed through seven editions. Yet the more it was read the more did the storm grow, with the Catholic republicans hailing it as a kind of charter for their program for the French Church and the conservatives and royalist Catholics maintaining that it contained the seeds of heresy which they characterized under the name of Americanism.

By the summer of 1897 the discussion had taken on such proportions that John A. Zahm, C.S.C., president of the fourth International Catholic Scientific Congress scheduled to be held in Fribourg, decided a clarification was needed and he asked Monsignor Denis O'Connell to read a paper on the subject. On August 20 O'Connell read his paper which he called "A New Idea in the Life of Father Hecker." He stated at the outset that in the mind of Hecker the term "Americanism" had a double significance, the one political and the other what he would call ecclesiastical. Under the first point O'Connell traced the basic ideas of the American government as they were embodied in the Declaration of Independence where the emphasis was on a government by the people with the ultimate source of all power and political rights in God. He stressed the prominence of the individual in the American system in contrast to the lack of

---

[138] Quoted by Vincent F. Holden, C.S.P., in "A Myth in l'Américanism," *Catholic Historical Review,* XXXI (July, 1945), 157. Holden discusses the origins of the French translation in some detail. The name of the French translator is incorrectly stated here as the Countess de Revillasc (p. 156). Cf. also Klein, *op. cit.,* pp. 15–29, which describes Klein's part in the undertaking.

rights enjoyed by the individual person in the Roman Empire, and although he confessed the American idea was not complete and exhaustive, he thought that as far as it went no one could say it was contrary to Catholic faith. In concluding his remarks on this aspect of the subject O'Connell recalled the words of praise uttered by Leo XIII for the American Constitution in 1887 when he had presented a copy of that document to the Pontiff from President Cleveland for his jubilee gift, and he went on to say that never did anyone surpass in force and eloquence Cardinal Satolli himself when he spoke at Chicago in 1893 and recommended the Gospel and the American Constitution taken together as the complete charter of human life.[139]

On the second point O'Connell confined himself to the relations of Church and State as they existed in the United States. In moderate language the monsignor insisted that union of the two could never exist in this country because it would be contrary to the Constitution. He remarked that however beautiful and true in theory union of Church and State might be, in practice it had, unfortunately, been only too often found to work to the grave injury of the Church by diminishing its liberty. The United States was defended against the charge of being a godless state, and O'Connell maintained, "Nowhere is the action of the Church more free, and the exercise of Pontifical authority more untrammeled."[140] He ended by saying that Americanism in this sense involved no conflict with either Catholic faith or morals, that despite repeated statements to the contrary there was no new form of heresy or liberalism here, and that when fairly considered Americanism meant nothing else than the loyal devotion which Catholics in the United States bore to the principles on which their government was founded, and their conscientious conviction that these principles afforded Catholics in this country favorable opportunities for promoting the glory of God, the growth of the Church, and the salvation of souls.

A week after his lecture O'Connell reported that the reception given to American ideas at Fribourg had been most cordial. The Germans, he said, were especially stanch in their friendship and they had no sympathy whatever for the narrow American faction

---

[139] *A New Idea in the Life of Father Hecker* (Fribourg, 1897), p. 8. O'Connell's paper was later published in pamphlet form.
[140] *Ibid.*, p. 10.

of which Monsignor Schroeder, professor of dogmatic theology in the Catholic University of America, was one of the leaders. He closed his remarks to Archbishop Chapelle by saying that he expected him and the other trustees of the university to relieve the faculty of the incubus of Schroeder at the next meeting of the board.[141]

When the text of O'Connell's lecture reached Cardinal Gibbons he was delighted. He told the monsignor that Abbé Magnien, too, was charmed with the text and would not alter a single word of it. Gibbons thought the reference to Satolli's memorable remark about the Bible and the Constitution was very happily chosen and that it ought to have a telling effect in Rome. Revealing his thorough sympathy with the statement of O'Connell's views on Americanism, the cardinal wrote:

> I regard its appearance as most opportune, & the paper itself is clear, precise in terms, giving a definition of "Americanism" to which every honest Catholic must subscribe. Every sentence conveys a pregnant idea, & the relations of Church & State are admirably set forth especially for the eye of Rome. "If this is treason, let them make the most of it," to use the word of Patrick Henry. I must congratulate you on your success. I have often written & spoken on the subject, but you have gone more profoundly to the root of the question.[142]

About two weeks later Archbishop Keane spoke at a dinner in Washington given in his honor at which the cardinal was present. Keane was eloquent on the subject of the United States and quoted the Pope as saying that it was "the land of hope, the land of the future."[143] The archbishop confessed a few days later that Gibbons was afraid of some of the things Keane had said, but that the cardinal could not help noticing that the points he dreaded most were the most vehemently applauded.[144] Gibbons was doubtless just as much in sympathy with Keane's sentiments as his most enthusiastic listener, but he was fearful lest the archbishop's flamboyant oratory give his enemies opportunity for further criticism.

Meanwhile O'Connell continued to receive warm commenda-

---

[141] AANO, O'Connell to Chapelle, Freiburg im Breisgau, August 27, 1897.
[142] ADR, Gibbons to O'Connell, Baltimore, September 27, 1897.
[143] *Church News* (Washington), October 16, 1897.
[144] ADR, Keane to O'Connell, Washington, October 15, 1897.

tion for his Fribourg address. *La Quinzaine* of Paris reprinted it with high approval, Vincenzo Cardinal Vannutelli pronounced it a "bravissimo discorso," and the first one to send him his thanks was Archbishop Corrigan! All of this was relayed to Gibbons, along with the monsignor's gratification that his effort had met with the Cardinal of Baltimore's pleasure.[145] In the flush of their heightened spirits O'Connell and Keane were intent that what they regarded as a strengthened position should be utilized, and with that in mind Keane, who had returned to Rome, urged Chapelle to impress upon Gibbons that Schroeder should be gotten out of the university. The Holy See, said Keane, had instructed the apostolic delegate that the Schroeder case should be settled in a way to satisfy the bishops; therefore, no compromise measures should be permitted and the professor's resignation should be demanded before the end of the scholastic year. It was apparent that Keane feared that for the sake of peace the cardinal might temporize with Schroeder and his supporters, and he was determined for that reason that Chapelle should make it plain to Gibbons that action was called for.[146] The campaign to rid the university of the German professor, who was one of the principal critics of the so-called Americanizers, was drawn out for a few more weeks, but by the middle of December Gibbons informed O'Connell that it was practically settled,[147] and on December 29 Monsignor Schroeder finally submitted his resignation and announced his departure for Münster where he had been offered a teaching position.[148] One of the most controversial figures was thus removed from the American scene, but he would be heard from again during the next two years in the agitation which characterized the movement on the opposite side of the Atlantic.

As the new year 1898 opened Keane informed Cardinal Gibbons, with an optimism that proved to be unwarranted, that affairs were peaceful in the Eternal City and no storm clouds

---

[145] 95-U-5, O'Connell to Gibbons, Genazzano, October 21, 1897. Chapelle congratulated O'Connell also and said of the address, "I subscribe to every word of it" (ADR, Chapelle to O'Connell, New York, October 23, 1897).

[146] AANO, Keane to Chapelle, Rome, November 17, 1897.

[147] ADR, Gibbons to O'Connell, Baltimore, December 14, 1897.

[148] For the details of the Schroeder case cf. Hogan, *The Catholic University of America, 1896–1903. The Rectorship of Thomas J. Conaty*, pp. 148–158. The whole question of Americanism as it touched the university is covered by Hogan in his chapter "Americanism and the University," pp. 138–172.

were visible. True, the French edition of Hecker's life and O'Connell's essay on Americanism had caused more attention to be directed to the subject than ever before and there was, said Keane, evidence of a spirit of narrowness but, he continued, "the bulk of sentiment is on our side." He called the cardinal's attention to a recent article in the *Civiltà Cattolica* which suggested that a republic would be a better form of government for Italy than a monarchy, and he regarded this first public utterance on the subject as highly significant since, in Keane's judgment, it could hardly have been published without the Pope's knowledge and approval. To the mind of the archbishop it was a further onward step in the Holy Father's policy and he concluded, "It ought naturally to prove favorable to Americanism."[149]

Although Gibbons would be pleased to hear a report of this kind from Rome, he was not quite so much an optimist as Archbishop Keane and he was still fretful over the carping cablegrams published in the American press on affairs in the Eternal City. For example, when a slighting reference to American churchmen in Rome appeared in connection with a dinner given in honor of William F. Draper, American ambassador to Italy, Gibbons felt that every reasonable and honest person in the United States would understand the propriety of such a social gathering as showing the friendly relations between the accredited ambassador and the American ecclesiastics resident in the Italian capital. Noting for O'Connell other recent samples of the same kind of thing which carried disrespectful references to Cardinal Vannutelli, O'Connell, and himself the cardinal was prompted to say, "there is some malicious creature in Rome who is disposed to distort & put a bad construction on everything done by those whom he [or she] does not like." True, a number of these stories in the press had no effect; nonetheless, the cardinal revealed his awareness of the damage they might do and he was plainly annoyed by them.[150]

As the campaign in France grew stronger against the ideas of Father Hecker and all the evil tendencies that were supposed to be embodied under the heading of Americanism, it became evident that the friends and supporters of the founder of the Paulists had a major battle on their hands. With a view to pre-

---

[149] 96-A-10, Keane to Gibbons, Rome, January 24, 1898.
[150] ADR, Gibbons to O'Connell, Baltimore, March 11, 1898.

paring as powerful a defense as possible, Elliott was urged by several to get a letter from Cardinal Gibbons in praise of Hecker and the Paulists which could be published in the next French edition of the biography. A letter of this kind from Gibbons would tell in France, said Keane, and he added, "but [it] will especially tell here in Rome."[151] Even before Keane's letter reached him, Elliott had approached the cardinal whose response left nothing to be desired. Gibbons stated that he was pleased to record his appreciation of Hecker and he went on to say he regarded him as a providential agent for the spread of the Catholic faith in the United States. Showing what he thought of the criticisms leveled against Hecker's orthodoxy, he wrote:

> His spirit was that of a faithful child of Holy Church, every way Catholic in the fullest meaning of the term, and his life adorned with the fruits of personal piety; but especially he was inspired with a zeal for souls of the true apostolic order, aggressive and yet prudent, attracting Protestants and yet entirely orthodox.

With words of the highest commendation for the Paulist Fathers and the manner in which they were carrying out their founder's ideals, Gibbons concluded, "I am pleased to learn that Father Hecker's apostolic career is every day more and more appreciated in Europe by the publication and circulation of his life and writings."[152]

The powerful endorsement of Isaac Hecker by the Cardinal of Baltimore was promptly dispatched to France where it was published on May 4 in the *Univers,* the journal of Louis Veuillot. It was hoped that it would head off the *imprimatur* of François Cardinal Richard, Archbishop of Paris, for a book being prepared by the Abbé Charles Maignen who for some time had been writing against Americanism under the pen name of Martel. The Abbé Klein was delighted with Gibbons' letter and he told Elliott that its publication was the best means of impressing Richard who disliked conflicts between bishops. "And thus," said Klein, "if a French bishop sides with Martel, he will have

---

[151] APF, Keane to Elliott, Rome, April 19, 1898. Keane told Elliott, "There is no use in approaching Cardinal Satolli on the subject. He has no more love for Heckerism and Americanism than the rest of them."

[152] *Ibid.,* Gibbons to Elliott, Baltimore, April 14, 1898. This letter was published in both English and French in the *Catholic World,* LXVII (June, 1898), 427–428, under the heading, "What the Thinkers Say." It also appeared in the sixth French edition of the life of Hecker.

the odium of opposing Cardinal Gibbons."[153] The Abbé Dufresne, who had suffered as a consequence of expressing admiration for Hecker's virtues by attacks on him in *La Vérité française* of Paris, was likewise grateful for what he called the "precious protection" given by Gibbons. In thanking the cardinal as well for a copy of *The Ambassador of Christ,* Dufresne concluded, "The name of Cardinal Gibbons is cited everywhere in Europe, and especially for the Catholics of Switzerland and France it is a true standard in showing how one is able to struggle for the Church on modern ground with a mingling of initiative and prudent judgment."[154]

A new cause for complaint against Americans was given to unfriendly European critics when in the last week of April, 1898, the United States declared war against Spain. Archbishop Keane told Gibbons that the feeling against this country seemed to intensify and it was hard to bear. He felt it all around him in Rome, and he remarked that although he was not aggressive with those who spoke to him about the war, yet they found him unflinching in standing up for his country. With more partisanship than an objective analysis of the facts would warrant, the archbishop continued:

> Weighing on the one side the old worn out "vested rights" that are being broken up, and, on the other, the interests of civilization which our cause represents, I could not, even as an impartial judge, hesitate as to which way my sympathies should go. I thank God ever more and more for being an American.

In concluding his letter Keane adverted to the choice which should be made for the vacant Archdiocese of Santa Fe, and he said, "I hope Your Eminence and the Archps. will make clear and strong representations to Rome. It is *in America* that wise solutions must be devised & urged, — then Rome will not resist."[155] There was no mistaking the patriotic fervor and inde-

---

[153] *Ibid.,* Klein to Elliott, Paris, May 5, 1898.

[154] 96-G-4, Dufresne to Gibbons, Hermance par Genève, May 7, 1898. When Dufresne suggested that the Paulists institute the preliminaries for Hecker's canonization, Elliott felt that would have to await further developments. He believed, however, that Dufresne was a devout and wise man and a good friend, and he told Gibbons, "I thank God that many Frenchmen are likeminded with him in their estimate of Father Hecker" (96-H-6, Elliott to Gibbons, New York, May 23, 1898).

[155] 96-H-1, Keane to Gibbons, Rome, May 15, 1898.

pendence of mind of men like Keane and Ireland, and that was
partly the reason why Gibbons felt so close a bond with them,
even though the cardinal was ordinarily not accustomed to expressing himself so forcefully as his two friends.

Meanwhile the enemies of Americanism like Charles Maignen,
Bishop Charles F. Turinaz of Nancy, and Georges Périès, the
last of whom had been dismissed from his chair of canon law
in the Catholic University of America two years before, continued
their campaign. Balked in their efforts to secure the *imprimatur*
of the Archbishop of Paris for the manuscript of Maignen, an
appeal was made to Alberto Lepidi, O.P., Master of the Sacred
Palace in Rome, who granted an *imprimatur,* and the book appeared early in 1898 under the title of *Etudes sur l'Américanisme:
le Père Hecker: est-il un saint?* It was published in both Rome
and Paris and before the year was out it had appeared in an
English translation from Rome. The essays of Maignen had been
published in part in *La Vérité française* of Paris during the early
days of 1898, and now additional material was added from the
French translation of Elliott's *Life of Hecker,* the writings of
Victor Charbonnel, and the speeches of men like Ireland, Keane,
and O'Connell. In the indictment drawn up against Americanism,
accusations were made to the effect that these men were limiting
the external submission to the Church, advocating a false liberalism in their dealings with non-Catholics, supporting a complete
separation of Church and State, opposing the evangelical virtues
and the older religious orders, and advocating the practice of the
active as against the passive virtues and the natural virtues as
against the supernatural. Gibbons was indignant at the Maignen
book, and shortly after receiving a copy he told O'Connell that
he had only glanced at it but had seen enough to perceive its
venom. He asked him to tell Keane that after reflection and
consultation he had decided to comply with his request by sending a protest. Gibbons concluded:

> I regard the attacks of Protestantism as mild compared with the
> unprincipled course of these so-called Catholics. Our mission is
> surely a hard one here. While trying to exhibit the Church in all
> her beauty, we are assailed by those who would exhibit her in an
> odious light. But truth will prevail.[156]

---

[156] ADR, Gibbons to O'Connell, Baltimore, June 16, 1898. Keane was among
the first of the Americans to see Maignen's book and he quickly warned Ireland

The story of the Maignen volume reached the public press, of course, and the Baltimore *Sun* of June 20, among many other papers, published a lengthy dispatch from Rome giving details on its publication and dealing very harshly with Maignen.

Despite the falsehoods which the book contained, those whom it indicted were genuinely alarmed at the effect it might have on the minds of some of the officials of the Holy See. O'Connell reported to Ireland that Bishop Sebastian G. Messmer of Green Bay was in Rome and was talking so much to the Pope, the cardinals, and the Jesuits against Heckerism that he feared for the worst. Ireland warned George Deshon, Superior-General of the Paulists, that O'Connell actually believed that the biography of Hecker would be put on the *Index,* and it was the opinion of the Archbishop of St. Paul that Deshon should send someone to Rome after consulting with Gibbons and Magnien, the Baltimore Sulpician, who were then at Southampton.[157] Bishop John S. Foley of Detroit was also vacationing with the cardinal and he, too, inquired of Elliott if any steps had been taken to prevent the book from reaching the *Index,* saying that he wrote not from mere curiosity but rather from an earnest desire to aid as far as he could.[158] Under the circumstances the Paulists did not feel there was much they could do to avert the impending condemnation of the life of their founder, but in the end they found a defender whose voice in Rome carried much more weight than their own.

During the summer of 1898 Cardinal Gibbons sought the counsel and advice of his friends in the matter, and by late August he was ready to forward to the Holy See the protest which he had promised to Keane and O'Connell in mid-June. He opened his lengthy letter to Cardinal Rampolla by saying that it was only after much thought, and impelled by the feeling of a serious and grave duty to be fulfilled in his capacity as an American bishop

---

that the Archbishop of St. Paul was pictured as the head of the American schismatical church, that Keane himself was described as a rationalist who would overthrow all dogmas for modern ideas; but as for Gibbons, as Keane wrote, "Against the Card. there was only a vein of *insinuation* . . ." (AASP, Keane to Ireland, Rome, June 4, 1898, copy).

[157] APF, Ireland to Deshon, St. Paul, July 30, 1898.

[158] *Ibid.,* Foley to Elliott, Southampton, July 31, 1898. Written across the letter in pencil was the following, "This was Card. Gibbons' way of reaching us. He was at Southampton & asked Bp. Foley to write. Answered we were powerless."

and a member of the College of Cardinals, that he was writing to protest against the book of Charles Maignen. The volume revealed, said Gibbons, the worst unfairness and the most violent hatred of Hecker and the congregation he had established. Americanism was spoken of as a quasi-heretical and schismatic doctrine, and the most ignoble insults were heaped upon American prelates whose love of the Church and of souls made them worthy of every respect and honor. His own name, said the cardinal, was associated with theirs in a more discreet manner, but to that he was resigned since he had enough confidence in the wisdom of Leo XIII and Rampolla to believe that they would render justice to those who deserved it. He was not writing to defend the orthodoxy of Father Hecker; that, as he said, would be judged with wisdom and justice at the Holy See, but he reminded Rampolla that judgment should be made on the basis of the English biography and not the inaccurate French translation. He then continued:

> I am writing you to denounce the part of the book where it treats of Americanism, to protest with all the energy in my soul and conscience against this incriminating tendency brought against us, against these perverse insinuations of which we are the object and these revolting calumnies against an episcopate and a clergy entirely devoted to the salvation of souls and filled with veneration for the Holy See and in particular for the sacred person of Leo XIII.

Gibbons stated that the impression created by the Maignen book was that Americans were hardly Catholics, that they lacked obedience to the teachings and directions of the Holy See, and that there was a strong spirit of schism among them. It was difficult to believe one's eyes when one read such atrocities or one's ears when one heard them. He had thirty years in the episcopate behind him, and the cardinal believed, therefore, that he could speak of the bishops and clergy of the United States with full knowledge. With that he asked Rampolla, "What do they mean when they talk about Americanism, in relation to this episcopate and this clergy?" And by way of answering his own question he continued:

> Of course we love our country and are devoted to it; we like its institutions because they allow us our whole liberty for goodness and allow us also to spread more and more the action of Religion and the influence of the Church. It is not here a matter of theory,

of system, of maxims set up like absolute principles, it is entirely a matter of practice. If that were what they call Americanism, wherein is the harm? But no, they are using the word like a scarecrow; they want to suggest a perverse tendency of a doctrine not only suspicious but clearly erroneous and even heretical, as people talk of liberalism, Gallicanism and other qualifications of the kind. Well, I can guarantee to Y.E. that all this is false, unfair, slanderous. No doubt, among us as everywhere else, there are differences of opinions or appreciation, but I have no hesitation in affirming, you have not in the whole world an episcopate, a clergy, and believers more fundamentally Catholic, firmer in their faith and more wholly devoted to the Holy See. In this, moreover, we are only following our traditions. The Sovereign Pontiff Pius IX was able to say in complete truthfulness that nowhere was he more completely the Pope than in the United States, and His Holiness Leo XIII could say the same. Nowhere in the world has the firm and wise direction he gave the Church been followed with better obedience and respect than it has among us.

The cardinal then came to the *imprimatur* of Lepidi for the Maignen work. He said he had known of the author's articles before and he had not attached any importance to them. But now matters were different. "The imprimatur of the master of the Sacred Palace," said Gibbons, "granted to this libel gives it the meaning of a serious work and one worthy of confidence." It was on account of the *imprimatur* that he believed it necessary to write as he was now doing. For many it would no longer be Maignen who accused the Catholics of the United States but rather the Holy See. The French edition had not yet circulated widely in this country but Gibbons had learned that an English translation of Maignen was being prepared and that it would be published with the pontifical *imprimatur*. The effect of an English edition bearing such an *imprimatur* would, said the cardinal, be disastrous both for the Catholics and the Holy See in the United States. "All kinds of motives and intentions," he wrote, "will be lent to it, and I fear that among our political men and others, the one meaning given to it will be a more or less hidden attack against the United States and a kind of revenge for Spain beaten in war by us." Gibbons closed his letter by a fervent appeal to Rampolla in the interests of the Church, and of the authority of the Holy See among American Catholics, to put an end to the war, to cause the *imprimatur* to disappear, and to allow them the peace they needed to spread the kingdom of God among Americans who up to that time had been so well disposed to listen to Catholics and to render them justice.[159]

But the peace for which Gibbons yearned was nowhere in sight in the last months of 1898. When Keane was quoted as having said that the Pope and Rampolla knew nothing of Lepidi's *imprimatur,* Father Brandi told Archbishop Corrigan that it was a fact that Leo XIII knew everything about it and that Lepidi had acted with the express consent of His Holiness. "On this point," said Brandi, "there is no doubt whatever."[160] Ireland at the time believed that the Vatican was disposed to regret the *imprimatur,* and he informed Gibbons that he recently had a letter from Rampolla reiterating his assurances that the Maignen book could safely be left to the Pope who would speak and act in due time. "The Cardinal's words to me," said Ireland, "in this last letter particularly, are such that I cannot believe they forebode any decision unfavorable to 'America.'"[161]

Up to this time the Cardinal of Baltimore had had no word concerning his protest to the Holy See on the subject, but early in October Rampolla's reply arrived. Leo XIII, said the Secretary of State, was grieved to learn of the distress of Gibbons and his colleagues over the Maignen book. The Pope desired them to understand that the authorization of the Master of the Sacred Palace meant nothing more than a negative statement to assure the faithful that the volume contained nothing against faith or morals, rather than an approval of the book's contents. If one kept that in mind he could not but see how unfounded were the fears which had been aroused. Needless to say, Gibbons fully understood the meaning of an ordinary *imprimatur.* It was against the special character of the one given to Maignen that he had protested as suggesting papal approval of the author's views. Yet of this Rampolla took no cognizance but continued that the Holy Father trusted the bad impression created would not last and that the bishops, so full of zeal, so active, and working so fruitfully in the Church would be comforted by the certainty that the esteem and good wishes which

---

[159] 96-M-6, Gibbons to Rampolla, Baltimore, August 27, 1898, copy in French in Magnien's handwriting. Alphonse Magnien of Baltimore is not to be confused with the Charles Maignen of Paris who wrote the book against Americanism.

[160] APF, Brandi to Corrigan, Rome, September 3, 1898, photostat.

[161] 96-N-4, Ireland to Gibbons, St. Paul, September 13, 1898.

the Pope had for them had not been diminished. "As for the rest," said Rampolla, "I am pleased to inform Your Eminence that His Holiness is taking it upon himself to write an official letter to Your Eminence about the doctrine of Fr. Hecker."[162]

The reply of Rampolla arrived about two weeks in advance of the annual meeting of the archbishops held at the Catholic University of America on October 12. Before he left New York Archbishop Corrigan was handed a lengthy protest against the calumnies on Father Hecker contained in Maignen's book. It had been written by Father Deshon, Superior-General of the Paulist Fathers, in the name of his community with the request that it be laid before the metropolitans. Deshon refuted in detail the main charges against Hecker's orthodoxy on the questions of devotion to the Holy Spirit, the matter of spiritual direction, and the taking of vows by religious.[163] Corrigan read the document for his colleagues, and then moved that since Gibbons had received a reassurance from Rampolla which promised that the Pope would send an official letter the American archbishops had no need to interfere. The motion was carried.[164] Some days after the meeting Abbé Magnien reported recent developments to Denis O'Connell, and he said that although Gibbons seemed to be pleased with Rampolla's reply, to him it had a very peculiar sound in that it ignored almost everything said in Gibbons' protest. Magnien remarked that the Secretary of State had told the cardinal that a letter from the Pope concerning Hecker's case would be sent. "What," asked Magnien, "is the meaning of that?" He wondered if it would contain a condemnation of Hecker's

---

[162] 96-N-6, Rampolla to Gibbons, Rome, September 23, 1898.

[163] The Deshon document was published by Holden, *op. cit.,* pp. 165–168.

[164] *Ibid.,* p. 168. The action of the archbishops was probably not pleasing to Keane and O'Connell who had both urged a strong joint protest of the metropolitans to the Holy See against the calumnies of Maignen. In July Keane had urged this on Ireland, although one could detect that he doubted it could be accomplished. He gave all his reasons and then asked Ireland, "But can it be brought about?" (AASP, Keane to Ireland, Houlgate [Calvados], France, July 21, 1898, copy.) Two weeks before the meeting in Washington, O'Connell told Ireland, "Please pull yourself together now and rally your forces for one supreme decisive effort — the protest" (AASP, O'Connell to Ireland, Freiburg, September 27, 1898). Keane was in Washington shortly after the meeting of the archbishops and he informed Ireland that the cardinal told him Archbishops Feehan, Ryan, Katzer, and Williams all supported Corrigan in his motion to lodge no protest. Ireland was absent from the meeting, and in his disappointment Keane concluded, "No strong voice there for truth & justice" (AASP, Keane to Ireland, Washington, October 18 [1898], copy).

doctrines or would it, for the sake of peace, state that nothing would be done. "I assure you, my dear friend," said Magnien, "that all this Roman rhetoric is at times very provoking."[165]

With Gibbons appearing to be pleased with Rome's answer to his protest and some of his friends frankly skeptical, there was no further progress until an Associated Press cablegram from Rome announced in early November that Leo XIII had ordered a silence imposed on American questions and had taken the whole matter into his own hands. Ireland was inclined to credit the report, for as he told Magnien, "I do not see what else the Pope could have done — if letters from Card. Gibbons & myself have weight any longer." Nonetheless, the Archbishop of St. Paul remained doubtful and for that reason he was going to Rome very shortly to see for himself.[166] Two days later brought word from Boeglin that the present tempest in Rome had blown over, but he counseled moderation on the part of Ireland and his friends and insisted that the archbishop come to Europe very soon so as to support this position. Ireland was working hard to get ready and, of course, he would visit Baltimore before he sailed.[167] In the midst of the uncertainty the Catholic papers sympathetic to the supporters of Hecker carried on bravely for their friends. For example, the San Francisco *Monitor* of November 19, which operated under the vigilant eye of Archbishop Riordan, hailed Gibbons, Ireland, and Keane as "the three noble representatives of an ecclesiastical method from which Rome has derived such profit."

Before long there was more substantial reassurance from the Eternal City for Cardinal Gibbons. Keane had arrived back in Rome and immediately had an interview with Rampolla who repeated to him that Leo XIII had taken the matter into his own hands and that nothing hurtful to American interests would be done. Keane stated that the protests sent in to the Holy See, and especially the letter of Gibbons, had done their work and the Pope now saw the seriousness of the situation and had withdrawn the case from those who, according to Keane, "were rejoicing in having it all their own way." The Pontiff had appointed a special commission to study the question and to report to him, and this

[165] ADR, Magnien to O'Connell, Baltimore, October 18, 1898.
[166] ACUA, Bouquillon Papers, Ireland to Magnien, St. Paul, November 6, 1898.
[167] *Ibid.*, Ireland to Magnien, St. Paul, November 8, 1898.

was considered in Rome as a defeat for the extremists who had been pursuing the so-called Americanists. Keane had that day had a visit from Serafino Vannutelli and the latter had related to him that in a recent audience he had asked Leo XIII not to publish the sentence against the book of their friend, Father Zahm, *Evolution and Dogma,* which had appeared two years before, and the Pope had granted his request. Furthermore, the Holy Father had outlined for Vannutelli the encyclical he was preparing on Americanism, saying it would touch on Church and State, individualism, and religious vows but, added Keane, "As to each, only the familiar warning not to represent the contingently useful as the *ideal.* So we hope there is no danger ahead."[168]

Some of the same information was confirmed a month later to Elliott by Monsignor O'Connell, but he enlarged upon it to say that during the vacation period everything was prepared for the condemnation of Hecker and the decree was actually placed on the Pope's desk for his signature. "Just at that time, however," he wrote, "a letter came from Card. Gibbons that 'shook him.' " When the Pontiff was pressed to sign he refused and announced that he would from then on handle the case personally. It was O'Connell's opinion, mistaken as it turned out, that Leo XIII's desire to do nothing to displease the Americans, plus his fear that Spain would resent compliments to its recent conqueror, had determined him not to publish a letter at all on Americanism.[169] It would seem clear, therefore, that if Gibbons' protest of the previous August had not brought the peaceful settlement for which he had hoped, it had at least given the Pope pause and had played a major part in preventing the condemnation of Hecker which had been drawn up by the opposition.

There had been, then, ample notice for some time that the Pope was preparing an encyclical on the controverted question.

---

[168] 96-S-8, Keane to Gibbons, Rome, November 9, 1898. On Zahm cf. Thomas F. O'Connor, "John A. Zahm, C.S.C. Scientist and Americanist," *The Americas,* VII (April, 1951), 435–462.

[169] APF, O'Connell to Elliott, Paris, December 10, 1898. Shortly before Christmas Gibbons was told by J. E. C. Bodley that the bogey of Americanism was still disturbing many of the French clergy. A good priest had recently visited Bodley and confided to him his misgivings about the American Church. Bodley happened to have a photograph of Gibbons which he showed to his visitor, and he told the cardinal that evidently the priest thought an American cardinal must be a desperate looking person, for in viewing the picture with evident relief he told Bodley, "Cependant il a l'air très doux" (96-U-6, Bodley to Gibbons, Biarritz, December 22, 1898).

The uneasiness felt over what it might contain had prompted Archbishop Ireland to make a hurried trip to Rome with a view to stopping it entirely if he could, and if that failed, at least exercising his influence concerning its contents. Yet in the end he did not succeed in either aim. According to the later testimony of Ireland and Keane, the special commission appointed by Leo XIII to draw up the document consisted of Cardinals Mazzella and Satolli and the original draft was a strong condemnation of Americanism. The Pope, however, softened its language and rewrote the beginning and the end in a way that took much of the sting out of it. On January 22, 1899, the Pontiff affixed his signature to the famous *Testem benevolentiae* and ten days later a copy of it was forwarded to Cardinal Gibbons by Rampolla.[170] Gibbons, of course, had been kept informed of the efforts to prevent the letter from being sent, and at the last minute he had added his own endeavor by cabling Rampolla to suspend its publication. In reply he was told that his cablegram had come too late since some copies had already been sent to other American bishops. Moreover, Rampolla added that the Pope could no longer delay in making his mind known on the subject, in view of the controversies which were raging among the Catholics of France and which were likely to create further dissension and division. "Rest assured then," he said, "that when Your Eminence sees the letter you will be immediately freed of any misgiving and will be perfectly satisfied."[171]

That frantic attempts had been made to head off *Testem benevolentiae* was certain. Keane conveyed the story to Magnien when he wrote:

> The sky has been full of *storm* these last two weeks. Ten fold efforts were made and the letter is gone! And gone under circumstances which show that they dodged and deceived Ireland. Rampolla told him it had not been sent; but between that evening and Ireland's seeing the Pope three or four days later, it had been sent! We have done our utmost, as you know, even now to hinder its publication, — but all signs indicate that they will be obstinate and we will fail. We have the consolation of knowing that we did our full duty. The blow will, I fear, be a sad one for the Paulists & for the memory of Hecker, and a blow to the Cardinal and Ireland who wrote in their

---

[170] 97-C-3, Rampolla to Gibbons, January 31, 1899.
[171] 97-D-1, same to same, February 9, 1899.

behalf. We must simply make the best of it, and carry on our game of explaining away to the American people the administrative blunders of our superiors.[172]

Two weeks later Archbishop Ireland furnished the Paulist superior-general with added details about how the Jesuits, Dominicans, and Redemptorists fought for very life to save the papal letter, and how a letter of congratulation from Archbishop Corrigan to Lepidi for the latter's *imprimatur* on Maignen's book was again and again, as he expressed it, "flung into my face." The Corrigan letter enabled the opposition to contend that the American hierarchy was divided on the question which naturally strengthened their position. True, Rampolla had told Ireland that the Pope had toned down the document in a way that would permit it to be said that the things condemned were never uttered or written in the United States, but all this offered small comfort to the Archbishop of St. Paul. He remarked to Deshon, "Fanatics conjured up an 'Americanism,' & put such before the Pope. Lepidi & Mazzella wrote the body of the letter. I cannot pray that God forgive them."[173]

Meanwhile the press got wind of the papal letter and Gibbons was approached by a reporter for his reaction, but the Baltimore *Sun* of February 23 informed its readers that until the text was published the cardinal had no comment to make on the subject. Two days later the *Catholic Mirror* of Baltimore carried the Latin and English texts of *Testem benevolentiae,* but not before its issue of March 11 was Gibbons' archdiocesan paper much more enlightening on the question of the encyclical. At that time it published Ireland's Roman statement of February 22 in which he had repudiated all the ideas condemned by Leo XIII, and said that all the bishops and faithful of the United States were ready to do the same. "We cannot but be indignant," said Ireland, "that such a wrong was done to us — to us bishops, to our faithful, to our nation — as to designate by the word Americanism,

---

172 ACUA, Bouquillon Papers, Keane to Magnien, Rome, February 11, 1899.

173 APF, Ireland to Deshon, Rome, February 24, 1899. Bishop Spalding expressed his sympathy for Elliott after the papal letter was published, but he was annoyed at the renewed talk of a red hat for Ireland. He told Daniel Hudson, C.S.C., "It is again announced that Abp. Ireland is to be made Cardinal. I should be glad to see him made anything that would keep him silent" (AUND, Hudson Papers, Spalding to Hudson, Peoria, March 1, 1899, photostat).

as some have done, errors and extravagances of this kind."[174]

What actually had Pope Leo XIII written in the letter of January 22 which he had addressed to the Cardinal of Baltimore? At the outset he stated that he had never ceased to profess a devoted affection for the Church in this country; yet it was not his present purpose to repeat the praise he had previously given but rather to point out certain things that were to be avoided and corrected. The life of Father Hecker, he wrote, had excited controversy on the score of opinions about the manner of leading a Christian life, but the difficulty over the biography had arisen, as the Holy Father expressed it, "chiefly through the action of those who have undertaken to publish and interpret it in a foreign language. . . ."[175] The principles on which these false opinions, under the heading of Americanism, were based reduced themselves to this, that the Church ought to adapt itself to advanced civilization, relax its ancient rigor, and show indulgence to modern popular theories and methods. There was a danger that the followers of these novelties judged that a greater liberty ought to be introduced into the Church in such a way that the exercise and vigilance of the Church's powers would be limited and each individual could then act more freely in pursuance of his own natural bent and capacity.

Stemming from these broad principles there were certain faulty conclusions drawn by some which the Pope declared were worthy of condemnation. He listed these as follows: first, that all external guidance should be rejected as superfluous for those who desired to devote themselves to the acquisition of Christian perfection; second, that the natural virtues should be extolled much more than formerly since they were in accordance with the ways and requirements of the present age; third, that the virtues

---

[174] Ireland's repudiation of the existence of the errors in the name of all aroused the ire of Archbishop Katzer and his suffragans who signed a letter to Leo XIII at Pentecost, 1899, accepting the fact that such errors did exist in the American Church, and expressing their pain and indignation that some did not hesitate to deny them. The letter of the bishops of the Province of Milwaukee was published in the *Tablet* of London on July 22, 1899. Archbishop Corrigan of New York, writing in the name of himself and his suffragans, thanked the Pontiff for saving the American Catholic faithful from the threatened errors in a way that made it clear that he, too, felt they were a reality. The Corrigan letter was printed *ibid.*, May 20, 1899. These letters appearing in English in the *Tablet* were translations of the original Latin or Italian which had appeared first in the *Civiltà Cattolica*.

[175] Wynne, *op. cit.*, pp. 441–442.

should be divided into active and passive, although the Pontiff insisted that there was not and could not be such a thing as a passive virtue; fourth, as a consequence of these attitudes there ensued a growing disdain for the religious life which showed itself in the expressions which advocates of these opinions used in regard to the vows taken by members of religious orders as being out of keeping with the spirit of the age and narrowing the limits of human liberty. "Hence," said Leo XIII, "from all that we have hitherto said, it is clear, Beloved Son, that we cannot approve the opinions which some comprise under the head of Americanism."[176]

However, if under the name of Americanism there should be designated the characteristic qualities which reflected honor on the people of the United States, just as other nations had special characteristics; or if there were implied the institutions, laws, and customs which prevailed in this country, then, said the Pope, surely there was no reason why these should be questioned or discarded. The Pontiff expressed his confidence that the bishops of the United States would be the first to repudiate and condemn as unjust to them and to their nation the ideas which he had outlined for censure, since these ideas raised the suspicion that there were, as he expressed it, "some among you who conceive and desire a church in America different from that which is in the rest of the world."[177] Although the papal letter had, therefore, clearly set forth the doctrines which the Holy Father censured, he had nowhere explicitly stated that these were held by American Catholics, and he had pointedly excluded from his consideration the political and social qualities of the people of the United States which were ordinarily meant in using the term "Americanism."

With the publication of *Testem benevolentiae* the Abbé Klein and the sincere Catholics among the French Americanists quickly submitted, the French edition of Hecker's biography was withdrawn, and as one historian has said, "theological Americanism was dead."[178] There were, it is true, some aftertones in the French press and periodicals but in Europe the storm subsided after a time.[179] But the wounds were a bit harder to heal in the

---

[176] *Ibid.*, p. 452.

[177] *Ibid.*

[178] McAvoy, *op. cit.*, p. 146, Klein published his own letter of submission of February 28, 1899, in his memoirs, *op. cit.*, p. 381.

[179] Cf. e.g., "A propos Américanisme," by Saint-Roman, *La Quinzaine*, XXVII

United States. From the first intimation that the papal letter had been sent to Cardinal Gibbons speculation was rife as to how he would receive it. For example, the *Catholic Citizen* of Milwaukee on February 25 noted the publication of the letter to Gibbons in the *Osservatore Romano,* which led them to wonder why there had been no word from the cardinal. The Milwaukee editor thought that the publication in the Vatican newspaper was either a discourtesy to Gibbons, for which an apology was owed, or it was an implied censure of him for withholding the letter from his people. Actually Gibbons' copy of *Testem benevolentiae* had arrived in Baltimore on February 16 and, as he explained to Monsignor O'Connell, it was the cabled abstracts from the *Osservatore Romano* published in the United States on February 22 that prompted him to release the text to the Baltimore *Sun* for its issue of the following day. Gibbons withheld the letter for a week, and it was the appearance of abbreviated versions of the text in the American newspapers which decided him to order a translation and full publication. What the cardinal really thought of the papal document we can gather from his statement to O'Connell. He wrote:

> It has excited scarcely any comment in the secular papers, & the Cath. papers as far as received have little to say about it except that they don't see its application to our country. Of course a few Cath. papers — badly disposed — will very probably make much ado about it. An abstract of Abp. Ireland's adhesion was published. It was, I think, timely, & I am glad he so cordially accepted it. But it is very discouraging to us that the American Church is not understood abroad, & that its enemies are listened to, & that they can lie with impunity. I do not think that any of the questions discussed was a living question here. But I suppose the H. Father had to act.[180]

It was apparent that Cardinal Gibbons regretted *Testem benevolentiae,* and it was doubtless for that reason that he maintained a complete silence on the subject insofar as the public was concerned. He could not, however, ignore the duty of an acknowledgment of the letter, and thus for a month he thought over the answer he would make and consulted with his

---

(March 1, 1899), 65–84, and George Fonsegrive, "Américanisme et Américains," *ibid.* (April 1, 1899), 306–318.

[180] ADR, Gibbons to O'Connell, Baltimore, March 2, 1899.

advisers before he addressed himself to Leo XIII. On March 17 his reply was ready and was dispatched to the Holy See. It read as follows:

> The letter in which Your Holiness reproves the errors which certain persons have represented under the name of Americanism reached me towards the middle of February. I had an English translation made which I published along with the Latin text.
>
> My feelings are too well known to Your Holiness for me to have to say that I thank you with my whole heart for having cast light on all these questions, which, in circles outside the United States, certain people seemed to enjoy complicating during the past year, but which in this country count for nothing in public opinion.
>
> This doctrine, which I deliberately call extravagant and absurd, this Americanism as it has been called, has nothing in common with the views, aspirations, doctrine and conduct of Americans. I do not think that there can be found in the entire country a bishop, a priest, or even a layman with a knowledge of his religion who has ever uttered such enormities. No, that is not — it never has been and never will be — our Americanism. I am deeply grateful to Your Holiness for having yourself made this distinction in your apostolic letter.
>
> I wanted to write at once to Your Holiness to thank you for this new act of kindness in our regard, but I preferred to wait in order to judge the effect which the papal document would have on public opinion and in particular on American Catholics. I am happy, Most Holy Father, to be able to tell you that the attitude which has been expressed, while mixed with certain surprise that such doctrines could have been attributed to American Catholics, has been one of the most profound respect for the mind of the Holy See, of lively gratitude for the kindness which you show us, of sincere appreciation for the distinction which Your Holiness so justly makes between the doctrines which we, along with you, reject, and those feelings of love for our country and its institutions which we share with our fellow citizens and which are such a powerful aid in accomplishing our work for the glory of God and the honor of Holy Church.[181]

---

[181] 97-E-8/1, Gibbons to Leo XIII, Baltimore, March 17, 1899, copy in French. The French original was published in the *Catholic Historical Review,* XXX (October, 1944), 347–348. Two weeks before Archbishop Williams had asked Gibbons, "In regard to the Pope's letter to Your Eminence, will you answer for all of us, or is it in order for us all to send an answer?" (97-E-1, Williams to Gibbons, Boston, March 3, 1899.) An effort to find Gibbons' reply in the AABo was unsuccessful.

Gibbons' letter spoke for itself. In polite and measured words he not only repudiated the false doctrines but he pointedly located their origin outside the United States, while the Pope's distinction between the errors which he condemned under the head of Americanism and the legitimate patriotism which the cardinal and his fellow Catholics felt for their country, won his gratitude. The Pontiff was also thanked for his fatherly guidance and there was no doubt that Gibbons appreciated the polite and considerate manner in which Leo XIII had phrased his counsels. Basically there was no conflict between the Pope's letter and the cardinal's reply, but the fact that the Holy See employed the term "Americanism" to designate the errors probably accounted for some of the disappointment which Gibbons experienced over the incident. He was at pains to state in his acknowledgment that the errors which had been censured did not exist in the American Church, and in this instance as in many others it was ultimately shown that the Cardinal of Baltimore understood the Church of his own land far better than some American prelates who sought to direct the policy of Rome toward American affairs.

The entire incident had proved a painful experience for Cardinal Gibbons and he had not yet seen the end of it. On March 16, 1899, the *Independent* of New York published a spurious interview which Gibbons was supposed to have granted three years before to Victor Charbonnel, an apostate French priest previously mentioned, in which the cardinal was quoted as having given his approval to mixed religious congresses, and at the same time voiced his criticism of the Church for having become a bureau of administrators instead of a group of apostles. Along with several more remarks of a like kind, reflecting unfavorably on Cardinal Richard and the French clergy, this incredible tale was reprinted on March 23 by Arthur Preuss, Catholic editor of the *Review* of St. Louis, accompanied by the editorial challenge, "We confidently expect His Eminence of Baltimore to give the lie to M. Charbonnel." It mattered little that Preuss professed not to believe the story, since his open hostility to the so-called Americanists during the recent controversy made it appear as a thrust at the cardinal.

In the *Review* of April 6 Archbishop Kain of St. Louis sharply chastised Preuss for publishing the supposed interview and said he had heard from Gibbons' own lips a denunciation of Charbonnel's lies even before the priest had apostatized. Likewise William Henry Thorne, convert editor of the *Globe,* was critical of Gibbons for not making public his answer to Leo XIII on Americanism, and although he, too, credited the cardinal with being pure minded and loyal to all the Church's dogmas, he maintained that for years Gibbons had been writing on Americanism in the manner of what he termed "a sort of 'me too Platt,' or undersecretary of the Archbishop of St. Paul."[182] As late as the summer of that year Preuss was still ruminating about the failure of Gibbons to make public his reply to the Pope on *Testem benevolentiae,* and in his issue of August 3 he stated that if the *Catholic Mirror* of Baltimore had, perchance, closed its columns to the cardinal, he would suggest that he use the *Review,* "than whose editor," he wrote, "despite Archbishop Kain, His Eminence has not a more well-meaning nor stauncher friend in all this blessed land."

Yet in the face of this severe provocation Cardinal Gibbons held his peace and said nothing for publication. Meanwhile plans were maturing for the annual meeting of the archbishops which was scheduled to assemble at the Catholic University of America on October 12. Nine of the fourteen metropolitans were present, but among the missing was Archbishop Katzer of Milwaukee. The Archbishop of San Francisco called attention to the letter of the bishops of the Province of Milwaukee of the previous Pentecost in which they had admitted to Leo XIII the existence of the errors outlined in *Testem benevolentiae.* Riordan and Kain felt the Milwaukee letter called for a protest in view of the fact that it constituted a direct charge of heresy on the part of some Americans. Ireland also deprecated it and moved that the entire hierarchy be asked to give an answer to two questions, namely, whether the errors existed in their dioceses or in other parts of

---

[182] "Was the Pope Fooled on Americanism?" *Globe,* IX (June, 1899), 132. The expression "Me too" owed its origin to an incident in May, 1881, when Roscoe Conkling, senior senator from New York, got into a dispute over control of the patronage in New York State. Thomas Platt, the junior senator from New York, whose fortunes were closely linked to those of Conkling, proposed that they both resign and stand for re-election by the state legislature as the best means of reasserting their power. The affair inspired Tom Nast, the cartoonist, to show Conkling strolling about with his head in his hand and Platt was following up behind in a similar pose and crying out "Me too," Matthew Josephson, *The Politicos, 1865-1896* (New York, 1938), p. 314.

the country and, second, if they did, to specify where they existed and by whom they were held. But Archbishop Corrigan was strongly opposed to Ireland's motion as disrespectful of the Holy See, a view which was shared by the Archbishop of Philadelphia. Ryan then offered a substitute motion that all the American bishops who had not yet written to the Pope on Americanism should do so. Ryan's substitute motion was lost by a tie and when Ireland's stronger resolution was put to a vote it was defeated five to four with Gibbons casting his vote against it.[183]

Officially speaking, therefore, the American controversy was closed in the United States and the cardinal had cast the vote that decided no further action should be taken on the subject by the American hierarchy. John Ireland was not pleased with the outcome. He told Denis O'Connell that Riordan, Kain, Alexander Christie of Oregon City, and himself had tried hard to push through a joint protest against the idea of existing doctrinal errors in the American Church but, as he expressed it, "Baltimore cried 'peace, peace, death even for the sake of peace' — and nothing was effected."[184] The cardinal had had more than enough of the problem, and not even the weighty pressure of his friend from St. Paul could shake him in his resolve not to reopen the case with Rome.

The ineffectiveness of his efforts to prevent the publication of *Testem benevolentiae* caused the Archbishop of Baltimore to undergo a temporary discouragement in regard to his relations with the Vatican. Early in November Keane reported to O'Connell that the cardinal was still steadfast on what Keane called "the burning questions," but as for Gibbons' attitude toward the Holy See, he remarked, "he is hopeless as to Roman conditions, & determined to waste no more words there."[185] Some weeks later the state of mind of the cardinal was described as serene and peaceful, and in reflecting the current rumors about Leo XIII's declining health, Keane added concerning Gibbons, "Nothing in Rome interests him save the coming end, — and

---

[183] 97-R-5, Minutes of the Meeting of the Archbishops, Washington, October 12, 1899.

[184] ADR, Ireland to O'Connell, New York, October 21, 1899.

[185] *Ibid.*, Keane to O'Connell, Baltimore, November 3, 1899.

the escape from what the papers first stated, Satolli's appointment as Vicar."[186]

But while Gibbons had, indeed, reasons for feeling depressed about his failure to win the Vatican to his way of thinking on Americanism, elsewhere there were elements in the situation which cheered him. In the summer of 1899 the *North American Review* published an article by the English church historian, William Barry, in which he reviewed the controversy in a manner altogether to the liking of the so-called Americanists. Barry stated that it would be to the everlasting honor of men like Gibbons, Ireland, and Keane that they had shown the world how they could be at once fervent Catholics and loyal Americans. "They can afford to be misunderstood," said Barry, "while their work prospers. But henceforth, though many assail, none will misunderstand them."[187] And when the Rector of the Catholic Institute of Paris published an unfriendly essay in the same journal the following March,[188] he was answered by one writing under the name of Etheridge who effectively demolished the Frenchman's arguments in a lengthy review of the whole case which ended with the summary judgment, "In Europe, Americanism was cradled as well as entombed; in America, it was unknown until it was condemned."[189] Articles like those of Barry and Etheridge appearing in one of the leading periodicals of the United States did much to put the matter in its proper light before the American public, a service which was appreciated by none more than the Cardinal of Baltimore.

Amid all the tension which marked the closing phases of the

---

[186] *Ibid.*, Keane to O'Connell, Washington, Christmas Day, 1899.

[187] " 'Americanism,' True and False," CLXIX (July, 1899), 48.

[188] P. L. Péchenard, "The End of 'Americanism' in France," CLXX (March, 1900), 420–432.

[189] J. St. Clair Etheridge, "The Genesis of 'Americanism,' " *North American Review,* CLXX (May, 1900), 693. Ireland, to whom the authorship of this article has been attributed, e.g., McAvoy, *op. cit.,* p. 134, was delighted with it. He told Denis O'Connell it could have been written only by one who had been on the inside, that the information was most exact, and that only diligent research could have accounted for several details. He said, "If you know the writer, give him my most sincere compliments" (ADR, Ireland to O'Connell, St. Paul, May 7, 1900). Unless Ireland was speaking facetiously, therefore, it would appear to be an error to assign the article to his authorship. The *North American Review* ceased publication with the winter number of 1939–1940 and an effort to trace the authorship through the office of the journal was unsuccessful.

controversy over Americanism the cardinal never wavered in the support he gave to those who were in the front line of battle. When, for example, a newspaper correspondent cabled from Rome that there was a doubt about Ireland delivering the panegyric on Joan of Arc at Orléans which had been announced to take place on May 8, Gibbons was quick to tell O'Connell, "He should *not* decline. A false interpretation would be put on his declination."[190] He was thoroughly pleased that Ireland carried out the engagement at Orléans and that he received so cordial a reception from other speeches delivered that summer. Gibbons, according to Keane, was delighted and was speaking warmly about Ireland's trip in Europe.[191] Nor was there a prouder American than the Archbishop of Baltimore in the following year when President McKinley chose John Ireland to be the spokesman of the United States at the unveiling of the statue of Lafayette which this country presented as a token of gratitude to France. Ireland's stirring address at Paris on July 4, 1900, delivered in French before the immense throng gathered in the Place du Carrousel, was filled with ringing phrases in praise of the French and American democratic way of life, sentiments which Gibbons shared with all his heart.[192] And later that summer when Ireland was invited by Leo XIII to give an address in Rome in the presence of the Pope and many members of the College of Cardinals, Gibbons remarked with gratification that it had attracted much attention in the United States. "It is an extraordinary honor," he said, "& I am anxious to have some details which the Abp. will probably send me."[193] Upon his return to this country in the autumn

---

[190] ADR, Gibbons to O'Connell, Baltimore, March 2, 1899. Ireland's sermon in the cathedral of Orléans can be found in his *The Church and Modern Society,* II, 31–65.

[191] *Ibid.,* Keane to O'Connell, Baltimore, November 3, 1899.

[192] For the text cf. Ireland, *op. cit.,* II, 9–28. John M. Hay, McKinley's Secretary of State, in congratulating Ireland on his selection by the President wrote, "No more eminent representative of American eloquence and patriotism could have been chosen" (LC, McKinley Papers, Hay to Ireland, undated, copy). The archbishop had received a letter from McKinley designating him to speak at Paris on July 4. He thanked the President and said, "Such a letter did me great honor before France and all Europe. Its good effects I feel very sensibly here in Rome" (LC, McKinley Papers, Ireland to McKinley, Rome, August 3, 1900).

[193] ADR, Gibbons to O'Connell. This was contained in the postscript of a letter the first page of which was lost. The fact that Gibbons mentioned the

Ireland visited the cardinal in Baltimore where he was pictured as overjoyed to see and hear him. Apparently the archbishop had inspired Gibbons with a brighter prospect over his relations with the Holy See, for Ireland remarked: "He will now surely go to Rome early in [the] spring to see for himself how much good his letter on 'Americanism' did. He is a new man."[194]

In the same manner that he stood behind Ireland, the cardinal upheld the cause of Archbishop Keane. Following the death of Archbishop Gross of Oregon City on November 14, 1898, he wrote a strong recommendation of Keane for the vacant see to Cardinal Ledochowski.[195] However, it was later decided by all Keane's friends that he could be of more service to the American Church in Rome at that time than he would be in Oregon and for that reason his name was withdrawn.[196] But a year and some months later the death of John Hennessy, Archbishop of Dubuque, on March 4, 1900, created another opening in the United States, and by this time conditions had so changed that all were agreed Keane should now be given a chance to return to his native land. With that in mind Cardinal Gibbons again addressed himself to Ledochowski, Prefect of the Propaganda, in Keane's behalf,[197] and on the same day he signed a lengthy appeal to Rampolla, Secretary of State, begging him to use his influence with the Pope to have Keane appointed to Dubuque.

Gibbons not only here reminded Rampolla of the promise given to Keane in 1896 that he would be appointed to an American see if his name appeared on the *terna,* but he quoted the exact words

---

obsequies for Humbert I of Italy would place its date soon after the assassination of the king on July 29, 1900. A year later Gibbons was in Rome and on the eve of his departure from the Eternal City he described his visit for Ireland. He spoke of his farewell audience of Leo XIII and he said, "He referred in glowing terms to your address before himself and the Cardinals, 'They said,' he remarked, 'that the Abp. was a liberal, but I told him to express his mind and we were delighted with his words' " (AASP, Gibbons to Ireland, Rome, June 20, 1901, copy).

194 ADR, Ireland to O'Connell, St. Paul, October 27, 1900.

195 97-B-9, Gibbons to Ledochowski, Baltimore, January 24, 1899, copy in French.

196 Keane recounted to Magnien the reasons why he should not leave Rome. He said, "While I would rather be in the humblest parish in the U. S. than in Rome, still I could not desert a post of duty simply because it was disagreeable." But he wished to repeat his gratitude to those who had worked, as he expressed it, "for my release from a painful situation" (ACUA, Bouquillon Papers, Keane to Magnien, Rome, February 11, 1899).

197 98-D-6, Gibbons to Ledochowski, Baltimore, April 15, 1900, copy in Latin.

of Leo XIII so that there would be no doubt about it. He stated further that Keane had already suffered much and he was still suffering from the position in which he found himself. While public opinion over his removal from the university had now calmed, nonetheless, there were many who did not understand why he was held so long in a situation which they regarded as humiliating for the archbishop, painful to many Americans, and vexatious for the welfare of the Church.[198] But the Holy See was not to be hurried, and it was not until September 12, his sixty-first birthday, that John Keane received official notification that he had been appointed second Archbishop of Dubuque. Thus one of the principal figures in the controversy over Americanism and one of Gibbons' closest friends had at last been vindicated after four years of practical exile during which he had undergone many severe trials.

By the turn of the century the last great internal struggle within the Catholic Church of the United States had for the most part run its course. Its origins lay far back in the century when the enormous influx of foreign-born Catholics raised tensions between various national groups and caused mutual embitterment over such questions as separate national parishes and foreign language schools for the children of the immigrants. Father Hecker and those who admired him like Gibbons, Ireland, and Keane were intent on the Americanization of the foreign-born Catholics. They were, moreover, convinced of the high destiny of the Church in this country and the favorable auspices which the democratic institutions of the United States afforded for the spread of the Catholic faith. The impressive strength which the American Church showed by the late century seemed in many ways to bear out their hopes, and in the power which American Catholicism revealed many of the harassed Catholics of Europe felt they had found a pattern worth following. That the enthusiasm of the progressive American churchmen may at times have carried them away and been responsible for action and words which were open to misinterpretation abroad, was true enough. But the effort which they were making to cultivate friendly relations with their non-Catholic fellow citizens, to attract converts to the Church, and to maintain cordial relations with the State contained nothing that was heretical. As

---

[198] 98-U-6, Gibbons to Rampolla, Baltimore, April 15, 1900, copy in French.

we have seen, it was the action of certain Catholics in Europe which made of Americanism something which gave to it an altogether novel meaning and turned it into a channel which was never intended by those whom they assailed.

In all of this Cardinal Gibbons never allowed himself to be intimidated or frightened off from the strong Americanism which he had always professed. To the cardinal the interpretation which was put upon the term in Europe was a distortion and an aberration of everything he understood and felt as an American Catholic. Through all the heated controversy he did his best to explain the issues and motives involved to the Holy See, to defend those most unfairly attacked, and to set at rest all doubts about the doctrinal orthodoxy of men whose integrity and soundness he highly esteemed. He waged a vigorous campaign to prevent the question from being given the dignity of a papal pronouncement, and in this he failed.[199] But the answer he returned to Leo XIII on *Testem benevolentiae* made it apparent that he had not retreated from his original position, even if he thanked the Pope for his solicitude in behalf of the American faithful. And it was only three years later that the Pontiff himself gave testimony to the reality of the exalted vision which Gibbons and his friends had entertained of the Church in this country. In the spring of 1902 Leo XIII celebrated the silver jubilee of his pontificate and at that time the cardinal addressed a letter of congratulations to him on March 2 in the name of the entire American hierarchy.[200] In acknowledgment of the congratulations the Holy Father replied on April 15 with the highest praise for the Church of the United States, and in referring to the suffering which the Church was then undergoing in Europe he spoke words which not only gladdened the hearts of all American Catholics, but which showed, too, that far from there being any lingering shadow over the Church of this land, its condition had become a source of consolation to the old Pontiff

---

[199] In the spring of 1901 Gibbons visited Rome and was very warmly received at the Holy See. It would please his friend in St. Paul when he learned of it, for Archbishop Ireland had recently referred to Gibbons' Roman journey and had remarked to Denis O'Connell, "I hope the Cardinal is well treated, & is happy. It were too bad if this were not so. He battled bravely when the Peries-Brandi wave was rolling over us, & he deserves to taste the joys of victory" (ADR, Ireland to O'Connell, New York, June 7, 1901).

[200] New York *Freeman's Journal*, May 10, 1902.

amid his many sorrows. On that occasion Leo XIII told Cardinal Gibbons and his colleagues:

> . . . Our daily experience obliges Us to confess that We have found your people, through your influence, endowed with perfect docility of mind and alacrity of disposition. Therefore, while the changes and the tendencies of nearly all the nations which were Catholic for many centuries give cause for sorrow, the state of your churches, in this flourishing youthfulness, cheers Our heart and fills it with delight.[201]

---

[201] Wynne, *op. cit.*, p. 514.

CHAPTER XVII

War and Its Aftermath

AT THE very time that Catholic theological circles in Europe were fretting over the problem of Americanism, there occurred an event which did more to focus the attention of the world upon the power and might of the United States than any previous fact in its history. Informed men everywhere had long been aware of the growing strength of the great Republic of the West, but it took the sudden and stunning victory of the United States over Spain in 1898, to convince them that a new world power had been born and that henceforth they would have to reckon with it seriously. This was Americanism of another variety, and those who had the responsibility for the conduct of international affairs found the new phenomenon no more to their liking than had some European theologians when they thought they had discovered heresy in the Catholic Church of the United States. Here was Manifest Destiny in a far more strident form than the imperialist ambitions for an Oregon boundary line or a province in Mexican California that had characterized the 1840's. The nation which had easily beaten an enfeebled Mexico and had won so vast a gain of territory in 1848 — only to suffer the humiliation of an enervating civil war a few years later — had within a generation more than regained its losses from that internal conflict, and in a few swift blows it had humbled Spain and cast an uneasy spell over the chancelleries of the old world which a few years before they would have thought impossible.

To be sure, there was no direct connection between the theological controversy over Americanism which reached its climax in Leo XIII's *Testem benevolentiae* of January 22, 1899, and the Spanish-American War which ended six weeks before in the treaty signed at Paris on December 10, 1898. Yet the coincidence of the American victory served to strengthen the impression among European churchmen and diplomats alike that a dangerous force was loose in the world and that it would need watching. In the eyes of some European Catholics, the bluster that had accompanied American reaction to theological criticism resembled the spirit of bravado with which Americans greeted their country's triumph over Catholic Spain and its entry into the race for world empire.

We have seen enough of the character of Cardinal Gibbons to appreciate the quality of his patriotism and the constant interest which he took in his country's welfare. But his love for his native land never blinded him to its defects, nor did it permit him to step out of his role as a religious leader to assume an aggressive and belligerent attitude in pressing the advantage of the United States at a time of crisis. Only three weeks after his ordination to the priesthood in the summer of 1861, when Americans were still in the early stages of the Civil War, he preached one of his first sermons on the subject of peace on July 21 in St. Joseph's Church in Baltimore. He dwelt upon the spiritual nature of peace, deplored the war, and stated that many causes had been assigned by statesmen for the conflict then raging, but he continued, "if we seek for the true & primary cause we will find it to consist in the sins of the nation."[1] Although his conduct during the next four years, as we have seen, was in every way admirable as a citizen of the North, he never lost sight of the fact that as a minister of religion his first duty was, insofar as he was able, to bind up the wounds in the souls and bodies of those in his charge, and to hasten by every means available to him the end of the unfortunate conflict which had divided his countrymen. It was a policy to which Gibbons steadfastly adhered during the next sixty years whenever the United States was at war.

A generation after the Civil War when the Archbishop of Baltimore had attained a national reputation among Americans, his support was solicited in the interests of a peaceful enterprise by Leo XIII's Secretary of State. Cardinal Rampolla asked him to use his influence to win the adherence of the United States to the Brussels Act for the elimination of the slave trade which had been signed on July 2, 1890, at the close of an international conference in the Belgian capital.[2] Gibbons explained to Rampolla

[1] 71-D-5, handwritten copy of the sermon on "Peace" which was preached in a revised form in the cathedral of Baltimore on Low Sunday, 1866.
[2] 88-L-2, Rampolla to Gibbons, Rome, March 11, 1891.

that the failure of the United States to ratify the act had been occasioned by no lack of good will; it was due rather to the pressure of work which confronted Congress at the time. In the short session which was scheduled for December, 1891, it would be brought up and then, said the cardinal, he would make prudent use of every means in his power to win the adherence of his country to the act for the extirpation of the traffic in slaves.[3] The senate at length approved the act on January 11, 1892, and it was ratified by the President a week later. The Cardinal of Baltimore promptly informed Rampolla of this action, and, without specifying the nature of his personal efforts, he said that he had not ceased to watch the progress of the matter and to employ whatever means were at his disposal to exercise a favorable influence over the outcome.[4]

Three years after the American ratification of the Brussels Act a serious dispute arose between Great Britain and Venezuela over the boundary between the latter country and British Guiana. The British and American newspapers took up the quarrel and fanned it to white heat, while the respective governments were exchanging sharp notes between Washington and London over their varying interpretations of the Monroe Doctrine. On December 17, 1895, President Cleveland delivered a spirited message to Congress in which he gave a strong reaffirmation of the American point of view, and by the close of the year matters looked really serious. On Christmas Eve the New York *World* telegraphed to Cardinal Gibbons for a statement of his views which they published the following day. Gibbons maintained that a war between Britain and the United States would be a calamity to the world and to Christian civilization and that there was no ground for an apprehension of war. "I regard the strictures on Mr. Cleveland's message by some American and English papers," said the cardinal, "as unjust and unwarranted, since he has shown himself a man of peace and conservative principles during both administrations." To Gibbons' mind the warlike interpretations put on Cleveland's message to Congress were forced, and the dispute, he felt, would

---

[3] 88-M-2, Gibbons to Rampolla, Baltimore, April 9, 1891, copy in French.
[4] 89-L-5, Gibbons to Rampolla, Baltimore, January 28, 1892, copy in French. A few weeks later the Belgian minister to the United States extended the official thanks of his government to Gibbons for the part he had played in behalf of American ratification (89-Q-10, Edouard Le Ghait to Gibbons, Washington, March 7, 1892).

be honorably settled, "not by the sword but by a mightier weapon — the pen."

The Venezuela boundary dispute threw a real scare into the hearts of all peace-loving people throughout the English-speaking world. Although the crisis eventually passed it served to emphasize the need for a tribunal of arbitration for differences of this kind between the United States and Great Britain. In this movement Cardinal Vaughan, Archbishop of Westminster, took a lively interest. Vaughan suggested to Gibbons that they issue a joint statement in favor of a tribunal of arbitration in the belief that the Catholic Church in both countries, united in sentiment upon the importance of substituting the use of reason for that of the sword, would have a salutary effect upon public opinion.[5] Gibbons agreed to join the English cardinal and meanwhile Vaughan got in touch with Michael Cardinal Logue, Archbishop of Armagh, who also expressed his willingness to sign such a statement.[6] Vaughan drafted the document and sent it for Gibbons' signature which the latter affixed. He returned it to Westminster with the understanding that it should be released on Easter Sunday.[7]

On April 5, 1896, the appeal of the three cardinals appeared in which they made their plea for a permanent tribunal of arbitration as a substitute among the English-speaking peoples for a resort to war. They recognized the practical difficulties with which such a project was beset, but they gave it as their belief that with good will such could be overcome. After outlining the advantages to be gained, the cardinals stated that the carrying out of the procedure for such a tribunal was, of course, the business of the respective governments, but since governments, as they said, were more and more becoming identified with the aspirations and desires of the people, their appeal in the first instance was addressed to the people. The statement explained the motive which had prompted the signers as representatives of the Prince of Peace and it closed by saying:

We therefore earnestly invite all to unite with us in pressing their

---

[5] 94-G-13, Vaughan to Gibbons, Westminster, January 18, 1896.

[6] 94-J-4, Vaughan to Gibbons, Westminster, February 24, 1896; 94-K-1, same to same, Westminster, March 3, 1896.

[7] Diary, March 6, 1896, p. 278. Gibbons remarked here that the statement was drafted by Vaughan.

convictions and desires upon their respective Governments by means of petitions and such other measures as are constitutional.[8]

The three cardinals were by no means alone at this time in their advocacy of a treaty of arbitration between the United States and Great Britain. In fact, the Venezuela affair had stirred up tremendous enthusiasm in behalf of an instrument of this kind for settling disputes between the two countries. As Vaughan told Gibbons two weeks after their statement had been issued, "I do not know that anything of a very important kind will be *done* by Governments; but all the same the Church has taken up a position of advantage before the world."[9] True, the Church had been put in its proper light by the joint appeal, although the statement of the cardinals had little if any effect upon the final outcome. Eventually tempers cooled on both sides of the Atlantic over the Venezuela affair, and when new and more threatening trouble arose for Britain among the Boers in South Africa, the London government agreed to accept the good offices of the United States as a mediator between itself and Venezuela. Through the late months of 1896 the dispute was gradually ironed out, and by the end of the year a settlement was in sight. Cardinal Gibbons followed the developments closely and when it appeared that an agreement had been reached he congratulated President Cleveland on what he called "the honorable & happy termination" of the Venezuela difficulty. "The opportuneness & wisdom of your message," said the cardinal, "are now recognized & applauded though at the time of its publication it raised a storm."[10] But the effort for an arbitration tribunal between the United States and Britain, although actually provided for in a treaty signed by the two powers on January 11, 1897, met with a hostile reception in the American senate. Despite a tremendous outpouring of sentiment in its behalf, the treaty failed to secure the necessary two-thirds majority when it was put to a vote on May 5 of that year.[11]

---

[8] 94-L-1, Statement of Cardinals Gibbons, Logue, and Vaughan, Easter Sunday, April 5, 1896.

[9] 94-L-7, Vaughan to Gibbons, Westminster, April 20, 1896.

[10] LC, Cleveland Papers, Gibbons to Cleveland, Baltimore, November 13, 1896.

[11] Cf. Thomas A. Bailey, *A Diplomatic History of the American People* (New York, 1942), pp. 477–492, for the background to the Venezuela dispute. When Gibbons was invited to attend a meeting in Washington on January 26, 1897, for the purpose of publicly attesting support of the arbitration treaty he regretted that a previous engagement would prevent him from being present, but he told

Two years before this happened there had begun a chain of events in Cuba which was destined to involve the United States in war. In February, 1895, a rebellion against Spain broke out in the island which won immediate sympathy from those Americans whose views were colored by the outcry of the yellow press that the Cubans should be free. During the strife which ensued in Cuba the sensational American papers continued to beat the drums, and with no effective solution of the trouble forthcoming from Spain, conditions grew more and more critical. By the early days of 1898 the insurrection had assumed such proportions that agitation arose in the United States to send part of the fleet for the protection of American lives and property. The battleship *Maine* was dispatched to Havana in late January and on February 15, 1898, a mammoth explosion sunk the ship in the harbor with a loss of over 250 officers and men. If the warmongers had up to that time lacked direct provocation for war, the sinking of the *Maine* now appeared to offer them the opportunity they had been seeking, and they did not fail to capitalize on it. Excitement rose to fever heat and the demand was heard on all sides for war with Spain to defend American honor. The jingoes were in no way impeded by the fact that there was no clear evidence as to who had caused the explosion; they wanted war and they thought the cause had now been provided.

Amid the tumult which had broken loose Cardinal Gibbons said nothing for publication until February 28 when a requiem Mass was offered in the cathedral of Baltimore for the victims of the *Maine*. On this occasion the cardinal preached the sermon. He first paid tribute to patriotism as a virtue, and remarked that we did not realize how much we loved our country until a crisis was upon it. He had words of sympathy for the bereaved families of the dead, as well as praise for the President, the cabinet, and the armed forces for their patient and dignified bearing in the emergency. But the most important part of the sermon dealt with the forbearance that all Americans should now exercise. The cardinal said:

> This nation is too brave, too strong, too powerful, and too just to engage in an unrighteous or precipitate war. Let us remember the

Teunis S. Hamlin that he was heartily in sympathy with the object of the meeting, and that he ardently hoped the promise held out by the treaty recently signed with Great Britain would be fulfilled (95-D-3, Gibbons to Hamlin, Baltimore, January 22, 1897, copy).

eyes of the world are upon us, whose judgment we cannot despise, and that we will gain more applause and credit for ourselves by calm deliberation and masterly inactivity than by recourse to arms.

He hoped that investigation would prove that the sinking of the *Maine* had been an accident and if that were true, Spain was not responsible. But even if some fanatical Spaniard had perpetrated this atrocious crime, it still would offer no necessity for war. The only circumstance which the cardinal believed would warrant hostilities would be the evidence that the Spanish government had connived at placing torpedoes or explosives in the harbor of Havana to destroy the vessel. But this he said he did not believe, and since an able commission had been appointed to investigate the matter, he urged his listeners to keep their minds open. "Let us calmly and dispassionately await the result of their verdict," he said, "and not anticipate their judgment."[12] Archbishop Corrigan appreciated the good sense manifest in Gibbons' words and wrote to thank him for them. "Coming at this time," said Corrigan, "they will help to allay the spirit of many throughout the Country."[13]

But the words of the cardinal and the many others who shared his belief that war was unnecessary were drowned out in the frightful din by which the yellow press kept the issue alive and whipped up sentiment for action. All through the month of March, 1898, tension continued to mount while the diplomats were attempting to adjust the differences between Washington and Madrid. During the first week in April the prospects for peace brightened a little when it was learned that the Spanish government, responding to the intercession of Pope Leo XIII, was preparing to grant an armistice in Cuba. On April 5 Spain met the second major American demand by instructing its military commander in Cuba to revoke the order for reconcentration of the rebels in camps. The name of the Pope began to appear more frequently in the news dispatches concerning the crisis, and it may have been that circumstance which inspired the story that Gibbons had called at the White House to discuss with President McKinley the trouble with Spain. On April 4 the cardinal issued a statement denying the visit. "There is not a word of truth in it," said Gibbons. "I have not seen the President for some time."

---

[12] *Church News* (Washington), March 5, 1898.
[13] 96-D-2, Corrigan to Gibbons, New York, March 1, 1898.

He went on to deplore the thought of war, and to say that conservative and thoughtful people evidently did not want a recourse to arms and seemed to be united in the belief that the whole question could be safely left to the President and, as he added, "in spite of a few excitable folk, to Congress as well."[14]

On Palm Sunday, April 3, Gibbons preached in his cathedral and took occasion to ask for prayers for peace and for divine guidance to the President, Congress, and the Spanish government so that their counsels might be directed to a peaceful solution of the problem which confronted the two nations. "Let us cherish the hope," said the cardinal, "that on Sunday next, when we celebrate the resurrection of Christ from the dead, we may also be cheered by the inauguration of the dawn of good will between Spain and our own beloved country."[15] On the following day the Washington papers gave the first information concerning the presence of Archbishop Ireland in the capital. As it was later learned, Leo XIII had asked the Archbishop of St. Paul to go to Washington as his representative in the hope that he might second the efforts of the Pope to avoid war. The New York *Herald* of April 5 stated that it would be regarded as remarkable that Ireland and not Gibbons had been chosen for the mission. By way of explanation, it was said that Ireland was younger and more vigorous than the cardinal; but the chief reason, in the mind of the *Herald*, was due to Ireland's Republican connections. They said, "The Cardinal, while a shrewd diplomat, does not stand in the same relationship to the present Administration as Archbishop Ireland, whose support of Mr. McKinley during the last campaign is well remembered." Ireland was at pains to keep his movements secret, but the news leaked out on April 4 and two days later the archbishop informed Gibbons of the purpose of his visit and the attempts he had so far made to further the cause of peace. He said he had wished to visit the cardinal but he had found no time, but before he returned to St. Paul he would see him and furnish him with details of the affair. The archbishop was at the moment still optimistic, and he told Gibbons, "In spite of all war clouds, I believe we are going to have peace."[16]

---

[14] Reily, *Collections in the Life and Times of Cardinal Gibbons,* V, 344–345.

[15] *Church News* (Washington), April 9, 1898.

[16] 96-F-3, Ireland to Gibbons, Washington, April 6, 1898. For full details on

But John Ireland's optimism proved to be unwarranted. By reason of a clumsy maneuver of Spain to make it appear that President McKinley had asked for the Pope's intervention and of the hysterical propaganda of the press, the atmosphere for peaceful negotiation was destroyed, and even though Spain capitulated to the American terms on April 9, the President took the fateful step two days later of submitting to a Congress eager for war a message in which he called for authority to use the army and navy to bring an end to hostilities in Cuba. True, Spain's peaceful gestures were not entirely ignored but reference to them was tucked away near the end of a very strong message so that the effect was almost entirely lost. On April 19 Congress passed a four-point joint resolution which was tantamount to a declaration of war on Spain and six days later the formal declaration was issued.[17] The United States thus entered a conflict which, in the judgment of all students of the question, could have been avoided had it not been for the poisonous influence of the war-mongers and the newspapers which served their purposes, as well as the lack of resolution on the part of the politicians.

In the last days of peace the presence of Archbishop Ireland in Washington gave rise to a number of fantastic tales. The *Church News* of Washington in its issue of April 9 took notice of these stories and tried to set the minds of its readers at rest when it said, "We have been assured by the most reliable authority that many of the statements contained in the secular journals relative to his mission are simply absurd." The Baltimore *Sun* of April 16 stated that Ireland had abandoned hope of peace on April 11, the day McKinley sent his message to Congress, and that he had gone to Baltimore that afternoon to confer with Cardinal Gibbons. "The two prelates," said the *Sun*, "after discussing the situation thoroughly, agreed that nothing more could be done." The *Sun*, which was ordinarily more reliable than most newspapers on questions relating to the Church, said that Ireland and his associates now felt they had done all they possibly could to avert the war. "If their efforts have failed," wrote the *Sun*, "it is not their fault. The case is now considered closed."

It was, indeed, closed although Ireland and Gibbons did not

---

the Ireland mission cf. John T. Farrell, "Archbishop Ireland and Manifest Destiny," *Catholic Historical Review*, XXXIII (October, 1947), 269–301.

[17] Bailey, *op. cit.*, pp. 494–510.

cease to experience annoyance at having their names bandied about in the secular press in a manner which caused them embarrassment and chagrin. The London *Daily Chronicle* was especially guilty of false reporting in this regard. For example, in a dispatch from its Paris correspondent which was published on April 16 in the Baltimore *Sun* it was stated that, "The smart plan of saddling Spain with the odium of the first shot by escorting merchantmen with relief for the reconcentrados is said to have been suggested by Cardinal Gibbons and Archbishop Ireland." A week later the Washington *Post* of April 22 carried an item from the Rome correspondent of the same London paper to the effect that Leo XIII had thanked Gibbons and Ireland for their peace efforts and had cabled Archbishop Martinelli, the apostolic delegate, "to preserve utmost prudence and strict neutrality." Gibbons' patience with these stories emanating from the London *Daily Chronicle* finally wore thin, and when the paper began to circulate reports which put the American Catholics in a false light in regard to the war effort, the cardinal issued a denial in which he said, "Catholics in the United States have but one sentiment. Whatever may have been their opinions as to the expediency of the war, now that it is on they are united in upholding the government."[18]

Knowing Gibbons as we do, it is not difficult to credit him with deep earnestness in the statement which appeared in the papers on May 4. All during the critical period leading up to the war the American Catholics had shown through their press, and the few public statements of the leaders of their Church, a very restrained and peaceful attitude. In this respect they were surpassed by no religious group in the United States unless it were by the Quakers and Unitarians.[19] When war came the Catholics responded to the call of duty by enrollment in the armed forces and once more the sisterhoods furnished the same unselfish service to the sick and wounded in the military hospitals which their predecessors had done during the Civil War.[20] The number

---

[18] Washington *Post,* May 4, 1898.

[19] For the attitudes of the various religious groups before and after the war cf. the chapter of Julius W. Pratt, *Expansionists of 1898* (Baltimore, 1936) entitled "The Imperialism of Righteousness," pp. 279–316.

[20] For the service of the Catholic sisters cf. the unpublished master's thesis, "The Work Done by the American Catholic Sisterhoods in the Spanish American War," by Sister M. Magdalen Wirmel, O.S.F., The Catholic University of America (1940).

of Catholic men engaged in the fighting with both the army and
the navy was so great that it became a problem to provide chaplains for their religious care. Early in July Cardinal Gibbons
called on the President and put before him the difficulties attendant on the insufficient number of Catholic chaplains in the armed
forces. The cardinal stated that in the lengthy conference he held
with McKinley they canvassed the problem thoroughly, and as
Gibbons remarked, "My interview was most satisfactory, but I
cannot now give any details as to how many or what particular
Catholic chaplains will be sent to the soldiers."[21]

All during the summer of 1898 the cardinal continued to be
preoccupied with problems arising from the war. Following the
victories at El Caney and San Juan Hill and the naval engagement at Santiago, the President called upon the nation to
express its thanks for the triumph of American arms. Gibbons
prepared a circular letter in response to McKinley's request
which was read in all the churches of the Archdiocese of Baltimore on Sunday, July 17, in which he asked his people to give
thanks to God for the victories and to pray for the souls of
those who had died in the fighting.[22] After the defeat of the
Spanish fleet at Santiago on July 3 Admiral Pascual Cervera
and a number of his officers were brought to Annapolis where
they were detained for some weeks. Arrangements were made by
Gibbons with Father James A. Kantz, C.Ss.R., of St. Mary's
Church in Annapolis for their spiritual needs,[23] and late in
August the cardinal went to the Maryland capital where he
called on Admiral Frederick V. McNair, Superintendent of the
Naval Academy, and paid a visit to Cervera and his men.[24] The
Spanish admiral was grateful for the courtesies extended to him
and his fellow countrymen by Gibbons, and shortly before their
departure for home they called to bid him good-by and were
shown through the cathedral by the cardinal.[25]

Gibbons likewise gave his close attention during the war to the
needs of the sick and wounded soldiers who had been returned
to the United States from the fighting fronts. On August 29

---

[21] *Church News* (Washington), July 16, 1898.

[22] Reily, *op. cit.,* V, 360.

[23] 96-K-4, Kantz to Gibbons, Annapolis, July 19, 1898; 96-K-5, Cervera to
Gibbons, Annapolis, July 22, 1898.

[24] Reily, *op. cit.,* V, 361.

[25] *Ibid.,* V, 362.

he visited the City Hospital in Baltimore where over 100 members of the fifth regiment had been placed after their service, and the following month he gave instructions to Father William A. Reardon of St. Peter's Church that he and his assistant priests should look after the spiritual wants of the sick soldiers in the University of Maryland Hospital.[26] When the cardinal learned that there was some danger that the sisters attending the men of the third division at Camp Thomas would be without the ministrations of a priest, he arranged for Father Francis T. McCarthy, S.J., to go to them from St. Francis Xavier Church in New York.[27] In the autumn rumors reached Gibbons that priests were not being admitted to the hospital tents at Camp Wikoff at Point Montauk, Long Island; whereupon he paid a personal visit to the camp which was amusingly described by Thomas Beer when he wrote:

> . . . a buzz passed under the brown canvas, through smells of typhoid, and the titular pastor of Santa Maria in Trastavere [sic] walked slowly down the line of cots, pausing to speak to a red-haired Unitarian youth of Celtic expression and bestowing a blessing which, he said, would do the boy no harm. He had been told that priests were being kept out of the place. It was a great relief to find that untrue.[28]

In ways such as these Cardinal Gibbons performed his duties to the nation while the fighting continued, and when active hostilities ceased after the protocol signed on August 12 there was no one who welcomed more heartily the end of the war than the Archbishop of Baltimore.[29]

Armed conflict, no matter how brief, leaves in its wake serious dislocations in the lives of those involved, and the Spanish American War was no exception. The American invasion of Cuba, Puerto Rico, and the Philippine Islands led inevitably to grave

---

[26] Ibid., V, 361–362.

[27] George Barton, "A Story of Self-Sacrifice. Being a Record of the Labors of the Catholic Sisterhoods in the Spanish-American War," Records of the American Catholic Historical Society of Philadelphia, XXXVII (June, 1926), 159.

[28] The Mauve Decade (New York, 1926), p. 148.

[29] In the terms of capitulation for Manila and its suburbs the American military guaranteed among other items that, "This city, its inhabitants, its churches and religious worship, its educational establishments and its private property of all descriptions, are placed under the special safeguard of the faith and honor of the American army." Correspondence Relating to the War with Spain (Washington, 1902), II, 757.

problems for the Catholic Church in these former possessions of Spain, and it was not long before the Cardinal of Baltimore was made aware of them. In the final week of the fighting he received a dismal picture of the state of the Church in Puerto Rico from a correspondent who said he felt bound in conscience to inform Gibbons of the frightful conditions in the island where in one area of around 9,000 kilometers containing eighty parishes there was only one priest, and in the city of Ponce with about 50,000 inhabitants there were but eight priests. With support from the government now cut off there were grave fears of further losses, and if help was not forthcoming from some source the future of the Church in Puerto Rico would, indeed, be very dark.[30] There was little that Gibbons at the moment could do about it, and within a few days word reached him of a situation in the Philippines that was much more pressing. The native forces, under the leadership of Emilio Aguinaldo had been struggling for two years for independence from Spain, and they had a deep hatred for the Spanish bishops and religious whom they associated with the former government. On August 18 the cardinal received a cablegram from Bishop Luigi Piazzoli, Vicar Apostolic of Hong Kong, which read, "Use influence in releasing one hundred priests prisoners of insurgents Cavite."[31] Gibbons immediately communicated with Archbishop Ireland who was then in Washington and who, in turn, saw the President and was told that General Wesley Merritt, commander of the American forces in the Philippines, had instructions to respect the lives and property of the natives and to hold no official communication with the insurgents. All this information was forwarded to Piazzoli by Gibbons,[32] but the painful situation created by the prisoners in the hands of the Aguinaldo forces meanwhile remained unsolved.

An interval of two months passed and the Vicar Apostolic of Hong Kong again reported to the cardinal that all efforts to win their release or a promise of better treatment for them, including that of three American Catholic chaplains, had ended in failure.[33] On October 19 Rampolla cabled Martinelli and asked him to confer with Gibbons to see if something could not be done to arouse public opinion in the United States against the barbarous treatment which he said was being shown toward José Hevia y Campomanes, Bishop of Neuva Segovia, and the 130 religious who were held prisoners with him.[34] Martinelli and Gibbons conferred in Washington and after their exchange of views the cardinal wrote a detailed explanation of the case to the Secretary of War, Russell A. Alger, in which he strongly urged that the American government take steps for the relief of the captives. He told Alger he understood very well that the relations between the American forces and the insurgents were such that the Americans could not exert the full power over Aguinaldo's faction that they might desire. Yet he felt confident that if the American authorities would assert the influence which their position gave them, they might compel the insurgents to act with greater consideration toward the prisoners and to refrain from every species of barbarity. Gibbons stated:

> It cannot fail to appear inconsistent to the world at large that we should be so deeply interested in the welfare of a distant and unknown people, and in freeing them from the hard rule of another nation, and, at the same time, be indifferent to the barbarities which that people uses toward its non-combatant captives.

For that reason he begged the American government through the Secretary of War to take, as he expressed it, "serious and effective steps to bring this disgraceful condition to an end."[35]

As a result of the cardinal's intervention, Secretary Alger dispatched messages to General Elwell S. Otis, who had meanwhile replaced Merritt, and to Admiral George Dewey in which he asked for a full investigation of the plight of the prisoners, and he added, "Use every means possible to secure their release, and

---

[34] 96-Q-4, Rampolla to Martinelli, Rome, October 19, 1898, cablegram in Italian, copy. A month before Rampolla had cabled Martinelli on September 13 with the request that the delegate "should present the matter to the Government of the United States and try to move it to take some opportune step regarding it." A copy of this cablegram was, as Secretary of State William R. Day expressed it, "left informally at the Executive Mansion by the secretary of the apostolic delegation with a request for such action as may seem proper." Day to Secretary of War Alger, Washington, September 16, 1898. *Correspondence Relating to the War with Spain*, II, 790–791. As a consequence Adjutant General Henry C. Corbin cabled the request to Otis in Manila on September 20 and added, "If under control your forces protect from inhuman treatment." *Ibid.*, II, 793.

[35] 96-K-1, Gibbons to Alger, Baltimore, October 24, 1898, copy.

care for them." Otis replied that he had endeavored with some success to obtain better treatment for the captives and he would continue to attempt to win their release. Copies of the communications were forwarded to Gibbons by Alger with the assurance that all would be done that was possible in the situation.[36] The cardinal told the Secretary of War that he was under great obligation for the marked courtesy which he had shown in the case. He would have the reply from Manila mailed at once to Cardinal Rampolla and he had no doubt that it would be gratifying to the Pope, "while it merits," added Gibbons, "the lasting gratitude of the suffering clergy in the Philippines."[37] All the facts in the case relating to the prisoners were likewise detailed for Rampolla by the apostolic delegate, who told him that Gibbons had seen McKinley on October 28 and that the President had assured the cardinal he had taken energetic action in behalf of the prisoners.[38]

The peace negotiations to bring the Spanish American War to a formal close were opened in Paris on October 1, 1898. Shortly after the armistice of August 12 there began the discussions looking to the choice of the personnel who would compose the American delegation. When the cardinal learned that the name of Associate Justice Edward D. White of the Supreme Court was being mentioned favorably as one of the commissioners, he wrote a recommendation of White to the President in which he stated that he would regard the selection as a happy choice which would give general satisfaction. He outlined briefly White's special qualifications and stated that he was writing without the justice's knowledge.[39] As it turned out, White was asked by McKinley to be a member of the commission but declined. He told the cardinal, without particularizing, that his decision was the result, as he said, "of as clear a conviction of duty as was ever mine." He was grateful to Gibbons for his recommendation and remarked that it gave him pain not to do as the cardinal had wished.[40]

---

[36] 96-R-7, Alger to Gibbons, Washington, October 31, 1898, enclosing copies of Alger to Otis, October 28, 1898 (96-R-5) and of Otis to Alger, Manila, October 30, 1898 (96-R-6). Cf. also *Correspondence Relating to the War with Spain*, II, 790–791, 793, 831.

[37] 96-S-3, Gibbons to Alger, Baltimore, November 1, 1898, copy.

[38] 96-S-2, Martinelli to Rampolla, Washington, November 1, 1898, copy in Italian.

[39] LC, McKinley Papers, Gibbons to McKinley, Baltimore, August 22, 1898.

[40] 96-N-2, White to Gibbons, Cooperstown, New York, September 7, 1898, *Personal*.

In the end McKinley chose Secretary of State William R. Day, three United States senators, and Whitelaw Reid, the well-known Republican journalist, as the members of the peace commission.

It was obvious, of course, that the Catholic Church would be vitally interested in the final settlement of affairs in the former possessions of Spain. As early as the previous May, Monsignor Denis O'Connell had cabled Archbishop Ireland from Rome, "Help hold Philippines." Although Ireland confessed he did not like the present war, he was ready to urge O'Connell's point of view. He felt the war would strengthen the American navy and extend the nation's power into new territories, and it was his opinion that if the Pope was to have any world-wide prestige in the future he would have to deal as never before with the United States. "Tell all this in Rome," said Ireland, and he went on, "even if we do not hold Cuba and the Philippines, the church there will be organized on the lines of Americanism."[41] Just what prompted the archbishop to believe that the Church would be organized on American lines in these territories if the United States did not retain them, it is impossible to say. On August 2, ten days before the end of hostilities, Rampolla first expressed the anxiety of the Holy See over the future of the religious orders in the Philippines when he asked Martinelli to confer with Gibbons in the hope that the latter might influence the President to regard the religious in a favorable way. The papal Secretary of State made it known that if there were abuses among the friars in the islands the Holy See was prepared to investigate them and if they should be discovered to adopt measures for their correction.[42]

Archbishop Martinelli likewise availed himself of the presence of the Archbishop of St. Paul in Washington to sound out the President on the future of the Church in the Philippines. Ireland was told by McKinley that in any territories annexed by the United States the Church would be separated from the State in conformity with the American Constitution without any implied hostility to the Church, and there would be guaranteed an absolute protection of ecclesiastical properties and persons.[43] At the time that McKinley was treating with Ireland a confidential

[41] ADR, Ireland to O'Connell, St. Paul, May 2, 1898.
[42] 96-M-1, Rampolla to Martinelli, Rome, August 2, 1898.
[43] 96-M-4, Martinelli to Rampolla, Washington, August 23, 1898, copy in Italian, enclosed in Martinelli to Gibbons, Washington, August 25, 1898 (96-M-5).

message was conveyed from the President to Archbishop Corrigan in New York, much to the same effect insofar as the Church in the West Indies was concerned. In regard to the Philippines, however, McKinley was said to have urged the Holy See to obtain every concession possible from Spain before the treaty of peace was signed. The President was represented as hoping that affairs between Rome and Madrid could be arranged quietly so as to preclude the possibility of sectarian clamor, for once the treaty was signed the United States would act simply on its principle of separation of Church and State and grant no concessions to Catholics any more than it would to Presbyterians or any other denomination. This information was forwarded by Corrigan to Cardinal Satolli with the added remark that it had reached him entirely unsought.[44]

With a view to having someone on the scene who could take in hand the Church's interests in Cuba and Puerto Rico, the Holy See on September 16 appointed Placide L. Chapelle, Archbishop of New Orleans, as apostolic delegate to the two islands with the further responsibility of looking after religious questions in the Philippines. Chapelle was then in Paris and on October 11 he informed Gibbons of his appointment by a cablegram, which he followed by a letter two weeks later in which he stated that he was ordered to remain in the French capital during the sessions of the peace conference. At that time the archbishop said matters were progressing very satisfactorily and he had well-grounded hopes that in the treaty the Church's interests would be properly protected.[45] Chapelle's optimism was in the main justified, insofar as the Church in Cuba was concerned, but the Philippines were another matter and there it would require greater effort. Cardinal Gibbons had early sensed the feeling in the Philippine Islands against the Spanish religious and when he met Martinelli in Washington on October 22 he warned the apostolic delegate of the prejudice against the friars on the part of many Americans, and he stated that the stories circulating recently about the religious, which could not be verified or denied, had only heightened the unfavorable view which many took to these men.[46]

In the first days after the conquest of the Philippines there

[44] AANY, Corrigan to Satolli, New York, August 21, 1898, *Riservata,* copy.

[45] 96-Q-1, Chapelle to Gibbons, Paris, October 11, 1898, cablegram; 96-R-4, Chapelle to Gibbons, Paris, October 25, 1898.

[46] 96-S-2, Martinelli to Rampolla, Washington, November 1, 1898, copy in Italian.

was considerable sentiment for giving the Filipinos their immediate independence, but as time went on opinion began to veer
in the opposite direction. The interest of businessmen became
aroused, there was a good deal of talk about the strategic importance of the archipelago, and even the churches, according to
one historian, "welcomed the 'little brown brother' as one to
whom the gospel should be carried."[47] In the meantime President
McKinley was perplexed as to what to recommend with the result
that he waited for opinion to crystallize, and thus he had an
opportunity to sound out certain men whose judgment he
respected. It was this circumstance that occasioned a message
to Cardinal Gibbons to come to the White House to speak with
the President. The cardinal was unaware of the reason why
he had been summoned, but he soon learned that it was with a
view to getting his ideas on the United States retaining the
Philippines. Gibbons assured McKinley that so far as the Church
was concerned he felt it was safer under the American flag than
anywhere else. He made it plain, however, that he had not wished
to see the United States take territories by force and he did not
now wish to see his country become a colonial power. He summarized his views for McKinley about holding the islands by
remarking, "Mr. President, it would be a good thing for the
Catholic Church but, I fear, a bad one for the United States."[48]
After hearing the advocates of both policies through some weeks
the President finally resolved his doubts, and on October 25 he
replied to the request of the peace commissioners for specific
instructions by saying that since the only alternatives were to
take all or none of the islands the United States would have to
take all. The Spaniards were naturally very reluctant to yield,
but the American offer of a payment of $20,000,000 helped to
win their assent, and on December 10 the Treaty of Paris was
signed which provided that Spain should relinquish sovereignty
over Cuba and cede the Philippines, Puerto Rico, and Guam outright to the United States.[49]

The Archbishop of Baltimore lost no time in idle laments over
the fact that the President had not chosen to follow his advice.
Instead he turned his attention to the problem of adjusting the

---

[47] Bailey, *op. cit.*, p. 518. For the attitude of the churches in reference to retaining the Philippines cf. also Pratt's chapter cited in note 20.
[48] Will, *Life of Cardinal Gibbons*, II, 611.
[49] Bailey, *op. cit.*, pp. 515–524.

Church to the new American regime in the island possessions with the intention of lending it all the assistance he could. Gibbons was pleased with Chapelle's appointment as apostolic delegate for two reasons: first, as he said, because he was an American, and second, as he phrased it, because "one was chosen who besides possessing the qualifications, was one to whom I am bound by so many ties." He remarked that when the archbishop called on him he would be able to supply useful information since he had received many items of important detail within the last few months from the several islands.[50] From these accounts that had been reaching Baltimore of late it was evident that Archbishop Chapelle's task would not be an easy one. For example, Father William D. McKinnon, an American chaplain in Manila, related to the Abbé Magnien that the islands were sorely in need of an apostolic delegate and the Church in general was in a bad plight. There was but one Catholic chaplain as against fourteen Protestant chaplains and, although McKinnon believed the Spanish friars were good men, he confessed that confusion reigned everywhere. He urged Magnien, therefore, to bring these matters to the attention of the cardinal in the hope that he might help to rectify them.[51] The press from time to time likewise carried disconcerting stories from the new possessions and on February 25, 1899, the *Catholic Mirror* of Baltimore deplored editorially the introduction by the American authorities in Cuba of the policy of racial segregation. "It remained," said the *Mirror*, "for Americans to draw the color line in Cuba and make it one of the first results of their occupation of the island."

Yet Archbishop Chapelle took a cheerful view of Cuban affairs insofar as they pertained to the Church and several months after reaching his post at Havana he told the cardinal that God had blessed his mission beyond his most sanguine hopes, and he felt that much had already been done for the protection of the best interests of both Church and State.[52] During the course of 1899 Gibbons continued to receive information both good and bad from the island possessions. An Episcopalian naval officer, Lieutenant W. E. Safford who was chief of staff to the Governor of Guam, made a strong plea to the cardinal for good priests for

---

[50] AANO, Gibbons to Chapelle, Baltimore, November 7, 1898.

[51] ASMS, McKinnon to Magnien, Manila, December 12, 1898.

[52] 97-E-4, Chapelle to Gibbons, Havana, March 13, 1899.

Guam. He had words of high praise for a certain old Father José Palmo but there were others, he said, whose lives were not edifying and Safford believed that if a group of American-born priests who could speak Spanish were sent, much good would be accomplished among the people of Guam.[53] Bishop James H. Blenk, S.M., of Puerto Rico was deeply grateful for Gibbons' check of $2,000 as a contribution of the Archdiocese of Baltimore toward relieving the destitute of that island, and four months later when the cardinal sent an additional $1,000 with words of encouragement Blenk went into more detail. While most people received baptism and extreme unction in Puerto Rico, he said there was a widespread disregard for the sacraments of penance and the Eucharist and, added Blenk, "Open concubinage is the great plague of the Island." Many of the priests were devoted to their duties and led exemplary lives but, as the bishop pointed out, the general corruption of morals cast suspicion upon all and in the case of not a few priests the suspicion had long since developed into conviction based on indisputable fact. Therefore, if he could only get recruits from among priests and religious of the highest moral qualities he felt something could be done.[54]

But bad as conditions might be in Guam and Puerto Rico they were even more critical in the Philippines, and in the last week of September, 1899, Chapelle received word from Rome that he had been formally appointed apostolic delegate there while retaining the same office for Cuba and Puerto Rico.[55] The feeling against the Spanish friars in the Philippines had grown very intense and this situation probably contributed to the discomfort of Bellamy Storer who had reached Madrid in June of that year as American minister. Mrs. Storer told Gibbons, "We find the task very hard of trying to bring about a kindly feeling between the United States and Spain. I doubt if we can do more than sow the seeds during our stay — hoping that they may grow and bear fruit."[56]

Of all the possessions taken from Spain the Philippines proved to be by far the most difficult to subdue. After assisting the American forces in their capture of Manila on August 13, 1898,

[53] 97-P-4/1, Safford to Gibbons, Agana, September 10, 1899.

[54] 97-P-5, Blenk to Gibbons, Washington, September 22, 1899; 98-B-1, same to same, Obispado de Puerto-Rico, January 13, 1900.

[55] 97-P-6, Chapelle to Gibbons, New Orleans, September 25, 1899.

[56] 97-S-5, Maria Longworth Storer to Gibbons, Madrid, November 6, 1899.

Aguinaldo's men broke with the Americans over the question of independence for the islands and on February 4, 1899, they raised the standard of revolt. For the next three years the fighting continued in sporadic fashion, and it was only in the spring of 1902 that the guerrilla warfare was finally wiped out. In the midst of the turmoil the Spanish friars were relentlessly pursued by the insurgents with a consequent serious loss in both lives and properties belonging to the religious. During the course of Spain's three centuries of occupation of the islands the Spanish religious had become extensive landowners and their wealth, together with the power they wielded over the lives of the masses, had made them the object of deep hatred on the part of the insurrectionists. This dislike had first been visited upon the friars at the time of the original Aguinaldo revolt in 1896, and through the succeeding four years they had continued to suffer great hardships. The abuse of their power by some of the friars lent an air of plausibility to the campaign against them, and by the time that the Americans took over there was a widespread opinion in the Philippines, which gradually began to spread in the United States, that the friars must go. The Treaty of Paris, it is true, had guaranteed the religious and property rights of persons and corporations, as well as insuring the rights of Spaniards to remain on in the islands without even the requirement that they become American citizens.[57] But the feeling against the friars was so intense that notwithstanding treaty guarantees their future in the Philippines offered little promise.

To make matters worse the Catholic Church of the Philippines was soon faced with a schism which was brought on in part by opposition to the friars. Among the close friends of Aguinaldo was Father Gregorio Aglípay, a priest of the Diocese of Nueva Segovia, a man of extreme nationalist views, strongly ambitious, and violently anti-friar. His repeated defiance of the recognized authorities of the Church led to his excommunication in April, 1899, and in October of the same year he broke entirely with the Filipino ecclesiastical authorities and by August, 1901, Aglípay and his followers had severed their connections with Rome and proclaimed the Filipino Independent Church. From the out-

---

[57] For a recent treatment of the preliminary stages of this case which embodies a thorough coverage of the sources cf. John T. Farrell, "Background of the 1902 Taft Mission to Rome. I," *Catholic Historical Review*, XXXVI (April, 1950), 1–31.

set the movement attracted a large following among the insurgent faction and those most opposed to the friars, and when Archbishop Giovanni B. Guidi, who arrived in Manila in the autumn of 1902 to replace Chapelle as apostolic delegate, published on December 2 the apostolic letter, *Quae mare sinico*, of Leo XIII addressed to the Filipinos, a new impetus was given to the schismatics.

The Pope had provided in his letter for a fresh start in the government of the Filipino Church but he had included no hint that the friars would be compelled to withdraw from the islands. As a consequence Aglipay and his party whipped the nationalist resentment to white heat and thousands flocked to join the rebellion against Rome. It is impossible to say exactly how many adherents the Independent Church had, but they would seem to have numbered at one time between 1,500,000 and 2,000,000 and to have secured the support of about 200 priests who joined the ranks. While the schismatics were without a compelling moral and religious force to hold their members together permanently, there ensued at the time a very disturbing situation over the possession of the parish churches and their properties which they had seized. In an effort to settle these troubles the American government in Manila in July, 1905, empowered the supreme court of the Philippines to render the final judgment concerning the ownership of the properties. After a long delay the court finally gave its decision in November, 1906, in favor of the right of the Catholic Church to the ecclesiastical edifices constructed originally for the use of its communicants, and within a short time thereafter the Aglípayan clergy were compelled to turn over the churches which proved a tremendous blow to the schismatic cause.[58]

---

[58] Cf. James A. Robertson, "The Aglípay Schism in the Philippine Islands," *Catholic Historical Review*, IV (October, 1918), 315–344; cf. also Donald Dean Parker, "Church and State in the Philippines, 1896–1906," an unpublished doctoral dissertation of the Divinity School, University of Chicago (1936), pp. 451 ff. Parker's work is heavily documented, but in matters pertaining to Filipino Catholicism the point of view of the Protestant missionary bodies is followed rather closely. Early in the fall of 1905 Alice Roosevelt, the President's daughter, visited the Philippine Islands. Someone sent Roosevelt a clipping from the New Orleans *Picayune* of October 2, 1905, which described a reception given for the young lady in Manila during which, it was said, she was engaged by Aglípay in conversation for a considerable time while the apostolic delegate was made to wait. Archbishop Agius, the delegate, was said to have reported the incident to Rome and to have expressed his dissatisfaction at the slight done to his dignity. The

It was into a situation such as this that there came in June, 1900, the second Philippine commission of the United States, headed by Judge William Howard Taft, after the Schurman Commission had wound up its business. The ultimate goal of the Taft Commission was the establishment of a civil government for the islands, but in the meanwhile the problem of the friars pressed for solution. Before Taft had been on the scene three weeks he informed Mrs. Storer, wife of the American minister to Madrid and an old friend of the Taft family in Cincinnati, that the evidence seemed overwhelming that the Filipinos were violently opposed to the friars' return to the parishes in which they had formerly officiated, and that with a few exceptions these religious would be killed if they moved about without the protection of the military. He had spoken with Archbishop Chapelle who had arrived in Manila six months before and, although the apostolic delegate argued cogently for the friars, he feared Chapelle did not see as clearly as he should the impossibility of the return of the religious. Taft spoke of the desirability of getting American priests to replace the Spaniards in the Philippines, and at the same time he gave assurances to Mrs. Storer concerning the policies of the commission in regard to the Catholic schools.[59] After conversing with several American Catholic chaplains in the Philippines, Taft was confirmed in his first impressions about the friars, and three weeks later he suggested to Mrs. Storer that she discuss the matter with Archbishop Ireland whom she was to meet that summer in Europe to see what could be done to obtain American priests.[60]

It is not easy, even at this late date, to arrive at exact conclusions regarding the question of the friars in the islands, but it is certain that their opposition to a break with Spain had created for them such strong political enemies that the vast good which they had accomplished in the archipelago during their long resi-

---

President grew very excited at the newspaper report, passed on the clipping to Taft, and remarked, "The Vatican ought to understand that I shall not tolerate any official recognition of any kind or sort being shown to any representative who comments upon what one of my children does. They have nothing to do with politics international or national, and if Mgr. Agius has said what is here represented he has been guilty of an unwarranted impertinence which I shall resent" (LC, Taft Papers, Roosevelt to Taft, Washington, October 5, 1905).

59 98-F-5, Taft to Maria Storer, Manila, June 21, 1900, copy. Several letters of Taft to Mrs. Storer in these months were later sent by her in copy to Gibbons.

60 LC, Taft Papers, Taft to Maria Storer, Manila, July 12, 1900, copy.

dence was lost to view in the current excitement. In the statement of the case propaganda was doubtless employed by both sides to win adherents, but there was one eyewitness of the friars' work in the Philippines in these critical months who had much to say in their behalf. Stephen Bonsal, a non-Catholic correspondent of the New York *Herald,* visited the islands and the evidence he found for the building of villages, churches, roads, and bridges by the friars impressed him. Not only had they taught Spanish to many of these untutored people, but they had instructed them in farming and had introduced into the islands every staple crop known to the Philippines with the exception of tobacco.

Moreover, the charges that there were no schools, or that the schools were bad, were met by Bonsal after personal observation with the statement that the facts were against both charges.[61] He likewise furnished evidence of their distinguished service as soldiers, and he cited the memorials to the Madrid government from the Spanish civil and military governors, with whom the friars were often at odds, as proof that the religious enjoyed high esteem even with the governors who had differed with them. As for the accusation that they had plundered the inhabitants, the writer stated that Taft and his fellow commissioners had put an evaluation on all friar properties in the Philippines at a figure considerably under $10,000,000, a figure which all were agreed was a generous estimate. Bonsal then remarked, "There are half a dozen foreign firms in Manila without the knowledge of the people and the islands which the friars possess, who have made as much money as this out of the Philippines within the decade."[62] He did not overlook the fact that during their long tenure of three centuries some of the friars had shown their human side and, therefore, that their history was not without stain; moreover, that in personal and political affairs, like other men, they had at times been swayed by passion. Nonetheless, the conclusion which Bonsal reached after his investigation was one with which the future historian of the friar question will in all likelihood concur. He wrote:

> But, when time has calmed the controversy to which the termina-
> tion of their mission in its mediaeval shape has given rise, it will

---

[61] Stephen Bonsal, "The Work of the Friars," *North American Review,* CLXXV (October, 1902), 455.

[62] *Ibid.,* p. 460.

be seen that under their guidance a large proportion of the Filipinos have reached a much higher stage of civilization than has been attained by other branches of the Malay family under other circumstances and in another environment. I believe the work of the friars is recorded in the golden book of those who have labored for their fellow men, and I am confident the credit of it, though dimmed to-day by partisanship and want of charity, will not escape history.[63]

During the summer and early autumn of 1900 a fairly lively correspondence ensued involving Taft, the Storers, and Ireland on ecclesiastical questions in the Philippines, the general tenor of which was that the good of the Church called for the removal of the Spanish friars, their replacement by American priests as far as possible, and the substitution of a more liberal and understanding man to act as apostolic delegate in the place of Chapelle.[64] So far as it is known, Cardinal Gibbons knew nothing at the time of this exchange of views. Late in June he endeavored to interest Archbishop Corrigan in the candidacy of Major George W. Fishback as secretary of the commission appointed by McKinley to revise the laws of Puerto Rico, since he had been reliably informed that although the major was not a Catholic he was friendly to the interests of religion.[65] But other than this there is no record of the cardinal taking active part in matters pertaining to the new possessions until the annual meeting of the archbishops.

On October 11 the metropolitans assembled at the Catholic University of America where they heard read a letter from Father Edward H. FitzGerald, an American chaplain in the Philippines, who emphasized the grave need of more priests to attend the thousands of American troops then in the islands who were presently served by only two Catholic chaplains. Several of the archbishops promised to try to find priests for this work. In addition to this plea for chaplains in the Far East, the only other item of business relating to the island possessions of the United States which was discussed at the meeting was the appeal of Donato Sbarretti, Bishop of Havana. Sbarretti begged the metropolitans to interest themselves in the difficulties of the Church in Cuba, and to urge on the government of the

---

[63] *Ibid.*

[64] For some of these letters cf. Maria Longworth Storer, *In Memoriam Bellamy Storer* (Boston, 1923), pp. 42–56, and Farrell, *op. cit.*, pp. 5–7, for a digest of others.

[65] AANY, Gibbons to Corrigan, Baltimore, June 29, 1900.

United States that justice be done to ecclesiastical properties there. The bishop feared that if the question was left to the constitutional convention soon to be held, the Cubans would almost certainly deprive the Church of its properties to the great detriment of religion.[66] What was done, if anything, in regard to the Cuban properties is not known, but on February 25, 1901, Gibbons saw President McKinley and proposed to him the names of seven candidates for chaplaincies with the armed forces. The President gave the cardinal hope that the Catholics would receive a fair share of the appointments to be made,[67] but Gibbons was careful to tell Archbishop Elder several weeks later that he anticipated the confirmation of only some of the names submitted.[68]

By the end of the year 1900 Judge Taft and his colleagues in Manila had finished their report on Philippine conditions and had submitted it to Secretary of War Elihu Root. In it, as Taft told Mrs. Storer, they had tried to make a clear distinction between the interests of the Catholic Church and those of the Spanish friars. The elimination of the latter from the islands was still on Taft's mind, and he did not hesitate to say that the report was mild on the abuses of the friars in comparison with what might have been said. As for the apostolic delegate, it was Taft's view that Chapelle had become absolutely identified with the friars and had won the disapproval of all Filipinos whether they were insurgents or in sympathy with the Americans. He did not think it necessary for Chapelle to have gotten himself into that position, but there he was, and while his ecclesiastical office compelled respect, politically, said Taft, "he has no force whatever."[69] Chapelle, on his part, remained convinced that the attitude taken by the Philippine Commission, as he expressed it, "unconsciously perhaps, indirectly surely," was hostile to the Church and its interests. Shortly before his departure from Manila for Rome and Washington, he informed Taft of his view

---

[66] 98-J-2, Minutes of the Meeting of the Archbishops, Washington, October 11, 1900.

[67] AANY, Gibbons to Corrigan, Baltimore, February 26, 1901.

[68] AAC, Gibbons to Elder, Baltimore, March 15, 1901. There is record of eleven Catholic chaplains having served with the regular army, eight with the navy, and six with the volunteer army from the outbreak of the war up to 1905. Cf. Aidan H. Germain, *Catholic Military and Naval Chaplains, 1776–1917* (Washington, 1929), pp. 136–155.

[69] 98-N-1, Taft to Maria Storer, Manila, December 4, 1900, copy.

and said that to his certain knowledge this was likewise the sincere belief of all the conservative, wise, and serious men both in the islands and in the United States with whom he had had any relations concerning his mission.[70] It was plain that matters had reached something of an impasse between the authorities of Church and State in the Philippines on the question of the friars and that it would have to be referred to Rome and Washington for final settlement.

On May 11, 1901, Cardinal Gibbons sailed from New York on the *Trave* for Rome where he arrived on May 22 in the company of Bernardino de Nozaleda, O.P., Archbishop of Manila. The cardinal remained in the Eternal City for a month, during which he had three private audiences of Leo XIII which gave him an opportunity to explain what he knew of Philippine affairs. Bellamy Storer, American minister to Spain, took the opportunity of Gibbons' presence in Europe to urge a visit to that country where, he said, Ciriaco Cardinal Sancha y Hervás, Archbishop of Toledo, was anxious to meet him. Storer described the wounded feelings under which the Spaniards were smarting in their defeat, and he was hopeful that a visit from the Archbishop of Baltimore would help to better relations.[71] But the cardinal for reasons best known to himself did not visit Spain that summer. Instead Gibbons remained on in Rome until late June where, as Denis O'Connell informed Archbishop Ireland, he was having a pleasant time and was much sought after. "Some how or other," said O'Connell, "he is hardly regarded as belonging to any side, and so all sides run to him."[72] The cardinal apparently found his role a pleasant one, for on the eve of his departure he told Ireland, "This was my most enjoyable visit to Rome."[73] These were agreeable details, to be sure, but they revealed

---

[70] LC, Taft Papers, Chapelle to Taft, Manila, April 13, 1901.

[71] 98-W-2/1, Storer to Gibbons, Madrid, June 4, 1901. Some weeks before Mrs. Storer had forwarded to Gibbons copies of several of Taft's letters from Manila, and she took occasion to say that her husband thought it was of the highest importance to replace Martinelli as apostolic delegate in Washington by a man who knew English well, would go out socially, and acquaint himself with American ways. "We have heard," she said, "that Monseigneur Zaleski fills all these conditions." Archbishop Ladislaus Zaleski was at the time Apostolic Delegate to the East Indies. It was the opinion of the Storers that the appointment by the Holy See of such a person to Washington would pave the way for a nuncio to be officially recognized in the future (98-V-5, Maria Storer to Gibbons, Biarritz, May 11, 1901).

[72] AASP, Ireland Papers, O'Connell to Ireland, Rome, June 6, 1901, copy.

[73] *Ibid.*, Gibbons to Ireland, Rome, June 20, 1901.

nothing of what Gibbons had accomplished toward settlement of the Church's problems in the Philippine Islands.

After visits to France, England, and Ireland the cardinal sailed for home on the *Etruria* and landed in New York on August 24. Upon his arrival he was interviewed by the reporters and the leading New York papers of the following day carried the accounts. The *Times* said, "He positively refused to discuss the subject of the Church in the Philippines," and the *Herald*, in referring to his audiences with the Pope, quoted Gibbons as saying, "I cannot say whether we discussed the situation in the Philippines or not. As to Cuba, that is not in my line." Following a visit to his friend, Major Keiley of Brooklyn, the cardinal proceeded to Baltimore where he was given a remarkable demonstration of welcome on August 26. An estimated crowd of between thirty and forty thousand people turned out to cheer him on his return home and acting Mayor Henry Williams and Charles J. Bonaparte gave the speeches of welcome. The Baltimore *American* of August 27 quoted Gibbons as saying in his response to their words, "In all sincerity I tell you that there is no country like America, no place like home, and no home like a home in Baltimore." After the reception at the station the cardinal suggested that they go to the cathedral to thank God for the blessing of a safe home-coming. Once more he revealed the deep affection he felt for his home city when he addressed the throng gathered to hear him in the cathedral. He said he was not attached to buildings or to brick and mortar, but rather to all that was good and upright among his fellow citizens without distinction of nationality or religion. "I have always enjoyed," said Gibbons, "the most friendly relations with all my fellow-citizens without distinction of race or creed, for I believe in the words, 'Behold how good and joyful a thing it is for brethren to dwell together in unity.' " In view of the fact that Cardinal Gibbons had made his journey to the Holy See mainly with a view to fulfilling his visit *ad limina,* and that no unusual triumph or spectacular event had distinguished his trip, the reception accorded him after an absence of three and a half months was, indeed, unusual, and the Baltimore *American* was probably not far wrong when it said that never before in the history of the city had a citizen received such a welcome upon his return home.

But if the Cardinal of Baltimore had little to say about what he had done on Philippine matters, the Archbishop of St. Paul was not so reticent. Ireland welcomed Gibbons back to the United States and said he had no doubt but that wondrous good would come of the cardinal's visit to Rome in making known the American point of view and in guarding the authorities there from what he termed, "future blunders in our regard." He had had several recent letters from Cardinal Rampolla about the Philippines, all of which led up to a formal request of the American government through Ireland that a representative be sent from Washington to treat with the Holy See about the friars' lands and other questions. The idea of regular diplomatic relations, he said, was clearly left out by Rampolla, and there was mention only of a temporary and restricted negotiation on special matters. The archbishop would have appreciated the counsel of Gibbons but in his absence he had done the best he could. Secretary Root was inclined to view the proposal with favor, but he was waiting for word from Taft in Manila before he made a decision. "From the general tone of Card. Rampolla's letters," Ireland told Gibbons, "I can see that Abp. Chapelle does not count for much," to which he added, "At any rate, the American government will be much displeased, as Mr. Root said to me, to see him return to Manila."[74] What reaction Gibbons showed to the growing impression of Chapelle's failure in the mission, to which the cardinal had originally been so pleased to see him assigned, we have no way of knowing.

Two weeks after Ireland gave this first intimation of a special American mission to the Holy See, President McKinley was struck down by an assassin's bullet at Buffalo on September 6 and died eight days later. When Theodore Roosevelt who succeeded immediately to the presidency issued a proclamation calling on the American people to gather in their churches on the following Thursday, September 19, the day of the funeral, Cardinal Gibbons responded at once and ordered memorial services in all the churches of his archdiocese. He personally presided in the cathedral of Baltimore on that occasion and preached the sermon. The cardinal extolled the virtues of the late President, expressed his sympathy and that of his people to Mrs. McKinley and the bereaved family, and took occasion to point a moral from the thousands of petitions which had been

---

[74] 98-Y-9, Ireland to Gibbons, St. Paul, August 25, 1901.

made to Almighty God to save the President's life. True, God had not seen fit to spare McKinley's life, but, said Gibbons:

> He has infused into the hearts of the American people a greater reverence for the head of the Nation, and a greater abhorrence of assassination. He has intensified and energized our love of country and our devotion to our political institutions.

The beautiful spectacle of prayers ascending from tens of thousands of temples throughout the land would not be lost in value. It had been a most eloquent recognition of God's superintending providence over the nation and such earnest and united prayers, said the cardinal, "will not fail to draw down upon us the blessings of the Almighty."[75]

With the advent of Theodore Roosevelt to the presidency there opened a span of years for Cardinal Gibbons during which he was probably on more intimate terms with the occupant of the White House than at any other time of his life. The day after McKinley's funeral he conveyed to the new President a message of condolence from Cardinal Moran of Sydney, and he availed himself of the opportunity to express the earnest hope that Roosevelt's administration would be creditable to himself and would redound to the material prosperity of the country.[76] Roosevelt replied that in thanking the Australian cardinal through Gibbons he wished to add a word of what he called "my regard for you and my appreciation of your attitude," and he hoped to see him soon.[77] Ten days later the President asked the cardinal to recommend a priest for a vacancy among the chaplaincies in the army and he outlined the qualifications which he thought the man should have.[78] Gibbons hastened to say that he would take immediate steps to select a priest who would fill all the requirements which Roosevelt so justly demanded for the office and

[75] Reily, *op. cit.*, VII, 1191, 1198–1200. At the annual meeting of the archbishops in Washington in November a formal resolution was passed in the name of all the Catholics of the United States lamenting the assassination of William McKinley and deploring the fact, as it read, "that in our land of enlightenment and liberty such a crime should have been possible." This resolution was followed by a second which invoked the benedictions of heaven on the administration of President Roosevelt (99-F-8, Minutes of the Meeting of the Archbishops, Washington, November 21–22, 1901).

[76] LC, Roosevelt Papers, Gibbons to Roosevelt, Baltimore, September 20, 1901.
[77] 99-B-5, Roosevelt to Gibbons, Washington, September 24, 1901.
[78] 99-C-3, same to same, Washington, October 5, 1901.

when the President was more at leisure he said he would call to pay his respects.[79] Thus was there begun a friendship between the two men that deepened with the passing of time and that was only ended seventeen years later by the death of Mr. Roosevelt.

Sometime late in October the cardinal went to Washington where he had a long conversation with the President on affairs in the Philippines insofar as they related to the Church. Roosevelt confessed that he found the problem of the friars' lands a baffling one, and that all the efforts so far made by Taft and himself had ended in failure. Gibbons inquired the terms on which he wished to make the settlement, to which Roosevelt replied that the most it seemed possible to pay for the lands, and still win the consent of Congress, was about $7,000,000. It was his idea that the lands should then be resold to other purchasers in small holdings so that the friars would no longer be a factor in the economic life of the islands. At the conclusion of their discussion Gibbons said, "I will undertake, Mr. President, to obtain a settlement for you on the terms which you state. I have no suggestion of my own on the subject."[80]

Some days after the interview with Roosevelt the cardinal informed Rampolla of his visit to the White House. He refrained entirely from giving any particulars and limited himself to statements of a general character which conveyed the impression of the good will obtaining on both sides. He told the papal Secretary of State that he had assured Roosevelt that the Holy See had constantly refused to have anything to do with the Aguinaldo party and, moreover, that the Roman authorities had full confidence in the sincerity and benevolent attitude of the American government. In turn, the President had asked him to make known to the Holy See his esteem for the Pope and Rampolla, that he knew and appreciated their good dispositions toward the United States, and that they could count on the most sincere and efficacious efforts being made to reach a solution on the problems of the Church in the Philippines that would be pleasing to Leo XIII and his Secretary of State. Roosevelt, said Gibbons, was very well disposed toward Catholics and toward the Church, and the

---

[79] LC, Roosevelt Papers, Gibbons to Roosevelt, Baltimore, October 7, 1901.

[80] Will, *op. cit.*, II, 615. The date of the interview is not given by Will. On the properties involved cf. Ambrose Coleman, O.P., "The Friars' Estates in the Philippines," *American Catholic Quarterly Review*, XXX (January, 1905), 57–79.

cardinal did not fear to go so far as to assure Rampolla that the Holy See would have nothing but praise for the action which the President would take in all these matters.[81] Having thus contributed to the creation of a cordial atmosphere in which the negotiations might be inaugurated, for the time being Gibbons let the matter rest there.

During the late autumn of 1901 the discussions continued in Washington between President Roosevelt and various parties about the best methods to be pursued in bringing a settlement to the troublesome friars' question in the Philippines. Archbishop Ireland, who spent much time in the capital that autumn in company with Bishop O'Gorman of Sioux Falls, saw the President on November 6 and went over the matter of a special mission to Rome for the friars' case, as well as the appointment of additional Catholic chaplains for the army. He reported to Gibbons that the idea in general of the mission was rather well received and, insofar as chaplains were concerned, the President had insisted that the priests to be appointed must be first-class men.[82] A month later John J. McCook of New York, a personal friend of Roosevelt's, visited the White House where he found the President still sorely perplexed about the friars' lands. He asked McCook if he had a suggestion by which the case might be brought to a practical conclusion. McCook replied that Roosevelt should confer with Gibbons as the highest representative in the United States of what he called the controlling authority, and in reporting this to the cardinal he said, "I assured him that you, and you only, were in a position to open the way to an early and complete adjustment of the matter, the importance of which could not, in my opinion, be overestimated."[83] On the same day

---

[81] 99-G-5, Gibbons to Rampolla, Baltimore, November 5, 1901, copy. Rampolla replied that Leo XIII was glad to hear of the favorable sentiments of the new President and thought they augured well for the Church and for the Catholics of the United States (99-F-7, Rampolla to Gibbons, Rome, November 21, 1901).

[82] 99-E-8, Ireland to Gibbons, Washington, November 7, 1901. The day before in New York the Archbishop of St. Paul, fresh from New Haven where he had been awarded an honorary LL.D. degree by Yale, told Monsignor O'Connell that Roosevelt was much more his [Ireland's] friend than McKinley. He remarked that Gibbons was still radiant of the sunshine of smiles poured upon him in Rome. "But so far as I can see," added Ireland, "it was only the sunshine of smiles" (ADR, Ireland to O'Connell, New York, November 6, 1901).

[83] 99-G-8, McCook to Gibbons, New York, December 10, 1901, *Personal & Confidential*.

that McCook communicated this news Gibbons dispatched the following letter to President Roosevelt:

> Having learned that you have under consideration the project of sending to the Vatican a representative of our Government to treat of Philippine questions, I am persuaded that such a course is very desirable.
>
> If a judicious representative were chosen, he would hasten the solution of Philippine matters. In Rome reside the Heads of all the Religious Orders who are subject to the Pope.
>
> I do not see any reasonable objection to such an embassy. It would be the action of one great Power treating with another on vital issues. The mission of course would be a specific & temporary one.
>
> I trust you will pardon me for the suggestion which is prompted by my interests in the welfare of our common country.[84]

In the meantime McCook did not let the matter drop. Upon his return to New York he once more took up the subject with Roosevelt and urged him to act, not only because a purchase of the friars' lands would be right in itself under American treaty obligations, but because he could think of nothing that would redound more certainly to the credit of the administration than a prompt solution to this difficult situation. "If you have not had the suggested conference at luncheon with the official who can do most to aid you in accomplishing this most important result," wrote McCook, "I earnestly beg, in the public interest, that it may not be long delayed."[85] Ireland, who saw the President on the evening of December 14, reported that Roosevelt was now enthusiastic about the mission to Rome and had brought into his counsels Senators William B. Allison of Ohio and John C. Spooner of Wisconsin who agreed to defend the project if it was attacked in Congress. Moreover, Ireland had been to New York where, at the suggestion of the President, he had seen Lyman Abbott, editor of the *Outlook*, and William H. Ward, editor of the *Independent*, and they had both written to Roosevelt strongly endorsing the plan. The archbishop remarked to Gibbons, "The President was much pleased with your letter."[86] On Christmas

---

[84] LC, Roosevelt Papers, Gibbons to Roosevelt, Baltimore, December 10, 1901, *Personal*.

[85] *Ibid.*, McCook to Roosevelt, New York, December 10, 1901, *Personal*.

[86] 99-H-4, Ireland to Gibbons, Washington, December 5, 1901. It was in a letter

Eve the cardinal informed Monsignor O'Connell of developments to date and said Roosevelt had promised to invite him to confer with him on the subject. "The secret was well kept here," he said, "but I see that it has leaked out in Rome."[87]

Archbishop Ireland was likewise disturbed by the news dispatches from Rome. In sending his greetings to Gibbons for the new year he remarked that the cables saying that the Vatican was more than ever hopeful of seeing a diplomatic representative in the United States were disquieting and might do harm. He had recently had another letter from Rampolla urging him to work and he was returning to Washington late in January to continue his mission.[88] Upon the completion of his stay in the capital the Archbishop of St. Paul left O'Gorman there to look after their interests and in introducing the bishop by letter to Judge Taft, he told him few others understood America and Rome better than O'Gorman, and he added, "anything I could say to you, Bishop O'Gorman will say as well as I could."[89] Simultaneously with these private negotiations various aspects of the friars' lands' question were aired in the press. The *Independent* of February 20, 1902, for example, carried an article of Salvatore Cortesi from Rome entitled, "The Vatican and the Philippines." Cortesi stated that in the early stages of the discussion McKinley had charged Attorney General Joseph McKenna to take the necessary steps about a settlement with the Holy See and, said Cortesi, "he found in Cardinal Gibbons, to whom he turned, a willing, enlightened and patriotic medium for the laying of the *desideratum* of the Executive before the Holy See." After a reference or two to the failure of Chapelle in Manila, the writer related that eight of the cardinals in the Roman Curia were either themselves religious or favorable to the friars' cause and for that reason, thought Cortesi, it would not be easy to win an agreement. He reported that the question had aroused in Vatican circles the hope of having one of their

to Bellamy Storer from Washington on December 8, 1901, that Ireland stated his visits to Abbott and Ward were made at the President's suggestion. Storer, *op. cit.*, p. 61. Chapelle arrived in Washington that same week and regretted that his time was so taken up by urgent business that he could not get to Baltimore to see Gibbons (99-H-8, Chapelle to Gibbons, Washington, December 19, 1901).

[87] ADR, Gibbons to O'Connell, Baltimore, December 24, 1901.

[88] 99-J-1, Ireland to Gibbons, St. Paul, January 1, 1902.

[89] LC, Taft Papers, O'Gorman to Taft, Washington, February 13, 1902, enclosing Ireland to Taft, Washington, February 12, 1902.

long-standing aspirations fulfilled, namely, an American representative at the Holy See, which prompted Cortesi to conclude
his article by asking if it were possible for the United States to
meet this desire without violating, "if not the word, at least the
spirit of the Constitution?"

News items of this kind — and there were many of a similar
type — were not helpful in preparing the American public for
the coming negotiations in Rome. Nonetheless, plans went forward and on March 13 O'Gorman announced to Cardinal Gibbons
that Ireland had managed to get for the bishop what he called
"the perilous honor" of appointment to Rome on Philippine affairs. O'Gorman thought it might prove perilous because the
United States was going to insist on some things which the
friar influence would not like to yield. "I know your letter to
the President about the matter," said O'Gorman, "had very
great influence with him."[90] With a view to enlightening public
opinion on the issues involved, Taft, who had been inaugurated
on the previous July 4 as the first civil Governor of the Philippines, published an article on "The People of the Philippine
Islands" which ran in the issues of May 1 and 8 of the *Independent*. In the latter issue he stated that the Christian Filipinos
belonged to two classes, the Spanish-speaking who numbered
about ten per cent and, secondly, the uneducated masses.
The Filipino, according to Taft, was a good Roman Catholic
but though he loved his Church he hated the Spanish friars because of the political and economic power they had exercised
in former years. "The feeling against the Friars," he said, "is
a political and not at all a religious one." The writer made no
distinction between those who disliked the friars for political
motives and those Filipinos who bore no ill will toward the
religious.

When the decision had finally been made to send an American
representative to the Holy See to treat of this question, the first
name considered to head the mission was that of James F. Smith,
associate justice of the supreme court of the Philippines and a
Catholic. But the President ultimately determined to make Governor Taft the head of the commission with Smith and Major
John Porter as members. Ten days before he sailed Taft paid a
visit to Gibbons in Baltimore where they held a lengthy con-

---

[90] 99-M-3, O'Gorman to Gibbons, Sioux Falls, March 13 [1902].

ference on the Philippines. The cardinal gained the most favorable impressions of Taft and in telling Monsignor O'Connell about it he said, "He is a splendid type of an American citizen, & he is disposed to be not only just but generous to the Catholic Church."[91] Bishop O'Gorman, who had preceded Taft to Rome, was awaiting the arrival of the governor, and in commenting on Leo XIII's joy at receiving Gibbons' letter of congratulations on his jubilee, he remarked, "The Taft Commission simply delights him."[92]

Governor Taft remained in Rome for about a month and by the middle of June, 1902, he was able to submit to Secretary of War Root the terms of purchase of the friars' lands and further details of his negotiations with the Holy See. On July 18 he had reached the closing stages of his mission when he informed Root that the Pope had agreed to instruct the Apostolic Delegate to the Philippines to work out the final details of agreement regarding the properties in question with the American government in Manila. Three days later Taft had his farewell audience of Leo XIII and made ready to depart for home.[93] The principles of a settlement which had been agreed to at Rome and the details which had to be determined later in Manila would, of course, have to be approved by Congress. All of this took time and it was only in December, 1903, that 410,000 acres of the lands of the Spanish friars in the Philippines were finally purchased by the United States for the sum of $7,239,000 in gold and with that the case was closed insofar as the Church was concerned.[94]

From the time the question had first been mentioned in the press, opposition to the purchase had been expressed by some in both the Catholic and secular journals. The President received

[91] ADR, Gibbons to O'Connell, Baltimore, May 7, 1902, *Private*.

[92] 99-R-6, O'Gorman to Gibbons, Rome, May 17, 1902.

[93] National Archives, Records of the Bureau of Insular Affairs, Taft to Root, Rome, July 21, 1902, cablegram, photostat. The Pope had asked Taft if he could accept a decoration, and when he replied in the negative he was presented with a mosaic for himself and an enamel piece for Mrs. Taft. Taft inquired of Root whether the gift should be accepted or returned and the Secretary of War replied that it could be retained, he thought, as personal. If the governor had further doubt he might ask the government, but Root felt to return it would be viewed as a discourtesy. He took occasion to congratulate Taft on the dignity and ability with which he had discharged his difficult duties in Rome. *Ibid.*, Root to Taft, Washington, July 21, 1902, cablegram, photostat.

[94] *Report of the Philippine Commission, 1903* (Washington, 1904), Part I, 43.

protests from certain Catholic groups against the injustice which they said was being done to the friars by the government. Articles such as that of John J. Wynne, S.J., called "The Friars Must Stay,"[95] appeared in some Catholic publications, while journals like the *North American Review* likewise carried defenses of the friars' position against the American government.[96] Roosevelt was puzzled by the Catholic criticism. He told Major John Crane that the government had only acted on the request of Archbishop Ireland and with the cordial approval of Cardinal Gibbons. In sending Taft to Rome he said he had feared anti-Catholic bias and that was why Taft had written for the *Outlook* and the *Independent,* thinking it was in that quarter that people would have to be convinced. But it had never entered his head, as he said, "that we should encounter Catholic hostility."[97]

In one Catholic editor, however, the government found a stanch defender. Herman J. Heuser of the *American Ecclesiastical Review* had little sympathy with the Catholic critics. He said the Taft Commission had done a fine work and that the express avowal of the Pope and Rampolla concerning the good dispositions of the United States should have stilled the criticism. Father Heuser struck out sharply at the Catholic press critics and especially at the Germans whose papers, he said, were in good measure conducted with the active assistance of the religious orders who were biased in the case. Moreover, in Heuser's mind some of the Catholic editors were guilty of publishing stories on such flimsy evidence that it simply made them falsehoods. "It is the *odium theologicum,*" said Heuser, "carried into the domain of social and political life by half-informed champions who see in their own interests the interests of a common cause."[98]

[95] *The Messenger,* XXXVIII (August, 1902), 211–229, which reprints correspondence and protests of certain Catholic groups to President Roosevelt. Ireland, no friend of the friar interests, told Bellamy Storer in a letter from New York of April 25, 1904, "It is admitted on all sides that the Friars received a generous price for their lands. Letters coming to me from Catholics in the Islands confirm this view." Storer, *op. cit.,* p. 109.

[96] Bonsal, *op. cit.,* CLXXV (October, 1902), 449–460.

[97] LC, Taft Papers, Roosevelt to Crane, Oyster Bay, New York, July 31, 1902, copy.

[98] "Catholic Journalism and the Friar Question," *American Ecclesiastical Review,* XXVII (September, 1902), 273. As late as 1906 the debate about the friars was still in progress in some Catholic circles when the *Western Watchman* of St. Louis on January 7 of that year defended the government against the friars' point of view, only to be answered by Ambrose Coleman, O.P., in the New York

The criticism of the administration by some of the Catholic papers, however, in no way affected the friendship of President Roosevelt and Cardinal Gibbons. When the President escaped without injury from an accident at Pittsfield, Massachusetts, in early September the cardinal thanked God and congratulated Roosevelt and the nation on his providential deliverance.[99] The President was grateful, thinking it characteristic of Gibbons to write him, and he expressed the hope that he would see him as soon as he returned to Washington.[100] O'Gorman also congratulated the President after the accident and said Rampolla had told him of Leo XIII's gratification in the same regard. The Bishop of Sioux Falls assured Roosevelt that he believed the Taft mission to Rome was no mistake and would do good to all concerned. Following his visit to Oyster Bay, O'Gorman had written a lengthy report to Rampolla and the papal Secretary of State had read it in full to the Pope. "The quietus that has fallen on our recalcitrant Catholics is owing," O'Gorman told Roosevelt, "in a good measure, to my report, for I did not spare them."[101]

Meanwhile Cardinal Gibbons did not forget the Church in the Philippines. When the Pope appointed Archbishop Guidi as

Freeman's Journal of February 17, 1906. Cf. also Coleman's "Do the Filipinos Really Hate the Spanish Friars?" *American Catholic Quarterly Review,* XXX (July and October, 1905), 449–461; 672–685.

[99] LC, Roosevelt Papers, Gibbons to Roosevelt, Baltimore, September 11, 1902.

[100] 100-A-6, Roosevelt to Gibbons, Oyster Bay, September 15, 1902. Their correspondence reveals the frequency and cordiality of their contacts. Cf., e.g., 100-D-2, Roosevelt to Gibbons, Washington, November 8, 1902, *Personal;* LC, Roosevelt Papers, Gibbons to Roosevelt, Baltimore, March 3 and 16, 1903.

[101] LC, Roosevelt Papers, O'Gorman to Roosevelt, Sioux Falls, October 17, 1902. LC, Taft Papers, contain a manuscript of eleven typed pages entitled "Memorandum of Bishop O'Gorman" which is undated but from internal evidence would appear to be of midsummer 1902. O'Gorman remarked that there was considerable private Protestant opposition to the Taft mission to Rome, and that in Catholic circles the chief criticism came from priests of St. Patrick's Cathedral in New York. He stated that the appointment of Donato Sbarretti by the Holy See as apostolic delegate to Manila was "for reasons which are not set down here" opposed by the Roosevelt administration. According to O'Gorman, the President went so far as to instruct Taft verbally to lodge a protest with the Holy See against the Sbarretti appointment. As for Ireland's role, O'Gorman said the archbishop had never struck a harder blow at the religious than the Taft Commission, and in referring to Ireland's somewhat sensational statements against the religious orders when he preached at O'Gorman's consecration in 1896, he called it, "The most eloquent peroration to my consecration sermon." The bishop felt Rome had made a mistake by urging that the settlement of the final details of the land purchase take place in Manila instead of in Rome, and he ended by remarking, "Wonder if Vatican realizes what it has lost in material profits and in diplomatic prestige."

the new apostolic delegate to the islands to succeed Chapelle the cardinal suggested to Rampolla that Monsignor Frederick Z. Rooker, secretary of the Apostolic Delegation in Washington, be named as secretary to Guidi since Rooker was an American of several generations' descent and was on excellent terms with the President and influential members of the American government.[102] But the suggestion, unfortunately, came too late as Guidi had already selected his secretary and it was not possible for Rampolla to second Gibbons' recommendation.[103] Some months later Gibbons was approached by Benjamin F. Tracy, former Secretary of the Navy, who told him that President Roosevelt and others would be gratified at the appointment of Thomas A. Hendrick of the Diocese of Rochester as Archbishop of Manila, and Tracy asked the cardinal to consider Hendrick's name. Gibbons summarized the qualifications of the priest for Cardinal Rampolla and included the data submitted to him on Hendrick by Bishop McQuaid of Rochester.[104] Once again the candidate about whom the cardinal had written to Rome was not selected, and in June Jeremiah J. Harty, a priest of the Archdiocese of St. Louis, was appointed Archbishop of Manila, although Hendrick was named Bishop of Cebu in the Philippines later that same summer.

Among the problems which faced the American government in Manila one of the most serious was that of education. In January, 1902, a Bureau of Education had been set up in the islands in the hope that through such an agency there could be inaugurated a system of schools which would reduce the exceedingly high illiteracy rate. The very meager provisions that had previously been made for elementary education had been the work of the Spanish friars, and with their removal from the Philippines the situation became even worse. The efforts to replace the Spaniards with American religious were very slow in getting under way and the departure of two American Augustinians,

---

[102] 100-A-8, Gibbons to Rampolla, Baltimore, September 22, 1902, copy in French.

[103] 100-B-7, Rampolla to Gibbons, Rome, October 13, 1902.

[104] 100-L-5, Gibbons to Rampolla, Baltimore, May 6, 1903, copy. Cf. also 100-K-7, Tracy to Gibbons, New York, April 15, 1903; 100-K-10, McQuaid to Gibbons, Rochester, April 23, 1903. At the beginning of March, Gibbons took lunch with the President and suggested that he felicitate the Pope on the silver jubilee of his pontificate and send a souvenir. Roosevelt took to the idea and sent through Gibbons a copy of the messages of the Presidents to the United States Senate (100-J-5, Gibbons to Rampolla, Baltimore, March 22, 1903, copy).

Daniel J. O'Mahoney and John McErlain, in the autumn of 1902 marked only the bare beginning of replacements.[105] The situation was known at the Holy See, of course, and in April, 1903, Cardinal Rampolla instructed Diomede Falconio, Apostolic Delegate to the United States, to appeal in the Pope's name to the hierarchy for teachers in the Philippines.[106] The archbishops took up the question in their meeting at Washington on April 23, but since negotiations had already been inaugurated with the government it was the view of the metropolitans that no new approach should be made. The archbishops asked Cardinal Gibbons to assure the Holy See that the attempt of the bishops to find teachers would be continued and extended to every part of the country where they could possibly be found.[107]

In this matter, as in so many other aspects of Philippine business, Archbishop Ireland took a leading role and two weeks after the meeting of the metropolitans he told Gibbons that he had just been authorized by cable from Manila by James F. Smith, Secretary of Public Instruction there, to secure 108 additional candidates for teachers' positions in the islands. Ireland outlined the procedure to be followed and urged the cardinal to secure as many applications as he could among prospective teachers.[108] The establishment of a school system and the knotty question of religious instruction caused, as was to be expected, some trouble in the Philippines. In late October, 1903, Smith reported to the President on the work of his office and in a detailed way he challenged the critics of his policies. Roosevelt thought the report so admirable as to be worth sending on to the cardinal.[109] Gibbons said he had read it with profound interest and satisfaction. He was happy to say that the suspicions and criticisms of the government by some religious journals in the United States were gradually diminishing in proportion as new light was thrown on the situation in the Philippines. He had every reason to hope that the religious conflict in the islands would be quieted before

---

[105] *Outlook,* September 27, 1902.

[106] 100-K-9, Falconio to Gibbons, Washington, April 21, 1903.

[107] Minutes of the Meeting of the Archbishops, Washington, April 23, 1903, copy.

[108] 100-L-2, Ireland to Gibbons, St. Paul, May 4, 1903. This information was conveyed to Monsignor Francesco Marchetti, auditor of the Apostolic Delegation, with a copy of the minutes of the archbishops' meeting (100-L-3, Gibbons to Marchetti, Baltimore, March 6, 1903, copy).

[109] 100-V-1, Roosevelt to Gibbons, Washington, December 1, 1903, *Personal.*

many months, and he set down the bases of his optimism as follows.

> The sources of my confidence lie in the judicial temper of Commissioner Smith, the arrival of the Bishops at their respective posts, and the calm conciliatory temper of Mgr. Guidi, the Apostolic Delegate; above all the earnest desire of yourself & your administration to be guided by a lofty sense of justice & impartiality in promoting peace & harmony among the conflicting elements that have to be dealt with in the Philippine Islands.[110]

But despite Gibbons' confidence, the Church of the Philippines continued to give trouble. By the end of 1903 the four American prelates who had been appointed by the Holy See to rule dioceses in the islands had reached their destinations. But the advent of Harty to Manila, Hendrick to Cebu, Rooker to Jaro, and Dennis J. Dougherty to Neuva Segovia had not been welcome to the insurgents and their sympathizers. In the middle of April, 1904, Gibbons received a cable from Bishop Hendrick requesting him to use his influence with the President in lending protection to the Church in Cebu. Neither the cardinal nor Roosevelt was at the time aware of the facts in the case, but the President stated that he would have inquiries made at once and report the result.[111]

Meanwhile, however, the President was upset at learning that Gibbons had signed a petition which requested that the United States promise ultimate independence to the Philippine Islands. He told the cardinal, "If such a promise was made by us one of the first consequences would be that the position of Bishop Hendrick and the other American Bishops would grow literally intolerable." The agitation for the petition, said Roosevelt, was playing directly into the hands of the very men who were intriguing against Hendrick and his fellow bishops, and it would render all the more difficult the task of Governor Luke E. Wright and his colleagues who were trying to protect the American prelates.[112] Gibbons sensed at once the mistake he had made. He explained that he had signed the petition under the influence of a declaration ascribed to Taft when he was governor in Manila that the future independence of the Filipinos would be assured

---

[110] LC, Roosevelt Papers, Gibbons to Roosevelt, Baltimore, December 2, 1903.

[111] Diary, April 19–20 [1904], p. 301.

[112] 101-F, Roosevelt to Gibbons, Washington, April 26, 1904, *Personal.*

and, too, with the understanding that this would not take place until the islands were ready for independence. "I should deeply regret," said the cardinal, "to do anything that would in the smallest way embarrass you in your delicate task & formidable burden of maintaining peace & order in those Islands."[113] From that time forward Gibbons resolutely opposed all efforts to hasten Philippine independence.

After filling out the unexpired term of McKinley, Theodore Roosevelt in November, 1904, stood for the presidency in his own right and won by a large majority. A week after the election Cardinal Gibbons wrote him, "I have waited till the first flash of victory had subsided to tender you my hearty congratulations. I pray God that your administration may redound to the peace, prosperity & development of our beloved country & to your own greater honor."[114] The President was gratified by the cardinal's message and thanked him as well for what he termed, "all your courtesy and kindness during the three years that have passed."[115] These two friends who found each other's company so congenial were happy at the prospect of four more years of association in the business affecting their common interests. There were still many unsolved problems in the island possessions of the United States which related to the Catholic Church, and it would take the best efforts of Roosevelt and Gibbons to see these matters to a satisfactory settlement.

The following June when Roosevelt appointed Charles J. Bonaparte of Baltimore as Secretary of the Navy, it gave great satisfaction to Gibbons. He told the President, "The choice is creditable to your head and your heart, and I think it will meet with the cordial approval of all the reflecting citizens of the United States. You have in Mr. Bonaparte," said the cardinal, "not only a devoted friend, but also a wise and prudent counsel-

---

[113] LC, Roosevelt Papers, Gibbons to Roosevelt, Baltimore, April 27, 1904, *Private*.

[114] 101-M, Gibbons to Roosevelt, Baltimore, November 14, 1904, copy.

[115] 101-P, Roosevelt to Gibbons, Washington, November 15, 1904. Roosevelt's regard for the cardinal had warmed considerably since the day in 1891 when he told his cousin in a letter of February 1, "My pleasantest dinner was one at Charles Bonaparte's to meet Cardinal Gibbons. The latter was very entertaining; the cultivated Jesuit [*sic*], with rather kindly emotions and a thorough knowledge of the fact that his Church must become both Republicanized and Americanized to retain its hold here." Anna Roosevelt Cowles (Ed.), *Letters from Theodore Roosevelt to Anna Roosevelt Cowles, 1870–1918* (New York, 1924), p. 113.

lor — a man sans peur et sans reproche."[116] If the appointment
of the distinguished Catholic lawyer did not meet with all the
cordiality that Gibbons had anticipated, he was right in predicting that Roosevelt would be well served by Bonaparte's wisdom
and integrity. The three men had long been close friends, and
it was in Bonaparte's home that the future President Roosevelt
and the cardinal had met many years before. But on principle
Bonaparte refused to take an active part in Catholic interests
before the government, since it was his belief that moves of
this kind would expose him and the Church to serious and reasonable criticism.[117]

One of the most difficult problems that arose in the Philippines
during Roosevelt's second administration was the adjustment
of the claims made by the Church for damages done to its buildings and properties during the time they were occupied by the
American military forces. In January, 1906, Archbishop Ambrose
Agius, O.S.B., who had become apostolic delegate in Manila
following the death of Guidi in June, 1904, appealed to Gibbons
to use his influence with the government to secure these claims.
Agius maintained that the ruling of Taft, who had in the interim
returned to Washington as Secretary of War, in excluding from
the assessment for damages all the destruction arising from acts
of war, looting, and other irregular actions of the military, had
reduced the figure to $363,030.19 which was totally inadequate
to repair the Church's losses.[118] The sum quoted by Agius was the
amount awarded by the board of church claims set up in Manila
by the government. President Roosevelt, too, thought that a
more generous settlement was owing to the Church and in early
March he told Taft, "I agree with you that this money is short
of what the Church in the Philippines is morally entitled to."

---

[116] LC, Roosevelt Papers, Gibbons to Roosevelt, Washington, June 3, 1905.

[117] Eric F. Goldman, *Charles J. Bonaparte, Patrician Reformer. His Earlier
Career* (Baltimore, 1943), p. 95.

[118] 103-A, Agius to Gibbons, Manila, January 19, 1906. About six years before
there had been agitation over the reported desecration of churches by the military,
and Henry C. Corbin, adjutant general of the United States, had then cabled an
enquiry to Otis, in which he said, "Enjoin on your officers special respect and
protection for all church property." Corbin to Otis, Washington, September 18,
1899, cablegram (*Correspondence Relating to the War with Spain*, II, 1070).
Otis cabled back the number of churches occupied as sixteen with three convents,
to which he added, "Church property respected, protected by our troops." Otis
to Alger, Manila, September 21, 1899 (*ibid.*, II, 1072).

Roosevelt was in favor of appointing another board which would report an additional sum to which the Church might claim an equitable right and which they could then ask Congress to appropriate.[119]

The Archbishop of Manila likewise became aroused about the matter and sent Gibbons a lengthy document which was sharply critical of the government, and which he asked the cardinal to forward to the President. The cardinal did as he was requested, stating that he hoped the case would appeal to Roosevelt's sense of justice and fair play and receive his favorable sentence. After paying tribute to Harty's zeal and wisdom, he said, "I am satisfied that by sustaining the just claims of the Archbishop of Manila you will strengthen and consolidate the authority of the American Government, for the Church will be the guardian and promoter of peace and good order in the Islands."[120] But the communication from Harty met with anything but a friendly reception at the White House. Roosevelt was distinctly annoyed by the strictures of the archbishop against the government's conduct and policies in the islands, and while he acknowledged that anything coming from Gibbons would have his careful consideration, the opening sentence of Harty's document, he said, prejudiced him against the whole of it. It was not surprising that the famous Roosevelt temper should have been stirred by the manner in which Harty launched his case. The President quoted back for the cardinal the offending sentence which read:

> From the time of American occupation of the Philippines the Catholic Church has been harassed and confounded with an apparently studied purpose on the part of the Government of the United States to control as its own if not to confiscate outright great charities of undoubted private origin.

Roosevelt maintained that such a statement was simply untrue. Moreover, he denied as false Harty's contention that the military commanders who had gone to the Philippines during the war had manifested persistent opposition to the Catholic faith, and he mentioned as examples of prominent Catholic officers John F. Weston who would soon succeed to command of the whole archipelago and James F. Smith who had originally entered the

---

[119] LC, Roosevelt Papers, Letterbook 32, Roosevelt to Taft, Washington, March 6, 1906.
[120] *Ibid.*, Gibbons to Roosevelt, New Orleans, February 11 [1906].

islands at the head of a California regiment and who had just been confirmed by the senate as Governor of the Philippines. Nonetheless, Roosevelt would submit the matter to Taft and if the latter deemed it wise he would forward it to Smith for study.[121]

Gibbons found in this case, as in so many others, that the role of mediator was not an enviable one. He informed Archbishop Harty that he had passed on his document to Roosevelt. "But in his reply," said the cardinal, "he was evidently displeased with the severe tone of the paper, & the manner in which the Administration was arraigned."[122] The following day he told the President that he regretted being requested to send him Harty's communication on account of the brusqueness of its language and the sweeping character of its complaints. "I have written to the Archbishop," said Gibbons, "to that effect. It was not in his usual style." He now enclosed the letter of Agius regarding the damages claimed, but added that he had no knowledge whatever of the merits of the case and, therefore, he merely submitted it to Roosevelt's sense of justice and benevolence.[123] The President thanked him for his kind and courteous letter and told Gibbons that he had taken up at once the complaints of Agius with Taft, Root, Bonaparte, and Bourke Cockran. All were agreed that when the report of the claims commission reached Washington it would be best to try first to get Congress to appropriate the amount actually awarded, and phrase a recommendation in such language that a later request for a further appropriation would not be blocked. Taft felt, said Roosevelt, that there was an equitable right to an additional appropriation for the benefit of the Church but, of course, the President had no idea whether Congress would act favorably or not on his recommendation.[124]

---

[121] 103-B, Roosevelt to Gibbons, Washington, February 15, 1906, *Personal*. An effort to find a copy of the Harty letter was unsuccessful. A letter which the archbishop addressed from Manila on February 27, 1906, to the Governor General of the Philippines and the Philippine Commission in which he complained bitterly about a threatened confiscation of San Juan de Dios Hospital, was kindly supplied in copy to the writer by Patrick H. Ahern from the Ireland Papers in the AASP, but this could not be the letter which incensed Roosevelt since the latter was sent to him by Gibbons from New Orleans on February 11.

[122] 103-B, Gibbons to Harty, Baltimore, February 27, 1906, copy.

[123] LC, Roosevelt Papers, Gibbons to Roosevelt, Baltimore, February 28, 1906.

[124] 103-C, Roosevelt to Gibbons, Washington, March 3, 1906. *Personal*. Gibbons quickly forwarded a copy of Roosevelt's letter to Agius, saying he was pleased

The presidential ire at the Archbishop of Manila was heightened when Harty published his letter and opened to public discussion the question of the American government's treatment of the Church in the Philippines. Not only was his letter published, but in the New York *Freeman's Journal* of April 14, 1906, he began an extensive and critical series of articles in rebuttal of the work of David P. Barrows, Superintendent of Public Instruction in the Philippines, called *A History of the Philippine Islands* which had been published the previous year. Others took up the case and the New York *Daily Tribune* of April 26 carried a notice of a meeting the preceding evening at the Catholic Club at which John T. McDonough, a former associate justice of the supreme court of the Philippines, had read Harty's protest and had stated that the archbishop wished his side of the matter to be known by the people of the United States. President Roosevelt was genuinely irritated at this publicity. He was sincerely in favor of the appropriation being made for the damage claims and he told Taft he would have sent a message to Congress on the Church's claims some time before had it not been for the publication of Harty's letter. If he acted now it would be construed as attempting to influence the fall elections, whereas he was determined to make it clear beyond a peradventure of a doubt that in dealing with the Church he was influenced solely by a sense of justice and equity. "A more unfortunate publication, from the standpoint of Archbishop Harty himself," said Roosevelt, "could not be imagined."[125]

Taft, too, was chagrined and for the same reasons as the President. He told Archbishop Ireland the reason for delay on the part of the administration in submitting the message about the claims to Congress, and he concluded, "I confess I am bitterly

---

with the President's response and he trusted Agius would also be pleased (103-C, Gibbons to Agius, Baltimore, March 5, 1906, copy).

[125] 103-J, Roosevelt to Taft, Washington, June 29, 1906, copy. Roosevelt told Taft two months before that Harty's letters seemed to show so unworthy an attitude on the archbishop's part as to make it difficult for the President to reconcile them with what he had previously known of his character. "The position," said Roosevelt, "is preposterous" (LC, Roosevelt Papers, Letterbook 33, Roosevelt to Taft, Washington, April 11, 1906). In the light of what happened later it is interesting to note that Roosevelt had suggested to Gibbons at the time of Guidi's death that he would like to see Harty named Apostolic Delegate to the Philippine Islands (101-H, Denis J. Stafford to Gibbons, Washington, June 29, 1904).

disappointed over Harty's attitude, and I must attribute it to the climate and some temporary aberration." Copies of this correspondence were immediately forwarded by Taft to the cardinal so that he might be kept abreast of developments.[126] Six months later Archbishop Agius was still imploring Gibbons to use his influence to obtain the appropriation by Congress of the damage claims. He maintained that although they were not due in strict legality they were due in equity, that the sums so far received were inadequate, and that he could conscientiously state that $3,000,000 gold would be far from covering the losses sustained by the Church; yet if that sum were granted it would put the authorities in a fair way to reorganize ecclesiastical affairs in the islands.[127] The final settlement, however, was nowhere near Agius' figure and in March, 1908, the sum of $403,030.19 was approved for payment to the Church in the Philippines which was only $40,000 above the original award made by the board of church claims in Manila.[128]

During the time that these negotiations were going on regarding the Filipino Church the cardinal was compelled to devote considerable attention to Puerto Rico and Cuba. Early in 1904 Bishop Blenk of Puerto Rico informed him of a conflict which had arisen between Blenk and the apostolic delegate, Archbishop Chapelle, over the latter's attempt to divide his jurisdiction into three dioceses. Blenk thought that such a move would work great harm in the island and this opinion, he said, was shared by the priests and people, as well as by the governor[129] who had just written to the President urging him to use his influence against it. What Gibbons did about the matter we do not know but, in any case, the projected division of the See of Puerto Rico was prevented at this time and came about only twenty years later.

More serious were the periodic threats which arose to the properties of the Church in the island. The changes in govern-

---

[126] 103-J, Taft to Gibbons, Washington, June 30, 1906, enclosing Taft to Ireland, Washington, June 30, 1906, *Personal.*

[127] 104-A, Agius to Gibbons, Manila, January 9, 1907.

[128] *United States Statutes at Large. Private Laws. 60th Congress, 1907–1909* (Washington, 1910), Vol. 35, Pt. 2, p. 1227. Two years later on April 21, 1910, the sum of $49,372.50 was approved for payment to be divided among the four religious orders in the Philippines, the Augustinians, Dominicans, Franciscans, and Recollects. *Ibid., 61st Congress, 1909–1911,* Vol. 36, Pt. 2, p. 1697.

[129] 101-H, Blenk to Gibbons, San Juan, June 15, 1904.

ment had entailed a good deal of confusion over land titles with the departure of the Spaniards and the arrival of the Americans, and when the archbishops met in April, 1907, an appeal was read from the successor of Blenk, Bishop William A. Jones, O.S.A., expressing the hope that the metropolitans would intervene with the United States government to have the disputed titles clearly vested in the Church so that the matter could be settled outside the courts.[130] If an effort was made by any of the archbishops in this regard it was apparently unsuccessful, for in the autumn of that year Gibbons informed Blenk, who had meanwhile become Archbishop of New Orleans on Chapelle's death, that he had just held a lengthy interview with a close friend of President Roosevelt's who had told him that the supreme court of Puerto Rico had given a favorable decision in the Church's property suit, but that the defeated litigants would appeal to the Supreme Court of the United States. Gibbons' informant hoped the latter court would not entertain the appeal but that was uncertain; for that reason the cardinal urged Blenk to engage a good lawyer and for this service he recommended the name of Edgar H. Gans of Baltimore.[131] Although the Supreme Court heard the appeal of the litigants in June, 1908, it handed down its decision upholding the previous judgment of

---

[130] 104-G, Minutes of the Meeting of the Archbishops, Washington, April 10, 1907.

[131] AANO, Gibbons to Blenk, Baltimore, September 21, 1907, *Private.* Just at this time the cardinal was appealed to by Roosevelt and Bonaparte to use his influence with Archbishop Blenk to have a mixed marriage involving Roosevelt's close friend, John A. McIlhenny, performed in a church in New Orleans. Gibbons sent the letters of the two statesmen to Blenk along with a copy of the *Acta Sanctae Sedis,* showing that in certain contingencies a bishop might permit a mixed marriage in a church, to which he added that the special request of the head of the nation was worthy of consideration and would not form a dangerous prescription. He said he hesitated to send the President's letter for fear Blenk would think him to be intruding, but, on the other hand, the suppression of the letter would, he thought, be disrespectful to the chief executive. "Liberavi animam meam," said Gibbons, "I will not even presume to make a suggestion unless Your Grace should ask it." Blenk asked the opinion of Archbishop Falconio and the apostolic delegate advised against the ceremony in a church. Gibbons told Blenk when he heard the decision, "I was & still am under the impression that you had the power of performing such a marriage without referring to the Holy See, by the reference to the Acta Sanctae Sedis, which I enclosed in a former letter. But I submit to the superior knowledge of the Ap. Delegate . . ." (AANO, Gibbons to Blenk, Baltimore, October 12, 1907, enclosing Roosevelt to Gibbons, Washington, September 28, 1907, and Bonaparte to Gibbons, Washington, September 28, 1907).

the Puerto Rico court in favor of the property rights of the Church.[132]

By reason of the measure of self-government allowed to Cuba there was, of course, far more leeway for the local politicians to make trouble for the Church there than in Puerto Rico. Following the regime of General Leonard Wood as military governor, a civil administration was gradually introduced and with the election of Tomás Estrada Palma in 1902 as President of Cuba the American troops were withdrawn. But Cuba was still far from enjoying internal peace. The Liberal Party was organized in opposition to Estrada Palma and soon the island was again in turmoil which by early 1906 led to a revolt and the re-entry of the American military forces. All of this put the Church in a bad way with the Liberals seemingly bent on confiscating its properties and restricting its freedom. Amasa Thornton, a New York lawyer, was alarmed at the way things were going in Cuba and the lack of what he believed to be a forceful representative of the Church who would lay its case before the government in Washington. Thornton thought the spiritual affairs of the island were safe in the hands of the Cuban bishops, but he was of the opinion that they were altogether too weak to make a fight for the properties. For that reason he appealed to Cardinal Gibbons to lend his assistance. "I never in my life have seen, Your Eminence," he told the cardinal, "such a neglect of business interest as has gone on in Cuba in the matter of church property."[133]

But no lasting remedy was applied to the difficulties of the Cuban Church at the time and when the Liberal Party won the elections of November, 1908, and took power with President José Miguel Gómez the situation grew worse. By the spring of 1910 a crisis appeared to impend and the Apostolic Delegate to Cuba

---

[132] Cf. Frederic R. Coudert, *The Status and Property Rights of the Roman Catholic Church in the American Spanish Possessions as Defined by the Supreme Court of the United States* (printed for private circulation, n.d.). Connolly Room, Mullen Library, The Catholic University of America, *Americana Catholica*, Vol. 10. On the litigation that arose over the Church's properties in both the Philippines and Puerto Rico following the American occupation cf. the summary of the principal law cases as they were decided by the courts from 1907 on in the chapter of Jorge R. Coquia's *Legal Status of the Church in the Philippines* (Washington, 1950), pp. 77–104, under the title of the Church as a "Juridical Personality."

[133] 102-F, Thornton to Gibbons, New York, March 10 and 13, 1905.

and Puerto Rico, Archbishop Giuseppe Aversa, informed the Holy See that the government was threatening to prohibit all external manifestations of religion and to forbid foreign priests and religious from entering the country. Once more the Holy See requested Gibbons to use his influence with the American government with a view to enlisting its good offices in behalf of the Church. The cardinal conferred in Washington with President Taft and Secretary of State Philander C. Knox, who were both sympathetic and willing to do all that was possible to avert the hostility of the Cuban regime toward the Church. A short time before, Taft had designated General Wood to represent the United States at the centennial of Argentine independence, and he now asked the general to make a stop at Havana on his way to Buenos Aires, ostensibly to pay his respects to President Gómez, and there to lodge an informal inquiry concerning the threatened legislation. After Wood had successfully executed his mission he informed Taft of Gómez' assurance that the legislation was not likely to pass, and that if it did it would be opposed by him. Taft passed this information on to the cardinal with the remark, "I hope you will regard this as ending the matter."[134]

Gibbons promptly summarized the developments in the case for Archbishop Falconio so that the apostolic delegate might, in turn, let Rome know that the danger had been averted.[135] Moreover, on April 29 the President sent General Carlos García Vélez and Elíseo Giberga, delegates of Cuba to the dedication of the new building of the Pan American Union in Washington, to Baltimore to give further assurance to Gibbons that the bill introduced into the lower house of the Cuban legislature prohibiting external religious manifestations would not pass. The Cuban delegates believed that if the measure should get by the lower house it would be killed in the senate, and even if both houses were to pass it, they felt certain President Gómez would veto it.[136] This welcome news was transmitted to Rafaelle Cardinal Merry del Val,[137] for which Gibbons received the gratitude of Pope Pius X and his Secretary of State for the leading role he had

---

[134] 106-F, Taft to Gibbons, Washington, April 19, 1910, enclosing Wood to Taft, aboard the *Montana,* April 14, 1910, copy.

[135] 106-G, Gibbons to Falconio, Baltimore, April 22, 1910, copy.

[136] 106-G, same to same, Baltimore, April 30, 1910, copy.

[137] 106-I, Gibbons to Merry del Val, Baltimore, May 25, 1910, copy.

played in averting the threat to which the Church in Cuba had been exposed.[138]

After the Philippine Islands and Puerto Rico passed under the sovereignty of the United States one of the responsibilities that devolved on the American Church was that of providing candidates for the episcopal sees in these possessions. In 1903 four American prelates had been appointed for the Philippine sees and seven years later when the Holy See erected the new Diocese of Zamboanga Father Charles W. Currier, assistant director of the Bureau of Catholic Indian Missions in Washington, was appointed as the first bishop. Currier, however, declined the office and enlisted the help of Gibbons to escape from what he characterized as "a calamity."[139] The cardinal understood the hardship which a long service in the islands might impose on the American churchmen, and for that reason he made representations to Rome in the hope of securing legislation that would shorten their time there. He was in the Eternal City for the conclave of September, 1914, and soon after his return home he informed Archbishop Harty that he had again urged the matter at the Roman Curia and, he added "[I] am pleased to say there is hope for success."[140]

Two months later Archbishop Riordan of San Francisco died on December 27, and Harty sought the help of Gibbons to be appointed to the vacant see. But when the *terne* of the bishops and priests were made out, Harty's name did not appear, and since in 1900 the Holy See had directed the archbishops not to

---

[138] Diary, June 20, 1910, p. 319. One of the final items of business which Gibbons was asked to undertake in behalf of the Church in Cuba was to intervene with the American government to prevent the Cuban government from declaring null and void canonical marriages and to put through a divorce bill (109-R, Peter G. Estrada, Bishop of Havana, to Gibbons, Havana, March 16, 1914; 109-V, Severiano Sainz, vicar-general of Havana, to Gibbons, Havana, April 30, 1914). Gibbons told Estrada to communicate with Archbishop Adolfo A. Nouel, Apostolic Delegate to Cuba and Puerto Rico, and to tell him, as he said, "that in a week or ten days, after some important business that I have on hand, I will [inform] him formally about this matter" (109-R, Gibbons to Estrada, Baltimore, March 23, 1914, copy).

[139] 106-K, Currier to Gibbons, Lima, Peru, June 25, 1910. Currier was making a tour of South America at the time where he said he found the state of religion in Peru and Bolivia "appalling" in contrast to the promising conditions in Brazil, Argentina, Chile, and Uruguay. He told the cardinal, "A passing cable in one of the newspapers here, reported the other day, that you were dead. I trust that it will be many years before such a report will be true."

[140] 110-J, Gibbons to Harty, Baltimore, October 20, 1914, copy.

add names beyond those on the *terne*,[141] there was nothing Gibbons could do about it. "Much as I would like to assist you in the desired appointment," said the cardinal, "I am helpless."[142] However, in less than a year Bishop Richard Scannell of Omaha died and on May 16, 1916, Harty was named as his successor. During that summer Harty visited Rome where, he said, Pietro Cardinal Gasparri, Secretary of State, had frequently remarked to him that no prelate in the United States possessed such an influence with the Holy See as the Cardinal of Baltimore. "Hence," said Harty, "your word will bring results as regards Manila. It would be a pity to place here a man unable to treat intelligently with three elements which must be considered, Rome, Washington, the Filipino people."[143] Another American prelate in the Philippines who had recently been transferred was Bishop Dougherty of Jaro who was promoted to the See of Buffalo in early December, 1915. Dougherty said he deemed it his duty to inform Gibbons of his appointment and, as he expressed it, "especially to thank you from my heart for the leading part which I have reason to believe you took in this gracious act of the Holy See. I will never forget your most kind interest in me; for which may Our Lord repay you!"[144]

One of the last major concerns of Cardinal Gibbons in regard to the Philippine Islands had to do with the question of independence. Early in 1912 there began a strong agitation among certain members of the Democratic Party to have inserted into their platform at the coming national convention a statement that would commit the party to early independence for the islands. When news of this reached Manila Archbishop Harty became genuinely alarmed. He hastened word to Baltimore in which he asked the cardinal to do everything he could to induce

---

[141] 98-J-2, Minutes of the Meeting of the Archbishops, Washington, October 11, 1900.

[142] 111-R, Gibbons to Harty, Baltimore, March 31, 1915, copy.

[143] 113-R, Harty to Gibbons, Manila, July 13, 1916. At the time that the See of Manila was still open Vance C. McCormick of the Democratic National Committee submitted a memorandum to President Woodrow Wilson suggesting that an American be named to the office (LC, Wilson Papers, McCormick to Wilson, Washington, August 10, 1916). In early September, 1916, the Holy See named the Irish-born and Spanish-trained Bishop of Zamboanga, Michael J. O'Doherty, to Manila who ruled the see until his death on October 14, 1949. He was then succeeded by the first native-born Filipino to be Archbishop of Manila, Gabriele M. Reyes.

[144] 112-V, Dougherty to Gibbons, Jaro, December 18, 1915.

the American hierarchy to work against independence. He said it was the consensus among all those of the white race in the Philippines that the natives were not yet ready to govern themselves and would not be ready for a long time to come. In the lengthy communication Harty detailed the reasons for his view and concluded by saying, "Sooner or later Japan would swoop down on the islands, annex them, and blot out any vestige of Christianity that might be found."[145] Two days later the archbishop wrote again, and this time he enclosed a corroborating statement against independence from a certain Martin Egan with whom the cardinal had conferred in Baltimore several months before. Harty remarked that if it were known in the islands that the American bishops were working against independence they would be compelled, as he said, "to get out of the Philippines by night — thankful if our lives were spared." Therefore, the utmost discretion should be exercised in the matter.[146]

But if the American hierarchy made any move to head off the commitment of the Democrats — and no evidence was found to show that they did — they were unsuccessful, for on June 25 at Baltimore the Democratic national convention wrote a plank into the platform favoring an immediate declaration of the purpose of the United States to recognize the independence of the Philippines as soon as a stable government could be established.[147] This policy was deeply deplored by President Taft, and even after he had been overwhelmingly defeated for re-election by Woodrow Wilson on November 5 of that year, he did not abandon his efforts to prevent what he believed would be a disastrous course for the American government to pursue. A week after the election the President informed Cardinal Gibbons that he would like very much to talk over the matter with him, and if he would let him know what day he could come to lunch at the White House he would set aside time for a discussion with him on the steps that should be taken. "You know," said Taft, "the Philippine policy is like the apple of my eye, and I am very sure that even the incoming President, if he understood the matter, would not permit such a gross departure from good policy as the present

---

[145] 108-D, Harty to Gibbons, Manila, March 14, 1912.

[146] 108-D, same to same, Manila, March 16, 1912, enclosing Egan to Gibbons, Manila, March 14, 1912.

[147] Porter, *National Party Platforms,* p. 332.

Jones bill now pending in the House would be if passed."[148]
The cardinal replied at once and set one of two dates on which
he could be in Washington, and in closing he remarked, "I take
this occasion to express to you my sincere regrets that you are
to leave Washington, and I know that this feeling is shared by
a great many others."[149]

The President and the cardinal lunched together on November 23 and went over all aspects of the question. As a result of
their conference it was determined that Gibbons should get in
touch with members of the American hierarchy and urge them
to work against the Jones Bill. In his letter to the bishops the
cardinal spoke of a cable message to him from Archbishop Harty,
of a visit he had from W. Cameron Forbes, who in November,
1909, had become Governor General of the Philippines, and of
his conference with the President. He outlined the reasons which
prompted all these men to oppose early independence for the
islands, and he stated that such action would be a serious blow
to the Catholic Church there and would place its properties in
dire jeopardy. Gibbons said that it was the President who had
suggested that the energy of the hierarchy should be bent upon
preventing an early grant of independence, and that their efforts
should be exerted quickly. The cardinal suggested, therefore, that
the bishops bring to bear all the influence at their command
upon their congressmen and other important citizens to stop the
Jones Bill from passing. "The President," he said, "was particularly emphatic in the expression of these views, adding that the
Catholic Church is the great bulwark against Socialism, the
wanton destruction of property, and the violation of property
rights, and that her power is sorely needed in the islands."[150] On
the same day Gibbons reported the situation to Cardinal Merry
del Val, saying he was hopeful that by concerted action the
calamity which threatened the Church in the Philippines could
be averted. "Any suggestion that Your Eminence may care to
make known to me," said Gibbons, "will be gratefully received,
and acted on to the best of my ability."[151]

---

[148] 108-P, Taft to Gibbons, Washington, November 13, 1912.

[149] LC, Taft Papers, Gibbons to Taft, Baltimore, November 14, 1912.

[150] 108-Q, Gibbons to the American hierarchy, Baltimore, December 2, 1912,
printed copy.

[151] 108-Q, Gibbons to Merry del Val, Baltimore, December 2, 1912, copy. On the
same day that Gibbons wrote to the hierarchy and to Merry del Val he informed

Both President Taft and Governor General Forbes were gratified at the action taken by the cardinal. Taft noted with pleasure
that he had written to the bishops on the question and he added,
"I thank you heartily for doing so."[152] Forbes forwarded a
package of documents on Philippine affairs to give Gibbons fuller
information on the subject,[153] and a few days later he told him,
"I am sure your action will have immense effect, and I am also
sure that if this matter is followed up, the bill can be killed in
its infancy."[154] Merry del Val was likewise pleased at the
efforts Gibbons had put forth and he, too, believed that it was
very doubtful if the Philippines were yet ready to govern themselves. He was certain that they were not prepared for their
own ecclesiastical government. To his mind a native episcopate
was not within sight and it would be only idle to hope for one
within his lifetime. If in spite of everything it proved impossible
to stop the movement in favor of independence in one form or
another, Merry del Val hoped that at least some sort of protectorate or supervision on the part of the United States could be
retained which would efficaciously safeguard the freedom of the
Church and the preservation of Catholic education in the islands.
"But if the Holy See is not entirely free in the nominations of
Bishops out there," said the Cardinal Secretary of State, "and in
any way obliged to select candidates among the native clergy, I
see nothing but disaster."[155]

Although the Jones Bill had a good many supporters there was
likewise a widespread opposition to the measure. James T. Williams, Jr., editor of the Boston *Transcript,* was vigorously op-

---

Harty of what he had done. The Archbishop of Manila was grateful for his
action and said, "I see the providence of God in the measures you have pursued
as His instrument solicitous for the welfare of the far away Philippine Islands.
I pray for and do not doubt that your efforts will save the serious danger with
which we are apparently confronted" (109-B, Harty to Gibbons, Manila, February
10, 1913).

[152] 108-Q, Taft to Gibbons, Washington, December 4, 1912.

[153] 108-Q, Forbes to Gibbons, Washington, December 5, 1912.

[154] 108-Q, same to same, Memphis, December 9, 1912. Senator James P. Clarke
of Arkansas succeeded in getting an amendment to the Jones Bill adopted by
the senate which would have given the Filipinos complete independence in not
less than two years and not more than four from the date of approval of the
bill. But the Clarke amendment was defeated in the House of Representatives,
according to Forbes, "very largely through the attitude of that wing of the Democrats associated with the Roman Catholic Church." W. Cameron Forbes, *The
Philippine Islands,* rev. ed. (Cambridge, 1945), p. 334.

[155] 109-A, Merry del Val to Gibbons, Rome, January 1, 1913.

posed to early independence for the Filipinos, and in his desire
to head off the bill before Congress he wrote confidentially to
President Taft to ask if he thought the Cardinal of Baltimore
would be willing to grant an interview to a representative of the
Transcript. "If you think Cardinal Gibbons would be willing to
talk or write on the subject," said Williams, "I would go to
Baltimore myself to see him."[156] The President communicated
the message to Gibbons and asked if he would be agreeable to
seeing Williams. The cardinal assented to the plan and on
February 19, 1913, the Boston *Evening Transcript* carried a
feature story entitled, "Cardinal Gibbons on 'Our Duty in the
Philippines.'" The article was prefaced by an introduction ini-
tialed by Williams in which he credited Gibbons with having had
more influence than anyone in the country in putting a stop to
the scandal of the Louisiana lottery, as well as having halted
the attempt of certain politicians in Maryland to put through a
Jim Crow law for that state.

In the interview itself the cardinal stated he was irrevocably
opposed to any move that would commit the United States to a
scuttle policy in the Philippines, "today, tomorrow or at any fixed
time in the future. . . ." He said he had maintained that taking
the Philippines in the first place was open to question, but once
in the responsibility devolved on the United States to finish the
job. It was evident that Gibbons' opposition to the measure was
not political but rather moral in character. He enumerated his
reasons for opposing the Jones Bill on the grounds that the Filipinos had not been consulted, and that even if a majority desired
independence he believed them utterly unprepared for the responsibility. Moreover, if the United States withdrew there was
danger of a lapse into barbarism and infidelity; withdrawal would
work an injustice on a large number of Americans who had
invested in the islands, and the President who was especially well
informed about the islands was altogether opposed. As an alternative there was suggested the appointment of a presidential
commission which should visit the Philippines and work out a
long range plan for education and training of the native population for self-government. In conclusion the cardinal said:

> I have no patience with the argument that the Philippine Islands
> are the source of an annual deficit to this country. Even were that

[156] 109-B, Williams to Taft, Boston, February 5, 1913, copy.

true, the fact would not warrant a cowardly abandonment of the clear and accepted duty of the American people toward the Filipinos.

The interview in the Boston *Transcript* created quite a stir. Some days after it appeared Gibbons told Cardinal Merry del Val that it had been published in almost every paper of importance in the country. "That it has had a good effect," said the cardinal, "is evident from the numerous letters I receive daily, congratulating me on the stand I have taken." He enclosed a copy of the interview and said he had purposely emphasized the aspects of law and order rather than the religious interests involved for fear of arousing sectarian bias. He thought that they could now reasonably count on a sufficient majority to defeat the Jones Bill. If it passed while Taft was in the White House, it would certainly be vetoed. The incoming President, it was true, was supposed to be in favor of it because of the pledge of his party platform but, said the cardinal, "he recently told a friend of mine that soon after his inauguration, he would call me in conference on the subject." He admitted to Merry del Val that one of the greatest evils of American rule among the thoroughly Catholic population of the Philippines was the establishment of the public school system, which no doubt would in a certain way work to the disadvantage of the Church. But comparing this evil with others of a more serious nature, he felt that the Catholics of the islands should be able to face it in the course of time by having their own parochial schools as had been done in the United States.[157]

One who expressed himself as pained by the Gibbons interview was Manuel L. Quezon, resident commissioner of the Philippine Islands in Washington. He was reluctantly led to believe, he said, that the interview really represented the cardinal's views, and he added that he had heard the Catholic bishops and clergy of the United States were striving to prevent independence for his country. He deeply regretted to hear this and he mentioned how the Spanish friars had lost prestige by working against a liberalizing regime in the islands; there was a danger, said Quezon,

---

[157] 109-C, Gibbons to Merry del Val, Baltimore, February 23, 1913, copy. Merry del Val expressed the gratitude of the Pope for the interview of Gibbons and said the Holy See was glad to learn the friendly reception given to it by the American press and public opinion (109-C, Merry del Val to Gibbons, Rome, March 12, 1913).

that the American churchmen would now suffer a similar loss of standing with the people. The entire letter breathed an air of hurt surprise, and Quezon concluded by drawing attention to a clipping which he enclosed showing a group of Filipino priests writing to President-elect Wilson asking for independence for their country.[158] In reply Gibbons reiterated the stand he had taken in the interview and told Quezon, "There is a great difference between independence and liberty. There are countries which have independence but no liberty or freedom, whereas the Philippine Islands, although for the present not enjoying independence, have freedom and liberty."[159] But if Quezon was disappointed by Gibbons' interview there were others to whom it brought real satisfaction, and of the latter Bishop Dougherty of Jaro was one of the most emphatic. Over a year later he told the cardinal:

> As to the Philippines, I believe that we can thank your Em. that we are not worse off than we are. Your stand on independence seems to have stayed the administration from granting it. The very thought of it checked the inflow of foreign capital and stagnated business here. It will probably be long before the march of progress be resumed.
>
> The natives now fear a war over China, between the U. S. and Japan. I am told that the dread of falling into Japan's hands has dampened the ardor of the Filipinos for independence.[160]

It was doubtless true that the opposition of the Cardinal of Baltimore had played a part in temporarily checking the Wilson administration from pushing the bill in Congress, but the cardinal would be the first to say that his influence at the White House was now much less than it had formerly been. Early in 1914 when Bishop Estrada of Havana appealed to him to help checkmate the threat of a bill declaring canonical marriages null and void and introducing divorce into Cuba, Gibbons sympathized with the bishop's disturbed state of mind, but he frankly told him, "I am sorry to say that I have not the same influence with the present administration, as with the preceding ones of Mr. Taft

---

[158] 109-C, Quezon to Gibbons, Washington, February 27, 1913.

[159] Quoted from the Manila *Daily Bulletin,* May 13, 1913, by W. Cameron Forbes, *The Philippine Islands* (Boston, 1928), II, 373. The date of Gibbons' reply to Quezon is given as February 28, 1913.

[160] 110-M, Dougherty to Gibbons, Jaro, November 7, 1914.

and Mr. Roosevelt."[161] In 1916 those behind the Jones Bill reopened the campaign in Congress and once again Taft, who was then dean of the School of Law at Yale University, wrote Gibbons to ask him if he would not exert his influence with the members of his Church to prevent the bill from passing.[162] In the interval the cardinal had in no way changed his mind about the issue of Philippine independence, and he informed Taft that he was in complete accord with his opinion. "Hence I shall be glad," he said, "to do all that I can to help in averting a course that would be injurious to the Islands and to our own country."[163] Yet despite the opposition of Taft, Gibbons, and the many others who shared their views, the Jones Bill was enacted into law on August 29, 1916. Practically speaking, it gave the Philippines a territorial status and declared it to be the purpose of the United States to grant independence as soon as a stable government could be established there.

Although Cardinal Gibbons had failed in his efforts to postpone the pledge of early independence for the Philippine Islands on the part of the United States, he had rendered notable services to his Church and to his country in the crisis occasioned by the Spanish American War and its aftermath. The judgment of posterity has long since been established that if the counsels of Gibbons and those who shared his views in the early days of 1898 had been followed, the United States might have been spared the ignominy of provoking an unjust war. But once war was declared the cardinal's conduct left nothing to be desired from the point of view of a loyal citizen. Insofar as he was able he endeavored to mitigate the suffering and sorrow of those who were personally involved, and by his alertness to the spiritual needs of the fighting men he showed himself a true moral leader. When the war was over and he was asked by the President for his judgment on whether the Philippines should be retained he replied with a show of wisdom that did credit to the deep attachment which he felt for both Church and State. In the difficult and delicate negotiations that ensued regarding ecclesiastical matters in Cuba, Puerto Rico, and the Philippines the adminis-

---

[161] 109-R, Gibbons to Estrada, Baltimore, March 23, 1914, copy.

[162] 113-A, Taft to Gibbons, New Haven, January 11, 1916, *Personal* and *Confidential*.

[163] LC, Taft Papers, Gibbons to Taft, Baltimore, January 12, 1916.

trations of Roosevelt and Taft had no more helpful and enlightened adviser than the Cardinal of Baltimore. Through Gibbons'
hands there passed many of the principal decisions affecting the
Church in the island possessions, and in all these matters the
cardinal proved himself to be of great assistance to the officials
of the government in Washington, to the Holy See, and to the
harassed bishops who were forced to grapple with the vexing
problems of ruling the Church in the newly acquired possessions
of the United States. All in all, therefore, the cardinal played the
role in which he was cast with striking success, and if in several
particulars he failed of his objective the experience proved rewarding, insofar as it prepared him for the larger role he was
destined to fill during and after World War I.

CHAPTER XVIII

Last Years as Chancellor of the University

AMID the anxieties which Cardinal Gibbons experienced in the years after the Spanish American War over the affairs of the Catholic Church in the new American possessions, he had the happiness for a part of that time of having close at hand his trusted adviser and friend, Monsignor Denis J. O'Connell. In January, 1903, O'Connell had been appointed as third Rector of the Catholic University of America. We have already spoken of the joy which this appointment brought to the cardinal when the news first reached him, and how eagerly he looked forward to welcoming O'Connell home from his long Roman exile.[1] The university was then in its fourteenth year of life but the period of stress and strain had not yet passed. Many of the hierarchy still withheld their support of the institution, the scars of the internal feuds had not fully healed, both students and financial resources were still scarce in the first years of the century, and these difficulties had produced a doubtful impression upon some of the officials of the Roman Curia concerning the university's future. It was no surprise, then, that apart from reasons of friendship the cardinal should welcome so wholeheartedly as rector one in whom he placed such great confidence.

Before he left Rome the rector-elect sent to Gibbons an optimistic account of the changed attitude which he now found at the Holy See toward the university, and he believed that all doubts regarding Rome's interest in the institution would soon be at an end. The principal interest of the Congregation of Studies and its prefect, Cardinal Satolli, remained, it was true, in the theological and philosophical faculties, but O'Connell assured the cardinal chancellor that there was no reason for apprehension

---

[1] Cf. I, 436–437.

about a major alteration in the nature and original character of
the university. "Indeed," said O'Connell, "I think the desire to
make it a real University is more earnest now than ever before. . . ." He was intent that news of the appointment of the
outgoing rector, Bishop Conaty, to the See of Monterey-Los
Angeles should become widespread before he appeared in the
United States, and he was likewise at pains to let Gibbons know
the appreciation which he felt for the attitude Conaty had taken
toward him. "Nothing could surpass," he said, "the unstinted
and generous manner in which he offered me his co-operation &
assistance." The monsignor planned to leave Rome the first week
in March and to arrive in Baltimore near the end of that month
where he would consult with Gibbons before taking up his duties.[2]

There were others besides the Cardinal of Baltimore who welcomed O'Connell's advent to Washington. Archbishop Ireland
remarked to Gibbons that even now it was difficult for him to
realize that the appointment had been made. "What a revolution
in the temper of Rome there is implied in his nomination!" said
the archbishop. The naming of O'Connell indicated to Ireland
that the feeling of the Holy See had become more friendly toward
him and his friends since the stormy days of the Americanism
controversy. He had recently received a letter from Cardinal
Satolli in which the latter had mentioned the more favorable atmosphere in Rome, and he had attributed it to the fact that
certain prelates had in the interval gone to a better life. "It would
look," said the Archbishop of St. Paul, "as if Satolli himself had
not been in his heart so much of an enemy of ours — but had
rather yielded to pressure from others, from which he is now
glad to recover."[3] Regardless of the motive for the change, it
was a welcome one to Gibbons and his associates, and the improved attitude at the Holy See toward things American seemed
to offer a happy augury for the university and its new rector in
the days ahead.

In the first weeks after his arrival in the United States Monsignor O'Connell stopped off for brief visits to the campus of
the university on several occasions and then traveled about the
East in an effort to interest various persons in the university's

---

[2] 100-H-9, O'Connell to Gibbons, Rome, February 28, 1903.
[3] 100-J-1, Ireland to Gibbons, St. Paul, March 2, 1903.

work.[4] Gibbons was cheered by news of success on a trip which O'Connell made to Atlantic City and by the friendly messages which the rector had received from the Archbishops of Boston and Philadelphia. "You are sowing the seed," said the cardinal.[5] On April 22 the new rector was formally inaugurated immediately after the semiannual meeting of the Board of Trustees. It had been evident for a long time that the university was in need of more ample sources of income than those yielded by occasional benefactions and student fees. In fact, the mounting deficits during the Conaty administration proved to be one of the principal reasons for the change in rectors. O'Connell lost no time in getting to the heart of the matter, and at the meeting on April 22 he presented to the trustees a highly detailed account of the university's finances from the time of its opening down to the present.

The report was not very encouraging, with current liabilities of $201,233.33 and only $56,251.11 to meet the obligations of the institution.[6] In order to overcome this debt and to build up an endowment, O'Connell proposed to the trustees that they petition the Holy See to order an annual collection for ten years in all the dioceses of the United States. The suggestion was not a new one, for Bishop Keane had endeavored at the very outset of the university's life to win support for an annual collection but without success. Now, however, the trustees agreed to the proposal and empowered O'Connell to go to Rome to present their request to Pope Leo XIII. Meanwhile the loyal friends of the university attempted to do what they could to bolster the failing finances. Bishop Spalding sent on a second installment of $1,000 as his subscription toward liquidating the debt, and he told O'Connell he would be looking for news of a big amount which he hoped he would soon get. "The whole trouble is lack of money," said Spalding, "and a good start will awaken new interest everywhere."[7]

---

[4] Colman J. Barry, O.S.B., *The Catholic University of America, 1903–1909. The Rectorship of Denis J. O'Connell* (Washington, 1950), p. 35. This work will be used throughout the early part of the present chapter for background to Gibbons' role as chancellor.

[5] ACUA, O'Connell Papers, Gibbons to O'Connell, Baltimore, April 13, 1903.

[6] Barry, *op. cit.,* p. 37.

[7] ACUA, O'Connell Papers, Spalding to O'Connell, Peoria, April 25, 1903.

In fulfillment of the mission entrusted to him by the Board of Trustees, the university rector sailed for Europe on July 1 but by the time he reached Rome the old Pope had entered upon his last illness and he died on July 20. Upon learning of the death of Leo XIII the Cardinal of Baltimore rushed to Rome to attend the conclave, and he arrived in time to be the first American to participate in the election of a Pope. With the choice of the College of Cardinals falling on August 4 on Giuseppe Cardinal Sarto, the Patriarch of Venice, the new pontificate of Pius X was begun while the chancellor and rector of the university were in Rome. Due to the period of transition through which the government of the Church was then passing, it was natural that some days should elapse before Gibbons and O'Connell could broach the subject of the university to the officials of the Holy See. But in due time the cardinal chancellor presented the university's case for an annual collection to the new Pontiff and on September 9 Pope Pius X addressed a letter to Gibbons in which he stated that the condition of the university had enlisted his "deepest sympathy and concern," and, as a result of the report which the cardinal had recently submitted the Pope, gave his permission for an annual collection to be taken up on the first Sunday of Advent in all the dioceses of the United States for a period of ten years.[8] Gibbons had meanwhile started for home soon after the coronation of the new Pope, but O'Connell remained on in Rome. After the rector had received a copy of the papal letter on the university he forwarded it to the cardinal and he told him, "Your letter, with the documents that accompanied it, made in the Vatican an excellent impression. It was said that whatever the divisions or indifference in the past, it was all unity and sympathy for the University now."[9]

The papal approval for the annual collection was, indeed, a great boon to the harassed administrators, but its success would depend on the response which the hierarchy gave to the idea. After receiving the document in late September Gibbons had Pius X's letter printed with an English translation and on October 8 he mailed it to all the bishops of the United States.[10] Upon O'Connell's arrival from Europe in early November the

---

[8] 100-Q-1, Pius X to Gibbons, Rome, September 9, 1903.

[9] 100-Q-4, O'Connell to Gibbons, Rome, September 13, 1903.

[10] Diary, October 8, 1903, p. 300.

cardinal asked him to wire from New York when he might expect him in Baltimore as he said he was anxious to have a long talk with the rector before he went to the university.[11] The cardinal was doubtless aware of the fact that the Pope's letter called for a pronouncement from him as chancellor, so that the university's case might be put as forcefully as possible before the hierarchy. With that in mind, and after he had conferred with O'Connell, he dispatched a letter to the bishops in which he called attention to the new Pope's first communication to the American hierarchy, seconded the idea of an annual collection, and stated that the American Catholics would wish to rival the generosity shown by their non-Catholic fellow citizens to educational institutions. Gibbons cited the example of the University of Louvain which had performed such noble service for the Church in Belgium and which, as he said, would have been unable to prosecute its work had it not been for an annual collection among the Catholics of that country. Summarizing the case for Louvain's sister institution in Washington, the cardinal said:

> The University has a plant and endowments amounting in all to about $2,000,000 contributed by the generosity of our clergy and laity. It is now necessary that we make good what has already been done, by adding such endowments, as will complete the Faculties, meet extraordinary expenses, and place the institution on a self-sustaining basis. . . .[12]

Ireland for one had grown worried lest Gibbons should not send a letter to the bishops and just before his copy reached St. Paul he urged O'Connell to have the cardinal write each bishop in his capacity as chancellor and ask his co-operation in the Holy Father's approval of the collection. "If this is not done believe me," said Ireland, "the great number of them will not respond. Insist on this. . . ."[13] In this case no insistence was necessary since Gibbons' letter was in the hands of the hierarchy by the third week of November, and it then remained to be seen what effect it would have in stimulating them to lend their support to the collection which had won the approbation of Pius X.

By reason of the papal letter, the appeal of the chancellor,

11 ACUA, O'Connell Papers, Gibbons to O'Connell, Baltimore, November 5, 1903.
12 100-T-6, Gibbons to the American hierarchy, Baltimore, November 13, 1903, copy.
13 ACUA, O'Connell Papers, Ireland to O'Connell, St. Paul, November 15, 1903.

and the publicity given to the subject by the bishops, priests, and Catholic press the university enjoyed in the late autumn of 1903 more general notice throughout the United States than it had ever before received. Interest was awakened by the pastoral letters on the annual collection by old friends like Archbishops Keane and Elder and Bishop Maes, while in other areas prelates like Ireland, Williams, and Spalding rallied nobly to the cause. Many of the Catholic newspapers came behind the movement strongly in an effort to interest their readers in giving generously to the collection. Typical of the spirit and enthusiasm which the campaign aroused was the comment of the Pittsburgh *Catholic* in its issue of November 26, 1903, when it said:

> The University is now in the hands of its reliable friends, the Catholic body en masse. The Catholic people never fail, once the appeal is made; and, as a rule, they are the court of final appeal for support.

So effectively had the publicity done its work, that it had even given cause for concern in certain Protestant circles as to just what lay behind all the activity in behalf of the university. The *Congregationalist* of December 3 warned its readers, "It behooves Protestant denominational educational societies, and friends of higher education among Protestants to be alive to what this institution in Washington means."

Meanwhile the returns from the collection began to arrive in Baltimore where Cardinal Gibbons kept a close watch on the results. During the early days of 1904 he would express from time to time his satisfaction or his disappointment to the rector with the amounts which reached him from various dioceses. For example, the $1,300 from the Diocese of Detroit[14] and the $951.27 from the Archdiocese of New Orleans did not, as he said, "come up to my expectations."[15] He likewise found disappointing $3,842.96 from the Archdiocese of Chicago which prompted him to comment, "The West supplies us with hot wind." But the unexpected sum from smaller and poorer sees such as $688.73 from the Diocese of Grand Rapids and $535.06 from the Diocese of Harrisburg helped, according to Gibbons, to make up for the deficiency.[16] Moreover, when loyal friends like Bishop Spalding

---

[14] *Ibid.*, Gibbons to O'Connell, Baltimore, January 24, 1904.

[15] *Ibid.*, same to same, Baltimore, February 19, 1904.

[16] *Ibid.*, same to same, Baltimore, March 1, 1904.

came through with the handsome sum of $4,000 from his small Diocese of Peoria there was reason for rejoicing.[17] In the opinion of Archbishop Glennon of St. Louis the appeal for funds had helped to quiet the criticism of the university by the German Catholics. Glennon believed that in time the Germans could be brought to support the cause, and he wondered if the Board of Trustees could not find some place for them in the work of the institution. "As a people," said the archbishop, "they serve well, if they are not allowed to dominate."[18] In the end the over-all result from the first annual collection proved to be very gratifying, and when the money was all in, the sum totaled $105,051.58.[19] All but three of the dioceses of the country had responded to the call and the most conspicuous of the three absentees was the Diocese of Rochester. Bishop McQuaid's early opposition to the university had not yet yielded to the point where he would permit a collection in its behalf among his people.

A further source of encouragement to the administrators of the university beyond the annual collection was afforded at this time in a large benefaction from the Knights of Columbus. As early as 1897 the knights in Mobile, Alabama, had launched a plan for the endowment of a chair of American history at Washington. The idea had gradually taken hold and K. of C. councils all over the land had responded, with the result that by the spring of 1904 the goal was reached and the formal presentation of the fund was scheduled for April 13. On that occasion over 10,000 Knights of Columbus traveled to the national capital where the supreme knight, Edward L. Hearn, presented to Cardinal Gibbons a check for $55,633.79 at a ceremony in front of McMahon Hall. In his speech Hearn emphasized the hope of the knights that the new chair in the university might prove helpful in eradicating anti-Catholic bias from the writing and teaching of American history.[20]

In accepting the benefaction the cardinal thanked the knights and assured them that their princely gift would be safely invested and sacredly devoted to the purpose designated by them. Gibbons stated that a professor would be engaged to fill the

---

[17] *Ibid.,* Spalding to Gibbons, Peoria, February 4, 1904.

[18] 101-B, Glennon to Gibbons, St. Louis, January 27, 1904.

[19] Barry, *op. cit.,* p. 54. Cf. pp. 260–264 of this work for a chart which gives the figures for the annual collections of the years 1903–1908 inclusive by dioceses.

[20] Barry, *op. cit.,* p. 208.

chair whose noble and genial theme it would be to tell of the leading part which the Catholic Church had played in the discovery and settlement of the continent of North America and of the assistance which it had given to the spread of civilization and Christianity among its inhabitants. "His task will be to vindicate the ancient Church from false aspersions," said the cardinal, "& to present her just claims for recognition to the tribunal of a discerning American people." He then said that the university had been gladdened by the contemplation of support from a united episcopate, by the generosity of the Catholic laity, and by the action of the Pope who had inaugurated his reign by sending a letter of sympathy and encouragement for the university's work. In an optimistic vein that was to be sadly belied within a short time, the cardinal chancellor remarked, "This present year is the most prosperous & auspicious that has dawned on the Catholic University since its foundation."[21]

Thinking in terms of the first annual collection and the splendid generosity of the Knights of Columbus there was, indeed, reason for confidence; yet these bright prospects were soon to be overcast by an event which would mark 1904 as one of the darkest years in the university's annals. The origin of the crisis which broke over the institution that summer lay far back in the administration of Bishop Conaty. As early as November, 1901, a special committee of the Board of Trustees, consisting

---

[21] 101-E, handwritten copy of Gibbons' speech accepting the K. of C. gift, Washington, April 13, 1904. The appointment of Charles Hallan McCarthy of Philadelphia to the chair of American history was not at all to the liking of Martin I. J. Griffin, one of the leading figures at the time in the American Catholic Historical Society of Philadelphia. He wrote Monsignor O'Connell repeatedly in an effort to have the university undertake the calendaring of the documents in the archives of the Archdiocese of Baltimore. To Griffin this would be putting to the best use the endowment given by the K. of C. "These archives are the foundation of United States Catholic History," he told the rector (ACUA, O'Connell Papers, Griffin to O'Connell, Ridley Park, Pennsylvania, October 28, 1907). When O'Connell stated that Gibbons had taken the archives in hand, Griffin was annoyed. He replied, "Oh! yes I know the Cardinal has 'taken the archives in hand himself' as far as the gathering and arranging and the preservation of them is concerned. But has he taken up the card cataloging, indexing and synopsis of the documents. I think not. Indeed I might ask Why should he? If he collects, arranges and saves the precious papers he has done his part right well" (ibid., Griffin to O'Connell, Ridley Park, November 11, 1907). But in spite of all Griffin's efforts the university did nothing to implement his suggestion which was not too surprising since the main purpose of the endowment was the teaching of American history.

of Archbishop Ireland and Bishops Spalding and Maes, had been appointed by Gibbons as chancellor to examine the unsatisfactory financial conditions, as well as to investigate the causes for the disgruntlement of some of the professors with the rector. At the meeting of the trustees in April, 1902, the committee reported its findings. According to the prelates the management of the university funds had revealed not only a lack of competency and of business methods, but there had likewise been present what they termed, "an almost culpable negligence. . . ."[22]

The investments of the institution had been from the beginning exclusively in the hands of the treasurer, Thomas E. Waggaman, a Washington lawyer and real-estate man. From the time in May, 1885, when Mr. Waggaman joined the committee for the future university he had been in almost constant attendance at the meetings of the Board of Trustees, and they had practically left all responsibility for the university's financial welfare in his hands without asking for an accounting of his transactions. Around the time that the investigating committee made its report rumors concerning the institution's financial instability began to circulate in the press, and they became sufficiently serious to draw a denial from Gibbons at the commencement in June, 1902. "As the chancellor, and speaking for the trustees," the cardinal was quoted as saying, "I wish to give our people to understand that there is no truth whatever in these rumors. . . ."[23] Perhaps, he did not at the time know as much about the financial affairs as he should have known or as he was to know later but, in any case, regardless of the chancellor's reported denial, there was enough substance to the stories about the finances and the general administration of the university to cause grave dissatisfaction with Conaty as rector and to accomplish his removal at the end of his first term of office.

As a consequence of the change of administrations in 1903 and the further scrutiny and recommendations of the trustees' committee — with Spalding taking the lead — a group of five outstanding Catholic lawyers, bankers, and businessmen was selected to advise the trustees on financial affairs. Early in 1904 Gibbons

---

[22] Hogan, *The Catholic University of America, 1896–1903. The Rectorship of Thomas J. Conaty,* p. 136. For details of this committee's work cf. p. 131 ff. of Hogan.
[23] *Evening Star* (Washington), June 4, 1902.

sent for Charles J. Bonaparte, Secretary of the Navy, and told
him of his desire that Mr. Bonaparte should assist the trustees
in an advisory capacity, and that if he were agreeable they should
like to count on his legal advice in matters which might come
before them. "He cheerfully assented to become a member," said
the cardinal in reporting to Monsignor O'Connell.[24] Also invited
to serve were Michael Cudahy of Chicago and Adrian Iselin,
Thomas Fortune Ryan, and John McCall of New York, all men of
means and long experience in the world of business. At a special
meeting of the Board of Trustees on January 28, 1904, all these
gentlemen were present and were voted in as members. In the
trying days that were before the cardinal the presence of Secretary Bonaparte and of Gibbons' close friend, Michael Jenkins of
Baltimore, who had served the university for many years, was a
source of great strength and consolation to the chancellor who
was then seventy years of age.

This is not the place to detail the full story of the financial
crisis which overtook the university in the summer of 1904.
Suffice it to say that a more thorough investigation of the institution's investments revealed that they had been "injudiciously
handled and insufficiently secured."[25] When the committee pressed
the treasurer for additional security for the funds, he was unable
to produce it. Large sums had been used in real-estate speculation in sections of the city of Washington which were as yet un-
developed in the neighborhood of the present Shoreham and
Wardman Park Hotels. The case grew more complicated as time
went on with additional difficulty and embarrassment arising over
Mr. Waggaman's failure to have his original bond of 1899 to the
university redrafted, as well as his failure to act when the committee of the trustees demanded a transfer in trust for the university of right, title, and interest in the properties in northwest
Washington as security for funds which the institution had placed
in his hands for investment.

Although the business methods of Waggaman left much to be
desired, the blame for the muddled state of affairs could not be
laid solely at his door, since the trustees and administrative officers had for years neglected to demand an accounting of the

---

[24] ACUA, O'Connell Papers, Gibbons to O'Connell, Baltimore, January 6, 1904.
[25] Barry, *op. cit.*, p. 83. Chapter III of this work gives the details of the
financial crisis through which the university was then passing.

institution's investments. Archbishop Riordan reflected this view when he urged Monsignor O'Connell to have the university's new legal counsel, George E. Hamilton, move quickly and energetically in demanding of Waggaman additional security for the funds. Riordan maintained that Gibbons and Jenkins might be willing to make up their share of the loss if a loss should occur, but the other trustees would not and could not if they would. "The Cardinal and the Presidents before you," said Riordan, *"must be held responsible* for the investment of the funds and no one else."[26] There was considerable truth in Riordan's view, for either Gibbons and the previous rectors had neglected to keep a close watch over the university's funds as they should have done, or they had displayed an unwarranted trustfulness in leaving these matters solely in the hands of the treasurer. At first, however, it seemed that Riordan's demands for action against Waggaman were precipitate, for on July 13 the treasurer entered into an agreement with the university to give as security a deed of trust on all of the unsold portion of the subdivision of real estate, as well as to sell his art gallery and credit the amount to the university. With this agreement in hand the university administrators breathed more freely and for a few weeks they were of the impression that the treasurer could work his way out of the difficulty.

But on August 22 all hopes were suddenly dashed when it became known that three Washington banks to which Waggaman owed money were prepared to enter involuntary bankruptcy proceedings against him. With the filing of the bankruptcy petition the news of Mr. Waggaman's predicament became public, and the university was now faced with the prospect of losing all its investments. It was a trying moment for Cardinal Gibbons. He wired for Father George A. Dougherty, secretary to the rector and a priest of the Archdiocese of Baltimore, to come to see him, and with Dougherty's assistance he hurriedly drafted a letter to the trustees in which he recounted the facts in the case. The cardinal explained that the entire indebtedness of Waggaman to the university amounted to $876,168.98, and he listed the collateral held by the institution as the deed of trust on the real estate in the Woodley section of Washington, a chattel mortgage

---

[26] ACUA, O'Connell Papers, Riordan to O'Connell, Greenwich, Connecticut, June 5, 1904.

on Waggaman's art gallery which was valued by its owner at $600,000, a bond of Waggaman's father-in-law and son for $200,000, and other securities amounting to $75,000. Gibbons then said:

> The blow which we have been anticipating has at last fallen. We know now the exact position of the University, and knowing this the sky has been cleared. We must confront the situation bravely and generously. As bankruptcy proceedings have been instituted against Mr. Waggaman, all revenue from that source has been cut off. The only regular source of revenue the University can depend on is the annual collection, which amounted last year to $104,023.86. . . .

He then came to his appeal for their help:

> The time has come now for the Trustees to exert themselves in an heroic manner and to preserve their honor and integrity before the world. The salvation of the University depends on the early action of the Board of Directors. What I would suggest is that each member of the Board who feels capable of raising that amount should contribute $50,000, payable in five or ten annual installments. . . .

Gibbons was happy to state that thus far no reproach had been cast by the press on the financial administration of the university, and he emphasized that at the fall meeting of the board and in the next appeal for the annual collection, the trustees must give the public assurance that the funds left to the university in trust would be religiously safeguarded by them.[27]

Although the tone of the chancellor's letter was calm, actually he had been dreadfully shaken by the blow. Father Dougherty wired O'Connell who was then in Seattle of what had happened, and he said, "Eminenza very distressed. Situation uncertain."[28] In a letter of the following day he went into detail about Gibbons' reactions, and he told the rector that when he first arrived in Baltimore in answer to the cardinal's wire he found him in a state bordering on collapse and suggesting that they suppress the Schools of Law and Technology and cut the salaries of the faculty. The cardinal was now feeling better, but Dougherty added, "when

---

[27]AABo, Gibbons to Williams, Baltimore, August 27, 1904.

[28] ACUA, O'Connell Papers, Dougherty to O'Connell, Washington, August 27, 1904, telegram.

the news was first published he went into a most pitiful condition. I was afraid he would not get over the shock."[29]

It is not difficult to understand why the disaster that had befallen his favorite institution should have been felt so keenly by the old cardinal, and why it should have taken him some time to recover his composure and to rally his spirits to face the unpleasant prospect that now confronted him. Yet despite the distress which he experienced as a consequence of the careless handling of the university's finances, Gibbons remained free from any trace of reproach or bitterness toward Waggaman when he had the unpleasant task of calling for his resignation on the day after the Washington banks had filed their petition of bankruptcy. A week later Mr. Waggaman sent in his resignation and he told the cardinal, "I thank you for your sympathy & hope you will remember me in yr. prayers, as I need them much."[30] In addition to the anxiety caused him by the university's plight, Gibbons had to suffer the humiliation of having his name bandied about in the press in a way that could only add to his discomfort. For example, the New York *Sunday Herald* on September 4 stated that the cardinal was, as they expressed it, "in a fair way to lose the greater part of his personal fortune" through the difficulties that had overtaken the university treasurer.

But regardless of pain and embarrassment, Cardinal Gibbons rallied nobly to the university's cause, and in its most severe trial to date the institution found no greater source of strength than the assurance of his loyalty and the prestige of his name. A striking example of the length to which Gibbons was prepared to go to save the institution was seen in his turning to a number of valued friends among the hierarchy and the laity to lend him $1,000 a year for five years so that he might be enabled, in turn, to give it to the university. The depth of the feeling which he experienced was revealed in the appeal he made, among others, to Bishop J. F. Regis Canevin of Pittsburgh, to whom he said, "It is not pleasant for flesh & blood to become a beggar in my declining years, but God wills it to Whom I bow in all humility."[31] The reactions to Gibbons' efforts to get additional funds from

---

[29] *Ibid.*, Dougherty to O'Connell, Washington, August 28, 1904.
[30] 100-L, Waggaman to Gibbons, Washington, September 1, 1904.
[31] 101-K, Gibbons to Canevin, Baltimore, August 30, 1904, copy.

the trustees and from personal friends varied with individuals. Archbishop Ryan believed it would be wiser to wait until they learned of the final decision about the deed to the Woodley property, although he stated he was willing to second any effort which Gibbons and the trustees might determine upon.[32] Williams of Boston wrote an encouraging letter which prompted the cardinal to say, "I will be personally responsible for $50,000 payable in 5 years, & besides I am making a special appeal to a few friends outside the diocese."[33] As the time neared for the new academic year to open Bishop Spalding suggested that it would be necessary to reduce the salaries of the staff, and with that in mind Gibbons requested the rector to ask the professors to come to see him as they arrived so that he might urge upon them the reasons for salary reductions.[34]

In addition to the worries over the finances, there were other problems relating to the university which were laid before the chancellor at this time. Archbishop Messmer of Milwaukee had warned Gibbons the previous spring that when he visited the campus for the meeting of the trustees he had heard criticism from the professors of O'Connell as rector, on the score that he was not abiding by the constitution in giving the academic senate and the faculty sufficient opportunity to voice their opinions regarding policies and decisions.[35] Messmer now wrote the cardinal again and suggested the names of four priests of German extraction who would be suitable candidates for the office of vice-rector, and he gave it as his opinion that the appointment of one of these men would please the German Catholics and do much to overcome their prejudice toward the university. He reported that the Waggaman failure had afforded a number of German Catholic newspapers a chance to attack the university administration and he feared, therefore, that the idea of money being squandered might lodge in the minds of many and do harm to the coming annual collection. Once more he returned to the subject of his previous letter and stated that he had recently read in the paper of "domestic troubles" at the university. What foundation there was for the report Messmer did not know, but

32 101-L, Ryan to Gibbons, Philadelphia, September 1, 1904.

33 AABo, Gibbons to Williams, Baltimore, September 4, 1904.

34 ACUA, O'Connell Papers, Gibbons to O'Connell, Baltimore, September 27, 1904.

35 101-G, Messmer to Gibbons, Milwaukee, May 8, 1904.

as he told Gibbons, "I do know that some gentlemen have complained of too much 'paternalism' or interference on the part of the rector."[36] There is no evidence that Gibbons took any cognizance of the criticisms of his favorite and O'Connell was not, of course, in any way responsible for a financial crisis that traced its causes to the previous administrations. Nonetheless, if the reports of internal dissension were proven true, the chancellor would have to contend with more at the university than a depleted treasury.

In view of the financial strain the second annual collection scheduled to be taken up on November 27, the first Sunday in Advent, assumed a more than ordinary importance. In preparing the letter to be sent to the hierarchy Gibbons readily followed a suggestion of Spalding's that a full and accurate account of the financial condition of the institution be embodied.[37] He termed the university's welfare "the most important undertaking of the Hierarchy in view of the general good," and then summarized for the bishops the amount of the previous year's collection from seventy-six dioceses, remarked that the university had no floating debt nor any deficit at the end of the previous year, and stated that the losses suffered through the bankruptcy of the treasurer were in part covered by securities. However, the Waggaman failure had deprived the university of revenues which had hitherto been available for its work, and even with the utmost economy the income was not sufficient to cover the necessary expenses. The cardinal pleaded strongly with the hierarchy to come behind the collection, and he concluded by saying:

> As I am prepared to do all in my power to build up the University, and determined to guarantee it against all loss, even at the sacrifice of all I possess, I feel assured that you and your clergy will aid this sacred cause by an earnest appeal to the generosity of the people under your charge, and by personal sympathy for the work to which this collection is applied.[38]

The Archbishop of New York expressed himself as delighted with the chancellor's appeal and its frank statement of the relations of the university with Waggaman. However, Farley was annoyed at the failure of trustees like Archbishops Ireland,

---

[36] 101-N, Messmer to Gibbons, Milwaukee, October 1, 1904.

[37] ACUA, O'Connell Papers, Gibbons to O'Connell, Baltimore, October 14, 1904.

[38] 101-N, Gibbons' letter to the hierarchy, Baltimore, October 22, 1904, copy.

Keane, and Riordan to respond with $1,000 personally to the guarantee fund, and he remarked to Gibbons, "I feel there is utter lack of the broad & public spirit I would expect to find in such men."[39] A day or two later the cardinal was told of Ireland's disappointment in learning that Farley was giving only $10,000 and Ryan of Philadelphia only $5,000. "The possessors of such large sees, each one with enormous revenues," said Ireland, "should have given much larger sums."[40] These reflections of the East and the West among the university trustees probably afforded to the harassed chancellor a moment of amusement amid his many serious concerns. He was careful, however, not to involve himself in the trustees' varying estimates of what their colleagues should contribute, but rather kept himself on the alert that no opportunity be lost to advance the university's interests.

When he went to Cincinnati the first week in November to attend the funeral of his old friend, Archbishop Elder, Gibbons took occasion to urge the collection and a subscription to the guarantee fund upon Henry Moeller, the new Archbishop of Cincinnati, and he reported to O'Connell, "I intimated that he might be invited to become a member of the Board of Trustees which seemed to please him."[41] Meanwhile Gibbons' letter to the hierarchy had produced a favorable impression in many circles and Edward J. Hanna, professor of theology in St. Bernard's Seminary at Rochester, wished to add his own word of praise to the general chorus that had greeted what he called "your strong, generous, uncompromising stand on the University." Hanna said he had always been interested in the university and he had become doubly interested since O'Connell had taken up the reins. "Your willingness to sacrifice all you have to further the Institution," he said, "ought to be an example and an inspiration to others."[42]

In the crisis which the university experienced in 1904 Archbishop Keane was as usual generous with encouragement and assistance. Speaking of the annual collection he told Gibbons, "No other influence can possibly count in this matter like the personal

---

[39] 101-N, Farley to Gibbons, New York, October 28, 1904.

[40] 101-N, Ireland to Gibbons, St. Paul, October 30, 1904.

[41] ACUA, O'Connell Papers, Gibbons to O'Connell, Cincinnati, November 7, 1904.

[42] *Ibid.*, Hanna to Gibbons, Rochester, November 21, 1904.

influence of your Eminence. The misfortune of the present moment is a great blessing, in having set you so earnestly to work for the gathering of funds." His own Archdiocese of Dubuque would, he believed, do as well as in the previous year and that, thought Keane, would be a victory, to which he added, "Your Eminence's zeal in the cause has certainly been the chief agency in securing it."[43] Keane had recently been delegated to call on Mr. George E. Hamilton, the university's legal counsel, to make a plea that his fees for the services he was rendering be moderate. Hamilton resented the suggestion that his fees might be unduly high, and he informed Gibbons that if they felt any apprehension on that score he would gladly resign and make way for someone else.[44] Bonaparte was likewise made aware of Hamilton's chagrin and he suggested to the cardinal that he "oil the feather" a little in Hamilton's regard since, he said, his plumage had been a good deal ruffled.[45] The chancellor promptly complied and assured Mr. Hamilton that the trustees were perfectly satisfied with his services and that they would not entertain for a moment the idea of his withdrawing from the work. "We have the highest confidence not only in your ability," said Gibbons, "but also in your professional integrity."[46] Whatever damage had been done by Keane's reminder about the fees was thus remedied and Hamilton stayed on the case.

In a further effort to win support for the university, Cardinal Gibbons made an appeal to the Knights of Columbus to contribute to the guarantee fund being gathered to overcome the recent losses. He praised the K. of C. for their generosity in endowing the chair of American history, and he now told them, "You will place me under special obligations by communicating my appeal to the Knights residing within your State or Territory, and by forwarding to me their contributions after they are collected."[47] In the assurance that the university's cause would be forcefully stated to the K. of C., the cardinal then turned to Archbishop Keane with the request that he address them at their next annual convention. Keane gave a wholehearted response and

[43] 101-R, Keane to Gibbons, Dubuque, December 7, 1904.

[44] 101-R, Hamilton to Gibbons, Washington, December 9, 1904.

[45] 101-R, Bonaparte to Gibbons, Baltimore, December 11, 1904.

[46] 101-R, Gibbons to Hamilton, Baltimore, December 12, 1904, copy.

[47] 101-R, Gibbons to the Knights of Columbus, Baltimore, December 12, 1904, copy.

remarked, "It would be a shame for any of us to refuse any effort, after the splendid example that you are giving us."[48]

Through the ensuing years Gibbons continued his exertions in behalf of the university's finances, and the encouragement and support which reached him from time to time were at least a partial reward for all the labor he had expended. For example, at the time that Archbishop Ryan sent $1,000 as a second installment of his subscription, he told the cardinal, "You have certainly shown yourself a devoted friend of the University."[49] That Gibbons appreciated the approval of others for what he was doing was made evident some years later when he expressed his thanks to Archbishop Farley for his check of $2,000 and, as he put it, "still more for the warm sentiments of commendation which accompany it regarding my efforts to save the University from an untimely death. The approval of my colleagues & especially of yourself is my highest reward."[50]

By the autumn of 1905 the chancellor was in a position to offer the university's friends a much brighter prospect. In acknowledging Ireland's recent check for $1,000 he remarked, "I am happy to inform you that the financial condition of the University is most encouraging."[51] A week later he mailed his letter to the hierarchy for the next annual collection, and at that time he went into some detail. He told the bishops that the entire debt of the institution was then only $50,000 and $355,000 was invested in first-class securities. "As the debt disappears," said the cardinal, "a large proportion of our annual income will be devoted to permanent investment. The University, freed from all liabilities, will be safely established upon what we may well call, the people's endowment."[52] The amount of the collection on this occasion reached the satisfactory sum of $100,551.30 and with the success of this endeavor, together with the gradually mounting guarantee fund, the cardinal could rightly feel that the worst of the storm had passed. In his appeal to the bishops in the autumn of 1906 he said:

With all my heart I thank you, your clergy, and the devoted people of your diocese for the aid and encouragement given me in

[48] AAB, unclassified, Keane to Gibbons, Dubuque, January 30, 1905.
[49] 102-F, Ryan to Gibbons, Philadelphia, March 17, 1905.
[50] AANY, Gibbons to Farley, Baltimore, April 16, 1908.
[51] AASP, Gibbons to Ireland, Baltimore, October 17, 1905, copy.
[52] 102-S, Gibbons to the hierarchy, Baltimore, October 24, 1905, printed copy.

these trying circumstances, and I shall remember it gratefully as long as I live. Now that the great trials of the University are over, it remains for us to push on by common endeavor, the development of this great work, having in mind the needs of our schools and colleges and the educational wants of our people.[53]

Meanwhile the special collection continued and ran on until 1910 when it had netted $136,229.14 and in that year it gave way to the fund to be raised for the Cardinal Gibbons Memorial Hall.[54] Insofar as the Waggaman case was concerned, it had become deeply involved in litigation and by March, 1906, there were eleven law suits pending in the courts of the District of Columbia as a consequence of creditors seeking to retrieve their losses. Eventually the university realized the sum of $361,589.08 from its claims against Waggaman which, it was true, was far from the $876,168.98 announced by Gibbons as the total indebtedness of the treasurer to the university when the bankruptcy proceedings were first made known. But all things considered it was, as the historian of O'Connell's rectorship has said in speaking of the improved financial condition by 1908, "more satisfying than anyone had dared to hope for in the dark days of August, 1904."[55]

Through the entire crisis Gibbons had fought valiantly for the institution he had come to love, and those who had followed the course of his words and actions during this trying period could attest that its strengthened position was due in no small measure to the energetic leadership he had displayed in its behalf. All who knew the cardinal would likewise attest the deep sincerity of his words when he told the bishops in his annual message of 1908:

> It is the pride of my heart to see every day the growing prosperity of our dear institution of learning, and it would be the crowning joy of my life to see its endowment completed before I close my eyes forever upon it.[56]

Those who were close to the university in the crisis saw the

---

[53] 103-Q, Gibbons to the hierarchy, Baltimore, November 6, 1906, printed copy.

[54] Barry, *op. cit.,* p. 96.

[55] *Ibid.,* p. 108. The fact that the lands which Waggaman had purchased became in time very valuable showed that he had not been without foresight in his choice of investments.

[56] 105-E, Gibbons to the hierarchy, Baltimore, October 15, 1908, printed copy.

extent of Gibbons' contribution and appreciated the extraordinary effort he had put forth. When the cornerstone of Gibbons Hall was laid on October 12, 1911, Archbishop Farley was one of the principal speakers, and at that time he said:

> But while Cardinal Gibbons thus rendered invaluable service from the beginning in every juncture, never in its history was his indomitable courage, the quality most needed in every vast undertaking, so notably shown as in the dark days of its greatest trial. . . . Then it was that he whom we delight to honor by these walls proved the bulwark of the people. "Never," he said, "while I have the power to wield a pen in appeal or lift a voice in pleading, shall this work of religion stop. God wills it; the work must go on."[57]

And in paying tribute to the chancellor on the occasion of the golden jubilee of his priesthood which occurred that year the rector, Monsignor Shahan, also alluded to Gibbons' services to the university at the time of the financial crisis. Shahan wrote:

> On all sides he rallied new friends to the support of the enterprise, pointed out more urgently than ever its rich promise, secured generous donations, and breathed into the situation a new life that has not ceased to put forth regularly fresh evidences of vigor and viability. Amid painful vicissitudes the University profited by the universal esteem in which the Cardinal was held. His protection was a tower of strength. . . .[58]

Fortunately, the relations of Cardinal Gibbons with the university were not all as troublesome as those growing out of the bankruptcy of its treasurer, even if time was to prove the cardinal too optimistic in 1906 when he spoke of the "great trials" as being over. To offset the reverses he had the satisfaction of witnessing the extension of the university's work and the gradual addition of new sources of strength and support from those who affiliated themselves with the institution. For example, on April 23, 1903, Gibbons laid the cornerstone of the Apostolic Mission House on the campus, a building intended for priests who would take special training in preparation for missionary labors in the United States, and on the same day he turned the first spade of earth for the College of the Immaculate Conception, the

---

[57] "Cardinal Gibbons Memorial Hall," *Catholic University Bulletin*, XVII (December, 1911), 775–776.

[58] "Cardinal Gibbons and the University," *Catholic University Bulletin*, XVII (October, 1911), 626.

house of studies of the Dominican friars, a structure which he dedicated on August 20, 1905. In the spring of the year 1905 he was likewise gladdened by the news that Michael F. Fallon, O.M.I., provincial of the Oblate Fathers, had purchased land across the street from the campus for a house of studies of that congregation.[59]

Two years before a proposal had been advanced which affected the religious society which the cardinal knew best, namely, the Sulpicians, to have them take over an undergraduate seminary at the university. The cardinal was agreeable to the plan, although nothing was done at the time to carry it out. But when the idea came up again in 1905 Gibbons expressed himself as opposed to moving St. Mary's Seminary in Baltimore in its entirety to Washington because of the adverse effect it would have on the clergy and city of Baltimore and, too, because it would deprive the Josephites of the assistance which the Sulpicians were rendering to their students there. As an alternative, he suggested that the course in philosophy be retained in Baltimore and that the theology classes be moved to Washington. In this way he would not altogether lose from his see city the old seminary on North Paca Street which had come to mean so much to the Catholic life of the community. But due to the decision of the Sulpician provincial council that they could not properly finance and staff both houses, the proposal was again set aside and it was not until September, 1919, that Gibbons dedicated the Sulpician Seminary at Washington, and then only as a strictly Sulpician project and not an integral part of the university.[60]

It was during the years of Monsignor O'Connell's rectorship that the university suffered the loss of one of its most loyal and helpful trustees when John Lancaster Spalding was incapacitated by a stroke of paralysis early in 1905. It was a loss which no one appreciated more keenly than the cardinal chancellor. Gibbons followed closely the progress of the bishop's illness and he was glad to be told by Spalding's companion, Father Daniel

---

[59] 102-F, Fallon to Gibbons, New York, March 17, 1905. The Oblate house of studies was formally dedicated by Gibbons on November 16, 1916.

[60] Barry, *op. cit.*, pp. 123–125. Cf. also the present writer's "Washington's St. Sulpice. Twenty-five Years." *The Voice*, XX (November, 1942), 17–19, 26, 28. For brief sketches of the religious houses of study around the university in these years cf. *Catholic University Bulletin*, XXIV (February, 1918), 21–37.

J. Riordan, that the prelate was hopeful and in the best spirits. "He has been greatly touched," said Riordan, "by the interest you have shown from the beginning of his illness and often speaks of it."[61] At the spring meeting of the trustees in that year the cardinal was asked to express to Spalding their sympathy in his illness. In conveying this message Gibbons wrote:

> I find it hard to say how warm & affectionate their words were. Yet one and all entertain the sweet hope that you will be with them on this occasion next year to aid & stimulate them by that enthusiasm & deep interest which you have always manifested in the University.
>
> And surely, dear Bishop, I need hardly say that I too feel most deeply all that they expressed, & with all my heart that your recovery will be rapid & sure, & that many years will yet be granted you to continue the many good works you have begun, & to add even greater lustre to a life that has shed so many blessings upon the American Church.[62]

Spalding's recovery proved to be only partial, although he did not for some time give up hope of remaining on the university board. In the fall of 1905 he expressed grateful appreciation for Gibbons' solicitude about his health, acknowledged how happy he was to receive the cheering news concerning the university, and said he had some reason to believe a family in his diocese might be induced to give $50,000 to the institution. "I greatly regret not being able to send the money I promised," said Spalding, "but my illness has been very expensive and has besides diminished my resources."[63] After an interval of two years he was compelled to admit that his health would not permit him to attend the meetings of the trustees, and for that reason he begged Gibbons to present his resignation to the board.[64] In telling Spalding of the reluctance with which the Board of Trustees agreed to his request, the cardinal said:

> In doing so, however, they recognized all your great services to the University in the past, and how in a sense you could be considered its founder and its ever-constant protector. The Board holds these great merits in grateful memory, and while returning to you

---

[61] 102-H, Riordan to Gibbons, Hot Springs, Arkansas, April 8, 1905.

[62] 102-K, Gibbons to Spalding, Baltimore, May 7, 1905, copy.

[63] 102-S, Spalding to Gibbons, Peoria, October 20, 1905.

[64] ACUA, O'Connell Papers, Spalding to Gibbons, Hot Springs, Arkansas, March 11, 1907.

its warm thanks for them, likewise expresses the hope that in course of time, your health being restored, you may be able to resume your accustomed place among us.[65]

Those who were acquainted with the university's history would be quick to second the tribute of the chancellor, for in all the American hierarchy there was no single bishop who had done more to bring the Catholic University of America into existence and to assist it during the first difficult years of its life than the Bishop of Peoria.

The role of the cardinal as Chancellor of the University involved him in a variety of matters that often taxed his powers of discretion and judgment. Among the most delicate of these duties was that of keeping the Holy See informed of the purposes and motives which lay behind certain developments at Washington. The day before the meeting of the trustees on November 17, 1904, Gibbons was presented with a communication from Cardinal Satolli, Prefect of the Congregation of Studies, in which the latter suggested that lay students should not be admitted to the university and that greater emphasis should be given to the School of Theology. Coming as it did so soon after the financial failure when the trustees were eagerly seeking sources of increased revenue, to say nothing of the fact that it would do injury to one of the purposes which the university was trying to fulfill, Satolli's letter met with a very unfavorable reception on all sides. The trustees discussed the matter at length, and finally resolved unanimously that Gibbons should reply in their name and thank the prefect for his solicitude for the university but tell him courteously that his suggestion could not be complied with.[66]

In framing his reply the cardinal expressed the trustees' gratitude for his abiding interest, but stated that he was sorry to have to inform him that his suggestion would run counter to the institution's best interests. Gibbons explained that the constitution of the university pledged it to the instruction of laymen, that

---

[65] 104-F, Gibbons to Spalding, Baltimore, April 30, 1907, copy. In the summer of 1908 Archbishop Ireland made a trip to Peoria to induce Spalding to resign as bishop of that see. Ireland reported that he did not meet with much opposition, and that Spalding had sent his resignation to the apostolic delegate. "He understands," said Ireland, "that his health is irreparably shattered, & that the work to be done in the Diocese demands an active bishop" (ACUA, O'Connell Papers, Ireland to O'Connell, St. Paul, August 7, 1908).

[66] Barry, *op. cit.,* pp. 128–129.

the appeal for the annual collection was based in part on this point, and that the religious communities had gathered about the university to prepare their members to teach lay students. The cardinal then remarked:

> It is to redeem that solemn pledge to the Country that Lay professors teach and Lay students study at the University with such striking results that other famed Universities admire the Christian and scientific results of such teaching. To suppress them would be to curtail the usefulness of the University, to be guilty of breaking its most solemn engagements to the Church, to wreck the confidence of the people in the Hierarchy of the United States and to jeopardize the very existence of the University.

Beyond this Gibbons reminded the cardinal prefect that the trustees would be liable to prosecution in the courts if they went against the intentions of the donors of the endowments. He assured Satolli that the trustees would continue their efforts to strengthen the School of Theology as the most important faculty of the university, and he concluded, "nor shall any effort be spared to make it the most efficient and equal to the best Theological Faculties of the World."[67] With this no more was heard of the incident, and in the autumn of 1905 the university was opened to lay undergraduates as well as to lay graduate students.

The crisis over the treasurer's bankruptcy had not only delayed by a year the admission of lay undergraduates, but it forced the curtailment of other activities of the university as well. Early in 1906 a discussion arose within the faculty over the participation of the university in intercollegiate athletics. The rector summarized the different points of view for Gibbons and said he was in favor of doing everything possible for intramural athletics, but he could not warm to the idea of sending competing teams around the country in view of the costs involved. However, before a final decision was reached O'Connell wished to know the opinion of the chancellor.[68] Gibbons replied that he was a firm believer in the necessity of athletics for young men studying in the university and the old and true saying, *mens sana in corpore sano,* was one to which he gave his adhesion. But he did not believe that the time had come for the university to compete in games

---

[67] ACUA, O'Connell Papers, Gibbons to Satolli, Baltimore, December 14, 1904, copy.

[68] *Ibid.,* O'Connell to Gibbons, Washington, February 20, 1906, copy.

with larger and better endowed institutions. "The small number of students that we have," said the cardinal, "the loss of study entailed and the crippled condition of our finances compel me to withhold my approval from the program as outlined."[69] It would be some time before the size of the lay student body and the financial resources of the university would be such as to warrant competition in intercollegiate athletics.

But if Gibbons felt the necessity of disapproving of inter-collegiate athletics because of the costs involved, he had plans which would add to the endowment of the institution and at a future date enable it to direct more of its income to purposes of this kind. Late in 1907 he urged upon Mr. Hearn, Supreme Knight of the Knights of Columbus, that the order implement its proposal to collect $500,000 for the university which had been suggested at the national convention the previous summer. In reply Hearn stated that there was not the enthusiasm for the work which one might expect but he promised that he would do all he could to make it succeed. His energy, he said, would be given to the project because of his regard for the cardinal, and in conclusion he remarked:

> I want you to know that the source of all my courage and strength in this great task is born of the affection I entertain for you, and the desire I have to see this enterprise a monument to your labors in the Catholic Church.[70]

However, Archbishop Glennon, who had made the original pro-posal for the endowment at the national convention, was not so sure that Hearn was advancing the cause as forcefully as he might do. He confessed that the source of his information was from knights who were hostile to Hearn and, therefore, he would not wish Gibbons to attach more importance to it than it de-served; yet rumors persisted that Hearn's delay in pushing the plan was due, as Glennon said, "to advices received from the Archbishop of Boston and the Jesuit Fathers. . . ." Glennon conceded that Hearn's course might be the wiser one and that the delay might really produce more favorable results, but he lamented the failure to take advantage of the enthusiasm of the last national convention of the K. of C. for the idea.[71]

---

[69] *Ibid.*, Gibbons to O'Connell, Baltimore, March 5, 1906, copy.

[70] 104-Q, Hearn to Gibbons, New Haven, December 7, 1907.

[71] 104-Q, Glennon to Gibbons, St. Louis, December 11, 1907, *Personal.*

Whatever the reason for the delay, the cardinal did not give up hope and when he was in Rome in the summer of 1908 he seized the chance to write a letter of congratulation to a newspaper editor who had praised the K. of C. Gibbons said the order was in need of a bond of unity, and to his mind no better bond could be found than the effort in behalf of the university. Reflecting, perhaps, his uneasiness with the failure of the campaign up to this time to take on more life, Gibbons stated, "We all expect something great and monumental of the society of the Knights of Columbus, and we should be sorry to see it fritter away its opportunities and its energies in little perishable dribs and drabs."[72]

At length the committee was appointed and Edward H. Doyle of Detroit was named chairman. Doyle had printed a circular letter for all the councils in which he recalled that at the national convention in Jamestown, Virginia, in August, 1907, and again at St. Louis the following year, the order had practically pledged itself to raise this endowment. A letter of Gibbons' was quoted and the knights were given instructions on how to proceed with the task of raising the money.[73]

During the course of the next few years Gibbons continued to encourage the K. of C. from time to time to complete their undertaking. In the spring of 1910 Philip A. Hart, one of the committee members for the endowment campaign, reported the progress to date, and he suggested to the cardinal that he write to the chaplains of the delinquent councils urging them to get behind the drive.[74] Gibbons gladly complied and sent out a letter in June to about 200 councils, and in pleading for the chaplains' co-operation in the matter, he said, "The Endowment Fund is the most important enterprise that the Knights of Columbus have yet undertaken, and places them in the front rank of the friends and supporters of Catholic Education."[75] By the end of the year 1913 the goal had been reached and on January 6, 1914, the

---

[72] "Cardinal Gibbons and the Knights of Columbus Endowment," *Catholic University Bulletin,* XIV (October, 1908), 723. The letter was dated Rome, August 15, 1908, and the person to whom it was directed was not identified beyond the fact that he was the editor of a paper called the *Register.*

[73] 105-L, Doyle and committee to the K. of C. councils, Philadelphia, April 29, 1909, printed copy.

[74] 106-I, Hart to Gibbons, Philadelphia, May 25, 1910.

[75] 106-J, Gibbons to chaplains of the K. of C. councils, Baltimore, June 11, 1910, copy; Diary, June 21, 1910, p. 320.

cardinal chancellor received from James A. Flaherty, the new supreme knight, a check for $500,000 at a ceremony in his residence in Baltimore where a group of distinguished clergy and laity had assembled for the occasion. The chairman of the order's endowment committee for raising the money, Mr. Doyle, credited the original suggestion for the benefaction to the speech of Archbishop Glennon delivered at the national convention of the K. of C. in 1907, and he stated that aside from the consideration of the encouragement it would give to Catholic education, the chief inspiration for the work had been the knights' knowledge of the pleasure it would bring to Cardinal Gibbons, "whose fondest hopes for the Catholic University," said Doyle, "are well-known to all."[76]

In reply the chancellor told the gathering that words failed him to express adequately his happiness at the accomplishment of the splendid task to which the knights had pledged themselves some years before. "I find only one parallel of your magnanimous deed," said Gibbons, "the building of a great mediaeval cathedral by the loyal and devoted merchants' guild of those former Catholic days." The cardinal then continued:

> While the Catholic people in the United States have in the past created great and memorable works of religion, monuments of divine worship, charity and education, we assist now for the first time at the conscious exercise of a vast power for common Catholic welfare by a Catholic association which finds in itself the inspiration, the courage and the means to do for common interest a work of supreme importance that must forever loom great and striking in the annals of our beloved country.[77]

The endowment was devoted to the purpose of providing fifty scholarships for lay graduate students to be distributed on the basis of competitive examinations and to be in the gift of Cardinal Gibbons during his lifetime. Knowledge of the university's good fortune was, of course, communicated to the Holy See, and a year later when the cardinal requested a letter from Pope Benedict XV for the approaching silver jubilee of the institution, he explained to Cardinal Gasparri, the Secretary of State, the disposition which had been made of the knights' money, and he

---

[76] "Knights of Columbus Endowment Fund," *Catholic University Bulletin,* XX (January, 1914), 75.

[77] *Ibid.,* p. 76.

said, "Indeed no event in our educational annals has so impressed the non-Catholic world with the profound faith of our Catholic laity as this great educational benefaction."[78]

In many other ways the cardinal protected and advanced the university's interests during the years of his chancellorship. In 1908 he was asked by the apostolic delegate, Archbishop Falconio, for his opinion regarding a petition of Bishop McQuaid to the Holy See for permission to grant degrees in canon law at St. Bernard's Seminary in Rochester. The delegate recalled that in 1901 McQuaid had obtained permission to grant degrees in philosophy and theology, but before he would answer Rome in the present instance he wished to have Gibbons' judgment.[79] The cardinal was opposed to giving the permission since, as he said, the university was much better equipped for advanced courses and, too, competition of this kind would do injury to the institution which needed the support of the whole American Catholic body.[80] Four years later, when Rome inquired his opinion on a similar petition for theological degrees to be granted by St. Vincent's Seminary at Latrobe, Pennsylvania, he again stated that it would detract from the university, to which the Holy See had directed the religious orders for founding houses of study. At present only St. Bernard's and St. Mary's in Baltimore enjoyed permission to grant theological degrees and if it were given to St. Vincent's other seminaries would demand it.[81] It was apparent that the cardinal was exercising a close vigilance to prevent encroachment upon the university's domain of graduate work in the sacred sciences.

In a similar manner Gibbons endeavored to assist the administrative personnel in Washington when it was a matter of the university's welfare or prestige. In 1909 the candidacy of Father George Dougherty was advanced for the office of vice-rector, but a possible obstacle presented itself in that he did not hold the doctor's degree. The chancellor wrote to the Holy See and detailed the priest's superior qualifications, gave a brief sketch of his education and administrative experience, and quoted the precedent of the first vice-rector, Philip J. Garrigan, who had

---

[78] 111-F, Gibbons to Gasparri, Baltimore, February 3, 1915, copy.

[79] 104-W, Falconio to Gibbons, Washington, April 13, 1908.

[80] AAB, unclassified, Gibbons to Falconio, Baltimore, April 14, 1908, copy.

[81] 109-C, Gibbons to Ascenso Dandini, Secretary of the Congregation of Studies, Baltimore, February 23, 1913, copy.

been given the degree by Rome. "As the need of a Vice-Rector for the University is very urgent," said Gibbons, "I would be particularly grateful to you if you could hasten the grant of this dignity."[82] Early in 1910 the Holy See acceded to the chancellor's request by conferring the S.T.D. degree on Dougherty and in April of that year he was elected vice-rector of the university.

But four years later, in the case of a suggested papal honor for another member of the administration, the prospective recipient was not enthusiastic. Rumor reached Edward A. Pace, dean of the School of Philosophy, that he was to be made a monsignor in recognition of the distinction he had brought to the university as one of the principal editors of the *Catholic Encyclopedia* which had been completed in 1912. Pace was strongly opposed to the honor and thought that it would do injury to his work. In his opinion there should be only one monsignor in the university, and he should be the rector; it had cost a great deal to attain something like unity among the professors and Pace was fearful that a papal honor for him might offer a pretext for what he called "a new split." He was grateful to Gibbons for the good will in his regard and he found the approval which the chancellor was pleased to give to his work most gratifying, but he begged to be spared the rumored dignity.[83] Seven years later, however, after Pace had distinguished himself anew by writing the original draft of the hierarchy's pastoral letter of September, 1919, he was raised to the rank of protonotary apostolic at the instance of Gibbons. In thanking the cardinal he said:

> In the honor which you have obtained for me, I am glad to recognize a new evidence of the Holy Father's good-will toward the University and a new reason for hoping that the work which means so much for Catholic education may speedily attain the ideals which you have cherished from the beginning.[84]

It was during the administration of Monsignor O'Connell that the theological movement known in the Church as modernism

---

[82] 105-T, Gibbons to "Your Eminence" [Satolli], Baltimore, November 13, 1909, copy.

[83] 109-G, Pace to Gibbons, Washington, June 13, 1913. Pace, Shahan, and the other editors of the *Catholic Encyclopedia* were awarded the medal, Pro Ecclesia et Pontifice, at the instance of Cardinal Farley this same year. *Catholic University Bulletin,* XIX (April, 1913), 351–352.

[84] 128-J, Pace to Gibbons, Washington, July 22, 1920.

reached its climax with the issuance of Pius X's encyclical, *Pascendi dominici gregis,* on September 8, 1907. The serious threat offered by the modernists to the integrity of Catholic doctrine naturally became a matter of grave concern in the Church's intellectual centers, and when the trustees of the Catholic University of America met on November 16 they gave their unanimous assent to the condemnation of the false doctrines enumerated in the encyclical and instructed the chancellor to write the Pope in their name to this effect. Moreover, at the same meeting a committee of five, consisting of Archbishop Ireland as chairman with Archbishops Farley and Glennon, Bishop Matthew Harkins, and Monsignor O'Connell, was appointed by Gibbons to make recommendations concerning books in the library of the university which might contain modernistic teachings.[85] In fulfillment of his duty the cardinal addressed a letter to Pius X in which he stated the adhesion of the Board of Trustees to the encyclical, and their firm resolve to give the fullest compliance in their power to its purposes. He also stated that he wished to add the spontaneous adhesion of all the instructors in the university and his personal assurance that in his capacity as chancellor he would exercise a rigorous application of his authority if such should prove necessary.[86]

The modernist movement was European in origin and extent and its application to the Church of the United States was on the whole slight and of relatively secondary importance.[87] It was true that the excitement aroused by the heresy was in part responsible for the death of the *New York Review,* a learned journal edited by several of the professors of St. Joseph's Seminary in New York, which began publication in June, 1905, but did not survive beyond the issue of June, 1908; and it was also true that in 1909 one casualty was counted in the American priesthood when William L. Sullivan left the Church at Austin,

---

[85] Barry, *op. cit.,* p. 177. At the meeting of the trustees on May 6, 1908, the committee appointed the previous fall to examine the books decided that all matters of this kind should be left to the vigilance of Gibbons as ordinary of the archdiocese. *Ibid.,* p. 177, n. 198.

[86] 104-P, Gibbons to Pius X, Baltimore, November 24, 1907, copy in Italian in O'Connell's handwriting.

[87] Cf. Anthony Viéban, "Who Are the Modernists of the Encyclical?" *American Ecclesiastical Review,* XXXVIII (May, 1908), 489–508. A recent discussion by a nontheologian is D. A. Binchy, "The Modernist Movement," *Cambridge Journal,* I (January, 1948), 220–232.

Texas. But in the main the controversy was confined to Europe, and in only one instance did the issues raised by the modernist movement become in any way serious in the university and call forth action from the cardinal chancellor. This is not the place to recount in full detail the complicated story of Henry A. Poels, associate professor of Old Testament Scripture, a scholar of Dutch birth, whose case indirectly involved the head of his department in the School of Theology, Charles P. Grannan.[88] We are interested in it here only insofar as it affected Cardinal Gibbons. Poels' difficulty grew out of the decision in June, 1906, of the Biblical Commission, of which he was a consultor, that Moses must be held to have been the main and inspired author of the Pentateuch. The professor was an exemplary priest, and the fact that he could not in conscience teach that Moses was the actual and immediate author of the first five books of the Bible worried him, although he never questioned the divine inspiration of the Scriptures and for that reason was never guilty of the modernist heresy. He made a trip to Rome in the summer of 1907 and had an audience of Pius X from which he gained the impression that the Pope had instructed him to follow the advice of Father Giovanni Genocchi and of Lawrence Janssens, O.S.B., secretary of the Biblical Commission. Poels later stated to the Board of Trustees that his two Roman advisers had told him not to abandon the teaching of Scripture, since it would become the source of adverse comment throughout the scholarly world and do injury to the university. In May, 1908, he secured a letter from Janssens in which permission was granted to him to continue his teaching, providing he did not contravene the decisions of the Biblical Commission. The professor gave the original of this letter to Bishop Maes, secretary of the Board of Trustees, and he sent a copy to Gibbons.

The next step in the case came in the summer of 1908. On July 18 Cardinal Gibbons sailed for Europe on the *Koenig Albert* in the company of Archbishop Farley, Bishop Foley, and Monsignor O'Connell.[89] For some time it had been well known in university circles that the rector was at serious odds over admin-

---

[88] Further details on the Poels case are given in Barry, *op. cit.,* pp. 177–183.

[89] Gibbons became ill in Europe on this occasion. Archbishop Ireland reflected his anxiety to O'Connell when he said, "I hope & pray that to-morrow's cablegram will announce his complete recovery" (ACUA, O'Connell Papers, Ireland to O'Connell, St. Paul, August 7, 1908).

istrative procedures with Grannan, head of the Department of Sacred Scripture. Yet when a question arose at the trustees' meeting in April, 1907, over Grannan's fidelity to some of the decisions of the Biblical Commission, O'Connell refused to make a statement against him and the trustees thereupon rescinded by a majority vote a resolution calling for Grannan's resignation. Shortly after his arrival in Rome in 1908 O'Connell had an audience of Pius X, during which he brought up the difficulty he was having with a Scripture professor who gave his students all the objections of liberal critics but did nothing to clear up the questions raised in their minds. But since no name was mentioned and the Pontiff had in mind the notice which had previously been brought to his attention about Poels, he understood that the rector was referring to the latter. This would probably account for Pius X's mention of his dissatisfaction with the Scripture professor in Washington when he received Cardinal Gibbons in audience about the same time.

In any case, nothing decisive happened until the meeting of the trustees on April 21, 1909. On that occasion Gibbons filed his letter of the previous November 22 which embodied his first annual report as Archbishop of Baltimore of the committee on vigilance for upholding Catholic doctrine in accordance with the instructions of the Holy See about modernism. The cardinal told Pius X that as a result of the committee's investigations nothing of an unfavorable nature had been discovered, except a doubt about the acceptance of certain decrees of the Biblical Commission on the part of Poels. He was careful to say that Poels was recognized as a man of eminent learning in Scripture and that his philosophical and theological principles were most correct. The matter would be further examined, said Gibbons, and then the subject would be referred to Rome for a final decision. The chancellor now called upon the trustees for action in regard to Poels. At the request of the board, the professor presented his case in writing on the following day and after listening to his history of the affair, including the episode of the mistaken identity in the papal audience, Poels was exonerated of blame by the trustees.[90]

---

[90] ACUA, Minutes of the Board of Trustees of the Catholic University of America. Volume I, 1885–1933, p. 174. A copy of the Latin letter of Gibbons to Pius X and of the Poels statement are contained in the accompanying folder.

Matters might have been allowed to rest there had not the visit to Rome in July, 1909, of the new Rector of the University, Dr. Thomas J. Shahan, brought to light a misunderstanding over what had happened in Poels' audience with the Pope two years before when the professor understood Pius X to have instructed him to follow the advice of Genocchi and Janssens. In his audience Shahan was now told that such had not been the understanding of the Pope. Thereupon Pius X wrote out an autograph memorandum for Shahan in which he expressed his admiration for the candor with which Poels had stated he could not in conscience admit the decision of the Biblical Commission on the Mosaic authorship of the Pentateuch, but the Pope added that if he remained firm in his position he could no longer continue to occupy his chair in the university. With this the Poels audience had been terminated without, as the memorandum read, "the Holy Father having advised him (as was natural) to consult any other person."[91]

A few days later this version of the audience was conveyed to Gibbons by Cardinal Merry del Val, the Secretary of State, who said that if Poels could not bring himself to submit a written statement under oath that he would accept and faithfully teach the doctrine and conclusions of the Biblical Commission he must resign his professorship. Merry del Val ended by saying, "Dr. Shahan is of course entirely of this opinion and he will fully explain the position to your Eminence."[92] The chancellor communicated with Shahan as soon as he received Merry del Val's letter and asked that he inform Poels in his name at once of the mind of the Holy See. As he explained, Gibbons could not say what form the statement by Rome would take until he saw it, but he would forward it immediately upon its arrival. "I would have written the Doctor myself," said the cardinal, "but as I leave for Salt Lake to-morrow, I am very busy now with my preparations."[93]

At this particular time Poels was visiting his home at Vernay in the Netherlands. Shahan now cabled him that Gibbons desired him not to return to the university until he had received a letter

---

[91] *Ibid.*, Pius X to Shahan, Rome, July 12, 1909, in Italian and an English translation.

[92] 105-P, Merry del Val to Gibbons, Rome, July 17, 1909, *Private.*

[93] AAB, unclassified, Gibbons to Shahan, Baltimore, August 1, 1909, copy.

which would follow. In the letter two days later Shahan explained the contents of Merry del Val's most recent communication to the chancellor, and stated that if Poels could not bring himself to declare under oath in a written statement that he would follow the decisions of the Biblical Commission he must necessarily resign. He also remarked that the Pope would himself draw up the statement and as soon as Gibbons was in receipt of it he would forward it. Shahan then concluded, "In the meantime he [Gibbons] informs you that it is of course useless to appear at the University before the terms of His Holiness are satisfactorily complied with."[94] Poels then cabled to Gibbons of his anxiety to see the statement he was asked to sign, stated his willingness to go to Rome, and asked what the cardinal advised him to do.[95] On the day that the cablegram was received Gibbons informed Merry del Val of all the recent developments and he told him that he had cabled Poels to the effect that if he wished to go to Rome he might well do so. The chancellor stressed the fact that unless Poels would subscribe to the desired statement he believed that the trustees at their November meeting would hesitate to allow the professor to resume his classes.[96]

Two days later the rector forwarded a lengthy communication to Merry del Val in which he stated that Gibbons' letter had been written in Italian so that it could be laid before the Pope if that was thought wise, and Shahan added that he had drawn it up himself with some caution and reserve. He then continued, "The Cardinal left it to me to state to you more fully his objections and mine to Doctor Poels' return to the University."[97] The rector then proceeded to give the various reasons why he and the chancellor were strongly opposed to Poels returning to Washington. First, there was the fact that he had withstood for two years what Shahan called a plain decision of the Holy See, a resistance which, he said, was being closely watched by other professors; second, even if Poels took the oath Shahan feared that many would not believe he earnestly accepted or would be able faithfully to teach the doctrines in question; third, he

---

[94] ACUA, folder accompanying the forty-second meeting of the Board of Trustees, Shahan to Poels, Washington, August 14, 1909, copy.

[95] *Ibid.,* Poels to Gibbons, Vernay, August 27, 1909, cablegram.

[96] *Ibid.,* Gibbons to Merry del Val, Baltimore, August 27, 1909, copy in Italian.

[97] *Ibid.,* Shahan to Merry del Val, Washington, August 29, 1909, copy. On the same day he signed a letter to Poels embodying similar information.

foresaw no little rejoicing among the modernists and their adherents if it should happen that Poels should blunt the decision of Pius X; finally, in the rector's opinion the best interests of the university would be gravely injured by the professor's return. The institution was then at a point where its future looked promising, and with prudent direction and hard work they were hoping to secure the friendly and vigorous support of the hierarchy. He had told Poels in a letter the same day, he said, that if it became known throughout the American Church that the university had retained on its faculty for five years a professor of Old Testament who was now obliged by the Holy See to take a special oath in order to keep his chair, he felt sure that the effect would be harmful. Therefore, Shahan begged Merry del Val to urge Poels to resign if he should visit Rome. Two weeks later the papal Secretary of State cabled to Gibbons that he had received his and Shahan's letters and that Pius X did not wish Poels to resume his teaching until after the November meeting of the trustees.[98]

But with the arrival of the professor in Rome matters took a new turn. On September 11 he had a somewhat unpleasant interview with Merry del Val in which he insisted that he had not knowingly contravened the instructions of Pius X; he was desirous of obeying ecclesiastical authority but he also wished to protect his honor as a priest, and if he was suddenly cut off from his teaching he would be suspect as a modernist in the eyes of the Catholic world. He regretted that he could not take the oath in the formula that Gibbons had forwarded unless he was allowed to add his own interpretation to the words, "sincere accepturum et fideliter traditurum" which it contained. But Merry del Val would not accede to this request and with that the interview ended.[99] Later Poels saw the Capuchin cardinal, Joseph Vives y Tuto, Prefect of the Congregation of Religious, who agreed with Poels' version of the case and volunteered to see Pius X and Merry del Val in his behalf. The professor likewise saw Leopold Fonck, S.J., President of the Pontifical Biblical Institute, who believed that there was such grave danger of an injustice being done to Poels that he went personally

---

[98] *Ibid.*, Merry del Val to Gibbons, September 12, 1909, cablegram.
[99] *Ibid.*, Poels' memorandum to the Board of Trustees, Washington, November 24, 1909.

to the Pope and made a plea for the professor. Fonck stated that the Pontiff was fully convinced of Poels' personal honor, and to safeguard it he would have Merry del Val inform Gibbons that no change was to be made in the professor's status that year. As for the points of doctrine in dispute, Fonck told Pius X that among the adherents of the broader tendency in exegesis Poels was certainly on the right side.[100]

The Pope did as he had promised, and in consequence on September 18 Gibbons received a cable from Merry del Val which stated that he had seen Poels, the situation was now somewhat modified, and the chancellor should await a letter before making a decision.[101] On the same day Poels informed Gibbons and Shahan from Rome that the Pope wished him to return to Washington, that he would be a bit late in arriving, but that as soon as he reached the United States he would furnish any information which they desired.[102] In the letter which followed his cablegram to Gibbons the Secretary of State said that Poels had made it quite clear that what Merry del Val termed "the serious misrepresentation" of the Holy Father's intentions and directions was not due to him. He paid tribute to Poels' sincerity and submissive spirit, and he believed it would not be fair to act abruptly and thus to cast a stigma on his honor as a priest. But since his intellectual position remained the same, the Pope had suggested that he should be allowed to resume his teaching on two conditions: first, that he would agree to abstain from any views not in complete conformity with the doctrine and guidance of the Holy See, and second, that during the course of the next academic year he would make arrangements to leave the university. Poels had agreed, said the cardinal secretary, to accept these conditions, and it was Merry del Val's wish that Gibbons should place this suggestion before the Board of Trustees.[103]

Poels arrived at the university on October 6 where he experienced a very cool reception from Shahan, who quoted to him the two conditions of Merry del Val's letter if he were to resume his

---

[100] *Ibid,* Fonck to Poels, Rome, September 18, 1909, translation in copy.

[101] 105-R, Merry del Val to Gibbons, Rome, September 18, 1909, cablegram.

[102] 105-R, Poels to Gibbons, Rome, September 18, 1909; ACUA, folder accompanying the forty-second meeting of the Board of Trustees, Poels to Shahan, Rome, September 18, 1909.

[103] 105-R, Merry del Val to Gibbons, Rome, September 19, 1909, *Confidential.*

teaching. The professor denied that the Pope had imposed the condition of resigning during the year when he had granted the audience to Fonck three weeks before. The next day Poels went to Baltimore where, as he put it, "His Eminence was most kind to me and gave me an opportunity to tell him what had happened in Rome."[104] Nonetheless, Gibbons, too, adhered to the stipulated condition and said he would have to lay it before the trustees at their next meeting. Poels was content when he learned that the cardinal did not question his honesty, and he told the chancellor that in the interval he would write to Rome to try to settle the difficulty himself. He hurriedly sent off word to Fonck and asked that he do everything possible to have Gibbons informed of the fact that Pius X had not imposed the condition of his resignation during the coming year. Apparently as a consequence of Fonck's efforts in Rome, the cardinal received from Merry del Val on October 19 a cablegram which stated that the Pope fully recognized the sincerity of Poels' explanation and, therefore, the Secretary of State begged Gibbons to keep his last letter, as the cable read, "entirely private and absolutely prevent all publicity."[105]

The next act in the story took place at the meeting of the trustees on November 17. After hearing a preliminary statement from Shahan the trustees asked that Poels be called in. In the detailed account he gave to the board, the professor held fast to his original position and cited the sentence from Fonck's letter in which the latter quoted the Pope as having declared repeatedly he would not have Gibbons instructed that a condition had been laid on Poels which required him to resign during the year, and further that he would have Merry del Val communicate this point to the chancellor.[106] After Poels' departure from the room the chancellor made it known that he did, indeed, receive a letter from Merry del Val in late September and that it was suppressed by cable some days later. At this point the minutes read, "Upon request to lay it before the Board, the Cardinal says he does not

[104] ACUA, Poels memorandum to the Board of Trustees, Washington, November 24, 1909.

[105] 105-S, Merry del Val to Gibbons, Rome, October 19, 1909, cablegram. The exact text of this cablegram read as follows: "Sincerity of Dr. Poels explanation being fully recognized by Holy Father I beg your Eminence to keep my last letter entirely private and absolutely prevent all publicity."

[106] ACUA, Poels' memorandum to the Board of Trustees, Washington, November 24, 1909.

feel at liberty to show it."[107] In view of Merry del Val's explicit instructions about secrecy, Gibbons' refusal was not surprising.

But there had been two cables from the Secretary of State which brought alterations in the case. The first was dated September 18 and declared the situation modified by Poels' interview of that day and requested Gibbons to await a letter before taking a decision; the second, October 19, instructed the chancellor to keep Merry del Val's confidential letter of September 19 entirely private. The second cablegram, as mentioned previously, was apparently sent as a sequel to the intervention of Father Fonck. The cardinal chancellor informed the trustees of the earlier cablegram, but for some reason best known to himself he remained silent about the second cablegram. Thereupon Bishop Maes made the following motion:

> In view of the explanations made by the Rev. Dr. Poels, considering that he has been permitted to teach since the beginning of the Scholastic year, and that there is some misunderstanding in the case, His Eminence having graciously promised to write again to Rome, Resolved that the Rev. Dr. Poels be allowed to continue to teach until a final answer is received from Rome.[108]

This motion was carried unanimously, Gibbons directed Maes as secretary of the board to write a letter to that effect to Poels, and with that the session was ended.

Two days after the meeting Cardinal Gibbons gave a detailed explanation of what had happened to Merry del Val. He recounted how the trustees had first heard the rector's report of his visits to the Holy Father and the Secretary of State, and how they had called in Poels and asked him to relate what had occurred on his last trip to Rome. Poels had responded to the request in detail and had submitted to them the letter of Fonck which, said Gibbons, as far as they could judge was of a purely private character. Poels was then asked to take the oath which he refused to do without adding his own interpretation, and with that the trustees determined to wait until the following June before they would ask him to withdraw from the university. Their reasons for delay were given as the fear of public scandal, the difficulty of getting another professor on such short notice, and the wish to avoid any stigma on Poels which an immediate with-

---

[107] *Ibid.*, Minutes of the Board of Trustees, November 17, 1909, p. 181.
[108] *Ibid.*

drawal would entail. Gibbons remarked that the trustees had endeavored to comply with the earnest hope that the Pontiff would give his approval to the decision and, as he expressed it, "thus put an end to a situation which, if continued, would prove detrimental both to the University and to the cause of religion."[109] In less than three weeks Merry del Val replied and said that Pius X commended and approved the action of the trustees in regard to Poels, subscribed to the decision that he should be kept on until June, and urged the necessity in the interim of watching carefully over his teaching lest any detriment come to his students.[110]

It is impossible to say, of course, what were the individual views of the trustees in this matter, but when Gibbons suggested to Archbishop Ryan that he write to the Pope and request that Poels be left on at the university until June; the Archbishop of Philadelphia replied that on reflection he thought it would be safer for the university if he left at Christmas. To Ryan's mind, Poels was a man with a grievance which he would be certain to ventilate before other professors and some favorite student friends. The archbishop was unfavorably impressed with his refusal to comply with the conditions which Ryan said had been laid down by the Pope and this was already known to many outside the university. Ryan had written to Merry del Val and had tried to lay both sides of the question before him, but he confessed that as he proceeded he felt there was only one side to it from the standpoint of the university whose interests were entrusted to the trustees' care.[111] But there were others among the trustees who were more inclined in Poels' favor. Bishop Harkins for one was annoyed at the chancellor's failure to reveal all the correspondence in the case to the trustees, and Harkins, a member of the visiting committee of the board, told the Bishop of Covington that when the committee met on March 8 he intended to ask for the minutes and the archives of the university in the hope that the latter might contain copies of the chancellor's letters. "I have no doubt," said Harkins, "but that His Eminence could settle the matter without any difficulty. . . ."[112]

[109] 105-T, Gibbons to Merry del Val, Baltimore, November 19, 1909, copy.

[110] 105-U, Merry del Val to Gibbons, Rome, December 8, 1909.

[111] 105-T, Ryan to Gibbons, Philadelphia, November 28, 1909.

[112] Archives of the Diocese of Covington, Harkins to Maes, Providence, January 23, 1910.

As for Poels himself, he was not content to allow the matter to drop without having a defense of his position printed for private circulation. The brochure appeared in the spring of 1910 and it was severe on the cardinal chancellor. Poels included in it certain correspondence among which was a letter of February 22 in which he told Maes that in his opinion Gibbons and Shahan were not looking for truth and justice, but, as he said, "merely try to please the Cardinal Secretary of State, even if I have to be wronged."[113] In another letter to Maes a month later Poels alluded to Gibbons' withholding the cablegram of Merry del Val from the trustees, and he said:

> No doubt, Cardinal Gibbons cannot fail to realize that in those circumstances, the carrying out of his plan would oblige me to disappear from the University grounds with my honor under a cloud. But His Eminence seems to be afraid that the vindication of my honor might entail certain consequences which would be disagreeable to others, whose honor and welfare, to his mind, are of greater importance.[114]

On April 6, 1910, the Board of Trustees held its semiannual meeting and at that time Gibbons reported receipt of the endorsement of the Holy See to their action of the previous November in relation to Poels. That the chancellor did not allow the case to take on new life was evident from the minutes, in which there occurred the sentence, "He deprecated all discussion." A motion was made and passed unanimously that whereas Poels' contract had expired in January, 1909, but he had been allowed to continue teaching by the permission of the trustees, the rector was now directed by the board to inform him that his relations with the university would expire at the close of the current academic year.[115]

It was obvious that the position of Cardinal Gibbons in the Poels case entailed a great deal of anxiety and worry. As Chancellor of the University he was responsible to the Holy See for the doctrinal orthodoxy of the institution, and at a time when

[113] 106-D, Henry A. Poels, *A Vindication of My Honor* (Washington, 1910), p. 63.

[114] *Ibid.*, p. 71.

[115] ACUA, Minutes of the Board of Trustees, April 6, 1910, p. 184. After his return to the Netherlands Poels became a leader in Catholic social movements, was made a monsignor, and died on September 7, 1948, at Heerlen.

there was such widespread uneasiness in Catholic circles over the dangers of modernism, the cardinal was more than ordinarily sensitive on this point. Moreover, as Gibbons had good reason to remember, less than fifteen years before the university had passed through two severe trials in the controversy over the schools which involved Professor Bouquillon and the Americanism trouble in which Bishop Keane was removed from the office of rector. It was not surprising, then, to find that the cardinal should agree with Shahan when the latter reasoned that the university could not well stand to have its orthodoxy questioned again. It was apparent that by the autumn of 1909 Gibbons had become convinced that for the good of the institution Poels should depart at the end of the school year, and that is why he refused to allow the case to be reopened before the trustees. It was perfectly natural, to be sure, that in this Dr. Poels should feel aggrieved. But in attributing the attitude of Gibbons to the latter's wish to please Merry del Val, the professor overlooked the effect which his continued presence would have on the university's reputation among those who had learned of the doubts entertained about him. True, Gibbons and Shahan wished to please Merry del Val, but that was not the sole motive for their action. Shahan was, indeed, a powerful factor in shaping Gibbons' judgment in the matter, and it was equally true that the rector was determined that Poels should go. But to imply that the chancellor showed himself insensible to Poels' good name was not in accordance with the facts, for if he had not wished to protect the priest's personal honor he could have urged his immediate withdrawal from the faculty. He not only did not do that but he even attempted to enlist the help of Archbishop Ryan in writing Rome to ratify the decision of the trustees that Poels' tenure be extended until June, rather than to have him dismissed immediately, or at Christmas as Ryan had suggested.

In withholding the final cablegram of Merry del Val from the trustees the chancellor may well have read more into its contents than was intended, since it did not explicitly withdraw the Pope's statement to Fonck that Poels need not resign during the year. But, on the other hand, Poels' informant was wrong in telling the professor that the cablegram allowed him to retain his chair and, as Poels' memorandum read, "was explicit in this

regard. . . ."[116] In failing to reveal the cablegram Gibbons' action
may have been open to blame, but he evidently believed that it
was for the university's best interests not to allow the long-
drawn-out case to be reopened; and in refusing to disclose to
the trustees the Secretary of State's confidential letter he was
only abiding by Merry del Val's strict instructions. All in all
it was a difficult decision to make. The chancellor was doubtless
aware that his final judgment did not result in universal satisfaction, but his conviction that the university's welfare would
be jeopardized by a further prolongation of the painful dispute
that had dragged on for nearly three years made him adamant
against any new appeals.

Yet the concern which the cardinal chancellor had in these
years over doctrinal orthodoxy and financial integrity were not
the only worries which plagued him in his relations with the
university. Within the first year of O'Connell's rectorship, as
we have seen, Archbishop Messmer warned Gibbons of discontent
in the ranks of the faculty over the rector's aloofness, his tendency to withhold information on matters of policy, and his
arbitrary way of dealing with the academic senate. This ill feeling
grew to such an extent that in May, 1905, a group of the professors, with Shahan as their spokesman, presented to the trustees an elaborate and detailed indictment of O'Connell as rector.
It resulted in the appointment of a committee of five professors
to study the university's constitutions with a view to placing the
jurisdiction of the rector, the academic senate, and the various
faculties on a clear and incontrovertible basis.[117]

During the months that the committee was holding its numerous meetings, there was no evidence of interference on the
part of the chancellor. But that his sympathies were with
O'Connell were obvious, when he optimistically observed to
Archbishop Ireland in the fall of 1905 that as far as he was
advised there was a spirit of harmony and good feeling at the
university. He then said:

> My conviction is that the Rector ought to be upheld in the legitimate
> exercise of his official duties. He will lose heart if he is hampered by

[116] *Ibid.,* Poels memorandum to the Board of Trustees, Washington, November
24, 1909.

[117] Cf. Barry, *op. cit.,* pp. 141–157, for the details of the controversy and its
final outcome.

unwarrantable interference or captious criticism. We took good care at the last Plenary Council to give the consultors only a consultative voice, & not the consensus. A Bp. could not do his duty with freedom if he was constantly opposed by Canons & Consultors. Let the Constitution be strictly observed which gives him full powers, subject to the Board of Directors.[118]

And in encouraging the rector to work hard to raise money before the next meeting of the trustees, Gibbons told his friend, "Your success, of which I am sanguine, will make me happy."[119] In his report to Pius X on the financial failure and the disaster it entailed to the university, the cardinal remarked that it was impossible to exaggerate the part played by O'Connell in these difficult circumstances by the extraordinary energy and by the humility and patience which he had shown.[120] Meanwhile the committee finished its work and the majority report was a strong enforcement of the rector's position. This was made known to the trustees at their meeting on April 25, 1906, and when the minority group attempted to dispute the majority's findings the minutes revealed that, "His Eminence feelingly pleaded for immediate and thorough action to put an end to the contentions and bickerings of the last year, a source of suffering and annoyance to him."[121] The majority's report was accepted, the rector had been vindicated, and the doubts concerning his jurisdiction were finally settled in a way which met with Gibbons' hearty approval.

Monsignor O'Connell went to Rome in the summer of 1906 where he found the officials of the Holy See in a very agreeable mood toward the university. He told Gibbons that he learned of a desire among some to accord him an official acknowledgment for what he had done, as well as to accentuate the position of the rector. Without mentioning directly advancement to the episcopacy, O'Connell quoted his Roman sources as having referred to the fact "that all his predecessors had that character," and he confessed that he found a certain gratification at these kind manifestations as they seemed to him to contain an element of equity. He assured Gibbons, however, that he had done

---

[118] AASP, Gibbons to Ireland, Baltimore, October 17, 1905, copy.
[119] ACUA, O'Connell Papers, Gibbons to O'Connell, Baltimore, December 6, 1905.
[120] 103-B, Gibbons to Pius X, Baltimore, February 27, 1906, copy in Italian.
[121] ACUA, Minutes of the Board of Trustees, April 25, 1906, p. 141.

nothing by word or act to initiate the movement.[122] The idea, of course, was altogether pleasing to the university's chancellor, and in the early winter of that year he wrote to Cardinals Satolli and Gotti with high praise of the rector and urged that he be made a bishop.[123] Rome did not respond to the original prompting, but Gibbons did not give up hope. He enlisted the aid of Archbishop Riordan who agreed O'Connell should be honored and he would be glad to sign his name to a petition for a titular bishopric for him.[124] In the autumn of 1907 the cardinal wrote again — this time to the Pope himself[125] — and a few weeks later Merry del Val informed him that the appointment would come in the next consistory.[126] At last the nomination of O'Connell to the titular See of Sebaste was announced and Gibbons was overjoyed. He told the rector:

> You may know, but hardly to its full extent, how happy I was made this morning by your elevation to the Episcopate. It is just a month today since I wrote to the Holy Father.
> Now you can say with Card. Newman: "At last I am vindicated." Thanks to God.[127]

[122] 103-L, O'Connell to Gibbons, Rome, August 25, 1906.

[123] 103-R, Gibbons to Satolli, Baltimore, December 6, 1906, copy; *ibid.,* Gibbons to Gotti, Baltimore, December 7, 1906, copy in Latin.

[124] 104-H, Riordan to Gibbons, San Francisco, June 11, 1907. It would appear from Riordan's letter that Gibbons must have alluded to O'Connell's going to San Francisco as coadjutor since Riordan was at pains to state his agreement that O'Connell should be honored, but he thought him too old to undertake the coadjutorship in San Francisco. An effort by the present writer to clear up the difficulty ended in failure. On March 20, 1950, Archbishop John J. Mitty of San Francisco informed him, "I have had two of my priests search the archives here but they can find no letter whatsoever that deals with the topic." When Riordan's *terna* for an auxiliary bishop came through later that summer, Gibbons informed the apostolic delegate that he did not know Richard Neagle of Malden, Massachusetts well, but his name having been on the *terna* for Boston would indicate that he had ability; John J. Lawler, Rector of the Cathedral of St. Paul in St. Paul, was unknown to the cardinal personally, nor had he heard much about him from any other source. But the third name he knew well and he gave a very strong recommendation to Edward J. Hanna of St. Bernard's Seminary, Rochester, who was finally named as auxiliary bishop to Riordan on October 22, 1912, and was appointed Archbishop of San Francisco on June 1, 1915 (104-K, Falconio to Gibbons, Washington, August 29, 1907; Gibbons to Falconio, Baltimore, August 31, 1907, copy).

[125] 104-P, Gibbons to Pius X, Baltimore, November 5, 1907, copy.

[126] 104-P, Merry del Val to Gibbons, Rome, November 25, 1907.

[127] ACUA, O'Connell Papers, Gibbons to O'Connell, Baltimore, December 7, 1907.

On May 3, 1908, Cardinal Gibbons consecrated his eighteenth bishop when he performed the ceremony for his friend, Denis O'Connell, in the cathedral of Baltimore. The elevation of O'Connell to the episcopacy gave further impetus to rumors that had been circulating from time to time that he would be taken by the cardinal as coadjutor with the right of succession to Baltimore.[128] A number of the rector's friends mentioned the possibility in their messages of congratulation to the new bishop and the *New Century* of April 25 published the rumor with the added comment, "Should this be true, the choice would fall upon none worthier the distinguished honor." That there was probably something to these rumors was revealed in the fall of 1908 when Gibbons urged Riordan to take O'Connell to San Francisco as auxiliary bishop. At that time he said, "I had entertained the idea of asking for him as Auxiliary and afterwards as Coadjutor, but was informed that I could not have two Auxiliaries at once, as I have one already."[129] In any case, O'Connell was not promoted to Baltimore and during the remaining months of his term as rector the idea disappeared from sight while he and the chancellor continued to concern themselves about university affairs.

One of the most pressing problems of the university for years had been the need to increase the size of the student body. In the year O'Connell came to Washington the enrollment had sunk to an alarmingly low point with only ninety-one students, but by dint of serious effort it had been raised to 224 for the academic year 1907–1908. In the summer of 1908 O'Connell and Gibbons composed an appeal to the hierarchy for more students which the chancellor signed. Gibbons reviewed the successful efforts that had been made to establish the financial security of the institution, acknowledged the many urgent needs which confronted the bishops in their dioceses, but reminded them that no good was ever effected in the Church without sacrifice. He begged, therefore, that they send more priests to the university, and he told them he made his plea not so much in favor of the University as in favor of the Church. He stated:

> We all know how much a clergyman's efficiency and influence are enhanced by higher education, and also how much in these days of

---

[128] Barry, *op. cit.*, pp. 241–242.
[129] 105-F, Gibbons to Riordan, Baltimore, November 10, 1908, copy.

general doubt and scepticism, priests of higher intellectual training are sorely needed everywhere.[130]

But in spite of the chancellor's urging, the enrollment continued for some time to be anything but satisfactory, and it was only in 1913 that the figure of 600 was reached.[131] Although the size of the student body was not what the administrative officers would have wished it to be, it had steadily increased since O'Connell took office, the financial crisis had been overcome, and the internal dispute over the constitutional position of the various officers and faculty groups had been resolved in the rector's favor. Yet he was not happy. The root causes of his discontent are not too clear, and probably only Gibbons knew the complete background that lay behind O'Connell's wish to depart at the end of his first term of office. From the answer which Archbishop Riordan had returned to Gibbons on June 11, 1907, it would appear the cardinal at that time had suggested to the Archbishop of San Francisco that he take O'Connell as his auxiliary or coadjutor bishop. Moreover, in the early stages of the candidacy of Bishop John P. Carroll of Helena for the rectorship the latter mentioned having discussed the matter with Gibbons in Baltimore in the summer of 1908.[132] Obviously, therefore, the likelihood of O'Connell leaving the university was known a few months in advance of the meeting of the trustees and before the end of his first term of office. The semiannual meeting of the Board of Trustees was scheduled for November 18 and at that time the question of the rectorship would come up. With that in mind three weeks before the meeting, Gibbons wrote to the trustees and asked them to give their opinion about a second term for O'Connell. Two things were evident from their replies: first, that they were unanimous in thinking he should remain in the office; second, that Gibbons had himself advocated a reappointment to the rectorship for his friend.[133]

---

[130] ACUA, O'Connell Papers, Gibbons to the American hierarchy, Baltimore, June 29, 1908, printed copy.

[131] *Catholic University Bulletin*, XIX (December, 1913), 669. Counting the summer session enrollment of 383 and that of Trinity College with 170, there was a total of 1,153 students that year.

[132] 105-E, Carroll to Gibbons, Helena, October 29, 1908.

[133] 105-F, James E. Quigley to Gibbons, Chicago, November 2, 1908. Quigley said, "I am one with Your Eminence in advocating the re-appointment of Mon-

A week before the meeting of the board the cardinal thanked Riordan for his letters on O'Connell and the rectorship question, and expressed his delight with what he called, "your judgment of Monsignor O'Connell and with your desire to have him as your Auxiliary." Actually the Archbishop of San Francisco had not said that he desired him, but rather that he would "most willingly receive him. . . ." Nonetheless, the cardinal continued that he had had a visit from O'Connell an hour or so after the letters arrived, and he had, as he phrased it, "communicated to him your wishes." O'Connell had, in turn, placed himself entirely in Gibbons' hands and would be guided by his counsel; therefore, the cardinal remarked to Riordan, "I promptly advised him to accept your proposal."[134] It was apparent that at the meeting the following week the putting forth of O'Connell's name for a second term would be hardly more than an empty gesture. The trustees assembled on November 18 and after an initial vote for O'Connell it was made known that he did not wish a second term; whereupon the balloting ended with a unanimous vote for John Carroll, second Bishop of Helena.

Gibbons promptly informed Carroll that in accordance with the university's constitution only his name would be forwarded to Rome.[135] He likewise told Riordan of the outcome of the meeting, and he gave further praise to O'Connell as one who would be a zealous co-worker, a devoted friend, and a person of particular assistance to the Archbishop of San Francisco in his relations with the Holy See. "After all the vicissitudes and disappointments to which Your Grace was subjected," said Gibbons, "I regard the turn in events providential in your regard." As soon as Riordan's letter asking for O'Connell would reach the Apos-

---

signor O'Connell to the Rectorship of the University." Riordan quoted with approval Gibbons' own words that it would be an injustice to put O'Connell aside without making any provision for him (105-F, Riordan to Gibbons, San Francisco, November 4, 1908). The above letter was intended for reading at the meeting of the trustees if Gibbons wished to do so. But on the same day the archbishop sent a private letter in which he told the cardinal he understood O'Connell was "most anxious" to leave the university and had, as he said, "expressed a willingness to come out here as Auxiliary Bishop to which Post he could be appointed without any difficulty." Riordan was quite willing to have him, but he thought that for the good of the university he should remain on where he was (105-F, Riordan to Gibbons, San Francisco, November 4, 1908).

[134] 105-F, Gibbons to Riordan, Baltimore, November 10, 1908, copy.
[135] 105-G, Gibbons to Carroll, Washington, November 19, 1908, copy.

tolic Delegation in Washington, he said, it would be forwarded
to Rome with a strong endorsement from the delegate.[136] Three
weeks later Gibbons learned that Falconio had sent the desired
recommendation to Rome, and the cardinal then addressed an
appeal to Merry del Val to further the appointment. Once more
there was the familiar praise of O'Connell as Rector of the University without any hint, however, as to why he had refused a
second term. The trustees, said the chancellor, would have requested the Holy See to continue him in office if no offer had
been made for his well-merited promotion. He then continued:

> But as this offer comes very opportunely at the end of his term of
> six years, they are unanimous in asking the Holy Father to grant
> the request of the Archbishop of San Francisco, and as soon as
> practicable, since Monsignor Riordan is much in need of an assistant
> to help him in the administration of his extensive diocese.[137]

At last the efforts of the cardinal ended successfully and on
Christmas Eve of 1908 the third Rector of the University was
named Auxiliary Bishop of San Francisco, the news of which
prompted Riordan to remark to Gibbons, "I need not tell you
how rejoiced I am over the appointment of our dear friend,
Bishop O'Connell."[138]

There would seem to be little doubt that there was more to
this case than meets the eye of the historian. Why Cardinal
Gibbons should be anxious to have one of his dearest friends so
far removed from him, why he should have made the extraordinary effort he did to get him out of the university where his
administration had met with the highest praise from the trustees,
and why O'Connell himself desired to be gone — all these questions pose a problem which it is impossible from the extant evi-

---

[136] 105-G, Gibbons to Riordan, Baltimore, November 20, 1908, copy. In referring
to Riordan's disappointments, Gibbons doubtless had in mind the fact that in March,
1903, Bishop George T. Montgomery of Monterey-Los Angeles had been appointed
Coadjutor Archbishop of San Francisco with the right of succession but he lived
less than four years, dying on January 10, 1907.

[137] 105-H, Gibbons to Merry del Val, Baltimore, December 10, 1908, copy. The
minutes of the Board of Trustees for November 18, 1908, make no mention of a
request that the Pope appoint O'Connell to San Francisco (ACUA, Minutes of the
Board of Trustees, November 18, 1908, pp. 170–171).

[138] Archives of the Archdiocese of San Francisco, Riordan to Gibbons, San
Francisco, January 13, 1909, copy. The writer is indebted to the Reverend Timothy
J. Casey of Serra High School, San Mateo, for copies of the correspondence from
these archives.

dence for the historian to answer with certainty. From the very outset of the negotiations Gibbons took the lead, but it is safe to say that he did so with O'Connell's knowledge and consent, for nothing occurred then — or later — to mar their friendship and thus provide the cardinal with a motive to wish to be rid of him. The air of mystery which surrounds the case may best be explained by the fact that O'Connell had made enemies within the university by the methods and procedures he had employed during his administration, and this hostility persisted after the question of conflicting jurisdiction between the rector and the academic senate had been settled in 1906 in the former's favor. But the atmosphere continued to be unfriendly to the rector and, perhaps, for that reason he indicated to his friend in Baltimore his desire to depart. Whatever the reason, the chancellor saw to it with Archbishop Riordan, the Holy See, and the apostolic delegate that the next few years of O'Connell's life would be led far from the university where the harassing problems of an academic administrator would not disturb his peace of mind.

Meanwhile Bishop Carroll was hurrying his preparations in Helena to finish the plans for his cathedral and college so that he might be free to take up his new duties in Washington when O'Connell's term would expire on January 11, 1909.[139] But a week after that date there arrived from Rome a cablegram in which the apostolic delegate was instructed to inform Gibbons that the Pope did not deem it opportune to transfer Carroll from his diocese and until candidates could be presented Pius X named Thomas J. Shahan as prorector.[140] Gibbons communicated at once with Carroll and confessed that this news was a great surprise and disappointment to him, but with his customary spirit of submission to the Holy Father he said, "I bow to the decision

---

[139] 105-J, Carroll to Gibbons, Helena, January 13, 1909; same to same, Helena, January 19, 1909.

[140] AANY, Gibbons to Farley, Baltimore, January 25, 1909, enclosing a copy of Merry del Val to Falconio, Rome, January 18, 1909, cablegram. The rumor began to circulate shortly after this cablegram was received that Edmund T. Shanahan, professor of dogmatic theology, not Shahan, had been named prorector. When word of this reached Rome, Merry del Val wrote to deny the rumor, and he said, "I therefore inform Your Eminence that the said rumors are false and fictitious, and I hasten to reaffirm the fact that Reverend Thomas J. Shahan was truly appointed and not Reverend Edmund Shanahan, of whom, in this matter, no mention of any kind was ever made" (ACUA, Minutes of the Board of Trustees, folder accompanying the meeting of April 21, 1909, Merry del Val to Gibbons, Rome, March 1, 1909).

of the Holy See, as an expression of the will of Divine Providence."[141] The Bishop of Helena stated that he was perfectly indifferent about the matter, but naturally he was curious. "What was the trouble?" asked Carroll. "Was I opposed in Rome and by whom?"[142] They were questions which at the moment Gibbons could not answer. But in an effort to avoid an embarrassing interval in the regular government of the university, the chancellor quickly wrote Merry del Val, quoted the article of the constitution which called for the sending of only one name for the rectorship, and stated that if three names were to be submitted, would the Holy See please let him know immediately as the matter was urgent.[143]

While awaiting final word from Rome preparations went forward for the formal departure of Bishop O'Connell and the inauguration of the prorector, a ceremony which took place on February 25 in the auditorium of McMahon Hall. In bidding farewell to the university over which he had presided for six years, O'Connell directed a special tribute to the chancellor. He said:

> While during my administration I may possibly have tried your patience a little, I now say that from the beginning to the end of my administration I never received from you anything but words of kindness and consolation to which were added those of wisdom, and you have been in the most literal sense of the word my counsellor, and I declare it is to you I owe whatever little success my administration may be credited with. You are surrounded as with a halo by the admiration and love of the American people that will follow you wherever you go. May you ever remain with a calm peace of soul which you so highly prize and may you live to see a very large measure of success for this grand institution of learning that is already in my mind infinitely indebted to you.[144]

In his reply Gibbons lauded the bishop for the ability he had shown in fulfilling his responsibilities in the trying days of the financial crisis, to which there was added a reference to the present promising condition of the finances and student enroll-

[141] 105-J, Gibbons to Carroll, Baltimore, January 22, 1909, copy.
[142] 105-J, Carroll to Gibbons, Helena, January 25, 1909.
[143] 105-J, Gibbons to Merry del Val, Baltimore, January 25, 1909, copy.
[144] "Installation of the Pro-Rector of the University," *Catholic University Bulletin*, XV (March, 1909), 316.

ment. He had words of praise as well for Shahan in formally introducing him to the audience, and he made a special plea for all to close ranks behind the prorector for the welfare of the institution. Then addressing himself to the faculty, the cardinal said:

> To the professors in particular let me say that without their coöperation the best equipped head can accomplish nothing. It is therefore from the very depths of my heart that I implore them to unite with Dr. Shahan in every effort to fulfill the original purpose of this Catholic University and to make it one day the perfect institution of learning which its founder intended it should be.[145]

In compliance with the wishes of the Holy See the trustees at their meeting on April 22–23, 1909, drew up a *terna* for the rectorship with Shahan in first place, Michael J. Lavelle, Rector of St. Patrick's Cathedral, second, and Denis J. Flynn, President of Mount Saint Mary's College, Emmitsburg, as the third name on the list. Gibbons forwarded the list to Rome and accompanied it with a powerful endorsement of Shahan for the office. He told Cardinal Satolli that not only was Shahan first but he had almost a unanimous vote, receiving eleven out of the twelve votes cast.[146] The chancellor was equally emphatic a few days later in his letter to Merry del Val, and after relating Shahan's qualifications he said, "I take the liberty of expressing that I personally have the utmost confidence in his ability to fill with satisfaction the position of Rector."[147] Without delay the appointment came through in a month's time, and in the early autumn the chancellor requested of the Holy See that Shahan be made a domestic

---

[145] *Ibid.*, p. 321. On the day that O'Connell was saying farewell to the university, Archbishop Riordan was writing him that he was glad he would deliver the lecture in San Francisco which he had requested. O'Connell had apparently submitted a title which included an allusion to the Circus of Nero. Riordan told him, "People out here know nothing about Nero. The only circus we know anything about is Barnum & Bailey's so I am going to call it something else; for instance 'A Roman Holiday in the Days of Nero' or some other title even shorter" (Archives of the Archdiocese of San Francisco, Riordan to O'Connell, San Francisco, February 25, 1909, copy). O'Connell reached his new home on March 29, and the archbishop reported to his brother in Chicago that the bishop was "in remarkably good spirits and ready for work" (*ibid.*, P. W. Riordan to D. J. Riordan, San Francisco, April 2, 1909, copy).

[146] 105-L, Gibbons to Satolli, Baltimore, April 27, 1909, copy.

[147] 105-M, Gibbons to Merry del Val, Baltimore, May 3, 1909, copy. Gibbons also wrote in Shahan's behalf to Cardinals De Lai and Martinelli (105-M, Gibbons to De Lai, Baltimore, May 7, 1909, copy; Gibbons to Martinelli, Baltimore, May 15, 1909, copy).

prelate, an honor which was likewise readily granted and with which Gibbons invested the new rector on December 16, 1909, in the chapel of Caldwell Hall.[148]

In all his undertakings for the university Monsignor Shahan found the same prompt and enthusiastic support from the chancellor which his three predecessors had experienced. As the time neared for the celebration of the golden jubilee of the cardinal's priesthood, Gibbons directed that the festivities should be pointed to the university so that it might reap the benefits of any expression of generosity from his friends and admirers. When Bishop O'Connell returned to San Francisco from a trip to the East and brought word of the cardinal's wishes for the university, Archbishop Riordan assured him he knew what the institution meant to him, and he said, "I have known you and loved you too many years not to be always ready to give you whatever assistance it may be in my power to render whenever you ask it."[149] Archbishop Ireland, too, knew Gibbons' mind and in accepting his invitation to preach at the jubilee, the Archbishop of St. Paul frankly stated that he thought he should have invited some other prelate whose financial resources were greater than his and who could, therefore, do more for the fund being raised for the university. "I am writing in all confidence & earnestly & sincerely," said Ireland, "because I desire success to your plans."[150]

But in spite of Ireland's misgivings the fund raising was not seriously impaired by the failure to choose another preacher and on October 12, 1911, the cornerstone was laid by Gibbons for the handsome Tudor Gothic residence building on the campus which bears his name, and which was intended as a lasting memorial to the half century of his priesthood. That same autumn Gibbons strengthened the position of Shahan when the latter went to Rome to ask for a renewal of permission for the annual collection. He addressed letters to Pius X and to a number of the cardinals, outlining the progress which the university had made, the promise that lay before it, and the urgent need it had for the revenue which accrued through the collection. To Merry del Val he said, "No work of Religion in our country is more

---

[148] Diary, October 8, 1909, p. 317.
[149] 107-D, Riordan to Gibbons, San Francisco, March 14, 1911.
[150] 107-E, Ireland to Gibbons, St. Paul, April 8, 1911.

dear to my own heart, knowing as I do that it will one day be a glorious light upon Holy Church in this country once it has out-lived the difficulties natural to the foundation of so great an enterprise."[151]

Shahan's trip to Rome ended in complete success and the Pope renewed the collection for a period of ten more years. The rector was so overjoyed that he could not wait to inform Gibbons when he would reach Baltimore. From on board the *Olympic* he summarized the contents of the papal letter and said he knew it would please the chancellor greatly. It contained words of praise for all who were associated with the institution, strongly encouraged the bishops to send students and the religious orders to establish houses of study, had a good word for the trustees and, as Shahan said, "of course a strong one for yourself. . . ." The rector remarked, "It is a long and warm letter, and will do us much good, *on the Board,* and among the clergy and the people."[152] This was good news, indeed, since the annual diocesan collection had become the main source of income for the university and it would have been a crippling blow to have been deprived of it. All through these years there were generous Catholics who from time to time earned the gratitude of the university by reason of their benefactions, but a few months after the papal letter good fortune came to the institution from an unexpected source. Max Pam, a prominent Jewish lawyer of Chicago, gave $1,000 for the first of five scholarships in social science which he accompanied by a statement to Gibbons of his motives. Pam told the chancellor he gave his donation in the

---

[151] 107-S, Gibbons to Merry del Val, Baltimore, November 6, 1911, copy. Copies of Gibbons' letters to Pius X and to Cardinals Vannutelli, Cassetta, and De Lai on the same date are in this file.

[152] 108-A, Shahan to Gibbons, on board the *Olympic,* January 16, 1912. In a concluding paragraph Shahan told Gibbons, "Everything looks favorable for your wishes in the matter of Richmond. . . . I rejoice most because it puts you at ease in this respect." The reference was to the appointment of Denis O'Connell as seventh Bishop of Richmond which was made on January 19, 1912. When the news of this reached San Francisco, Riordan informed Gibbons that O'Connell was very much pleased with the promotion. He then said, "To me his appointment brings not joy but sorrow. We have lived so happily together these three years, and he is so agreeable and genial all the time, that it will be difficult to find one to replace him. He will be an element of strength in your province, and I am sure should you need anyone to help you, you could not rely on a more loyal and true friend" (Archives of the Archdiocese of San Francisco, Riordan to Gibbons, San Francisco, January 23, 1912, copy).

belief that scholarships of this kind would help to advance the American principle of "live and let live" and, too, because, as he said:

> The Catholic Church holds to the traditions of the past; it is conservative; it stands for authority, for government, for the rights of the individual and for the rights of property, and these to my mind are the chief elements that enter into individual and national happiness. . . .[153]

All in all matters were in a much better state by the autumn of 1912 than they had been at any time in the university's history, and in his annual appeal to the hierarchy the chancellor could tell the bishops that the student body had now reached 1,000, the library had increased to 80,000 volumes, the faculty numbered fifty-six, and the Sisters College which had opened only a year before had fifty students.[154] Moreover, at the beginning of that year it had been announced that the university had no debts and the investments of the institution then amounted to $1,178,825.43[155] In view of these developments, Gibbons had no hesitancy in recounting the accomplishments of Monsignor Shahan as rector for Gaetano Cardinal De Lai, Secretary of the Congregation of the Consistory, and recommending that Shahan be made a bishop.[156] Nothing came of the request at this date, however, but early in 1914 Gibbons was informed confidentially by David Fleming, O.F.M., who was attached to the Congregation of the Holy Office, that both Pius X and Merry del Val were sympathetic and only awaiting word from him and the apostolic delegate. Fleming told Gibbons, "I ascertained in the most confidential manner the view taken at the Vatican before troubling your Eminence. . . ."[157] The cardinal then renewed his request, Shahan was named as titular Bishop of Germanicopolis on July 24, and on the following November 15 the cardinal consecrated the rector in the cathedral of Baltimore.

---

[153] 108-H, Pam to Gibbons, New York, June 1, 1912.

[154] 108-P, Gibbons to the American hierarchy, Baltimore, November 3, 1912, copy. The enrollment continued to increase steadily up to World War I, and it was announced in the fall of 1914 that the university was opening "with the largest student body ever within her walls." *Catholic University Bulletin*, XX (October, 1914), 568.

[155] *Ibid.*, XVIII (January, 1912), 79.

[156] 108-P, Gibbons to De Lai, Baltimore, November 1, 1912, copy.

[157] 109-Q, Fleming to Shahan, Rome, February 12, 1914.

From the time the university had first been suggested it had few friends who were as loyal to its interests as Archbishop Ireland. But as he grew old he found the trips to Washington for meetings of the Board of Trustees more difficult, and for that reason at the fall of 1913 he resigned his place on the board. His friend in Baltimore was loath to have him depart, and he asked in the name of the trustees if Ireland would not reconsider and continue as one of them. The archbishop was grateful for the compliment, wished for the university from his heart strength and prosperity, and said he rejoiced in the wondrous growth it had attained. But he begged that the trustees definitely pass him by. He said:

> In the early days, I served it on two notable occasions. Together with Bishop Spalding I fought valiantly, and successfully, to hold it in Washington, when powerful efforts were being made to put it in New Jersey or in Philadelphia — and again, in Rome, I kept the infant well alive, when even its eminent sponsor & the chosen rector were timidly viewing the grave the enemies had opened beneath it. To-day it has grown & is growing of its innate power. I am not needed — & yield to the command of years, to stay at home.[158]

Those who knew the services which the Archbishop of St. Paul had rendered to the institution regretted, as Gibbons did, his withdrawal but they probably recognized, too, that he had earned his rest.

In November, 1914, the Catholic University of America reached its twenty-fifth anniversary. It was decided to postpone the celebration of the silver jubilee until the following April when it could be held in connection with the meeting of the trustees. In anticipation of that event Gibbons requested of Cardinal Gasparri, the Secretary of State, that the Pope write a letter of congratulations. The chancellor stated that such a letter, urging the bishops' support, suggesting that they send promising young priests for study, and encouraging Catholic parents to send their sons to the university would prove a great

---

[158] 109-R, Ireland to Gibbons, St. Paul, March 23, 1914. On April 22, 1914, there was presented to the university by Michael Jenkins of Baltimore, treasurer of the institution, a bronze bust of Cardinal Gibbons which was the work of J. Maxwell Miller of Baltimore. The unveiling of the bust took place at a ceremony in which the principal speech was delivered by Patrick C. Gavan, Chancellor of the Archdiocese of Baltimore, in the presence of the university's trustees and other guests. *Catholic University Bulletin,* XX (May, 1914), 414–416.

assistance. Reflecting the war then raging in Europe, the cardinal thought that it would also be an excellent occasion for the Holy Father to say a few words to the entire American Catholic body in favor of Christian education as the sole anchor of mankind amid what he called "the disturbances and ruins which purely secular interests and passions are everywhere creating or increasing."[159]

The celebration of the silver jubilee drew to Washington the three American cardinals, nine archbishops, and twenty-one bishops besides a large representation from various colleges and universities. Cardinal Farley was the celebrant of the pontifical Mass at St. Patrick's Church on April 15 and Cardinal Gibbons was the preacher. In his sermon the chancellor paid tribute to the interest and sympathy shown by the popes since the university's founding under Leo XIII, to the American hierarchy generally, and especially to Archbishops Keane and Spalding. There was need at the outset, said Gibbons, for a man whose soul was filled with what he called "a holy, creative enthusiasm," and he was found in the person of John J. Keane, the first rector. He saluted Keane who was present, and he now rejoiced with him as he looked upon the fruit of his labors. "Thou O beloved brother," said the cardinal, "didst sow the seed amid the snow and rains of trial and adversity. Thy worthy successor is reaping the harvest."[160] Of Spalding, who was not able to be present, he remarked that all outstanding works had their inception in the brain of some great thinker, and God had given such a brain and such a man in Spalding. If the university was then an accomplished fact all were indebted in no small measure for its existence in that generation to what Gibbons called, "the persuasive eloquence and convincing arguments of the Bishop of Peoria."[161] As for his own part in the university's history, the cardinal regarded it as a special favor granted to him by God

---

[159] 111-F, Gibbons to Gasparri, Baltimore, February 3, 1915, copy. There was no record of a response from the Pope to this request. However, on the occasion of the cardinal's golden jubilee celebration as a bishop, Benedict XV sent a letter wherein generous mention was made of the university (121-D, Benedict XV to Gibbons, Rome, April 10, 1919, printed copy).

[160] *A Retrospect of Fifty Years* (Baltimore, 1916), II, 194. Gibbons dedicated these two volumes to the rector, faculty, and benefactors of the university. The incorrect date of 1916 is given here (p. 190) instead of 1915.

[161] *Ibid.*, II, 195.

that he had been permitted to devote so much of his time to this sacred cause. In conclusion he stated:

> From the beginning, the University has been for me an object of deepest personal concern. Through its growth and through its struggles, through all the vicissitudes which it has experienced, it has been very near to my heart. It has cost me, in anxiety and tension of spirit, far more than any other of the duties or cares which have fallen to my lot. But for this very reason, I feel a greater satisfaction in its progress. I feel amply compensated for whatever I have been able to do in bearing its burdens and in helping it through trial to prosperity and success. I thank Heaven that my hopes have not been in vain, and I rejoice that the future of the University is now assured.[162]

The principal item of business at the meeting of the trustees which preceded the jubilee celebration was to make provision for the rectorship, since Shahan had now reached the expiration of his first term of office. On the *terna* drawn up Shahan was given a unanimous vote for first place, Pace was put second, and Shanahan third. Gibbons forwarded the list to Benedetto Cardinal Lorenzelli, Prefect of the Congregation of Studies, with a strong recommendation that Shahan should be reappointed, and within a few weeks the Holy See confirmed the rector in office for another six years.[163] Although the chancellor was eighty-one years of age that summer he had continued to make himself available whenever possible for visits to the university if his presence was desired. Ever since the inauguration of the summer session in July, 1911, he had appeared on the campus to lend encouragement to the professors and students in their summer work, and when Dr. Pace invited the cardinal for the session of 1915 he told him, "We have always looked forward to your visit as the most pleasant incident of the whole session. . . ."[164]

The love which Gibbons had for the university had long since become well known among the American bishops, and they knew that there was nothing that would please him more than to

---

[162] *Ibid.,* II, 204–205.

[163] 111-T, Gibbons to Lorenzelli, Baltimore, April 28, 1915, copy in Italian.

[164] ACUA, Pace Papers, Pace to Gibbons, Washington, July 6, 1915, copy. Gibbons paid his visit on July 12 and Pace told Shahan he "appeared to be in the best of health and humor; he took luncheon with us and met a number of the Instructors, lay and clerical." *Ibid.,* Pace to Shahan, Washington, July 13, 1915, copy.

manifest an interest in his favorite institution. For example, when the cardinal sent a generous donation for St. Mary's Home and Orphanage in Jacksonville, Florida, Michael J. Curley, Bishop of St. Augustine, and destined to be Gibbons' successor as the university's chancellor, thanked him and said he regretted he could not do more for the university due to the poverty of his diocese. Probably anticipating the pleasure it would afford Gibbons, he said, "My interest in that great Catholic Institution antedates by years my elevation to the Episcopate, and I hope to see the day when the Catholic University of Washington will come into its own, and will be the very sun in the firmament of Catholic Education in this country."[165] And yet the cardinal's interest in the Catholic University of America did not cause him to overlook the good work being done by other American Catholic universities. As the time approached for the University of Notre Dame to celebrate its diamond jubilee in June, 1917, Father John Cavanaugh, the president, sent an urgent invitation to the old cardinal that he celebrate the Mass of thanksgiving. Cavanaugh realized the difficulty a trip of this kind would entail for a man of Gibbons' age and he, therefore, said he would arrange to have a special car bring him from Baltimore and would see that every detail of the journey was made as comfortable and as free from fatigue as possible.[166] Gibbons replied that while he did not usually accept such invitations, yet the solemn occasion, the wide influence of Notre Dame, and the high esteem he had for Father Cavanaugh inclined him to agree to be present, and unless some unforeseen obstacle should intervene, "you may," he said, "put me down as accepting."[167]

By the time that Notre Dame had entered its year of jubilee the clouds of the European war were gathering more ominously in the direction of the United States, and by the spring of 1917 it was obvious that little short of a miracle would prevent American intervention in the conflict. On March 16 and 17 three American ships, homeward bound, were attacked without warning and sunk by German submarines and four days later President Woodrow Wilson summoned Congress to meet in special session on April 2. Bishop Shahan quickly responded to the

---

[165] 113-B, Curley to Gibbons, St. Augustine, January 19, 1916.

[166] 114-R, Cavanaugh to Gibbons, Notre Dame, January 16, 1917.

[167] AUND, Presidents' Papers, Gibbons to Cavanaugh, Baltimore, January 20, 1917.

crisis before the country, and in a letter to the President he said, "In view of the present emergency, the Catholic University of America has the honor to offer itself to you for such services as the Government of the United States may desire from it."[168] Wilson thanked the bishop for his generous letter and told him he was grateful for his pledge of co-operation and support.[169] It was an action on the part of the rector which met with the chancellor's warmest approval. Shahan's letter to the President proved no empty gesture, for during the war which followed several of the university buildings were turned over to the government for use, over 800 of the alumni saw service in the army and navy, of whom thirteen gave their lives, and around fifty of the clerical alumni acted as chaplains to the armed forces.[170] The chancellor combined his love of country and of the university by subscribing $10,000 to the fourth Liberty Loan drive and sending the bonds to the university, with the information that during the remainder of his life the interest should be paid to him, but at his death the bonds would become the property of the institution free of all conditions whatsoever.[171]

The trying experiences of World War I afforded to Gibbons an opportunity to emphasize in his annual university letter in the fall of 1918 the value which the institution had for American Catholics. He told the bishops of the government work going on in the Maloney Chemical Laboratory, as well as of the presence of 500 young men on the campus who were enrolled in the S.A.T.C. "I am truly proud," said the chancellor, "of the war record of the Catholic University, and I gladly commend it to the gratitude of our Catholic people." He remarked that God had spared him to celebrate his golden jubilee as a bishop, and it was his firm belief that the chief service of his episcopacy had been the help he had given to the university.[172] The date of the jubilee fell on August 16, 1918, but the celebration was postponed until the autumn and when that time came Baltimore was suffering so badly from the epidemic of influenza that the

---

[168] *Catholic University Bulletin,* XXIII (March, 1917), 33. Shahan to Wilson, Washington, March 28, 1917.

[169] *Ibid.,* Wilson to Shahan, Washington, March 30, 1917.

[170] *Ibid.,* XXVI (January, 1920), 7–8.

[171] 121-M, Gibbons to the Catholic University of America, Baltimore, May 9, 1919, copy.

[172] AAC, Gibbons to Henry Moeller, Baltimore, November 5, 1918.

festivities were held to a minimum. The principal commemoration was, therefore, delayed until February 20, 1919, at Washington.

On that date there assembled at the Franciscan Monastery for the pontifical Mass, besides Gibbons, two cardinals, O'Connell and Begin, the special envoy of Benedict XV, Archbishop Bonaventura Cerretti, the apostolic delegate, ten archbishops, and fifty-eight bishops together with a large gathering of clergy and laity. The preacher was Archbishop Mundelein of Chicago, who in emphasizing Gibbons' affection for the university, said:

> And the friends who are nearest to him and who enjoy his confidence will tell you that no institution in his diocese or elsewhere is as dear to his heart as the Catholic University of America. Other names were associated with his in its inception and its foundation, but none other can be placed with his in its growth and progress.[173]

The foreign guests likewise sensed the cardinal's feeling for the university, and Bishop Frederick W. Keating of Northampton, who represented the English hierarchy, later described the deep impression made upon him by his visit to the university which he called Gibbons' "most ambitious and most anxious undertaking."[174] It had, indeed, been a most anxious undertaking since that day in the spring of 1885 when he had presided for the first time at a meeting of the committee for the establishment of a university. But as the years went on Gibbons' interest intensified and in the last summer of his life he was still found rallying the American hierarchy to the university's support. In

---

[173] *Catholic University Bulletin*, XXV (April, 1919), 197–198. Three weeks before his golden episcopal jubilee, Gibbons consecrated on March 30 the last of a long line of twenty-three bishops for the American Church in William Turner, professor of philosophy in the university, who had been named sixth Bishop of Buffalo.

[174] F. W., Bp. of Northampton, "Impressions of Catholic America," *Dublin Review*, CLXIV (April-June, 1919), 170. When Gibbons outlined the duties for the administrative committee of the newly established National Catholic Welfare Council he was again mindful of the university. He cited for the four bishops the fields of American Catholic endeavor, and he said, "Our greatest single hope is in the Catholic University which in its short existence has already been of the greatest service in many ways that even the Catholic public, perhaps is not aware of. . . . If it is to obtain and hold its place among the leading universities of the United States, a greater interest in its welfare and success must be aroused among our Catholic people. It ought not to be difficult to double or treble, at least, the annual contribution. Our Committee should consider ways and means of effecting this" (121-L, Gibbons to Bishops Muldoon, Schrembs, Glass, and Russell, Baltimore, May 5, 1919, copy).

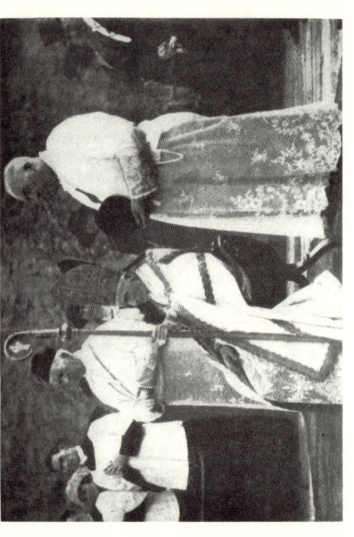

Cardinal Gibbons presides over one of the last of many national ecclesiastical ceremonies in his lifetime. The occasion was the laying of the cornerstone on September 23, 1920, of the National Shrine of the Immaculate Conception on the campus of the Catholic University of America. At the cardinal's right is the Right Reverend Edward J. McGoldrick, pastor of St. Cecilia's Church, Brooklyn, and at his left the Right Reverend Francis J. Van Antwerp, pastor of Our Lady of the Rosary Church, Detroit.

the final letter which he wrote in preparation for the annual collection of 1920 he included many of the familiar phrases about the services which the institution had bestowed upon the Church and the nation, and in conclusion he remarked:

> The years of my earthly life are drawing to a close, and in the way of nature I must ere long appear before my judge. I could have no greater happiness in these remaining years than to know that the Catholic University of America was placed on a solid basis for the present, in keeping with its admitted needs, with its encouraging growth and progress, and with the educational interest of our Catholic people.[175]

Six months before he died Cardinal Gibbons presided at the second annual meeting of the American hierarchy which was held on the university campus. On September 21, the day preceding the meeting of the hierarchy, he occupied the chair for the last time as president of the university's Board of Trustees. He was encouraged by the rector's report that the annual collection of the year before had amounted to $150,000, that generous donations had been received for the National Shrine of the Immaculate Conception on the university campus, that the faculty now numbered eighty-seven, and that owing largely to the end of the war there was an increase of 336 students over the previous year. Shahan likewise told the trustees that the cardinal's donations to the university during the year just ended had amounted to $16,000.[176] Two days later Gibbons laid the cornerstone for the great church recently begun on the campus and the special joy which the occasion brought him was evident when he told Father Bernard A. McKenna, the rector's secretary, on the following day, "I cannot deny myself the pleasure of telling you how impressed I was with the ceremony of Wednesday. Not only was it a grand affair in every respect, but the uncommon smoothness with which the ceremony was carried through was a source of genuine satisfaction."[177] It was the last important function over which the aged chancellor presided at the university, and within a few weeks thereafter he entered upon an illness from which he never fully recovered. Yet even in the

---

[175] AAC, Gibbons to Moeller, Baltimore, July 8, 1920.

[176] ACUA, Minutes of the Board of Trustees, Washington, September 21, 1920, pp. 264–266.

[177] 129-H, Gibbons to McKenna, Baltimore, September 20, 1920, copy.

final weeks of his life the university was on his mind. One day while seated in his invalid's chair in his room the cardinal suddenly turned to one of the priests of his household and without warning he said:

> Father, I wish I could tell you the full story of the Catholic University. There was a time in its history when some of my closest friends begged me to desert the work, but I would not. Night after night, I sat at the desk there, and with my own hand wrote letter after letter. "We must go on with the work," I wrote. All the time my heart was heavy. Those nearest to me were falling away one by one and I was facing the future alone. The University was the child of my old age, and like children begotten in old age, its beginnings caused me much pain.[178]

When the Board of Trustees assembled on April 1, 1921, for its sixty-fifth meeting it was one of the few times in nearly thirty-six years that the chair was not occupied by James Gibbons. Bishop Shahan reported that in the financial crisis of 1904 there had come to the institution through the late chancellor's efforts $189,025.34 and since that time he had contributed $314,127.21, a total of over $400,000 in seventeen years. But the rector added that the cardinal's financial aid was surpassed by his devotion to the cause and by what was termed, "the prestige with which his amicable personality and nobility of life endowed this center of Catholic education." Cardinal O'Connell, who presided at the meeting, appointed Archbishop Moeller, Bishop O'Connell, and Mr. Walter George Smith as a committee to draft resolutions of respect and condolence for the departed chancellor. In a lengthy communication the committee reported to the trustees at their next meeting, and in summarizing Gibbons' contribution to the university they said, "How well he succeeded in this grand enterprise will not be entirely evident until the University's history is written. Then it will appear how his masterful direction, coupled with his brave optimism, carried it through its formative years to the success it has now attained."[179]

True, the full story of the role played by the cardinal in the university's life would have to await the historian; yet long

---

[178] Albert E. Smith and Vincent de P. Fitzpatrick, *Cardinal Gibbons, Churchman and Citizen,* p. 127.

[179] ACUA, Minutes of the Board of Trustees, April 1, 1921, p. 268; folder accompanying the meeting of September 20, 1921.

before he died the leaders of the American Church were aware of the place it occupied in his affections and the inestimable debt of gratitude which they all owed to him as its first chancellor. One of those who for many years had worked at his side as a trustee and who had supported the cardinal in every effort for the institution's welfare was John J. Glennon, Archbishop of St. Louis. It was, therefore, from knowledge and experience that Glennon spoke in his sermon at the funeral of Gibbons in saying that were he to speak, he would, Glennon believed, leave as a heritage "his body to Baltimore, his heart to the University and his soul to God."[180] Fifteen years later, on October 22, 1936, the university had the honor for the first time in its history of entertaining a papal Secretary of State in the person of Eugenio Cardinal Pacelli who visited the campus and delivered an address. The future Pope Pius XII paid tribute to the founder of the university, Leo XIII, and in recalling that Pontiff's efforts in its behalf, he pronounced a judgment which found an immediate echo in the hearts of the vast audience who heard him. He said:

> At the side of the luminous figure of the Pontiff stands that of the co-founder of the University, one of the noblest and grandest men whom this country has given to the Church and whom the Church has given to this country — James Cardinal Gibbons.[181]

---

[180]*Catholic University Bulletin,* XXVII (March, 1921), 22.

[181] Eugenio Cardinal Pacelli, "The Catholic University and the Church," *Catholic University Bulletin,* V., N.S. (January, 1937), 4. The speaker recalled the invitation which Bishop Shahan had extended to him years before to teach Roman law in the university and how he was prevented from accepting by Pius X. *Ibid.*

CHAPTER XIX

World War I

ABSORBING as were the affairs of the Catholic University of America for its chancellor in the early years of the twentieth century, there were other problems at this time of a more critical and far-reaching character that weighed upon his mind. To one of the temperament of Cardinal Gibbons even the suggestion of armed conflict between nations was abhorrent, and for that reason he never lost an opportunity to speak out in behalf of peaceful measures when he felt that his words might prove helpful. For example, during the months preceding the drawing up of an arbitration treaty between the United States and Great Britain in 1911, there was considerable public discussion on the subject. Gibbons seized the chance of his address before the third National Peace Congress at Baltimore in May of that year to urge such a treaty on the grounds of common language, similar constitutional governments, and the benefits that would derive not only to the two principals but to the whole civilized world. "The time," said the cardinal, "seems to be most auspicious for the consummation of this alliance."[1]

---

[1] Baltimore Evening *Sun,* May 3, 1911. Some months before Gibbons' attention had been called by Archbishop Farley to the warlike remarks of an unnamed clergyman, and Farley had indicated that he was going to speak out in behalf of peace. Gibbons replied, "I am glad you are going to speak, & in the interests of peace. Your remarks will counteract the ominous & warlike notes of our friend. The evil effects of predictions of coming strife between ourselves & other countries are two-fold. They arouse & intensify the apprehensions of the people at large, & they justify & compel the enormous expense of armaments which are so pleasing to our military men as well as to the manufactures of warlike equipments.

"The Prelates of the Catholic Church are looked to as the greatest power to tranquilise the bellicose agitation, & to say to the world: 'Peace be still.' They should never add fuel to the flame" (AANY, Gibbons to Farley, New Orleans, March 1, 1911). An effort to find the original of Farley's letter in the Gibbons Papers failed and no copy could be found in the AANY among the Farley Papers.

But when the treaty of 1911 reached the United States Senate it became so encumbered with amendments that the good effect was completely lost. Nonetheless, Gibbons in company with others of a similar mind did not lose heart, and two years later they rejoiced that the Secretary of State in the new administration, William Jennings Bryan, should inaugurate discussions for treaties of conciliation with Britain and other nations. During the course of these negotiations there occurred the centennial of the Treaty of Ghent between the United States and Britain. Gibbons regretted his inability to be present at the commemorative ceremonies, but he took occasion to tell Alton B. Parker of his strong desire for an arbitration treaty between the two English-speaking powers. He summarized the arguments he had used two years before, and he added that in his belief the United States and Great Britain had been more successful in adjusting and reconciling legitimate authority with personal liberty than any other countries in the world. In conclusion the cardinal stated:

> Let Britannia and Columbia join hands across the Atlantic and their outstretched arms will form a sacred arch of peace which will excite the admiration of the nations, and will proclaim to the world the hope that with God's help the earth shall never more be deluged with blood shed in fratricidal war.[2]

Among the problems inherited from the Taft administration by President Woodrow Wilson when he assumed office in March, 1913, there were, to be sure, far more serious ones than the failure of a satisfactory arbitration treaty with Great Britain. Ever since the overthrow of President Porfirio Díaz of Mexico in May, 1911, there had been increasing trouble south of the border, and it was obvious that the internal revolution through which Mexico was then passing held the gravest threat to the thousands of Americans resident there and to the millions of dollars of property owned by American business firms in Mexico. Moreover, the fall of the Díaz regime brought on a persecution of the Catholic Church which grew in intensity as one revolutionary junta succeeded another at Mexico City. Wilson at first followed the policy of noninterference and nonrecognition of the

---

[2] 109-E, Gibbons to Parker, Baltimore, April 27, 1913, copy. A month or so later Gibbons sent Secretary Bryan a copy of his letter to Parker as he had promised on the occasion of their recent meeting (National Archives, Department of State Archives, Gibbons to Bryan, Baltimore, June 14, 1913).

government of Victoriano Huerta, but as American lives continued to be lost and American property destroyed sentiment mounted in the United States for armed intervention, and by the spring of 1914 a war hysteria, "the like of which had not been seen in the United States since 1898," was sweeping the nation.[3]

In all of this Cardinal Gibbons felt the deepest anxiety. Not only did he deplore the prospect of war, but he was likewise distressed by the suffering which the Church in Mexico was experiencing. What made matters more difficult for him at the moment was the fact that he was scheduled to sail for Rome on business just at the time when the crisis seemed to be at its worst. On the eve of his departure from Baltimore he wrote a pastoral letter to his people in which he made a plea for their prayers during the May devotions that were about to begin. "I am leaving you," said the cardinal, "at a time when there is danger of a war which is desired by no one but yet may be forced upon us by circumstances we cannot control."[4] On the same day Gibbons addressed a letter to José Mora y del Rio, Archbishop of Mexico, in which he suggested that they unite their faithful in a crusade of prayer for peace. "Your nation and mine ardently desire to avert the calamity of war," he said, "and to persevere in the relations of friendship and mutual respect which have hitherto united us. Let us humbly but confidently hope to obtain from the God of peace these inestimable blessings."[5]

Although by late June Argentina, Brazil, and Chile had succeeded in mediating the dispute between the United States and Mexico and several weeks later Huerta's regime gave way to that of Venustiano Carranza, peaceful relations between the two countries were by no means restored. Moreover, the Church in Mexico was compelled to endure even greater hardships. Among those at whom the hatred of the revolutionary movement was especially directed were the Jesuits, and in the face of the threat that they would be expelled entirely from Mexico the general of the society, Franz X. Wernz, made an appeal to Gibbons to

---

[3] Bailey, *A Diplomatic History of the American People,* p. 607.

[4] 109-W, pastoral letter of Gibbons to the Archdiocese of Baltimore, Baltimore, May 1, 1914, copy.

[5] 109-W, Gibbons to Mora, Baltimore, May 1, 1914, copy.

protect them.[6] The cardinal, who was in Switzerland at the time, promised Wernz that after his return to Baltimore he would do all in his power to help the Mexican Jesuits.[7] Gibbons arrived in New York on July 13 aboard the *Berlin* and ten days later, on the occasion of his eightieth birthday, he gave an interview to the press in which he emphatically denounced Carranza and his rival, Francisco Villa, for their depredations against the clergy.

In the interview the cardinal stated that by force of circumstances the United States was in a position where it must practically speak for the rest of the world in regard to the Carranza government, since it was obvious that it was the only first-class power that could be expected to take the initiative in recognizing the present Mexican rulers. Americans, said the cardinal, were especially watching the Constitutionalist Party in three particulars: the treatment accorded to foreigners and their property; an amnesty for political and military opponents of the Carranza rule; and finally, the treatment of the Catholic Church and its representatives. Nothing, said Gibbons, would shock the civilized world more than punitive or vindictive action toward priests or ministers of any Church, whether Catholic or Protestant. "The treatment already said to have been accorded priests," he remarked, "has had a most unfortunate effect upon opinion outside Mexico." He was quoted as entertaining slight hope of a restoration of peace through the triumph of the Constitutionalists since they represented largely a conflict of the outs to get in, with nothing better in prospect than counterrevolutions in almost any event.[8]

The Gibbons interview was widely disseminated throughout the United States and brought a quick response from the government in Washington. Two days after it appeared in the press Blair Lee, United States Senator from Maryland, called on the cardinal at the request of President Wilson and Secretary Bryan. Lee brought a copy of a dispatch which the American government had sent to Carranza and Villa regarding the persecution of the Church, and it was stated that an American representative

---

[6] 109-XYZ, Wernz to Gibbons, Rome, June 5, 1914.

[7] 109-XYZ, Gibbons to Wernz, Territet, Switzerland, June 7, 1914, copy.

[8] Baltimore *American,* July 24, 1914. The published interview differs in a number of particulars from the typed copy (110-A).

in Mexico had informed the administration by wire that it was not Villa but rather one of his subordinates who seemed to be involved in the killing of two priests. "The President and the Secretary of State," said the memorandum, "desire to advise the Cardinal that they feel reasonably sure of being able to prevent any objectionable recurrence."[9] While this was gratifying news to Gibbons, he did not fail to tell Senator Lee that the President should be reminded that the records of Carranza and Villa were so bad that their protestations would have little weight before the discerning public until they were supplemented by deeds. He referred to the anxiety of the bishops and religious of Mexico, and he promised Lee that he would see Secretary Bryan in this connection as soon as he had anything of importance to communicate.[10]

Soon after the interview with Lee the cardinal sent word of it to Archbishop Mora of Mexico and requested the prelate to inform him immediately if any open persecution on the part of the Constitutionalist regime should take place.[11] At the same time Father Anthony J. Maas, Maryland provincial of the Jesuits, submitted to Gibbons data on the number and condition of the many Mexican religious exiles arriving at the Jesuit house in El Paso, Texas, and stated that the Mexican Jesuits had declared that the best service Gibbons could render to the cause of the Church in Mexico would be to induce the American government to insist on protection of life and property for all priests and religious. The cardinal was able to offer some hope to Maas by summarizing for him the substance of his interview with Lee.[12] Evidence that an impression had been made on the Mexican officials by Wilson's dispatch — prompted by the Gibbons press interview — was found in the fact that Carranza instructed his Washington agent to call on Monsignor William T. Russell, pastor of St. Patrick's Church and the cardinal's representative in the capital, with reassurances for Gibbons that the rights of the Church in Mexico would be protected and there would be no

---

[9] 110-A, memorandum to Gibbons delivered by Lee, June 26, 1914. No copy of the Wilson dispatch to Carranza was found in the archives.

[10] 110-B, Gibbons' personal memorandum on the interview with Lee, Baltimore, July 27, 1914.

[11] 110-C, Gibbons to Mora, Baltimore, August 1, 1914, copy.

[12] 110-B, Maas to Gibbons, New York, July 31, 1914; 110-C, same to same, New York, August 3, 1914.

violation of ecclesiastical property. All this information the cardinal relayed to the papal Secretary of State, Cardinal Merry del Val, in order that the Holy See might be kept abreast of developments.[13]

Two days after his letter to Merry del Val the cardinal received a call from Hubert L. Hall of the Department of State who came at the instance of Secretary Bryan and bore a letter of introduction from Monsignor Russell.[14] Hall, who had lived for some years in Mexico, was believed to be thoroughly familiar with the situation there, and he informed Gibbons that Carranza had repudiated and condemned Villa's conduct toward the Church and had promised to carry out Wilson's instructions about the protection of its interests. The cardinal was willing enough to credit Carranza with sincerity, if not from benevolence, as he said, at least from self-interest, but he was not at all sure that Carranza could keep Villa and other rebellious agencies in check. He laid before Hall the plight of the exiles at El Paso and asked him to tell Secretary Bryan that no government in Mexico could long endure which followed the policy of religious persecution, and that if the rulers behaved toward the Church there with the justice and charity that marked the conduct of the government of the United States, they would find their best support in the Catholic religion and the hierarchy.[15]

Meanwhile Cardinal Gibbons was content to await developments in Mexico in the hope that a change would be brought about by Wilson's representations in behalf of the Church. For this reason he cautioned Father Maas that *America,* the Jesuit weekly, should refrain from expressing apprehensions over the dire consequences that might follow from Carranza's arrival in Mexico City. He felt it would be pleasing to the administration in Washington if the representatives of the Church would now

[13] 110-C, Gibbons to Merry del Val, Baltimore, August 4, 1914, copy.

[14] 110-C, Russell to Gibbons, Washington, August 4, 1914.

[15] 110-D, Gibbons to Maas, Baltimore, August 7, 1914, copy. It was on the occasion of Hall's visit that Gibbons received confirmation of the press reports concerning the grave illness of Mrs. Wilson. He wrote the President immediately, "to assure you," as he said, "of my heartfelt sympathy & of my fervent prayers for her speedy recovery" (LC, Wilson Papers, Gibbons to Wilson, Baltimore, August 6, 1914). Mrs. Wilson died some days later, and in thanking the cardinal for his letter of sympathy the President remarked, "It gave me peculiar pleasure that you should think of me in my sorrow and I particularly valued such an evidence of your friendship" (110-D, Wilson to Gibbons, Washington, August 18, 1914).

abstain from harsh criticism, follow what he called "a benevolent though vigilant attitude," and give Carranza an opportunity to fulfill his promises. The cardinal even entertained the hope that Carranza's conduct might assume a favorable and constructive tendency and that Mexico might enter upon an era of peace.[16]

But his hopes were almost immediately belied when he received word from Bishop Michele de la Mora of Zacatecas of the continuing persecution of the clergy in his diocese. He forwarded the bishop's letter to Wilson with an appeal for his help, in which he said, "I feel quite sure that just one word from you to the Constitutionalist leaders would have a great effect and would relieve the sad condition of affairs."[17] But the President was under no illusions concerning the influence he might wield over the Mexican rulers, and he was sorry to say that it was not true that he could affect a change in Mexican policy since he had spoken again and again on the subject. Wilson assured the cardinal that he would continue to exert his best efforts and he hoped it might be with increasing effect, but for the present they would have to await the subsidence of the passions which had been aroused in Mexico.[18] Nor was Gibbons' information from the Department of State more reassuring. Bryan told him that Vice-Consul John R. Silliman had telegraphed from Zacatecas that while there might not be so many expulsions of priests as heretofore, it was not expected that the Catholic schools would be permitted to reopen there in the near future.[19]

At this juncture the attention of Cardinal Gibbons was once more distracted from the Mexican troubles by the death on August 20 of Pope Pius X which entailed for him another journey to Rome to attend the conclave. The cardinal left almost immediately and did not return to the United States until September 24, reaching Baltimore just two days in advance of the opening of the thirteenth annual convention of the American Federation of Catholic Societies in his see city. On the day before the convention closed Gibbons met with Bishops James A. McFaul of

[16] 110-D, Gibbons to Maas, Baltimore, August 13, 1914, copy.
[17] LC, Wilson Papers, Gibbons to Wilson, Baltimore, August 18, 1914.
[18] 110-D, Wilson to Gibbons, Washington, August 21, 1914, *Personal*. In the absence of Gibbons on the high seas, Eugene J. Connelly, acting chancellor of the Archdiocese of Baltimore, told Wilson he was forwarding his letter that day (LC, Wilson Papers, Connelly to Wilson, Baltimore, August 22, 1914).
[19] 110-E, Bryan to Gibbons, Washington, September 1, 1914.

Trenton and Joseph Schrembs of Toledo and Richard H. Tierney, S.J., editor of *America,* and gave his approval to the statement which the leaders of the federation had framed on the Church in Mexico. The statement, which was presented to President Wilson by a delegation that called at the White House, was reported to have denounced the persecution and the silence of the American press concerning it. No text was given out since, according to the Baltimore *Catholic Review* of October 3, the delegates decided that the very strongly worded paper should first be in the hands of the President before it was given any publicity. In any case, the committee was graciously received by Wilson who told them that he was already acting along the lines suggested.[20]

Two weeks after the close of the Baltimore convention, McFaul stated that it had been proposed that he get in touch with the American hierarchy to lend their support to the federation's stand on Mexico. However, recent reports that Carranza might have to resign and make way for a new government had given pause to the Bishop of Trenton, and he was puzzled as to what steps he should take in view of the changes which were said to be imminent in Mexico. "Be good enough," he told the cardinal, "to send me your opinion."[21] Gibbons lost no time in recommending a policy of watchful waiting. He summarized his reasons by saying that the changing character of the Mexican political scene gave room for caution, that Wilson had written him several times of his efforts to help in the way that the federation had already suggested, that there was some evidence for believing there had been exaggerations in the statements concerning the evil deeds in Mexico, and finally, that the American Catholics must keep in mind that the sufferings visited upon their coreligionists were at the hands of the faithless children of their own Church, not from pagans, Protestants, Jews, or Mohammedans. Therefore, he concluded, it was the part of wisdom to refrain from constant and annoying attacks upon the President

---

[20] 110-G, McFaul to Gibbons, Trenton, October 2, 1914. Apparently the committee that called at the White House had no bishop with it. McFaul told Gibbons that Charles Warren Currier, Bishop of Matanzas, Cuba, had wished to accompany the committee, but McFaul insisted that if any bishop was to go it should be Schrembs or himself. McFaul remarked, "He [Currier] was very stubborn, so I had to tell him that he could not represent Federation. That settled it, but I fear he's my enemy now."

[21] 110-G, McFaul to Gibbons, Trenton, October 15, 1914.

and his cabinet, veiled under the cover of petitions and resolutions. "The effect of this ceaseless harassing," said Gibbons, "might probably result, not in securing any assistance in our cause, but in setting the entire Administration against us."[22]

The attitude of forbearance which the Cardinal of Baltimore had assumed at this time was doubtless motivated by the best of intentions, but it was not shared by all American Catholics. Neither did he persist in it, as we shall see, when he got nearer to the scene of the trouble and talked to some of the victims of the persecution. Among those who felt there was need for stronger action on the part of the Catholics of the United States was Father Francis C. Kelley, editor of *Extension,* the monthly magazine of the Catholic Church Extension Society. During a trip through Texas Kelley interviewed a large number of the Mexican exiles and he forwarded to Gibbons a lengthy account of their sufferings. He believed that American Catholics had an opportunity to insist that no government be recognized in Mexico unless it guaranteed religious liberty. "If we weaken in this demand," he said, "the Church (and again, I speak from information received from the Bishops) will be wiped out of existence."[23]

This letter arrived at a time when the cardinal was in no happy mood toward Father Kelley. Gibbons had just read the trenchant editorial which he had written in *Extension* on the Mexican situation in which the editor made a plea for money to relieve the exiles from the persecution, and in the editorial he had placed the blame for the conditions there squarely at the doorstep of the Washington government. In pointed questions he had asked, "Who has brought this state of things about? Ourselves! Who insisted upon the non-recognition of a government lawfully in charge according to the Constitution of Mexico? Ourselves! Who upheld the hands of Carranza and Villa? Ourselves!" Kelley stated that it was not too late for the American government to redress the wrongs suffered by the Church in Mexico, by insisting that the Catholics of that country should enjoy the free exercise of their religion and that all seized ecclesiastical property be restored to its owners. In this way, he thought, the American people could make some amends for the

---

[22] 110-J, Gibbons to McFaul, Baltimore, October 16, 1914, copy.
[23] 110-K, Kelley to Gibbons, San Antonio, October 26, 1914.

evil that had been done.[24] It was not surprising that statements of this kind emanating from an American Catholic magazine should displease Gibbons. He told Kelley of the good will manifested by the President and of his efforts to relieve the situation, and in referring to the editorial and its accusations concerning American guilt, he remarked, "This is a serious charge and one that has been felt keenly at Washington. It is one that can be made only after very careful investigation and with sufficient proof."[25] It was fairly plain that the cardinal did not think Kelley had the proof, and that he had made a grave error by writing in this fashion.

The differences which Cardinal Gibbons had with Father Kelley over the latter's public statements, however, in no way affected his response to the appeal for funds which had been made by the editor of *Extension*. Some days after his letter to Kelley, he sent off a personal donation of $250 to Bishop John W. Shaw of San Antonio with the request that he distribute it among the Mexican refugees according to the manner he deemed best.[26] He followed his check by a letter of sympathy which he signed in the name of the American hierarchy to the hierarchy of Mexico for the suffering they were experiencing, wherein he stated that those who antagonized the Church had at best only a crude idea of popular government. In the United States the Church enjoyed freedom. Therefore, the American people would not consistently favor any movement that would interfere with the liberty of the Church in Mexico. "They will not, I am sure," said Gibbons, "deliberately assent to the establishment on their borders of a system of misrule based on the worst of tyrannies, the tyranny of the State over soul and conscience."[27] Meanwhile Kelley was at pains to assure the cardinal that he had meant no disrespect to President Wilson in the offending editorial, but he was in possession of so much irrefutable evidence from Mexico that he felt sure of his position. Wilson, Kelley believed, had been deliberately misinformed by his representatives below the

---

[24] Editorial, "Where the Gates of Hell Are Open," IX (November, 1914), 3–4.

[25] 110-L, Gibbons to Kelley, Baltimore, October 29, 1914, copy.

[26] 110-N, Gibbons to Shaw, Baltimore, November 10, 1914, copy. For Benedict XV's letter of March 17, 1915, thanking Gibbons for the alms given to the victims of the Mexican persecution cf. Harry C. Koenig (Ed.), *Principles for Peace* (Washington, 1943), pp. 158–159.

[27] 110-N, Gibbons to Mora, Baltimore, November 19, 1914, copy.

border, and in the volume of documents which the Catholic
Church Extension Society had just authorized for publication
the facts would be set forth in defense of the Church and that
could be done, as he said, without hurt to or direct criticism of
the President.[28]

There were others besides Father Kelley who were uneasy
over the silence in American Catholic circles regarding the
Mexican persecution. Archbishop Messmer, for example, wrote
in the name of the bishops of the Province of Milwaukee to ask
if it would not be wise for the three American cardinals to issue
a solemn protest.[29] Gibbons viewed an action of this kind, addressed to the ruling element in Mexico, as entirely useless in
light of the reception given to the previous protests of the
American government. As for directing such a document to the
administration in Washington, he believed it was problematical
how much good would be accomplished. He conceded that many
right-thinking men felt a move of this kind would result in the
United States bringing pressure to bear that would alleviate the
situation, and he also admitted it would have the effect of proving
to everyone, including fair-minded Protestants, that the American
hierarchy were not indifferent to the sufferings of their Mexican
coreligionists. Yet from the language he employed it was evident
that Gibbons did not feel ready to commit himself to a decision
in regard to the proposed protest, and he ended by not answering
Messmer's inquiry in any direct way. He told the archbishop
that Wilson had no doubt realized before this that a blunder
had been made in not recognizing Huerta and in giving aid to
his enemies who later proved to be our own. But he believed
the President was doing all he could to rectify the mistake, except
to go to war which no peace-loving man could contemplate.[30]

On the same day the cardinal outlined the Messmer proposal
to Archbishop Ireland and, without specifically asking for his
advice, he went on to say that he believed Wilson now had reason
to deplore his repudiation of Huerta, his secret aid to Carranza
and Villa, his rejection of the advice of the American minister
at Mexico City, and his employment of secret agents like John

28 110-N, Kelley to Gibbons, Chicago, November 13, 1914. The work to which
Father Kelley referred was later published by him under the title, *The Book of
Red and Yellow* (Chicago, 1915).

29 110-W, Messmer to Gibbons, Milwaukee, December 23, 1914.

30 110-XYZ, Gibbons to Messmer, Baltimore, December 26, 1914, copy.

Lind.[31] But if Gibbons felt hesitation about the protest from the cardinals, Ireland did not. The Archbishop of St. Paul thought the letter of sympathy sent a month before to Archbishop Mora should suffice for all purposes. A letter from the three American cardinals was, in the opinion of Ireland, too solemn a document to be put forth without pressing need and without assurance of success, and in this judgment Archbishop Keane of Dubuque, who was with him as he wrote, agreed. To Ireland the Archbishop of Milwaukee and his suffragans were what he called "fussy" people, unconscious of American public opinion, and ready to embroil the Church in difficulties of any and every kind.[32] For all these reasons he could not subscribe to the idea of a protest from the cardinals, and in the end none was made.

Meanwhile Father Kelley continued his efforts in behalf of the Mexican Catholics. Early in 1915 he went to Washington where he saw the President, Secretary Bryan, and others, and in reporting the results of his visit he told Gibbons, "I think they are on the way to conviction of the right of our position, and I am preparing documents for the President now, which I hope will lead him to make a declaration regarding liberty of conscience in Mexico."[33] During the same winter the cardinal received his first direct evidence of the Mexican persecution from some of its victims on the occasion of his annual visit to his brother in New Orleans. He met there Archbishop Mora and others who told him of the frightful conditions under which the Church was laboring, and upon his return to Baltimore late in March Gibbons gave an interview to the press. He spoke emphatically about the lawlessness prevalent in Mexico, stated that Carranza and Villa were disgraces to their country, approved the nonintervention policy of the Wilson administration, said he would see Secretary

---

[31] AASP, Gibbons to Ireland, Baltimore, December 26, 1914, copy.

[32] 110-XYZ, Ireland to Gibbons, St. Paul, December 31, 1914.

[33] 111-D, Kelley to Gibbons, Chicago, January 26, 1915. A quarter century later Kelley, by now Bishop of Oklahoma City-Tulsa, described his visit to Washington in his memoirs, *The Bishop Jots It Down* (New York, 1939). But the intervening years had brought either a lapse of memory or a new light on the interviews with Wilson and Bryan. Speaking of the former, he said that after a quite unsatisfactory talk Wilson suggested he see Bryan, to which Kelley added, "but I knew that it would do no good" (p. 192). After describing an equally unsatisfactory interview with Bryan, the bishop wrote, "Outside the door of the State Department I dropped a cherished illusion about the binding force of liberty of conscience in our ideal of democratic government" (p. 194).

Bryan with whom he had been in correspondence, and hinted that a worthy candidate for the presidency of Mexico would come forward who would bring lasting peace to that country. The interview was widely copied and called forth editorials in papers like the Baltimore *Sun* and the New York *Times*, which in the main approved the cardinal's views but expressed curiosity concerning the unnamed candidate for the Mexican presidency.[34]

The strong condemnation of both Carranza and Villa contained in Gibbons' interview of March 24 naturally drew opposition. Several weeks later Enrique C. Llorente, confidential agent of the Villa-Zapata faction in Washington, published a statement in which he defended the action taken against the Church, and remarked that the cardinal's statement had been made after conferring with Archbishop Mora. Referring to Gibbons' interview, Llorente said, "It is to be regretted that this usually discreet and respected Prince of the Church has intimated a purpose to enter politics in Mexico. . . ."[35] Another one who resented Gibbons' strictures on Carranza was John Lind who since 1913 had been acting as Wilson's personal agent in Mexico and who had consistently championed the recognition of Carranza by the American government. Lind was confident that Wilson's delay in recognition would ultimately win out. The delay had been due to political reasons but, on the other hand, it was his opinion that "Cardinal Gibbons' indiscretion in coming out in open hostility to the Constitutionalist movement made any other course suicidal for the Administration."[36]

In the midst of the excitement aroused over the cardinal's

---

[34] New York *Times,* March 25, 1914, and an editorial on March 26; Baltimore *Sun,* March 25, 1914, with an editorial entitled, "The Cardinal on Our Mexican Policy." The Mexican leader to whom Gibbons was referring was probably General Felix Díaz to whom Father Kelley referred in his letter of January 26, 1915, regarding a testimonial of character for Díaz sent by Archbishop Mora to Gibbons (111-D). On the subject of American intervention in Mexico, the cardinal changed his mind some months later. In an interview given to a reporter at Southampton, New York, he deplored action of this kind, yet he added, "but I believe that some form of intervention by this country is the only solution to the reign of anarchy that has existed there for several years." He alluded to the American protectorate over Cuba and the good it had accomplished and, although it would be more difficult in Mexico, he wondered if it might not offer a solution to the problem. Washington *Post,* August 1, 1915.

[35] New York *Times,* April 5, 1915.

[36] George M. Stephenson, *John Lind of Minnesota* (Minneapolis, 1935), p. 299.

interview he received a request from Archbishop Giovanni Bonzano, Apostolic Delegate to the United States, for his judgment
on a suggestion that had recently been made to him. It had been
proposed that great good might come of sending an outstanding
American priest or prelate to Mexico as apostolic delegate in
the belief that such a person might receive the support of the
American government. Bonzano gave his considerations for and
against such a move, and then stated that he would be obliged
if Gibbons would express his opinion on the subject.[37] It was the
belief of the cardinal that after peace had been restored in
Mexico it would be an excellent idea to have an American appointed as delegate there. He felt that after the restoration of
peace the government at Mexico City would naturally look to
the United States as a model for reforming and re-establishing
its affairs and would be guided in very large measure by American ideas. "Such being the case," said Gibbons, "I would think
that a prudent, energetic prelate or priest of this country, who
has some knowledge of the Spanish language, could do a great
deal of good for the Church in Mexico."[38] But in the troubled
years that followed for the Church in its relations with the
Mexican government there was little opportunity offered for real
peace between them and nothing came of the suggestion.

Despite his continued efforts the cardinal was able to note
very little success in his attempt to improve the lot of the
Mexican Catholics. On September 2, 1915, he had an interview
with President Wilson on this and other matters, but his brief
reference to the subject made it evident that no progress had
been made. Gibbons wrote, "We discussed Mexico without finding a solution."[39] How much the cardinal knew of the tendency
of the Wilson administration at the time to recognize Carranza
it is impossible to say, but it is certain that the *de facto* recognition which came on October 19 did not have his approval. He had
upheld Wilson's policy of watchful waiting and had discouraged
attacks by Catholics that might reflect on the President's handling
of the problem, but after his trip to New Orleans early in 1915
Gibbons was outspoken in his denunciation of Carranza's attacks
on the Church.

---

[37] 111-T, Bonzano to Gibbons, April 22, 1915, *Strictly confidential*.

[38] 111-U, Gibbons to Bonzano, Baltimore, May 1, 1915, copy.

[39] 112-G, Gibbons' memorandum of the interview with Wilson, September 2,
1915.

Other American Catholics who felt as Gibbons did naturally took up his words, and months later a certain John F. McGee of Minneapolis got out a circular letter indicting the Wilson administration for its Mexican policy in which he said, "no one has more accurately stated the net result of the almost criminal conduct of the administration in Mexico than His Eminence, Cardinal Gibbons, in interviews given by him to the public press. . . ."[40] That Gibbons' strictures were justified, was more than proven true in the succeeding two years. Not only was the armed intervention of the United States in 1916 in an effort to capture Villa rendered futile, but the withdrawal of American troops in February, 1917, and the formal recognition of Carranza on March 3 of that year did little either to restore peaceful conditions within Mexico or satisfactory relations with the United States. Carranza was, as one historian has said, "tyrannical, stubborn, and inefficient, not to say corrupt,"[41] and all the efforts of the American government to favor him in view of the increasing gravity of the European war yielded little if any return.

Meanwhile the persecution of the Church continued unabated and when Carranza struck at the persons of Archbishop Francisco Orozco of Guadalajara and Bishop Michele de la Mora of Zacatecas, Pope Benedict XV made a direct appeal by cable to President Wilson in their behalf.[42] The Pope was assured through the apostolic delegate that the American government would make representations to Carranza about the case, but no assurance could be given that anything would be done. In the spring of 1917 a constituent congress met at Querétaro and framed a

---

[40] Quoted in Stephenson, *op. cit.,* p. 324, as support of Lind's belief that Catholic propaganda was making a great impression. For evidence of Lind's unfriendliness toward the Church in Mexico cf. *ibid.,* pp. 227, 281.

[41] J. Fred Rippy, *Historical Evolution of Hispanic America* (New York, 1940), pp. 298–299.

[42] LC, Wilson Papers, Benedict XV to Wilson, Rome, January 26, 1917, cablegram. Wilson asked the opinion of Secretary of State Robert Lansing concerning the form which his answer to the Pope should take. Lansing submitted a memorandum to Joseph P. Tumulty, Wilson's secretary, in which he said he could find no precedent for a Pope addressing a President directly, and if the President sent a direct reply it would undoubtedly give trouble with the Italian government. Therefore, he suggested that Tumulty answer in Wilson's name either to the apostolic delegate or to Cardinal Gibbons. Lansing concluded, "I think this is the best way out of the embarrassment caused by the action of His Holiness in addressing the President directly" (LC, Wilson Papers, Lansing to Tumulty, Washington, January 27, 1917, *Personal and private*).

constitution for Mexico which was signed on May 1. Its articles relating to religion and education embodied serious violations of the rights of religious liberty and the freedom to educate in religious schools. At the meeting of the American archbishops in Washington on April 18 a committee consisting of Gibbons, Archbishop Moeller of Cincinnati, and Walter George Smith, a prominent lawyer of Philadelphia, was appointed to draw up a protest in the name of the metropolitans against the antireligious clauses of the constitution.[43] Smith made the preliminary draft of the document and sent it to the cardinal for his approval. It might, he said, seem too severe, but he had gone over it repeatedly and found nothing but a plain statement of facts. As to the expediency of sending it directly to the President, he was in favor of it, although he left the final judgment on this point to the cardinal.[44]

Gibbons thought over the matter for several weeks and then informed Smith that in view of the many difficulties under which Wilson was laboring on account of the outbreak of the war with Germany, he felt the protest might be interpreted as a willingness to add to his burdens.[45] But if he was disinclined to address the protest to the White House, he had little hesitation in having it published in the Baltimore *Catholic Review* of May 19. The statement of the archbishops maintained that it was in no sense their wish to enter upon a domain which was outside their jurisdiction, but they felt justified in observing that the United States had recognized the government of Mexico that was responsible for a constitution containing grave violations of the rights of the individual to liberty of worship and to religious education. They regarded it, therefore, as their duty to speak out in protest against such infringements of the rights of their coreligionists in Mexico.

Smith was delighted to see the publication of the protest, and he hoped all the Catholic papers in the country would copy it, even though, as he said, "it seems too much to hope that the secular papers will give any attention to it." He had received reliable information that negotiations were soon to begin for the grant of a large loan to Carranza, and if this were true it would

---

[43] 115-G, Minutes of the Meeting of the Archbishops, Washington, April 18, 1917.
[44] 115-H, Smith to Gibbons, Philadelphia, April 25, 1917.
[45] 115-M, Gibbons to Smith, Baltimore, May 15, 1917, copy.

consolidate and strengthen the Mexican leader to the point where he could crush all opposition. It appeared to Smith that before such a loan was granted representations should be made that the constitution of Mexico be amended so as to remove all obnoxious provisions relating to religion.[46] A week later he provided more detailed information on the terms of the projected loan, and in an attempt to offset the damage that the loan would cause, he suggested that the protest of the Mexican hierarchy against Carranza's persecution of the Church, as well as the protest of the American archbishops, should be republished with additional protests if possible from the American Federation of Catholic Societies to the speaker of the House of Representatives and the president of the United States Senate.[47] Gibbons heartily agreed with the idea, and he stated that in view of the fact that he was on the eve of his departure from home for a visit to Indiana, he would wish Smith to take up the matter for him.[48] That Mr. Smith's information had a basis in reality was evident when in August Secretary Lansing let it be known to Ambassador Henry P. Fletcher at Mexico City that the United States would not veto a loan to Carranza from American bankers, although he believed that there should first be some guarantee of financial reforms.[49] Needless to say, the decision of the Department of State to permit Carranza to float a large American loan was unaccompanied by any suggestion of change in the clauses of the Mexican constitution concerning religion and education.

For over three years, therefore, the Cardinal of Baltimore had endeavored to be of help to the harassed bishops, priests, and religious of Mexico but with very little success. In the early stages of the conflict he had put his faith in the protests of the American government to the Mexican rulers, and had tried to restrain public criticisms of the Wilson administration on the part of American Catholics. But as time went on the cardinal realized

---

[46] 115-N, Smith to Gibbons, Philadelphia, May 21, 1917.

[47] 115-Q, same to same, Philadelphia, June 1, 1917.

[48] 115-Q, Gibbons to Smith, Baltimore, June 2, 1917, copy.

[49] *Papers Relating to the Foreign Relations of the United States 1917* (Washington, 1926), p. 1014, Lansing to Fletcher, Washington, August 8, 1917, telegram. Some months later Lansing told the ambassador that the Department of State "would look with favor upon a loan by private bankers to Mexico," providing guarantees were given concerning American property there. *Papers Relating to the Foreign Relations of the United States 1918* (Washington, 1930), p. 653, Lansing to Fletcher, Washington, April 25, 1918, telegram.

the futility of expecting that the Washington government could or would do much to alleviate the suffering of the Church in Mexico. He then became more outspoken in his own public utterances concerning the outrages perpetrated below the border; yet neither the policy of forbearance nor that of open criticism worked for the improvement of conditions among the Mexican Catholics. Villa's excesses were only slightly worse than those of Carranza, his rival, and the Wilson administration was in time furnished with ample proof that the denunciation of both men by Gibbons in the spring of 1915, when he declared that neither was to be trusted and that the people had no confidence in them, was altogether justified.[50] Nonetheless, the increasing gravity of American relations with Germany in these years prompted the President to give support to Carranza, and in the crisis that was upon the United States by early 1917 the Mexican leader was allowed to pursue his tyrannical policies toward the Church without serious hindrance from Washington. Amid the clamor of World War I the voices of protest raised by Catholics were drowned out, and thus the Mexican revolution continued to run its course.

When one considers the magnitude of the war which engulfed Europe in the first week of August, 1914, it was small wonder that the mounting fury of the conflict should cause the importance of Mexico and its revolution to recede in men's minds. As previously mentioned, Cardinal Gibbons sailed for Rome the last week of that fateful month to attend the conclave that was to elect a successor to Pius X. But in spite of his efforts to reach the Eternal City in time he failed, and a few hours before Gibbons presented himself at the Vatican on September 3 the cardinals had elected Pope Benedict XV. After being accorded the distinction of having the first audience granted by the new Pontiff in his reign and remaining for some days in Rome, the cardinal set out for home and landed at Boston from the *Canopic* on September 24. In the interview which he gave upon his return he refused to comment on the causes of the war, but stated that it was the general opinion among those to whom he had spoken that Italy would eventually become involved and would enter the conflict on the side of the allies. Gibbons paid high tribute to Thomas Nelson Page, United States ambassador to Italy, and the

---

[50] *Catholic Messenger* (Davenport), April 1, 1915.

other American officials in Europe for the help they had given to stranded Americans, and he likewise had words of praise for the efforts which the President and the Secretary of State had exerted in their behalf.[51]

The importance of influencing public opinion in the United States was, of course, recognized from the very outset by the European belligerents. Moreover, by 1914 Cardinal Gibbons was eighty years of age and had for some time enjoyed an international reputation. It was not surprising, therefore, that the propaganda agencies of the warring nations should endeavor to win his favorable judgment on their part in the conflict. A few weeks after his return from the conclave, the cardinal received a communication from Sir Gilbert Parker, who had been placed in charge of publicity for the United States by the British government, in which he stated that the German press bureau in this country had been making efforts to throw the responsibility for the war on the allies. "It is important," said Parker, "that those who influence public opinion in America shall have access to documents which give a true narrative of the events leading up to the war," and with that in mind he was forwarding to the cardinal the official white papers of the British government.[52] A few months thereafter he received a similar letter with documents enclosed from Jules Cambon, who had been French ambassador to Berlin up to the outbreak of the war.[53]

Nor were American officials insensible to the position which Gibbons occupied and the roles he had played in behalf of peace in recent years. Secretary Bryan told him that as a token of his appreciation for what he termed, "your long and earnest devotion to the cause of international peace," he was sending a paperweight which was identical with those he had given to the ambassadors and ministers who had signed with him the thirty treaties providing for investigation of disputes.[54] The European

[51] New York *Times,* September 25, 1914. A clipping of his interview from the Baltimore *Sun* was sent by Gibbons to Wilson who stated that he had read it "with interest and appreciation" (LC, Wilson Papers, Eugene J. Connelly to Wilson, Baltimore, September 25, 1914; Wilson to Gibbons, Washington, September 28, 1914, copy).

[52] 110-G, Parker to Gibbons, London, October 7, 1914.

[53] 111-C, Cambon to Gibbons, Paris, January 22, 1915.

[54] 110-W, Bryan to Gibbons, Washington, December 23, 1914. In thanking him Gibbons told the Secretary of State, "it shall be treasured because of the donor

war likewise brought an increase to the requests for press interviews from Gibbons and frequently his opinion was solicited
concerning real or rumored moves on the part of the Church
which related to the warring powers. For example, early in 1915
he was asked by a reporter why the Vatican was looming up so
conspicuously on the diplomatic side of the war. To Gibbons
this was necessarily so by reason of the thousands of Catholics
involved on both sides. But the reporter was not entirely satisfied,
and he remarked, "There were evidently other reasons in the
mind of the Cardinal, of which he did not deem it prudent at the
moment to speak."[55]

There were, indeed, a number of subjects on which Gibbons
did not deem it prudent to speak during the course of the war,
and one of them was the issue of home rule for Ireland. He was
naturally interested in seeing the Irish people win their political
freedom, but he had been repelled by the periodic threats of
violence which had disrupted Irish life for several years preceding the outbreak of fighting on the continent. Late in March,
1914, he expressed himself rather forcefully when he said:

> To my mind, it appears that the Government is to blame for not
> taking the upper hand and restoring peace. It could do this if it went
> about it in the right way. There is only a small proportion of the
> population in Ireland engaged in the present uprising, and I cannot
> understand why the Government permits it to dictate what should be
> done and what should not be done.[56]

Some months later the cardinal visited Ireland on his way home
from Rome and he was favorably impressed by the conditions
he observed in Wexford where so many of the former tenants
were being transformed into landowners. But when questioned
about the agitation in Ulster, it was reported that he smilingly
replied, "As an outsider, it is quite evident that I cannot talk
of Ulster. . . ."[57] Three weeks thereafter Great Britain was at

---

and the history of the gift itself" (LC, Bryan Papers, Gibbons to Bryan, Baltimore,
December 24, 1914).

[55] New York *Times,* January 9, 1915.

[56] *Ibid.,* March 23, 1914.

[57] *Ibid.,* July 14, 1914. On June 14, 1950, the present writer spoke with Thomas
Canon O'Malley at Partry, Ireland, who told him that he met Gibbons on the
occasion of this final visit to Ireland at the Hollymount railroad station. In reply
to a question concerning his views on home rule, the cardinal was quoted as having

war with Germany, and in the crisis which ensued John E. Redmond, leader of the Irish Nationalist Party in the House of Commons, pledged the support of his followers to the crown. It was a gesture which delighted Gibbons and on the occasion of Redmond asking him to circulate a pastoral letter of Cardinal Mercier in the United States, the Cardinal of Baltimore told him of the gratification and admiration he felt for his speech. "Your words," he said, "were most timely and golden and have added immeasurably to the esteem in which you are held by right thinking men."[58]

But the pledge of loyalty given by Redmond did little to still the political storm in Ireland, and as the war went on matters remained critical. After the entry of the United States into the European conflict and President Wilson's statement of the ideals of democratic government which motivated American action, Redmond made an appeal to Gibbons for assistance in inducing Britain to put into immediate effect the principles laid down by Wilson for the self-government of small nations.[59] The cardinal communicated with Sir Cecil Spring Rice, British ambassador to Washington, and asked what he would suggest in response to this appeal.[60] At this point the evidence breaks down, since the ambassador put the case into the hands of Father Sigourney Fay, a convert priest who was Gibbons' agent in the matter, and Sir Eric Drummond and Mr. Cecil J. F. Dormer, two Catholic members of the British Commission to the United States.[61] The two Englishmen lunched with the cardinal some days later, but there was no evidence of what was said other than the press statement that they had discussed home rule for Ireland "informally."[62]

Meanwhile matters were growing more desperate in Ireland with the Sinn Féin being supplied with large funds from the United States, and Redmond's Nationalist Party being without the money necessary to fight an election campaign which might soon be upon them. He appealed, therefore, to Gibbons to help

---

replied, "What this country needs is a wider distribution of land and more temperance."

[58] 111-J, Gibbons to Redmond, Baltimore, February 17, 1915, copy. The letter was made public in London and cabled to the United States. Cf. New York *Times*, March 5, 1915.

[59] 115-H, Redmond to Gibbons, London, April 25, 1917, cablegram, *Confidential*.

[60] 115-H, Gibbons to Spring Rice, Baltimore, April 27, 1917, *Confidential*.

[61] 115-K, Spring Rice to Gibbons, Washington, April 29, 1917.

[62] New York *Times*, May 6, 1917.

them raise a sum of around £25,000 in the hope that they could then win the election and bring self-government to the Irish people, whereas a victory by the Sinn Féin would make a settlement with England impossible. The situation was so serious that Redmond felt it called for great sacrifices on the part of the lovers of Irish freedom in the United States. The time was, as he said, "perhaps, the most crucial moment in the fortunes of Ireland during the last half-century."[63]

The reply of Cardinal Gibbons to this appeal must have been very discouraging to the Irish leader. He said he regretted that he could not be of assistance in the manner suggested since, as he put it, "In all my years in public life I have never contributed any money towards a political fund and do not feel disposed to depart from this rule." Moreover, he had followed the custom of never asking others to do this, and if money was to be raised in the United States for the Irish election campaign, the Archdiocese of Baltimore was hardly the place to make a start since New York, Boston, Chicago, Philadelphia, and other cities had a far larger number of Irish and their descendants than Baltimore. He had gathered from recent reports that there was a feeling of discouragement over the prospects of home rule and a disposition to consider further efforts of little avail. "It is reasoned," said Gibbons, "that since Ireland has not received, in this crisis of the English Government, the Home Rule which she has been contending for, she has practically no hope for the future."[64] With this severe dash of cold water it was not surprising that no more should be heard of the subject as far as Gibbons was concerned.

However, a year later when he was asked by Ralph M. Easley, director of the League for National Unity, to sign a plea to the Irish people to refrain from withholding support to England in the war, he refused. He had his secretary reply that his position as a cardinal made the situation extremely delicate for him, and he would be reluctant to say any word that would have the appearance of entering upon the politics of Ireland. The problem was rendered more difficult because it would make it seem that he was at variance with the Irish hierarchy, who were opposed to the conscription campaign and whose knowledge of their country's

---

[63] 115-L, Redmond to Gibbons, London, May 2, 1917, *Confidential*.
[64] 115-N, Gibbons to Redmond, Baltimore, May 21, 1917, copy.

troubles was greater than those who lived thousands of miles away. "Taken in itself," it was said, "the plea would meet with no objection if it came just from the laymen composing the League."[65]

At the close of World War I Ireland's political peace was far from attained, and at a meeting of the American archbishops late in 1918 Gibbons was asked to inquire in their name of Cardinal Logue, Archbishop of Armagh, in what form the Irish hierarchy desired home rule. In compliance with the request, he asked Logue if their objective for Ireland was to remain under England's dominion with control of their internal affairs, or was it absolute independence. He then added, "If I might be permitted to express my own opinion, I prefer the first." But he assured the Irish cardinal that he had never given public expression to this view because of his high regard for the judgment of the Irish bishops, in whose decision he would abide.[66] In reply Logue stated that he believed he knew the views of the Irish hierarchy sufficiently well to speak for them. He thought the bishops and their people would be satisfied with, what he termed, *"complete control* of their internal affairs, including their finances. . . ." This, he believed, would restore peace to Ireland but nothing short of that would. True, some of the younger and more ardent spirits were holding out for complete independence, and they carried the people with them because the British government was playing fast and loose with the reasonable demands of Ireland. Nonetheless, said Logue, "I don't believe that absolute independence is practically attainable and I am not sure that it would be for our good if it were attained."[67]

Moderate demands such as these doubtless met with the entire approval of Gibbons. Two months later an Irish Race Convention held in Philadelphia on February 22–23, 1919, drew over 5,000 delegates from all parts of the country and more than twenty bishops were in attendance. The cardinal arrived for the second day, and it was he who put before the convention at its closing session the resolution demanding self-determination for Ireland, a resolution which was adopted by acclaim amid scenes of wild

---

[65] 117-S, Easley to Gibbons, New York, June 12, 1918; Eugene J. Connelly to Easley, Baltimore, June 14, 1918, copy.

[66] 119-T, Gibbons to Logue, Baltimore, December 7, 1918, copy.

[67] 119-W, Logue to Gibbons, Armagh, December 27, 1918.

enthusiasm. In presenting it Gibbons said, "The nations of the earth are clamoring for liberty. And why should not freedom-loving Ireland join in the general cry."[68] Yet Gibbons never put himself in the forefront of American movements for Ireland's freedom. He was first and always an American, and in the excitement which swept many American-Irish in these days he was never conspicuous. He was vigorously opposed to the violence which intermittently racked Ireland after 1914, and with the entry of the United States into the war on England's side three years later, he became even more sensitive on the subject lest any word or action of his might contribute to weakening the allied cause.

The war on the continent was not long in progress before the inevitable suffering it entailed brought appeals for relief of the victims. In the early winter of 1914 the cardinal received an urgent cablegram from Sir Gilbert Parker in behalf of the starving Belgians. "A word from Your Eminence to the American people," he said, "will touch the hearts and open pockets of thousands, who if they knew the terrible devastation and desolation of innocent Belgians, would for humanity's sake give freely."[69] Gibbons acted at once and $2,500 from the Archdiocese of Baltimore was turned over to the Maryland Committee for Belgian Relief.[70] In time the number and variety of appeals for help caused a slackening in the contributions for Belgium, and late in 1916 George Barr Baker, a member of the Commission for Relief in Belgium, made a trip to Rome and laid the plight of the Belgian children before Benedict XV. The Pope endorsed the plan for soliciting funds from the children of the world, said he

---

[68] Philadelphia *Public Ledger*, February 24, 1919. Gibbons was not the only American bishop of Irish descent who refrained from becoming too closely involved in the question. For example, Bishop Muldoon of Rockford who attended the Philadelphia convention, a few days later wrote in his diary under date of February 27, 1919: "Several times have I been asked during [the] past month to consider going to Paris on a committee to discuss the cause of Ireland. I have refused as I did not think it best for a Bp. to be on the committee" (Archives of the Diocese of Rockford). A summary of the role played by Gibbons in the preliminary arrangements for the Irish convention of February, 1919, in Philadelphia may be found in Patrick McCartan, *With De Valera in America* (New York, 1932), pp. 81–86.

[69] 110-S, Parker to Gibbons, Maastrict, Netherlands, December 1, 1914, cablegram.

[70] 110-S, Robert Garrett to Gibbons, Baltimore, December 3, 1914. Four days later a receipt was signed for Gibbons acknowledging $200 which he had given to the ambulance fund of the American Hospital in Paris. *Ibid.*

would write Gibbons requesting that he interest the American hierarchy in the project, and as an earnest of his intentions he would forward 10,000 lire to the Cardinal of Baltimore.[71]

As a consequence of the publicity given to the plan in the *Literary Digest* and other journals, Gibbons soon began to receive dozens of responses from men in all walks of American life. Among them Thomas J. Bensley, Rector of Christ Episcopal Church at Palmyra, New York, alluded to his Episcopalian faith, but said he and his people felt that this appeal of the children came to all irrespective of religious differences.[72] In about two weeks the contributions amounted to $5,000, and in thanking the cardinal for his check in this amount, the chairman of the commission stated he did not believe Gibbons could realize what high hopes were based on the letter of the Pope, and the enormous influence of the cardinal's endorsement of the work. He apologized for dwelling on these points but, as he said, "my excuse is that I know your high place in the public estimation, and can't resist the temptation to plead the children's cause, even when writing to thank you for your already generous work."[73]

The efforts of Cardinal Gibbons for relief of the victims of war were not, however, confined to the Belgians. When Harry Friedenwald, chairman of the American Jewish Relief Committee, appealed for the vast numbers of Jewish people who found themselves in dire straits, Gibbons assured him of his heartfelt sympathy for them and instructed his secretary to inform Friedenwald that he was confident the Catholic people of the United States would respond generously to this latest appeal to help their brethren who were enduring so much suffering.[74] Late in the war Benedict XV asked Gibbons to appeal to President Wilson to use his good offices for getting American Red Cross aid in to the starving Serbians. The cardinal laid the proposal before the President and was immediately assured that Wilson had given the matter a great deal of thought and he was sincerely

---

[71] "The Cry of the Belgian Children," *Literary Digest,* LIV (January 6, 1917), 22–23.

[72] 114-P, Bensley to Gibbons, Palmyra, January 8, 1917.

[73] 114-R, A. J. Hemphill to Gibbons, New York, January 19, 1917. For a copy of Benedict XV's letter of October 28, 1916, to Gibbons exhorting alms from the children of the United States for the starving Belgian children cf. Koenig, *op. cit.,* pp. 218–219.

[74] 113-C, Connelly to Friedenwald, Baltimore, January 21, 1916, copy.

anxious to help. The difficulties in the way were many, chiefly because it was found that the promises of the enemy powers to transmit and distribute relief could not be relied upon. "But you may be sure," said Wilson, "that if any way can be found, I shall be glad to find it."[75]

Before World War I was a year old the Germans resorted to submarine warfare with the consequence that American lives were lost in increasing numbers. Resentment naturally heightened and when the *Lusitania* was sunk off the Irish coast on May 7, 1915, with the loss of 128 American citizens the press rang with denunciations of the atrocity. Gibbons was asked for a statement, and after expressing sorrow for the families of the victims and prayers for divine guidance for the President, he urged Americans to be calm and prudent. "Popular sentiment," he said, "is not a standard to be followed too hastily."[76] But calmness was difficult to maintain on either side of the Atlantic during the spring and summer of that year. A week after the sinking of the *Lusitania,* the apostolic delegate communicated to Gibbons the fears of the papal Secretary of State that revolutionary disturbances in Italy were threatened and, therefore, the American College and its students should be placed under the official protection of the United States.[77] The cardinal got in touch immediately with Secretary Bryan who, in turn, cabled Ambassador Page at Rome to place the college under American protection if that should prove necessary. Page did not believe that there was serious danger of an outbreak; nonetheless, he had some time before informed the Rector of the American College that his students and all Americans in Rome "could under all circumstances count on all possible protection."[78] It was an assurance that met with the prompt and warm thanks of the cardinal and the apostolic delegate.[79]

The uneasiness of Cardinal Gasparri concerning the American

[75] LC, Wilson Papers, Gibbons to Wilson, Baltimore, December 19, 1917; 116-M, Wilson to Gibbons, Washington, December 20, 1917.

[76] New York *Times,* May 11, 1915.

[77] 111-V, Bonzano to Gibbons, Washington, May 14, 1915.

[78] 111-V, Gibbons to Bonzano, Baltimore, May 14, 1915, copy; William T. Russell to Gibbons, Washington, May 15, 1915; Bryan to Russell, Washington, May 15, 1915; same to same, Washington, May 17, 1915.

[79] 111-W, Bonzano to Gibbons, Washington, May 18, 1915; Gibbons to Bryan, Baltimore, May 19, 1915, copy; 111-XYZ, Gibbons to Bryan, Baltimore, May 28, 1915, copy.

College reflected the critical relations then existing between the Vatican and the Quirinal. During the previous December, Prince Bernhard von Bülow, former Chancellor of Germany, had paid a visit to Rome in what proved to be a futile effort to hold Italy in line with the Central Powers. During his stay he had an audience of Benedict XV which set off a series of quite unverified speculations in the press as to the role that the Pontiff was playing, and after Italy's indecision was finally resolved in a declaration of war on Austria-Hungary on May 23, they continued to be published. For example, on June 13 the New York *Times* reported from London that von Bülow had tried hard to influence the Pope in behalf of Germany but he had failed, and in summarizing the reasons it was said, "One of the most powerful agencies against German influence was that of the American Cardinals, especially Farley and Gibbons, who pointed out what a disastrous effect might be produced in America." It was only one of a number of such reports for which there was no substance in truth.

In most of these cases Gibbons sensibly followed the policy of ignoring them, but in the late summer of 1915 when a cable from the London *Morning Post* reported that he and Cardinal O'Connell of Boston were calling a conference of neutral cardinals and bishops in Switzerland with a view to launching an effort for peace, he felt he should not maintain silence. From Southampton where he was vacationing at the time, Gibbons issued a statement in which he said, "The dispatch in the morning papers in which my name is mentioned in connection with a projected conference of prelates to be held in Switzerland is without foundation."[80] The fact that a source close to the President, the Department of State, and Cardinal Farley all denied knowledge of the conference emphasized the seriousness with which the report was regarded. As a matter of fact, Gibbons and his coreligionists in the United States were generally speaking careful not to embarrass the administration by proposals of this nature, or by open espousals of one side or the other in the European war. In this connection one who investigated the opinions of ministers of religion in the United States at the time stated, "The Catholics before the days of April, 1917, were, in their pulpit utterances, loyal to the President, and refrained, appar-

---

[80] New York *Times*, August 14, 1915.

ently, from the type of criticism so prevalent among the Protestant churches."[81]

In spite of the instructions given by the German government to its submarine commanders to spare large passenger liners, one commander violated these instructions and on August 19, 1915, sank the *Arabic,* a British ship, with the loss of two American lives. Excitement again ran high and the danger of a diplomatic break between the United States and Germany was for some days real. In the new emergency Gasparri cabled Bonzano that he should request Gibbons to inform President Wilson that the Holy See had advised Germany to settle the question over the *Arabic* in a friendly manner and refrain from sinking similar ships in the future. It was stated that the Holy See had confidence that its advice would be followed by Berlin, and the cardinal was instructed to carry out his mission in a strictly confidential way.[82] Four days later Gibbons called at the White House and read Wilson the Pope's dispatch, with which the President expressed pleasure and requested the cardinal to convey his thanks to Benedict XV. Wilson had no objections to the publication of the document, but he left that decision to the discretion of the papal authorities. Gibbons took occasion to praise the President's efforts to maintain peace, and he stated that after reading the New York papers on the *Arabic* case he felt Wilson had great provocation to assume a warlike attitude, to which the chief executive replied that he did not read papers. Secretary of State Lansing also had words of praise for the Pope's dispatch and told Gibbons that it probably had much influence in the amicable decision which the German government had made in the matter.[83]

The decision to which Lansing referred had reached the Department of State the day previous to Gibbons' visit when Count Johann H. von Bernstorff, German ambassador to Washington, had assured Lansing that warning to ships and safety provisions for noncombatants would be given in case of future submarine shelling of passenger vessels. The purpose of the cardinal's visit to Washington, then, had to do with the Holy See's efforts to bring a peaceful settlement to the situation growing out of the

---

[81] Ray H. Abrams, *Preachers Present Arms* (Philadelphia, 1933), p. 32.

[82] 112-F, Bonzano to Gibbons, Washington, August 29, 1915.

[83] LC, Wilson Papers, Notes made on interview of Gibbons with Wilson, Washington, September 2, 1915. Cf. also 112-G, memorandum of Gibbons of his interview with the President.

sinking of the *Arabic;* but once more the press went astray and reported that Gibbons had carried a message from the Pope asking the President to tender his good offices in some form to the belligerents to bring about an armistice. The cardinal refused to disclose the purpose of his visit, other than to acknowledge that he had brought a message from Benedict XV to Wilson and that it had an "indirect bearing" on peace between the warring nations. In spite of the care with which Gibbons chose his words, the Baltimore *Sun* for September 3 and the New York *Times* and other papers for several days thereafter continued to speculate on the possibilities of an armistice through the concerted action of the Vatican and the White House. The *Sun* supplied its readers with a reason why Wilson would have to initiate the negotiations since, as it said, Gibbons was understood to have told Lansing, "The Vatican is handicapped by its isolation through Italy's participation in the war." Any hope the cardinal might have entertained to clear up the confusion by publishing the Pope's message on the *Arabic* case, was dashed when he received a cablegram instruction through Bonzano that the Holy See held it inopportune at the present to make public anything regarding Gibbons' visit to the White House.[84]

It was only natural that the increasingly grave character of the European conflict, and the growing danger of involvement by the United States, should have touched off a variety of plans and schemes for averting the menace to American peace. With some of these ideas Cardinal Gibbons had genuine sympathy; from others he withheld his support. For example, in the days before Henry Ford's ill-starred peace ship sailed for Scandinavia in the hope of bringing about an armistice through the neutral nations, Gibbons was quoted as seeing no hope in Ford's scheme and refusing to sanction it.[85] And although the cardinal was certainly desirous of his country remaining clear of the war, it was not at the cost of adopting the principles of pacifism. A petition against the preparedness campaign of Wilson was circulated by the Reverend Frederick Lynch, secretary of the Church Peace Union, and a copy was sent to Gibbons. In declining to give his signature he made it known that, although he was always a peace-loving man, he would take no step that might embarrass the

---

84 AAB, unclassified, Bonzano to Gibbons, Washington, September 7, 1915.
85 New York *Times,* November 25, 1915.

President in what he called, "his conscientious efforts to make reasonably secure the honor of our country. . . ."[86]

But patriotic as he was the cardinal would not compromise his religious faith to demonstrate that patriotism. An effort to win his endorsement for a statement entitled "The American," which was being circulated by Howard Knight of Livermore & Knight Company, failed due to its closing sentence which read, "He counts politics, creeds, ancestry, as nothing beside the great fact — HE IS AN AMERICAN." Gibbons instructed his secretary to inform Knight that the Catholic creed summarized religious truths which Catholics held most dear, nor did those truths interfere with loyalty to country any more than loyalty to country interfered with religion. "For these reasons," it was stated, "he feels that we cannot count our creed as nothing beside the great fact that we are Americans."[87] But the League to Enforce Peace which had been organized in June, 1915, with William Howard Taft as its president, was a group to which the cardinal could give wholehearted approval. The platform of the league advocated arbitration of disputes between nations, but it left room for a nation to resort to war if that proved necessary. Therefore, when Taft invited Gibbons to be present at the league's meeting in Washington in May, 1916, he regretted that previous engagements would keep him away, but he sent a letter of approval in which he said, "The plan is a sane one for it does not make the mistake of disregarding the fact that human nature in the future will be very much the same as today and yesterday."[88]

With the acceleration of Wilson's preparedness campaign in the spring of 1916 the problem of the war came before the American archbishops for the first time at their annual meeting

[86] 113-D, Connelly to Lynch, Baltimore, February 6, 1916, copy. The opinion of Gibbons on this question was shared by his fellow bishops and priests of the Catholic Church. In a survey made on pacifist ministers of religion in the United States during 1917–1918 Abrams could find no Catholic clergymen to list. His somewhat wry comment was, "The Catholics, with a discipline of obedience, give no room for non-conformity" (*op. cit.,* p. 197).

[87] 113-K, Knight to Gibbons, Providence, Rhode Island, May 4, 1916; 113-L, Connelly to Knight, Baltimore, May 7, 1916, copy.

[88] LC, Taft Papers, Gibbons to Taft, Baltimore, May 6, 1916. At the same time Gibbons instructed the Vice-Rector of the Catholic University of America to hold himself in readiness to be present at the meeting on May 26–27 to read his letter before the league members (ACUA, Pace Papers, Connelly to Pace, Baltimore, May 7, 1916).

over which Gibbons presided on May 3. At that time Father
Lewis J. O'Hern, C.S.P., who had been designated by the hierarchy to take charge of matters concerning the armed forces,
submitted a report in which he stated the need for more chaplains
and the difficulty he was experiencing in finding them. As a
result of O'Hern's appeal, the metropolitans passed a motion to
communicate with their suffragans and to take steps to increase
the number of priests who might serve with the expanding army
and navy personnel.[89]

Meanwhile, despite the assurances given by the German government that it would employ precautions in submarine warfare,
allied vessels carrying American passengers continued to be
sunk. The torpedoing of an unarmed French ship, the *Sussex,*
on March 24, 1916, with injury to several Americans occasioned
a new crisis between Berlin and Washington. On April 18 Lansing
dispatched a note in which he threatened the rupture of diplomatic relations unless the Germans immediately declared an
abandonment of their present methods of submarine warfare.
Once more the Holy Father communicated with Wilson and
Emperor William II in an effort to effect a settlement. He asked
the President to suspend his decision on the question, since he
saw the possibility of a peaceful solution and hoped that no
American incident would embarrass his effort.[90] After the passage
of a week without a reply Gibbons informed the President that
he had received a cable from Benedict XV asking him to inquire
concerning an answer.[91] Three days later Wilson forwarded a
copy of his reply to the Pope which had been sent through
Archbishop Bonzano, the apostolic delegate.[92] Actually the effort

---

[89] 113-K, Minutes of the Meeting of the Archbishops, Washington, May 3, 1916.
A year later Gibbons informed O'Hern that in addition to his appointment as
official representative of the hierarchy for matters pertaining to chaplains, the
archbishops had now designated him as their official representative on the national
committee for safeguarding the morals of the soldiers, the providing of halls for
religious services, and all similar matters calling for relations with the government
(115-N, Gibbons to O'Hern, Baltimore, May 19, 1917, copy).

[90] Benedict XV to Wilson, n.d., enclosed in Wilson to Lansing, Washington, May
15, 1916, asking for Lansing's suggestion "as to the manner and substance of my
reply." *Papers Relating to the Foreign Relations of the United States. The Lansing
Papers* (Washington, 1939), I, 15.

[91] LC, Wilson Papers, Gibbons to Wilson, Baltimore, May 12, 1916.

[92] 113-K, Wilson to Gibbons, Washington, May 15, 1916. In thanking Gibbons
for his action in the matter, Bonzano explained that he had immediately sent
Wilson's answer to the Pope by ciphered cablegram without being obliged, as he

The cardinal in 1916 at the age of eighty-two.

(Courtesy of the Most Reverend John M. McNamara)

of the Holy See had come too late to be of any assistance, for on May 4 the German government acceded to the American demands in a manner which Wilson accepted. The President expressed his appreciation to Benedict XV for the friendly sentiments that had prompted his cable and he stated, "I am gratified to say that before the receipt of your message the discussion had already entered upon a stage of satisfactory understanding."[93]

There were few periods in the long life of Cardinal Gibbons in which the extraordinary qualities of leadership which he possessed showed to better advantage than during the years of World War I. In the steadily deepening crisis which enveloped the country, his voice was listened to with a respect accorded to few if any Americans outside official circles of the government. By the summer of 1916 he had reached his eighty-second birthday and the thirtieth anniversary of his appointment as a member of the College of Cardinals. Long before this Americans of every creed and walk of life had come to admire his wisdom, his patriotism, and his moral leadership. It was not, therefore, an exaggeration when the Baltimore *Sun* of June 8, 1916, hailed Gibbons on the anniversary of his cardinalate in an enthusiastic editorial called "A Great American." The *Sun* said at that time:

> There are other Catholics in this continent, but there is only one Cardinal Gibbons; the Catholic Church has given many distinguished prelates and priests to its work in this country, but none who has inspired the same general confidence and the same earnest esteem. . . . We doubt whether anywhere in the world-wide territory in which his church has raised the cross there can be found any other Cardinal or any other priest who touches humanity at so many points, who exercises such an influence among persons of every class and condition, believers and unbelievers, Catholics and Protestants, Jews and

put it, "to expose the original of the President to the danger of being opened by transmitting it through the mails" (113-B, Bonzano to Gibbons, Washington, May 22, 1916).

[93] *Foreign Relations. . . . Lansing Papers,* I, 16, containing Lansing's undated draft of Wilson's answer to Benedict XV. Gibbons' letter of May 12 was delivered by Monsignor Russell to Tumulty, the President's secretary. Russell saw Lansing beforehand and indicated that there was "some feeling" on the part of the cardinal that no reply had yet been made to the Pope, since Wilson had said he would answer on May 8. Lansing apparently wished the reply to go through Gibbons rather than Bonzano, since he told the President, "I have also drafted a reply to Cardinal Gibbons which provides for the transmission of your answer to the Pope's communication through him" (LC, Wilson Papers, Lansing to Wilson, Washington, May 15, 1916, *Personal and confidential*).

Gentiles. To all he seems to speak in their own tongues by some Pentecostal power, or by some subtle affinity that makes nothing human foreign to him. . . .

This was strong language, tinged no doubt by the pride of Baltimore for its most distinguished citizen, but there were thousands of Americans all over the land who subscribed to it. By the close of that year Gibbons had become the senior bishop of the Catholic world, a fact brought to light by the recent consistory at Rome and made known to its readers by the New York *Times* on December 13. But the reason for the deference shown to him was not because of age, but rather that the public had been won by the gentle and kindly manner, the sound judgment, and the expansive affection with which he seemed to embrace all his fellow citizens. Surely there were others in the American Church at the time who were more effective public orators, as an incident during the summer of 1916 was to prove. Prompted by the rising tide of anti-Catholic feeling represented in the *Menace* and the resuscitated Ku Klux Klan, there was held a series of meetings in New York in observance of Catholic Week. At the great gathering in Madison Square Garden on August 20 which drew the three American cardinals and an audience of around 20,000, Cardinal O'Connell delivered a powerful address on the complete religious liberty owing to Catholics in the face of the current bigotry, a claim which he based on American democratic principles and the record which Catholics had shown for loyalty to their country in all its wars. It was said that seldom had a New York audience been more affected and, as it was expressed, "Time and again Cardinal Gibbons's thin hand, stretched out over the people, had stilled their tumult in an instant. This time even his quiet authority was powerless."[94] It was apparent that O'Connell was the hero of the evening, and that the simple speech of Baltimore's cardinal was no match for the majestic eloquence of the Cardinal of Boston. But in the realm of public relations, Gibbons found no serious rival among the American bishops of his day.

A year later the war with Germany recalled to memory Gib-

---

[94] New York *Times,* August 21, 1916. The anxiety felt by the archbishops over the anti-Catholic movement at the time was clearly reflected in their meeting in the spring of that year. Cf. 113-K, Minutes of the Meeting of the Archbishops, Washington, May 3, 1916.

bons' stand against the efforts of some of the German Catholic
extremists thirty years before. On Sunday, June 3, the New York
Times Magazine carried a feature article entitled "How Cardinal Gibbons Fought Pan Germans." The article rehearsed the
cardinal's opposition to the efforts of Cahensly and his followers
for separate bishops, parishes, and language schools, and it was
stated that the war had brought into strong relief the real proportions of what, perhaps, was to be "the chief public service
performed by Cardinal Gibbons — his long fight for 'Americanism' in the organization of the Catholic Church in this country."
The movement against which Gibbons fought was described at
some length, together with the threat it would then have constituted had it won its goal. It was stated that many who recalled
the struggle of the 1880's and 1890's did not hesitate to say that
it was due to Gibbons, "more than to any other man that the
United States is going to war with so great a degree of solidarity
against the Government of one of the great peoples from which
the American Nation has sprung. . . ."[95]

Yet the prestige which the cardinal enjoyed was not due to
the fact that he always espoused popular causes. On the contrary, he sometimes gave his public support to measures with
which numerous Americans were in disagreement. For example,
in the summer of 1916 he favored the movement for universal
military service, for which he earned the prompt gratitude of
ex-President Roosevelt who stated that he wished as an American
to thank him most cordially for what he had said.[96] Gibbons'
reasons, contained in a letter to H. H. Sheets, secretary of the
Association for National Service, and by him made public, were
that discipline such as the young men would receive would help
to develop their character and improve their physical condition,
as well as to instill into them the idea of obedience to lawful
authority. Alluding to the President's preparedness campaign, the
cardinal said he was persuaded that such military preparation
would make for peace rather than for war. Any nation thinking

---

[95] The copy of a letter Gibbons wrote to Allen Sinclair Will, his biographer,
from Deal Beach, New Jersey, on October 29, 1918, proved that Will was the
author of the unsigned article (119-K). Will was on the staff of the New York
Times at this time.
[96] 113-T, Roosevelt to Gibbons, New York, August 11, 1916.

of an attack would be deterred, he said, "by recognition of the fact that our country is prepared for every emergency."[97]

But if Gibbons believed in a modified militarism to meet the present emergency, he had by no means abandoned his hope for an armistice in the European war. When President Wilson on December 18, 1916, sent identical notes to the belligerents asking them to state specifically what they were fighting for in the belief that it might possibly lead to an armistice, the cardinal was overjoyed. He declined to give an extended statement to the press, but he did say that he thought Wilson's action increased the hope of peace, for the President would not have moved had he not possessed information that led him to believe that good might come from it. The German peace proposal of a few days before, the reply of Prime Minister David Lloyd George — all encouraged Gibbons, and he was quoted as saying, "The prospect for peace is bright."[98] But the cardinal's enthusiasm was not shared by his friend, Archbishop Ireland, who told him he feared the appeal for a European armistice would not produce the desired result. "The war will be fought out," said Ireland with more accurate prophecy, "until the victories of the Marne & Verdun shall have swept their way beyond the banks of the Rhine."[99]

---

[97] New York *Times,* October 8, 1916. Sheets thanked Gibbons for what he had written and said that he believed his letter would be of much value "to help mold public opinion favorable to a system of Training, and awaken a consciousness of the need of the spirit of service among our people" (113-W, Sheets to Gibbons, Washington, October 11, 1916).

[98] New York *Times,* December 22, 1916. Benedict XV congratulated Wilson on his note to the belligerents, and the Spanish ambassador to Washington, Don Juan Riaño y Dayangos, said he had been told to convey the message personally to the President (LC, Wilson Papers, William Phillips to Tumulty, Washington, December 27, 1916).

[99] 114-L, Ireland to Gibbons, St. Paul, December 28, 1916. Several weeks later Albert W. Dennis, one of the editors of the *Massachusetts Magazine,* told Wilson he was writing a book in which he wished to make reference to the high personal character of Cardinal Gibbons, and he thought Wilson had some time before paid public tribute to the cardinal. He now asked if the statement could not be sent to him (LC, Wilson Papers, Dennis to Wilson, Salem, Massachusetts, January 18, 1917). Wilson attached a memorandum to the letter to Tumulty and requested him to reply. In it Wilson said, "Please explain to Mr. Dennis how extremely invidious it would be for me to attempt things of this sort. I have a real admiration for Cardinal Gibbons, but I do not remember anywhere expressing that admiration in public" (*ibid.,* Wilson to Tumulty, Washington, January 24, 1917).

Regardless of the prospects at Christmas of 1916 there was no real hope for peace, and with the German announcement of unrestricted submarine warfare early in the new year the United States severed diplomatic relations on February 3. Several American ships were sunk during the succeeding weeks, and on April 2 the President delivered his war message to the senate and four days later war was declared on Germany. The conflict that Wilson had striven so hard to avoid was now upon the country, and Cardinal Gibbons rose to the occasion. In a prepared statement for the press, written, it was said, in response to requests that had reached him from distinguished statesmen in Washington and others, the cardinal made known his views in the following words:

> In the present emergency it behooves every American citizen to do his duty, and to uphold the hands of the President and the Legislative department in the solemn obligations that confront us.
>
> The primary duty of a citizen is loyalty to country. This loyalty is manifested more by acts than by words; by solemn service rather than by empty declaration. It is exhibited by an absolute and unreserved obedience to his country's call.
>
> Both Houses of Congress with the Executive are charged and sworn to frame those laws that are demanded by the present crisis. Whatever, therefore, Congress may decide should be unequivocally complied with by every patriotic citizen. The members of both Houses of Congress are the instruments of God in guiding us in our civic duties. It behooves all of us, therefore, to pray that the Lord of Hosts may inspire our national legislature and Executive to frame such laws in the present crisis as will redound to the glory of our country, to righteousness of conduct and to the permanent peace of the nations of the world.[100]

The cardinal's statement was widely publicized and elicited favorable comment from many quarters. Senator Joseph E. Ransdell felt it had made a forcible contribution to the cause of patriotism, and he sincerely hoped, as he said, "that all our Bishops and Archbishops throughout the country will follow your example in this respect."[101] Theodore Roosevelt wired from Oyster Bay, "With all my heart I thank you as an American for your noble and patriotic appeal."[102] Ten days later Gibbons

---

[100] 115-E, Gibbons' statement on the outbreak of war, April 5, 1917, copy.

[101] 115-E, Ransdell to Gibbons, Washington, April 6, 1917.

[102] 115-E, Roosevelt to Gibbons, Oyster Bay, New York, April 7, 1917, telegram.

made known to Francis Cardinal Bourne, Archbishop of Westminster, the aims that had motivated the entry of his country into the European conflict, and he said the United States was happy, therefore, to unite with Great Britain and every other nation to insure the loyal acceptance by governments of the world of what he called, "those principles of peace and justice which are the sole guarantees of the permanence of our Christian civilization."[103]

In the altered circumstances which now confronted the American Catholics along with their fellow citizens, it became necessary for the authorities of the Church to offer leadership to their people in the war effort. The archbishops of the United States assembled at Washington on April 18 under the presidency of Gibbons where they drafted a statement to the President assuring him of the support and loyalty of Catholic citizens in the tasks that lay before him.[104] Cardinal Gibbons communicated the message to Wilson on the following day and it was likewise released to the press.[105] A week later the chief executive begged pardon for the delay in acknowledging the message due to the pressure of official duties, but he wished Gibbons and his colleagues to know his gratitude for what he termed "the very remarkable resolutions" of the archbishops. Their statement, he continued, "warms my heart and makes me very proud indeed that men of such large influence should act in so large a sense of patriotism and so admirable a spirit of devotion to our common country."[106] At the same meeting that drew up the resolutions to Wilson, the archbishops moved to hasten action on the part of the entire hierarchy in nominating priests to fill the quota of Catholic chaplains in the armed services, and a committee was likewise appointed to investigate the question of exemption of priests and seminarians from the draft.[107]

As the war progressed Gibbons was as good as his word about

---

[103] 115-F, Gibbons to Bourne, Baltimore, April 15, 1917, copy.

[104] 115-G, Minutes of the Meeting of the Archbishops, Washington, April 18, 1917.

[105] 115-G, Gibbons to Wilson, Baltimore, April 19, 1917, copy.

[106] 115-J, Wilson to Gibbons, Washington, April 27, 1917.

[107] 115-G, Minutes of the Meeting of the Archbishops, Washington, April 18, 1917. Archbishop Glennon of St. Louis reported to Gibbons three days later that through the courtesy of Senator James A. Reed of Missouri a special meeting of the senate committee had been held and they had agreed to an insertion among the exemptions covering priests and seminarians (115-G, Glennon to Gibbons, St. Louis, April 21, 1917).

the need for implementing one's loyalty to country. Late in May, 1917, he directed a pastoral letter to the priests and people of the Archdiocese of Baltimore in which he urged that they subscribe to the liberty loan drive. "The seriousness of the situation cannot be overestimated," said the cardinal. "It is something of personal interest coming home to each one of us. Let it not be said that we were weighed in the balance of patriotism and found wanting."[108] William G. McAdoo, Secretary of the Treasury, was naturally gratified with what he termed "your admirable statement," and he hoped the cardinal's patriotic example would be followed by all the hierarchy.[109] Late in the same month Henry P. Davidson, chairman of the American Red Cross War Council, visited Gibbons at Baltimore to elicit his support for their work, and the cardinal's strong endorsement of the Red Cross was later given to the press and brought the warm thanks of Davidson.[110] Herbert C. Hoover also came to Baltimore the same week and won Gibbons' assistance for the food conservation drive, with the exception that he was opposed to the "bone dry" amendment in the food administration bill.[111]

A few days after Hoover's visit the cardinal addressed a pastoral letter to his people, in which he confidently called on them to give the fullest co-operation to the government in its laudable endeavors to conserve the food resources of the country.[112] Yet the cardinal's desire to be of help to the government officials in the war did not cause him to overlook what he regarded as the Church's best interests. In June, 1916, Newton D. Baker, Secretary of War, had given his approval to the distribution of army chaplaincies on the basis of the strength of the various denominations. However, a year later this decision was reversed in favor of the old basis of allotting to the Catholics 16/67 of the total. When this news reached Gibbons he informed Baker of his disappointment, stated that Catholics had not been given

---

[108] Baltimore *Catholic Review,* June 2, 1917.

[109] 115-Q, McAdoo to Gibbons, Washington, June 2, 1917. In reply Gibbons hoped his letter would have a wider reaching effect in awakening patriotism, to which he added, "I could not have done less than I did" (115-Q, Gibbons to McAdoo, Baltimore, June 5, 1917, copy).

[110] 115-S, Davidson to Gibbons, Washington, June 19, 1917. Cf. New York *Times,* June 20, 1917.

[111] New York *Times,* June 26, 1917.

[112] 115-T, Gibbons' pastoral letter on food conservation, Baltimore, June 26, 1917, copy.

their just proportion, and alluded to the unfortunate timing of this decision when Catholics were manifesting so fine a spirit of loyalty. The cardinal concluded by saying he was convinced there would be a heartier response to every sacrifice demanded of American Catholic boys, if they felt that their government was doing its utmost to furnish them the spiritual and moral helps they needed in the camp and in the field.[113] Baker meanwhile conferred with Father O'Hern who was in charge of chaplaincies for the bishops, and he presumed O'Hern had informed the cardinal of the latest order on chaplain distributions. "It does not do all that Father O'Hern thought justice under the circumstances," said Baker, "but it does make a substantial approach even to what he felt abstractedly just. . . ."[114]

But the preoccupation of Cardinal Gibbons with matters directly relating to the government did not cause him to lose sight of the war efforts of private Catholic groups. He took time to write his congratulations to the Knights of Columbus for the plans they had launched in aid of the servicemen, and in acknowledging the cardinal's good wishes Supreme Knight James A. Flaherty said they would be a stimulant to push their work with ardor and earnestness.[115] Later in the summer of 1917 the cardinal fully endorsed the meeting which was held on August 11–12 at the Catholic University of America under the chairmanship of John J. Burke, C.S.P., of the Chaplains' Aid Association of New York, and which had been called with a view to organizing Catholic war efforts on a more unified scale. Father Burke was in close touch with Cardinal Farley in the succeeding months on the business in hand, and he likewise consulted frequently with the Cardinal of Baltimore.[116] In November Gibbons addressed a letter to the American hierarchy, in which he explained that an informal discussion had taken place on the occasion of the recent meeting of the trustees of the university concerning the need of a more permanent organization to supervise Catholic interests in the war. He outlined the many aspects of the work wherein unity was needed and asked the bishops

---

[113] 115-S, Gibbons to Baker, Baltimore, June 15, 1917, copy.

[114] 115-T, Baker to Gibbons, Washington, June 23, 1917.

[115] 115-T, Flaherty to Gibbons, New Haven, June 23, 1917.

[116] The genesis and development of this movement are described in the popular work of Michael Williams, *American Catholics in the War* (New York, 1921), pp. 88–153. The definitive history of the N.C.W.C. remains to be written.

if they would consent to the formation of the National Catholic War Council by the metropolitans.[117]

The response to Gibbons' appeal was generally favorable, and some weeks later the cardinal invited four bishops to act as an administrative committee for the archbishops in this work. Those selected were Peter J. Muldoon of Rockford, Joseph Schrembs of Toledo, William T. Russell of Charleston, and Patrick J. Hayes, Auxiliary Bishop of New York.[118] After having won the consent of the four prelates to serve, Gibbons outlined for them on January 12, 1918, the authority they possessed, the aims they should keep before them, and the various groups within the American Catholic body whose assistance they should enlist. "Your task," he said, "will be to direct and control with the aid of the ordinaries, all Catholic activities in the war."[119] Four days later the administrative committee of the National Catholic War Council met at the Catholic University of America with Bishop Muldoon as chairman and John F. Fenlon, S.S., as secretary, and from that time to the close of the war the numerous and difficult problems which beset it were canvassed at regular intervals with Cardinal Gibbons and the other archbishops of the country.

As the embattled peoples of the world neared the end of the third year of fighting the sentiment for peace ran fairly high in all countries. This was true not only in Europe, where a feeling of exhaustion was widespread, but even in the United States there was a growing weariness with the struggle. It was shortly after the failure of the Austrian peace proposals carried on through Prince Sixtus of Bourbon that Pope Benedict XV made his famous attempt to end the war. After informal soundings in Berlin and the allied capitals he addressed a note on August 1, 1917, to all the belligerents. The Pontiff proposed a definite set of points on which peace might be made which included disarmament, arbitration of disputes, freedom of the seas, evacua-

---

[117] AAC, Gibbons to Moeller, Baltimore, November 21, 1917. For a printed copy of Gibbons' letter to the hierarchy cf. Williams, *op. cit.*, pp. 144–146.

[118] Williams, *op. cit.*, pp. 146–148, for Gibbons' letter of December 18, 1917, to Muldoon.

[119] *Ibid.*, p. 149. Gibbons' letter of January 12, 1918, to the four bishops is published on pp. 148–152. On January 16, 1918, Muldoon confided to his diary: "The committee of Bps. is a most agreeable and delightful one" (Archives of the Diocese of Rockford).

tion and restoration of occupied territories, renunciation of indemnities, and the conciliatory examination of conflicting claims such as those relating to Alsace-Lorraine and the Trentino.[120] At the time that the papal note was made known Cardinal Gibbons was on holiday at Deal Beach, New Jersey. Father Fenlon, President of Divinity College at the Catholic University of America and a close friend of the cardinal's, at once strongly urged Gibbons to speak out in favor of an acceptance of Benedict's proposals. Fenlon reflected the sentiment of those Americans who wished to end the war, and it was his belief that the people were now in need of a leader to voice their desires and, he said, "your voice for the initiation of peace negotiations would have a greater effect than the voice of any American except the President."[121] The apostolic delegate, too, communicated a summary of the papal note to Gibbons with the purpose, as he said, that the cardinal might endeavor with his usual tact and prudence to exert his influence toward favorably disposing the government of the United States to the papal program.[122]

It was apparent, therefore, that the Cardinal of Baltimore was expected to put the peace note of the Pope before the government and the public in the best possible light. He sensibly refrained, however, from an extended statement until he had seen the text, although he told the press that every rational citizen would acknowledge that the Pontiff was actuated by the loftiest motives, and for that reason his suggestions deserved to be received with the attention due to any document emanating from so august a source. Gibbons had no doubt that the government of the United States would give to them the respectful consideration which they deserved.[123] Meanwhile he assured Bonzano that he would do everything in his power to further the wishes of the Holy See in the matter, and he would use to the utmost whatever influence he might possess to induce the government and the public toward a favorable consideration of the Pope's note.[124] After Gibbons had read the text and taken some measure of public opinion on the question, he issued a fuller

---

[120] For the English text of Benedict XV's note, *Dès le début,* cf. Koenig, *op. cit.,* pp. 229–232.

[121] 115-W, Fenlon to Gibbons, Washington, August 14, 1917.

[122] 115-W, Bonzano to Gibbons, Washington, August 15, 1917.

[123] New York *Times,* August 16, 1917.

[124] 115-W, Gibbons to Bonzano, Deal Beach, New Jersey, August 17, 1917, copy.

statement in which he commented on the individual points raised by Benedict XV and sought to meet the principal criticism leveled against the papal proposals, namely, that they favored Germany. "If anybody calls this a pro-German document they must use words without meaning," he said, "for they include the destruction of Germany's military power, and subjection of her in future to a board of arbitration which would be able to coerce her if she tried to evade her obligations. . . ." He granted that the Pope's effort might be called noble idealism which might or might not be realizable in fact, but the cardinal thought the principles laid down by the Pontiff offered the only solution to the permanent peace of the world.[125]

In the meantime Benedict XV's note was being considered in Washington. After consulting with Secretary Lansing and others the President at length forwarded his reply on August 27. He praised the motives which had prompted the papal message, but as to the methods suggested for ending the war, the President was not in agreement. "Our response," said Wilson, "must be based upon the stern facts and upon nothing else." Benedict XV's desire for the *status quo ante bellum* to be effected on the principles enunciated in his note would, in Wilson's view, involve a recuperation of Germany's strength and a renewal of its policy. No faith could be placed in the present German government, and for that reason its word must be accompanied by conclusive evidence of the will and purpose of the German people themselves.[126] Although the President's reply represented an under-

---

[125] 115-W, Gibbons' statement to the press on Benedict XV's peace note, August, 1917. The American press was in general unfriendly toward any serious acceptance by the United States of the Pope's proposals. Cf. the New York *Times,* Philadelphia *Inquirer,* and Washington *Post,* all for August 15, and the Chicago *Tribune* and Boston *Evening Transcript,* August 17, 1917.

[126] *Papers Relating to the Foreign Relations of the United States 1917,* Supplement 2 (Washington, 1932), I, 177–179. Between August 13–27 the President was guided principally by Colonel Edward M. House in drafting his reply to Benedict XV, although Secretary Lansing, several of the allied ambassadors, and a group of United States senators were likewise consulted directly or indirectly. It was evident that Wilson was less inclined to be conciliatory toward the Pope's proposals than House was (LC, Wilson Papers, House to Wilson, Magnolia, Massachusetts, August 15, 1917, and Wilson to House, Washington, August 16, 1917, copy. Cf. also Charles Seymour's chapter, "The Pope's Peace Proposal," *The Intimate Papers of Colonel House* ([Boston, 1928], III, 149–173). Lansing sent the President's reply by cable to Walter Hines Page, American ambassador in London, who was instructed to give it to the Pontiff "for the President, as there is no papal legate accredited to the United States" (Lansing to Page, Washington, August 27,

standable point of view, it made any working arrangement on the basis of the Pope's proposals impossible. It was an instance wherein Gibbons' indirect influence proved of no avail, although there was no evidence of any direct approach on his part to the White House. The allied governments were determined to abolish the German imperial government before they would end the war, and thus the well-intentioned effort of Benedict XV came to naught.

Yet Gibbons' failure to win more favorable consideration for the papal peace note in no way deterred him from continuing his war efforts. In the autumn of 1917 he agreed to make a public announcement in favor of military training for youths of nineteen and twenty after the war, and in expressing his gratitude for this latest contribution of the cardinal to the training program, the secretary of the National Association for Universal Military Training told him that his war work, as well as that of Archbishop Ireland, the Knights of Columbus, and the Catholic sisterhoods was setting what he called "a magnificent example of patriotism, unity, and national solidarity" which he trusted would be followed by all other organizations within the country.[127] The growing antiwar feeling mentioned previously led in October, 1917, to' the organization by a group of nationally known citizens of the League of National Unity of which the cardinal was made honorary chairman. It was intended that

1917, cable, *ibid.,* I, 177). Lansing cabled the American diplomatic representatives in allied countries on August 18 to find out the opinion of the governments to which they were accredited on the papal peace note since this information was desired by the President. For the replies cf. *ibid.,* I, 165 ff. Fifteen years later Jules Jusserand, who was French ambassador to Washington in 1917, in speaking of Wilson's reactions to the Pope's peace note, stated in a letter to the editor of the *American Historical Review,* "The President plainly showed me his ill-humor at Benedict's wanting to 'butt in' (his own words)" (XXXVII [July, 1932], 818). Article 15 of the secret Treaty of London of April 26, 1915, barring the Pope from the peace negotiations, apparently disabled the signatories of that treaty from replying to Benedict XV's note of August 1, 1917, since Britain and France sent no answers. Cf. H. W. V. Temperley (Ed.), *A History of the Peace Conference of Paris* (London, 1921), IV, 291. Among the allied and associate powers besides Wilson only Belgium and Brazil sent a reply. "The reception of the Pope's overtures by the Entente had indeed been frigid in the extreme" (Humphrey Johnson, *Vatican Diplomacy in the World War* [Oxford, 1933], p. 34). Austria's reply was conciliating, and even Turkey and Bulgaria answered the papal note, which led Johnson to remark that in general the Quadruple Alliance "Shewed a punctilious correctness in its relations with the Holy See, which was lacking in the opposing camp." (*Ibid.,* p. 33.)

[127] 116-A, Sheets to Gibbons, Washington, October 3, 1917.

through this medium Americans of all creeds, classes, and occupations could be aroused to the need for prosecuting the war to a successful finish. In this connection Gibbons told the President:

> We are working to the end that our countrymen may see the folly and grave disobedience of unjust and ill-tempered criticism of national policies. We are bending our efforts to point out to our fellowmen that they in all probability see the present situation from only one angle, whereas the Government sees it from every viewpoint, and is therefore alone in the position to judge of the expediency of national affairs.[128]

For obvious reasons Wilson felt grateful and said that Gibbons' letter had brought him cheer and reassurance. He wanted the cardinal to know, moreover, that he appreciated his consenting to preside over the important and influential group of men and women who composed the league, and who had so generously undertaken to support the administration in its efforts to make the character and purpose of the war clear to the American people.[129]

The designation by President Wilson of Sunday, October 28, as a day of prayer for the success of American arms was, of course, the sort of thing which met with the warm response of Gibbons. He preached on the occasion in his cathedral, and he took the opportunity to insist upon the paramount duty of obedience on the part of citizens to their government, and the caution they should exercise in criticizing its policies in wartime. The cardinal had no doubts about the endurance of the Republic; it had come through storms before and it would triumph over the storms that then assailed it. But, said Gibbons, if the United States was to endure it must rest on a stronger foundation than the genius of statesmen, the patriotism of the people, and the wisdom of the law. It must be based on a devout recognition of the overruling Providence Who created, governed, and directed the affairs of nations and of men. "We have no union between church and state," the cardinal stated, "but this does not imply any antagonism between the two powers. Church and state amicably move in parallel lines, helping one another in their respective field of labor."[130]

---

[128] LC, Wilson Papers, Gibbons to Wilson, Baltimore, October 6, 1917.
[129] 116-B, Wilson to Gibbons, Washington, October 9, 1917.
[130] Washington *Post,* October 29, 1917.

On the same day the cardinal dedicated the Knights of Columbus building at Camp Meade where he addressed the soldiers and counseled them to trust in God, to lead clean lives in body and soul, to be obedient to lawful authority, and to help their fellow men.[131] The New York *Sun* was deeply impressed by the sermon at Camp Meade, and in an editorial the following day stated that the cardinal's words constituted "one of the most powerful and stirring messages uttered to the people of any belligerent nation since the war began, and in the elevation of its tone, the practicableness of its wise counsel and the clarity of its form it certainly has been outdone by none. . . ." The *Sun* thought Gibbons' sermon should be reprinted by the government and circulated in every city, town, and hamlet in the land, since the obligation of the citizen to the United States and the worthiness of the country to demand the fulfillment of this obligation were set forth, according to the New York editorial writer, "with a simplicity, a directness, and a convincing force that are seldom combined in the outgivings of any man." Others besides the New York *Sun* appreciated the address, and Father Burke of the N.C.W.C. staff wished to republish it at once for distribution throughout the army camps in the belief that it would do an immense amount of good.[132]

The role that the cardinal had played in public affairs since the outbreak of the war was not lost on observant men. Secretary of State Lansing was aware, of course, of Gibbons' message to Wilson as honorary chairman of the League of National Unity, and on the occasion of the cardinal's asking the Department of State to facilitate the departure of Father Sigourney Fay for Italy on a mission for the Red Cross, Lansing told Gibbons he welcomed an opportunity to be of service to him at a time when his support of the administration had been so generally commended. "I need not tell your Eminence," he said, "that the letter you have already received from the President is in accord with the high regard which the American people and their Government have for your patriotic service in behalf of your country."[133] As the new year approached Archbishop Ireland sent his annual greeting to the cardinal, in which he said that

[131] Baltimore *Sun,* October 29, 1917.
[132] ANCWC, Burke to Gibbons, n.p., November 5, 1917, copy.
[133] 116-F, Lansing to Gibbons, Washington, November 14, 1917.

Bishop Carroll of Helena had visited him recently and had told him that on his trip to Baltimore he had found Gibbons "running up and down stairs as fast as in previous years." Ireland was happy to learn his health was so good, and he remarked, "It is delightful to notice how you are holding the Church in the foreground in these meaningful days of war. May God bless you and reward you."[134] Gibbons reciprocated his friend's good wishes for the new year, and by way of comment on his war activities he replied, "I am trying to do all that I can that the Church may be of full service to the country during these trying days, and that no ground will be left after the ordeal is over upon which the enemies of the Church might endeavor to raise up unfair charges against her."[135]

But in spite of all that Gibbons and his fellow Catholics in the United States and the other belligerent countries did to place the position of the Church and the true neutrality of the Holy See before the public, insinuations and unfair charges continued to be made in certain quarters. Early in the year 1918, for example, the *Red Cross Magazine* carried a poem by Rudyard Kipling in which there appeared an offensive reference to Benedict XV which linked him to the cause of the kaiser. Protests were immediately made, and the head of the American Red Cross called on Gibbons to apologize for the incident, said that the poem had been published without the knowledge of the authorities, and a public apology would be made. The issue of the magazine three months later printed the apology, and the editors stated that they hoped Catholics would understand that the appearance of the Kipling poem was purely the result of an oversight. They further expressed the appreciation of the Red Cross for the part that Catholics were playing in the army, navy, the Knights of Columbus work in the camps, and in the Red Cross itself.[136]

---

[134] 116-N, Ireland to Gibbons, St. Paul, December 28, 1917.

[135] AASP, Gibbons to Ireland, Baltimore, December 31, 1917, copy.

[136] 117-E, Gibbons to Gasparri, Baltimore, March 24, 1918, copy in Italian and translation. The poem was entitled "The Holy War," and with reference to John Bunyan, Kipling had written:

> "The Pope, the swithering neutrals,
> The Kaiser and his Gott
> Their roles, their goals, their naked souls —
> He knew and drew the lot!"

So persistent, however, were the criticisms of the Holy See's action in the war, that Cardinal Gibbons undertook to answer them in an article for *America* entitled "The War Policy of the Pope." He first paid tribute to the justice and fair-mindedness of Americans in having a decent regard for the opinion of others, and of possessing a willingness to listen to both sides of a question and to judge it on its merits. He then proceeded to outline the extremely delicate position of the Pontiff as the common spiritual father of so many children at war with one another. The cardinal met the charge of papal silence by citing the numerous occasions on which Benedict had spoken for peace, in behalf of prisoners of war, and against the cruelties perpetrated against noncombatants. In the same manner he cited the expressions of sympathy for Belgium, whose sufferings the Pope had been accused of overlooking, and as evidence of the feeling about papal policy in the camp of the enemy, he quoted the Hamburg *Fremdenblatt* of January 29, 1917, to the effect that in their opinion the one belligerent power against which the Vatican had spoken was Germany. Speaking of the terrible ordeal through which the Pope was passing, Gibbons remarked, "Every act of his is watched, scrutinized by jealous, critical, hostile eyes, only too ready to find fault and to register blame." For that reason the Pontiff needed more than ever before the support of his loyal children. In closing the cardinal congratulated the American people on the generosity with which they had rallied to the support of the President, paid high tribute to Wilson for his ideals, and expressed confidence that the people would continue to support the chief executive in a spirit that would be, as he said, "an earnest of complete victory and of a return of the happy peace for which he and the Holy Father are earnestly laboring, each in his own sphere."[137]

The Gibbons defense of the position of the Vatican in the war was widely reprinted in the American press, and carried as well in a number of the European newspapers. Copies were, of course, sent to Rome and Archbishop Bonaventura Ceretti of the Secretariat of State presented a copy to the Holy Father. According

---

Red Cross Magazine, XII (February, 1918), 49. The apology was carried in the issue of May, 1918 (p. 76).

[137] *The War Policy of the Pope* (New York, 1918), p. 8, a reprint in pamphlet form of the article in *America,* XVIII (February 23, 1918), 487–488.

to an Associated Press dispatch to the Philadelphia *Public Ledger* of March 21, the Pope ordered the article to be translated and distributed, considering it to be, as it was said, "the most able exposition that had been given of the circumstances of his unique and difficult position." A month after it appeared Gibbons alluded to the article in a letter to the papal Secretary of State, in which he said it had been copied by all the larger secular dailies and he trusted it would go far in removing false impressions regarding Benedict XV's attitude. To this Gasparri replied that the Pope had read it with the greatest satisfaction and had entrusted to him the agreeable duty of thanking him for the article.[138]

But the current propaganda against the Holy See was a stubborn thing, and was not to be silenced easily. In the same spring of 1918 Ralph H. Graves, Sunday editor of the New York *Times,* informed Gibbons of charges arising in England against the Church and many of its high dignitaries, to the effect that they were hampering the cause of the allies in Ireland, Italy, Austria-Hungary, and Canada. Certainly, said Graves, no such state of affairs existed in the United States, and for that reason the *Times* would like very much to print an authentic interview with a cardinal who was known to be a stanch friend of the allied cause.[139] But the sensitiveness which, as we have seen, Gibbons felt about the Irish question prompted him to decline the interview. Lloyd George had just announced the decision to impose military conscription in Ireland, and the situation was then extremely tense. With that in mind, the cardinal informed Graves that he was in receipt of many letters relative to Ireland which were filled with contradictory stories. Since the matter was of such grave importance and had so many delicate phases he concluded, "I am reluctant to give an interview based upon the reports that have reached us here."[140] As the end of the war neared the propaganda against the Vatican showed no sign of abating, and when Gasparri cabled asking the cardinal to try to

[138] 117-E, Gibbons to Gasparri, Baltimore, March 24, 1918, copy in Italian and translation; 117-K, Gasparri to Gibbons, Rome, April 27, 1918.

[139] 117-K, Graves to Gibbons, New York, April 29, 1918. The distress felt at the Holy See by these false reports arising in England was shown when Thomas Nelson Page, American ambassador in Rome, cabled Lansing on November 28, 1917, to the effect that the Vatican had asked Cardinal Bourne to make a reply to a recent attack on the Holy See in the London *Morning Post. Foreign Affairs . . . 1917,* Supplement 2, I, 326.

[140] 117-L, Gibbons to Graves, Baltimore, May 2, 1918, copy.

offset these false stories, Gibbons assured him that he had missed no occasion to speak out in condemnation of the calumnies against the Holy See and in calling attention to the exploits of Catholics in the war.[141]

The closing months of the war offered no surcease to the variety of demands made upon the energy and time of the Cardinal of Baltimore. As the date approached for the Philadelphia convention of the League to Enforce Peace, its president, ex-President Taft, again solicited the cardinal's support. Gibbons stated that he would recommend active participation on the part of the Catholic clergy in the meetings in view of the league's sane program and high aims. And in adumbration of his future support of the League of Nations, he agreed with Taft concerning the need of an organization between nations to provide the machinery by which peace might be maintained. "Personally I feel," said the cardinal, "that the inauguration of such a league as you plan is essential at this stage in the world's history, otherwise we are likely to see retrogression instead of further progress in human affairs." He promised that he would write a formal letter to the convention and would likewise appoint Bishop Shahan, Rector of the Catholic University of America, to represent him.[142]

Some days after his letter to Taft the cardinal presided at the meeting of the archbishops in Washington, where their sessions were devoted in the main to problems arising out of the war. Preliminary plans were laid for a national collection to finance the work of the N.C.W.C., the need for more chaplains in the armed services was canvassed, and the metropolitans heard the reports of Bishop Muldoon and his colleagues on the progress thus far made in co-ordinating the efforts of Catholic groups in behalf of the war.[143] In addition to these broad general problems Gibbons kept in mind the interests of individuals whose lives were adversely affected by wartime regulations. For example, when the proclamation was issued ordering all aliens out of the District of Columbia it imposed a hardship on some of the sisters who were born in Alsace-Lorraine and Poland and who were employed at the Catholic University of America and vari-

---

[141] 118-H, Gibbons to Gasparri, Baltimore, August 2, 1918, copy in Italian.

[142] LC, Taft Papers, Gibbons to Taft, Baltimore, March 29, 1918.

[143] 117-G, Minutes of the Meeting of the Archbishops, Washington, April 10–11, 1918.

ous other institutions of the Church. The cardinal appealed to the President for exemptions for these women, due to the character of their secluded lives and the absence of any fear that their presence might work harm to the country. Wilson consulted Attorney-General Thomas W. Gregory and let him know that he would like to do what the cardinal requested if that were possible. Gregory counseled that the President might assure Gibbons every effort would be made to deal as liberally as possible with all cases, insofar as it did not conflict with the proclamation and the rules that had already been applied in the cases of over 150 women who had asked for similar exemptions.[144] But the cardinal's intervention proved of no avail, and the sisters were compelled to leave the federal district for a period of some months.

The extraordinary precautions taken to insure the national safety by measures of this kind were understandable, even if they did occasion temporary inconvenience to innocent people. But when the threat appeared to bar the teaching of the German language from American schools, Gibbons felt this was going too far. He was asked for an expression of opinion and he stated emphatically that he thought such a regulation would be a pity for the reason that German was one of the means of enriching the mind. "We should no more dismiss that language from our curriculum because of the danger of Prussianism," said the cardinal, "than we should do away with the pagan classics, Latin and Greek, because of the fear of our children becoming contaminated with paganism." He conceded, however, that the government had every right to examine the textbooks used in German to see if they contained anything laudatory of Prussianism to the hurt of American principles and, furthermore, to test the loyalty of the teachers. And he took occasion at this time to make a strong plea for the teaching of English to the children of immigrants. On this point he felt strongly. "As a bishop, whose contact with these people has been daily, running over a period of fifty years, I know whereof I speak," he said. In learning English the immigrant children would breathe in an American atmosphere and imbibe sentiments that would make for a united and

---

[144] LC, Wilson Papers, Gibbons to Wilson, Baltimore, May 15, 1918; Wilson to Gregory, Washington, May 16, 1918, copy; Wilson to Gibbons, Washington, May 16, 1918, copy; Wilson to Gibbons, Washington, May 22, 1918, copy.

devoted people. In this manner they would be gradually weaned from their ancestral hostilities and prejudices and attached more and more to American ideals.[145]

Insofar as the strength of his eighty-four years permitted, the Cardinal of Baltimore continued right up to the end of the war to assist at as many public functions as possible. In early June, 1918, he preached at a military Mass at Camp Meade before a large assembly of men about to embark for the front. He emphasized for the soldiers the bond of their common citizenship and common goal in the war, and once more he counseled obedience to their officers and courage in the fighting that lay before them. In conclusion he said:

> Go, then, my friends, unhesitatingly and serene at heart. Whether you come back with wounds or without them, we will be glad to welcome you and accord you the meed that is a hero's due. Remember, such wounds as you may receive will be honorable. You will be proud of them and will boast of them and will want to show them in years to come. It is with such wounds that you will prove that you possessed the souls and hearts of brave men. Remember what Lord Nelson said on the eve of his great victory, "England expects every man to do his duty." America expects every one of you to do your duty. Go forth to battle and victory, and God be with you![146]

Nor did Gibbons' enthusiasm for winning the war cause him to be unmindful of the bereaved families of those who had given their lives on the battlefield. When he learned the news of the death of Quentin Roosevelt, the son of his close friend, the ex-President, he wired his condolences to the father. Roosevelt replied, "Your telegram touched me very deeply. You know how I believe in you, and it meant much to have you think of me and mine."[147]

It was his concern for the maintenance of high morale among the troops, as well as for the respect due to the symbol of the Christian faith, that prompted the cardinal about this time to protest to Secretary of War Baker against the rumored removal of the cross from the uniforms of the chaplains and the substitution of the shepherd's crook. Gibbons spoke forcefully on the

---

[145] 117-P, Gibbons to F. W. Reynolds, director of the Service Bureau, Baltimore, May 21, 1918, copy.

[146] 117-R, manuscript copy of Gibbons' sermon at Camp Meade, June 9, 1918.

[147] 118-E, Roosevelt to Gibbons, Oyster Bay, New York, July 23, 1918.

matter. The presence of 1,400 Christian chaplains in the armed forces should, he said, carry more weight than the desires of fifteen or twenty chaplains who might wish the change. Not only should the cross not be removed from the uniforms but chaplains, according to the cardinal, should be rewarded with promotions in the same manner as doctors and dentists. In conclusion he told Baker, "you must surely recognize the moral effect of the chaplains upon our American soldiers. They are the inspiration of the men, not only aiding and urging them to lead clean, wholesome lives but encouraging them to do manfully and bravely their duty in this terrible crisis. . . ."[148]

In the same spirit of upholding the hands of those who were bearing the heaviest burdens, Gibbons sent a stirring appeal to the hierarchy in the early autumn of 1918 asking them to support the drive to be made for funds to carry on the work of the N.C.W.C. The bishops, he said, would soon be called upon to carry through one of the most serious and arduous public undertakings in the history of the American Church. The honor of the hierarchy was at stake and all the bishops must come behind the prelates of the administrative committee of the National Catholic War Council. "They are doing our work," he said, "the work of the American Hierarchy, and they deserve the best we can give them." The success of the administrative committee would mean the accomplishment of the greatest good for the American servicemen and the honorable war record of the Church, but this success depended principally upon the bishops since the people would follow their leadership.[149]

In one of the final and most trying experiences of the war years Gibbons displayed his unflagging interest in whatever touched the welfare of the fighting men. In the closing months of the war there appeared in the United States the devastating influenza epidemic, which soon invaded the training camps and threatened to take more lives than all the battle fronts combined. News reached the cardinal that the suffering at Camp Meade was especially severe and that the emergency had taxed the nursing force to the limit of endurance. In these circumstances he informed General Jesse McI. Carter who was in command that if

[148] 118-G, Gibbons to Baker, Baltimore, July 30, 1918, copy.
[149] Archives of the Diocese of Mobile, Gibbons to Edward P. Allen, Baltimore, September 12, 1918.

he found it possible to use some of the nursing sisters from the Catholic hospitals of Baltimore, he was sure the sisters would gladly volunteer their services. Carter was, of course, deeply grateful and asked for seventy-five nurses at once.[150] A month later when the epidemic had somewhat abated the general thanked Gibbons for sending priests and sisters to Camp Meade, and he spoke of the "noble service" they had rendered in assisting the chaplains and nurses at the base hospital and in administering spiritual consolation to the sick and dying officers and soldiers of the camp. "In writing this letter of gratefulness," he said, "I speak not only for myself, but for the entire personnel of my command in our warm appreciation of what you did for us."[151]

Just two weeks before the armistice Cardinal Gibbons demonstrated again the sacrifice he was willing to make in order to assist the cause of the armed forces. On Sunday, October 27, there was held in Madison Square Garden in New York a mass meeting which drew around 15,000 people to further the united drive for war-camp activities. Monsignor Joseph F. Mooney, administrator of the Archdiocese of New York, sent a pressing invitation for the cardinal to be present, saying that the committee in charge were desirous of having national representation, and they particularly wished Gibbons to be there as the foremost leader of the Church in the United States.[152] The old cardinal confessed that his first inclination was to ask to be excused from making the journey to New York, as he had been working hard and felt the strain of his labors and was looking forward to a few days' rest. But he would attend in the hope of contributing to the success of the drive, although he was glad Mooney had not asked him to make an address since it was imperative that he conserve his strength.[153]

By this time it was evident that the end of the war was not far off. On October 4 Germany and Austria-Hungary had appealed to Wilson for an armistice on the basis of his fourteen points, and the negotiations going on between the world capitals pointed to an imminent cessation of the fighting. News of the armistice negotiations was transmitted officially to the Holy See

---

[150] 118-V, Gibbons to Carter, Baltimore, October 1, 1918, copy; Carter to Gibbons, Camp Meade, Maryland, October 2, 1918.

[151] 119-G, Carter to Gibbons, Camp Meade, Maryland, October 29, 1918.

[152] 119-B, Mooney to Gibbons, New York, October 18, 1918.

[153] 119-G, Gibbons to Mooney, Baltimore, October 21, 1918, copy.

by the Austrian government and the Pope cabled an appeal to the President in which he begged that Wilson hasten the end of the ruthless scourge that had too long afflicted humanity. The message of Benedict XV was sent to the apostolic delegate, but Cardinal Gibbons was requested to see the President and to urge that he should give consideration to the Austrian appeal and thus have the glory of bringing a speedy end to the conflict.[154] The cardinal did as he was asked, although he chose to write a letter instead of calling personally at the White House since, as he said, he did not wish to trespass on Wilson's valuable time then engrossed by such weighty cares, nor did he wish to offer, as he expressed it, "any occasion for comment which would likely be caused by my calling on you personally."[155]

The President was grateful for the consideration of his time, although, as he said, "I must say that even amidst the rush of these days it would have been a welcome relief to have the pleasure of seeing you in person once more. . . ." He had every inclination of the heart to respond to the suggestion of Benedict XV and he hoped the Pope did not doubt that. But American relations with Austria-Hungary had become greatly complicated since his address on the fourteen points of the previous January, by reason of recognition of Czechoslovakia on September 3 and of the national aspirations of the peoples of Yugoslavia, thereby creating obligations in honor toward them. Consequently Wilson concluded by merely stating the hope that Gibbons would convey to the Pope his great appreciation for the message and the spirit that had prompted it.[156] This information was cabled to Rome,[157] and within a few days a further cablegram from Gasparri again urged Gibbons to see the President and to exhort him to bring about an armistice. Certain principles for a settlement were outlined, and Gasparri concluded, "Your Eminence may add that

---

[154] 118, Bonzano to Gibbons, Washington, October 10, 1918; AAB, unclassified, Benedict XV to Wilson, Rome, October 9, 1918, copy.

[155] LC, Wilson Papers, Gibbons to Wilson, Baltimore, October 12, 1918.

[156] 119-B, Wilson to Gibbons, Washington, October 18, 1918. The day before his letter to Gibbons the President answered the Pope through the apostolic delegate. He stated the desire of the United States for peace and that he would use every endeavor to pursue such a course as would bring to the world the blessings of a lasting peace. "I warmly appreciate," said Wilson, "the generous confidence you express in my personal influence in this time of tragedy and travail" (LC, Wilson Papers, Wilson to Benedict XV, Washington, October 17, 1918, copy).

[157] 119-G, Gibbons to Gasparri, Baltimore, October 21, 1918, cablegram in copy.

all humanity places its hope in the ability and impartiality of the President."[158] Less than a week before the armistice on the western front, Gibbons conveyed to Wilson the latest message from the Holy See and emphasized once more the hopes the world had placed in his ability to affect a settlement.[159] By this time, however, the negotiations between the allies and the defeated enemies had gone too far, and it is doubtful if the action of the Holy See played any part in the terms agreed upon.

The exhaustive ordeal of World War I was at last brought to a close with the armistice of November 11 which stopped the fighting on the western front, and there was no noncombatant who welcomed the end with more sincerity than the Cardinal of Baltimore. He ordered his priests to substitute the oration of thanksgiving in the Mass in place of the oration for peace, and to make certain that the victory would be celebrated in a fitting manner he gave instructions that a solemn service should be held in all the churches of the archdiocese on Thanksgiving Day, November 28, at which the Church's official prayer of jubilation, the *Te Deum,* should be sung.[160]

The era of World War I brought out more strikingly than ever before the unique position which Cardinal Gibbons had come to occupy in American public affairs. The difficulties with Mexico, the troubles in Ireland, and the myriad problems arising out of the European war and American participation therein — all served to emphasize that his influence and leadership far transcended the boundaries of his own archdiocese or even of his own country. Shortly before the end of hostilities, Jules Jusserand, the French ambassador to Washington, presented to Gibbons in the name of the French Republic the decoration of grand

[158] 119-L, Bonzano to Gibbons, Washington, October 30, 1918, enclosing copy of the Gasparri cable in Italian and an English translation.

[159] 119-M, Gibbons to Wilson, Baltimore, November 5, 1918, copy. Gasparri had suggested as the three principles on which the armistice should be based the following: first, Wilson and the allies should be in accord on the principal conditions of peace with Germany so as to avoid further misunderstandings; second, these conditions should be such as not to leave germs of reconquest and revenge, and hence they should be moderate and compatible with the honor of Germany; third, the conditions of peace should be the conditions of the armistice. In conveying these ideas to Wilson the cardinal stated the first and third very much as Gasparri had expressed them, but in regard to the second point, his letter read "that the peace should be stable and permanent, which cannot be if it is to be a merely punitive peace."

[160] Baltimore *Catholic Review,* November 16, 1918.

officer of the Order of the Legion of Honor. He alluded to the
fame and respect which the cardinal enjoyed in the United States,
and he said, "The same are felt for you in France where your
great influence, ever exercised in favor of noble causes, and in
these latter years, in favor of the noblest of all, that of the reign
of justice in this world, have won for you the admiration of
everyone."[161] Later a similar honor was paid to him when King
Albert I of Belgium conferred on Gibbons the grand cordon of
the Order of Leopold II.[162]

Cardinal Gibbons' sound and unruffled judgment, his love for
his Church and country, and his willingness to expend his time
and talents in behalf of public causes won him the confidence
of men of all shades of religion and political opinions on both
sides of the Atlantic. He knew and loved the Church and the
American Republic with an intensity that was excelled by no
American of his age, and it was this thorough understanding of
and affection for both that enabled him with such success to
draw the two societies closer in a common enterprise where their
welfare was at stake. True, he did not always attain the goal
he had set for himself as, for example, in his hope that through
the government of the United States the persecution of the
Church in Mexico might be mitigated, but his was the Catholic
voice that carried the greatest weight in the America of his day
with government officials of the highest rank, and if he did not
always obtain his objective, he at least placed before the State
the claims of the Church in a strong yet respectful manner. And
to his fellow Catholics no claims of the State upon their loyalty
and service were ever expressed and won so universal a hearing
as those voiced by the Cardinal of Baltimore. The tribute paid
by a recent historian to one aspect of the role he played would,
therefore, be sustained by those who knew his life. It was said
that Cardinal Gibbons did more, perhaps,

> than any other person in the past hundred years to commend the
> Roman Catholic Church to the people of the United States, and to
> interpret its views and adjust its work so as to make them
> effective under the conditions of religious freedom in our American
> democracy.[163]

---

[161] 119-A, Jusserand to Gibbons, Washington, October 16, 1918.

[162] 128-V, M. Costermans to Gibbons, Brussels, August 23, 1920.

[163] Anson Phelps Stokes, *Church and State in the United States* (New York, 1950), II, 363.

CHAPTER XX

Problems of the Peace

THE return of peace in November, 1918, ushered in a period of inevitable adjustments which seriously affected both Church and State. If the victory over Spain in 1898 had made the United States a world power, the defeat of Germany and Austria-Hungary twenty years later projected American leadership into the counsels of the old world in a manner that left no doubt that henceforth its responsibilities to the community of nations would be of a much graver character. For a brief moment the President of the United States enjoyed an unparalleled eminence as the international champion of the peoples of all lands, until the cold light of reality began to dawn over the peace conference in Paris and the subsequent struggle which he encountered when he presented the treaty settlements to the United States Senate. But before the disillusionment had set in Wilson's idealism had captured the imagination of the world, and all eyes were turned toward him in the hope that he might lead war-weary humanity to a better day. The Catholic Church, sorely tried by the four-year conflict, likewise appreciated the enhanced position of the United States and its President, and during the next two years the Pope and his Secretary of State sought on more than one occasion to secure American assistance in the postwar problems that faced the Church in Europe. For any approach on the part of the Holy See to the American government, the Cardinal of Baltimore continued to be, of course, the ideal medium, and from the end of the war up to his death Gibbons held the prime position he had won in this regard.

It was not long after the fighting ceased before the men in the armed services began to return, and among the first of the home-coming troops to arrive in Baltimore were several hundred soldiers and sailors who assembled in the Cathedral of the Assumption on Sunday, December 15, for a special religious service arranged in their honor. Cardinal Gibbons addressed them on that occasion, praising the motives that had led the United States to enter the war, thanking the defenders of the nation for their brave deeds, and counseling them to trust always in God who had given them their victory. In greeting the servicemen he said, "My dear boys, and this is what I prefer to call you, I had to make an effort to be here this afternoon. I have just come from confirming in the suburbs. But I want to say what a pleasure it is to me to meet the saviors and defenders of our beloved country. . . ." After the sermon and benediction the soldiers and sailors were received by the cardinal in the parlors of his residence where he shook hands and exchanged a few words with each man.[1]

One of the most immediate and pressing problems of the period following the armistice, was to make provision for the thousands of persons in Germany and the other defeated countries who were in danger of starvation. Petitions for relief were received with increasing urgency by the Holy See, and with a view to invoking the help of the United States, Cardinal Gasparri cabled asking Gibbons to intercede with the President in behalf of the victims of the famine in Germany.[2] The United States Food Administration had already accomplished wonders in the conservation of food for export, and the remarkable achievements of Herbert C. Hoover as food administrator were now turned to relieving the plight of the peoples of central and southeastern Europe. Gibbons was aware of Hoover's impending mission, and for that reason when he informed Wilson of the Pope's appeal he stated that he had assured the Holy See that the American authorities were fully alive to the seriousness of the situation.[3]

The President was not unmindful of the conditions described by the Pontiff, and he asked Gibbons to inform Gasparri that the papal request would receive the most considerate attention possible in the circumstances.[4] In a further move to lend assist-

---

[1] Baltimore *American,* December 16, 1918.

[2] 119-P, Bonzano to Gibbons, Washington, November 15, 1918.

[3] LC, Wilson Papers, Gibbons to Wilson, Baltimore, November 16, 1918; 119-P, Gibbons to Bonzano, Baltimore, November 16, 1918, copy.

[4] 119-Q, Wilson to Gibbons, Washington, November 18, 1918. The President's reply was communicated to the apostolic delegate who, in turn, relayed it to the Holy See (119-R, Gibbons to Bonzano, Baltimore, November 21, 1918, copy; Bonzano to Gibbons, Washington, November 25, 1918).

ance to the drive for food for the starving of Europe, Gibbons ordered Hoover's message to be read in all the churches of his archdiocese on Sunday, December 1. It was an action for which he was told, "Mr. Hoover and the entire Food Administration deeply appreciate the cordial support that you have continually given to our efforts since our work was first undertaken."[5] And a month later when the war activities of the Food Administration were closed down, the cardinal again received an expression of thanks. A member of the staff said, "Mr. Hoover, who is abroad studying the future food needs of the world, desires that we express to you his personal gratitude for what you have done."[6]

The needs which Hoover surveyed during his visit to Europe late in 1918 proved to be far beyond the original calculations. A year later, therefore, he made a fresh appeal through Gibbons for a letter from Benedict XV to relieve in particular the plight of over three million children. "Remembering the enormous stabilizing value of the letter sent you by his Holiness in 1916," said Hoover, "I feel sure you will recognize the importance of help from such an authoritative source."[7] Gibbons acted at once and asked Archbishop Cerretti, Secretary of the Congregation for Extraordinary Ecclesiastical Affairs, to lay the matter before the Pope and to obtain a strong letter endorsing the American relief drive.[8] The Holy Father promptly complied with the request by forwarding a warm recommendation of Hoover's efforts in appealing to the generosity of all Americans irrespective of creed or party. It was a charity that embraced all who were in need without distinction and, he added, especially did the suffering of the innocent children of those who were the enemies of yesterday commend itself. The Pontiff took occasion to compliment Hoover on the providential work he was still carrying on, news of which, he said, had reached him through Cardinal Gibbons.[9] The Hoover request was only one among dozens of such appeals which reached the cardinal in the last year of his life from relief organizations in many lands. Typical of the support which he gave at this time was his letter to Princess Julia

---

[5] 119-R, H. Alexander Smith to Gibbons, Washington, November 19, 1918.

[6] 119-V, illegible signature to Gibbons, Washington, December 20, 1918.

[7] 124-D, Hoover to Gibbons, Washington, December 19, 1919.

[8] 124-D, Gibbons to Cerretti, Baltimore, December 20, 1919, copy.

[9] 124-K, Benedict XV to Hoover, January 9, 1920, copy; 124-H, Hoover to Gibbons, Stanford, California, January 2, 1920.

Cantacuzene in behalf of the American Central Committee for Russian Relief. In commending the committee to the generosity of the American people, he remarked, "Russia should certainly enlist the aid of our Christian people, for the reason that by such help will the menace of Bolshevism be overcome and atheism halted in its attacks on religion."[10]

Not only did Gibbons lend his endorsement to these campaigns to help the needy, but he often made personal contributions as well. For example, when Archbishop Cerretti was returning to Rome in the spring of 1919 after having represented the Pope at the cardinal's golden episcopal jubilee, he sent the Pontiff a sum of $5,000 for his charities.[11] He likewise forwarded the proceeds of a collection taken up in the Archdiocese of Baltimore to the Catholic Institute of Lille and recommended its cause to the American Red Cross.[12] But it was Belgium and its Catholic University of Louvain which seemed to have a special appeal for the charity of Cardinal Gibbons. On the occasion of his golden jubilee Louvain had conferred upon him the honorary degree of doctor of theology in recognition of his attainments and in gratitude for his assistance, and during the months that followed he continued his benefactions to the university and to other Belgian charities. The cardinal was made a sponsor of the national committee for the restoration of the library at Louvain, and in sending $200 for this fund to President Nicholas Murray Butler of Columbia University, he remarked that the many appeals reaching him at the time, including those from Belgium, prevented him from giving a larger contribution.[13] For his part in promoting Louvain's cause the authorities of the university were naturally grateful, and Monsignor Adolphe Hebbelynck, rector emeritus, who was directing the campaign in the United States, let Gibbons know how much his patronage had meant to them.[14]

The particular affection which Gibbons showed for Belgium was probably motivated in part by the plucky stand which the

---

[10] 124-M, Gibbons to Cantacuzene, Baltimore, January 14, 1920, copy.

[11] 121-A, Gasparri to Gibbons, Rome, April 1, 1919.

[12] 126-B, Emile Lesne, Rector of the Catholic Institute of Lille, to Gibbons, Lille, April 5, 1920.

[13] 121-P, Gibbons to Butler, Baltimore, May 17, 1919, copy.

[14] 121-J, Hebbelynck to Gibbons, New York, May 1, 1919; 123-M, Hebbelynck to Gibbons, New York, October 14, 1919.

little country had made through the war years, and by the noble bearing of Désiré Joseph Cardinal Mercier, Archbishop of Malines. Mercier displayed an extraordinary leadership during the crisis which enveloped his native land, and the fearless resistance which he offered to the German invaders had won for him a world-wide fame long before the war had ended. Mercier felt deeply grateful for the assistance which the United States had given to Belgium during its great trial, and in token of his gratitude in the early spring of 1919 he sent from his meager resources $1,000 as a subscription to the liberty loan drive which was then on. At the time that he forwarded his money for the purchase of a bond, the Cardinal of Malines thanked Gibbons for his invitation to visit the United States but stated that the pressure of his duties would delay his coming until the autumn.[15] He was once more assured of a heartfelt welcome and Gibbons asked that he be informed well in advance of the date of his arrival so that he might send a delegation to New York to meet him and escort him to Baltimore. "Your Eminence's subscription of $1000.00 to the Victory Loan," he said, "has made a profound impression on the people of this country and has excited most favorable comment."[16]

At length Cardinal Mercier and his party arrived in the United States on September 9, and after a day in New York they traveled on to Baltimore where Gibbons and an immense crowd met them at the station. On Sunday, September 14, the two cardinals were present in the sanctuary of the cathedral for the solemn Mass during which Bishop Patrick J. Donahue of Wheeling preached a sermon which carried many graceful allusions to the honored guest and to his country. The next evening between 25,000 and 30,000 Baltimoreans filled the Fifth Regiment Armory to welcome the Cardinal of Malines, and again on the evening of September 16 an overflow audience gathered in the Lyric Theater to hear his address. In introducing Mercier the Cardinal of Baltimore remarked that he had been presented as a priest, a prince of the Church, and as Archbishop of Malines. Therefore, he would present him under another title, namely, "as an ardent patriot and fearless champion, who vindicated and upheld the honor, the sovereignty, the independence of his coun-

---

[15] 120-R, Mercier to Gibbons, Malines, March 9, 1919.
[16] 121-L, Gibbons to Mercier, Baltimore, May 6, 1919, copy.

Cardinal Gibbons and his guest, Cardinal Mercier of Malines, on the occasion of the latter's visit to Baltimore, September 14, 1919.

(Courtesy of the Baltimore *News Post*)

try at the risk of fines, of imprisonment, of death itself." Following his visit to Baltimore Mercier went to Washington where he called at the White House and was received by the President, and on September 23 he was present when Gibbons dedicated the Sulpician Seminary at the Catholic University of America.[17] After a few days in the capital the Belgian cardinal visited a number of other cities throughout the country where the same general enthusiasm greeted him from the throngs who gathered to pay tribute to his peerless leadership.

On the eve of Mercier's departure from the United States, he told Gibbons that the absorbing nature of his tour had left him little or no time to write his thanks for the cardinal's hospitality and kindness. But the sole pleasure of having passed some precious hours in the intimacy of Gibbons' company was sufficient recompense for all the physical fatigue of his travels.[18] Mercier was assured that Gibbons understood perfectly why he had not written, and he wondered how he had been able to stand the trying ordeal so well and so graciously. The Cardinal of Baltimore had followed him in thought along his journey and, as he said, "[I] appreciate every honor done to you by our warm hearted people as an honor to myself." The visit of the Archbishop of Malines to Gibbons' home would be treasured for all time with its heritage of happy memories, and in closing the cardinal stated, "It brings a deep sense of comfort to observe that your journey through the United States will have a far reaching and lasting effect in allaying prejudice and bringing God's children closer together in the bond of love."[19]

Many months before the two cardinals had had an opportunity to meet and become better acquainted, they had been in touch with one another on a question which was regarded as vital to the interests of the Holy See. The problem owed its origin to the actively hostile attitude of the Italian government

---

[17] Baltimore *Catholic Review*, September 13, 20, 27, 1919.

[18] 123-L, Mercier to Gibbons, New York, October 11, 1919. Franz, the Flemish valet of Mercier, accompanied the cardinal to the United States and kept a diary of his trip. Among the items the following is of interest: "Here at Mgr. Gibbons', we have black servants who have to work, and white ones who only make believe they do. They all eat a great deal, and meat everyday, except of course, on Fridays. We have three sisters who look after bedrooms. Two black servants are dressed as finely as the King's servants at home." John A. Gade, *The Life of Cardinal Mercier* (New York, 1935), appendix, p. 295.

[19] 123-M, Gibbons to Mercier, Baltimore, October 17, 1919, copy.

toward the Vatican in recent years, and the efforts which the Italian officials put forth to prevent any settlement of the Roman Question by influences outside Italy. The policy of the Italian government was clearly revealed to the world when the Bolshevik government of Russia made public in *Izvestia* of November 28, 1917, the secret commitments entered into by the czar's regime. Among these confidential documents was the secret Treaty of London of April 26, 1915, in which France, Great Britain, and Russia had agreed to certain conditions in order to bring Italy into the war on the side of the allies. Article 15 of that treaty read as follows:

> France, Great Britain and Russia shall support such opposition as Italy may make to any proposal in the direction of introducing a representative of the Holy See in any peace negotiations or negotiations for the settlement of questions raised by the present war.[20]

It was apparent, therefore, that if Italy had its way there would be no papal representative at the peace conference, nor would any solution to the incongruous position occupied by the Pope since 1870 be entertained by any of the signatories of the secret treaty. On the other hand, it was equally obvious that unfair discrimination of this kind would be resented by the officials of the Vatican and that if the occasion presented itself an attempt would be made to remove it.

One of the earliest efforts at finding a way out of the awkward situation in which the Holy See had labored for nearly half a century, was inaugurated through the medium of a young American priest, Father Sigourney W. Fay. After some years as a minister of the Protestant Episcopal Church he had become a convert to Catholicism in 1908 and two years later he was ordained to the priesthood by Gibbons as a subject of the Archdiocese of Baltimore. Early in the winter of 1917 Fay sailed for Europe as a deputy commissioner of the American Red Cross in Italy with the rank of a major in the United States Army.[21] Doubtless one of the reasons why he was selected for the delicate

---

[20] W. Henry Cooke and Edith P. Stickney (Eds.), *Readings in European International Relations since 1879* (New York, 1931), p. 457. Various versions of the text of the article appeared in different places after the first publication in *Izvestia* which involved contradictions over the exact wording.

[21] 116-F, Lansing to Gibbons, Washington, November 14, 1917.

task of ecclesiastical diplomacy — aside from the confidence which Gibbons placed in his ability — was that he was on friendly terms with Arthur James Balfour, Foreign Minister of Great Britain, and with Sir Eric Drummond and Mr. Cecil Dormer, members of the British Commission in Washington. At any rate, Fay arrived in Rome on January 15, 1918, and he soon began to supply the cardinal with lengthy accounts of his experiences which were sent through the British diplomatic pouch. During his first week in the Eternal City he had interviews with Cardinal Gasparri, Archbishop Cerretti, Ambassador Page, and Count John F. C. de Salis, British minister to the Holy See. On January 22 he was with Gasparri for an hour, during which the Secretary of State spoke of the great esteem which he knew the American government had for Cardinal Gibbons and expressed a curiosity to learn the reaction of American Catholics to the clause in the secret Treaty of London.

Fay was informed by Gasparri of the grief of the Holy Father at the constant misrepresentations of his neutrality and of the restraint which the Holy See had exercised in replying to these attacks even in its own defense lest it might embarrass the allied governments. As an example, Gasparri cited the fact that the secret clause had been known at the Vatican for some time before the Russians published it, but the Holy See had held its peace and trusted in God for fear of raising difficulties for the allies. Now, however, there were two points on which the Vatican had determined to act in its own interests, and in these the papal authorities would ask the assistance of Cardinal Gibbons. First was the clause in the secret treaty pertaining to the Holy See which should be stricken out or allowed to fall into desuetude, and second, whatever influence was possessed by Catholics in the allied countries should be brought to bear to get a representative of the Pope into the peace conference. Gasparri wondered if Gibbons might not persuade President Wilson to intimate to the British government that it would be well to drop the clause, and he likewise spoke strongly of the good effects which he believed would follow from a protest of the hierarchy against it. As to the second point, it was Gasparri's view that there were two cardinals to whom the whole allied world looked with unqualified admiration, namely, Gibbons and Mercier. A protest toward the end of the war from these two churchmen against excluding the Pope from the peace conference would not, he thought, fail to have its effect.

In reply to the proposals of the Secretary of State, Fay let it be known that any direct approach of Gibbons to Wilson on the matter of the treaty clause would be very difficult, but he suggested that through the cardinal's influence at the Foreign Office in London something might be done. He likewise told Gasparri that before leaving the United States he had discussed the matter with Gibbons and with the British ambassador in Washington, and the latter had given it as his private opinion that a properly timed protest from Gibbons and Mercier would have an excellent chance of success. At this Gasparri expressed the wish that as soon as Fay had finished his work for the Red Cross, he should go to London and sound the Foreign Office on the matter. The American priest summarized for Gibbons his friendly interviews with Ambassador Page and Count de Salis to whom, however, it would seem he did not reveal the purpose of his business with the Holy See. He closed his long letter by saying that Gasparri had said the Vatican liked to deal with frank and straightforward people, and that was why they liked to treat with the English. Fay was amused at the remark, since it reminded him of something that Gibbons had once said to him. "You may remember telling me," he wrote, "that you thought my greatest protection in Rome would be what Your Eminence was pleased to call my frank manner." It was gratifying to him to find that Gasparri seemed pleased that he should have spoken quite frankly and openly to him about the various aspects of the case.[22]

It was just a week before the arrival of Father Fay in Rome that President Wilson made his famous address to Congress on January 9, 1918, outlining the fourteen points on which a peace might be concluded. During the weeks that followed the replies of the belligerents were watched with deep anxiety by all who hoped for an end to hostilities. On February 11 the President addressed Congress again on the subject, "War Aims of Germany and Austria." He stated that the reply received to his peace proposals from Vienna was uttered in a friendly tone and Count Ottokar Czernin, the Foreign Minister of Austria-Hungary, had found in his statement a sufficiently encouraging approach to the views of his own government to justify him in believing, as

---

[22] 116-S, Fay to Gibbons, Rome, January 23, 1918. *Strictly confidential.*

Wilson said, "that it furnishes a basis for a more detailed discussion of purposes by the two Governments." But the reply of Count Georg von Hertling, Chancellor of Germany, was described as vague and confusing.[23]

There was none who followed these efforts to reach an understanding for an armistice more closely than Pope Benedict XV, and when he received Father Fay in audience following Wilson's address of February 11 he made that clear. The Pope remarked to Fay that he was glad to see the United States and Great Britain in accord with the principles he had laid down in his note of the previous August, and he frankly told the American priest that the timing of his note had been ill chosen. Fay was at pains to convey a precisely correct impression to Gibbons on this point, and with that in mind he said, "I think that perhaps I had better give Your Eminence His Holiness's exact words: 'But as to the time I issued my note there can be no doubt, my son, that the moment was ill-chosen.'" The Pontiff then made a searching inquiry concerning the manner in which Archbishop Bonzano was fulfilling his duties as apostolic delegate to the United States, and he left Fay under the impression that he thought Bonzano should have told him that it was not the proper time to issue his peace note. Benedict XV had words of high praise for Gibbons and Mercier, and he felt that if the two cardinals would protest to the British government — as the only allied government except Belgium having a diplomatic representative at the Vatican — the clause barring the Holy See from the peace conference could be gotten rid of. For that reason he wished Fay to go to England as soon as his Red Cross work was concluded in Italy. After his audience, Fay compared his impressions with those of Aidan Cardinal Gasquet, the English Benedictine, who had been received in audience two days before, and he found that the Pope had spoken much more plainly to Gasquet about the German reply to Wilson than he had to him. Gasquet received the impression that if the allies should attempt to pry Austria-Hungary loose from Germany the Pope would be willing to help. On the basis of all this information, Fay composed a telegram which he first showed to Cerretti and then sent to Balfour and

---

23 Ray Stannard Baker and William E. Dodd (Eds.), *War and Peace. Presidential Messages, Addresses, and Public Papers (1917–1924) by Woodrow Wilson* (New York, 1927), I, 177.

which, according to Fay, the British foreign minister later cabled to Wilson. It was this circumstance which led Fay to remark to Cardinal Gibbons, "On the 12th [*sic*] the President, as Your Eminence has seen, rose to the bait in his message in which he says that the Allies may come to terms with Austria."[24]

Upon receipt of Father Fay's letter the cardinal acted at once. On February 24 he had an interview in Washington with Lord Rufus Reading, the British ambassador who had replaced Spring Rice following the latter's sudden death. In this interview Gibbons stated the motives behind the suggestion which he ventured to make that the clause excluding the Pope from the peace conference be eliminated. He acted, as he later told Balfour, on the grounds that he felt a public reparation was owing to the Holy Father on account of the premature publication of the secret treaty by Russia and, second, for the sake of England and its allies. Under the heading of the second point the cardinal advanced the following reasons: (1) the large Catholic proportion in the American armed forces which was at least thirty-five per cent in the army and even more in the navy; (2) the bad impression caused by the publication of the clause among American Catholics would be entirely neutralized by its elimination; (3) as signal as the patriotism of American Catholics had been shown to be, the removal of the clause would bring their feelings even to enthusiasm; (4) it would be a gracious act on the part of His Majesty's government to take the initiative in this matter; (5) the elimination of the clause would appeal to the Catholics of the British Empire as well as to those of the United States; (6) the possibility that the American archbishops might require Gibbons at their Easter meeting to forward their protest against the implied insult to the Holy See; (7) such a protest would naturally lead to counterprotests which would produce one of those divisions of opinion which they were most anxious to avoid during the war; (8) it had been his policy since the outbreak of the war to foster among the American people good feeling toward the allies, believing such to be best for the future of the United States. In conclusion Gibbons said, "In making this personal request for the elimination of the clause, I firmly believe

---

[24] 116-V, Fay to Gibbons, Rome, February 12, 1918. *Strictly Private*. The Pope quizzed Fay closely about the public influence of Archbishop Ireland in the United States, and remarked that he had been informed he was an old and broken man. It led Fay to comment, "Somebody has been telling lies about Mgr. Ireland."

that I am asking for what is best for the future welfare and relations of England and the United States."[25]

Before a reply could be received by the cardinal from Balfour, Lord Reading had cabled the substance of his interview with Gibbons and had received word of the debate in the House of Commons on the official interpretation given by the British government to the controverted clause. Reading sent a record of this debate of February 14 to the cardinal and stated that it made clear that the British government, as he expressed it, "have not bound themselves to any policy which would entail a disregard of any efforts which His Holiness may make in the future, as he has in the past, in the general interest of mankind." In addition to the public debate, Reading informed the cardinal that he had word from Balfour that the matter had been taken up by the Vatican directly with His Majesty's government, and the British minister at the Holy See had been instructed to inform Cardinal Gasparri that the terms of Article 15 as published in Russia were entirely misleading, and that the British government had never contemplated and would never contemplate binding itself to a foreign government to obstruct what Reading called "any activities which the Holy See may wish to initiate on any subject connected with Peace or War."

Moreover, as Reading further stated, Count de Salis had been told to emphasize that the attitude of the British government toward Benedict XV's peace note of August 1, 1917, was in no way connected with the existence of Article 15. The clause had never been viewed in London as indicating anything further than what Reading termed, "a limitation of the membership of the eventual peace conference to the actual belligerents."[26] Quite apart from the lofty sentiments expressed by the British ambassador in the first part of his long letter, the real significance of his communication was to be found in the sentence which made it clear that the British government would not sponsor the admittance of the Pope's representative at the conference of peace. Nonetheless, the cardinal thanked Reading for his courteous communication and informed him that he was forwarding its contents immediately to Cardinal Gasparri.[27] Without com-

---

25 117-A, Gibbons to Balfour, Baltimore, March 6, 1918, copy.
26 117-C, Reading to Gibbons, Washington, March 19, 1918.
27 117-E, Gibbons to Reading, Baltimore, March 23, 1918, copy.

mitting himself in any way on the letter of Reading, Gibbons sent a copy of it to the papal Secretary of State and concluded by assuring Gasparri that he was doing everything in his power to make the Papacy appear in the proper light before the American public, and that he was always ready to comply with any instructions which he might wish to send him.[28]

Meanwhile Gibbons received word of the fine impression created in Rome by Father Fay and the discreet manner in which he had carried out his difficult assignment. Shane Leslie, who was attached to the British Embassy in Washington, furnished this information to Father Louis R. Stickney, chancellor of the Archdiocese of Baltimore, and in commenting on the line which Fay's future efforts might take he said, "It practically comes down to this that the position of the Holy Father politically will be what the Cardinals of Malines and Baltimore are able to request for him."[29] Yet it was not to be so simple a matter as Leslie anticipated, for the British foreign minister contented himself in replying to Gibbons with an allusion to Reading's explanation of some weeks before concerning the official British attitude toward Article 15, to which he added:

> I can assure you that I personally would gladly see the clause eliminated or profoundly modified not only for the very cogent reasons given by Your Eminence but also on the merits of the case. Your Eminence will, however, realize from Lord Reading's explanations that it is a matter of great delicacy for us to take further action in this direction at present, though any steps Your Eminence may think proper to take will have my cordial goodwill.[30]

Nor was the Holy See satisfied with the explanations given by the British government in regard to Article 15 of the secret treaty. Gasparri assured Gibbons of the Pope's approval and gratitude for what he had said to Lord Reading, but he emphasized that although the version of the clause given out in London was less injurious than the one published in Russia, it was still unfavorably regarded at the Vatican since it excluded the Holy

---

[28] 117-E, Gibbons to Gasparri, Baltimore, March 24, 1918, copy in Italian and translation.

[29] 117-F, Leslie to Stickney, Washington, Easter Sunday [March 31], 1918, *Private.*

[30] 117-F, Balfour to Gibbons, London, April 3, 1918, *Private.* Gibbons sent Gasparri a copy of his letter of March 6 to Balfour, as well as a copy of the latter's reply (117-J, Gibbons to Gasparri, Baltimore, April 22, 1918, copy).

See alone among the neutrals from the peace conference. Therefore, Benedict XV requested the cardinal to insist on this point with the British ambassador, and when opportunity presented itself with President Wilson.[31] On the following day Father Fay informed Gibbons that he was now ready to leave Rome for London where he was being sent on business for the Red Cross and to fulfill a mission for Gasparri. Fay was grateful for the honor of being made a domestic prelate with the warm approval of his ordinary, and he told the cardinal, "I am bringing a letter to Your Eminence from Cardinal Gasparri which will give you an idea of how much the Holy Father appreciates the great work you have done for the cause of religion in this crisis."[32]

At this point there occurred an incident which, perhaps, revealed the strain under which Cardinal Gibbons was then laboring, and which gave evidence of one of the very few times in his long life that he assumed a sharp tone in his correspondence. Maria Longworth Storer, wife of the former American ambassador to Vienna, approached Bishop Shahan with the suggestion that the entire American hierarchy appeal in a body to President Wilson to provide a representative of the Pope at the peace conference. Shahan was perplexed about how he should answer, since Mrs. Storer had been a benefactor of the university and he should like to write her a fair and pleasing letter. Yet, as he said, "The good lady seems to think that such a step can be taken without proper forethought and regular consultation." But if there was hesitation in the mind of Shahan, there was none in the mind of the cardinal. Gibbons strongly reprobated the suggestion as most impolitic and one that would result in a serious blow to the prestige of the hierarchy. If such a move seemed wise to the bishops, they would inaugurate it in good time and when it would be welcomed by the civil authorities. As for Mrs. Storer, she had been what Gibbons termed "a mischief-maker for years," and he was not surprised at this latest imprudent action. He referred to her efforts of some years before to secure a red hat for Archbishop Ireland, and stated that her

---

[31] 117-K, Bonzano to Gibbons, Washington, April 27, 1918, enclosing a copy of a cable from Gasparri; *ibid.*, Gasparri to Gibbons, Rome, April 27, 1918.

[32] 117-K, Fay to Gibbons, Rome, April 28, 1918. A week before Gasparri had cabled Gibbons saying a papal distinction had been asked for Fay, and the Holy See wished to know whether and what distinction the cardinal desired to have bestowed upon him (117-J, Gasparri to Gibbons, Rome, April 20, 1918, cablegram).

meddling in ecclesiastical affairs had been the cause of much embarrassment. With this forceful expression of his reaction to the Storer suggestion, the cardinal concluded, "I shall leave it to your good judgment as to how to answer best the communication which I am returning to you herewith. But you will be guided by remarks noted above."[33] It was apparent that Gibbons was taking no chances on a repetition of the fiasco that had attended Mrs. Storer's attempts to win a cardinalate for Ireland.

Meanwhile the negotiations concerning the offending clause in the secret Treaty of London continued. Gibbons was informed of the gratification felt at the Holy See when it became known that Secretary Lansing had told Count Vincenzo Macchi di Cellere, the Italian ambassador to Washington, that the American government desired that the feelings of American Catholics should be no longer offended by the circulation of propaganda against the Holy See in the United States. The Pope was convinced that it was Gibbons who had given the suggestion for this action to the President, and he wished the cardinal to know his gratitude. Moreover, it was now stated that when Gibbons should next see Wilson it was the wish of the Pontiff that he should speak to him about Article 15 and tell him that it was insulting not only to the Holy See but to the Catholic hierarchy and people as well. The Cardinal of Baltimore was reminded that Mercier and Louis Cardinal Dubois of Rouen had already issued protests and that the hierarchy of the United States might likewise do so. But since protests of this kind might injure the military efficiency of the allies, the President could be told that the American bishops had up to the present refrained from taking any action. All difficulty, however, would be removed if Wilson would let it be known to Baron Sidney Sonnino, Italian foreign minister, through the American ambassador at Rome that Article 15 should be either suppressed entirely, or at least modified in such a way as not to exclude only the Holy See among the neutrals from representation at the peace conference. Such action, according to Gasparri, would give just satisfaction to the Holy See, to the Catholic hierarchy and faithful of the world, and to the British government. "Only the President of the United

---

[33] 117-N, Shahan to Gibbons, Washington, May 15, 1918; 117-P, Gibbons to Shahan, Baltimore, May 21, 1918, copy.

States," he said, "can say a friendly and at the same time an efficacious word to the Italian government."[34]

In reply Gibbons promised to take the first opportunity to explain Gasparri's ideas on the elimination of the treaty clause to President Wilson and Secretary Lansing. However, it should not be forgotten, said Gibbons, that a danger existed in Wilson speaking out at that moment on a matter relating to the internal affairs of an allied power, and just at present the President was very preoccupied with serious problems of the war and with major domestic issues. Furthermore, the papal Secretary of State was informed that there was on foot a move for a third term for Wilson and, although such would run counter to American tradition, it might happen and this, too, must not be lost sight of.[35]

Within a few weeks a new development arose when the Belgian government officially demanded that Article 15 be modified in such a way as not to permit any neutral state to be represented at the peace conference without the signed consent of the allied powers. Gasparri thereupon called this to Gibbons' attention and said that the Belgian suggestion would remove the injurious character of the disputed clause insofar as the Holy See was concerned, that the English government desired it should be done, but Sonnino refused to agree. Once more he thought a word from Wilson to the Italian government would accomplish the end desired, and he begged Gibbons to ask the President to speak it,[36] to which the cardinal again promised that he would grasp the first opportunity to lay the matter before Wilson.[37] At this point the evidence is not clear. Whether the cardinal saw Wilson or not it is impossible to say but, at any rate, ten days after his

---

[34] 117-T, Gasparri to Gibbons, Rome, June 18, 1918. Actually the Holy See was the only neutral completely barred from the conference. The question of who should compose the personnel was a matter of prolonged discussion. One of the leading works on the conference has stated, "It was finally determined to admit all those who had declared war on, or had broken off relations with Germany, though the neutrals were to be allowed to take part in discussions which affected their special interests." H. W. V. Temperley (Ed.), *A History of the Peace Conference of Paris* (London, 1920), I, 247.

[35] 118-F, Gibbons to Gasparri, Baltimore, July 24, 1918, copy in Italian.

[36] AAB, unclassified, Bonzano to Gibbons, Washington, August 1, 1918, enclosing a cable of Gasparri received the previous day.

[37] *Ibid.*, Gibbons to Bonzano, Baltimore, August 2, 1918, copy. Cf. 118-H, Gibbons to Gasparri, Baltimore, August 2, 1918, copy in Italian.

reply to Gasparri he wrote him again and outlined why he thought it would be impossible for the President to follow the suggestion offered by the Vatican.

The Belgian proposal, said Gibbons, would entail grave embarrassment for Wilson since he had declared on a number of occasions that at the end of the war all the neutral nations, great and small, but especially those of South America, were to be represented at the conference of peace. But if the Belgian formula were accepted it would mean that the President could not follow his own will in the matter, but would first have to secure the signatures of the allied belligerents before admitting any neutrals to the conference table. It was impossible, thought the cardinal, that Wilson would wish to bind his hands in this fashion or to abandon his liberty of action. Gasparri was reminded of the political coloring that would be put on Wilson's action in view of the approaching congressional elections in the autumn, and for that reason it seemed better to Gibbons for the time being to trust to the future and if a favorable opportunity presented itself he would not fail to advance the wishes of the Holy See.[38] Although between mid-August and the close of the war the cardinal had occasion to approach Wilson several times on the question of an armistice, he apparently made no move to urge upon the President any action in regard to admitting a representative of the Pope to the peace conference.[39]

By the early autumn of 1918 it must have become evident to even the most sanguine officials at the Vatican and in the Church at large that nothing could or would be done to effect the elimination or substantial modification of Article 15. It was probably with that conviction that Cardinal Bourne suggested to Cardinal Gibbons that their efforts be concentrated on a full consideration in the peace conference of the need for the independence of the Holy See in relation to the Italian government. Bourne alluded to the rectifications that were likely to take place in regard to Poland, Schleswig-Holstein, and Alsace-Lorraine, and he felt that the question of the Holy See's independence might well be associated with these problems as one item in a

---

[38] *Ibid.*, Gibbons to Gasparri, Spring Lake, New Jersey, August 13, 1918, copy in Italian in Denis J. O'Connell's handwriting.

[39] LC, Wilson Papers, Gibbons to Wilson, Baltimore, October 12, 1918; 119-M, same to same, Baltimore, November 5, 1918, copy.

long series of injustices. He was writing quite independently, he said, but he was anxious to learn if Gibbons shared his opinion and would be willing to urge the matter upon the American government and, if necessary, to awaken American Catholic sentiment in support of such a demand. "Probably no other similarly favourable occasion is likely to arise at any future period," said Bourne, "and I think that we ought to do all in our power to seize this occasion of obtaining for the Holy See just and adequate freedom."[40]

Gibbons delayed answering the English cardinal until, as he said, he could give his suggestion careful consideration. By the fortunate turn of events in the termination of the war a favorable solution seemed to be shaping itself on such questions as those of Alsace-Lorraine and Poland. He had been in frequent communication with President Wilson on matters of vital interest to the Holy See and he felt the President would be interested in its just claims. Should Wilson extend his European trip to Rome it was Gibbons' hope that he would get a deeper insight into the position of the Holy See if he visited Benedict XV as the cardinal had requested him to do. Without committing himself to any definite measure, Gibbons told Bourne that he would have his hearty assistance in such action as the Archbishop of Westminster should deem expedient and he held himself ready for him to command his co-operation.[41] Bishop McDonnell of Brooklyn was likewise of the opinion that something ought to be done to insure the question of the Pope's independence being brought before the peace conference. He was in favor of a world-wide petition of the Catholic hierarchy, if this be pleasing to the Vatican, and he said, "Now is the time for united effort on the part of the Catholics of the United States that some measure of freedom be secured for the Pope in dealing with his world-wide flock without the interference of the Italian government. . . ."[42] Gibbons thanked him for his warm interest in the question and said he had been in correspondence with Cardinal Bourne about it. "We are awaiting," he said, "the proper moment to take action." The cardinal gave it as his

---

[40] 118-W, Bourne to Gibbons, Westminster, October 12, 1918, *Confidential.* Bourne's letter was delivered by Monsignor Maurice E. Carton de Wiart, one of his secretaries, to whom, said Bourne, Gibbons might speak in full confidence.

[41] 119-U, Gibbons to Bourne, Baltimore, December 12, 1918, *Confidential,* copy.

[42] 119-V, McDonnell to Gibbons, Brooklyn, December 20, 1918.

personal opinion that the best policy would be to have the nations of the world guarantee the liberty of the Holy See since, as he said, any effort to restore the temporal power such as it was would be filled with the greatest difficulties and would be doomed to meet with failure.[43]

Three weeks later there took place on January 18, 1919, the formal opening of the conference of peace in Paris where seventy delegates gathered as the representatives of twenty-seven victorious powers. On the day that the conference opened Cardinal Gasparri cabled instructions through the apostolic delegate to Cardinals Gibbons and O'Connell that they should immediately signify to Cardinal Mercier that he demand of the peace conference in the name of the American hierarchy and their faithful the territorial sovereignty of the Pope.[44] Gibbons promptly complied with the request and, in addition to a cablegram, he sent Mercier a letter which outlined his ideas on the subject.

The Cardinal of Baltimore remarked at the outset that the great respect and esteem which the Cardinal of Malines had gained throughout the world during the past four years would naturally cause any proposal of his to be given due consideration. Since the conference proposed the settlement of all questions likely to disturb the peace of the world and the removal, if possible, of all those causes which tended to create division among peoples, it was Gibbons' firm conviction that among such questions which should be settled once and for all was that of the independence of the Holy See. He mentioned the unsatisfactory position which the Pope had occupied for many years,

---

[43] 119-V, Gibbons to McDonnell, Baltimore, December 21, 1918, copy.

[44] 120-C, Bonzano to Gibbons, Washington, January 18, 1919, enclosing a copy of Gasparri's cablegram. During the previous week Gibbons lost his trusted agent in these matters when Monsignor Fay died suddenly in New York on January 10 on the eve of his departure for England to continue his mission (New York *Herald,* January 11, 1919). Four months before his death Fay had published an article in which he had endeavored to counteract the propaganda against the Holy See as being pro-German. He mentioned that the Pope was the only non-belligerent who had protested the rape of Belgium, the bombing of unarmed towns, the unrestricted submarine warfare, and the deportation of the Belgians. "In spite of this official disapproval of Germany's methods of warfare," he said, "the Pope's attitude has constantly been misrepresented in every Allied country, and every effort has been made to represent him and the Church over which he presides as one of the principal means of Germanizing the world" ("The Voice of the Vatican," *The Chronicle,* IV [September, 1918], no pagination).

and he said, "Against this present state of affairs the conscience of the whole Catholic world protests and will not be satisfied until full independence be given to him." With that end in view he requested Mercier in his own name, and in the names of the American bishops and their people, to place the matter before the delegates at Paris, since the American Catholics like the Catholics of the entire world felt they had a right to be heard in a matter of such importance to them. In asking for a solution to the Roman Question the Cardinal of Baltimore emphasized that he was in no way suggesting the impairment of the unity of Italy. On the contrary, he desired the removal of those conditions which had caused a division in the past and which had proved so harmful to Italy. And in committing his request for action to Mercier he concluded, "no one better than Your Eminence could make himself the interpreter of this desire, as you so nobly proved yourself to be the great champion of liberty and justice."[45]

Although the effort of the cardinals to have the Roman Question discussed at the Paris peace conference proved ineffectual against the hostility of the Italian delegation and the opposition or indifference of the other great powers, a final attempt was made which was of interest in light of the solution of the question ten years later. Early in 1919 Father Kelley of the Catholic Church Extension Society decided to go to Paris in what proved to be a vain attempt to get a clause into the covenant of the projected League of Nations guaranteeing liberty of conscience. On May 10 he held a private conversation with Cardinal Mercier at Malines in which the latter told him of his anxiety to do something about the independence of the Holy See. Mercier was reluctant to go to Paris unless he had assurance ahead of time that President Wilson and his associates would be willing to receive him and talk over the matter with him; in the latter case he would be quite willing to make the trip. Upon Kelley's return to the French capital he sought out Colonel Edward M.

---

[45] 120-C, Gibbons to Mercier, Baltimore, January 20, 1919, copy. Gibbons was in touch with Cardinal O'Connell during these days on the subject, and after the latter had explained his own approach to Mercier, he remarked, "I shall await with anxiety any information which Your Eminence wishes to convey to me with regard to the furtherance of this idea" (120-C, O'Connell to Gibbons, Boston, January 20, 1919; Gibbons to O'Connell, Baltimore, January 20, 1919, copy).

House, the President's confidential adviser, and broached the subject of the cardinal's visit. Father Kelley later described House's reaction as follows:

> He at once said that the President certainly would see His Eminence, but doubted if he would discuss the Roman question. He thought that the President would not wish to have it brought up. It was, after all, somewhat out of the line of American interests, and there were our religious divisions at home to consider.[46]

It was quite apparent, therefore, that nothing could be hoped for from the American delegation. On the same day as his interview with House, the American priest accidentally met on the street the Marquis Giuseppe Brambilla, counselor of legation in the Italian peace delegation. At Brambilla's suggestion an informal meeting was arranged between Premier Vittorio Orlando of Italy and Father Kelley in which the former made it known that he was willing to discuss the question of the Papacy. Encouraged by this fact, Kelley hurried to Rome and put the matter into the hands of Archbishop Cerretti who, in turn, consulted with the Pope and Cardinal Gasparri. As a consequence Cerretti and Kelley returned to Paris, and on June 1 the Vatican diplomat met Orlando and laid before him the proposals of the Holy See in the form of a written statement by Gasparri in which he asked that the character of a state be accorded to the Holy See for the inclosure of the Vatican with a guarantee of the independence and sovereignty of the Pope. The bright prospects which seemed to offer themselves were soon shattered, however, owing to the bitter quarrel that had broken out in the peace conference itself between Wilson and the Italian delegation over the territorial ambitions of Italy. As a result of this disagreement Orlando left Paris on June 10, and nine days later the vote which he provoked on the subject in the Italian parliament went against him and his government resigned. Francesco Nitti then succeeded as premier and Tommaso

---

[46] Kelley, *The Bishop Jots It Down*, p. 266. For Cerretti's part in the negotiations cf. the very sketchy account in Elvira Cerretti, *Il cardinale Bonaventura Cerretti, Memoria* (Rome, 1939), pp. 215–231. There is no adequate biography of Mercier and the works so far published make no mention of his part in these negotiations. Cf. *Cardinal Mercier's Own Story* (New York, 1920); Henry L. Dubly, *The Life of Cardinal Mercier* (Cork, n.d.); and John A. Gade, *The Life of Cardinal Mercier* (New York, 1935).

Tittoni came in at the foreign office. But the lowered prestige of the Italians at Paris and the rising threat of revolt within Italy provided a poor atmosphere in which to continue the conversations which Orlando and Cerretti had inaugurated, even if there had been a disposition on the part of the new Italian government to do so, which there was not. Consequently nothing further came of the matter at that time. Ten years later in commenting on his role in the preliminary steps with Cerretti in 1919 Orlando wrote:

> I said that America influenced in two ways this attempt of agreement: Positively and negatively. Positively, because the suggestion which brought about the interview came from an American prelate. Negatively, because, without my tragic dissension with President Wilson, my prestige as head of the government which had won the war and concluded the peace would have remained untouched, and the Italian people would have been peaceful and contented. The two conditions whose absence prevented the conclusion of the agreement would then have been fulfilled.[47]

Every attempt made, then, before and during the peace conference in Paris to have the obnoxious clause removed or modified in the secret Treaty of London, to win a hearing at the conference table on the question of the Pope's independence, and to get an assurance of the restoration of his sovereignty had failed on the part of Gibbons and the other churchmen who tried. Nonetheless, there was one minor point which, it was hoped at the time, might have an indirect bearing on the question, and in this particular the cardinal succeeded. Some time before the departure of President Wilson for Europe Gibbons requested him to visit the Pope if he should go to Rome. The cardinal repeated what he had stated on previous occasions concerning the high esteem in which the Pontiff held Wilson, and he then said:

> My dear Mr. President, as an American as well as a Catholic, as one who is bound to you by the bonds of patriotism as I am bound to the Holy Father in the bonds of religion, I ask you in the strongest and most affectionate manner of which I am capable not to leave Rome without paying a personal visit to the Pope. I ask you to do this not only because it will be a great consolation to the Holy Father who so admires and trusts you, not only because it

---

[47] Vittorio E. Orlando, "The First Agreement between Italy and the Holy See," *Saturday Evening Post,* CCI (May 4, 1929), 206.

will bind the hearts of Catholics to you forever, but because it will delight the hearts of all good men, who whether they agree with the Holy Father in religion or not, at least recognize him as the representative of the greatest moral authority left in the world, and because you, Mr. President, in the opinion of all men, are the one who raised the late war from the plane of national jealousies into the plane of idealism and made it a conflict and a struggle for justice, for righteousness, for liberty and for nothing else. I say then that this will give delight to all men of good will to know that you have not disregarded or slighted the representative of the moral order.

I feel sure that I have only asked you to do what you have already determined in your heart to do, but which I felt it was nevertheless my duty to put before you.[48]

In reply Wilson stated that he was turning aside in the midst of a very busy day to say how sincerely he appreciated the personal thought of him and of the interests of the whole world which had prompted the cardinal to write. "I beg to assure you," he said, "that it carries the greatest weight." He had formed no plans about what he was to do in Europe, except that he would devote every energy to the peace settlement, but he concluded, "it will give me real pleasure to have your suggestions in mind if I should go to Rome."[49] Wilson in fact

---

[48] LC, Wilson Papers, Gibbons to Wilson, Baltimore, November 27, 1918. Further instances of Gibbons making requests of Wilson in matters of interest to the Church can be found. For example, in the spring of 1919 the cardinal wrote the President when the latter was in Paris asking that he interest himself in the holy places in Palestine. Wilson acknowledged his letter of April 15 and said the information about the holy places was novel to him, but he added, "I shall try to make myself acquainted with the problem in the most sympathetic way" (LC, Wilson Papers, Wilson to Gibbons, Paris, May 6, 1919, copy). Nearly a year later the cardinal interceded in behalf of the Christians — both Catholic and Protestant — who were being persecuted in Transylvania, and he stated to Wilson, "I respectfully ask that you cooperate with the British Government, and exact from Rumania the promise to give a fuller share of religious liberty to the inhabitants of Transylvania" (*ibid.*, Gibbons to Wilson, Baltimore, March 26, 1920).

[49] 119-S, Wilson to Gibbons, Washington, November 30, 1918. Gibbons sent copies of the correspondence exchanged with Wilson on this point to Bonzano and Gasparri (119-T, Gibbons to Bonzano, Baltimore, December 2, 1918, copy; Gibbons to Gasparri, Baltimore, December 7, 1918, copy). Bonzano congratulated him on his letter to Wilson and said that if the dispatches in the press could be credited, Gibbons' efforts would be fruitful of good results, for the Associated Press cables had announced that the Italian papers were already publishing it as a certainty that the President would visit the Pope (119-T, Bonzano to Gibbons, Washington, December 4, 1918).

did visit Benedict XV on January 4 at the end of his stay in Rome, and later the same day the Pontiff received in audience the American newspaper men attached to the President's suite during which he paid a high tribute to the American chief executive.[50]

But if Cardinal Gibbons experienced a disappointment on the score of his failure to win a rectification from the Paris peace conference of the injustice done to the Papacy in 1870, President Wilson was destined to suffer an equally great one in the defeat of his favorite scheme for a league of nations. Even before the United States entered the European conflict the President, strongly influenced by the League to Enforce Peace, had become convinced that a league binding all the nations of the world together offered the greatest hope for the future peace of mankind. It was an idea which Gibbons shared and, as we have seen, he had actively co-operated with the League to Enforce Peace, of which he was a vice-president, in furthering the cause before the American public.

---

[50] New York *Herald,* January 5 and 6, 1919. By the summer of 1919 the situation within Italy had become extremely grave. The heavy losses sustained by the war, the failure to secure the territorial gains that had been promised, the inflationary prices, and the widespread economic suffering contributed to a resurgence of the socialist and communist elements, and by midsummer the likelihood of revolution was regarded at the Holy See as real. In the emergency the Vatican became anxious concerning its financial securities and through the medium of Monsignor Charles A. O'Hern, Rector of the American College, a request was made of the American Embassy that the treasure be housed there for safekeeping. Peter A. Jay, chargé d'affaires, cabled to Frank L. Polk, Acting Secretary of State, deprecating the move but stating that O'Hern had intimated that Cardinal Gibbons could secure the permission of the President if that were necessary. The Vatican feared a communist overthrow of the Italian government, and while Jay was inclined to think the Holy See unduly alarmed over the Bolshevik menace, he closed his lengthy cable by saying, "it has additional importance as throwing a somewhat startling light on general Italian situation as understood by Vatican which has, especially in this Catholic country, special sources of information" (National Archives, Department of States Archives, 866.51, Jay to Polk, Rome, July 15, 1919, *Very confidential,* cablegram). In reply Polk approved Jay's attitude in general, but stated that if O'Hern wished, he might deposit the treasure in the embassy's chancery for safekeeping on condition that he himself would assume responsibility for it; the embassy was to be held responsible only so long as its premises were not violated or otherwise disturbed. Polk suggested, however, that O'Hern might find a more suitable place in the American College than in the embassy, especially, as he said, "since the American flag could be raised over the premises of the College if at any time events should develop making it desirable to take such action" (*ibid.,* Polk to Jay, Washington, July 18, 1919, *Confidential,* cablegram in copy).

After the war was over the cardinal continued his efforts in this regard and upon a visit paid to him by William H. Short, secretary of the league, Gibbons discussed the matter of the assistance which the Catholic Church might give and invited the co-operation of the National Catholic War Council in the league's work. In introducing Short to Father Burke, chairman of the Special War Activities Committee of the N.C.W.C., in December, 1918, the cardinal stated that the next few months would witness the treaty of peace framed and acted upon by the United States. "We shall then know," said Gibbons, "whether we are to have a league of nations for the maintenance of justice and peace or whether the world will go back to the condition of armed rivalry which has obtained hitherto." The League to Enforce Peace was planning to carry on a vigorous campaign during this period with the object of crystallizing public opinion in favor of a league, and the question had now arisen as to how the Church might meet its responsibilities and share in the movement. The suggestion had been made, said the cardinal, that the most effective instrumentality for this would be the N.C.W.C., and in this view he heartily concurred. "It is logically a necessary feature of the work for which the Council was created," he said, "and would indeed be the very crown of its activities since a just and lasting peace was America's motive in entering the war." Therefore, he hoped Burke would confer and co-operate with Short to advance this aim.[51]

There was little question about the need for a publicity campaign in favor of the League of Nations, for opposition to the idea of the United States entering such an organization grew steadily during the spring of 1919, and long before the proposal was laid before the senate there were formidable forces arrayed against it. Gibbons, however, did not allow his support to slacken and in early April he gave a press interview in which he advo-

---

[51] ANCWC, Gibbons to Burke, Baltimore, December 10, 1918. William Howard Taft, president of the league, asked Gibbons to be present at a convention in New York to open the meeting with an invocation or an address. "We would be delighted to have either or both," he said (119-XYZ, Taft to Gibbons, Washington, December 31, 1918). The cardinal replied that it pained him to refuse the invitation because of his extreme age; only the day before he had written Short cheerfully lending the use of his name to the cause. "Thus you see," he said, "I am heart and soul for the League, and will do all in my power to have its measures carried out. Perhaps a letter from me might serve you?" (120-A, Gibbons to Taft, Baltimore, January 3, 1919, copy.)

cated a league of nations and deplored the idea of delaying a ratification of the peace treaty.[52] Friends of the league were, of course, aware of his views, and the anxiety they felt at the widespread criticism of the organization among those American-Irish who opposed it on the ground of the failure of the peace conference to provide for Irish freedom, made them desirous that Gibbons' favorable opinion should receive the widest publicity. William J. Sullivan of Boston was one who shared this desire, and in writing to Joseph P. Tumulty, secretary to President Wilson, he asked, "would it not be well at this time to have the attitude of the most powerful and influential man in all America, particularly among those of Irish blood, brought more sharply and conspicuously to the attention of the people? I refer, of course," said Sullivan, "to the great Cardinal Gibbons. . . ."[53]

In the meantime the Treaty of Versailles was signed on June 28 and the American President departed soon thereafter for home where on July 10 he submitted the treaty, embodying the covenant of the League of Nations, to the United States Senate for ratification. On the same day the cardinal welcomed the President home, and in doing so he said, "You have had a most trying and important mission abroad and I beg to congratulate you on your accomplishments."[54] The mission had, indeed, been a trying one but it had not been so severe as the one immediately ahead of Wilson, for the treaty had no sooner been placed before the senate than the pent-up opposition of months broke loose among the senators and before long was reflected in the country at large. Within a very short time it was apparent that the President had the major battle of his political life on his hands to save his cherished league.

In the fight that ensued the administration sought to marshal every possible aid to win ratification of the Treaty of Versailles. On the eve of his departure for Paris to replace Wilson as head of the American Commission to Negotiate Peace, the Undersecretary of State, Frank L. Polk, asked Monsignor Cornelius F. Thomas, pastor of St. Patrick's Church in Washington, to ascertain if the cardinal would not issue a statement for publication in favor of the League of Nations. Gibbons was reminded

---

[52] New York *Times,* April 4, 1919.

[53] LC, Wilson Papers, Sullivan to Tumulty, Boston, June 26, 1919.

[54] *Ibid.,* Gibbons to Wilson, Baltimore, July 10, 1919.

that some of the American hierarchy had come out against the league because of the failure to mention or uphold self-determination for Ireland while other bishops had insinuated that religious prejudice had operated in depriving the Irish cause of a hearing at Paris. Polk expressed the fear that the element of religious prejudice might be introduced into the coming congressional elections, based on what the league had failed to guarantee. For that reason, Thomas told the cardinal, "He thinks that if your Eminence would publicly say a word in defense of the League, the testimony would be used as an offset to any anti-League agitation because of Catholicity."[55] Gibbons was at the time spending his eighty-fifth birthday at the home of the Shriver family at Union Mills, Maryland, and his response came in the form of a birthday interview to the press in which he said:

> It is my firm conviction that after thorough and honest discussion in both houses of Congress, both parties will finally arrive at a common agreement, based upon a just and sincere league of nations that will give us a reasonable guarantee against the horrors of war in the future as well as well-grounded assurance of lasting peace without in any way impairing American sovereignty or surrendering any American right and without involving us in entangling alliances. I am sure that an early adoption of the league of nations will infuse intense joy throughout the United States without distinction of party and will be hailed with satisfaction by the allied powers of Europe.[56]

If Gibbons' prediction that adoption of the league would infuse intense joy throughout the country proved quite erroneous, there was no doubt about the joy his interview brought to the White House. After reading the statement of the cardinal in the Washington *Post,* the President wrote him as follows:

> It is with the deepest pleasure that I learn from this morning's Washington Post of your statement with regard to the League of Nations. You have perceived, as is habitual with you, the really profound interests of humanity and of Christianity which are in-

---

[55] 122-R, Thomas to Gibbons, Washington, July 23, 1919. *Private.* On the basis of various reports reaching him Tumulty, Wilson's secretary, believed that the influence of Cardinal O'Connell and Archbishop Hayes was being thrown against the league. Cf. H. C. F. Bell, *Woodrow Wilson and the People* (Garden City, New York, 1945), p. 333.

[56] Washington *Post,* July 25, 1919.

volved in the issue of the adoption of the League Covenant, and it is with profound pleasure that I find myself aligned alongside of you in this great cause, to which the anxious and prayerful thought of every Christian man, it seems to me, must turn with hope that will permit no denial.

Even a serious delay in the adoption of the League will do much to institute anxiety throughout the world, not excepting Europe, and I know of what significance it will prove to be that you should lend your great influence to prevent giving even an added opportunity to the forces of disorder and of evil.[57]

Due to an absence from home and his feeling that Wilson was too heavily burdened for correspondence, Gibbons did not reply until a month later. At that time he expressed the hope that the fruit of the President's labors would quickly be seen and that he and the senate would soon arrive at a satisfactory conclusion of the weighty questions then confronting them.[58] Polk in time learned of Gibbons' response to his suggestion, and he expressed his appreciation from Paris by saying he felt certain the beneficial effects of the cardinal's interview would be far reaching.[59]

Cardinal Gibbons continued to the close of his life to do what he could to convince his fellow countrymen of the wisdom of the United States adopting the League of Nations. In the winter of 1919 he joined with a group of distinguished Americans in petitioning the President to accept the amendments offered by Senator Henry Cabot Lodge to the Treaty of Versailles, in order that the League of Nations might not be entirely lost.[60] When Pope Benedict XV issued on May 23, 1920, his encyclical, *Pacem Dei munus pulcherrimum,* in which he expressed the desire that the nations unite in a league to maintain their own independence and safeguard the order of human society, the Cardinal of Baltimore was highly pleased. In an interview which he granted to Stephen Bonsal of the Baltimore *Sun* the following autumn, he called attention to the Pope's words and said that one feature of the league covenant which he especially

[57] 122-S, Wilson to Gibbons, Washington, July 25, 1919, *Personal* and *Confidential.*

[58] 123-C, Gibbons to Wilson, Baltimore, August 23, 1919, copy.

[59] 123-F, Polk to Gibbons, Paris, September 9, 1919.

[60] Charles Seymour (Ed.), *The Intimate Papers of Colonel House* (Boston, 1928), IV, 507, note 2.

admired was the provision for delay when a crisis threatened, and he liked as well the right of any nation to bring to the attention of the assembly or council any circumstance that might be thought to threaten good international relations.[61]

About the same time a local newspaper in Oklahoma reported Gibbons as endorsing the League of Nations without any regulations safeguarding American interests and a critic of the league wired him to ask if he had been correctly reported. The cardinal telegraphed in reply, "I am incorrectly quoted. Recommended *a* league of nations with proper reservations and constitutional safeguards."[62] But despite all reservations, the treaty failed to command a majority when a vote was first taken in the senate in November, 1919, and on March 20, 1920, it failed a second time, even though it was modified by fifteen reservations framed by Senator Lodge. Although the failure of the senate to adopt the league was a disappointment to Gibbons, he was not prepared to place all his trust in that organization to preserve the peace. Just a few weeks before the first senate vote he was asked to give his opinion again on the subject of universal military training for American youth. The cardinal advanced the familiar arguments of the good to be derived from discipline and obedience to superiors; but he added that he was convinced that military training was essential for the welfare and security of the nation. "In the recent war," he said, "we had the trained armies of our Allies to lean upon until our soldiers were prepared for the battlefield. We cannot always depend upon such a favorable circumstance in the event that we are drawn into war again."[63]

One of the questions which strongly influenced the thinking of American Catholics — especially those of Irish descent — on the League of Nations was the failure of the Paris peace conference to do anything positive for the freedom of Ireland. Even

---

[61] Baltimore *Sun,* October 21, 1920.

[62] 130-D, Charles Standard to Gibbons, Tulsa, October 29, 1920, telegram; Gibbons to Standard, Baltimore, October 29, 1920, telegram, copy.

[63] 123-P, Louis R. Stickney to Howard H. Cross of the Universal Military Training League, Baltimore, October 22, 1919, copy. On April 11, 1920, Gibbons officiated at a ceremony in his cathedral when he presented to Admiral William S. Benson, Chief of Naval Operations, the Order of St. Gregory the Great which had been conferred on him by Benedict XV. Secretary of the Navy Josephus Daniels was present for the occasion. Josephus Daniels, *The Wilson Era. Years of War and After, 1917–1923* (Chapel Hill, 1946), pp. 583–584.

before the conference opened many of these people had made public their views, and among them Bishop Shahan, Rector of the Catholic University of America, petitioned President Wilson to interest himself in the self-determination of Ireland when he reached Paris.[64] But nothing was done to settle the matter at the peace conference, and meanwhile the armed resistance led by the Irish Republican Army created a state of virtual civil war in Ireland throughout the year 1919. We have already seen the cautious policy which Cardinal Gibbons pursued on the Irish question and, although he did lend his presence to the Irish convention in Philadelphia in February of that year and granted an interview to Éamonn de Valera, the leader of the Sinn Féin Party, the following summer,[65] he continued his attitude of reserve. For example, when Evelyn Wrench of the English-Speaking Union who was attached during the war to the British Ministry of Information, sought to win his adherence to a statement on Ireland, the cardinal replied that he thought it more advisable for him to remain silent in view of the agitation and disquietude prevailing in that country. "I fear the attachment of my name," said Gibbons, "would be misconstrued, and might involve me in embarrassing correspondence."[66]

But if Gibbons felt reluctant to commit himself on Irish affairs, there was a Catholic churchman on the other side of the world who experienced no such hesitation. Daniel Mannix, Archbishop

---

[64] Shahan to Wilson, Washington, November 30, 1918, *Catholic University Bulletin*, XXV (February, 1919), 172–173. Wilson had little sympathy with the cause of Irish freedom. In his diary of the Paris peace conference Stephen Bonsal noted under date of March 23, 1919, the President had informed the peace commission that before leaving the United States he had been visited by a delegation who had asked him to pledge himself to work for Ireland's freedom at Paris. Wilson was quoted as having said, "My first impulse was to tell the Irish to go to hell, but, feeling that this would not be the act of a statesman, I denied myself this personal satisfaction" (*Unfinished Business* [London, 1944], p. 138).

[65] New York *Times,* August 26, 1919. Gibbons gave De Valera a friendly suggestion that the meeting scheduled for Baltimore that evening should be characterized by wisdom, judgment, and discretion, "so that it may enlist," as he remarked, "new friends to your cause." He stated that he remembered as a boy the help given to Ireland by the United States. "I shall never forget," he said, "the arrival of a ship filled with corn." For a recent treatment of De Valera's American tour from June, 1919, to December, 1920, cf. Mary C. Bromage, "De Valera's Mission to America," *South Atlantic Quarterly,* L (October, 1951), 499–513.

[66] 126-H, Gibbons to Wrench, Baltimore, April 20, 1920, copy.

of Melbourne, was Irish-born and a forceful advocate of the freedom of Ireland from English rule. Late in the spring of 1920 Mannix left Australia for Ireland to visit his old mother. He had been so outspoken on the subject of the English overlordship of his native land that he had won an international reputation in this regard. When the *Ventura* on which Mannix was travel-ing reached Honolulu, a Hawaiian band at the wharf played "America" which had the same air as "God Save the King." A group of passengers formed a ring around the archbishop while the anthem was being played, and they sang the words of "God Save the King." Mannix refused to rise. Asked if he did not know it was the national anthem, he replied that he did, but as an Irishman sailing on an American vessel under the American flag he did not deem it necessary to rise in the circum-stances. He later explained that he had risen for the "Star Spangled Banner," but insofar as the English national anthem was concerned, he remarked, "I don't think I am bound to rise when some ill-bred person sings an anthem to embarrass me."[67] Unfortunately, the news dispatches from Honolulu and the *Ventura* were colored against Mannix and the incident left an unhappy impression in the United States, although it did not prevent him from receiving a tremendous welcome from his many admirers in San Francisco when he landed on June 7. One of the passengers on the *Ventura* joined ten other Americans in signing a protest against Mannix' action and sent word of it to Gibbons. The fact that there were several Catholics who signed the protest proved, according to the author of the letter, that there was no religious feeling involved, and that it was purely and simply a case of protesting disrespect to the American flag.[68]

It can easily be imagined that Cardinal Gibbons would be disturbed by the action of a Catholic churchman such as was described by the press and in the letter of his correspondent. After Mannix had been in the country about three weeks the cardinal received a telegram from him in Chicago saying he gratefully accepted Gibbons' invitation to visit him on July 24.

---

[67] Frank Murphy, *Daniel Mannix, Archbishop of Melbourne* (Melbourne, 1948), pp. 86–89, describes the incident and cites the *Irish World* of New York for July 24, 1920, for Mannix' explanation before an audience at the Catholic Summer School at Cliff Haven, New York.

[68] AAB, unclassified, Marsilis C. Parsons to Gibbons, New York, June 23, 1920.

Since Gibbons had issued no invitation of the kind, he was naturally puzzled and he wired in reply:

> I am at this moment in receipt of a telegram signed by you stating that you will be here July 24th. I fear there must be a mistake. I will indeed be most happy to see you, but as is my custom, I will be absent from the city during the whole month of July and part of August. Anytime after these dates a visit from you will be most acceptable.[69]

Five days later from Detroit the Archbishop of Melbourne informed the cardinal that the wire had been sent by mistake; it had been meant for Cardinal O'Connell. "If an opportunity had offered," said Mannix, "I should have deemed it an honour and a duty to pay my respects to Your Eminence. But I sail from N. York July 31."[70] Nonetheless, Mannix found time before sailing to come to Washington and on July 25 he was driven with his party in the company of Father Patrick J. Healy, professor of church history in the Catholic University of America, and Mr. Frederick V. Murphy who taught architecture at the university, to Westminster, Maryland, to see the cardinal.

Gibbons had left Baltimore some time before and was spending a holiday at the home of the Shriver family at Union Mills a few miles from Westminster. The prelates met at St. John's Rectory in Westminster and were entertained at luncheon at the home of Mr. and Mrs. Joseph N. Shriver. No mention was made of the question of Irish freedom, and the cardinal confined his brief speech at the luncheon to a word of welcome to the guests, several polite references to Melbourne, and to the happiness which the Shrivers had afforded him for many years by their friendship and hospitality. In reply Mannix alluded to the joy he had experienced on his American visit, and he was quoted as saying that his trip would not have been a success, "either from my own point of view or from the viewpoint of those to whom I shall relate my experiences, had I not enjoyed the privilege now mine of meeting and conversing with Cardinal Gibbons."[71] The meeting was later described as rather strained and not very

---

[69] 127-XYZ, Mannix to Gibbons, Chicago, June 30, 1920, telegram; Gibbons to Mannix, Baltimore, June 30, 1920, telegram in copy.

[70] 128-B, Mannix to Gibbons, Detroit, July 4, 1920.

[71] Baltimore *Catholic Review*, July 31, 1920.

pleasant.[72] A non-Catholic in New York heard of the incident and congratulated Gibbons on the stand he had taken on the occasion of the archbishop's visit. The cardinal's correspondent agreed that the Irish should have their own government, but insofar as Mannix was concerned he remarked, "I think how much better if, as a great churchman, he had brought a ringing spiritual message to the American people and left the work of trying to free Ireland to the laymen."[73]

Yet in spite of appearances, the Cardinal of Baltimore was not unsympathetic to the aspirations of the Irish people nor insensible to their sufferings. The arrest in March, 1920, of Terence MacSwiney, Lord Mayor of Cork, and his subsequent hunger strike elicited his sympathy, and when he was visited by Rowland A. C. Sperling, head of the American department of the British Foreign Office, he let that be known. Sperling was impressed by what Gibbons had said at their interview and he asked the cardinal if he would put it in writing. The latter complied by saying that it was a matter of deep regret to him that Prime Minister Lloyd George had not been more magnanimous in his treatment of MacSwiney. "Such an act of magnanimity," said Gibbons, "would have won the affection of the Irish people and put them in a more receptive mood for any overtures of conciliation." He hoped that this expression of views would not be considered presumptuous, but since Sperling had asked for them he gave them, having in mind the interests of Britain as well as Ireland.[74] One of the final episodes relating to the Irish question in the life of Cardinal Gibbons occurred through the disappointment of Father Michael A. McFadden, pastor of St. Richard's Church, Swanton, Ohio, at the failure of the hierarchy to discuss the political troubles of Ireland at their annual meeting in the fall of 1920. In reply to the complaint, the cardinal had his secretary state that the meeting had a crowded agenda which allowed of very little discussion of outside matters. Toward

---

[72] Interviews of the writer with Miss M. Madeline Shriver, Union Mills, Maryland, July 9, 1945, and with Mr. Frederick V. Murphy, Washington, August 17, 1950.

[73] 128-Q, Frank Lee to Gibbons, New York, August 1, 1920. Gibbons was not the only churchman who tried to avoid a meeting with Mannix. When the latter reached London, Cardinal Bourne declined to receive him, for which the Archbishop of Westminster incurred the charge of being anti-Irish. George A. Beck, A.A. (Ed.), *The English Catholics, 1850–1950* (London, 1950), p. 177.

[74] 130-L, Gibbons to Sperling, Baltimore, November 15, 1920, copy.

the close of the meeting Gibbons had been approached by certain archbishops, whose loyalty to Ireland was beyond question, and who advised against permitting the Irish question to be introduced. The cardinal was of the same opinion for the reason that the business in hand had not been finished. At the next annual meeting the sessions would be extended if necessary to admit treatment of this and other matters outside the program laid down in the agenda. In conclusion it was stated with evident exaggeration, "Will you be good enough to say that Ireland has no more ardent champion than the Cardinal of Baltimore. In his own quiet way he is working constantly for the happy outcome of Ireland's struggle for freedom."[75]

One of the most important problems facing the American Church upon the return of peace was that of determining the future status of the National Catholic War Council. Although this is not the place to tell the early history of what ultimately became the National Catholic Welfare Conference, the central position which that organization has assumed in the development of twentieth-century American Catholicism will warrant the risk of some repetition of what has already been said concerning Cardinal Gibbons' part in its beginnings. With the entrance of the United States into World War I in the spring of 1917 it became apparent to the leaders of the American Church that some form of organization should be set up for unifying and strengthening Catholic war activities. The Knights of Columbus were the first in the field when the Supreme Board of Directors met in Detroit on June 24, and there ratified unanimously an appeal made to the order by the supreme officers for a million dollar fund to be expended for religious and recreational purposes for the benefit of the men of all religious faiths in the armed services.

Apart from this notable effort, there was an increasing need for the provision of chaplains and other safeguards for the morals

---

[75] 131-A, Albert E. Smith to McFadden, Baltimore, December 1, 1920, copy. That Gibbons did work for Ireland's welfare was acknowledged on the day he died when Morgan J. O'Brien of New York sent condolences in the name of the American Committee for Relief to Ireland to Bishop Owen B. Corrigan and said, "Foremost in all enterprises of mercy and charity his last act signed by the dying hand that was never raised but in benediction was his appeal to the American people whom he loved and trusted on behalf of striken Ireland" (133-R, O'Brien to Corrigan, New York, March 24, 1921).

of the troops. With that in mind Father John J. Burke, C.S.P., editor of the *Catholic World*, established under the auspices of Cardinal Farley in New York the Chaplains' Aid Association which soon had chapters covering the entire country. Burke co-operated closely with Lewis J. O'Hern, C.S.P., who had been designated by the hierarchy to deal with the government on the subject of Catholic chaplains, with Father William J. Kerby, professor of sociology in the Catholic University of America, and others to further the work. With a view to co-ordinating the war activities of all Catholic groups, Burke proposed to Gibbons that a general meeting of all Catholic societies be held which would bring about this result. The cardinal gave his consent and suggested that he seek the counsel of Cardinals Farley and O'Connell before proceeding. During the succeeding weeks Burke obtained the approval of the Cardinals of New York and Boston, wrote a letter to the entire hierarchy asking that they appoint one clergyman and one layman from their dioceses, and finally contacted the officers of all the Catholic lay societies of a national character as well as representatives of the Catholic press.

As a consequence of this appeal the representatives of sixty-eight dioceses and twenty-seven national Catholic organizations gathered on August 11–12 at the Catholic University of America, where there was founded the National Catholic War Council with Burke as the first president and representatives of various dioceses and societies among the other officers. It was this council which joined with representatives of other religious faiths, at the suggestion of Burke, in establishing an interdenominational committee for the safeguarding of the morals of the American fighting men in the camps and at the battle fronts. Much good was accomplished for the cause during the ensuing months, but the need was felt for an organization which would operate directly under the hierarchy, and in the government of which the bishops would take more direct responsibility than could be assumed by the priests and laymen. It was with that in mind that Gibbons wrote to the hierarchy on November 21 saying that at the meeting of the trustees of the university the previous week the question had been discussed and it was the unanimous opinion of the prelates present that the hierarchy should act in concert on the important matters growing out of the war effort. He outlined the main problems to be solved and asked the bishops if they would agree to the formation of a war council by the board of archbishops.[76]

One of those who had been present at the meeting of the university trustees was Archbishop Glennon of St. Louis. After his return home he exchanged views with some of the western bishops, and he informed Gibbons that James J. Keane, Archbishop of Dubuque, had suggested that since the metropolitans were too dignified and ponderous a group to function effectively as a war council, he thought Gibbons should give the whole matter over to a committee composed of Bishops Thomas F. Hickey of Rochester, Thomas F. Lillis of Kansas City, Peter J. Muldoon of Rockford, and William T. Russell of Charleston.[77] The cardinal was grateful for the suggestions but he said that a few hours before Glennon's letter arrived he had sent a communication to the hierarchy along the lines proposed, and he added, "As the work is so large we will appoint a sub-committee, whose membership will include two of the four Bishops whom you mentioned."[78] Meanwhile in response to an inquiry from Burke the cardinal sanctioned his continuing co-operation with the interdenominational committee, and he told him that the old N.C.W.C. would not go out of existence completely but would continue its activities under the council to be organized by the hierarchy.[79]

During December, 1917, the replies to Gibbons' letter to the bishops proposing a Catholic war council under the metropolitans were received and they were almost universally favorable. Acting upon this sanction, three days after Christmas Gibbons informed Bishops Muldoon, Russell, Joseph Schrembs of Toledo, and Patrick J. Hayes, Auxiliary Bishop of New York, that with the endorsement of the archbishops they had been selected to compose the executive committee of the newly organized National Catholic War Council. If they gave their consent to serve, the cardinal desired that they be present at a meeting to be held at the Catholic University of America early in January. The four bishops agreed to the proposal, and on January 12, 1918, Gibbons

---

[76] The story of this movement with the texts of the principal pertinent documents can be found in Michael Williams, *American Catholics in the War,* pp. 97–153.

[77] 116-H, Glennon to Gibbons, St. Louis, November 21, 1917.

[78] 116-H, Gibbons to Glennon, Baltimore, November 24, 1917, copy.

[79] 116-H, Burke to Gibbons, New York, November 23, 1917; ANCWC, Eugene J. Connelly to Burke, Baltimore, November 26, 1917.

outlined for them the authority they possessed under the metropolitans, mentioned the old N.C.W.C. and the K. of C. as
groups with whom they should consult, and summarized in a
general way the problems which they were expected to handle.[80]
Four days after the cardinal's letter was signed, the meeting
took place at the university and formal organization was given
to the newly created council. The N.C.W.C. was to be composed
of the fourteen archbishops of the United States, an executive
committee of the four bishops mentioned previously who derived
their authority from the metropolitans, and a more general committee numbering the four prelates, along with six members of
the K. of C. Committee on War Activities, and six members of
the Committee on Special War Activities of the old N.C.W.C.

Two months after he had made his first appeal for support to
the hierarchy for the new organization, the cardinal thanked
the bishops for their encouraging response to the suggestion.
"The unanimity and cordiality of the replies," he said, "were not
only most gratifying, but are a sure prophecy of the success of
the Catholic War Council." He mentioned the meeting held at
the university on January 16, had words of praise for the report
later submitted to him, and remarked, "They handled the situation, I think, in a masterly manner." In closing Gibbons expressed the hope that the American bishops would give the four
prelates on the executive committee the benefit of their advice
and co-operation, for now that the work was well started it would,
with God's help and their assistance, carry on to a successful
finish.[81] Through the remainder of the war the cardinal continued
to act as the central figure around which the work revolved, and
when it approached the time for the spring meeting of the archbishops in 1918, he submitted to them an outline of suggestions
from the executive committee of the N.C.W.C., and asked that
they give it their serious consideration before the meeting scheduled to convene on April 10.[82] Gibbons presided over the sessions
of the meeting on that date and Muldoon reported that the
N.C.W.C. would need fifteen million dollars to conduct its war
activities up to July, 1919. Means were suggested for raising the
money, and a motion was passed that Gibbons should draft a

[80] Williams, *op. cit.*, pp. 146–152.

[81] Shahan Papers, Holy Angels Rectory, Philadelphia, Gibbons to Shahan,
Baltimore, January 30, 1918.

[82] ANCWC, Gibbons to the archbishops, Baltimore, March 14, 1918, copy.

letter to the hierarchy seeking their help in collecting the funds. Bishop Hayes reported the grave need for more chaplains, and the archbishops approved a motion that this subject should be included in Gibbons' letter to the hierarchy, as well as a request that the cardinal petition the Holy See to hold the new *Code of Canon Law* in abeyance insofar as the rule demanding four years of theology for seminarians was concerned.[83]

On August 16, 1918, Cardinal Gibbons reached the fiftieth anniversary of his episcopal consecration, but the celebration was postponed until October. At that time, however, the influenza epidemic was at its height so the ceremonies in Baltimore were reduced to a minimum, and it was planned to have a more formal celebration at a later date. In recognition of the event Bishop Muldoon was instructed by the executive committee of the N.C.W.C. at its meeting in New York to extend to the cardinal their congratulations. He said:

> We, the National Catholic War Council, realise very clearly that without your assistance and cooperation very little could have been accomplished.
> For your words of encouragement, for your direction, for the letters that you have honored us with, and for your willingness to aid us at every turn, we desire in this feeble way to express our deepest appreciation.
> If the National Catholic War Council accomplishes anything worth while, to you must be given the credit. . . .[84]

If Gibbons had proved helpful during the wartime organization and service of the N.C.W.C., his assistance was still needed after the coming of peace. No undertaking so vast as the activities of the N.C.W.C. could hope to escape without difficulties, and in the solution of its problems friends of the organization turned on more than one occasion to seek the counsel of the cardinal. For example, a certain amount of feeling arose within the ranks of the K. of C. because it was thought that their work was being hampered by the N.C.W.C., and that they were not altogether welcome as an affiliated group of the council. Father John J. Wynne, S.J., grew alarmed at the rumors of an impending break and he appealed to Gibbons to lend his aid since, as he said, he

---

[83] 117-G, Minutes of the Meeting of the Archbishops, Washington, April 10–11, 1918.

[84] 119-H, Muldoon to Gibbons, New York, October 22, 1918.

knew how proud the cardinal was of the solidarity of American Catholicity.[85] Unfortunately, Gibbons' reply is not extant, but he encouraged Wynne to come to Baltimore at a later date to talk over the matter with him.[86] Some opposition to the N.C.W.C. had arisen likewise within the ranks of the hierarchy, and when Gibbons asked Muldoon to co-operate with the League to Enforce Peace the bishop replied that he feared the program was too expensive and would involve too many hands. He added, "Some of the Bishops, as you know, do not look any too kindly on the National Catholic War Council and might be very willing to take our approval of the League as indicating that we were over-stepping our charter."[87]

But in spite of these minor drawbacks, the work progressed and at the formal celebration of Gibbons' golden jubilee in Washington on February 20, 1919, a step was taken which was destined to give the N.C.W.C. a new and more far-reaching character. On that occasion there was present as the personal representative of Pope Benedict XV to the Gibbons jubilee Bonaventura Cerretti, Archbishop of Corinth and Secretary of the Congregation for Extraordinary Ecclesiastical Affairs, as well as a large number of the bishops of the United States. Cerretti addressed the hierarchy in the chapel of Caldwell Hall at the Catholic University of America. He spoke at some length of the impartiality of the Pope during the recent war and the suffering he had experienced by reason of that conflict, and he expressed the Pontiff's wish that the American bishops should join him in his efforts for a just and lasting peace and for the adjustment along the lines of Christian ethics of the many difficulties in the world of education and of labor. Gibbons was complimented for the outstanding role he had played during the war, and Cerretti remarked that his being sent as a special envoy to a jubilee of this kind was without precedent. The cardinal's fame was world wide, said the archbishop, and during his days as Apostolic Dele-

---

[85] 119-T, Wynne to Gibbons, New York, December 2, 1918. The same week Supreme Knight Flaherty sent Gibbons a lengthy report on the K. of C. budgetary needs, but aside from an oblique reference to the misrepresentation of enemies of the order, he said nothing directly about the strained relations with the N.C.W.C. (119-T, Flaherty to Gibbons, New Haven, December 5, 1918).

[86] 119-T, Wynne to Gibbons, New York, December 5, 1918. An effort to find the letter of Gibbons among the Wynne Papers was unsuccessful (John J. McMahon S.J., to the writer, New York, August 24, 1950).

[87] 119-XYZ, Muldoon to Gibbons, Rockford, December 29, 1918.

gate to Australia he had found that there, too, as he expressed it, "the name of Cardinal Gibbons was a household word and a source of inspiration."[88]

Later the same day a committee was appointed by the cardinal to investigate the best means of carrying out the Pope's desires as expressed by Cerretti. On the following day at the meeting of the archbishops the report of this committee was read. They recommended that in the future the entire hierarchy assemble in an annual meeting, which would include not only the metropolitans but all the American ordinaries, auxiliary bishops, and the Rector of the University if he were a bishop. Moreover, it was likewise recommended that a standing committee of five bishops be appointed by Gibbons to represent the hierarchy in supervising general Catholic activities and interests, and that the secretary of the present gathering be instructed to write to the absent prelates asking for their adherence to whatever should be determined upon. The report was unanimously adopted, and pursuant to its recommendation the cardinal temporarily appointed the four prelates of the N.C.W.C. executive committee, with himself as chairman, to constitute the suggested committee, at the same time making it clear that this membership would be provisional until the next meeting of the hierarchy when he would propose that a permanent committee be elected by ballot.[89]

Not long after the return of Archbishop Cerretti to Rome the Pope on April 10 addressed a letter to the American hierarchy, in which he stated that his representative had brought their greetings and the communication in which the bishops had signified their intention to set up commissions to deal with educational and social problems as well as to hold an annual meeting. "This is truly a worthy resolve," said Benedict XV, "and with the

[88] Details of the jubilee and the visit of Cerretti were covered by the Baltimore *Catholic Review,* February 22 and March 1, 1919. Cerretti was very close to Gibbons in the last years of his life, and among the Gibbons Papers there are numerous examples of how the cardinal turned to Cerretti to transact his Roman business for him. For example, in July, 1920, he asked the archbishop to oversee the payment of certain repairs on his titular church of Santa Maria in Trastevere and at the time he explained that the canons had lately asked for money to improve the music in the basilica. The cardinal informed Cerretti that he was then receiving numerous letters from all over the world asking for bread to eat. Referring to the canons, he remarked, "It would be well for them to know of this fact" (128-F, Gibbons to Cerretti, Baltimore, July 16, 1920, copy).

[89] 120-L, Minutes of the Meeting of the Archbishops, Washington, February 21, 1919.

utmost satisfaction We bestow upon it Our approval."[90] Meanwhile Gibbons proceeded to appoint Muldoon, Russell, Schrembs, and Hayes as the committee to serve under his chairmanship on general Catholic interests.[91] However, the fact that Hayes had been named Archbishop of New York on March 10 caused him to beg to be excused because of his increased responsibilities, and, therefore, at the suggestion of Archbishop Hanna of San Francisco, the cardinal chose in his place a prelate to represent the Far West, namely, Joseph S. Glass, C.M., Bishop of Salt Lake City.[92]

After the appointment of the provisional committee had been made Gibbons communicated with his fellow metropolitans and outlined for them the steps that had thus far been taken. He remarked that the joy of his jubilee had been enhanced by the knowledge that it had been made the occasion for inaugurating measures which he regarded as the most important for the Church since the Third Plenary Council of Baltimore. Especially gratifying to the cardinal was the appointment of the committee on general Catholic interests. Hitherto, he said, through the courtesy of his colleagues in the hierarchy and because the national capital was within the limits of the Archdiocese of Baltimore, the burden of the Church's general interests had in great measure rested on him. "My experience has made me feel keenly," said Gibbons, "the necessity of such a committee which with adequate authority and the aid of sub-committees could accomplish more than any individual, however able or willing he might be." It was recognized by all that the Catholic Church in the United States, partly through defective organization, was not exerting the influence which it should in proportion to the numbers and individual prominence of many of the American Catholic people. The diocesan units were, indeed, well organized but the American Church as a whole was, in the opinion of the cardinal, suffering from what he termed "the lack of a unified force that might be directed to the furthering of those general policies which are vital to all." Therefore, an episcopal committee vested

---

[90] "The September Meeting of the American Hierarchy," *Ecclesiastical Review*, LXI (July, 1919), 4. The letter of Benedict XV is reprinted here along with several subsequent letters of Gibbons to the hierarchy.

[91] 121-G, Schrembs to Gibbons, Toledo, April 24, 1919.

[92] 121-C, Hayes to Gibbons, New York, April 4, 1919; 121-K, Gibbons to Glass, Baltimore, May 4, 1919, copy.

with full authority and confidence could accomplish much to remedy the situation. Gibbons then sketched his ideas of how a permanent committee should be chosen by secret ballot at the meeting of the entire hierarchy, with a view to having represented as far as possible the interests of the Church at large as well as the various sections of the country. A meeting of the temporary committee would be held soon, and among the important matters which imposed themselves for consideration were a collection for the financial needs of the Holy See, a continuation of the activities of the old N.C.W.C. as far as it might be deemed expedient, measures to safeguard Catholic interests in national legislation, the vital needs of Catholic education, and the awakening concern over the needs of the home and foreign missions. The cardinal and his committee would, therefore, appreciate suggestions on any or all of these matters from the archbishops.[93]

A few days later the Cardinal of Baltimore submitted to the bishops of the committee some of his own thoughts on the subjects which should engage their attention, along with suggestions that had been made to him by different members of the hierarchy. After outlining the topics in much the same order as he had done to the archbishops, Gibbons remarked that it was evident the committee would need a headquarters and clerical assistance and before long steps should be taken to establish such a bureau. He said he regarded the suggestion for their committee, growing out of the visit of Cerretti, as a divine call to summon their best thought and maximum energy in order that the kindling of religion in the hearts of American Catholics might be organized and properly directed. In the opinion of the cardinal, probably no other Church in history had so grand an opportunity to challenge it as had the American Church at that moment, and it was his belief that the formation of the committee would launch a new epoch in the Church of the United States. "On us, and particularly on your younger and stronger arms," he said, "devolves the duty of surveying the field and planning the great work."[94]

---

[93] 121-J, Gibbons to the archbishops, Baltimore, May 1, 1919, printed copy.

[94] 121-L, Gibbons to Muldoon, Schrembs, Glass, and Russell, Baltimore, May 5, 1919, printed copy. Gibbons was in favor of all the proposals made to him by Muldoon when the latter visited him on May 19, except the item of raising a fund of twenty-five million dollars to finance the hierarchy's program. The cardinal did not think that could be done. On September 6, when Muldoon and Fenlon called on him again, he was still skeptical about the financial drive, although

During the course of the next four months the bishops, with
Father John F. Fenlon, S.S., acting as their secretary, held three
meetings in which they laid the plans for the future structure
of the N.C.W.C., and prepared the reports which were to be
submitted to the hierarchy at its first annual meeting in September. At New York on August 28 Bishop Glass proposed that the
permanent name of the organization should be the National
Catholic Welfare Council, and his proposal was carried.[95]
Although Gibbons was not able to be present at these meetings,
he assisted the committee by keeping the hierarchy informed in
their name of the progress of the work so that when they assembled in Washington in the autumn they would be familiar
with what had been done.[96] By the end of August the committee
was ready to lay before the archbishops their preliminary recommendations for the various departments into which the work of
the N.C.W.C. should be divided, postponing until September the
plan for financing these units. After stating that they had called
into consultation qualified men in each particular field, they
listed — following closely the outline submitted to them by
Gibbons four months before — the projected departments as
follows: missions, education, press and literature, social service,
and Catholic societies and lay activities. The bishops told the
metropolitans:

> Our guiding idea has been the thought expressed by so many
> bishops at the gathering last spring, that we have urgent need now
> of organizing on broad national lines for the welfare of the whole
> Church and that the organization to be formed should have the
> authority and support of the whole Hierarchy and be subject to its
> direction and control. The departments of the organization follow
> the broad lines of the Church's work and needs in this country,
> practically as suggested in His Eminence's letter of May fifth last.[97]

he left the proposal in their hands and said that if the general meeting of the
hierarchy would accept the budgetary proposals he would fall in line (Archives of
the Diocese of Rockford, Diary of Bishop Muldoon, May 19 and September 6,
1919).

[95] ANCWC, Minutes of the Meetings of the General Committee on Catholic
Affairs and Interests, New York, May 9, 1919; Notre Dame, July 22–24, 1919,
and New York, August 28, 1919.

[96] 121-P, Gibbons to the American hierarchy, Baltimore, May 17, 1919, printed
copy; 121-R, same to same, Baltimore, May 24, 1919, printed copy.

[97] 123-E, Muldoon, Schrembs, Glass, and Russell to the archbishops, New York,
August 30, 1919, printed copy.

As the date approached for the first annual meeting of the American hierarchy Cardinal Gibbons issued an appeal to all the bishops that they should solicit the prayers of their people for the success of the gathering, a copy of which he likewise gave to the Catholic press. "The prospect is that we shall have a very large meeting," he remarked, and he added, "Already, I am told, seventy bishops have replied in the affirmative, none in the negative, and only one doubtful."[98] Archbishop Glennon, who had served for some years as secretary of the meetings of the metropolitans, submitted his resignation in advance of the meeting since, as he said, he presumed that the annual assembly of the archbishops would now give way to the new order. "I wish to felicitate Your Eminence even in advance of the meeting itself," said Glennon, "on the evident success which with God's Grace is sure to attend the forthcoming meeting of the American Hierarchy."[99] The evening before the bishops were to convene, Gibbons sent for Bishop Muldoon and reviewed with him the entire agenda for the meeting. The bishop later stated, "His last words were 'Sit with me tomorrow and guide me through the proceedings,' " to which Muldoon added, "For his age the Cardinal is extremely bright and misses no point."[100]

On September 24, 1919, there gathered at the Catholic University of America ninety-two of the 101 ordinaries of the United States, and at the opening session Cardinal Gibbons gave the welcoming address. He stated that this was the largest meeting of bishops in the history of the American Church; only the Third Plenary Council of Baltimore approached it in size, and he was the sole survivor of that council as well as of the Vatican Council a half century before. The cardinal expressed his high hopes for the outcome of their deliberations, and he once more stated his conviction that their present assembly held an extraordinary significance for the future of American Catholicism. Upon the acceptance of the resignation of Glennon as secretary, Denis J. O'Connell, Bishop of Richmond, was elected to the post, and

---

[98] Archives of the Diocese of Mobile, Gibbons to Edward P. Allen, Baltimore, September 11, 1919, printed circular.

[99] 123-H, Glennon to Gibbons, St. Louis, September 20, 1919.

[100] Archives of the Diocese of Rockford, Diary of Bishop Muldoon, September 23, 1919. The bishop added that since Gibbons had been entertaining Cardinal Mercier for the previous week he was then much fatigued.

the meeting then heard the report of Bishop Muldoon on the N.C.W.C. and proceeded to discuss the question.

Only one serious objection to the acceptance of the report was raised and that came from Bishop McDonnell of Brooklyn. McDonnell believed that an organization such as Muldoon had outlined would conflict with the constitution of the Church, according to which no bishop could exercise jurisdiction in the diocese of another bishop without delegation from the Holy See. He further stated that he thought the letter of Benedict XV of the previous April, giving papal approval to the establishment of episcopal commissions and an annual meeting, had not been prepared in Rome but rather in the United States. Even according to the terms of the Pope's letter, said McDonnell, the two commissions mentioned were recognized only as advisory in character, and they had no power to enter into the diocese of a bishop and to exercise any activity there. In reply Muldoon explained that no legislation was intended that would conflict with the jurisdiction of the ordinaries and, as far as the two committees mentioned by the Pope were concerned, he saw no prohibition against adding to their number. The Bishop of Rockford reported that the discussion of the first morning session produced a discouraging effect upon Gibbons and he feared nothing worthwhile would be accomplished. But Muldoon told him not to worry, that affairs would take a turn for the better, and that with the possible exception of the financial budget, the entire program would be finally accepted. And the bishop then added, "This seemed to cheer his good old heart."[101] After further discussion, Bishop Canevin of Pittsburgh moved that the report be accepted giving the hierarchy's approval to the N.C.W.C., Archbishop Keane of Dubuque seconded the motion, and it carried. On the following day the hierarchy elected by secret ballot the members of the administrative committee of the N.C.W.C., and Edward J. Hanna, Archbishop of San Francisco, was chosen as chairman with Dennis J. Dougherty, Archbishop of Philadelphia, Austin Dowling, Archbishop of St. Paul, Muldoon, Schrembs, Russell, and Canevin named to serve under him.[102]

About two weeks after the meeting Gibbons wrote an account

---

[101] *Ibid.*, September 24, 1919.

[102] ANCWC, Minutes of the First Annual Meeting of the American Hierarchy, Washington, September 24–25, 1919. At this time the name of the executive committee of the N.C.W.C. was changed to administrative committee.

of the sessions to the Holy Father. He thanked the Pope for his letter of approval of the annual meeting which had been read at the sessions, and he remarked that the most cordial harmony had prevailed among the ninety-two bishops present. He then outlined what had been done to establish the N.C.W.C. by listing its projected departments and the personnel of its administrative committee, and he stated:

> In this way the Hierarchy is now well organized to care regularly and efficiently and immediately for every important Catholic interest in the United States, and to this work of organization the bishops gave most of the time and the wisdom of the meeting. Nearly the entire Hierarchy was present, and all returned to their sees deeply impressed with the importance of their action and the brotherly charity which prevailed over the counsels of so large a body.[103]

One of the ways in which the N.C.W.C. proved almost immediately useful to Gibbons was in the matter of appeals from Europe for relief. During the September meeting the cardinal had spoken in behalf of Ludwig von Pastor, historian of the Papacy, and had thanked the bishops for their response to the collection taken up for him. This was the kind of service which might hereafter be handled through the N.C.W.C. With that in mind, in early November the cardinal asked Father Burke for lists of organizations in different countries to which appeals for relief might be directed since, as he stated, he was continuing to receive begging letters from all over. "The writers seem to imagine, because of my position," he said, "that I have at my disposal funds for these various purposes. The truth is, that I have not."[104]

Meanwhile further details of the N.C.W.C. were being worked out, and at a meeting on December 9–10, 1919, at the university the need for a central office for its activities was examined and agreed upon, and Father Burke, chairman of the Committee on Special War Activities of the old organization, was unanimously elected executive secretary to preside over the headquarters in Washington.[105] Before very long Burke had reason to complain

---

[103] AAB, unclassified, Gibbons to Benedict XV, Baltimore, October 11, 1919, copy in translation of the original Italian text.

[104] ANCWC, Gibbons to Burke, Baltimore, November 10, 1919.

[105] *Ibid.*, Minutes of the Meetings of the General Committee on Catholic Affairs and Interests, Washington, December 9–10, 1919. At a meeting in Washington on April 14, 1920, Burke's title was changed from executive secretary to general secretary of the administrative committee.

to Gibbons concerning the editorial policy of his archdiocesan newspaper. On December 20 the Baltimore *Catholic Review* carried an editorial signed by John I. Barrett, an assistant at St. Patrick's Church in Washington where Monsignor Thomas, the editor, was pastor. The editorial was entitled "Luxurious Welfare Work." Barrett credited the Y.M.C.A., the K. of C., and the N.C.W.C. with having done good work during the war, but he questioned the manner in which they had handled their funds. He said millions of dollars had been spent and he asked, "Where have they gone? Was the best use made of the money? How much has been wasted?" Moreover, he disliked the purely secular tone of recent welfare enterprises which left no room for religion and spiritual values. In conclusion Barrett stated, "The whole proposition smacks of the fad, and fads seldom accomplish much. Give us the old-fashioned Catholic methods of looking after man and his welfare and we know that much good will result."

Burke was irked by the editorial which he called unintelligent, unfair, and likely to give a false impression concerning the finances of the N.C.W.C. and the K. of C. He reminded Gibbons that the hierarchy of the country under the guidance of His Eminence had recently established the National Catholic Welfare Council, and in conclusion he remarked, "Certainly that movement deserves the support not the censure of the Catholic press."[106] If the cardinal was disturbed by the erring ways of his weekly newspaper, his reply did not show it. He had his secretary answer that he had not seen the editorial in question, to which the secretary added, "He suggests that you write the editor, Monsignor Thomas."[107] But Gibbons took another matter relating to the N.C.W.C. more seriously. When his secretary informed him that Bishop McDonnell had stopped over in Baltimore the previous week to visit his seminarians at St. Mary's Seminary without calling on the cardinal, Gibbons was at pains to let the bishop know his disappointment. There had run through his mind more than once, he said, the possibility that McDonnell felt there might be some coldness or unfriendliness as a result of the discussion over the N.C.W.C. in the meeting at Washington some months before. He told the Bishop of Brooklyn that he would be very sorry if their friendship of many years would be lessened

---

106 *Ibid.*, Burke to Gibbons, Washington, December 26, 1919, copy.
107 *Ibid.*, Albert E. Smith to Burke, Baltimore, January 1, 1920.

by that incident, and he concluded, "I want you to feel that my home is your home, to which you are always welcome, and in which there are rooms at all times for you and your secretary."[108]

One of the final services rendered to the N.C.W.C. by Cardinal Gibbons was to win from the Paulist superior-general permission for Father Burke to devote his full time to the office of general secretary. Bishop Russell had spent a week in Washington trying to set up the press department of the council, and had experienced great difficulty in the absence of Burke who was in New York attending to his duties as editor of the *Catholic World*. The Bishop of Charleston, therefore, appealed to Gibbons to ask the Paulist superior for the good of the Church if he would not release Burke from all other obligations.[109] The cardinal promptly complied by telling Father Thomas Burke, the superior-general, that no one was more familiar with the work than his brother, no one was more congenial to the administrative committee of bishops, and more agreeable to the government officials in Washington. For that reason as a personal favor he asked, "will you be good enough to acquiesce in this request?"[110] The superior gave his consent and shortly thereafter Father Burke took up permanent residence in Washington.

Formal notification to the American Catholic people of the establishment and objectives of the National Catholic Welfare Council was given in the pastoral letter of the hierarchy which was published late in February, 1920. At the meeting of the bishops the previous September, Gibbons had appointed a committee consisting of himself, Cardinal O'Connell, and Bishop Shahan to supervise the writing of the first general pastoral of the hierarchy since 1884.[111] The actual drafting of the document was turned over to Monsignor Edward A. Pace, professor of philosophy in the Catholic University of America. After he had finished the first draft, Pace sent it to the Cardinal of Boston who went over it carefully and offered detailed criticisms, for which Pace thanked him in the name of Shahan and in his own name. "Your approval of the document as a whole is most en-

---

[108] 124-T, Gibbons to McDonnell, Baltimore, February 3, 1920, copy.

[109] 124-XYZ, Russell to Gibbons, Greenville, South Carolina, February 13, 1920.

[110] 125-B, Gibbons to Thomas Burke, C.S.P., Baltimore, February 18, 1920, copy. Written across the top: "Agreed to by Superior & letter sent to Russell."

[111] ANCWC, Minutes of the First Annual Meeting of the American Hierarchy, Washington, September 24–25, 1919.

couraging," he said, "and I shall do my best to bring the last sections into line with the rest."[112] In the section of the pastoral devoted to the N.C.W.C., it was stated that in view of the good results obtained through merging Catholic activities for the time and purpose of war, the bishops had determined to maintain for the ends of peace the spirit of union and the co-ordination of their forces.[113] Although he had nothing to do with the preparation of the text, Gibbons signed the document in the name of all the bishops as the dean of the American hierarchy.

The pastoral created an excellent impression, and within a few days after its publication the cardinal received evidence of the fact. Archbishop Hayes for one expressed his pleasure and remarked what a privilege and consolation it must have been for Gibbons to affix his name to this historic document a full generation after the last council of Baltimore.[114] And from another quarter the Reverend Wilbur M. Smith, pastor of the First Presbyterian Church at Ocean City, Maryland, on the basis of the quotations he had read from it in the secular papers, pronounced it "a magnificent epistle" and asked for a copy of the entire text.[115] While Gibbons could claim no direct credit for the pastoral, he was doubtless gratified at its favorable reception, for it summarized much of the progress of American Catholicism during the previous thirty-five years in which he had been an active participant as the first-ranking dignitary of the American Church.

In the last summer of his life the Cardinal of Baltimore was given the opportunity to read another kind of summary when in August, 1920, he was presented with the proof sheets of Michael Williams' book, *American Catholics in the War,* which described the developments that led through the wartime emergency to the organization of the National Catholic War Council. Gibbons was asked to write the preface to the volume, and in reviewing the contributions which American Catholics had made to their country in the war, he stated that Williams' book might in truth be called the "promise fulfilled" since it told the story of how the hierarchy, the priests, and the Catholic people had fulfilled

---

[112] ACUA, Pace Papers, Pace to O'Connell, Washington, December 19, 1919, copy.
[113] Guilday, *The National Pastorals of the American Hierarchy* (*1792–1919*), p. 296.
[114] 125-E, Hayes to Gibbons, New York, February 23, 1920.
[115] 125-E, Smith to Gibbons, Ocean City, February 23, 1920.

the promise made by the archbishops in April, 1917, to President Wilson that the Catholic Church of the United States would do its part to win the war. The cardinal spoke of the splendid work of the K. of C. and the National Catholic War Council and, in referring to the latter, he stated that it had brought into national expression the Catholic principles of justice and of fraternal service that bespoke the continued prosperity and happiness of the United States as a nation. Moreover, it had opened the way for its successor, the National Catholic Welfare Council, to win, as he said, still greater achievements in the days of peace for God and for country.[116]

In less than a year thereafter Cardinal Gibbons was dead, but the contribution he had made to the founding of the present National Catholic Welfare Conference fully warranted the resolution of sympathy which was voted by the administrative committee at its meeting on April 5, 1921. There they spoke of the cardinal as the originator and first chairman of the council, and they expressed the desire that the administrator of the Archdiocese of Baltimore should know their appreciation for the cardinal's inestimable services.[117]

---

[116] Williams, *op. cit.*, pp. vii–viii.
[117] ANCWC, Minutes of the Meeting of the Administrative Committee, Washington, April 5, 1921.

CHAPTER XXI

The International Churchman

THERE could be little question that the stirring events of World War I and the years that followed noticeably enhanced the international reputation already enjoyed by Cardinal Gibbons. The part he played in behalf of the arbitration of disputes between nations, his efforts to alleviate the suffering of the Church in Mexico, the strong leadership he gave to American Catholics once their country had entered the European war, and the manner in which he bestirred himself in such measures as the representation of the Holy See at the peace conference and the relief of the victims of famine in the countries of war-torn Europe — all served to focus attention upon the Cardinal of Baltimore as one of the striking world figures of his time. And yet for a quarter century before World War I his deeds and personality had made his name a familiar one to many in distant parts of the world. From the time that he received the cardinal's hat in March, 1887, and delivered his memorable sermon on Church and State in his titular church in Rome, Gibbons had commanded an ever widening public notice abroad, and the circumstances of his defense of the Knights of Labor, his opposition to the Church's condemnation of Henry George, and his vigorous championing of Archbishop Ireland in the controversy over the schools brought to him an audience in the European press which no American Catholic churchman had received up to that time. It is with the international relationships of the cardinal, which lay outside these major matters which we have previously discussed, that we are presently concerned.

We have already seen something of the interest which Gibbons retained in the affairs of Ireland where he had spent his boyhood years. It is true that his singleness of purpose in serving the allied cause during World War I, and his doubts concerning the wisdom of complete Irish independence, had restrained him from espousing the goal of freedom with all the ardor that character-ized some other Americans of Irish descent. But the cardinal was never insensitive to the political wrongs of Ireland, nor did he turn a deaf ear to the appeals for help which periodically reached him from that country. In the spring of 1889 when dis-sension was still rife in Ireland over the failure of Gladstone's first home rule bill and the Irish were unnerved by the trial of Charles Stewart Parnell, leader of the Nationalist Party, nu-merous arrests were made by the British in an effort to crush the opposition. E. Dwyer Gray of the staff of the Dublin *Free-man's Journal,* informed Gibbons of the injustices that had been perpetrated in treating those arrested purely on political grounds as common felons, and he made an appeal for a protest from the cardinal which, he thought, would serve to correct the evil.[1] In reply the cardinal stated that as far as opportunity enabled him to judge, it was the general sentiment of thoughtful Americans that the treatment of political prisoners in Ireland had been, as he said, "exceedingly harsh & wantonly severe, & in that view I am compelled to concur." Yet he hoped that this might prove only a passing episode in view of the prospects of home rule which seemed then, according to Gibbons, to be hard within Ireland's grasp.[2]

Unfortunately, however, home rule was still far from the grasp of the Irish, and within a year the failure of the potato crop and the threat of famine minimized the political disabilities under which they labored. Gibbons' old schoolmate of Ballinrobe, Bishop Francis McCormack of Galway, was one of the first to send him direct word of the emergency which now confronted them, and he remarked that the present tendency seemed to be to put pressure for relief on the British government rather than to appeal to the United States.[3] Matters did not improve and by early winter the situation in some parts of the country had grown desperate. John Lyster, Bishop of Achonry, made a touch-

[1] 85-S-12, Gray to Gibbons, Dublin, March 9, 1889.
[2] 85-W-1, Gibbons to Gray, Baltimore, April 6, 1889, copy.
[3] 87-W-5, McCormack to Gibbons, Galway, September 20, 1890. Six weeks before Cardinal Newman had died on August 11, and it prompted McCormack to add, "The death of the great English Cardinal has been the occasion of a chorus of universal admiration and eulogy by the Press of the three Kingdoms. Seldom or ever was such tribute paid to any man in Church or State."

ing appeal to Gibbons in the name of his stricken people, and he remarked, "Their last potato will be gone before New Year's Day; then we are face to face with the grim reality of want."[4] The cardinal responded generously to this and further requests which he received from other sources, and within a few weeks' time he distributed £1,220 to various Irish bishops whose dioceses were the hardest hit by the famine.[5] Nor did he fail to be helpful to old Irish connections in other ways. When another schoolmate of Ballinrobe, Major Robert H. Tighe, interceded with him to assist his nephew, William J. de Blacquiere, in finding a job in Baltimore, the cardinal had the young man appointed as business manager of the *Catholic Mirror,* a position in which he served for a number of years.[6] Gibbons' assistance to Ireland was not forgotten, and on the occasion of the silver jubilee of his episcopacy Cardinal Logue of Armagh commented on the unusual demonstration of affectionate regard with which Americans had greeted the anniversary, and he added, "Indeed the joy, affection and veneration was [*sic*] not confined to Americans. In the short cablegram which I sent I could only hint at the pleasure with which Irish Catholics, cleric and lay, hailed the auspicious event."[7]

---

[4] 88-E-11, Lyster to Gibbons, Ballaghadereen, County Roscommon, December 18, 1890.

[5] Diary, February 12-March 21, 1891, p. 251. Early in his career Gibbons began sending financial aid to Ireland. For example, in February, 1878, a certain Honorie Byrne, writing from the workhouse in Ballinrobe, thanked the archbishop for sending money to help save the house of her brother's widow and orphans (73-N-13, Byrne to Gibbons, Ballinrobe, February 4, 1878). All through the remainder of his life Gibbons continued to be generous to the poor and afflicted in Ireland. One of the clearest memories of the cardinal retained by those who met him on his many visits to that country was his generosity to relatives and old friends in need, whom he never failed to call upon and help. Interview of the writer with Thomas Canon O'Malley and Mrs. Catherine Casey, a distant cousin of Gibbons, at Partry, County Mayo, June 14, 1950.

[6] 90-T-3, Tighe to Gibbons, Kingston-on-Thames, Surrey, August 28, 1892; Reily, *Collections in the Life and Times of Cardinal Gibbons,* V, 470–471.

[7] 92-U-6, Logue to Gibbons, Armagh, December 7, 1893. Other testimonies of the regard in which he was held abroad reached Gibbons at the time of his jubilee. For example, Canon William Barry, the English church historian, told him that many Catholics thought as he did, that Providence had raised Gibbons up as a champion in their behalf, a man, as he said, "to whom the love of Light and Freedom comes by instinct, and who sees in such enthusiasm not the danger but the promise of the Christian Faith" (92-A-3, Barry to Gibbons, Dorchester, Wallingford, October 5, 1893). Father Francis E. Ryan of the staff of St. Michael's Cathedral, Toronto, remarked, "Your Eminence's name is a household word in

The Cardinal of Baltimore was, of course, always well acquainted with conditions in Ireland, but as his fame spread he was frequently drawn into developments in other parts of the world with which he was not familiar. During the summer after his jubilee there broke out in the Anatolian provinces of the Ottoman Empire the first of a series of shocking massacres of the Armenian subjects of the sultan. The world was outraged at the cruelties perpetrated by the Turks, and an American committee was established to inform opinion in the United States and to lend assistance to the victims. Gibbons offered his good offices to Daniel C. Gilman, President of the Johns Hopkins University, who was a member of the committee, and Gilman assured the cardinal that his co-operative words would be conveyed to the committee and at a later date they might have occasion to seek his counsel.[8] Matters steadily grew worse for the Armenians and a year later Etienne Pierre Azarian, Armenian Patriarch of Constantinople, forwarded to Gibbons letters of Cardinal Rampolla showing the Holy See's deep concern over the suffering of these people, supplied him with a lengthy description of the horrors committed against his flock, and begged for his help.[9] The cardinal promptly offered his aid and said he would publicize the cruel treatment of the Armenians in the United States. The patriarch was grateful for the encouragement and for the money sent by Gibbons, but after a few weeks he warned him that the Turkish government had prohibited appeals to the outside world; therefore, the cardinal and his fellow bishops in the United States were asked not to publish his letter, although they might make use of the facts he had submitted.[10] Azarian likewise felt compelled to inform Gibbons some months later that the money contributed by the American hierarchy had been of no profit to the Armenian Catholics, for the reason that all the funds had been distributed by Bible House, an agency in Turkey

Canada, and your words and works are here a wonderous power for good, and for the glory of God and His Church" (92-L-1, Ryan to Gibbons, Toronto, October 18, 1893).

8 93-P-1, Gilman to Gibbons, Baltimore, January 2, 1895.

9 94-J-1, Azarian to Gibbons, Constantinople, February 15, 1896. Azarian sent Gibbons at various times copies of Rampolla's letters to him, e.g., of December 17, 1895 (94-F-2), January 3 and 27, 1896 (94-G-2 and 14), and February 5, 1896 (94-H-3).

10 94-K-9, Azarian to Gibbons, Constantinople, March 31, 1896.

for the American Bible Society, which had seen to it that relief was given entirely to the Protestant Armenians and Georgians.[11]

In cases such as that of the afflicted Armenians, Gibbons frequently employed the device of publicizing in the press and pulpit the facts pertaining to situations abroad, in the hope that the sympathy and generosity of the people of the United States might thus be drawn to them. When Cardinal Lavigerie of Algiers sought his advice on the best method to use in reaching the American public on the movement he was leading for the eradication of the slave trade in Africa,[12] Gibbons told him that he would have his discourses on the subject translated and published in the *Catholic Mirror* and from that source other papers would reproduce them. In this manner, he thought, Lavigerie's work would receive wide publicity and elicit the sympathies of American readers.[13] The traffic in slaves was a subject in which the Cardinal of Baltimore retained a lively interest over a period of many years. After the Brussels Act had been signed by the colonial powers in July, 1890, pledging its signatories to work for a systematic extirpation of the trade in Negroes, the cardinal, as we have seen, exerted his influence to win ratification of the act by the United States, and when that came about in January, 1892, he informed Cardinal Rampolla of the efforts he had put forth to effect a favorable vote on the measure in the United States Senate.[14]

There was another matter which related to the Negro population in Africa some years later which involved Gibbons in some trouble. During the 1870's the Anglo-American journalist and explorer, Henry M. Stanley, had interested King Leopold II of Belgium in the exploitation of the extensive rubber resources of the Congo region of central Africa. The king organized a private commercial company with himself as president and chief stockholder, entered into agreements with the native chieftains for turning over their lands to the company, and at an international conference on African affairs held in Berlin in the winter of

---

[11] 94-T-6, Azarian to Gibbons, Constantinople, November 24, 1896.

[12] 84-U-7, Lavigerie to Gibbons, Paris, August 6, 1888. Lavigerie said he welcomed the opportunity to associate himself with Gibbons whose career he had followed and admired for a long time.

[13] 84-W-7, Gibbons to Lavigerie, Baltimore, August 24, 1888, copy in French.

[14] 89-L-5, Gibbons to Rampolla, Baltimore, January 28, 1892, copy in French.

1884–1885, Leopold secured the recognition of the powers for the establishment of the Congo Free State of which he was formally declared sovereign in May, 1885. Within a few years the Belgian ruler earned a huge personal fortune from the venture and, in an age when the imperialistic policies of the European powers were at so high a pitch, this fact excited criticism, especially when it became known that grave abuses were being perpetrated against the native population and that practical slavery was the lot of many of the Congo inhabitants.

Agitation over the issue grew stronger as time went on, and in March, 1904, there was founded in England the Congo Reform Association which had as its main objective to arouse world opinion against the regime of Leopold II and to compel reform. The problem was rendered more complicated by the fact that there existed great jealousy and ill feeling between the Protestant and Catholic missionaries in the Congo, with charges by the former that the Catholics winked at the abuses because they were favored by the king's government.[15] The Congo Reform Association was intent upon gaining American opinion to its side, and in the spring of 1904 it sent a petition to the United States Senate which was presented by Senator John T. Morgan of Alabama. The association decided to renew its effort in the autumn of that year by delegating its secretary, Edmund D. Morel, to present a petition to President Roosevelt and to carry its case before the thirteenth International Peace Congress which was scheduled to be held in Boston the first week in October.

Cardinal Gibbons was drawn into the matter at this point by the Belgian government. They had learned of the intention to bring the question before the congress in Boston, but they had not been invited to send a representative to present the king's side of the case. The government of Leopold II, therefore, had recourse to the good offices of Gibbons to support their demand

---

[15] Arthur Berriedale Keith, *The Belgian Congo and the Berlin Act* (Oxford, 1919), pp. 222–223. Cf. the chapter, "Social Progress," pp. 217–235, of this work for a discussion of the religious and educational phases of the problem. In May, 1906, a concordat was signed between the Holy See and the Belgian authorities in the Congo under which the missions were established by common accord of the two principals with the provision made for the Catholic missionaries that they should receive 100 — or in special cases 200 — hectares of arable land on condition that they would instruct the children of the natives; priests who acted as chaplains would be paid by the colonial government (p. 222).

that the question should be kept off the agenda.[16] The cardinal agreed to lend his assistance to the cause by writing a letter to the Reverend Edward Everett Hale, minister of the South Congregational Church in Boston and one of the leading officials of the congress, who read it at one of the sessions. Gibbons stated his regret that he could not attend the meeting in person, and he remarked that if he were present he would regard it as his duty to say a word in vindication of the policy of Leopold II in the Congo. He cited the recognition given to the regime at the Berlin conference twenty years before, quoted the Italian and British delegates to that conference in admiration of the king's policies, and attributed the present prosperity of the region to Belgian toil and sacrifice. With all these factors in mind, the cardinal said he would regret to have a congress bearing the name of peace discuss a question which was calculated to arouse enmity and strife, and he added that it would likewise be unfair since no representative of the Belgian government had been invited to present the king's case.[17] But despite Gibbons' effort to prevent a discussion of the question he failed, and the day after his letter was read Morel assailed the Congo regime in the congress and was answered by George Herbert Head, a delegate from Cambridge, England.

When word of the action taken by the cardinal reached King Leopold II he promptly instructed his minister at Washington to thank him in his name,[18] and the gratification of Pope Pius X was likewise expressed to Gibbons through Cardinal Gotti, Prefect of the Propaganda.[19] Yet the storm raised by the treatment of the Congo natives was not allowed to die out and during the agitation over the question Gibbons did not escape criticism for his intervention in the case. Morel reproached him for not knowing or examining the facts, and in reply the cardinal was quoted as saying that his information had been based upon reports from missionaries. Since it was not probable, said Gibbons, that Morel would convert him to his way of thinking and, on his side, he had not convinced his opponent, he felt it would be better to

---

[16] 101-S, Gibbons to Gerolamo Cardinal Gotti, Baltimore, December 16, 1904, copy in French.

[17] New York *Herald*, October 7, 1904.

[18] 101-M, Baron Ludovic Moncheur to Gibbons, Washington, October 12, 1904.

[19] 101-Q, Gotti to Gibbons, Rome, November 24, 1904.

discontinue any further exchange of views.[20] A good deal of ill feeling had been engendered by the affair and for some time religious groups in the United States continued to disagree over their interpretations of events in the Congo.[21]

During the succeeding months further exposés revealed more damaging evidence against Leopold II's handling of his responsibility and in December, 1906, Senator Henry Cabot Lodge of Massachusetts espoused the cause of the Congo natives against their sovereign in the United States Senate.[22] Shortly thereafter the Reverend H. Gratton Guinness publicly attacked Gibbons in a Presbyterian church in Baltimore as "the strong hand in this country who prevented the government from noticing the atrocities in the Congo."[23] Although the credit attributed to the cardinal's persuasive powers was probably exaggerated, he had, nonetheless, come out strongly for Leopold's interests, nor was he disposed at this point to back down. He prepared a statement for the press in which he took cognizance of the attack that Guinness had made upon him, and he stated that his position in the case had always been clear. He had had access to the facts from Catholic missionaries on the scene in the Congo, and from that source he had been informed that the stories of abuse were greatly exaggerated. Gibbons credited Leopold II with being a wise and humane ruler who promptly redressed cruelty when he learned of it, and the king's recent decrees giving the natives additional lands and ameliorating the condition of the laborers were cited as evidences of his good will. "I fear," said the cardinal, "that this agitation against King Leopold's administration is animated partly by religious jealousy and partly by commercial rivalry." He hoped that it would not succeed in stirring up the great powers against little Belgium. But he made it clear that

---

[20] Fritz Masion, *Histoire de l'état indépendant du Congo* (Namur, 1912), I, 150–151. The Congo Reform Association published for some time a series of special monthly issues of the *West African Mail* in order to publicize their campaign. Unfortunately, the file of the Library of Congress on this journal did not have the particular issues of these months, and a thorough search of the AAB failed to reveal any trace of the Gibbons-Morel exchange of letters.

[21] Keith stated that the Catholic hierarchy permitted itself to be led to accept the view that, as he expressed it, "the interests of the faith demanded the denial of the wrongs of the Congo and thus quite unnecessarily religious animosities were imported into the discussion." *Op. cit.*, p. 130.

[22] *Ibid.*, p. 129.

[23] New York *Herald,* December 16, 1906.

he was not criticizing the attitude of the American government, for the American consul general had recently gone to the Congo and the cardinal gave it as his belief that the consul's report would set at rest the false accusations brought against the Belgian sovereign. Gibbons disclaimed any personal interest in the affair, and in reiterating his motive as that of wishing to defend a small nation in the interest of fair play, he concluded by saying, "I would willingly make the same defence in behalf of Holland, Sweden, Denmark or any of the weaker Powers if circumstances demanded."[24]

It was to be expected that the cardinal's action would earn the gratitude of the Belgian king, and in acknowledging the Christmas greetings of Gibbons which cardinals were accustomed to address to the heads of Catholic states, he took occasion to make known again his thanks for the support that had been given to the Congo government. The king spoke of the frightful barbarism which existed in some parts of Africa, but he said he was glad to tell the cardinal that the two great scourges from which the Negro race suffered there, namely, the slave trade and alcoholism, had disappeared from the Congo.[25] Over a year later the King of the Belgians proposed Gibbons for the Grand Cross of the Order of the Crown for what he had done, and in accepting the distinction the cardinal stated that in his defense of Leopold II's Congo regime he had only sustained a right which had been unjustly attacked.[26]

In regard to the differences over the king's administration of the Congo Free State, it was doubtless true that amid the sordid imperialism of the period some of the interests that had identified themselves with the demand for reform acted from other than altruistic motives. As Gibbons had suggested, religious jealousy and commercial rivalry had played their part in the movement once the question had entered into the public consciousness after 1903. But allowing for this fact, the evidence still pointed strongly against the government of the Belgian king as having been guilty of serious exploitation of the natives and, too, at times of inhuman treatment of the Negro population. Not only were

---

[24] *Ibid.*

[25] 104-A, Leopold II to Gibbons, Laken, January 8, 1907.

[26] 104-U, Gibbons to the Secretary of State of Leopold II, Baltimore, February 24, 1908, copy in French.

the writings of Secretary Morel of the Congo Reform Association and the reports of Sir Roger Casement, the British consul, extremely damaging to Leopold II, but even the report of November, 1905, issued by a three-man commission appointed by the king himself, was unfavorable to many aspects of the regime and further contributed to popular indignation. All through the next three years the clamor kept up and finally in October, 1908, by an act of the Belgian parliament the Congo was annexed to Belgium, effective control of the colony passed for the first time out of royal hands, and with this change the abuses began to be uprooted and public agitation of the issue gradually ceased.

In all that pertained to Gibbons' role in the affair, there was no question of the motives which prompted him to lend his support to Leopold's administration. He acted, as he stated during the controversy, from no personal interest but rather in behalf of what he considered an unjust attack upon a small country and in the interests of the Catholic missions. But the cardinal had not been fully informed of what was taking place in the Congo, and his apparently complete reliance for information on the word of the king's government and the reports which reached him periodically from the missionaries, in the end betrayed him into a position which proved difficult to defend. It was an instance where Gibbons' judgment was given on a distant and confused situation with which he was not fully acquainted, and when he was challenged he presumably did not see a sufficiently cogent reason for reversing his position. His willingness to intervene at the request of the government of Leopold II in what he believed at the time to be an injustice against a small state was understandable and, within limits, admirable. But his failure to inform himself adequately of the facts in the case, rather than to base his opinion solely on the evidence of one side, was one of the few times in his long life where Gibbons' normally keen judgment went astray and exposed him to the charge of partisanship and ignorance of the facts governing an issue. In view of the history of Leopold II's stewardship in the Congo and of Gibbons' meager knowledge of conditions there, it would have been better for the cardinal had he remained clear of the case entirely.

One of the features in the life of the Catholic Church which of recent years had drawn attention to its international character was the series of eucharistic congresses held at intervals in different countries of the world. The movement had begun with the meeting at Lille in France, in June, 1881, and in 1907 it was decided to hold a congress for the first time in an English-speaking country with the gathering scheduled for London in September, 1908. Nine years before Cardinal Vaughan had exacted a promise of the Cardinal of Baltimore to be present and to preach at the dedication of the Cathedral of the Most Precious Blood at Westminster, and he had then told him, "The sermon is being looked forward to as of international interest."[27] But as the time neared for the opening of the new cathedral, Vaughan entered upon his last illness and it happened that the imposing edifice whose construction he had overseen was used for the first time for the English cardinal's own requiem in June, 1903. With that in mind, his successor, Archbishop Bourne, four and a half years later sent a pressing invitation to Gibbons months in advance of the eucharistic congress, reminding him of the circumstance that had prevented the fulfillment of his previous promise and stating that in a certain sense the English Catholics still had a right to hear his words within the walls of the cathedral at Westminster. Bourne was anxious that there should be a good representation of the English-speaking bishops of the world, and he begged Gibbons, therefore, to accept and to do all that he could to arouse interest in the congress among his colleagues of the American hierarchy.[28] At first the cardinal demurred at making the trip to London, but as he later said he found Bourne's second letter so persuasive that it had wrought in him a change of heart. In spite of his many engagements he would endeavor to be there and to preach on the closing Sunday of the congress if his health permitted. Gibbons revealed the value he attached to these international gatherings when he told the archbishop:

> If I were to consult the rules of prudence I would stay at home & not assume this duty at my period of life. But I must make a personal sacrifice for the sake of our Lord, & to strengthen the bonds of fellowship between the Episcopate of England and the United States, & I remember that the English Church was represented at our centennial celebration in Baltimore in 1889.[29]

---

[27] 97-U-4, Vaughan to Gibbons, Westminster, December 7, 1899.

[28] 104-Q, Bourne to Gibbons, Westminster, December 8, 1907.

[29] 104-U, Gibbons to Bourne, Baltimore, February 17, 1908, copy.

On board the *Koenig Albert* for Europe

This picture was taken at New York on July 18, 1908, and shows Cardinal Gibbons seated in the center with Bishop O'Connell and Archbishop Farley of New York on his right and the ship's captain and Bishop Foley of Detroit on his left. The priests standing behind the prelates are unidentified.

(Courtesy of the Archives of the Archdiocese of New York)

The success of the eucharistic congress in London was marred by only one incident which left an unhappy memory. After the congress had opened on September 9, Prime Minister Herbert Asquith sent word indirectly to Archbishop Bourne that the government would be obliged if he would cancel the plan to hold an outdoor procession of the Blessed Sacrament on the closing day, since they feared it would upset Protestant susceptibilities and give rise to disorders in the streets. Bourne tried hard to win a reversal of the government's request but they were unwilling to yield and, consequently, it became the archbishop's unpleasant duty to announce Asquith's decision to the great audience that had assembled in the Albert Hall for the program on the evening before the final day of the congress. Naturally there was keen disappointment on the part of thousands of Catholics who had traveled to London from all parts of the British Isles, and whose numbers made it impossible for them to be accommodated within the cathedral at the closing services. Nonetheless, the Archbishop of Westminster urged that all should show a spirit of obedience to the government's wish and in the end matters passed off without incident.[30]

The final pontifical Mass was celebrated by the papal legate, Vincenzo Cardinal Vannutelli, and it was at this Mass on Sunday, September 13, that Gibbons preached his sermon. The announcement of the previous evening lent more than ordinary significance to several of the ideas expressed by the American cardinal. He sketched the links which bound the Catholics of the United States to those of Great Britain, and in doing so he instanced not only their common religious faith but their language, their literature, and the constitutional similarities of their governments; but he mentioned as well how much the Church in the two countries owed to the Irish and to the French. The cardinal took note of the consecration in 1790 in England of John Carroll, the first American bishop, and in tracing the steady advance of English Catholicism through the period of over a century since that event, he complimented the English bishops, clergy, and people on the notable progress they had made amid surroundings that were often hostile. Nor did he fail to include

---

[30] Ernest Oldmeadow, *Francis Cardinal Bourne* (London, 1940), I, 373–398, discusses the episode of the forbidden procession and reprints some of the correspondence that passed between Bourne and the government officials.

an especially graceful tribute to Cardinal Newman. But it was Gibbons' reference to Maryland that his audience probably found of special interest, due to the news that had broken the previous evening. The preacher stated that this colony had been founded by English Catholics and, said the cardinal, it was Maryland that was "the first to establish on American soil the blessings of civil and religious liberty."[31] He went on to sketch the broad toleration of the Maryland government in welcoming Puritans and Anglicans alike, and he quoted the American historian, George Bancroft, to the effect that it was in colonial Maryland that Protestants were sheltered from Protestant intolerance. His words doubtless suggested to many of his listeners a contrast between the spirit that had animated the Asquith government in banning the outdoor procession and that shown by the Maryland pioneers of nearly 300 years before.[32]

Just two years later a eucharistic congress was held for the first time in the new world where Paul Bruchesi, Archbishop of Montreal, played host to representatives of the Church from every corner of the globe. Bruchesi was intent that Gibbons should be present, and long before the event he extended to him an urgent invitation. Gibbons informed the archbishop that he would regard it not only as a pleasure but a duty to attend, and he remarked that when he learned at London that Montreal was selected for the twenty-first international congress he was highly gratified, for he considered it the ideal city of the North American continent by reason of the deep Catholic spirit and sentiment of its people. "I will most certainly do all that is in my power," he said, "to enlist the cooperation of my Colleagues, and will, as requested by you, address a letter to the faithful urging them to take an interest in the Congress."[33] As the date approached for the opening Gibbons invited Archbishop Farley of New York to accompany him in the private car of Leonard F. Loree, President of the Delaware and Hudson Railroad, which the latter had placed at his disposal. He stated that it was his intention to

---

[31] Gibbons, *A Retrospect of Fifty Years,* II, 56. The text of the sermon can be found here, pp. 47–67.

[32] Oldmeadow, *op. cit.,* I, 380, speaks of this passage of the sermon as "an ironical coincidence."

[33] Archives of the Archdiocese of Montreal, Gibbons to Bruchesi, Baltimore, February 20, 1910, copy sent to the writer through the kindness of Robert Canon Mitchell, Chancellor of the Archdiocese of Montreal.

arrive in Montreal after the preliminary celebrations which were scheduled for September 6–7, and he remarked to Farley, "I imagine you would not regret it much were you to miss those social and civic festivities."[34]

On the closing day of the congress, September 11, Gibbons preached the sermon at the pontifical Mass in St. James Cathedral which was celebrated by the papal legate who again was Cardinal Vannutelli. It was for the most part a spiritual discourse devoted to the subject of God's numerous benefactions to man which were crowned by the gift of His divine Son in the Eucharist. Near the end of his sermon he addressed the legate and spoke of the account which Vannutelli would give to the Holy Father on his return to Rome where he would recount the wonderful manifestation of faith which he had witnessed during the preceding days in Montreal. Alluding to the incident in London two years before, Gibbons concluded, "You will speak of the solemn and public processions through the streets of Montreal, not only without let or hindrance, but with the cordial approval and cooperation of the civic authorities, and the piety and enthusiasm of its devoted people."[35]

While the presence and sermons of Cardinal Gibbons at functions of the Church in foreign lands, such as the eucharistic congresses of London and Montreal, no doubt contributed to the enhancement of his prestige as an international churchman, it was the services he rendered in matters directly relating to the Holy See that emphasized most clearly his position in that regard. In the years before the establishment of the Apostolic Delegation at Washington in 1893 Gibbons was called upon in a number of cases to act as the official agent of Rome in the settlement of disputes in the American Church. Mention has already been made of several instances where he served in this capacity in Louisiana and Colorado,[36] but there were others of a similar nature which were destined to absorb a great deal of the cardinal's time and energy in the years before the arrival of Archbishop Satolli. These were matters which would normally fall to the office of a nuncio or delegate of the Holy See, and they not only consumed a great deal of Gibbons' energy in travel and corres-

---

[34] AANY, Gibbons to Farley, Baltimore, August 18, 1910.
[35] Archives of the Archdiocese of Montreal, photostat copy of the sermon.
[36] Cf. I, 272–281.

pondence, but as we shall see in the case of the Diocese of Cleveland, they sometimes proved a severe personal trial. One such example arose out of a controversy between Rupert Seidenbush, O.S.B., Vicar Apostolic of Northern Minnesota, and a number of French-speaking priests whom he had brought in to care for the French-Canadians in his vicariate. One of these men had been guilty of giving grave scandal, and when the bishop sent another priest to replace him he raised a scene and for a time refused to yield his church to the newcomer. In the case of another, trouble ensued over Seidenbush's attempt to divide his parish against his will.

There had been considerable dissatisfaction with the bishop's administration apart from these two instances and ultimately through the medium of Father Charles Boucher, pastor of St. Louis Church, Fond du Lac, Wisconsin, several of the malcontents carried their cases to Rome. As a consequence, early in the summer of 1887 Cardinal Simeoni asked Gibbons to investigate the difficulties of the Church in northern Minnesota and to report to the Holy See, an assignment which the cardinal agreed to perform on the occasion of a projected visit to the Northwest later that year.[37] Gibbons informed Seidenbush of his appointment well in advance of his visit, and in replying that he would calmly await the cardinal's arrival, the bishop detailed some of the wrongs which he felt he had suffered at the hands of several of the priests, and he declared, "A quire of foolscap would not suffice to relate all their ugly doings."[38] In October Gibbons spent several days in St. Paul on his way to the Pacific Coast, and he used the opportunity to interview the principals to these conflicts, a summary of which he then forwarded to Simeoni.[39] That there had been faults on both sides seemed clear from

---

[37] 83-A-9, Gibbons to Simeoni, Baltimore, July 6, 1887, copy in Latin; Diary, July 18, 1887, p. 218. The Archives of the Diocese of St. Cloud and of St. John's Abbey, Collegeville, were searched by Vincent Tegeder, O.S.B., who in a letter of November 9, 1950, kindly supplied the writer with some of the information that was missing in the AAB.

[38] 83-D-3, Seidenbush to Gibbons, St. Cloud, July 22, 1887.

[39] Diary, September 24 [sic], 1887, p. 220. This date is in error as Gibbons did not reach St. Paul before September 28 at the earliest. Box 83 in the AAB is filled at this point with correspondence relating to various phases of the troubles in Minnesota, but no copy of Gibbons' account to the Holy See could be found.

the fact that a year later Archbishop Ireland informed the cardinal with evident satisfaction that Rome had cabled Seidenbush calling for his resignation,[40] and shortly thereafter the departure of the bishop from his post was publicly announced.[41]

Even more unpleasant than the troubles in Minnesota was an assignment which Gibbons received in the spring of 1888 to act as arbitrator between Bishop Richard Gilmour of Cleveland and the Sisters of Charity or Grey Nuns of St. Vincent's Orphan Asylum in Toledo who for some time had been quarreling over the title to the asylum's property. Simeoni appreciated the burden that this would impose on Gibbons but since, as he said, all previous efforts to reach a settlement had ended in failure, he would be grateful if the cardinal would undertake to investigate the matter on the spot and endeavor to adjudicate it for the Holy See.[42] Although he did not in the least welcome the task, Gibbons agreed to carry out the wishes of Rome and he stated that he would visit Toledo later in the summer.[43] The trouble owed its origin to the fact that at the time the orphan asylum was built in 1855 Gilmour's predecessor, Bishop Amadeus Rappe, had transferred the title to the sisters in the belief that if it were held in their name, rather than that of the diocese, the property would be more likely to remain in the nontaxable category. However, from the outset the asylum was supported by funds collected from the faithful of the Diocese of Cleveland, and Rappe had regarded the transfer of title as a formality and not as making the asylum the actual property of the Grey Nuns. The sisters, however, felt differently about the matter, and when Bishop Gilmour sought to gain the title back on the grounds that the asylum had been supported by the diocese, they refused to yield and maintained that the ownership of the property was

---

[40] 85-I-6, Ireland to Gibbons, St. Paul, November 23, 1888.

[41] 85-O-5, Ireland to Gibbons, St. Paul, January 11, 1889. A week before Ireland told the cardinal he was glad that the latter had declined to reply directly to A. Lemay, one of the disgruntled priests, whom Ireland characterized as a "very dangerous man." The archbishop had been named administrator of the vicariate at Seidenbush's resignation and, although he recognized the difficult nature of the task that lay before him, he thought "the occasion will be afforded to do something toward giving a right impulse once for all to religious matters in Northern Minnesota" (85-N-5, Ireland to Gibbons, St. Paul, January 3, 1889).

[42] 84-L-7, Simeoni to Gibbons, Rome, May 15, 1888.

[43] 84-O-7, Gibbons to Simeoni, Leonardtown, Maryland, June 8, 1888, copy.

theirs by right as well as by law. Neither were they persuaded that they were wrong in learning that all the pastors of the city with one or two exceptions agreed with the bishop.[44]

Cardinal Gibbons found his task a very distasteful one. He confessed to Archbishop Elder that he knew nothing of its merits, and in asking that he outline for him the main points at issue and suggest the best means of effecting a reconciliation or compromise, he frankly stated that he was not sanguine of success.[45] Nonetheless, he proceeded to acquaint the bishop with his appointment by Rome and received in return a full statement of Gilmour's side of the case. The Bishop of Cleveland rejoiced that at last there was a prospect of an examination where all would have a chance to be heard and the facts exposed. He maintained that for over nine years he had tried in vain to discuss the matter with the sisters and that it was during his absence in Rome in 1875 that they had built a hospital and mortgaged the asylum as part security for the debt incurred. It was his belief that the case turned about the answer to the question: whose money had built the orphan asylum? If it was proved that it had been the money of the sisters, then the property was undoubtedly theirs, but if it was shown that the land had been bought and the building constructed by money collected by the Diocese of Cleveland for a diocesan institution, it was his contention that it should be in the name of the diocese.[46] Meanwhile the cardinal received messages of welcome to Toledo from the sisters, as well as from the theologian, Dr. James A. Corcoran, who was there on other business and who took occasion to submit a rather damaging report on Gilmour's administration of his see.[47]

Since the cardinal had promised to attend the celebration in honor of the golden jubilee of Father Edward Sorin, C.S.C., Superior-General of the Congregation of Holy Cross, which was

[44] George F. Houck, *A History of Catholicity in Northern Ohio and in the Diocese of Cleveland* (Cleveland, 1903), I, 130–132, treats this case briefly as well as a similar one involving St. Vincent's Asylum in Cleveland. The forthcoming history of the Diocese of Cleveland by Michael J. Hynes will probably throw additional light on the case.

[45] ACC, Gibbons to Elder, St. Charles College, Ellicott City, Maryland, July 8, 1888.

[46] 84-S-4, Gilmour to Gibbons, Cleveland, July 12, 1888.

[47] 84-T-2, Sister Fernand to Gibbons, Toledo, July 21, 1888; 84-T-1, Corcoran to Gibbons, Toledo, July 21, 1888.

to be held on August 15 at the University of Notre Dame, he decided to combine the mission to Toledo with his attendance at this event. Archbishop Ireland and Bishop Gilmour were also present at the Sorin jubilee, and Ireland reflected something of Gibbons' frame of mind about what lay before him when he told Monsignor O'Connell, "I assure you he was more afraid of Richard, than Richard was of James, and he started out from Notre Dame for Toledo in fear and trembling."[48] After reaching Toledo, Gibbons established himself at St. Vincent's Hospital where he heard the evidence in the dispute. The bishop acted as his own advocate and the advocate for the sisters was Patrick F. Quigley, pastor of St. Francis de Sales Church in Toledo who, as we shall see, had already proved himself a sore trial to Gilmour on other counts.[49] After gathering all the facts as presented by both sides, the cardinal returned to Baltimore and for the next few weeks he continued to be the recipient of a considerable amount of correspondence from the interested parties.[50] All the while Denis O'Connell remained in close touch with Gibbons in order to keep him abreast of the various opinions on the case as held by the Roman officials, and he indicated the difficulty with which the situation was viewed in Rome when he remarked, "If you can succeed there, you will lose nowhere."[51] By the first week in October the cardinal had finished weighing the evidence and was ready to pronounce judgment, but before dispatching his final word to Gilmour and the sisters he called in the consultors of the Archdiocese of Baltimore, reviewed the points at issue with them, and asked for their opinion, which was given unanimously in favor of Gibbons' decision.[52]

The substance of the judgment rendered by the cardinal was as follows. The legal title to the property in question was to

---

[48] ADR, Ireland to O'Connell, St. Paul, August 18, 1888. It was on this occasion that Gibbons bestowed on Ireland the pallium of his new rank as first Archbishop of St. Paul which Bishop John J. Keane, also present at the Sorin jubilee, had recently brought from Rome. Cf. Arthur J. Hope, C.S.C., *Notre Dame, One Hundred Years* (Notre Dame, 1943), p. 239.

[49] Houck, *op. cit.*, I, 132.

[50] The Gibbons Papers in the AAB at this date contain numerous letters relating to the Gilmour-Grey Nuns case. E.g., 84-W-3, Sister Deschamps to Gibbons, Toledo, August 21, 1888; 84-W-10, Corcoran to Gibbons, Toledo, August 26, 1888; 85-A-8, same to same, Toledo, September 7, 1888.

[51] 85-A-2, O'Connell to Gibbons, Sorrento, September 4, 1888.

[52] Diary, October 5, 1888, p. 228.

remain with the sisters and the Bishop of Cleveland was to allow them to make such collections in the diocese as he deemed necessary and sufficient for the proper support of the orphans. On the other hand, the sisters were to renounce all pecuniary claims of every kind against the Diocese of Cleveland, including claims for expenses incurred in defending the present suit. Moreover, they were not to sell, alienate, mortgage, or otherwise encumber the property without written permission of the bishop, nor were they to make any notable improvements or changes in the property without his written permission. The bishop's written permission would also be necessary if the sisters should ever wish to use the property for any other purpose than an orphan asylum, and they were further directed to make an annual written report of the finances of the institution to the bishop which, if he so desired, was to be audited by two competent persons of his own choice.[53] On all points, therefore, except the first and most important, involving as it did the question of legal title, the decision favored Gilmour, and in this particular Gibbons remarked that he feared he would be disappointed. He had been instructed several times from Rome that he should be guided by the prescriptions of Leo XIII's constitution, *Romanos pontifices,* of May 8, 1881, which regulated the relations between bishops and religious and which had been applied to the American Church in September, 1885.[54] He reminded Gilmour of this fact, and stated that since the document did not authorize the transfer to the bishop of property such as that in question but only required a faithful account of its administration to be made to him, the decision which he was forwarding was the only one he could reasonably render. "Until our legislation in this subject is radically changed," he said, "I see no possibility of obtaining the redress you have so ably contended for."[55]

---

[53] ADC, Gibbons to Gilmour, Baltimore, October 5, 1888, enclosing a copy of the decision. A copy was also sent to the sisters (85-E-7), and one in Latin to Simeoni on October 6, 1888 (85-E-11).

[54] 85-B-9, O'Connell to Gibbons, Rome, September 15, 1888; 85-C-4, Simeoni to Gibbons, Rome, September 17, 1888.

[55] ADC, Gibbons to Gilmour, Baltimore, October 5, 1888. According to the diocesan historian, the sisters "of their own accord" transferred St. Vincent's Orphan Asylum to Gilmour's successor, Ignatius F. Hortsmann, in December, 1900, "thereby vindicating Bishop Gilmour's contention." Houck, *op. cit.,* I, 132, note.

The Grey Nuns were entirely satisfied with the cardinal's decision, and they told him that if he could have witnessed their joy in reading it he could have formed an estimate of the gratitude they felt toward him.[56] But the Bishop of Cleveland was anything but happy over the outcome. He believed that the consequences would be serious and would extend far beyond the limits of the orphan asylum and, according to Gilmour, the future would now inherit a legacy which he had hoped to prevent and against which he had worked for sixteen years. Yet in spite of his disappointment, he wished the cardinal to know, as he said, that "the result in no way changed the pleasant and I hope lasting kindness that has grown up between us."[57] The receipt of this letter brought great relief to Gibbons' mind. He revealed the tension under which he had been working when he told his friend in Cleveland:

> Ever since I sent the Decision, I experienced a sadness & melancholy which interfered with my work & even impaired my health, fearing lest the judgment should impair our friendship, or cool your affection which I appreciate so much.
>
> Your words have touched my heart. The magnanimity with which you bear the decision & the renewal of your expression of friendship for myself have increased my admiration for you, & I hope the Lord will give me an opportunity of proving my affection.[58]

Although he felt consoled by Gilmour's letter, Gibbons continued to be anxious over this and other aspects of the matter as Bishop Keane informed O'Connell some weeks later.[59] One thing that disturbed him was that he had learned too late that the Pope would have preferred to have him merely investigate the case and report it to Rome for final adjudication. Leo XIII was now quoted as believing that it would have been better to have used the Toledo case as an occasion for clarifying the *Romanos pontifices* constitution on the point of the tenure of church property by religious.[60] But, unfortunately, a terse cablegram from O'Connell, asking that the decision be held, and stating that a letter from Simeoni was on the way, did not help matters for Gibbons. He immediately adverted to a letter of Simeoni's that

[56] 85-F-6, Sister Deschamps to Gibbons, Toledo, October 10, 1888.

[57] 85-F-11, Gilmour to Gibbons, Cleveland, October 12, 1888.

[58] ADC, Gibbons to Gilmour, Frederick, Maryland, October 15, 1888.

[59] ADR, Keane to O'Connell, Baltimore, November 2, 1888.

[60] 85-F-4, O'Connell to Gibbons, Grottaferrata, October 8, 1888.

had arrived only a few days before O'Connell's cablegram and which had repeated that a decision should be rendered on the basis of *Romanos pontifices*. Interpreting the matter in this manner, Gibbons proceeded to hand down his judgment, not knowing that a second communication had already been dispatched which outlined for him the new procedure which the Holy Father wished to have followed. When he learned the true state of affairs in Rome the cardinal was greatly upset, and he was at pains to explain to both Simeoni and O'Connell the circumstances which led to his mailing the decision the day before he received the latest instructions from the Holy See.[61]

It was entirely understandable why he had acted as he did but, nonetheless, the latest turn of events only added to his uneasiness of mind. Sensing Gilmour's discontent, and knowing that Gilmour had been one of the strongest supporters behind the decree — later disallowed by the Propaganda — four years before in the council for strengthening the bishops' hand in cases of property of this kind, Gibbons now consulted four of the American archbishops and learned that they were in favor of petitioning the Holy See to incorporate the abrogated decree in the Baltimore legislation. He immediately informed Gilmour of this fact, added his own endorsement, and said that Archbishop Riordan who was then in Rome also favored it.[62] Obviously he was hopeful that this news would help to take the sting out of the decision which he had felt compelled to render against Gilmour over the title to the orphanage. Meanwhile Simeoni received Gibbons' judgment of the Toledo dispute, and the acknowledgment of his gratitude for the solicitude and prudence which the cardinal had exercised in the matter gave no indication that the Holy See regarded Gibbons' decision as other than final. The Prefect of Propaganda had been informed by the Grey Nuns of the full satisfaction with which they had greeted the

---

[61] 85-F-5, Gibbons to O'Connell, Baltimore, October 9, 1888, copy; 85-F-8, Gibbons to Simeoni, Baltimore, October 11, 1888, copy in Latin.

[62] ADC, Gibbons to Gilmour, Baltimore, November 13, 1888. The decree of 1884 to which Gibbons referred, and which would have ecclesiastical properties administered by religious but acquired or built by funds collected from the faithful in a diocese, to be held in the same form and name as other diocesan properties, can be found in *Acta et decreta concilii plenarii Baltimorensis tertii* (Baltimore, 1886), p. lxvii. The writer wishes to express his thanks to Dr. Jerome D. Hannan, Vice-Rector of the Catholic University of America, for his kindness in reading certain sections of this biography dealing with canonical questions.

terms of settlement, but he remarked that up to the time of writing he had received no word from the Bishop of Cleveland.[63]

Considering the amount of trouble that he had already been caused as a result of the Toledo orphanage case, it is easy to appreciate the disagreeable feeling which Cardinal Gibbons experienced at the close of the same year in receiving a request from Simeoni that he act for the Holy See in investigating a dispute of long standing between Bishop Gilmour and Father Quigley, one of his Toledo pastors. If there was anything that Gibbons would have wished at that time to do it was to stay clear of all difficulties in the Diocese of Cleveland, and he made that quite evident in announcing to Gilmour his most recent delegation from Rome. He summarized his reasons for not wishing to go there, the chief of which was on Gilmour's own account. "Evil-disposed persons," he said, "would draw extravagant & false conclusions from such a visit, as has been done already, and might try to make inferences hurtful to your dignity and episcopal authority which I am desirous of upholding and vindicating." The cardinal desired, if at all possible, to settle the matter without the form of a judicial process, and he stated that if Gilmour would visit him and outline what he regarded as a just and reasonable solution of his difficulty with Quigley, he would then try to induce the latter to assent to it if, as he hoped, his own views coincided with those of the bishop.[64] A few days later he informed Quigley of his appointment by the Holy See and asked him to come to Baltimore sometime between a given set of dates, a request with which the priest promptly complied.[65]

---

[63] 85-H-9, Simeoni to Gibbons, Rome, November 16, 1888. Gilmour found more agreement with his position in quarters nearer home than he would have experienced in corresponding with Simeoni. When he solicited the opinion of Archbishop Corrigan, he received a confirmation of his own views. Corrigan, too, thought Gibbons should have given the title to the orphanage or to the pious cause of which the bishop was the representative and guardian, and he added that he had reached the same conclusion from a study of the underlying principles of *Romanos pontifices* (ADC, Corrigan to Gilmour, New York, December 17, 1888, *Private*). The Bishop of Cleveland was naturally gratified at learning this, and in thanking Corrigan he remarked that the archbishop's interpretation, according to both the common law and the *Romanos pontifices,* "is & ever was mine . . ." (AANY, Gilmour to Corrigan, Cleveland, December 24, 1888).

[64] ADC, Gibbons to Gilmour, Baltimore, January 7, 1889, *Private*.

[65] 85-N-12, Gibbons to Quigley, Baltimore, January 10, 1889, copy; 85-O-10, Quigley to Gibbons, Toledo, January 14, 1889.

The quarrel between Gilmour and Quigley had developed out of a series of differences in which the latter had disregarded the bishop's admonitions concerning such things as abuse of his parishioners from the pulpit and his tendency to fight out his battles in the public press. Quigley, who was described by one as having a "well known eccentric character,"[66] had, however, enlisted the assistance of an able defender in Dr. Corcoran, probably the leading Catholic theologian in the United States at the time, who was convinced that Gilmour's manner of administering his diocese had often been in violation of canon law.[67] One of those who felt aggrieved at Quigley for what he regarded as reflections on his good name from the pulpit was a certain Denis Coghlin who threatened to go to law to gain his point. Gibbons summoned Coghlin to Baltimore on the same day that Quigley would be there with the intention of settling the matter as quietly and informally as he could. "I am far more concerned," he told Gilmour, "about your good standing & influence in Rome than an incident like this."[68]

The Bishop of Cleveland knew, of course, that his diocesan troubles had been reported to the Holy See and he was prompt to express his gratitude for Gibbons' attitude in the Quigley affair, and above all for his kindness in speaking a word to Rome. "For this latter I am deeper indebted to you," he remarked, "than perhaps I need say. . . ." And at this point Gilmour gave vent to his feelings concerning his relations with Rome. He made the rather revealing statement that in the seventeen years he had been Bishop of Cleveland he could count in less than ten the letters he had written to the Holy See, and he confessed that in this he may have been at fault since he had been told that Rome liked to be consulted. But having no need of assistance from that quarter he had not troubled the Roman officials, and if they did not now think him worthy to receive an inquiry about Quigley he would not offer explanations of his side of the matter. He knew that Corcoran had reported him to the Holy See and he felt humiliated that Gibbons should have

---

[66] Houck, *op. cit.*, I, 155. Speaking of the Quigley case, Houck said, "It thus reached the newspapers, and through them, the country at large, with the result that much criticism, adverse to the Bishop's action, was aroused." *Ibid.*, I, 156.

[67] 84-T-1, Corcoran to Gibbons, Toledo, July 21, 1888; 85-A-8, same to same, Toledo, September 7, 1888.

[68] ADC, Gibbons to Gilmour, Baltimore, January 16, 1889, *Personal & Private*.

to be tormented by what he termed "the shame of Dr. Quigley & the dotage of Dr. Corcoran. . . ." Conscious as he was of the unfavorable impression that this sort of writing might make on Gibbons, the bishop ended his letter by saying, "Please excuse this partial outturning of the inner man — in your kindness it has its being."[69]

In all the unpleasant business relating to the Diocese of Cleveland the cardinal was able to bring a peaceful solution to at least one source of the friction. He heard Mr. Coghlin's charges against Father Quigley on the score that the latter had upbraided him from the pulpit for bad morals, for getting money in an illicit way, and for controlling the Democratic Party in Toledo. But since Coghlin was unable to prove that he was the party whom Quigley had in mind in his remarks, Gibbons decided that he had no case and before they parted at his residence in Baltimore the cardinal succeeded in bringing about a reconciliation between the two men and they shook hands as a token of restored peace.[70] In informing Simeoni of the happy outcome of the matter some weeks later, Gibbons described the Quigley-Coghlin affair as one of the principal causes which had led to the trouble between Quigley and his bishop.[71] But the differences between Gilmour and the Toledo pastor had gone too far to enable the cardinal to head off a crisis and on March 19, 1889, the bishop suspended Quigley for a period of three months and removed him from his pastorate. Gilmour later outlined his procedure to Cardinal Simeoni, but he put himself in wrong in the eyes of Rome by giving no specific reasons for the penalties he had inflicted on the priest.[72] The result was that Quigley went to Rome where he won a restoration to his status as pastor with a restitution of salary to be made to him from the date of his suspension. Simeoni reported this action to Gibbons and stated that it was due to the fact that Gilmour had not followed the forms of procedure demanded by canon law in such matters. The Prefect of Propaganda added that the Holy See had heard rather alarming reports about the administration of the Diocese of Cleveland and the officials of

---

[69] 85-P-6, Gilmour to Gibbons, Cleveland, January 19, 1889.

[70] 85-T-5, Gibbons' summary of the Quigley-Coghlin case, Baltimore, March 12, 1889.

[71] 85-V-8, Gibbons to Simeoni, Baltimore, April 5, 1889, copy in Latin.

[72] Houck, *op. cit.*, I, 155–156.

the congregation would, therefore, be grateful if he would gather the necessary data so that they might have exact knowledge of affairs there and thus form a true idea of the condition of the Church in that diocese.[73] By this time Gibbons was doubtless tempted to wonder if he would ever be rid of the troubles in that see.

Meanwhile Rome gave instructions to Archbishop Elder, the metropolitan, to execute the reinstatement of Quigley in his parish, and likewise to send a report covering Gilmour's administration. Elder was plainly worried over how to go about the job and he, therefore, communicated with Gibbons several times to gain his advice. In a second letter he was able to tell the cardinal that Gilmour would place no obstacle in the way of Quigley's reinstatement.[74] Gibbons rejoiced to hear this news, and he told Archbishop Elder that the esteem he had always entertained for the bishop now rose higher as a result of his wise and magnanimous action. Through all the trouble Gilmour had found a stanch friend in the Archbishop of Cincinnati, and the cardinal was glad to associate himself with Elder's defense of the bishop before the Holy See. He said:

> I intend also to write to Rome showing the good the Bishop has done — his strong faith & zeal — the discipline he has established or developed, his well-ordered chancery, the progress of religion, etc. I would be pleased if you would have no objection to send me an outline of your letter that I may add to, & confirm it.
> His good qualities are obscured in some quarters on account of these controversies in which he has been involved.[75]

Although Gibbons had been asked in early August to send Rome his opinion of Gilmour's administration, it was almost four months before he replied. Without going into details, he stated that if the Holy See felt the Diocese of Cleveland should be investigated he believed that it would better satisfy public

---

[73] 86-G-8, Simeoni to Gibbons, Rome, August 5, 1889. That Rome was in a bad mood toward Gilmour at this time was evident from a letter of O'Connell to Gibbons three weeks before. He said he had written the bishop to desist, and he added, "They are in a temper here to act gravely. Abp. Elder sustains him but it does not seem to avail" (86-E-10, O'Connell to Gibbons, Rome, July 16, 1889).

[74] 86-J-5, Elder to Gibbons, St. Martin's, Brown County, Ohio, August 21, 1889; 86-K-4, same to same, Cincinnati, August 26, 1889.

[75] AAC, Gibbons to Elder, Baltimore, August 28, 1889.

opinion there if it were done in a formal and juridical manner rather than by a private investigation. Therefore, he judged it wiser and more opportune not to make inquiries concerning affairs in Cleveland, for if he attempted to do that it would become known and matters would not be helped. As for the bishop himself, Gibbons contented himself with saying that he regarded Gilmour as a just man whose management of the temporal affairs of his diocese had put them in a prosperous state, although in his personal relations he had, perhaps, at times been too severe.[76]

Yet while retaining the friendship of Gilmour and offering a sympathetic explanation of his difficulties to Rome, Gibbons did not lose the high regard of one of the bishop's chief adversaries, for when Quigley learned in the Eternal City of the death of Dr. Corcoran on July 16 he wrote to the cardinal in the friendliest spirit and said that for years he had known something of the relations that had obtained between Gibbons and Corcoran. During the latter's prolonged stay in Toledo a year before, Quigley maintained that Corcoran had manifested his great love for the cardinal and had spoken of him daily. "I doubt if any one in the Church of great America," said Quigley, "rejoiced more, or gloried more in your exalted position and in your services to Holy Mother Church."[77] Three months later Quigley returned to the United States and was reinstated in his parish at Toledo, but within a very short time he and Gilmour were at odds again over the bishop's order that the orphans in his parish should be moved to Cleveland. Quigley sent Gibbons a long telegram explaining the matter and appealing to him for his judgment. The cardinal promptly wired back "Obey";[78] and some days later he told the priest that since he feared it might involve a new issue he did not feel warranted in rendering a decision unless instructed to do so by the Holy See.[79] He had

---

[76] 86-U-6, Gibbons to Simeoni, Baltimore, November 22, 1889, copy in Latin.

[77] 86-N-2, Quigley to Gibbons, Rome, September 14, 1889.

[78] 86-W-2, same to same, Toledo, December 21, 1889, telegram. Gibbons wrote across the wire, "My answer dated Dec. 21, 89 was 'Obey.'"

[79] 87-A-6, Gibbons to Quigley, Baltimore, January 4, 1890. In November, 1888, Gilmour had dismissed John B. Primeau, pastor of St. Louis Church, Toledo, from his parish. Primeau, who had not been incardinated into the Diocese of Cleveland, appealed his case to the metropolitan, Archbishop Elder. When Elder sought Gibbons' advice about the matter, the cardinal did not think there was any fear of Rome settling the case over Elder's head, nor did he think Rome

seen more than enough of the Cleveland troubles and he was not
going to be drawn in again unless by the orders of Rome. A
little over a year later Bishop Gilmour died on April 13, 1891,
at a time when Gibbons was in New Orleans. The cardinal had
known and admired the Bishop of Cleveland on many counts in
no way related to the recent troubles. For that reason, in
extending his regrets to Archbishop Elder that he could not attend
the funeral he could honestly say, "I regarded him as a great man
whose talents & logical mind would command admiration in any
assembly whether lay or clerical. It will be hard to find a man
to *fill* his place."[80]

At the very time that Cardinal Gibbons became so deeply
involved as the somewhat reluctant agent of Rome in the troubles
of the Diocese of Cleveland, the Holy See had entered upon a
new and acute crisis in its relations with the Italian government.
Ever since 1870, of course, those relations had been strained but
in July, 1887, Francesco Crispi became Prime Minister of Italy
and with his advent to power a campaign of open hostility
toward the Church was inaugurated. Implications for the
Papacy's temporal power could be seen in a penal code which
was enacted by the government in June, 1888, whereby anyone
who was judged guilty of doing anything to put the state or
any part of it under foreign domination, or of altering the unity
of the state, was condemned to perpetual imprisonment at hard
labor. Any clergyman who abused his office by exciting criticism
of Italian laws or institutions, or who made attacks upon the
public authorities, was to be fined and temporarily deprived of
his benefice, and any priest who performed acts of public worship
contrary to the rules laid down by the government was to be
fined and imprisoned for three months. Decrees were likewise
issued against religious education in the Italian schools, and in
time the properties of the religious confraternities and charitable
societies were seized by the government under the pretext of

---

would refer it to him, to which he added, "I hope I am done with them." But
in case the Holy See should refer it to him, the cardinal said he would inform
Propaganda of Elder's willingness to act as a court, and he would remind Rome
of its promise to refer cases of this kind to the metropolitans and of the evil
consequences that would follow from depriving the metropolitans "of the small
remnant of appelate jurisdiction which is left to them" (85-U-5, Gibbons to
Elder, Baltimore, March 21, 1889, copy). Elder ultimately heard the Primeau
case and decided against him in December, 1890. Cf. Houck, *op. cit.,* I, 157–163.
   80 AAC, Gibbons to Elder, New Orleans, April 19, 1891.

laicizing charitable works throughout Italy. It was apparent that the radical elements who supported the Crispi regime were determined if they could to paralyze the power and influence of the Church in Italian life. Individual bishops and priests denounced the penal code, and in the month that it became law Pope Leo XIII issued a solemn protest against it in a papal allocution.

Actions such as these could not help but prove painful to Catholics in all parts of the world. Four years before when the Italian government had threatened to seize the American College in Rome, along with the other properties held in the name of the Congregation of the Propaganda, the American bishops, as we have seen, intervened with the government of the United States to save the college, Gibbons issued a pastoral letter in protest against the seizure of Propaganda's properties, and a protest meeting was held in Washington with his blessing.[81] In the present instance Catholics in several of the European countries had made public protests against the treatment accorded to the Holy See, and certain officials of the Vatican let it be known that they would like to see similar manifestations from the Catholics of the United States. Monsignor O'Connell conveyed this desire to Cardinal Gibbons and informed him that he had been called by Archbishop Mario Mocenni, substitute Secretary of State, who wished Gibbons to know that he spoke in the name of Cardinal Rampolla.[82] The Archbishop of Baltimore replied at once that he would lay the proposal before the prelates who would be gathered for the consecration of John Foley as Bishop of Detroit a few weeks hence and by this method, he thought, concerted action would be secured. He mentioned the devotion of the American hierarchy to the Holy See, the concern which they all felt for the wishes of the Pope, and in referring to the procedure he proposed to follow in carrying out the suggestion of Rome, he added, "Of course I am unable to foresee how far it will aid the end which is desired."[83] Actually Gibbons was skeptical from the outset about the wisdom of attempting any public demonstrations in the United States on this subject and in informing Archbishop Ireland of what he had just learned

---

[81] Cf. I, 269–272. For Italy's campaign against the Church in these years cf. Eduardo Soderini, *Leo XIII, Italy and France* (London, 1935), pp. 3–120.

[82] 85-D-8, O'Connell to Gibbons, Grottaferrata, September 27, 1888.

[83] 85-G-4, Gibbons to O'Connell, Baltimore, October 18, 1888, copy.

from Rome he said he had "grave doubts" that agitation of this kind would do any good.[84]

Yet in spite of his misgiving, the cardinal followed his customary practice of consulting as many of his fellow bishops as possible and at the consecration of Foley on November 4, and at a meeting of the bishops who composed the committee for the university ten days later, he sounded out opinion on the advisability of protest meetings against Italy's treatment of the Church. He later related to Ireland their general agreement that public agitation would do no good, but he stated that they were likewise agreed that a warm and affectionate letter should be addressed to the Holy Father which would express their conviction that he should enjoy complete liberty in the exercise of his exalted office.[85] In fulfillment of his promise to his colleagues, Gibbons sent a communication to all the archbishops whom he had not seen personally, and he there summarized the request made by the Vatican Secretariat of State. He said he had spoken to the Archbishops of Boston, New York, and Philadelphia and they were unanimous in their opinion that the time was quite inopportune for holding public meetings on this question, and that such gatherings would very probably result in provoking counterdemonstrations on the part of the opponents of the temporal power. "With the views of these archbishops," said Gibbons, "I entirely concur." He added that they were agreed that a letter should be sent to the Pontiff which would express the filial affection and sympathy of the American Catholics, and which at the same time would forcibly though temperately declare that the interests of the Catholic world demanded that the Pope be absolutely free and untrammeled and enjoy full autonomy in his government of the Church. If these suggestions met with the approval of the archbishops, Gibbons stated that he would then have a draft of the letter submitted to them for their signatures and later forward it to the Holy Father.[86]

---

[84] AASP, Gibbons to Ireland, Baltimore, October 19, 1888, copy. When Mocenni read the sentence in the cardinal's letter expressing uncertainty as to how far the protest meetings would contribute to the effect intended, O'Connell said, "He burst out: 'this will contribute a great deal. Know that America is one of the greatest countries in the world'" (85-G-13, O'Connell to Gibbons, Rome, October 31, 1888).

[85] AASP, Gibbons to Ireland, Baltimore, November 14, 1888, copy.

[86] 85-I-10, Gibbons to the Archbishops of the United States, Baltimore, November 24, 1888, copy.

The archbishops replied within a week and they were unanimous in their belief that it would be ill advised to hold the proposed public meetings, and all but one were agreed that a letter bearing their names should be dispatched to the Pope. On the latter point Archbishop Kenrick of St. Louis told the cardinal, "I also decline to sign any letter to His Holiness in which the question of the Temporal Power would be introduced. The sooner that it becomes known to the Holy Father that there is a diversity of opinion on that subject among the Bishops, the better will it be for Religion."[87] Most of the metropolitans merely stated their agreement with Gibbons' proposals very briefly and let the matter rest there, but Archbishop Gross of Oregon City went into considerable detail. He doubted that the majority of the American Catholics could be made to see the necessity for the autonomy of the Pope. He wrote:

> So many years have elapsed since the King of Italy has made Rome his capital; during this period everything seems in the eyes of the public to have gone on as quietly in the Church; that the Bishops have perfect freedom in their intercourse with the Holy See; that great assemblies have been held; that the Holy Father has spoken and written just as freely as in other days; — and His Government of the universal Church seems to the public to pursue its even course as unimpeded as in by-gone times, that the Catholic public in our country at least, seems almost to have settled down to the belief, that the Head of the Church is doing very well under existing circumstances.

Gross deeply regretted that such was the condition of the public mind on the question, and as for himself, he was ready to do all in his power to obtain the autonomy of the Holy See but, as he added, "I believe it to be my duty to state candidly my opinion."[88]

Although the Vatican authorities, faced as they then were by the openly hostile measures of the Crispi government, would doubtless have found it exceedingly difficult to understand views such as those expressed by Gross, it should not be forgotten that at this particular time anti-Catholic bigotry was steadily on the rise in the United States with the recently founded American Protective Association. For that reason, Gibbons and

---

[87] 85-J-5, Kenrick to Gibbons, St. Louis, November 26, 1888.
[88] 85-K-2, Gross to Gibbons, Portland, December 1, 1888.

his colleagues were more than ordinarily sensitive to anything that might offer further weapons for the hands of the Church's enemies. In the environment of that day public protest meetings by American Catholics on the subject of the Italian government's treatment of the Papacy, or the necessity of restoring the temporal power, would have been immediately seized upon and used against them. Knowing the temper of the American people as well as he did, Gibbons endeavored, therefore, to steer a middle course. He was glad to learn from Bishop Keane who was then in Rome that the latter approved of his associating the other archbishops with him in the letter to the Pontiff, and he was even happier to be told that Keane would suggest that after a delay of a few months some sort of public utterance in vindication of the Holy Father's independence and freedom of action be made which need not even mention the temporal power. "I am assured here," he said, "that such declarations would be acceptable & useful."[89]

Meanwhile the hierarchy's letter to Leo XIII was drafted. It denounced the persecution of the Church by the Italian government and stated that the suffering which it had brought to the Holy Father was deeply lamented in the United States. The American hierarchy was likewise represented as holding the conviction that the Pontiff could not properly fulfill his functions unless he were entirely free. On the subject of the temporal power, the letter spoke only in general terms. It recalled the horror with which the American clergy and laity had heard the news eighteen years before of the seizure of the papal domain and the protests which had been expressed in the United States at that time in public meetings and in the press. The recent laws which had profaned religion in Italy were deplored, as well as the growing fury and hate by which the enemies of God and His Church persecuted His followers. These men, it was said, were not satisfied with their victory in fraudulently occupying the city and lands of the Holy Father, but they now defiled good morals by their attacks upon the institutes and foundations of religion.[90] After they had read the text a number of the metropolitans expressed

---

[89] 85-L-9, Keane to Gibbons, Rome, December 18, 1888.
[90] 85-P-5, American hierarchy to Leo XIII, Baltimore, January 17, 1889, copy in Latin.

their pleasure with the letter, and Gross told the cardinal that, as he expressed it, ". . . in this as on so many other occasions Your Eminence has most decidedly succeeded in voicing the opinions of the entire body of the American Episcopate."[91]

The letter which Gibbons had sent to Rome apparently took care of the situation for the time being. However, the campaign against the Church in Italy grew in intensity and in June, 1889, a fresh insult was offered the Holy See when a statue of Giordano Bruno, the sixteenth-century Dominican friar who had been burned at the stake for heresy, was unveiled in Rome and elaborate ceremonies which drew delegations of the Masonic lodges from all over Italy, and for days the streets of the Eternal City rang with denunciations of the Pope and the clergy. The Vatican naturally felt deeply offended, and in the absence of Denis O'Connell, Father Farrelly of the American College informed Gibbons of the wish of the Holy See that the Catholic press of the United States remonstrate against the incident and, if possible, the secular press should be induced to do likewise.[92] In reply the cardinal stated that the American Catholic papers had already carried a number of condemnations of the insult offered to the Holy Father and if he could lay his hands on the particular issues he would forward them. As for the secular press, he observed that with few exceptions they had taken no notice of the subject beyond brief dispatches which merely mentioned the unveiling of the statue. He believed that the great mass of American readers, as well as the newspapermen themselves, knew nothing of Bruno's history and had not taken the trouble to inquire who he was. "The event," he said, "did not excite a ripple of commotion in this country." He feared, therefore, that it would be next to impossible to persuade the secular papers to revert to it, and he thought it probable that agitation of the incident would on the whole do more harm than good.[93] It was evident that the cardinal was not sympathetic to any effort to bestir the American press on the question of the Bruno statue.

---

[91] 85-P-4, Gross to Gibbons, Portland, January 16, 1889. Reflecting the spread of the A.P.A., Gross remarked that since the November elections there was abroad in Oregon what he called "quite a Know-Nothing spirit," although in his opinion it would not do any serious harm.

[92] 86-B-10, Farrelly to Gibbons, Rome, June 6, 1889, *Private*.

[93] 86-D-4, Gibbons to Farrelly, Baltimore, June 20, 1889, copy.

Later in the same summer the Pope's independence again became a matter for discussion among the American bishops, as plans gradually matured for the Catholic congress which was to be held in Baltimore in connection with the centennial of the hierarchy. They felt that it was necessary to devote one of the papers to this theme, and after a meeting of the committee in Detroit, Bishop Foley stated that they agreed that the man selected to read the paper should be chosen by Gibbons.[94] About the same time the cardinal was informed from Rome that Mocenni and others had seen the wisdom of not expecting the American press to go back and pick up the Bruno incident for comment. But in the interval the tension with the Italian government had in no way abated, and he was told that the Vatican officials found comfort in the thought that the congress in Baltimore would say something in defense of the Holy Father. That there was grave anxiety at the Holy See was evident, and O'Connell commented, "The question of the Pope's leaving Rome was discussed at a secret consistory, but it is questioned if the idea be seriously entertained."[95]

Gibbons appreciated and sympathized with the position of the Pontiff and he suggested, therefore, that Archbishop Ireland confer with Thomas O'Gorman, Rector of St. Thomas Seminary in St. Paul, about writing a paper to be read at the congress that would express the need for the Pope's independence in a strong and vigorous way. The cardinal then revealed the dual point of view which he had kept uppermost in all the direction he had assumed of American Catholic reaction to the feud between the Vatican and Italy. He advised that in writing the paper O'Gorman should bear in mind what he termed, "the wishes of the Holy See and the temper of our own country which should not be antagonized."[96] Ireland assured him that O'Gorman would write the paper in a way that would be entirely satisfactory to him,[97] and William J. Onahan of Chicago, one of the leading lay members of the arrangements committee, felt that O'Gorman would justify the high estimate implied by the cardinal's suggestion of his name.[98]

[94] 86-E-6, Foley to Gibbons, Detroit, July 11, 1889.
[95] 86-E-10, O'Connell to Gibbons, Rome, July 16, 1889.
[96] AASP, Gibbons to Ireland, Cape May, New Jersey, July 18, 1889, copy.
[97] 86-F-1, Ireland to Gibbons, St. Paul, July 24, 1889.
[98] 86-F-7, Onahan to Gibbons, Chicago, July 29, 1889.

At the congress which was held on November 11–12, 1889, the paper entitled "The Independence of the Holy See" was actually read by Charles J. Bonaparte, a prominent Catholic lawyer of Baltimore who had distinguished himself as a member of the National Civil Service Reform League. The history of the temporal power of the Papacy was first briefly reviewed with mention being made of the many benefits it had conferred on Italy and Europe in general. In regard to the Law of Guarantees passed by the Italian parliament in 1871, the question was posed whether or not the Catholics of the world would accept it. A negative answer was given since, as it was said, the pretension of a national parliament to legislate regarding the Holy See involved a denial of its independence, and since the Pope was not a citizen of Italy, he was not subject to the law. The speaker declined to say how the problem might be solved, although a settlement by treaty of the great powers which would carry an international sanction was suggested as a step in the right direction. In conclusion American Catholics were cautioned against crude projects, petulant complaints, and sweeping and uncharitable denunciations for the reason that these would not help the Pope. But they were likewise told that they would do less than their duty if they failed to say that the Holy Father had been wronged, and that against this wrong they now temperately but firmly protested and would continue to protest.[99] These were sentiments to which Cardinal Gibbons subscribed, of course, with a full and hearty assent.

On the day preceding the opening of the centennial celebration in Baltimore the *Catholic Mirror* of that city published an editorial on the temporal power of the Pope which drew com-

---

[99] *Souvenir Volume Illustrated. Three Great Events in the History of the Catholic Church in the United States* (Detroit, 1890), pp. 30–32. In all likelihood Bonaparte simply read the paper that had been written by O'Gorman, although its tone would be entirely congenial to him. He was a man of independent mind on Church questions, but he shared the views held by Gibbons and his associates on matters of this kind. For example, four months previous to the congress Bonaparte delivered an address at Ridge, Maryland, in which he spoke strongly in behalf of separation of Church and State. Deploring the price which the Church had often had to pay for official union with the State, he said: "Moreover Caesar does not work for nothing; he must be paid for his protection; if he makes heresy treason, he asks that she make treason heresy, and this is little less than a ruinous price for a less than doubtful service." Goldman, *Charles J. Bonaparte. Patrician Reformer,* p. 19.

ment both at home and abroad. It stated that the Pontiff had, indeed, been unjustly despoiled of his property and that the Catholics of the world wished him to have complete independence, and for that reason the great powers should concert to free him of all dependence upon Italy. But the editorial then continued:

> We think we voice the intelligent sentiments of American Catholics, at least, when we say that it is not desired to interfere with the geographical lines that at present define the boundaries of the Kingdom of Italy. The kingly prerogative that formerly inhered in the pontificate in relation to the temporalities that constituted the Papal dominions is neither essential nor indispensable to the spiritual authority or spiritual dominion of the Pope. The Holy Father, as Vicar of Christ and visible Head of the Church, has no absolute need for extensive territory wherein to wield the power and exercise the rule of an earthly kingdom.[100]

In the press of business attendant upon the festivities, Gibbons did not see the editorial until someone called his attention to it a week after it was published. Regardless of the fact that the editorial may in all likelihood have represented the opinion of a considerable number of American Catholics at that time, the cardinal realized at once the painful impression it would create in Vatican circles, and with that in mind he instructed Monsignor O'Connell who was then in Baltimore to call on the lay editor and, as he later explained in answer to Farrelly's inquiry from Rome about the matter, to "reprimand him for his indiscretion, not to use a stronger phrase." He further explained that the *Mirror* had carried an editorial in the issue following his rebuke which, he thought, had in great measure atoned for the former one. He reminded Farrelly that the American bishops in plenary council had publicly disclaimed responsibility for the views of the Catholic papers, and that these weeklies were for the most part not official organs. In the cardinal's judgment most of the mistakes of the lay editors had been made through misconception rather than through malice or intentional disobedience, and this being the case, their errors did not excite any scandal or even arouse any great interest. Nonetheless, he wished it to be known that O'Connell had

---

[100] *Catholic Mirror*, November 9, 1889.

charged the editor of the *Catholic Mirror* in his name never to publish anything in the future on the subject of the temporal power of the Papacy without first submitting it to him.[101]

Throughout all the storm and stress that characterized the relations between the Holy See and Italy at this time, the sympathies of Cardinal Gibbons, it need hardly be said, were entirely with the Pope. Sixteen years before Crispi forced the present crisis upon the Vatican, Gibbons as a missionary bishop in North Carolina had made the temporal power of the Holy See the subject of his first pastoral letter. In that document he had sought to prove the Pope's claim through a review of the Church's history, and to establish title to the temporal sovereignty on the basis of long possession, legitimate acquisition, and a just use of the original grant confided to the Papacy.[102] The tone of the pastoral was firm and clear, although the language was sufficiently restrained as to offer no opportunity for criticism to fair-minded Americans outside the Church.[103] In

[101] 86-W-7, Gibbons to Farrelly, Baltimore, December 28, 1889, copy. In the issue of November 23, 1889, the *Catholic Mirror* carried an editorial entitled "The Roman Question" in which they called for the "absolute independence of the Holy See in the city of Rome." Since, as it was said, the despoiling of the Pope's properties was a wrong, it was impossible to contemplate an acknowledgment or concession of any character from the Pontiff that would reinvest Italy with what was called "that honor and integrity which were cast aside when it unlawfully annexed the Pontifical States." The American Catholics' profound loyalty to the Pope was stressed, and whatever influence they could bring to bear to right the wrong that had been done him was both an obligation and a duty. The editorial concluded, "The Catholic press can have no grander theme, no more lofty mission, than the vindication of the rights of the Sovereign Pontiff and the dignified assertion of the correct sentiment of the American people which, without unwarrantable obtrusion, is freely offered to aid in the solution of the difficulties and dangers which surround the Supreme Head of the Catholic world."

[102] *A Circular Letter on the Temporal Power of the Popes Addressed to the Clergy and Laity of the Vicariate Apostolic of North Carolina* (Baltimore, 1871). The letter was dated the feast of St. John Chrysostom (January 27) and ran to fifteen pages.

[103] Gibbons' pastoral offered an interesting contrast to one issued eleven years before on the same subject by John Hughes, Archbishop of New York. Hughes practically made the temporal power essential to the Holy See, and the fearless language he employed in arraigning the Church's enemies was the subject of considerable comment. Some days after its publication Hughes told a Roman friend, "Our Catholic laity needed such a document to brace them up, since all manner of evil has been said and published in Protestant journals against the government of the Holy See." (Hughes to Bernard Smith, O.S.B., January 30, 1860, published in John R. G. Hassard, *Life of the Most Reverend John Hughes* [New York, 1866], p. 419.) The Hughes document emanated from the Second Provincial Council of New York and was signed on January 19, 1860.

the intervening years Gibbons had grown more acutely conscious of the temper of his own country, and for that reason he was adverse to public demonstrations which he feared might give further provocation to groups like the A.P.A. and in the end accomplish little real benefit for the Holy See.

Insofar, then, as the leadership of American Catholics on this question was dependent upon his directives, he endeavored to enunciate the principles for which they stood in a dignified manner and to express their sympathies by means of the letter to the Pope and the paper read at the centennial congress in a way that would properly convey to the Vatican their sentiments, without at the same time affording unnecessary grounds for opposition from their non-Catholic fellow citizens. Such continued to be the cardinal's policy in the matter, and when a few years later he received an elaborate proposal for solving the vexing problem from Mariano Soler, Bishop of Montevideo, he again made his position very clear.[104] Soler asked that he support him in trying to win the governments of the world to bring moral pressure to bear on Italy through Austria-Hungary. Contrary to his usual custom, Gibbons waited for over six months before he replied. He then offered the pressure of work as an apology for his delay, and at the outset he stated that, to be sure, he wished nothing left undone to win complete freedom for the Pontiff. But any means taken toward that end must, he said, be actually effective and must be adapted to the genius of each people. The cardinal stated that after the most mature consideration he doubted very much that the American government would ever consent to exercise pressure of this kind on Italy. Intelligent statesmen would doubtless realize that an official manifestation, such as the one suggested by Soler, would not entirely compromise their impartiality, but the spirit of the masses would strongly resent even the appearance of interference in religious matters. He reminded the bishop that the American citizen considered it one of his proudest boasts that the State had no relation whatever with the Church, and that it did not interfere with any form of religion. He explained the two-party system governing American political life, and he added that neither of the parties would venture to compromise its chances of success at the polls by taking a step which, as he remarked,

---

[104] 89-M-9, Soler to Gibbons, Montevideo, February 10, 1892, *Confidential.*

would seem to identify its policy with the special interests of the Catholic population of the United States. "Hence," the cardinal concluded, "whilst endeavoring to avail ourselves of every opportunity to speak out our mind on the inalienable rights of the Holy See, we deem it useless to try to induce the Government to interfere in this matter."[105]

Whereas the Latin American prelate had sought the intervention of Gibbons with the government of the United States in behalf of the Papacy, there were, on the other hand, some of the cardinal's own fellow citizens who thought that he might use his influence for their benefit with several governments in Latin America. Two years after Soler's proposal a group of Methodist ministers in the United States asked him to call the attention of the Holy See to certain civil disabilities which their coreligionists were experiencing in Peru, Ecuador, and Bolivia.[106] On the occasion of his visit to Rome in the spring of 1895 Gibbons consulted Cardinal Rampolla about the matter, and as a consequence the Secretary of State asked the papal representatives in the countries involved for information on the subject.[107] Rampolla later explained that the laws on marriage, about which complaint had been made, were governed by constitutional provisions in these states but that the Methodists had private chapels wherein they were permitted to bless marriages after a civil ceremony had been performed.[108] Under the circumstances, therefore, the cardinal felt that he had done as much as could reasonably be expected to satisfy the petitioners. There were times, too, when he sensibly refused to interfere at all in an affair in these distant regions. For example, in October, 1902, Archbishop Riordan of San Francisco won a decision from the Permanent Court of Arbitration at The Hague for the payment by Mexico of the claims owing to the Church in California from the Pious Fund. The cardinal was asked by Archbishop Eulogio Gillow of Oaxaca to induce Riordan not to press for payment,

---

[105] 90-E-2, Gibbons to Soler, Baltimore, September 1, 1892, *Confidential*, copy.

[106] 93-T-7, John Lee to Gibbons, Chicago, April 22, 1895; 93-U-3, same to same, Chicago, May 20, 1895.

[107] 93-V-2, Gibbons to Lee, Rome, June 4, 1895, copy.

[108] 94-D-9, Rampolla to Gibbons, Rome, November 30, 1895. On the constitutional restrictions relating to the Protestant denominations in the three countries mentioned cf. Edwin Ryan, *The Church in the South American Republics* (Westminster, Maryland, 1943), pp. 53–54: 63–68; 71–73.

since he feared the Mexican government would place the blame for its loss on the Church of Mexico and force it to make the payments. But in spite of the archbishop's plea, Gibbons declined to approach Riordan on the matter.[109]

About five years later Cardinal Gibbons was the recipient of a request from the Holy See relating to the Church in South America which he found easy to grant. Cardinal Merry del Val, Secretary of State, notified him that a Catholic congress was to be held in Brazil and that word had reached the Holy See that the Cardinal of Baltimore was going to be invited to preside as papal legate. Merry del Val explained that the nomination of Joaquim Cardinal Arcoverde de Albuquerque Cavalcanti, Archbishop of Rio de Janeiro, two years before to the College of Cardinals as South America's first cardinal had excited the jealousy of Argentina and Chile. Under these circumstances, if a papal legate were to visit the Brazilian capital the Holy See would incur bad feeling in the other republics and, as Merry del Val said, "we shall be worried to death with the reproach that all Pontifical honours are being granted to Brazil whilst the other Republics are being left out in the cold. . . ." For that reason the Holy See would appreciate it if Gibbons were to find plausible reasons for declining the invitation.[110] The cardinal had no hesitation in assuring Merry del Val that his advanced age, his ignorance of the Portuguese and Spanish languages, and his many pressing duties would offer him cogent excuses, and thus the Vatican would be saved the threatened embarrassment if the invitation should materialize.[111]

On a matter of more fundamental importance to the welfare of religion in South America, however, Gibbons showed himself to be quite active. When Venezuela separated from Colombia in 1830 it had retained the law of 1824 which had declared that the right of patronage of the Church was vested in the republic. According to article thirty-nine of that law, all members of the

---

[109] 100-C-3, Gillow to Gibbons, Oaxaca, October 27, 1902. Another example of Gibbons declining to be drawn into a troubled situation in a distant area was his refusal to use his influence at Rome on the selection of a successor to Alexander Christie in the See of Vancouver Island after Christie was named Archbishop of Oregon City in February, 1899 (97-H-2, Gibbons to F. Verbek, Baltimore, May 9, 1899, copy).

[110] 104-T, Merry del Val to Gibbons, Rome, January 24, 1908, *Private*.

[111] 104-V, Gibbons to Merry del Val, Baltimore, March 5, 1908, copy.

hierarchy had to be native-born and all clergymen either natives or naturalized citizens.[112] Despite the many constitutional changes in later years, this law was retained and when a new constitution was to be drafted in 1914 Archbishop Carlo Pietropaoli, Apostolic Delegate to Venezuela, sought Gibbons' assistance in having the clause stricken out in the hope that thereby the great shortage of priests might be relieved from outside. The cardinal conferred with Secretary of State Bryan in Washington on the subject and he, in turn, discussed it with President Wilson and then cabled to Preston McGoodwin, American minister to Caracas, to indicate to the Venezuelan government the interest of the United States in winning permission for American clergymen to exercise their ministry in the republic.[113] But despite the expression of American interest in the case, the new constitution of

---

[112] Mary Watters, *A History of the Church in Venezuela, 1810–1930* (Chapel Hill, 1933), p. 236. The text of the patronage law of July 22, 1824, is given here in translation, pp. 222–237.

[113] 109-U, Bryan to Gibbons, Washington, April 16, 1914. Cf. also Gibbons to Bryan, Bonzano, and McGoodwin, Baltimore, April 17, 1914, copies; 109-V, Gibbons to Merry del Val, Baltimore, April 29, 1914, copy. Another example of an appeal to Gibbons from Latin America was that of Guillermo Rojas, C.M., Bishop of Panama, who described the failure of the government of Panama to honor the payments due to the Church under the concordat between the Holy See and Colombia and, too, the laws of the congress of Panama against Christian marriage. Rojas said he submitted these cases to the cardinal, "praying Your Eminence to make use of your influence with the Government of the United States in our favor . . ." (111-R, Rojas to Gibbons, Panama, April 5, 1915). Whether Gibbons took any action in the case is not known. Early in 1913 Gibbons made a direct appeal to Senators Elihu Root and Henry Cabot Lodge to favor a settlement of the long-standing dispute between the United States and Colombia over the amount of money to be paid to the latter for its loss of Panama in 1903. The cardinal urged it, as he told Root, in the conviction that an amicable adjustment would result in "more friendly and intimate relations between the two countries concerned and will create good feeling with the other South American Republics" (111-D, Gibbons to Root, Baltimore, January 25, 1915, copy). But both Root and Lodge were opposed to a ratification of the treaty in its present form, since it would reflect on the policies of former President Roosevelt (111-D, Root to Gibbons, Washington, January 27, 1915; 111-N, Lodge to Gibbons, Washington, March 8, 1915, *Personal*). It was not until April 20, 1921, that the senate finally gave approval to the treaty with Colombia after oil had been discovered in the latter country in which the United States wished to share. An historian of American diplomacy has said of this incident, "One of the most striking aspects of this whole unfortunate affair is that if the $25,000,000 finally paid to Colombia had been offered in 1903, a vast amount of unpleasantness would almost certainly have been avoided." Bailey, *A Diplomatic History of the American People*, p. 546.

Venezuela as finally framed in 1914 held to the provision of 1824 concerning the nationality requirements of churchmen.

A movement of greater significance to the Universal Church wherein the Cardinal of Baltimore was asked to lend his support was that of the Society for the Propagation of the Faith. This society had been of immense help to the world-wide missions of the Catholic Church since its establishment in 1822 and the American Church had benefited enormously from the funds it had contributed to the spreading of the faith in the United States.[114] But by the end of the nineteenth century many of the dioceses of the American Church had outgrown a missionary status and were in a position to make a return for the cause of the faith in less favored countries. Cardinal Gibbons reflected this fact shortly after the close of the Third Plenary Council when he thanked the society in the name of the entire hierarchy for all that it had done for American Catholicism. At that time he stated that if the seed planted on American soil had now grown into a mighty tree it was, as he said, "mainly to the assistance rendered by your admirable Society that we are indebted for this blessing."[115] Yet the bright prospects of greater financial support from the United States were not forthcoming, and with that in mind Charles Harmel, president of the Paris central council of the society, made a direct appeal some years later to Gibbons. He said they regarded him as their special protector in the United States, and he asked, therefore, that the cardinal bestir his colleagues in the hierarchy to greater efforts.[116]

Gibbons reported Harmel's dissatisfaction to his fellow arch-bishops at their meeting in St. Louis a month later, but for several years nothing much seemed to be done about it.[117] Finally in October, 1896, positive action was taken when the metropolitans adopted unanimously the suggestion of Archbishop

---

[114] Cf. Edward J. Hickey, *The Society for the Propagation of the Faith. Its Foundation, Organization and Success (1822–1922)* (Washington, 1922), and Theodore Roemer, O.F.M.Cap., *Ten Decades of Alms* (St. Louis, 1942). Gibbons' own Archdiocese of Baltimore had received $56,757 from the society in the years between 1823 and 1865. Hickey, *op. cit.,* p. 188.

[115] Gibbons to the directors of the society, Baltimore, December 6, 1884, *Annales de la propagation de la foi* (Paris, 1885), LVII, 121.

[116] 89-B-3, Harmel to Gibbons, Paris, October 20, 1891.

[117] 89-D-5/1, Minutes of the Meeting of the Archbishops, St. Louis, November 29, 1891.

Riordan that a priest be appointed as national director for the society's work in the United States.[118] This proposal had come about partly as a result of an agreement reached in Paris earlier in the year between the society's central council and the Superior-General of St. Sulpice, to the effect that the Sulpician Fathers in Baltimore would act as the society's American agents if this should prove acceptable to the bishops.[119] Gibbons informed Harmel on November 1 that the suggestion was entirely agreeable to the prelates, and he then outlined the proposed organization which would have its headquarters at St. Mary's Seminary in Baltimore. Alphonse L. Magnien, S.S., consented to serve as director and Father Henry Granjon was assigned to assist him. The society was likewise incorporated under Maryland law and Gibbons became the chairman of the board of directors. Therefore, when Cardinal Rampolla made inquiries in the society's behalf the following spring, Gibbons could report progress and say that he looked forward to greater financial returns as a result of the new organization.[120]

The Paris officials were gratified, of course, to hear of the new start made in the United States, and in expressing their thanks they recalled that the Paris central council had sent to the American missions since 1822 over $5,400,000; for that reason it was thought that in some measure it was a matter of justice that the American Catholics should now contribute more to the Church's missions in poorer lands.[121] In order to give a further impetus to the cause, Rampolla asked Gibbons to convey to the hierarchy the pleasure which Leo XIII had felt in learning of their recent reorganization, and likewise the confidence which the Pontiff placed in their zeal to further this great missionary enterprise. The Archbishop of Baltimore had copies of Rampolla's letter sent to all the archbishops, and he expressed the hope that the work recommended therein would meet with their sympathy and receive their hearty and needed co-operation.[122] Ten days later the annual meeting of the archbishops assembled in Wash-

---

[118] 94-S-3, Minutes of the Meeting of the Archbishops, Washington, October 22, 1896.

[119] Hickey, *op. cit.*, pp. 123–124.

[120] 95-Q-3, Gibbons to Rampolla, Baltimore, June 13, 1897, copy in French.

[121] 95-R-4, Harmel and Alexandre Guasco, secretary of the society, to Magnien, Paris, July 15, 1897.

[122] AAC, Gibbons to Elder, Baltimore, October 10, 1897.

ington and the plans submitted at that time by Magnien and Granjon to advance the work were unanimously adopted.[123] The receipts of the society from the American Church soon showed a notable increase. In 1897 there had been collected $34,196.31 while the following year brought $55,511.79 and from that time on the sums rose steadily and for 1921, the year of Gibbons' death, the collection from the United States amounted to $1,245,403.53.[124]

One series of events that served to emphasize the role which Cardinal Gibbons had come to play in the life of the Universal Church was the celebration of the silver jubilee of the reign of Leo XIII, the death soon thereafter of the aged Pontiff, and the conclave which elected his successor. Long before the time of the actual anniversary, the American archbishops in their meeting of November, 1901, had authorized the cardinal to salute the Holy Father in their name.[125] In carrying out their request he reviewed the accomplishments of the pontificate in the Church throughout the world, and then stated that among the exalted offices which occupied the Pontiff's watchful care there had been scarcely one that he had not deigned to employ for the peculiar and special advantage of the Church in the United States.[126] In the same week the cardinal addressed a letter to the pastors of the Archdiocese of Baltimore in which he asked that Sunday, April 6, be set aside as a day of general observance of the jubilee in all the churches.[127] On the designated Sunday Gibbons himself delivered the sermon in his cathedral on Pope Leo's long reign. He mentioned that he had first seen the future Pontiff in the Vatican Council in 1869, and he then described some of his characteristics which he had observed in the frequent audiences granted to him by Leo XIII in the years since 1880. But the subjects upon which the cardinal spoke with the greatest warmth, were the notable contribution which the Pope had made in his encyclical, *Rerum novarum,* and the joy and satisfaction

---

[123] 95-U-6, Minutes of the Meeting of the Archbishops, Washington, October 21, 1897.

[124] Hickey, *op. cit.,* p. 126.

[125] 99-F-8, Minutes of the Meeting of the Archbishops, Washington, November 21–22, 1901.

[126] 99-L-2/2, Gibbons to Leo XIII, Baltimore, March 3, 1902, copy.

[127] 99-L-5, Gibbons to the pastors of the Archdiocese of Baltimore, March 6, 1902, copy.

he had given to the English-speaking world when he had created John Henry Newman a cardinal in 1879.[128] Nearly a quarter of a century of the thirty-four years that Gibbons had then been a bishop had been lived under Leo XIII, and during that time his numerous audiences and almost constant communications with the Holy Father on American ecclesiastical problems made him feel especially close to the old Pontiff.

Many times within recent months there had been alarming reports concerning the failing health of Pope Leo XIII, but in each case he had rallied and renewed his energies for the great burden of his office. However, in the summer of 1903 when he had reached his ninety-third year it became evident that he could not revive again and that the end was not far off. On July 8 Gibbons received a cablegram from Rampolla that the Pope was not expected to live, and at this news the cardinal quickly made arrangements to sail with Patrick C. Gavan, his chancellor, who would serve him as conclavist at the approaching conclave.[129] They landed at Le Havre on July 16 and then proceeded to Paris where they were the guests of the Sulpicians. Gibbons had arranged to meet Monsignor O'Connell in Lucerne, and on all details such as the timing of his arrival in Rome and the ecclesiastical robes he would need for the ceremonies there, he told him he would be guided by his advice. "Please to keep me advised regarding the Pope's condition," he said, "for it is hard to get exact news from the papers."[130] Three days later Leo XIII died on July 20, and the cardinal then set out for Rome where he was to have the distinction of being the first American to take part in the election of a Pope.

The conclave opened on the evening of July 31 with all but two of the sixty-four cardinals present, illness having prevented Pietro Cardinal Celesia, Archbishop of Palermo, from attending while Cardinal Moran of Sydney lived at too great a distance to arrive on time. On the two first scrutinies the voting ran strongly in favor of Cardinal Rampolla, and it appeared that he might be elected. In fact, as Gibbons later related, prospects appeared so favorable for the Secretary of State that after the

128 99-P-1/4, Gibbons' sermon on the silver papal jubilee of Leo XIII, Baltimore, April 6, 1902.
129 Will, *Life of Cardinal Gibbons,* II, 634–635.
130 ADR, Gibbons to O'Connell, Paris, July 17, 1903.

second scrutiny the Cardinal of Baltimore who was seated at his right turned and congratulated him.[131] But before the third scrutiny on August 2, John Cardinal Puzyna, Bishop of Cracow, rose in the conclave and pronounced the veto of the Emperor Francis Joseph of Austria-Hungary against Rampolla's candidacy. The imperial veto produced a profound impression in the conclave, and brought forth vigorous protests against this interference in the affairs of the Church by a lay state from Rampolla himself, as well as from Luigi Cardinal Oreglia, dean of the sacred college, and Adolphe Cardinal Perraud, Bishop of Autun. Nonetheless, whatever chances he had had for the Papacy were now destroyed, and the balloting began to incline toward Guiseppe Cardinal Sarto, Patriarch of Venice.[132]

At this point, however, a difficulty arose when Sarto made it known to his colleagues that he wished them to pass him by. His reluctance to be considered threatened a stalemate, and while affairs were in this uncertain state Cardinal Satolli paid a visit to Gibbons' room. What happened then is best told in a summary of Gibbons' own words. After conferring for some time with Satolli he volunteered a suggestion, which he later said he hoped was an inspiration. He told the cardinal to go to Sarto and beg him for the love of God to bow to the selection and to yield to the action of the Holy Spirit. Gibbons asked Satolli to get the Patriarch of Venice to say positively "yes" or "no" and then to return to him before the next session for, as he expressed it, "I do not know what to do." The Cardinal of Baltimore waited until the middle of the afternoon, but Satolli did not return. When they had again assembled in the conclave, however, he came and whispered to Gibbons "accepit." The latter reminded Satolli that while they understood this, the

---

[131] AWC, Notes taken by I. Barrett, S.J., from a private lecture given by Gibbons to the students of Woodstock College on November 4, 1903.

[132] Merry del Val, who was secretary of the conclave, later stated, "It is my certain conviction that the latter [Rampolla] would have never been elected in any case, for the majority of the electors was firmly intent upon choosing some other candidate." Cardinal Merry del Val, *Memories of Pope Pius X* (London, 1939), p. 1. For two recent contributions to the subject of the imperial veto cf. Friedrich Engel-Janosi, "Zwei Studien zur Geschichte des österreichischen Vetorechtes," in Leo Santifaller (Ed.), *Festschrift zur feier des Zweihundertjährigen Bestandes des Haus-Hof-und Staatsarchivs* (Vienna, 1951), II 283–300, and the same author's article, "L'Autriche au conclave de 1903," *Revue belge de philologie et d'histoire*, XXIX (1951), 1119–1141.

other cardinals did not. Satolli then sought out Oreglia, the dean, communicated Sarto's answer to him in private, and thereupon the news was made known to all the cardinals that Sarto would accept the Papacy if elected. At the next scrutiny he received thirty-five votes and, as Gibbons concluded, "All left the conclave like boys out of school for they felt the end was near."[133] The end was, indeed, near for on the following morning, August 4, in the seventh scrutiny Sarto received fifty votes, was declared elected, and took the name of Pius X. "Thus was the voice of an American," said Gibbons' first biographer with some exaggeration, "heard for the first time in a Papal conclave, potent in bringing about a decision."[134] In any case, the American cardinal was granted an audience by the new Pope on the evening of the day the conclave ended, and Pius acceded to his request that he receive some American pilgrims who felt disappointed at the prospect of leaving Rome without having seen the Pope. Pius X likewise received Gibbons in another private audience before he left the Eternal City, and on this occasion he gave his approval to an annual collection for the Catholic University of America and to a proposal for an exhibit from the Vatican for the exposition being planned for the following year in St. Louis to commemorate the centennial of the Louisiana Purchase.[135]

On the day of Pius X's election Gibbons had cabled Archbishop Ireland, "Pope man of God!" But Ireland was not consoled. He felt keenly what he regarded as a defeat for his friends, Rampolla and Serafino Vannutelli, and in expressing that sentiment to Denis O'Connell, he commented, "either one would have done me for 'a man of God.' "[136] But the Archbishop of Baltimore was sincerely elated with the choice, and not long after his return home he preached a sermon in the cathedral in which he manifested his pleasure and described the qualities of the new Pontiff which had so deeply impressed him. Gibbons regretted the absence of such men as Newman, Manning, Taschereau, and Vaughan, all of whom had died some time before, and he voiced the wish that the time might come when every country in the world would be represented in a papal conclave. Moreover, he said he would not be at all surprised if in a subsequent conclave the United

---

[133] AWC, Barrett notes on Gibbons' talk, Woodstock, November 4, 1903.
[134] Will, *op. cit.*, II, 647.
[135] *Ibid.*, II, 648–651.
[136] ADR, Ireland to O'Connell, St. Paul, August 4, 1903.

States would have several representatives so that the number of American cardinals, as he remarked, might be commensurate with the population, grandeur, and commanding influence of the nation. He praised the perfect freedom which the cardinals had enjoyed in the conclave, and he said he found more freedom there than he had witnessed when he listened to debates in the British and French parliaments and the American Congress. In describing the climax of the conclave and the reluctance of the future Pontiff to assume the Papacy, he said, "So little did Cardinal Sarto expect to be the choice of his colleagues, that on setting out for Rome he purchased a return ticket to his home in Venice."[137]

Nearly three months elapsed before Pius X named a Secretary of State and then on October 18 he chose Monsignor Merry del Val and in the consistory of November 4 he created him a cardinal.[138] The new Secretary of State was of Spanish and English blood and had received part of his education in England. Gibbons was plainly delighted with the selection, and in congratulating Merry del Val he said he did so, not only because of his eminent qualities of mind and heart, but because of his intimate knowledge of the English language and his deep understanding of the temperament of the English-speaking peoples. "To me, then, & to the entire English-speaking world," he said, "the selection of your Eminence has been especially pleasing & full of interest, and I pray God your administration may be long, successful, peaceful and happy."[139] In connection with the appointment, however, the Cardinal of Baltimore suffered an embarrassment when a dispatch published in the London *Times* stated that he had previously conferred with the government in Washington relative to the choice of Merry del Val. Gibbons was quick to repudiate the report which had been copied by a number of American newspapers, and he explained to Thomas F. Kennedy, Rector of the American College in Rome, how completely false the whole story was and asked him to offer his regrets to Merry del Val. Kennedy did as he was directed and, after reading Gibbons' letter to the Secretary of State, the latter told him to

---

[137] 100-R-1, Gibbons' sermon on the conclave, Baltimore, October 4, 1903.
[138] Merry del Val, *op. cit.*, pp. 15–18.
[139] 100-U-1, Gibbons to Merry del Val, Baltimore, November 17, 1903, copy.

assure the cardinal that he attached no weight or credence to the newspaper story.[140]

If during the days of the conclave of August, 1903, the mind of the Patriarch of Venice had turned toward France, it could easily be understood why he should have been adverse to assuming the tiara at that time. Ever since the advent of the ministry of René Waldeck-Rousseau in June, 1899, relations between the Church and State had grown steadily more critical, and the last years of Leo XIII were darkened by the campaign of the French government against the religious orders and schools. Under Waldeck-Rousseau's successor, the apostate religious and active Freemason, Emile Combes, a program of annihilation of the Church's influence was inaugurated which led to France's severance of diplomatic relations with the Vatican in July, 1904; and finally under the leadership of Aristide Briand there was promulgated in December, 1905, the law of separation of Church and State. The American bishops had been following the crisis in the Church of France, and in the spring of 1906 Bishop Maes of Covington suggested to Gibbons that they address a letter of sympathy to the French hierarchy in the trial through which they were passing.[141] The cardinal chose the opportunity offered by the annual meeting of the metropolitans two weeks later and, after gaining their permission to speak in the name of all, he expressed the sympathies of the American hierarchy in a letter of May 1 which he sent to François Cardinal Richard, Archbishop of Paris.[142]

Although the effective labors of the French Church had already been crippled in good measure by the radical legislation, the fury of its enemies seemed to know no bounds. René Viviani, Minister of Labor, was heard to say in the Chamber of Deputies, "We have snatched the human conscience from belief in a future life. . . . Do you think that the work is at an end? No, it is but beginning." Moreover, in the summer of 1906, Briand, Minister of

---

[140] 100-U-5, Kennedy to Gibbons, Rome, November 28, 1903.

[141] 103-E, Maes to Gibbons, Covington, April 10, 1906.

[142] 103-F, Gibbons to Richard, Baltimore, May 1, 1906, copy in French; 103-E, Minutes of the Meeting of the Archbishops, Washington, April 26, 1906. A resolution of sympathy for the Catholics of France was likewise sent by the executive committee of the American Federation of Catholic Societies, New York *Freeman's Journal,* May 12, 1906.

Justice and Education, addressed a congress of teachers at Amiens, in which he stated that the time had now arrived to root up from the minds of French children the ancient faith which had served its day and to replace it with the light of free thought.[143] It was a piece with his even more shocking pronouncement of two years before at Lisieux, where he had declared that God having been chased from the schools, hospitals, and prisons of France it was now necessary to chase Him from the government.[144]

It was not difficult to imagine the impression of horror which statements of this kind would produce on the mind of Cardinal Gibbons. He held his peace, however, until the end of that year, and he then gave out a lengthy interview on the conflict of the Church and State in France. At the outset Gibbons denounced the conduct of the French anticlericals, and he maintained that he was weighing his words when he attributed it to their hatred of Christianity. As an old man he said he knew well the sense of fair play of the American people, but he regretted to say that in reporting the crisis in France, the press of the United States had shown itself to a considerable extent to be the reflex of the Parisian radical journals.[145] He took occasion to praise the relations of Church and State in the United States where the government permitted perfect freedom to the Church to carry on its divine mission unhampered by restrictive legislation. Gibbons

---

[143] *Saturday Review of Politics, Literature, Science, and Art* (London), CII (August 18, 1906), 194. Years later René Viviani was in Washington on a mission for the French government in March, 1921, when Gibbons died. According to the Abbé Ernest Dimnet, the latter wrote him that he should attend the cardinal's funeral in the interests of better Franco-American relations. Viviani immediately accepted the suggestion and was present in the cathedral of Baltimore on March 31 for the obsequies, after which he asked the Sulpicians to show him St. Mary's Seminary and some of the sights of the city. Dimnet tried to excuse Viviani's boasted atheism of the early century on the grounds that it had been occasioned in good measure by a youthful enthusiasm for Jean Jaurès whose rhetorical outbursts against Christianity the younger man had imitated. Ernest Dimnet, *My New World* (New York, 1937), pp. 285–286.

[144] *Ibid.*, CII (August 25, 1906), 222.

[145] The stricture which Gibbons made about the reporting of the American press was also expressed by the *Saturday Review* concerning the English newspapers. They stated editorially in their issue of August 18, 1906, that not the least melancholy feature of the whole unhappy affair was the English sympathy for the anti-Christian side. They felt that the Pope was in every way the injured party, and that the cause for which he was fighting was the cause of Christendom. But according to the *Saturday Review*, the English press in general suppressed the exhibits of the real French radical attitude toward Christianity.

then quoted several of the most damaging statements of leading French politicians to prove his charge that they had acted from motives of hatred, and he also reviewed the spoliation which the Church had endured at the time of the French Revolution, as well as the losses it had suffered there in recent years. He condemned the law of separation and stated that it was not only this law which the Pope repudiated, but also the tyranny cloaked in the guise of separation. He had confidence in the faith of the French clergy and people, and for that reason he did not believe that they would tamely allow religion to be strangled in France. In conclusion the cardinal remarked, "The view of the case as I have given is based on the facts and the documents. We need only leave it to an impartial and liberty loving people to decide which party is responsible for the present miserable conflict."[146]

The interview was widely copied in the United States and was likewise carried in part in many European papers. Congratulations on his stand soon began to reach the cardinal from various sources both at home and abroad,[147] and the *News and Courier* of Charleston, South Carolina, made it the subject of an editorial on December 17 in the thought that the French government's attack on the Catholic Church was an attack on all the Christian denominations. Archbishop Riordan was pleased with the interview, but he thought the American bishops should now proceed to issue a pointed and solemn protest. "The question," he said, "is not understood by the non-Catholic people of our country and should be given to them in an authoritative way."[148] Gibbons was in favor of the proposal of Riordan, but upon consultation it was found that several of the other metropolitans were not warm to the idea and in the end nothing came of it.[149] Meanwhile

---

[146] Baltimore *Sun,* December 14, 1906.

[147] 103-T, Archbishop Ryan to Gibbons, Philadelphia, December 10, 1906; Martin Maloney to Gibbons, Philadelphia, December 17, 1906. Paul la Rocque, Bishop of Sherbrooke, said the interview had been reproduced in the Canadian papers and he thought Gibbons had spoken clearly and firmly to the point (103-U, La Rocque to Gibbons, Sherbrooke, December 26, 1906).

[148] 103-T, Riordan to Gibbons, San Francisco, December 20, 1906; 103-U, same to same, San Francisco, December 27, 1906.

[149] 103-V, Glennon to Gibbons, St. Louis, December 29, 1906. Glennon was personally favorable to the idea, but he said he gathered the impression from speaking to Archbishops Ireland and Keane at the funeral of Bishop Henry Cosgrove of Davenport that they were unwilling to risk the excitement which such a protest might arouse.

the apostolic delegate, Archbishop Falconio, expressed his congratulations for the interview and his report of it to the Holy See soon brought the thanks of Pius X and Cardinal Merry del Val.[150]

In France itself those who showed any reaction to the Gibbons interview naturally reflected their own sympathies in relation to the quarrel between the Church and State. For example, the distinguished Catholic layman, Albert de Mun, who was a member of the Chamber of Deputies, was delighted with what he read of it, and requested the cardinal to furnish him with the full text and to recommend an American periodical to which he might send an article that would explain the origins and nature of the conflict so that Americans might have access to the true facts.[151] But another Frenchman was of a quite different mind about Gibbons' statement. Paul Sabatier, whose sympathies lay with the anticlericals and who had recently published a volume entitled *Disestablishment in France,* stated that the French newspapers of all shades of opinion had carried extracts from the interview, but he had not been able to secure the complete text; therefore, he, too, asked that it be sent to him.[152] The cardinal complied with the request and some months later Sabatier thanked him and enclosed the copy of an open letter which he had just finished in reply to Gibbons. He felt the interview would lead public opinion astray, not only by what he termed its errors in fact but also by Gibbons' silence on the liberties which, according to Sabatier, the law of separation had assured to the Church.[153]

The London *Times* of May 17, 1907, announced the appearance of Sabatier's publication in terms of praise for its knowledge of the facts, and stated that there was more to the affair than what they termed the "fiery pages of Cardinal Gibbons or encyclicals of Pius X." Sabatier's letter was written in an urbane style, in which he protested the regard which he, a non-Catholic, had for the Church of France. He made much of the fact that some of the French clergy were willing to give the law of sepa-

---

[150] 103-V, Falconio to Gibbons, Washington, n.d., but the letter contained his greetings for Christmas; AAB, unclassified, Falconio to Gibbons, Washington, January 6, 1907, enclosing a copy of a cablegram from Merry del Val instructing him to thank Gibbons in the name of Pius X; 104-A, Merry del Val to Gibbons, Rome, January 7, 1907.

[151] 104-B, de Mun to Gibbons, Paris, January 12, 1907.

[152] 104-A, Sabatier to Gibbons, Chantegrillet près Crest, Drôme, January 5, 1907. Sabatier's volume appeared in an English translation in London in 1906.

[153] 104-E, same to same, Assisi, Umbria, March 28, 1907.

ration a trial but that Rome had refused and, while he admitted the impropriety of Viviani's public statements, he maintained that they did not represent the official view of the French government and he contended that Briand had not uttered the sentiments which Gibbons had attributed to him. In regard to the cardinal's statement that the concordat of 1801 had made provision for the state to pay the salaries of the clergy as a compensation for the spoliation of the Church's properties at the time of the revolution, the author begged the question by saying that the concordat contained no express guarantee of salaries under the guise of compensation. Sabatier likewise held that Gibbons had been greatly deceived when he had spoken of the French government in terms of official atheism in his letter of sympathy to Cardinal Richard, and he professed to find it difficult to understand how the American cardinal could be so proud of separation of Church and State in his own country when the Holy See had condemned such an arrangement.[154]

When word of Sabatier's attack upon his interview reached him the cardinal was in New Orleans to confer the pallium upon Archbishop Blenk. The only point on which he replied was that relating to his views on Church and State in the United States. He said he did not presume to speak for other countries and other conditions insofar as advocating separation for them, although he would venture the opinion that whatever the view of the French episcopate might be in regard to separation, he thought it would be better for that country if they could enjoy the real separation of Church and State as it existed in the United States. He did not relinquish his well-known stand in the face of Sabatier's challenge, and the New York *Freeman's Journal* of April 27 quoted Gibbons as having said:

> I am, therefore, unalterably attached to the separation of Church and State in this country, and have always expressed my belief and satisfaction in it. I so expressed myself in its favor thirty years ago, I did so later on in Rome itself, and I have no hesitation in expressing the same solemn belief today.

One of the consequences of the spoliation of the French Church by the radical party in control of the government, was the in-

---

[154] Paul Sabatier, *An Open Letter to His Eminence Cardinal Gibbons apropos of His Interview on the Separation of Church and State in France,* translated by John Richard Slattery (Boston, 1908).

ability of the French Catholics to contribute as they had done in the past to the financial support of the Holy See. Partly as a result of this situation Domingo Merry del Val, brother of the papal Secretary of State, was sent to the United States to consult with some American bankers concerning the reorganization of Vatican finances. Shortly before his departure from the country, Merry del Val expressed to Gibbons the gratitude he felt for the courtesy and aid which the cardinal had extended to him during his visit.[155] Meanwhile the revenues which were necessary for the Holy See to conduct its administration in the proper manner, and to afford relief for the many calls upon its charity, did not prove adequate and a plan was, therefore, evolved to have Bonaventure Broderick, until recently Auxiliary Bishop of Havana, establish an office in the United States in order to promote the collection of the Peter's Pence.

When news of this plan reached Gibbons he was strongly opposed to it and he determined to make a very firm but polite protest against it. He told Cardinal Merry del Val that when the first rumors of the affair were heard they were received with incredulity by the bishops, but since the reports persisted he felt it his duty to inform the Holy See that the proposal had aroused a very deep and intense feeling. In the first place, it was greatly feared that the establishment of such a bureau would be construed as a reflection on the loyalty and devotion of the hierarchy to Rome and would, perhaps, tend to lessen their zeal and cool their ardor for the Holy Father's financial needs. Second, the apostolic delegate had already inaugurated a movement to increase contributions from the American Church, and for that reason a new arrangement might only create confusion and conflict. Finally, the selection of Bishop Broderick for such a task was not, in the cardinal's mind, a happy choice since there were repeated rumors — whether true or false, he did not know — concerning Broderick's mistakes in Havana. The fact that there were very close and constant communications between Washington and Havana, and that the bishop had already begun negotiations to secure a residence in Washington, would be, according to Gibbons, hazardous to the whole undertaking. In conclusion the cardinal stated, "I sincerely trust that Your Eminence will pardon this intrusion, and at the same time, will assure His

---

[155] 100-U-6, Merry del Val to Gibbons, New York, November 29, 1903.

Holiness of our devotion to him, & our determination to aid him to the best of our ability & at all times."[156] It is not likely that Gibbons would have expressed himself so strongly if he had not been certain of the support of his fellow bishops, and in one case at least he was left in no doubt when Archbishop Ireland the same week sent his hearty approval of the cardinal's stand.[157]

Gibbons' letter to Merry del Val received an immediate and detailed reply. The Secretary of State was at pains to explain that the mission which had been entrusted to Bishop Broderick had been solely intended to assist those bishops in the United States who cared to avail themselves of his services. Far from wishing to reflect on the well-known loyalty of the American bishops to the Holy See, the project had been based exclusively upon the conviction of that loyalty. As for the person chosen, the selection had been made out of consideration for Broderick's request that he be permitted to return to the United States to reside, but under the circumstances Merry del Val had now sent him orders to suspend all action until further notice.[158] With that the plan was ended and no more was heard of it. But about the same time Archbishop Falconio called on Gibbons and suggested the possibility that Bishop Broderick might establish his residence in Washington and assist the cardinal in episcopal functions in that city. Gibbons explained that he and his auxiliary bishop, Owen B. Corrigan, could take care of these functions without any difficulty, and there was no need, therefore, for Broderick's services in the capital. It was added that since the bishop knew Spanish well he could, perhaps, be of help to the Church in the Philippines or Cuba.[159] In any case, it was evident that the

---

[156] 102-F, Gibbons to Merry del Val, March 16, 1905, copy. The false accounts concerning the Vatican's great wealth caused the apostolic delegate to make public the exact amount of Peter's Pence from the United States in recent years in order to still these rumors. Falconio stated that from 1895 to 1905 the Apostolic Delegation had received $828,708.66 from American dioceses or an average of $75,337.15 a year. Allowing for the fact that some bishops made their payment personally on the occasion of their *ad limina* visits, he maintained that the total from the United States in any one year surely did not exceed $100,000. The delegate stated that he was glad to observe an increase in Peter's Pence after his appeal of the previous year, but he was anxious that the exaggerated stories of the wealth of the Holy See should be corrected. *Catholic Mirror*, May 12, 1906.

[157] 102-G, Ireland to Gibbons, St. Paul, March 22, 1905.

[158] 102-G, Merry del Val to Gibbons, Rome, March 30, 1905, *Confidential*.

[159] 102-G, Gibbons to Merry del Val, Baltimore, March 31, 1906, copy.

ordinary of the Archdiocese of Baltimore would not consider him a welcome guest within his jurisdiction.

But if the American hierarchy did not take kindly to the idea of a special agent in residence for the promotion of Peter's Pence, that did not mean that they were indifferent toward the Holy See's needs. At the meeting of the metropolitans in April, 1907, over which Gibbons presided, Archbishop Keane introduced the subject and remarked the losses suffered as a result of the crisis in the French Church, and the need there was to scotch the ridiculous statements that appeared from time to time concerning the great wealth of the Vatican, whereas it had scarcely enough revenue to meet its ordinary expenses. The metropolitans moved that a strong letter should be drafted by Archbishops Ireland and Keane which would be sent to the entire hierarchy urging a more generous collection for the Holy Father.[160] Apparently the results of this move were not entirely satisfactory, for a year later Ireland again made a plea for a continuous and persistent support that would insure a definite amount being forwarded each year to Rome, and as a result of further suggestions from Archbishops Ryan and Farley it was moved to submit the subject once more to their suffragans and then to draw up a general plan of action that would embody the various suggestions that had been put forth.[161] From these efforts a more systematic and generous support for the Holy See from the American Church was attained, and the last time that the subject was mentioned in the annual meetings of the metropolitans it was stated that the priests should be exhorted to give to Peter's Pence along with the laity, and Gibbons was authorized to address the bishops with a request that they issue instructions to this effect.[162]

Although the contacts of Cardinal Gibbons with Pope Pius X were neither as frequent nor of so long a duration as had been his relations with Leo XIII, nonetheless, Pius appreciated the prestige which the Archbishop of Baltimore had brought to the Universal Church during his long and eventful life. When Father Gavan, Gibbons' chancellor, visited Rome in the summer of

---

[160] 104-G, Minutes of the Meeting of the Archbishops, Washington, April 10, 1907.

[161] 104-Y, Minutes of the Meeting of the Archbishops, Washington, May 8, 1908.

[162] 107-F, Minutes of the Meeting of the Archbishops, Washington, April 27, 1911.

1911 he had a private audience of Pius X, and at that time the Pontiff spoke of the cardinal with special warmth. He expressed his pleasure at hearing that Gibbons was well and remarked that he hoped he would live for years to continue the wonderful work he had accomplished in the United States. The Pope mentioned the esteem which the cardinal enjoyed in his own country, and how much he had done to make religion honored and respected in the great Republic of the West, a fact which prompted Pius to lament that the same could not be said for Italy. The day of the audience happened to be the Pope's seventy-sixth birthday, and in hearing that Gibbons was then approaching seventy-seven, he remarked that this was not old, to which he added, "we are both *giovanotti* yet." The audience was concluded by a command to Gavan to inform the Pope some weeks in advance of the celebration of Gibbons' golden jubilee as a bishop so that he might send him a letter of congratulation.[163] In November of that year Pius X held a consistory at which a number of new cardinals were created, among whom were Archbishops Farley and O'Connell and the Apostolic Delegate to the United States, Diomede Falconio, who was a naturalized American citizen. The event signalized the growing importance of the American Church, and in thanking the Pontiff for the new honor paid to the United States, Gibbons stated that it had rejoiced not only the American Catholics but their non-Catholic fellow citizens as well since it was viewed as a recognition of their country.[164]

In the spring of 1913 the world press carried such alarming reports of the illness of Pius X that Gibbons began making preliminary arrangements to leave for Rome. He consulted Cardinal Farley and said that if death ensued he would wish to accompany him to the conclave; for that reason he felt it would be well for Farley to engage passage for them on a ship leaving New York within the next few days. The cardinal remarked that he felt a great delicacy in mentioning the subject, and he earnestly prayed that the press notices of the Pope's condition were exaggerated; yet he believed they should be prepared.[165] Farley agreed with Gibbons and he, therefore, made reservations for them and their

---

163 107-H, Gavan to Gibbons, Rome, June 3, 1911.

164 108-E, Gibbons to Pius X, Baltimore, April 24, 1912, copy in Latin.

165 AANY, Gibbons to Farley, Baltimore, April 10, 1913; same to same, Baltimore, April 14, 1913; Louis R. Stickney to Farley, Baltimore, April 17, 1913.

secretaries on the *George Washington* which was scheduled to sail the following Saturday. They were entirely dependent upon the newspapers for information as neither cardinal had received any direct word from the Vatican. The Archbishop of Boston was apparently of the same mind as his colleagues, for at the close of Farley's letter he remarked, "A friend met Cardinal O'Connell yesterday in the Plaza Hotel where he is staying. He is, I presume, waiting like ourselves, and has come on to New York where he can find more frequent steamers than in Boston."[166] But in the end the Pope recovered in 1913 and lived for over a year.

In the spring of 1914 Gibbons had important business to transact with the Holy See concerning his archdiocese, about which we shall see later. He announced to Merry del Val his approaching visit some months in advance, and at that time he said, "Considering my age it may be the last time I shall have the privilege of seeing the venerable Pontiff to whose august person I am bound by so many ties of duty and affection. . . ."[167] The cardinal sailed on May 5 on the *Princess Irene,* and as it happened this visit to Rome was the last time that he would see Pius X alive. After finishing his business in the Eternal City he traveled on to several other countries in Europe and arrived home on July 13. After having taken care of the work that had accumulated in his absence, the cardinal left Baltimore on August 19 for a holiday at Spring Lake, New Jersey, where he was to be the guest of the Marquis Martin Maloney. But the intended vacation was cut short within a few hours when news arrived that Pius X had died on August 20. Having returned from Europe only five weeks before, the old cardinal who had just passed his eightieth birthday was reluctant to make the long journey again. But his new chancellor, Father Louis R. Stickney, persuaded him that accommodations could be secured for them to sail the following day and that as the dean of the American hierarchy it was his duty to be present at the conclave. Stickney won his consent and then rushed to New York where he made arrangements to have the *Canopic,* which was sailing from Boston that day with Cardinal O'Connell aboard, come to New York to pick up the Cardinal

---

[166] 109-E, Farley to Gibbons, New York, April 16, 1913.
[167] 109-Q, Gibbons to Merry del Val, Baltimore, February 28, 1914, copy.

of Baltimore.[168] On August 21, therefore, the day after the Pope's death, the two American cardinals set out in the hope that they might arrive in time to participate in the election of the new Pontiff. Cardinal Farley, who happened to be in Switzerland at the time, was thus in advance of his fellow countrymen.

The dramatic character of the trip on the *Canopic* was heightened by the fact that World War I had broken less than a month before with Austria-Hungary's declaration against Serbia on July 28. Moreover, the strain was increased for Gibbons and O'Connell by their knowledge that at that time the law governing a papal conclave stipulated that the cardinals should begin their sessions ten days after the death of the Pope. In ordinary circumstances it would have been very close timing, but with an allied ship having to calculate the hazards from German submarines, the chances of arriving on time were further reduced. Nevertheless, Gibbons and his companion tried to keep their spirits high but when they landed at Naples on the morning of September 3 they were greeted by Monsignor Cerretti who had come to meet them and he was not encouraging about their chances of casting a ballot in the conclave. O'Connell and his secretary hired an automobile and started for Rome in the hope of gaining time, while Gibbons and Father Stickney took the train. But neither method of travel proved successful. The conclave had opened on August 31, and on the morning of the fourth day, September 3, the choice had fallen on Giacomo Cardinal della Chiesa, Archbishop of Bologna. When Gibbons reached the Eternal City, therefore, he found the crowds rejoicing in the election of the new Pope Benedict XV. He rushed to the Vatican where he was told the Pontiff was only then being clothed in his change of habit from red to white, and the tension under which the old cardinal had been living in recent days apparently had told on him, for O'Connell whom he met in the

---

[168] Interview of the writer with Monsignor Louis R. Stickney, Baltimore, July 16, 1947. Cardinal O'Connell, too, had returned from Europe only a few days when the Pope died. He had sailed from Hamburg on a German ship just as World War I was breaking in western Europe, and in his memoirs he remarked the danger in which the ship stood from British or French submarines. He said, "For ten days we zigzagged across the ocean and during all the voyage no lights were permitted on the steamer." William Cardinal O'Connell, *Recollections of Seventy Years* (Boston, 1934), p. 337.

papal palace, later remarked that Gibbons looked quite worn. After the Pope had finished his change of dress the Cardinal of Baltimore was ushered in along with O'Connell, and the two Americans offered their congratulations in a brief audience and then retired to their respective hotels to await the coronation. After participating in the ceremonies which inaugurated the new reign and after only nine days in Rome, Gibbons sailed again on the *Canopic* from Naples and arrived home on September 24.[169]

It was the last time that Cardinal Gibbons saw Rome. He was to live on to less than a year from the end of the pontificate of Benedict XV, but the exigencies of the war and his advanced age precluded the possibility of his visiting the Holy See again. Through the twenty-eight years since he had been created a cardinal he had served Leo XIII and Pius X in various important capacities, and in the years that were left to him the distinguished position which he had long since attained as one of the Church's foremost figures, enabled him to be of outstanding service to Benedict XV in the international crisis created for the Holy See by World War I and the first years of peace. Every member of the College of Cardinals is in a sense an international churchman, but by reason of the commanding prestige he enjoyed in the United States and throughout the world, this was especially true of James Gibbons of Baltimore.

---

[169] O'Connell, *op. cit.*, p. 338; Will, *op. cit.*, II, 807. When O'Connell failed a second time in February, 1922, to reach Rome for a papal election, he lodged a protest with the new Pope Pius XI who shortly thereafter extended the time of the opening of a conclave to fifteen days after the death of the Pope. O'Connell, *op. cit.*, pp. 344–345.

CHAPTER XXII

The Leader of the American Church

THE established position which Cardinal Gibbons had won in the counsels of the Universal Church by the early years of the twentieth century, and the international fame which had come to him in circles outside the Church, were predicated in part upon the extraordinary qualities he had displayed in contributing an enlightened leadership to the Catholic Church in his own country. By reason of the fact that after October, 1877, James Gibbons was the occupant of the premier see of the United States, and that for a period of a quarter of a century he was the only American churchman who held the dignity of a cardinal, his prestige was naturally enhanced and it offered to him unique opportunities to exercise leadership over his colleagues in the hierarchy. Yet granted these advantages, a lesser man than Gibbons might easily have failed to fulfill the promise they held out. It was by virtue of the confidence he inspired in others through his sound judgment, his wise counsel, and his supreme tact that the accidents of high office and dignity were made to serve the ends of religion in uniting around him his fellow bishops for the common welfare of American Catholicism. The manner in which Gibbons employed his gifts in handling the major problems and controversies of the Church in the United States, has already been set forth in detail. There remain to review now matters of lesser importance, which further reflect the policies of the Cardinal of Baltimore in relation to the Church of which he was the recognized leader for so many years.

In his dealings with the Holy See on questions pertaining to the American Church Gibbons was, as we have seen, at all times respectful of the supreme pontifical authority; yet that did not mean that he responded to every hint and suggestion that emanated from circles close to the Roman Curia. For example, a

few weeks before he received the red biretta of his rank as a
cardinal he had a visit from Robert Fulton, S.J., provincial of
the Maryland province of the Society of Jesus, who informed him
that he had been instructed by Rome to take an active interest
in raising a special collection in the United States for the golden
jubilee of Leo XIII's priesthood. It was not the first suggestion
of this kind to have reached Gibbons, and he was frankly opposed to it. As he stated to Archbishop Williams, the bishops
had pledged themselves in the Third Plenary Council to a collection for the Pope to be taken up sometime before the summer
of 1887; there was likewise the annual Peter's Pence, and in his
judgment three collections in one year for the same purpose
would prove demoralizing and would fatigue the people. The
fact that Fulton mentioned that if he hesitated there would
probably be pressure brought to bear upon him from Rome, did
not disturb the cardinal, for as he remarked to Williams, "I
replied that I would wait for the pressure." He had already consulted the Archbishops of New York and Philadelphia who were
in agreement with him, and he now proposed to the Archbishop
of Boston that at the proper time they should all join in a letter
of felicitation to the Pontiff, make his jubilee the occasion for
increasing the Peter's Pence, and reply to all requests for pecuniary aid from whatever source that they had agreed on a
fixed policy. "I think it is very important," he said, "that we
should act in concert on this matter, and agree on a basis of
action."[1] In the end the proposals made by Gibbons were adopted
and carried out.

The method which the cardinal pursued in this as in so many
other instances, namely, to first consult with his colleagues before reaching a decision, was responsible in part for strengthening their confidence in him and for rendering them much more
amenable to his suggestions. And when previous consultation was
combined with moderation of views, it was made all the more
attractive. When, for example, the Holy See signified its readiness
to modify the regulations governing the lenten fast for the United
States, Gibbons late in 1886 again sought the advice of the
American archbishops and stated that the suggestion of one of
their number, to the effect that there should be no black fast
whatever in Lent was, in his opinion, a wise one since, as he

---

[1] 81-B-9, Gibbons to Williams, Baltimore, June 7, 1886, copy.

remarked, the American climate and customs would make its enforcement very difficult.[2] The same sense of moderation was shown several years later on an entirely different subject. Bishop Maes of Covington proposed to Gibbons that he sign a petition asking the Holy See to advance the devotion to St. Joseph to the rank of *protodulia*, that is, to a place between that accorded to the Mother of God and to the saints in general.[3] After consulting several theologians about the matter, he informed Maes that upon mature reflection he was determined not to sign the petition but rather to oppose it. He set down his reasons in detail and ended by saying that this hitherto unknown devotion in the Church would, as he expressed it, "put us to our wits' end to explain the matter to our people & especially to Protestants who would charge us with creating a new object of worship."[4] Of his opposition there could be no doubt, but lest the Bishop of Covington feel that he had been too brusque in his refusal, he suggested a month later that he might bring the matter before the annual meeting of the archbishops. He did not wish, as he said, that his opposition should be interpreted as restraining Maes' freedom of action in trying to obtain the assent of the other bishops.[5] Nothing further was heard of the proposal concerning the devotion to St. Joseph, but it served to illustrate not only the cardinal's spirit of conservatism and moderation on questions of this kind but, too, to show the almost instinctive opposition with which he often reacted toward suggestions of a new and somewhat radical character.

But if Gibbons was slow to be won to new ideas of a speculative order, he revealed no such reluctance in the realm of practical affairs where he unquestionably felt more at home. And there was no set of circumstances where the cardinal was more alert than in directing the practical relations of the Holy See with the American Church. Following the death of Cardinal Simeoni in January, 1892, he waited for some months until he could form a judgment concerning the attitude of his successor, Cardinal Ledochowski, on American questions. He then con-

---

[2] AAC, Gibbons to Elder, Baltimore, December 31, 1886.

[3] 87-T-3, Maes to Gibbons, Covington, August 18, 1890.

[4] Archives of the Diocese of Covington, Gibbons to Maes, Woodstock, Maryland, August 23, 1890.

[5] *Ibid.*, same to same, Baltimore, September 20, 1890.

gratulated him on the enlightened and wise manner in which he was handling the business of the American Church. He said he sensed from the outset that Leo XIII had found in Ledochowski a man who was conciliatory yet firm, and his actions to date had clearly shown that the new Prefect of Propaganda comprehended and appreciated the situation of the Church in the United States. Gibbons expressed his happiness and at the same time his hope that Ledochowski would continue to manifest the same benevolence, being persuaded, as he remarked, "that a liberal and wise policy will contribute very much to the strengthening of the Church in this country, while narrow views will only retard its progress and compromise the conversion of the Protestants."[6] It was apparent that whatever could be done by way of a word from Baltimore, would be used to guide the new prefect's conduct into the paths of moderation and sympathetic consideration for the American scene. Thus, in imparting to the Roman official the counsels of which he was himself a master, did Gibbons render a service to all the bishops of the United States who had to deal with Ledochowski.

Before the new Prefect of the Propaganda was long in office he was confronted with a situation in the American Church with which he was not prepared to deal. Mention has already been made of the financial disaster that overtook the Archdiocese of Cincinnati in 1878 when Father Edward Purcell, brother of the Archbishop of Cincinnati, failed in his private banking business.[7] After some years a number of the creditors were not yet satisfied with the settlement that had been made, and they appealed to the Holy See. Their appeals were referred by the Pope to the Propaganda, and Ledochowski, unfamiliar as he was with the subject, asked Gibbons if he could suggest a way of quieting these demands.[8] Before making any reply the cardinal communicated with Archbishop Elder and said he would take no action until he had heard Elder's side of the case. Since a visit on his part to Cincinnati might arouse suspicions, he suggested that Elder come to Baltimore and that he bring facts and figures from which he could compose a satisfactory letter to the prefect, one, as he

---

[6] 89-Y-8, Gibbons to Ledochowski, Baltimore, June 21, 1892, copy in French.
[7] Cf. I, 89, 143, 185, and note 79.
[8] 90-A-6, Ledochowski to Gibbons, Rome, July 7, 1892.

said, that would show how earnestly Elder had tried to settle the debts.[9]

After conferring with the Archbishop of Cincinnati in the fall of that year the cardinal summarized matters for Ledochowski by explaining that the civil courts of Ohio had declared against granting the creditors money out of any except a few of the properties of the archdiocese. The old archbishop had made the mistake of saying that the creditors would be paid in full, thinking his brother had used the funds for diocesan purposes. But upon investigation it had been found that for the most part he had used the money for secular concerns. Therefore, the Archdiocese of Cincinnati was not responsible in justice to these creditors. As for charity, much had already been done through collections and gifts for the neediest cases. When some of the creditors refused a compromise and turned to the civil courts, they found that they lost more in the end through court expenses, a fact which, according to Gibbons, must be attributed to their own obstinacy. True, there had been great scandal when the news first broke and harm had been done to religion. But when it was learned that only five institutions of the archdiocese had profited from Purcell's funds — and the remainder had been sustained by the charity of the faithful — the good sense and fair judgment of the American people had seen the point. Therefore, if some still persisted in taking scandal it could not be helped, and Gibbons concluded by declaring that he did not see how the Archbishop of Cincinnati could have done more for these creditors than he had done.[10] He thus came strongly behind his friend in Cincinnati, and in informing him of what he had written to Ledochowski he remarked truly that his statement of the case embodied a vindication and justification of Elder's action.[11]

But in another case involving American Catholic interests which came before Cardinal Ledochowski the Cardinal of Baltimore was not successful in effecting a solution that was satisfactory to himself and his fellow bishops. Early in 1897 Gibbons was informed that the general chapter of the Brothers of the Christian Schools in Paris had under discussion the question of

---

[9] AAC, Gibbons to Elder, Brighton, Massachusetts, August 12, 1892.

[10] 90-M-2, Gibbons to Ledochowski, Baltimore, October 28, 1892, copy in French.

[11] AAC, Gibbons to Elder, Baltimore, October 28, 1892.

forbidding Latin to be taught in their schools in the United States since it was against their rule. He immediately wrote to the president of the chapter and explained how important it was that the brothers should not be prevented from offering Latin in their curriculum, since it would prove harmful to the schools' reputation with the educational authorities of the various states who demanded that Latin be taught in most places.[12] Others besides Gibbons were opposed, and Archbishop Kain of St. Louis was especially aroused because he depended on the Christian Brothers' college to give his boys their preparatory training for the priesthood. Kain was irked at the French visitors of the order coming to the United States to dictate policies with which the hierarchy were not in agreement, and he hoped. Gibbons would talk strongly to them when they appeared in Baltimore.[13]

The following autumn at the meeting of the metropolitans Kain renewed his interest in the case and, with all the archbishops in agreement, Gibbons was authorized to name an American bishop who would take their petition to Rome in person.[14] The cardinal gave advance notice to Ledochowski that he had appointed Bishop Thomas S. Byrne of Nashville to handle the matter for the archbishops.[15] But after a stay of over six months in the Eternal City the Bishop of Nashville was still without a decision. He told the cardinal he had recently submitted to Propaganda the signatures of 638 Christian Brothers in the United States who wished to have Latin taught in their schools. He had done this since the superior-general of the brothers had said there were only twenty brothers who were in favor of their teaching Latin. "As all the Hierarchy are committed to this question," said Byrne, "it is important it should not go against them."[16]

Meanwhile the archbishops were growing impatient with the delay and at their meeting in October, 1899, Archbishop Ireland expressed himself strongly on the subject, and they ended by unanimously approving a renewed attempt at Rome by Arch-

---

[12] 95-J-1, Gibbons to "President of the Chapter," Baltimore, March 1, 1897, copy.

[13] 96-E-3, Kain to Gibbons, St. Louis, March 14, 1898.

[14] 96-Q-2, Minutes of the Meeting of the Archbishops, Washington, October 12, 1898.

[15] 97-A-1, Ledochowski to Gibbons, Rome, January 3, 1899, acknowledging Gibbons' letter of December 6, 1898.

[16] 97-J-2, Byrne to Gibbons, Rome, June 12, 1899.

bishop Riordan who was soon to visit the Holy See.[17] But despite Riordan's efforts, the cardinals of the Propaganda ruled against the petition of the American hierarchy on December 11 and three weeks later their decision was approved by Leo XIII. In communicating the result to Gibbons, the Prefect of Propaganda stated that the archbishops might make a formal request to the superior-general of the brothers, but the Holy See felt it must uphold the perfect observance of the rule of religious orders, even though Rome favored the study of the classics.[18] As an earnest of how seriously the American prelates regarded the ban on Latin in the schools of the Christian Brothers, they addressed a petition directly to Pope Pius X in 1906 giving reasons why it should be lifted.[19] Nonetheless, not until two years after Gibbons' death did the Holy See initiate a request to the superiors of the brothers and finally bring about a change in their rule.[20]

While the case of the Christian Brothers offering Latin was under consideration, there arose another problem in which the cardinal was vitally interested. During the last half of the nineteenth century there had grown up numerous Catholic organizations of a fraternal and charitable nature, all of which were concerned in one way or another with the advancement of the Church and its works in the United States. After the founding of the A.P.A. and the launching of an organized campaign against Catholicism, members of the Church were naturally more sensitive to these attacks and more alert to discrimination against them as Catholics. One of those who felt keenly on this subject was Bishop McFaul of Trenton who was extremely active in the affairs of the various Catholic lay orders and societies. Through the initiative of the Knights of St. John at their Cleveland convention of June, 1899, there arose the idea of federating all the Catholic groups with a view to strengthening their forces and producing a united front on questions of vital concern to American Catholics. McFaul was heartily in favor of the idea

[17] 97-R-5, Minutes of the Meeting of the Archbishops, Washington, October 12, 1899.
[18] 98-A-7/1, Ledochowski to Gibbons, Rome, January 11, 1900.
[19] 103-E, Archbishops of the United States to Pius X, Washington, April 25, 1906, printed copy.
[20] Angelus Gabriel, F.S.C., *The Christian Brothers in the United States, 1848–1948* (New York, 1948), pp. 478–490, discusses the case briefly.

of federation, and in speeches and articles he constantly urged it upon all who would listen to or read his words.

In an article in the *North American Review*, the Bishop of Trenton outlined the areas in which discrimination was practiced against Catholics, pointedly insisted that the remedy was not a Catholic political party, but just as strongly maintained that American Catholics would not go on tolerating an abuse of their rights. His conclusion doubtless sounded a bit ominous to many readers when he asked the question as to what channel the movement he had in mind would take, and then proceeded to state:

> This question will be answered in due time. Able leaders will determine upon legitimate, honorable, and Constitutional methods, as the cause grows and prospers, and passes beyond the stage of theory and suggestion to that of practice and action.[21]

Although McFaul had specifically disclaimed the idea of a political party and although he was answered the following month by Father Thomas H. Malone, a member of the Colorado State Board of Charities and Corrections, there was still a certain amount of uneasiness even in Catholic circles. Malone contended that McFaul's statements had been framed in such a way as fairly to subject them to the charge of suggesting political unity along religious lines, an interpretation which a considerable number of people had given to the bishop's words.[22]

Needless to say, to all this the Cardinal of Baltimore gave the closest attention, for there were few subjects which aroused and sustained his interest more than the relationship of American Catholic citizens to their non-Catholic fellow countrymen. Late in November, 1900, a meeting was scheduled for New York at which it was intended that the preliminary plans should be laid for federating the Catholic societies. A few days before the meeting Archbishop Ireland wrote to the cardinal about it, and in reply Gibbons expressed himself clearly and forcefully. He acknowledged that it was premature to pronounce a judgment until they would see what would happen, but he added, "a priori,

---

[21] "Catholics and American Citizenship," CLXXI (September, 1900), 332.

[22] "Catholic Citizens and Constitutional Rights," *North American Review,* CLXXI (October, 1900), 599.

I have serious misgivings regarding the wisdom of the measure." If the leaders of federation had in the beginning restricted the union to purely religious and moral purposes, he thought its effect would be beneficial; but from the outset there had been inserted a political note which enemies of the Church had seized upon and severely criticized. True, the promoters of federation had disclaimed any intention of having the organization subserve political ends further than defending Catholic interests; yet in the mind of the cardinal their disclaimer had come rather late and enemies would continue to quote the earlier emphasis indefinitely. Revealing how gravely he viewed the projected federation, Gibbons told Ireland:

> I fear that the effect of the proposed coalition will be to unite the neutral population as well as the sects against us. Attacks on the Catholic Church are always popular. A pretext is eagerly seized, & public feeling is easily aroused. The public will deny that we have such grievances as call for so formidable a phalanx. They will say that we are better treated than in France or Italy, & it may be harder for us to elect Catholics to office than ever at the present time.
>
> I say nothing of the danger of politicians perverting the organization to their own selfish ends.[23]

Whether the note of caution sounded by Gibbons and others, or the criticisms of the A.P.A. and their following, influenced the gathering in New York is not known. But in any case, they steered away from any expression likely to arouse suspicions on political grounds, and in reporting the aims of the American Federation of Catholic Societies, the *Catholic News* of December 1 mentioned that the principal object was "the cementing of the bonds of fraternal union among the Catholic societies of the United States." A year later the first annual convention of the federated societies was held in Cincinnati and Gibbons' fears were sufficiently allayed by that time for him to send a letter of greeting which was read to the convention on the second day. Bishop McFaul was present and spoke, and in taking cognizance of the criticism of the A.F. of C.S. on the score of political aims, he stated, "The opposition has therefore sounded an alarm which is quite unnecessary, as we are in perfect agreement as to the

---

[23] AASP, Gibbons to Ireland, Baltimore, November 23, 1900, *Private,* copy.

necessity of avoiding the domain of partisan politics."[24] A statement of this kind helped to reassure Gibbons, and in the years of its active life the A.F. of C.S. gave him no further cause for concern on the ground of its participation in politics.

Some years later in a matter which likewise concerned the entire American Catholic body, the cardinal felt no such hesitation in giving his approval to the activity of the laity. Archbishop Bonzano, the apostolic delegate, had received a complaint from a certain diocese concerning the euchre and dancing parties that were being held for the benefit of the parish churches. He inquired if this was not prohibited by the Third Plenary Council legislation, and what was Gibbons' opinion on the question.[25] The latter was at pains to reply in some detail. He stated that social conditions had been greatly modified during the preceding generation, especially among the poor whose long work hours gave them little chance for recreation. Dancing among Americans, said Gibbons, was a universal form of relaxation, and if the decree of 1884 were to be taken literally Catholic young people would be driven to non-Catholic and even anti-Catholic social centers. He instanced the growing slum areas of the large cities and the enticement of the socialists to the young, and he maintained that in conditions such as these the young must have the priest as their friend. But if the priest were to ban dancing entirely, he would lose them. Likening the problem to that of the drink evil, he remarked, "Strict prohibition of the sale of liquor usually works greater evils than a moderate regulation." The same rule applied to dancing. According to the cardinal, the council of 1884 had referred to public halls of unsupervised dancing, and it did not mean decently conducted dances under ecclesiastical supervision with parents and relatives present who could see all and easily censure or discourage any excesses. That was the mind of the council Gibbons knew, for he had presided over the deliberations of that assembly. If the Church was too severe in this respect, Catholic marriages might easily diminish. The cardinal concluded his very sensible judgment on the case by saying that he had read the excellent letter of an

[24] *Proceedings of the Convention of the American Federation of Catholic Societies held at Cincinnati, December 10, 11, 12, 1901* (Cincinnati, 1902), p. 13. The text of Gibbons' letter is not given.

[25] 109-E, Bonzano to Gibbons, Washington, April 28, 1913.

unnamed American bishop recently sent to Bonzano, and he entirely agreed with the bishop in the motives that had led him to the actual toleration of dancing under the conditions and safeguards which Gibbons had described above.[26]

The strong disinclination of Cardinal Gibbons to have the Church employ disciplinary measures of a harsh and sweeping nature, except in cases of grave necessity, was well illustrated in his attitude toward the American Catholic press. For many years Catholic newspapers, which were independent enterprises and functioned without the official approbation of the local bishops, had given trouble from time to time by reason of items that they published. At the time of the Second Plenary Council in 1866 the bishops sought in their decrees and pastoral letter to distinguish between papers that were official organs of the dioceses and those that were not, with insistence on the point that the ordinaries were not responsible for what appeared in the latter.[27] But this legislation did not remedy the situation, and some months before the plenary council of 1884, as we have seen, Gibbons received a complaint from Father Andrew A. Lambing of Pittsburgh who wished to have the council devote its attention to the subject. In reply Gibbons deplored the fact that items such as Lambing had mentioned should appear in a newspaper having a Catholic name, but he was doubtful that legislation concerning these nonofficial papers would be very helpful, and as evidence he cited the failure of the decrees of 1866 to overcome the abuse. Although he said he might bring the subject to the attention of the council, it was evident that he was not warm to the suggestion, for as he told Lambing, "I think that the vigilance of the Ordinary is the most effective means of checking the evil of which you justly complain."[28] In any case, the council of 1884 legislated anew on the subject in a number of decrees which elaborated on the laws of eighteen years before, and the bishops on this occasion included a paragraph in their pastoral letter in which they urged the faithful to support the Catholic press.

---

[26] 109-F, Gibbons to Bonzano, Baltimore, May 3, 1913, copy. For a discussion of the varying interpretations given to Decree 290 of the 1884 council on the subject of dancing cf. John R. Schmidt, "Attendance of Priests at Dances," *The Jurist*, XI (January, 1951), 77–99.

[27] *Concilii plenarii Baltimorensis II. . . . decreta*, pp. 256–259; Guilday, *The National Pastorals of the American Hierarchy, 1792–1919*, pp. 213–214.

[28] Letterbook, Gibbons to Lambing, Baltimore, May 2, 1884, p. 74.

But in their exhortation they took cognizance of the objectionable type of Catholic newspaper which, as they said, was Catholic in name or pretense but "uncatholic in tone and spirit, disrespectful to constituted authority, or biting and uncharitable to Catholic brethren."[29]

With all of this the cardinal was, of course, in agreement, even if he remained skeptical about the effectiveness of legislation to cure the evil. That he sincerely regretted the excesses of the Catholic press wherever they occurred we know, for a year after the council in Baltimore he headed a group of American bishops in sending a message of adherence to Leo XIII for the letter the Pontiff had recently addressed to Joseph Cardinal Guibert, Archbishop of Paris, in reference to the abuses of certain Catholic newspapers in their severe criticism of the hierarchy.[30] The question was still on Gibbons' mind some years later when he received an inquiry from Herman J. Heuser, editor of the *American Ecclesiastical Review*, concerning the Catholic press of the United States. The cardinal had one of the priests of his household reply in his name by saying that the great majority of Catholic papers were faithfully fulfilling their mission, although a few were not imbued with the Catholic spirit, and these latter not only failed to advance the cause of religion but proved to be a real hindrance to the spread of Catholic truth. In his answer to Heuser, he made further observations on the American Catholic press which were worthy of note. It was stated as his deliberate conviction that the multiplication of diocesan weekly papers in the United States was far from desirable. He felt that the supply greatly exceeded the demand and that the division of effort induced weakness and invited failure; for this reason he urged consolidation and concentration of effort under enlightened direction as calculated to attain the high purposes which Catholic journalism was intended to subserve. In the cardinal's mind a leading weekly of the dignity and scholarship of the London *Tablet* would meet all requirements, and he believed that no fairer field could be desired for such a paper than the United States. As for a Catholic daily paper, his opinion was contained

[29] Guilday, *op. cit.*, p. 252. For the decrees of 1884 cf. *Acta et decreta concilii plenarii Baltimorensis tertii*, pp. 126–129.

[30] Diary, November 12, 1885, p. 190. Cf. also AAC, Gibbons to Elder, Baltimore, December 19, 1885.

by implication in what he had already said about a weekly. The opportuneness and practicability of a Catholic daily might later be discussed in the light of the experience which the establishment of a weekly such as he envisioned would afford.[31]

Insofar as he was concerned, personally, for one who was a leading public figure for so many years and the ranking dignitary of a Church which was often maligned in the public prints, Cardinal Gibbons on the whole fared very well at the hands of the press. Yet he, too, had suffered from misrepresentation, and for that reason when Andrew Carnegie grew indignant at a letter published in the Buffalo *Catholic Union and Times,* in which his work for world peace was imputed to base motives, the cardinal could appreciate how he felt. Carnegie sent the clipping to Gibbons and the latter assured him of his sympathy, for as he said, "I know from personal experience how much it hurts to have one's actions, falsely interpreted."[32] And yet, in spite of the abuse which certain publications heaped upon the Church and upon him personally, Gibbons did not see the remedy in suppression. For example, when in 1914 Bishop McFaul showed a disposition to further the resolution of the American Federation of Catholic Societies to the effect that the *Menace,* an anti-Catholic paper begun three years before, should be barred from the mails, Gibbons was of quite another mind.[33] He replied that he had never been very desirous for the suppression of the *Menace* because there were a half-dozen anti-Catholic papers in circulation which were just as bad. Moreover, the American public were, as he maintained, unutterably opposed to interference with a free press since such action was contrary to their idea of liberty. True, they often confused liberty with license, but were the bishops to try to suppress the *Menace* it would result in the creation of bitter feeling against the Church on all sides, the other anti-Catholic papers would become more offensive, and the *Menace* would raise its head in a short time under a new name. For these reasons, therefore, the cardinal was opposed to any attempt to carry out the resolution of the A.F. of C.S.[34] Knowing him as we

---

[31] ACHSP, Heuser Papers, William A. Fletcher to Heuser, Baltimore, September 24, 1898.

[32] LC, Carnegie Papers, Gibbons to Carnegie, Baltimore, November 8, 1913.

[33] 110-G, McFaul to Gibbons, Trenton, October 15, 1914.

[34] 110-J, Gibbons to McFaul, Baltimore, October 16, 1914, copy.

do, it is not surprising to find him preferring to endure the calumnies of papers of this kind, rather than to run the risk of stirring up a hornets' nest on the score that the Church was tampering with the freedom of the press.

Moreover, there was never any doubt about the cardinal's appreciation of the role the press could play in the life of the Church both in his own country and at the Holy See. In a chapter of his book, *The Ambassador of Christ,* which he entitled "Instruction and Reception of Converts," he explicitly urged the American priests, for whom the book was mainly intended, to be mindful of the uses to which the secular press could be put for the good of religion. Through this medium he believed priests could profitably expound the salient points of Catholic doctrine or correct erroneous statements by striking down, as he said, "the foul bird of religious calumny in its flight." To him the press was the great vehicle of public thought which daily confronted everyone and which could not be ignored. Since even on religious questions, it was regarded by many as an oracle and went far toward molding the opinion and forming the judgment of millions who had only vague ideas of Christianity, Gibbons counseled his priest readers to be alive to its usefulness and to keep themselves in touch with its movements.[35] With a similar idea of having the Roman Curia properly served by the press, the cardinal responded at once to a request of Secretary of State Bryan, for a recommendation in behalf of the United Press correspondent in Rome.[36] He addressed a letter to Cardinal Gasparri, the papal Secretary of State, in which he explained that the U.P. was a reputable news-gathering agency which enjoyed a good reputation and was held in high esteem by the government officials of the United States. The U.P. would like to have the same facilities for news as those given to other agencies and for that purpose Gasparri was asked to help bring this about.[37] It was an action for which the cardinal received the prompt and cordial thanks of the U.P. representative in Washington.[38]

Any discussion of the relations of Gibbons to the press naturally raises the question of how he dealt with the Catholic paper

---

[35] *The Ambassador of Christ,* pp. 343–344.
[36] 111-A, Bryan to Gibbons, Washington, January 9, 1915.
[37] 111-B, Gibbons to Gasparri, Baltimore, January 12, 1915, copy.
[38] 111-C, Carter Field to Gibbons, Washington, January 21, 1915.

published in his own see city. When he came to Baltimore as archbishop in 1877 he found the *Catholic Mirror,* which had begun publication in January, 1850, with Father Charles I. White as editor, carrying on as the private enterprise of a group of laymen. The new archbishop was fully acquainted with the *Mirror* from his previous residence in the city, and from the fact that during his years in North Carolina and Virginia it had served him and his people as a channel for Catholic news when they had no newspaper of their own. That fact that Baltimore was the premier see and, too, that by the middle of the 1880's its archbishop had taken on a national stature, gave to the *Catholic Mirror* an importance which it would probably not otherwise have attained. At the risk of some repetition it will be pertinent to review here some aspects of the relations of the Archbishop of Baltimore to the weekly which was published in his see city, since it was not infrequently quoted on national problems as reflecting Gibbons' views, although he did not make it the official organ of his archdiocese until ten years before it suspended publication.[39]

That Catholic news originating in Baltimore was carefully watched by some, there was no doubt. Very early in his Roman career Dr. O'Connell cautioned Gibbons to determine who it was that was sending letters from Baltimore to the *Osservatore Romano.* True, there had not appeared to date anything objectionable, but O'Connell felt the archbishop ought to be more vigilant lest an unfair statement about him or his archdiocese should appear in Rome.[40] Nothing developed to cause Gibbons concern

---

[39] There were two other Catholic papers published in the Archdiocese of Baltimore in Gibbons' time. The *Church News* of Washington, edited by Milton E. Smith, a layman, began publication on October 3, 1886, and ran into the early years of the twentieth century with its name later changed to the *New Century.* In Baltimore the German weekly, *Katholische Volkszeitung,* first appeared in 1859 under the editorship of Joseph and Christopher Kreuzer and lasted down to October, 1914.

[40] 79-L-17, O'Connell to Gibbons, Rome, May 29, 1885. O'Connell had heard that it was a Baltimore Redemptorist who was sending the news stories to Rome, and he thought it would be well if Gibbons would seek information about the matter from Elias F. Schauer, C.Ss.R., the provincial. Some months later Bishop McQuaid of Rochester grew disturbed at the leaks of confidential matters pertaining to the Third Plenary Council which he said had been traced to a Catholic layman in Baltimore who was heading his information as coming from Dublin, Ireland, and which had been published in the London *Tablet* (80-D-9, McQuaid to Gibbons, Rochester, January 28, 1886). The American hierarchy was not the

so far as we know on the score of the news items forwarded from Baltimore to the *Osservatore Romano*. But he was soon to experience embarrassment from another quarter by the *Catholic Mirror's* attacks on Anthony M. Keiley of Richmond as unfit for the position of American minister to Austria-Hungary, to which he had been nominated by President Cleveland. In expressing his regret over these attacks to Keiley's brother in a letter which was published in the New York *Herald* of July 16, 1885, Gibbons revealed his relations to the *Mirror* when he said, "I have no official organ, and . . . I do not hold myself in any wise responsible for the editorials which have appeared in a Baltimore paper reflecting on your brother. . . ." He was probably hopeful that this public disclaimer of his responsibility for the *Mirror* would serve to obviate future difficulties over policies which the paper might espouse.

The Baltimore weekly had been for many years a spirited paper on public questions, and as a result of differences of opinion it had more than once earned the ire of James A. McMaster, editor of the New York *Freeman's Journal*. There were others besides McMaster who believed that the *Catholic Mirror* was at times guilty of conduct unbecoming a Catholic paper and, with the old rivalry in mind, one of McMaster's correspondents invited his attention to it about a year after the Keiley incident, and stated that it was parading under false colors as a Catholic weekly and was deserving of a castigation from his pen.[41] Likewise in Rome O'Connell continued to be uneasy and he suggested to Gibbons that he thought it would be worth while for some priest now and then to give the *Mirror* a hint about "what things to write up and what to write down."[42] Two years later a grievance

---

only one that experienced difficulties on the score of its business being aired in the newspapers. Some years before when the controversy over the Montreal branch of Laval University and other questions were agitating the Canadian hierarchy, Bishop Lynch of Toronto complained to Archbishop Taschereau of Quebec about the injurious spectacle of religious differences being made public. The Bishop of Toronto felt religion was suffering and that tepid Christians were being given an excuse for their shortcomings by pointing, as he said, "to the clerical squabbles and unbecoming proceedings even of dignitaries of the Church" (Archives of the Archdiocese of Toronto, Lynch to Taschereau, Toronto, November 24, 1872, copy).

[41] AUND, McMaster Papers, an unsigned and undated letter to McMaster which by internal evidence reveals that it was written after the *Mirror's* issue of August 14, 1886.

[42] 81-W-1, O'Connell to Gibbons, Grottaferrata, September 25, 1886.

of another kind reached the cardinal from Rome when the *Mirror's* editor, William J. O'Brien, dropped the paper's Roman correspondent, Eduardo Soderini. Soderini was greatly perturbed and sought from Gibbons the name of an American paper to which news stories might henceforth be cabled from the Holy See. He apparently felt the cardinal would not interfere to have him reinstated with the *Mirror,* since he did not ask to have that done. But in thanking him for past favors Soderini may have been disclosing that Gibbons had told him something of his problems with the paper when he remarked that he now saw better the difficult time the cardinal had in dealing with the gentlemen of the *Mirror.*[43]

Yet throughout all these years there was no evidence that the complaints and suggestions he received about the weekly caused the Archbishop of Baltimore to take any steps to restrict the editorial freedom of the *Catholic Mirror.* Only when the paper published an editorial unfriendly to the temporal power of the Holy See, and he received a remonstrance from Rome, did he move. When that occurred in the autumn of 1889 he sent O'Connell, as we have seen, to the editor with the message that he was never to publish anything in the future on that subject without first submitting it to him. Even in this case, however, he excused the imprudent utterances of Catholic papers edited by laymen on the grounds that no malice was intended and that since their statements were invested with no authority except their own, they did not excite any scandal or arouse any great interest. Showing that up to that time he had kept himself strictly aloof from the *Mirror's* editorial policies he stated, "As a matter of fact, the Editor of the Mirror has never consulted me before

---

[43] 86-C-8, Soderini to Gibbons, Paris, September 22, 1888. Earlier that year a former staff member of the *Catholic Mirror* was the occasion of further embarrassment to Gibbons in his relations to Archbishop Corrigan. Hugh P. McElrone had asked and obtained a letter of recommendation from Gibbons to Corrigan so that he might have better facilities for gathering Catholic news for his paper, the New York *World* (AANY, Gibbons to Corrigan, Baltimore, January 20, 1888). But McElrone was soon in trouble with Corrigan and his vicar-general, Monsignor Preston, over his reporting of the McGlynn case, and Gibbons felt compelled to apologize to the Archbishop of New York for having recommended him (AANY, Gibbons to Corrigan, Baltimore, March 27, 1888). The incident put a further strain on the relations between the two archbishops, even though McElrone wrote a detailed explanation to Gibbons which gave evidence that he had been shabbily treated by Preston (84-G-8, McElrone to Gibbons, Brooklyn, March 31, 1888; 84-G-6, Corrigan to Gibbons, New York, March 30, 1888).

writing any article for that paper. . . ."[44] It was apparent that the cardinal was not disposed to interfere with the way the editor was conducting the paper's affairs unless he was practically compelled to do so. The instance just mentioned is one of the very few of which there is record in which he spoke in this manner. In other words, Gibbons practiced toward the Catholic paper in his own archdiocese the liberal attitude which he recommended toward the press in general.

In 1891 a stock company was organized to publish the *Catholic Mirror* after the Baltimore Publishing Company went out of business, and at that time Gibbons became one of a large number of stockholders in the new company, and in 1898 with Father Matthew O'Keefe, pastor of St. Francis Church, Towson, as editor the paper became for the first time the official organ of the Archdiocese of Baltimore. Through the years that followed many names figured in its affairs but one of the most prominent and enduring was William J. de Blaquiere to whom the paper was leased in January, 1902. At that time the stock was valued at $15,325, of which the cardinal held the paltry sum of $9.00.[45] Obviously under the revised management his control was not very close, although there were those who wished that it might be otherwise. For example, shortly after the organization of the stock company in 1891, Maurice Francis Egan of the University of Notre Dame, who had previously served under McMaster on the *Freeman's Journal,* had told the cardinal that when it was suggested some years before that he buy an interest in the *Mirror* he had demurred because the cardinal was not then in a position to direct its policy. Egan had now come to believe that Gibbons' policies on American Catholic questions would, as he said, be the salvation of the Church in the United States, and the news

---

[44] 86-W-7, Gibbons to John P. Farrelly, Baltimore, December 28, 1889, copy. Three years later in the midst of the press excitement over Rome's decision on the school controversy of Archbishop Ireland, the cardinal told Bishop Maes of Covington that he had instructed the *Catholic Mirror* to express no views other than to publish the official declarations that might come from Rome in the matter (89-V-4, Gibbons to Maes, Baltimore, June 16, 1892, *Personal,* copy). Likewise in February, 1910, he reprimanded Humphrey J. Desmond of the *New Century* (Washington) for an editorial in its issue of February 12 criticizing the Vatican for not granting a papal audience to former Vice President Fairbanks (AAB, unclassified, Desmond to Gibbons, Washington, March 3, 1910).

[45] Diary, January 24, 1902, p. 296. On the affairs of the *Catholic Mirror* cf. Reily, *Collections in the Life and Times of Cardinal Gibbons,* V, 470–471.

of a change in the management of the *Mirror,* therefore, had given Egan renewed hope for the paper. He stated:

> Now is your chance to give it a powerful position. The Catholic papers in New York have no influence. The Boston *Pilot* is too far away to control the Southern and Middle States. The *Catholic Standard* [Philadelphia] is content to be merely respectable; the Western papers have more vitality, but that does not concern you.[46]

But in spite of the glittering prospect held out for the cardinal to have the *Mirror* set the pace for American Catholic journalism, nothing was done to have the paper essay the role of leader. In this Gibbons may, indeed, have made a mistake, for a weekly published under his auspices in the favored location of Baltimore, and with the talent of the university at Washington to draw on, might have evolved into something akin to the *Tablet* of London of which the cardinal spoke so admiringly to Heuser some years later. In fact, when the publishing firm of de Blaquiere closed down in the summer of 1908 and the *Catholic Mirror* was issued for the last time on June 13 of that year, an interval of nearly five and one half years intervened during which the Archdiocese of Baltimore had no English-speaking Catholic paper in its see city. The announcement made by the *Mirror* in its final issue that there would soon be a successor in which the clergy would take a much more active part, was not fulfilled until November 29, 1913, when the first issue of the *Catholic Review* appeared. The new paper carried a letter of warm approbation from the cardinal who strongly exhorted his priests and

---

[46] 89-L-1, Egan to Gibbons, Notre Dame, January 29, 1892. A few years later a group of twenty-four Catholic newspapermen in New York extended a joint invitation to the cardinal to preach at the tenth anniversary of the printers' Mass which Archbishop Farley was to celebrate. As Catholic men of the press, they felt there was a word to be spoken on the relations of the press to the people and the people to the press, and they believed Gibbons was the man to do it (107-C, New York Catholic newspapermen to Gibbons, New York, January 21, 1911). Although the cardinal was unable to accept the invitation, he sent a letter to Father Luke J. Evers, pastor of St. Andrew's Church, who had inaugurated the printers' Mass in 1901, and this letter was read at the anniversary celebration on May 7. Gibbons stated that he would have taken particular pleasure in being present, but as that was not possible he wished to extend his greetings. Among other things he said, "As it is the duty of the press to be an agent of good and not of evil, so it is the duty of the people to give their support to such papers as are conspicuous for their elevating tone, and to do everything in their power to lessen the great evil results of those which have an influence for bad." New York *Herald,* May 8, 1911.

people to support the *Review;* and its management did, indeed, show a much closer affiliation with the clergy when it listed the names of six priests and three laymen as the board of directors with Father Cornelius F. Thomas, pastor of St. Ann's Church in Baltimore, as the new editor.

Yet even now the Archbishop of Baltimore did not change his attitude of general aloofness toward editorial policies that had characterized his relations to the *Mirror.* When, as we have seen, Father Burke of the National Catholic Welfare Council complained late in 1919 about an editorial in the *Review* that was critical of that organization, Gibbons' secretary was instructed to reply that His Eminence had not seen the offending editorial and, therefore, suggested that Burke communicate with the editor.[47] On the whole he had consistently followed a liberal policy in regard to what was published by the Catholic papers in his archdiocese, and he apparently saw no reason for changing his attitude at this late stage of his life. The extraordinarily cordial relations which existed for years between the cardinal and the management of the Baltimore *Sun* enabled him to have access to its columns at any time he wished for an interview or pronouncement. It was a relationship which afforded to Gibbons a more effective outlet than that of the Catholic weeklies for ideas to which he wished to give public expression. This may, indeed, have accounted in part for the seeming lack of interest which he showed at times toward the Catholic press and its problems.

If the relations of Cardinal Gibbons to the press were on occasion the subject of some annoyance to him, there were other matters pertaining to the American Church and its welfare which gave him far more anxiety. We have already seen the part he played in having the Bureau of Catholic Indian Missions at Washington reorganized after the plenary council of 1884 and an annual national collection launched for its support. This was done in the hope of making the bureau a more efficient agency and an improved intermediary between the federal government and the Indian missions.[48] But the problems surrounding the Catholic Indians were by no means solved by these measures. The fact that the Catholic Church had more Indians in its charge than any denomination, and had been much more successful

---

[47] ANCWC, Albert E. Smith to Burke, Baltimore, January 1, 1920.
[48] Cf. I, 283–285, 470.

This photograph was taken beside the cathedral in Baltimore on December 3, 1920, two days before the cardinal suffered a relapse in his final illness at Emmitsburg. The occasion was the annual meeting of the Board of Directors of the Commission for Catholic Missions among the Colored People and the Indians. Reading from left to right is Father Eugene J. Connelly, chancellor of the Archdiocese of Baltimore, Archbishop Dougherty of Philadelphia, Father Louis R. Stickney, rector of the cathedral, Cardinal Gibbons, Father Edward R. Dyer, S.S., secretary of the board, Archbishop Hayes of New York, Monsignor William H. Ketcham, secretary of the commission, and Father William J. Hafey of the cathedral staff.

than the Protestant churches in the schools it had established on the various Indian reservations, excited Protestant jealousy. Since the government contributed annually on a per capita basis for the support of the Indian children receiving their education in the schools erected by the different churches, the Catholics naturally received by far the largest share of these appropriations. Added to the friction which arose on this score, was the fact that from time to time agents of the government's Office of Indian Affairs in the field fell to quarreling with the Church's missionary personnel over the handling of the funds and the general administration of policy. In situations such as these Gibbons was appealed to more than once to help iron out the difficulties. Archbishop Gross for one confessed that repeated attempts on his part to reach the President concerning the abuses of an agent in his archdiocese had failed and, therefore, he made a plea for the cardinal's intervention.[49] Gibbons forwarded Gross' grievance to President Cleveland with the recommendation that a new agent be appointed to replace the one with whom the Archbishop of Oregon City was having trouble, and he likewise took the opportunity to state that it would be a consolation to the Indians if the sisters who had been removed from their schools would be restored as teachers.[50]

But the incident of the Oregon agent was minor in comparison to the dissension which broke out after the appointment of General Thomas J. Morgan as Indian commissioner by President Harrison in 1889. Morgan was a former Baptist minister who had strong notions about the principle of separation of Church and State in administering the affairs of his office, and despite opposition from both churchmen and politicians he insisted that the Indian schools should be placed upon the same basis as the public schools. Shortly after assuming office Morgan sought an interview with Gibbons, and at that time he expressed his appreciation for the Church's interest in Indian education and for the work which had already been done by Catholics in this regard. He pledged himself to be fair to all concerned and stated that he needed and felt that he would have the sympathy and co-operation of all good people who, like the cardinal, sensed the importance and urgency of educating the Indians.[51] These were gratifying

[49] 83-Y-3, Gross to Gibbons, Portland, December, 1887.
[50] 83-V-3, Gibbons to Cleveland, Baltimore, December 16, 1887, copy.
[51] 86-R-9, Morgan to Gibbons, Washington, October 22, 1889.

sentiments and Gibbons welcomed the chance for a conference, but he urged that Morgan come soon, for the grievances of some of the bishops were so grave that they had decided to hold a meeting at his residence in the following month with a view to taking action on the situation.[52] It turned out that Morgan was unable to get to Baltimore before the bishops' meeting, but meanwhile he lodged a vigorous complaint with the cardinal against the articles which had appeared in the Catholic press reflecting, as he said, on his personal character and official policies. He regarded the criticisms he had seen as entirely without foundation and some of them he thought were false and slanderous.[53]

The Catholic press had, indeed, taken up the issue and in some instances had resorted to intemperate attacks that in the end only made matters worse. Regardless of the fact, therefore, that fair-minded men recognized the superior results attained by the Catholics in educating the Indians and that in the light of their numbers they had not for years been accorded full justice,[54] the question became so embittered on both sides that it was difficult to arrive at a calm and judicious settlement of the differences. One of those who was especially indignant at Morgan's way of doing things was Archbishop Ireland. He was among the prelates who attended the meeting in Baltimore, and some days later the archbishop and several others held a lengthy conference with President Harrison at which Secretary of State Blaine and William Windom, Secretary of the Treasury, were present. According to Ireland, the two cabinet ministers plainly showed their sympathy to the position of the committee, and he stated that while no conclusions had been reached, he felt that as far as they could read through Harrison's words an impression had been made on him and that the conference would result in some good. But Ireland remained harsh with regard to Morgan and maintained that he had no confidence in him.[55]

Actually the interview of Ireland and his associates with the President yielded no permanent results in settling the difficulties between the Office of Indian Affairs and the Bureau of Catholic

---

[52] 86-S-1, Gibbons to Morgan, Baltimore, October 24, 1889, copy.

[53] 86-T-2, Morgan to Gibbons, Washington, November 2, 1889.

[54] Loring B. Priest, *Uncle Sam's Stepchildren. The Reformation of United States Indian Policy, 1865–1887* (New Brunswick, 1942), p. 24.

[55] 86-U-5, Ireland to Gibbons, Washington, November 20, 1889.

Indian Missions. The attacks of some of the Catholic papers continued, and Morgan published a defense of himself in which he denied that he had discriminated against Catholic teachers in the Indian schools and that, despite his personal opposition to granting public money to sectarian schools, he had, nonetheless, given increased amounts to the Catholic Church. He made clear his belief that this practice was contrary to the spirit if not the letter of the Constitution and it was contrary as well to public policy. To Morgan the business of educating the Indians belonged to the government, and he thought it unwise for the government to evade its duty by farming it out to the churches.[56] Although Gibbons was not in sympathy with this view, he did not share in the excess of zeal with which some Catholics sought to gain their point over Morgan through the public press.

For example, when a personal attack on the commissioner appeared in the New York *Sun* of June 28, 1891, by a former employee of the Catholic bureau, the cardinal expressed his regret and told Morgan he was opposed to personal charges of that character. He regretted it all the more since he understood that prior to its appearance friendlier relations had been insured between Morgan's office and the Catholic agency. But now he learned that Morgan had announced that he would completely sever relations between the two offices, and decline to enter into contracts with the Catholic bureau for the education of Indian children. "This, I submit," he said, "is a very grave step, and one that I fear will be fraught with much embarrassment to all concerned in the great and necessary work of educating our Indian wards. . . ." The cardinal stated that he felt it would be a mistake to carry out the announced change and, therefore, he asked that the commissioner reconsider the matter and agree to carry on as before. He assured Morgan of the good intentions of the Bureau of Catholic Indian Missions, and in an effort to re-establish harmony he added, "I will say that I will use my influence to prevent any one connected with that bureau indulging in attacks upon you of a malevolent or personal character."[57] In acknowledging receipt of Gibbons' request, the com-

---

[56] Thomas J. Morgan, *The Present Phase of the Indian Question* (Boston, 1891), pp. 12–13. This is a pamphlet of twenty-three pages.

[57] LC, Benjamin Harrison Papers, Gibbons to Morgan, Cape May, New Jersey, July 12, 1891, copy. The writer is indebted to Harry J. Sievers, S.J., for copies of a number of letters in this collection.

missioner enclosed further clippings of press attacks upon him from Catholic sources and then went on in considerable detail to defend his decision and to lay the blame for the break upon the Catholic bureau. His belief in the cardinal's fair-mindedness and the great respect he held for his personal character must, he said, be his apology for writing at such length. Morgan remarked that he would have taken neither the time nor the pains to make so full a statement to anyone else, and he could only regret that Gibbons' kind and authoritative offices did not sooner intervene to prevent the action which, as he phrased it, "the unwise, unchristian course of the Catholic bureau forced upon this office."[58]

Once the policy had been announced there was little chance of having it reversed, and in the circumstances the cardinal

---

[58] Morgan to Gibbons, Washington, July 16, 1891, in *Sixtieth Annual Report of the Commissioner of Indian Affairs to the Secretary of the Interior* (Washington, 1891), p. 170 of appendix. Some of the correspondence that passed between Placide L. Chapelle, vice-president of the Bureau of Catholic Indian Missions, and Morgan is also printed here. Cf. also LC, Harrison Papers, Morgan to Gibbons, Washington, July 18, 1891. Morgan remarked to a friend at this time that the controversy with the Catholics, the extreme heat, and the grippe made him wish he had a lodge in "some vast wilderness." He added, "I am in no mood to enter the race for the Presidency, where the work is so vastly harder than mine, although I think the Catholics would run me if they could!" (LC, Harrison Papers, Morgan to E. W. Halford, Washington, July 20, 1891, copy.)

Gibbons' failure to take a strong stand with Morgan on this question brought keen disappointment in certain Catholic quarters. For example, Father Joseph A. Stephan, director of the Bureau of Catholic Indian Missions, told Mother Katharine Drexel, "I am deeply sorry that our Bureau was so outrageously treated by Com. Morgan; but a man like him, who was found guilty by a court martial . . . and always was a bitter enemy of Catholics could not be expected to give us justice. Instead that good and noble Cardinal wrote to this hypocrite Morgan; he ought to have spoken a decisive word to the President and not expose himself to get snubbed by a perjurer and understrapper" (Archives of the Sisters of the Blessed Sacrament, Cornwells Heights, Pennsylvania, Drexel Papers, Stephan to Drexel, Washington, August 31, 1891, copy through the kindness of Harry J. Sievers, S.J.). A year later the Catholic resentment played a part in the election of 1892. It was aired in the Catholic press, and among others the *Catholic Citizen* of Milwaukee in its issue of September 24, 1892, stated:

"The trouble with the Catholic Indian Bureau is that Cardinal Gibbons and Archbishop Ireland do not seem to have endorsed its fight against Commissioner Morgan and the Catholic public are not clear as to the facts in the case. Archbishop Ireland made some sort of peace with Commissioner Morgan over Father Stephan's head. Certainly Catholic Republicans cannot, with present information, be urged to vote against their party on this issue." For a fuller treatment of the subject cf. Harry J. Sievers, S.J., "The Catholic Indian School Issue and the Presidential Election of 1892," *Catholic Historical Review,* XXXVIII (July, 1952), pp. 129–155.

decided to make the best of it and to do what he could to quiet the storm it had raised in Catholic circles. The *Catholic Review* of New York on August 1 carried a statement from Gibbons of two days before in which he said he was now in a position to dispel fears and encourage hopes regarding the Catholic Indian missions. He believed undue importance had been given to the recent controversy between Morgan and the Catholic bureau. At his request Archbishop Ireland had visited the commissioner that day and had come away satisfied as to Morgan's position. In order to expedite business in the future all contracts were to be signed by the respective superintendents of the Catholic Indian schools, rather than by the director of the Bureau of Catholic Indian Missions. Ireland had been assured that all contracts of the previous year would be continued and that in view of new applications recently made to Morgan the latter would appropriate an additional sum of $40,000 over and above the amounts heretofore assigned for the support of the Church's Indian schools. Gibbons' statement had a pacifying effect, and the *Independent*, the leading Protestant weekly of New York, had high praise for the cardinal's good sense in an editorial of August 6.

While the new way of signing contracts with the Catholic Indian schools removed the Catholic bureau from the picture insofar as the federal government was concerned, the experience with Morgan had been sufficiently unpleasant to prompt Archbishop Ryan to suggest at the time of the commissioner's resignation that Gibbons should try to have John H. Oberly, a former commissioner with whom the Catholics had gotten on well, appointed in his place.[59] The cardinal immediately acted on the suggestion in writing President-elect Cleveland, but his request was not successful and in April, 1893, Daniel M. Browning received the appointment.[60] By this time the campaign of the A.P.A. against the Catholic Church was beginning to gain momentum, and they found in the appropriations for the Catholic Indian schools a suitable target for their propaganda and mis-

---

[59] 91-D-9, Ryan to Gibbons, Philadelphia, January 26, 1893.

[60] 91-D-10, Gibbons to Cleveland, Baltimore, January 30, 1893, copy. A similar effort by Gibbons in 1912 to secure the appointment of J. George Wright as commissioner in succession to Robert G. Valentine was unsuccessful as Cato Sells was named (LC, Taft Papers, Gibbons to H. C. Phillips, secretary of the Board of Indian Commissioners, Baltimore, July 8, 1912, with copy to Taft).

representation. For the next few years more and more was heard about the violation of the principle of separation of Church and State in relation to the Indian schools, and gradually the agitation of the A.P.A., joined by some of the Protestant sects, made itself felt in government circles. As a consequence, the system was denounced by Secretary of the Interior Hoke Smith in 1894 and three years later Congress passed a law abolishing it. Thus after June 30, 1900, the date specified by Congress, the Church was to be thrown entirely on its own in supporting its missionary schools for the red man.

But when the process of secularization advanced another step and sought to compel all Indian children to leave religious schools and to enroll at government schools where no religion was taught, the hierarchy decided upon strong action. At the meeting of the archbishops in October, 1898, they unanimously authorized Gibbons to inform all the American hierarchy of the threat and to urge them to petition Congress against such a move. The cardinal dispatched a letter in which he reviewed the facts and suggested that the bishops write to their congressmen, and he further suggested that they seek to have the whole question of the contract schools reopened and Indian education finally determined on a basis that would be fair to both the government and religious schools. In communicating copies of his petition to the bishops, he added that they, too, should write their congressmen, and it was apparent that the cardinal felt somewhat aroused, for he remarked:

> We were too quiet, and, with a mistaken confidence that the hostility to our Indian work, instigated by the A.P.A.'s and seconded by the sects, was but for a day and would soon disappear, allowed matters to drift with little or no effort to stem the tide of opposition to us.[61]

In this instance the action of Gibbons and his colleagues was to more effect, for despite the continued propaganda the Indian children were not only not removed from the Catholic schools, but the cardinal's contention that appropriations for these schools could be made out of the Indians' tribal funds was allowed.

[61] 96-U-2, Gibbons to the bishops of the United States, Baltimore, December 5, 1898, printed copy. A few days later the cardinal told Archbishop Elder that it had been suggested that his letter and the report of Monsignor Joseph A. Stephan on the Catholic bureau which he enclosed should be kept confidential (AAC, Gibbons to Elder, Baltimore, December 10, 1898). Cf. also Will, *Life of Cardinal Gibbons,* I, 495–496.

President Roosevelt accepted this solution after receiving an opinion from the attorney general that it was legally sound, and the President then sanctioned new contracts in cases where the Indians expressed the wish by petition to have a portion of their funds allotted to this purpose. There was a further outcry from the opposition against Congress allowing the tribal funds to be used for support of religious schools, but the practice was maintained and in May, 1908, the action of Roosevelt was sustained by a decision of the Supreme Court. The success which marked this particular endeavor raises the question as to whether more forceful action by the cardinal at an earlier date might not have brought better results. To be sure, his attempts at conciliation of Morgan and others were well intentioned, but they bore no real advantage in the end. The thought suggests itself that had Gibbons rallied the hierarchy sooner to joint action as he did in October, 1898, a more equitable settlement for the Indian mission schools might have been gained and the Catholic Church, identified for over three centuries with the religious instruction of the red man in North America, might thus have found itself in a stronger position in relation to the federal government.

However, the Church had meanwhile to make renewed efforts to support its Indian schools without the aid of direct government grants. One method used was the organization of the Society for the Preservation of the Faith among Indian Children, in the furtherance of which Gibbons addressed an appeal in October, 1901, to the American clergy for their generosity, and he personally contributed $1,000 that year to the cause.[62] Although the Catholics had experienced and would continue to experience certain grievances against the federal Office of Indian Affairs, the blame for the trouble had not all been on one side. That fact was emphasized at the time that Father William H. Ketcham, director of the Bureau of Catholic Indian Missions, issued his report for 1902. The financial agent of the bureau, Father Henry G. Ganss, complained to Archbishop Ryan of Ketcham's lack of tact in including criticisms of the Indian commissioner in his published report. Reflecting on the inept manner in which the bureau had often conducted its business, Ganss

---

[62] *Indian Sentinel, 1902–1903* (Washington, 1903), p. 26. Gibbons' letter of October 8, 1901, was carried on the inside front cover through several numbers of this annual volume.

considered the Ketcham report as only one more addition to a list of blunders committed by the agency, and he went so far as to say he thought the bureau ought to be abolished entirely as it had lost the confidence of the government officials. Since Gibbons and Ryan were members of the board that controlled the bureau, he felt that they ought to be made aware of mistakes of this kind that might compromise them.[63]

In addressing the Archbishop of Philadelphia, Ganss was speaking to one who had official connections with both the federal and Catholic agencies, for in February, 1902, the cardinal had recommended to President Roosevelt that Ryan be made a member of the Board of Indian Commissioners and the recommendation had been accepted.[64] Ryan served in the advisory capacity assigned to members of this board until his death in 1911, and at that time Gibbons was appointed by President Taft to replace him. But the cardinal had little time to devote to the work, and about the only extant record of his activity was an introduction to the President for Charles S. Lusk, secretary of the Catholic bureau, in order that he might lay before Taft certain conditions in the Office of Indian Affairs affecting the interests of the Catholic Indian schools and missions, which Gibbons wished to have placed before the President, and if possible remedied.[65] The cardinal served on the board for nearly two years and then submitted his resignation because of his preoccupation with other duties, an action which he accompanied by a recommendation that Ketcham be appointed in his stead, and shortly thereafter that was done.[66]

This endeavor for the Catholic Indians was the most remote from his own jurisdiction of all the varied missionary enterprises of the American Church to which Cardinal Gibbons gave attention during his years as Archbishop of Baltimore. With the Negroes, on the other hand, he had had a firsthand acquaintance that extended over virtually his entire mature life. His residence as a young man in New Orleans and Baltimore, the nine years he spent as a bishop in North Carolina and Virginia, and his removal to Baltimore in 1877 — all placed him in areas where the number of Negroes was relatively large, and where

[63] 100-D-7, Ganss to Ryan, New York, November 24, 1902.
[64] Diary, February 29, 1902.
[65] LC, Taft Papers, Gibbons to Taft, Baltimore, July 8, 1912.
[66] 108-P, Taft to Gibbons, Washington, November 30, 1912.

he acquired a far closer insight into the problems of the colored than he had ever had with the Indians. The Archdiocese of Baltimore, comprising as it did the State of Maryland and the District of Columbia, contained a fairly high proportion of Negroes, and during and after the Civil War this number was augmented by the many colored persons who moved north. It would be impossible to determine with exactitude how many of these people were Catholics, but judging from the fact that there was only one parish each in Baltimore and Washington for colored Catholics in 1877, when Gibbons came as archbishop, one could assume that they were not very numerous.[67] In the counties of Maryland their numbers were even less distinguishable in the sense that they attended church with the white people. But the tendency in the cities was toward separate parishes, and that the number of Catholic Negroes in Washington was increasing we know, for Gibbons was archbishop only about six months when he received a petition from a committee which claimed to represent from 800 to 900 colored Catholics in the eastern part of the city, who asked for a church of their own in that neighborhood. Archbishop Bayley had assigned all the colored Catholics in the capital to St. Augustine's Church where the pastor, Felix Barotti, had exclusive charge of their spiritual welfare.[68] For reasons that are not clear, nothing was done for some years to carry out their wishes for a second parish of their own and the colored Catholics continued to go to St. Augustine's or to one of the white churches.

Yet the failure of Gibbons to establish a new colored parish in Washington at this time was no indication of lack of sympathy or interest on his part. Each year he contributed $500 toward paying off the debt on St. Augustine's Church, and in thanking him the pastor, Michael J. Walsh, remarked that his kindness toward his colored flock had been fruitful of many graces for them and, he thought, fruitful as well of encouragement to those who labored all over the country for the Negro Catholics.[69] That the cardinal's reputation for kindness to the colored was

---

[67] The difficulty of finding reliable statistics on the Negro Catholics of the Archdiocese of Baltimore in these years was made clear by John T. Gillard, S.S.J., *Colored Catholics in the United States* (Baltimore, 1941), pp. 97–98.

[68] 73-R-4, Committee of Negro Catholics of Washington to Gibbons, Washington, April 22, 1878.

[69] 80-B-3, Walsh to Gibbons, Washington, January 7, 1886.

widespread, became evident several years later when Father
Augustus Tolton, pastor of St. Joseph's Church, Quincy, Illinois,
the only colored priest in the United States up to that time,
told him of the esteem he had won by reason of being, as he
said, "such a lover of our poor down trodden race."[70]

Further evidence of Gibbons' sympathetic interest was shown
in the warm welcome he extended in December, 1881, to the
Franciscan Sisters of Mill Hill who came to Baltimore from
England to open St. Elizabeth's Home for the colored, the first
white religious in the United States to devote themselves entirely
to the Negro apostolate. Moreover, he extended every facility
to the Josephite Fathers in their work for the colored at St.
Francis Xavier Church in Baltimore, and in 1888 he sponsored
the opening there of St. Joseph's Seminary to train American
young men for a missionary career among the Negroes of the
United States. He dedicated the seminary on September 9 of
that year after it had begun with three students, and a year
later Gibbons welcomed the opening of Epiphany Apostolic College
by the Josephites in his see city as a preparatory seminary
for the society's candidates. In 1891 the cardinal had the satisfaction of witnessing the first fruits of his hopes for native
vocations among the colored when he ordained Charles R.
Uncles, a Josephite, the first Negro priest ordained in the
country.[71] On the occasion of the first congress of American
Catholic Negroes which opened with a Mass on New Year's Day,
1889, at St. Augustine's Church in Washington, the cardinal
was present and preached the sermon. He spoke of the different
types of liberty which men enjoyed and he emphasized the importance of the moral liberty which God had given men to
choose right from wrong. Gibbons foretold that the congress
would mark an era in the history of the American Catholic
colored people by reason of the strength they would derive from
their unity. But he struck a note of warning when he said,
"Remember the eye of the whole country is upon you. It is
not the eye of friendship, but the sharp eye of criticism." Therefore, he would have them be on their guard to lead good lives,

---

[70] 84-T-5, Tolton to Gibbons, Quincy, July 24, 1888.
[71] John T. Gillard, S.S.J., *Catholic Church and the American Negro* (Baltimore, 1929), pp. 41, 85, 143–144. Cf. also *Society of Saint Joseph of the Sacred Heart, 1893–1943* (Baltimore, 1943), pp. 10–11.

support Christian education, and co-operate with their pastors.[72]

These were salutary words, to be sure, but they did not solve the problem of the increasing numbers of Catholic colored in Washington, who were unable to find proper accommodations in the white churches of their neighborhoods and who continued to petition for another separate parish. Father James M. O'Brien, pastor of St. Peter's Church, seconded their appeal to Gibbons and strongly urged a church and a school for them since, as he said, if they could not occupy places other than those in the back rows in the white churches, they would gradually drop out and not go to church at all. O'Brien maintained there were then about 1,500 in and around Capitol Hill who had $3,000 with which to start, and he believed a beginning ought to be made.[73] After some further delay St. Cyprian's Church at 13th and C Streets, S.E., was finally opened in 1893 for the colored with James R. Matthews as the first pastor, and within three years the parish had prospered to the degree that it was able to establish a large and flourishing parochial school under the Oblate Sisters of Divine Providence. Meanwhile the see city of the archdiocese made provision for its growing Catholic colored population, and to St. Francis Xavier Church there were added in time St. Barnabas and St. Peter Claver Churches which were exclusively for the Negroes and which were cared for by the Josephite Fathers. In all these five city parishes of the Archdiocese of Baltimore there were parochial schools for the colored children.[74]

On the subject of education for the Negroes, Gibbons was strongly in favor of provisions being made to teach them trades. If they were to become a factor in their country's prosperity, to make their presence felt, and to exercise any influence in bettering their status he maintained that it was necessary that they should be taught to be useful citizens besides having a sound religious training. For this purpose it was the cardinal's opinion that institutions should be founded wherein they could

[72] *Three Catholic Afro-American Congresses* (Cincinnati, 1893), p. 10. The text of the sermon is carried on pp. 5–11.

[73] 87-S-10, O'Brien to Gibbons, Washington, August 17, 1890.

[74] These five parishes of Baltimore and Washington, exclusively for the colored, were all that were opened during Gibbons' lifetime. But the year after his death his successor, Archbishop Michael J. Curley, established two more parishes in Washington for the Negroes, Holy Redeemer and Our Lady of Perpetual Help.

learn useful trades; thus equipped he thought the colored population could look hopefully to the future.[75] With this in mind,
he bought a tract of land not long before he died near Ridge,
Maryland, and although he did not live to see the plan developed,
the year after his death there opened on this property the
Cardinal Gibbons Institute with thirteen students who formed
the original student body under an exclusively colored faculty
for what later became a trade school along the lines of the
Hampton-Tuskegee plan.[76]

Nor did the cardinal feel that the backwardness of many of
the colored in education should be allowed to interfere with their
rights as citizens. When the question of an amendment to the
Maryland constitution arose in 1909 which would bar the Negroes
in large numbers from voting, Gibbons gave an interview to the
press in which he made his position very clear. He stated that
if the stories of abuses at the polls were true, the way to
remedy the evil was to enforce the voting laws of the state on
both the whites and Negroes; if, on the other hand, as he had
heard, the proposed amendment was intended as a device by
the Democrats to prevent the Republicans from winning an
election, then the measure was plainly unjust. Asked if his
experience with Negroes in North Carolina and Maryland caused
him to believe that they were sufficiently well educated to use
their voting privileges in the proper manner, Gibbons made a
distinction. From his knowledge he would say that in North
Carolina in his time the colored were not prepared to vote,
but in Maryland they were vastly superior, and while they
might fall short of some of the requisites of good citizenship,
they possessed many fine traits which time would improve
under proper treatment. The cardinal concluded the interview
by saying:

> Moreover, the laws of the land give the negroes the right to vote
> and to deprive them of that right is, in my opinion, an open violation
> of the spirit, if not of the letter, of the Constitution of the United
> States, and, for that reason, if there were no others, I am opposed
> to the adoption of the proposed amendment.[77]

---

[75] Joseph Butsch, "Catholics and the Negro," *Journal of Negro History*, II
(October, 1917), 407, quoting an undated letter of Gibbons.

[76] Gillard, *Catholic Church and the American Negro*, pp. 186–188.

[77] Baltimore *American*, January 25, 1909.

Gibbons' championing of the Negroes' right to vote was ill received by many, and one correspondent told him that although he had the greatest respect for his wisdom, he feared that he did not understand the conditions that confronted the white people of southern Maryland, for regardless of the choice offered to the Negroes, they would always vote Republican despite the virtues of Democratic candidates for public office.[78]

The experience which Gibbons gained from his dealings with the colored people in his own archdiocese enabled him to treat more intelligently with problems pertaining to the Negroes and the Church on a national scale. While there was never any doubt about his personal sympathy for the colored, and the reasonably adequate provision which he made for their spiritual welfare, that situation was apparently not true elsewhere in the United States. In any case, the Holy See had been informed that the Catholic Negroes in some dioceses were placed in a humiliating status in relation to white Catholics, and even to their bishops and pastors. For this reason Cardinal Gotti, Prefect of the Propaganda, asked the apostolic delegate to call the matter to the attention of Gibbons with a view to having the archbishops take steps to remedy matters.[79] At their meeting in April, 1904, Gotti's complaint was laid before the metropolitans by Gibbons and they discussed it at some length. It was agreed that since it was a matter depending on local circumstances, the cardinal should communicate the prefect's letter to all the bishops and add to it the request of the archbishops that if such abuses existed they should be corrected. Gibbons was asked to make a report to Rome on the question, and when it was pointed out that far more was being done for the Indian missions than for the colored, the cardinal appointed a committee consisting of Archbishops Ryan, Ireland, and Glennon to investigate the matter during the year and to report at the next meeting.[80]

In replying to Gotti the Cardinal of Baltimore stated the action that had been taken, and he went into some detail to explain what was being done for the colored Catholics in his

---

[78] AAB, unclassified, William J. Frey to Gibbons, Tompkinsville, January 27, 1909.

[79] 101-F, Gotti to Falconio, Rome, January 18, 1904, copy of which was enclosed by Gibbons to the American hierarchy, Baltimore, April 22, 1904.

[80] 101-E, Minutes of the Meeting of the Archbishops, Washington, April 14, 1904.

own jurisdiction and to give praise to the missionaries and parish priests who were working among them.[81] A year later Archbishop Ryan, as spokesman of the committee to the metropolitans, recommended the establishment of a bureau with a priest in charge for the colored missions similar to the one for the Indians. He likewise recommended that a committee of bishops of both the North and South be named by Gibbons with the cardinal as chairman, and that this committee be given power to select the priest and to supervise for the hierarchy the work of his office.[82] At the meeting in April, 1906, a committee consisting of Gibbons as chairman with Ryan, Farley, and Bishops Byrne of Nashville and Edward P. Allen of Mobile was approved, and they were authorized to name the director of the bureau and to proceed with its establishment.[83] They chose John E. Burke, pastor of St. Benedict the Moor Church in New York, who opened an office there, and through this medium a more systematic effort was made in the succeeding years to gather funds for the colored missions and to promote their well-being.[84]

Despite the increased revenues which were made available for this cause, and the greater number of priests and religious who each year devoted their time and labor to the conversion of the American Negroes, reports continued to reach the Holy See that not enough was being done by the Church in the United States for the colored people. When Gaetano Cardinal de Lai, Secretary of the Consistorial Congregation, relayed to Gibbons the comments of an unnamed prelate to this effect, the cardinal made a detailed reply. He explained the Protestant predominance in the South where the bishops were handicapped by a lack of priests, and he recounted, too, all that had been done by

---

[81] 101-G, Gibbons to Gotti, Baltimore, May 14, 1904, copy in Latin. His statement that there were around 40,000 Catholic colored in the Archdiocese of Baltimore in 1904 was either in error, or a severe leakage occurred during the next quarter century. At the time of the first official national census of Catholic Negroes in the United States in January, 1928, there were only 21,927 reported for the archdiocese. Gillard, *Catholic Church and the American Negro,* p. 48.

[82] 102-K, Minutes of the Meeting of the Archbishops, Washington, May 4, 1905.

[83] 103-E, Minutes of the Meeting of the Archbishops, Washington, April 26, 1906.

[84] 104-G, Minutes of the Meeting of the Archbishops, Washington, April 10, 1907.

the Josephites, Jesuits, and others in the field, as well as by the hierarchy through the decrees of the plenary councils and the establishment of the bureau for financing the colored missions. In view of these facts Gibbons contended that the American bishops had made strong efforts for the evangelization of the Negroes. Taking into account all the obstacles they had to overcome, it was his opinion that the Catholic endeavor in this regard was not without its promising outlook. He agreed that all possible means should be used to encourage native vocations among the Catholic colored people, but he concluded by saying that there was nothing mentioned by the prelate who had spoken to De Lai that the bishops of the United States had not already tried.[85]

As Cardinal Gibbons reached the celebration of the golden jubilee of his episcopacy his work in behalf of the colored race was recalled by one of their number, who stated that through his life the cardinal had distinguished himself as the Negro's friend. This man appreciated Gibbons' kindness to his people, and he hoped God would spare him to consecrate and send forth more zealous clergymen of the Negro race who, like the lowly Nazarene, would not disdain to live, for better or for worse, among their fellow men and to teach them to rise morally.[86] The final endeavor put forth by the cardinal to advance the conversion of the colored came at the second annual meeting of the hierarchy in September, 1920, when he introduced a discussion of the question. He had been visited a short time before

---

[85] AAB, unclassified, Gibbons to De Lai, Baltimore, March 28, 1914, copy. There is no evidence to show what Gibbons' attitude on segregation of the races might have been. In all probability he was content to continue the policy of segregation in the churches, to which he was accustomed during all his early life and which he found in vogue in the Archdiocese of Baltimore when he became the ordinary in 1877. The seeming hint on this subject from the Holy See in 1904 was passed by without comment when Gibbons sent his reply to Cardinal Gotti's inquiry about the treatment of the Negroes in the Church of the United States (101-G, Gibbons to Gotti, Baltimore, May 14, 1904, copy in Latin). The nearest approach to the subject by the cardinal that was found was his statement ten years later to the sixth annual conference of the National Association for the Advancement of Colored People meeting in Baltimore, a statement which the New York *Times* of May 4, 1914, quoted as having heartily endorsed the movement to uplift the Negroes and having urged prayer and faith in God as the means of bringing about conditions, as it was said, "to bridge the gap which divides Christianity and pride."

[86] 119-B, Archibald A. Herrick to Gibbons, Newark, October 19, 1918.

by a clergyman who had recently come from Rome, and the latter had reported that Benedict XV was distressed to learn of the tremendous number of American Negroes and the relatively small percentage of Catholics among them. The Pope was quoted as suggesting that seminaries be established for them and, perhaps, that Negro bishops be introduced. Gibbons was opposed to bishops for the colored, but he was in favor of expanding the facilities for seminary training for their missionaries, and he had words of high praise for the institutions in his own archdiocese which were carrying out this purpose. He asked the bishops to give their blessing to seminary education for the Negro apostolate, and the discussion ended with the subject being referred to the hierarchy's committee on missions.[87]

The Cardinal of Baltimore devoted a considerable amount of his time and labor through the years to the improvement of the missions for the Indians and the Negroes in the United States, but toward another missionary enterprise of the American Church his attitude remained cool. In the early years of the twentieth century Francis C. Kelley, pastor of Immaculate Conception Church at Lapeer, Michigan, conceived the idea of a national missionary organization that would advance the faith in backward areas of the United States. The receipt of a circular letter from Abbé Magnien of Baltimore in behalf of the Society for the Propagation of the Faith strengthened his resolve, not, as he said, that he was moved so much by gratitude for the great society that had done so much for the American missions as by the thought that, as he put it, "we had a duty to vindicate our Catholicity in missionary action within and even beyond our borders."[88]

Father Kelley realized from the outset that the hope of translating his dream into reality would depend upon his success in finding a powerful patron. His first choice was Archbishop Farley, but he declined and so did Archbishop Ryan. In his judgment Archbishop Williams was too old and he felt the same about Cardinal Gibbons who, he believed, would not consider adding further to the burdens he was already bearing.[89] He

---

[87] ANCWC, Minutes of the Second Annual Meeting of the American Hierarchy, Washington, September 22–23, 1920.

[88] Kelley, *The Bishop Jots It Down*, p. 114.

[89] *Ibid.*, p. 118.

finally approached Archbishop Quigley of Chicago who was sympathetic to the idea, and as a consequence on October 18, 1905, at a meeting in Quigley's residence there was organized the Catholic Church Extension Society. A number of prominent clerical and lay Catholics were asked to lend their support to the society, and when Secretary of the Navy Bonaparte asked Gibbons' advice in the matter, the cardinal replied that he knew nothing of the organization beyond what was contained in the pamphlet that had been sent to him. But since he considered the scheme of Kelley as rather vague and immature and its aims as very ambitious, he stated, "I would be sorry to see your name associated with it, at least in its present indefinite form." He suggested, therefore, that Bonaparte excuse himself on the plea of engrossing duties, which he thought would be a reasonable and inoffensive reply.[90]

But Kelley was not a man to be put off. The following spring the Archbishop of Chicago came before the annual meeting of the metropolitans primed with data supplied by the pastor of Lapeer concerning the aims and objectives of the new society. Moreover, Kelley was on hand with Bishop Charles J. O'Reilly of Baker City and two laymen to supplement the remarks of Quigley. After hearing the statements of these gentlemen, Gibbons suggested that the subject be referred to a committee consisting of Quigley as chairman with Archbishops Keane, Glennon, and Messmer as members with the idea that they should study the project further and report back the following year.[91] Since the minutes of the meeting of 1907 made no mention of the project, it apparently received no further backing from the metropolitans at that time. Yet despite the lack of official support from the archbishops, the society grew and in November,

---

[90] LC, Bonaparte Papers, Gibbons to Bonaparte, Baltimore, October 28, 1905. The cardinal concluded his letter by saying, "I am not acquainted with Rev. Fr. Kelly [sic]." Gibbons had apparently forgotten that in 1888 he had met Kelley at Chicoutimi, Canada, when the latter was a seminarian looking for an American bishop to adopt him. Thomas J. Broydrick, pastor of St. Martin's Church, Baltimore, who was traveling with the cardinal had suggested that he be incardinated into the Archdiocese of Baltimore, but Gibbons said he already had enough students studying for his archdiocese, although he seemed pleased later at the news that Kelley had been accepted by Bishop Foley for the Diocese of Detroit. Kelley, *op. cit.*, pp. 47–49.

[91] 103-E, Minutes of the Meeting of the Archbishops, Washington, April 26, 1906.

1908, there was held under its auspices in Chicago the first American missionary congress. By 1910 Father Kelley had won the approval of Pope Pius X, and that year there was collected nearly $200,000 for building chapels and equipping missionary churches throughout the West and South.[92] As the work expanded the demands for assistance increased, and to meet these numerous requests Kelley made a proposal to the hierarchy for a national collection in the society's behalf. Gibbons was opposed to the idea of a national collection, and he let this be known in soliciting the opinions of the other archbishops. Archbishops O'Connell and Farley agreed with him that there were already too many national collections,[93] and Riordan of San Francisco regretted giving his signature to Kelley's petition for several reasons. He said he felt some misgivings concerning Kelley's business acumen and, furthermore, he had signed only after receiving Kelley's promise that he would first consult with Gibbons. Now he had learned that the cardinal had not been previously approached on the question of a national collection, and he was going to order his name to be withdrawn from the petition.[94]

Gibbons did not allow his opposition to be confined to the American metropolitans. The petition of Father Kelley had stated that it was being forwarded to the Holy See, and with this in mind the cardinal made known his position to the papal Secretary of State. He told Merry del Val that since the plenary council of 1884 the American hierarchy had followed the custom of consulting together before any such national project as this was undertaken, but that Kelley's petition was the first he had heard of it. Gibbons then enumerated the national collections which were already authorized, and it was his opinion that a further appeal on a national scale would do harm to those made for the Holy See, the Catholic University of America, the Indian and Negro missions, the Holy Land, and the Society for the Propagation of the Faith. Therefore, he thought it would be well for Rome to delay any decision until the archbishops had time to discuss the matter fully and, he added, that even if the metropolitans were to agree to a collection of this

[92] Francis C. Kelley, *The Story of Extension* (Chicago, 1922), pp. 116–117, 128–130.

[93] 107-A, O'Connell to Gibbons, Boston, January 2, 1911; Farley to Gibbons, New York, January 7, 1911.

[94] 107-D, Riordan to Gibbons, San Francisco, March 14, 1911.

kind, the gathering and distribution of such a fund ought to be left to the hierarchy, and not to any society however worthy it might be. "Otherwise," he said, "I foresee difficulties that I forebear to describe in detail."[95] Two days later he informed Kelley that any movement in which Archbishop Quigley was interested was calculated to arouse his sympathy and co-operation, but before taking action, he deemed it an act of courtesy to the metropolitans on his part that he should first consult them, and this he intended to do at their next meeting.[96]

This delaying tactic brought the subject before the archbishops when they assembled in Washington on April 27, 1911. There took place at this time a lengthy discussion of the question of a national collection for the Catholic Church Extension Society, but since no agreement was reached on the advisability of petitioning the Pope for his approval, the metropolitans ended by merely commending the work in general and deferred any further action.[97] This was the last that was heard of the subject, insofar as the minutes of their meetings reveal. Although the project for an annual collection for the society was thus killed, the good work of the organization was not seriously impaired, for in October, 1914, it held the second missionary congress in Boston where it was demonstrated how much had been accomplished by the society in spreading the faith in the United States, and by 1919 its annual collection amounted to over $500,000.[98] The reluctance of Gibbons to give his full support to this agency was probably due to a number of factors. First, he had not been personally approached at the outset by Kelley, nor had the plan been originally presented to the metropolitans. In addition, his aversion toward increasing the burdens of the American Catholics by adding to the number of national collections also accounted in part for his reaction to the idea. The further factor that Father Kelley, as we have seen, became involved during the Wilson administration in the troubled situation of the Church in Mexico in a way that the cardinal did not always approve, may likewise have contributed to his attitude of aloofness toward the society.

---

95 107-A, Gibbons to Merry del Val, Baltimore, January 3, 1911, copy.

96 107-A, Gibbons to Kelley, Baltimore, January 5, 1911, copy.

97 107-F, Minutes of the Meeting of the Archbishops, Washington, April 27, 1911.

98 Kelley, The Story of Extension, pp. 116–117.

But if that were so in regard to the Catholic Church Extension Society, there was no faltering when the Cardinal of Baltimore was approached some years later with a plan for furthering the participation of the American Church in the foreign missions. For some time this subject had engaged the attention of several priests, and by the spring of 1911 they had reached a point where they were ready to seek the official approbation of the hierarchy. The two persons chiefly responsible for the plan were Fathers Thomas F. Price of the Vicariate Apostolic of North Carolina and James A. Walsh, director of the Society for the Propagation of the Faith in the Archdiocese of Boston. Both had already distinguished themselves in what they. had done for the missionary cause, and when they met at the eucharistic congress in Montreal in September, 1910, their similar aspirations and hopes prompted them to pool their endeavors. They immediately set about visiting some of the leading bishops, and among the first whom they approached was the cardinal.[99] Gibbons was well acquainted with Price from his days in North Carolina where years before he had given this first native priest of the state his first Communion, confirmed him, and shown him great kindness in the pursuit of his vocation.[100] He knew Price's zeal for the conversion of non-Catholics, and the hopes he had entertained some years before to found a missionary congregation.[101]

It was, therefore, no stranger who presented himself on Charles Street in the early spring of 1911 to seek the cardinal's approval of the plan for the foreign missions. Gibbons gave him a warm reception and suggested that he consult Archbishop Falconio, the apostolic delegate. Shortly thereafter he likewise composed a lengthy letter which he addressed to the metropolitans, in which

---

[99] For the background to this question cf. George C. Powers, *The Maryknoll Movement* (Maryknoll, New York, 1920); the popular biographies of the co-founders, Daniel Sargent, *All the Day Long* (New York, 1941); John C. Murrett, *Tar Heel Apostle* (New York, 1944); and Raymond A. Lane, *The Early Days of Maryknoll* (New York, 1951).

[100] 81-H-12, Price to Gibbons, Wilmington, June 28, 1886. Price was ordained ten days before Gibbons received the red biretta.

[101] 101-G, Leo Haid, O.S.B., to Gibbons, Belmont, May 10, 1904. Bishop Haid asked for Gibbons' advice concerning Price's desire to found a religious congregation and it was evident that Haid himself was not in sympathy. Unfortunately, no copy of the cardinal's reply could be found.

he cited the need for a seminary in the United States to train priests for the foreign missions, and he remarked that, at the time of writing, out of more than 17,000 American priests scarcely sixteen were engaged in this work. He noted Cardinal Manning's observation concerning the increase of vocations in England after the Church there had bestirred itself for the missions abroad, quoted Vaughan's warning to the American hierarchy at the time of their centennial in 1889 that the prosperity of the American Church would hardly endure if they failed to assume their share of the missionary endeavor in foreign lands, and also noted that the American Protestants had been in the foreign mission field for over a century.

Gibbons also submitted at this time a practical plan of action. He suggested the establishment of a missionary seminary that would be independent of any diocese and would be directly under the Congregation of the Propaganda like those of Mill Hill, Paris, and Milan. He stated that since there were sufficient funds already at hand to make a humble beginning, and the promise of several burses, the question of money would prove no immediate obstacle. The cardinal included brief sketches of the lives of Fathers Walsh and Price, who were already known to most of the archbishops, the former as editor of the *Field Afar* and the latter of *Truth*. The apostolic delegate was quoted as saying that, as soon as the hierarchy gave its approval, the two priests would visit the principal foreign mission seminaries and apply to the Holy See for approval. Upon receipt of Rome's permission, they would then return to the United States to begin the work. The cardinal concluded by asking the archbishops if they would commend the proposed idea to their suffragans and, in the event of their favorable consideration, he asked that they suggest one or more desirable locations from which a choice might be made for both a provisional and a permanent seminary.[102]

A month later the metropolitans gathered for their annual meeting, and at that time Gibbons sponsored the proposal and won their unanimous agreement. The minutes read:

> We warmly commend to the Holy Father the two priests mentioned
> as organizers of this Seminary, and we instruct them to proceed to

[102] 107-D, Gibbons to the Archbishops of the United States, Baltimore, March 25, 1911, copy.

Rome without delay for the purpose of securing all necessary authorization and direction from the Propaganda for the proposed work.[103]

Walsh and Price lost no time in carrying out this mandate. In Rome they were kindly received by Pius X and Cardinals Merry del Val and Gotti. As Price said, the doors were thrown wide open to them owing to Gibbons' and Falconio's letters of recommendation. One thing remained to be decided at once, and that was the name the new society should take. Price told Gibbons that he and Walsh had talked over the matter and it was, as he expressed it, "our united desire that you should have the honor of naming it." He then suggested as a name the Catholic Foreign Mission Society of America so that it would emphasize that the Catholic Church of the United States was now actively in the field. The cardinal approved the name and it was, therefore, adopted. Price concluded by saying that the Prefect of Propaganda had instructed them to communicate through Gibbons for all further details, as he would write to the Archbishop of Baltimore and give whatever directions he had for their future guidance.[104]

Upon their return to the United States the cofounders of Maryknoll, as it is more familiarly known, consulted once more with Gibbons, Falconio, and Farley and in December, 1911, they settled temporarily at Hawthorne, New York, where they remained for almost a year. In September, 1912, they moved to a location near Ossining on the Hudson, and in that month the seminary opened with six students and five priests as teachers, with a discipline that was based in the main on the rule of St. Sulpice. Three aspirants to the brotherhood were also on hand, and in a private house at one corner of the grounds a group of eight women gave domestic assistance and formed the nucleus out of which the Maryknoll Sisters would later grow.[105] The young society prospered and on September 8, 1918, Father Price set out for China as the superior of a group composed of himself and three other priests, the first of the many Maryknoll missionaries to devote their lives to spreading the

---

[103] 107-F, Minutes of the Meeting of the Archbishops, Washington, April 27, 1911.

[104] 107-K, Price to Gibbons, Rome, July 5, 1911.

[105] 108-Q, Walsh and Price to Gotti, Ossining, December 8, 1912, copy to Gibbons.

faith in the Orient. Due to the conditions occasioned by World War I news was slow in reaching China, but by early summer of 1919 Price had heard of the celebration in honor of the cardinal's golden jubilee. He did not wish to let it pass — late as he was — without sending his congratulations. He remarked that, at the time Gibbons was installed as a bishop in North Carolina fifty years before, he was a lad of eight, but he remembered the occasion vividly. He continued:

> From that day to this I have ever felt that you acted towards me as a kind father and that when occasion presented itself you never failed to do for me whatever you thought the circumstances permitted. Whatever has come to me on earth & which I hold in esteem has come to me largely through you.[106]

The life of Father Price was not to last for long thereafter, for three months later he was stricken with acute appendicitis while alone at the mission in Yeungkong. He managed with great difficulty to reach Hongkong where he died on September 12, just a year and four days after leaving the Maryknoll headquarters. Word of his death was delayed in reaching the United States but on September 21 Father Walsh telegraphed the sad news to the cardinal.[107] Gibbons had assisted at the birth of this first foreign mission society of the American Church, and he had now outlived one of its founders. By the time of his own death a year and a half later its promise was already bright, and less than six months after the cardinal died there departed from Maryknoll for China five priests, one brother, and a first group of sisters, six in number.[108]

The leading role which Cardinal Gibbons played in such matters as the missionary enterprises of the Church of the United States was only one phase of the influence he exercised in directing the course of American ecclesiastical affairs. By the late nineteenth century his power was so universally recognized that there was hardly a major problem that arose in any diocese in the land that he was not consulted for his advice and assistance. It would be impossible to record in detail all these cases, but a summary of several of the more significant ones will serve to illustrate the type of calls made on Gibbons and

---

[106] 121-V, Price to Gibbons, Yeungkong, Province of Kwangtung, June 5, 1919.
[107] 123-H, Walsh to Gibbons, Ossining, September 21, 1919, telegram.
[108] Powers, *op. cit.,* pp. 145–146.

the success he had in handling them. One such case involved the affairs of the Archdiocese of St. Louis. Early in 1891 Archbishop Ryan reminded the cardinal that at the end of that year the old Archbishop of St. Louis would reach the golden jubilee of his episcopacy, the first time in the history of the American Church that a bishop had served a half century. Ryan was anxious that the Pope should signalize the Kenrick jubilee by some striking honor and he suggested that it might be fitting to make him a cardinal. Gibbons was asked, therefore, if he would inform the Pontiff about the approaching jubilee and see what could be done.[109]

The Cardinal of Baltimore complied by telling Leo XIII of the desire expressed by a number of American prelates that Kenrick should be honored in a manner that the Pope would judge fitting, noting at the same time the unique character of the jubilee for the United States, and giving generous praise to the archbishop's outstanding qualities and service. No specific mention of the cardinalate was made, and the closest Gibbons came to the topic was to say that in honoring Kenrick the Pope would be honoring the American Church and the entire nation.[110] But Leo XIII did not see fit to bestow the red hat in this case, and at the celebration in St. Louis on November 30 the Cardinal of Baltimore responded to the toast to the Pontiff, and at the end of his speech presented Kenrick with a medallion likeness of Leo framed in gold which the Holy Father had sent to him as a gift.[111]

By this time Archbishop Kenrick had reached the age of eighty-five and was in need of assistance. Without following the canonical procedure of consulting his suffragans, the old man chose the name of his vicar-general, Philip P. Brady, and asked if Gibbons would sponsor his nomination as coadjutor before the metropolitans at their meeting in November, 1892. The archbishops refused to pass on Brady because of the violation of the rules governing such cases and it, therefore, became the unpleasant duty of the cardinal to inform Kenrick in as delicate a manner as possible of the procedure he must follow. He told

---

[109] 88-J-7, Ryan to Gibbons, Philadelphia, February 17, 1891.

[110] 88-P-8, Gibbons to Leo XIII, Baltimore, May 18, 1891, copy in French.

[111] 89-D-6, unnamed newspaper clipping of Gibbons' speech, St. Louis, November 30, 1891.

the archbishop that he must first consult his suffragans and have a *terna* of names drawn up. He endeavored to mitigate the disappointment as tactfully as he could when he said:

> I unite with my colleagues in expressing our sorrow for your enfeebled health and your absence from our deliberations which you would have enlightened by your wisdom and experience. I also express the hope that the early selection of a coadjutor will prolong your life & give you in your declining years that rest and tranquility which your labors & merits amply deserve.[112]

The archbishop did as he was instructed, and within a few weeks Gibbons was asked by one suffragan, Bishop Richard Scannell of Omaha, for his opinion on the three names that the irremovable rectors of St. Louis had put forth, namely, Bishops Kain of Wheeling, Spalding of Peoria, and Fitzgerald of Little Rock. Scannell added that there were no consultors in St. Louis, the situation there was a difficult one, and for that reason he was desirous of having Gibbons' advice if he should be pleased to give it.[113]

The cardinal had no hesitation in giving his opinion. He thought all three bishops were worthy of consideration, but since he knew Kain best he gave him the strongest recommendation.[114] After the suffragans met Scannell sent word that their votes were cast for Spalding in first place, Kain in second, and Bishop Chatard of Vincennes in third.[115] Meanwhile the cardinal received further expressions of favor for Kain from several St. Louis pastors,[116] and by the end of the month he was ready to express his choice to the Holy See. He explained to Cardinal Ledochowski that Spalding did not wish the position, that Chatard had not been proposed in any way by the clergy of St. Louis, which would make him less acceptable, and that for these reasons Kain was the most desirable name on the *terna* and he would strongly recommend, therefore, that Kain be chosen.[117] These recommendations bore weight in Rome, and in

---

[112] 90-R-3, Gibbons to Kenrick, Baltimore, November 20, 1892, copy.

[113] 90-U-6, Scannell to Gibbons, Omaha, December 9, 1892.

[114] 90-V-2, Gibbons to Scannell, Baltimore, December 12, 1892, copy.

[115] 90-V-3, Scannell to Gibbons, Omaha, December 16, 1892, *Personal*.

[116] 90-V-7, James J. McCabe, pastor of Sacred Heart Church, and James McCaffrey, pastor of St. Patrick's Church, to Gibbons, St. Louis, December 19, 1892.

[117] 90-W-7, Gibbons to Ledochowski, Baltimore, December 27, 1892, copy in Latin. Three days later Gibbons wrote Ledochowski again to second the petition

the early summer of 1893 the Bishop of Wheeling was named Coadjutor Archbishop of St. Louis.

When the news had first reached Kain that he was being considered for St. Louis, he let Gibbons know that he was far from being free of apprehension,[118] and he was not long in his new home before he had reason to believe that he had judged correctly. Kenrick treated him politely, but insofar as the financial affairs of the archdiocese and the appointment of priests were concerned, the old archbishop gave him nothing to say or to do and the newspapers were beginning to spread false rumors about a rift between the two prelates. Kain had heard that faculties making him apostolic administrator had been forwarded from Rome, but they had not yet appeared and he was definitely worried.[119] Having in the meantime been advised by Archbishop Ryan to await developments, the cardinal did nothing.[120] But matters grew steadily worse and Kenrick displayed such unmistakable signs of mental enfeeblement that Kain begged Gibbons to intercede at Rome in his behalf.[121] The cardinal lost no more time in urging Ledochowski to enlarge Kain's faculties since, as he said, Kenrick had grown both mentally and physically unfit to rule, yet obstinately continued to try to hold the reins of ecclesiastical government.[122] Actually the Prefect of Propaganda had already moved before Gibbons' letter arrived, but he said he would be obliged if the cardinal would use all the means at his disposal to induce Kenrick to cede the administration into the hands of his coadjutor.[123] About the same time

---

of the bishops of the Province of St. Louis that Dubuque be made a metropolitan see (Diary, December 30, 1892, p. 263). He had been asked by Bishop John Hennessy of Dubuque to do this, and after learning the action that Gibbons had taken, Hennessy thanked him for the pointed and forceful way that he had communicated his approval of the move to the Holy See. Hennessy hoped God would give him length of days, as he said, "to edify by your bright example and guide in your wisdom the hierarchy and clergy of our favored country" (91-A-4, Hennessy to Gibbons, Dubuque, January 4, 1893), The Archdiocese of Dubuque was erected on June 15, 1893.

[118] 90-V-4, Kain to Gibbons, Wheeling, December 17, 1892.

[119] 91-W-5, Kain to Gibbons, St. Louis, September 26–27, 1893. Ryan had spoken to Kenrick about sharing his powers with Kain, but the coadjutor had little confidence in the effectiveness of Ryan's intervention. As he said, "The truth is Archbp. R. is too timid — perhaps I might put it — too *reverential.*"

[120] 91-W-7, Ryan to Gibbons, Philadelphia, September 27, 1893.

[121] 92-V-6, Kain to Gibbons, St. Louis, December 18, 1893.

[122] 92-W-2/1, Gibbons to Ledochowski, Baltimore, December 22, 1893, copy.

[123] 93-A-7, Ledochowski to Gibbons, Rome, January 13, 1894.

Kain received the documents containing his faculties from the Holy See, and from that time on the coadjutor was able to rule the see with real as well as nominal power.[124] Archbishop Kenrick resigned in May, 1895, and lived on to March 4 of the following year when he died some months short of his ninetieth birthday.

Archbishop Kain was destined for no such lengthy tenure of office in St. Louis as his predecessor. In fact, only nine years after he assumed full control his health began to fail and he was in need of assistance. With Kain's consent, his physician informed the cardinal of the archbishop's condition and suggested that he should have help to carry out his episcopal duties.[125] Gibbons quickly communicated this information to Cardinal Gotti in the hope, as he said, that the latter would hasten the nomination of an auxiliary bishop for St. Louis since the need appeared to be urgent.[126] Later, however, it was decided to petition the Holy See for a coadjutor with the right of succession, rather than for an auxiliary bishop, and when the *terna* was forwarded it contained the names of Bishops John J. Hennessy of Wichita, Edward J. Dunne of Dallas, and John J. Glennon, Coadjutor Bishop of Kansas City. Archbishop Riordan was emphatic in his belief that Hennessy and Dunne were not suited for St. Louis, and with this in mind he urged the cardinal to send to Rome a forceful recommendation of Glennon as the only one on the list who was equal to the position.[127] Gibbons was of a similar mind, for before Riordan's letter had time to reach Baltimore he had dispatched to Gotti the warmest approval of Glennon which was accompanied by conventional remarks concerning the other two candidates.[128] On April 27, 1903, Glennon received the appointment and the last six months of Kain's life were thus eased by the presence of one who relieved him of many of the burdens of his office.

If the last years of Archbishop Kenrick gave cause for concern the final days of Archbishop Feehan of Chicago were even more troubled. By 1899 Feehan, in uncertain health and seventy years of age, had reached the time when he required assistance

[124] 93-A-8, Kain to Gibbons, Wheeling, January 15, 1894.
[125] 100-B-4, John P. Boyson to Gibbons, St. Louis, October 8, 1902.
[126] 100-C-2, Gibbons to Gotti, Baltimore, October 22, 1902, copy in French.
[127] 100-G-5, Riordan to Gibbons, San Francisco, January 19, 1903.
[128] 100-G-6, Gibbons to Gotti, Baltimore, January 22, 1903, copy in Latin.

in the discharge of his episcopal duties. The consecration of one of his pastors, Alexander J. McGavick, as auxiliary bishop in May of that year, brought no real relief because McGavick soon became incapacitated through illness. What made matters so difficult in the choice of a new auxiliary was the fact that internal factions had arisen among the clergy over the administration of the archdiocese. Out of this situation their developed a bitter opposition to Peter J. Muldoon, the candidate of Feehan, who since 1888 had been his chancellor. The opposition to Muldoon was concentrated mainly among a group of Irish-born priests who resented the young American's favored status with the Irish-born archbishop.

Father Muldoon was a close friend of Abbé Magnien, superior of St. Mary's Seminary in Baltimore, under whose regime he had finished his priestly studies in 1886, and he was also admired by Gibbons. Therefore, when the cardinal went to Rome in the spring of 1901, the opponents of Muldoon became alarmed lest the influence of Baltimore be used to secure the appointment. As Hugh P. Smyth, pastor of St. Mary's Church, Evanston, told Monsignor O'Connell, "No one questions His Eminence's devotion to religion, but it is feared that he is misinformed as to the true state of things here."[129] Some weeks thereafter it was announced that Muldoon had been appointed Auxiliary Bishop of Chicago. That Gibbons had favored his candidacy, there was no doubt, for after the cardinal's return home Muldoon thanked him for what he had done in Rome, and he remarked, "We all appreciate how much your word meant, and certainly it is difficult to say how long the appointment might have been delayed, were it not for your kindly interest."[130]

In an effort to demonstrate to all that Muldoon had the strong support of the authorities of the Church, the apostolic delegate, Sebastiano Martinelli, who had been created a cardinal three months before, came to Chicago to consecrate the new bishop on July 25. Feehan was likewise grateful for Gibbons' assistance

---

[129] ADR, Smyth to O'Connell, Evanston, May 21, 1901. Six weeks later Smyth told O'Connell that should the appointment of Muldoon be made, the cardinal would be blamed because it was known that he had taken sides without inquiry and that during a visit to Chicago he was under the guidance of Edward A. Kelly, pastor of St. Cecilia's Church, one of the main Muldoon backers (ADR, Smyth to O'Connell, Evanston, July 8, 1901).

[130] 98-Y-11, Muldoon to Gibbons, Chicago, August 29, 1901.

in the case, and he stated that it had not only proved helpful to him personally but it had rendered a service to religion and to the future welfare of the Archdiocese of Chicago. "If the men in question had had their way," said Feehan, "the government of this diocese would have become practically impossible."[131] Yet the opposition did not take its defeat in good grace and, in fact, in October of that year Jeremiah J. Crowley, pastor of St. Mary's Church, Oregon, Illinois, one of the ringleaders, was excommunicated by Feehan after refusing to accept the conditions of submission laid down by the apostolic delegate.[132] Unfortunately, the whole sad business was aired in the press, and the grave scandal caused Bishop Spalding to beg Gibbons to intervene to put a stop to it.[133] Whether or not he made any attempt to play the role of peacemaker is not known. In any case, two weeks later there occurred the Crowley excommunication, and the ugly situation continued to embarrass the Catholics of the Archdiocese of Chicago through the remaining months of Feehan's lifetime.

The Archbishop of Chicago died rather suddenly on July 12, 1902, and some days after the funeral the consultors and irremovable rectors and the bishops of the province met to draw up their respective *ternae*. Spalding was placed first on both lists, with the priests giving Muldoon the next highest number of votes and assigning Bishop Quigley of Buffalo to third place. The results were immediately communicated by Spalding to the cardinal, with the statement that it was the conviction of the bishops of the Province of Chicago as well as the general feeling among the most intelligent and religious priests and laymen that the appointment of Muldoon would be, as he characterized it, "an irreparable calamity."[134] Regardless of his esteem and affection

---

[131] 99-A-8, Feehan to Gibbons, Chicago, September 16, 1901.

[132] Cornelius J. Kirkfleet, O.Praem., *The Life of Patrick Augustine Feehan, Bishop of Nashville, First Archbishop of Chicago, 1829–1902* (Chicago, 1922), pp. 378–380, reprints two documents on the Crowley case in an appendix. Unfortunately, there is no discussion of the case in this work.

[133] 99-C-5, Spalding to Gibbons, Peoria, October 11, 1901. Spalding enclosed a letter from Father Smyth of Evanston which he asked to have returned. By way of clarifying an allusion by Smyth to Baltimore, Spalding said, "The Abbe Magnien is bitterly hated by many priests in the West as a meddler and intriguer. . . ."

[134] 99-U-3, Spalding to Gibbons, Peoria, July 25, 1902. Gibbons kept no copy of his reply, but he wrote across the top that it had been answered on July 29.

for Muldoon, the cardinal sensed the gravity of the situation in Chicago, and for that reason he sent a forceful recommendation to Cardinal Ledochowski that the Bishop of Peoria should be named to the vacant see. He did not fail to speak highly of Muldoon, but it was his judgment that at this juncture of affairs in that disturbed area of the Church, he was not the man to heal the still open wounds.[135] If he had any lingering doubts about how critically matters were viewed there by some, they were dissipated after Michael Cudahy, one of the city's most prominent Catholic laymen, bared further details to him and made an earnest plea that he support Spalding.[136] The serious differences that had arisen over filling the vacancy doubtless contributed to the delay in naming an archbishop, and it was not until early 1903 that the issue was decided. At that time the Holy See chose James E. Quigley, Bishop of Buffalo, a selection that may well have been made in the belief that he was uncommitted to any of the quarreling factions in Chicago.

For the first five years of Archbishop Quigley's administration Muldoon continued to serve as his auxiliary until the erection of the Diocese of Rockford in September, 1908, when he was named as first bishop of the new see. The Archbishop of Chicago died on July 10, 1915, and at that time Bishop Muldoon was placed second on the priests' *terna,* although his name did not figure in the list drawn up by the bishops.[137] Archbishop Bonzano, the apostolic delegate, furnished the cardinal with all the necessary data and asked for his judgment on the candidates proposed.[138]

The archives of the Diocese of Peoria contain little or nothing of Spalding's correspondence with other bishops.

[135] 99-W-2, Gibbons to Ledochowski, Baltimore, August 15, 1902, copy.

[136] 100-B-1, Cudahy to Gibbons, Chicago, October 1, 1902.

[137] 112-D, Muldoon to Gibbons, Chicago, July 17, 1915. The priests' *terna* consisted of Edmund M. Dunne, Bishop of Peoria, Muldoon, and McGavick, Auxiliary Bishop of Chicago, in the order named; the bishops' *terna* carried the following names in the order named: John P. Carroll, Bishop of Helena, John J. Glennon, Archbishop of St. Louis, and Thomas F. Lillis, Bishop of Kansas City. (112-F, Bonzano to Gibbons, Washington, August 18, 1915). Five years before Rome had issued instructions that all who were connected in any way with episcopal *ternae* were bound *sub gravi* to keep the information secret. There had been abuse of confidence in some of these cases, and the publication of the names in the newspapers had a tendency to impair the freedom of the Holy See's judgment (AAB, unclassified, De Lai to Gibbons, Rome, March 30, 1910, printed copy).

[138] 112-F, Bonzano to Gibbons, Washington, August 18, 1915.

In this instance Gibbons was unhesitatingly for the Bishop of Rockford. He told Bonzano:

> This because he is a native of Chicago, is well acquainted with the needs of that Diocese, and also because his appointment to Chicago would be a vindication for him of the unjust persecution against him whilst he was Auxiliary of Chicago. Regarding the other two mentioned on this terna I have nothing to say.[139]

The cardinal's preference for Muldoon on this occasion was shared by Archbishop Messmer of Milwaukee who urged Gibbons to use his influence with the Holy See to the end that he would be named, and he proposed that he communicate with Rome directly rather than through the apostolic delegate.[140] The cardinal promised to write to De Lai in Muldoon's favor,[141] but once more Gibbons' candidate for Chicago failed to win final approval and in December, 1915, George W. Mundelein, Auxiliary Bishop of Brooklyn, was named third Archbishop of Chicago.[142] The appointment was not well received by many, and Muldoon told the cardinal:

> Chicago clergy and laity are stunned, and feel very, very keenly the fact that Chicago has had no voice, or at least the voice of Chicago, through her elected officials, was utterly ignored.

He wanted Gibbons to know the affectionate gratitude that he felt for the latter's kindness toward him in all that had pertained to the matter, and he concluded by saying, "I wish to assure you that I am very happy and contented, and have no feeling, except one of sorrow that some one that had been presented had not been selected."[143] Doubtless the cardinal, too, was disappointed at the outcome, but thereafter that feeling in no way

---

[139] 112-G, Gibbons to Bonzano, Baltimore, September 1, 1915, copy.

[140] 112-H, Messmer to Gibbons, Milwaukee, September 4, 1915.

[141] 112-H, Gibbons to Messmer, Baltimore, September 6, 1915, copy.

[142] Another example wherein Rome had not followed Gibbons' recommendation and had chosen a bishop whose name appeared on neither the priests' nor the bishops' *terna* had occurred some years before. The cardinal had espoused the candidacy of Bishop Matthew Harkins of Providence for the coadjutorship of Boston on the grounds of his being first on both *ternae*, that he was the most acceptable name to Archbishop Williams, and, too, because of Harkins' personal qualifications (101-F, Gibbons to Gotti, Baltimore, April 22, 1904, copy in Latin). Yet in February, 1906, William H. O'Connell, Bishop of Portland, was appointed as Williams' coadjutor with the right of succession.

[143] 112-T, Muldoon to Gibbons, Rockford, December 4, 1915.

lessened his cordial co-operation with Chicago's new archbishop for the general welfare of the American Church.

Criticism such as Cardinal Gibbons met for his part in the tangled affairs of the Archdiocese of Chicago at the turn of the century was probably paralleled on other occasions, but the consummate tact which he displayed in most instances, together with his eminent fairness and sound judgment, saved him from the fate that befalls those of lesser genius in the realm of personal relations. No man of high station in either civil or ecclesiastical life who exercises great power and influence over the affairs of others, can hope to escape entirely from criticism of his actions and policies. In this respect the cardinal was no exception, although he came off remarkably well when one considers the length of time that he was the dominant personality of the Church in the United States. Not only did Gibbons enjoy a reputation among his fellow bishops for solid piety and common sense, but his unfailing kindness and consideration of their desires served to draw them about him in a manner that offered an unmistakable recognition of his leadership. This was the situation as early as 1893 when the cardinal celebrated the silver jubilee of his episcopacy, and by 1918 the esteem and affection for him as the leader of American Catholicism was so deep and widespread that the completion of his fifty years as a bishop was marked by one of the most extraordinary demonstrations that a churchman has ever received from his associates and admirers.

One of the ways in which the personality of Gibbons was favorably impressed upon the American hierarchy, their clergy, and people was through his graciousness of presence at their ecclesiastical functions. It would be idle to pretend that the cardinal did not thoroughly enjoy these affairs; nonetheless, there were times when long journeys and absence from his normal duties were undertaken only with considerable sacrifice of his personal convenience. He always found a special pleasure in visiting New Orleans where his brother and two sisters resided, and there were few major events in the life of the Archdiocese of New Orleans at which he did not assist. At the celebration of its centennial in April, 1893, he was present and spoke at both the Mass and the banquet, but he had insisted beforehand that Archbishop Janssens should sing the pontifical Mass and give the blessing regardless of what the rubrics might say. As he remarked, "You

Cardinal Gibbons on a visit to his family. The cardinal is seated with his brother, John T. Gibbons, on the latter's front porch in New Orleans.

(Courtesy of Mrs. Margaret Gibbons Start)

represent your spouse, the diocese of New Orleans, & you ought to represent her fully."[144] Three years later he preached at the centennial of St. Louis Cathedral in that city and in April, 1907, he conferred the pallium on Archbishop Blenk as he had done for Janssens eighteen years before. Gibbons' lively interest in New Orleans continued to the end of his life, and not long before he died he expressed that interest in a practical way by forwarding a check for $1,000 to Archbishop John W. Shaw for the projected Notre Dame Seminary three months before the formal drive for funds was launched.[145] It was among the last of many favors and courtesies which over a period of more than forty years the six archbishops who ruled the See of New Orleans had experienced at his hands.

A prelate for whom the cardinal entertained a very high regard and whom he often consulted on questions of policy, was Archbishop Williams of Boston. At the time of Williams' death in August, 1907, Gibbons was unwell, and for that reason he felt compelled to decline the invitation of the coadjutor, William O'Connell, to preach the funeral sermon, although he wired that he would try to pontificate if O'Connell so desired.[146] He made the trip to Boston, therefore, and on September 4 he celebrated the requiem for the old archbishop, at which the coadjutor preached after Bishop McQuaid, Williams' intimate friend, had replied that he was unequal to the task.[147] While the cardinal had never been close to the new Archbishop of Boston, their relations had not been unfriendly. Four years after Williams' death Gibbons welcomed O'Connell into the College of Cardinals, and he remarked the coincidence of their being the same age when they received the red hat, to which he added the wish that O'Connell's years as a cardinal might be as long as his own and that they might bear more abundant fruits than he had been able to show.[148] In thanking him for the greeting, the cardinal-

---

[144] AUND, New Orleans Papers, Gibbons to Janssens, Baltimore, February 18 and 20, 1893.

[145] 129-R, Gibbons to Shaw, Baltimore, October 11, 1920, copy.

[146] AAB, Gibbons to O'Connell, Baltimore, August 31, 1907, telegram, copy.

[147] In his memoirs O'Connell related that both Gibbons and McQuaid declined his invitations through reasons of health, and he then remarked, "So I decided that I, myself, with God's help, would undertake to sing the Mass and preach the sermon" (O'Connell, *Recollections of Seventy Years*, p. 267). No mention was made in this account of the fact that Gibbons finally offered the funeral Mass.

[148] 107-R, same to same, Avondale, Maryland, October 31, 1911, copy.

elect revealed something of their previous relationship when
he said:

> I shall prize forever the letter of Your Eminence received this
> day. It is the latest of so many proofs of interest in my career and
> work, for the first momentous step in which I owe so much to you.
>
> I do not forget that my nomination as Rector of the American
> College came chiefly from you. And that was the beginning of all
> that has come to me ever since.
>
> No one can ever divide or weaken the strong hold that Your
> Eminence has upon the heart of this great nation. Happy if we who
> follow after you, can retain what you have so gently yet so valiantly
> won.
>
> I am deeply grateful for your kind sentiments. I think you know
> how attached I am to you, and how much I appreciate being in some
> measure associated with all that you stand for. Boston and Baltimore
> will be even more united now than ever.[149]

It may have come as something of a surprise to Gibbons to have
so much attributed to his influence but, in any case, through the
years of his lifetime that remained Baltimore and Boston worked
in harmony for the good of the Church.

In a position such as he occupied it was inevitable that Gibbons should be the recipient of requests for recommendations of
those who aspired to promotions in both Church and State. At
times he seemed to have more than his share of them, for although
the cardinal was generally cautious about whom he recommended,
his instinctive kindness precluded the possibility of a rebuff and
laid him open to numerous petitions of this kind. A case in point
was Monsignor Robert Seton, grandson of the famous Mother
Elizabeth Seton and cousin of Archbishop Bayley. Seton was

The naming of O'Connell as a cardinal was not popular in some circles. Archbishop Riordan stated to Gibbons, "I do not wish to allude to the appointments
that have recently been made for the United States, and which will be confirmed
tomorrow in the Eternal City. One of them is above all understanding, and it
is better perhaps to keep silence than to express my views on it. Our old friend
of St. Paul would have been the choice, I think, of nearly all the best minded
of our people, but he will only have to bear this humiliation as best he can. I
have not written to him because I dare not trust myself to write just as I feel"
(107-V, Riordan to Gibbons, San Francisco, November 29, 1911). Three years
later Ireland reflected the same view when he acknowledged the cardinal's letter
from Rome after the conclave, and concluded with the statement, "I hope that
Benedict XV asked no counsel from your friend of Boston" (110-G, Ireland to
Gibbons, St. Paul, October 5, 1914).

[149] 107-S, O'Connell to Gibbons, Boston, November 1, 1911.

aggrieved that for years he had been made to suffer what he considered an unmerited neglect in the Church, and during his residence in Rome he consequently brought the matter to the attention of Cardinal Rampolla. Rampolla was quoted as saying that there must have been some sinister influence at work and that he would seek an opinion from Gibbons; meanwhile Seton was to say nothing himself.[150] But the monsignor, taking no chances on a slip, communicated his grievances to the Cardinal of Baltimore and asked that he recommend him for a titular archbishopric.[151] Gibbons requested of Rampolla that the honor be conferred and in June, 1903, Seton was named Archbishop of Heliopolis.[152] But this was not the end, and three years later the cardinal compliantly submitted the suggestion to Pius X that Seton be made a canon of St. Peter's.[153] This time, however, the appointment was not forthcoming, and for several years thereafter Seton continued to fret about his failure to gain the canonry which he attributed in good measure to what he called Gibbons' lack of "back-bone" in pushing his petition.[154]

---

[150] Robert Seton, *Memories of Many Years* (*1839–1922*) (London, 1923), p. 225.

[151] 100-E-7, Seton to Gibbons, Rome, December 26, 1902.

[152] 100-H-6, Gibbons to Rampolla, Baltimore, February 2, 1903, copy in Latin. Seton stated that on Feehan's death the year before Satolli had suggested he be named Archbishop of Chicago, but he had declined (*op. cit.*, p. 224), although six years later he expressed his disappointment at not being given a see in his native country (AUND, Edwards Papers, Seton to James F. Edwards, Prague, August 22, 1908).

[153] 103-F, Gibbons to Pius X, Baltimore, May 9, 1906, copy in Latin.

[154] AUND, Edwards Papers, Seton to Edwards, Rome, November 4, 1906; January 28, 1907; Prague, August 22, 1908; and Rome, December 29, 1908. In the letter from Prague in speaking of Gibbons he said, "He does not push things, follow up things and allows himself to be snubbed like a regular caterpillar-back to use one of Grant's words for such a character." Another instance wherein Gibbons refused to "push" for a favor at the papal court involved the desired reinstatement of Francis A. MacNutt in his rank as a papal chamberlain. In 1904 Bishop William H. O'Connell of Portland had sought the intervention of Gibbons at Rome that MacNutt might be appointed to the post of *cameriere di numero* which MacNutt desired (101-H, O'Connell to Gibbons, Portland, June 15, 1904). The cardinal at that time was happy to comply and authorized O'Connell to cable the Holy See in his name. He said he knew and esteemed Mr. MacNutt, and he added, "at my request he recd. his present appointment" (AABo, Gibbons to O'Connell, Baltimore, June 17, 1904). Meanwhile, however, MacNutt had fallen into disfavor at Rome and in 1906 the cardinal was advised by Monsignor Kennedy, Rector of the American College, against writing a letter in MacNutt's behalf. Eight years later Gibbons replied to MacNutt's plea for reinstatement that he would be pleased to speak for him if the cardinals in Rome who were said

Among the many bishops who frequently looked to Baltimore in these years for help in various undertakings was Archbishop Riordan of San Francisco. By the time his auxiliary bishop, Denis J. O'Connell, left him for Richmond in January, 1912, Riordan was over seventy years of age and wished to have a coadjutor. Among those whom he first considered was Monsignor Russell, pastor of St. Patrick's Church in Washington, and his inquiry about him to the cardinal brought an enthusiastic answer that he regarded Russell as an ideal man and one eminently fitted for the position.[155] In the meantime, however, Cardinal De Lai informed Riordan that his reasons for a coadjutor were not sufficient, but that he might have another auxiliary bishop. Riordan was disappointed, for he had his heart set on a coadjutor, and for that reason he applied again to Gibbons to make a special plea to De Lai that he be allowed to have Bishop Dennis J. Dougherty of Jaro in the Philippines who had signified his willingness to accept the coadjutorship.[156] There is no record of Gibbons' response to this request, and for the time being Dougherty remained at his post in the Philippines. Two months after his appeal for Dougherty the Archbishop of San Francisco sought the assistance of Gibbons in getting Edward J. Hanna, professor of theology in St. Bernard's Seminary, as auxiliary bishop.[157] The cardinal gladly complied and wrote a very favorable letter to De Lai on the qualifications of Hanna for the office,[158] and toward the end of that year he was appointed. Riordan lived on until December, 1914, and at the time that Hanna acknowledged Gibbons' message of condolence at Riordan's death, he stated that the cardinal had, perhaps, known the late archbishop better than anyone else, and he added, "How often he talked of you, and of the hard days that have gone!"[159] When the *ternae*

---

to have befriended him would recommend to Gibbons that he ask for the favor that MacNutt desired. Insofar as the records show, that was the last that was heard of the matter (103-F, Gibbons to Kennedy, Baltimore, May 6, 1906, copy; 103-H, Kennedy to Gibbons, Rome, June 9, 1906; 110-G, MacNutt to Gibbons, Brixen, Tyrol, October 8, 1914; 110-N, Gibbons to MacNutt, Baltimore, November 9, 1914, copy).

[155] 108-B, Riordan to Gibbons, San Francisco, January 23, 1912; 108-C, Gibbons to Riordan, Baltimore, February 2, 1912, copy.
[156] 108-E, Riordan to Gibbons, San Francisco, April 3, 1912.
[157] 108-E, same to same, San Francisco, June 10, 1912.
[158] 108-E, Gibbons to De Lai, Baltimore, June 24, 1912, copy.
[159] 111-A, Hanna to Gibbons, San Francisco, January 9, 1915.

for San Francisco arrived and Hanna's name was found first on both lists, it gave Gibbons a chance to express his high admiration for the bishop to the apostolic delegate and to make plain his preference that he should receive the see.[160] On June 1 of that year Hanna was appointed third Archbishop of San Francisco.

Although Bishop Dougherty had not been made San Francisco's coadjutor in 1912, his tenure of office in the Philippines was then drawing to a close. In June, 1915, the papal Secretary of State informed Gibbons that he had heard Dougherty's health in the islands was not good and that he wished to return to the United States. He asked, therefore, if the cardinal would see to it that his name be placed on a *terna* for an American diocese.[161] Gibbons assured Gasparri that he would bring the matter to the attention of the metropolitans at their next meeting, and that he would recommend Dougherty for consideration as a candidate.[162] The death of Bishop Charles H. Colton of Buffalo on May 9 had left that important see without an ordinary, and in early December the Bishop of Jaro was transferred to Buffalo. Dougherty had learned of what Gibbons had done and he desired, as he expressed it, "to thank you from my heart for the leading part which I have reason to believe you took in this gracious act of the Holy See. I will never forget your most kind interest in me; for which may Our Lord repay you!"[163]

The cardinal was ready enough to entertain suggestions concerning the promotion of bishops to American sees from a source such as Gasparri, but he was considerably more reserved when they originated in less official circles. That became evident upon the death of Archbishop Edmond F. Prendergast of Philadelphia in February, 1918. Patrick S. McHale, C.M., provincial of the Vincentians, stated that he had been asked by some priests of Philadelphia to say a word in favor of Bishop Dougherty of Buffalo as Prendergast's successor. Considerable support had developed in Philadelphia in favor of the auxiliary bishop, John J. McCort, and there was some feeling on the subject. While McHale had words of praise for McCort, he believed that Dougherty

160 111-H, Gibbons to Bonzano, Baltimore, February 13, 1915, copy. The name of Peter C. Yorke, prominent priest of San Francisco and for some years editor of the *Monitor,* as third on the priests' list, did not meet with Gibbons' favor.
161 112-B, Gasparri to Gibbons, Rome, June 12, 1915.
162 112-D, Gibbons to Gasparri, Baltimore, July 13, 1915, copy in Italian.
163 112-V, Dougherty to Gibbons, Jaro, December 18, 1915.

would add more luster to the see by reason of his greater experience and his pronounced success in governing three other dioceses.[164] The cardinal was aware, of course, of how things stood in Philadelphia, and with the current situation in mind he replied as follows:

> The tribute you pay the Auxiliary of Philadelphia is a just one and most deserved. His zeal and piety are too well known to need any words of commendation from me. As for the other mentioned in your esteemed letter, his work in his very important Diocese makes him fit to adorn any See in this whole country. So that any choice that might be made by the Holy See will but carry on the glorious achievements of the late Archbishop.[165]

It was an interesting example of how Gibbons could combine the amenities of polite intercourse with a completely noncommittal attitude, and upon the appointment of Dougherty to Philadelphia three weeks later McHale doubtless remained none the wiser as to where the cardinal had stood on the question.

The year 1918 took a heavy toll among the close associates of Cardinal Gibbons in the American hierarchy. The death of Prendergast in February was not a severe personal loss to him, for although their relations had been cordial, they had never been intimate friends. But in the deaths of four other bishops that year his grief was deep and real, and their passing seemed to leave him standing almost alone among the generation of prelates with whom his name was linked in the history of the Church. One of these was John S. Foley, Bishop of Detroit, a man whose association with Gibbons extended over a period of more than sixty years since their days together at St. Charles College. Like so many others, Foley had sought in his advanced years the intervention of his friend in Baltimore to have a coadjutor appointed for him, but Rome had not seen fit to grant the request.[166] Foley died on January 5 and his death removed one whose friendship Gibbons had deeply cherished and whose company he had enjoyed more than once on prolonged holidays in Canada and in Europe.

---

[164] 117-F, McHale to Gibbons, Brooklyn, April 3, 1918.

[165] 117-G, Gibbons to McHale, Baltimore, April 9, 1918, copy.

[166] 112-T, Foley to Gibbons, Detroit, December 1, 1915. On the same day Foley's auxiliary bishop, Edward D. Kelly, petitioned Gibbons for the same cause. *Ibid.*

But a prelate who had played at Gibbons' side a much more prominent role in American ecclesiastical life than Foley was John J. Keane. We have already seen how he and the cardinal had worked together on the major issues that had confronted the Church in the last years of the nineteenth century, and how earnestly Gibbons had striven to vindicate the reputation of Keane when it had been attacked in Rome. No one was happier than the cardinal, therefore, when Keane was finally named Archbishop of Dubuque in 1900, and it was with a full heart that he traveled to Dubuque in April, 1901, to confer the pallium on his old friend. Keane fully appreciated all that Gibbons had meant to him, and in his sermon on that occasion he said:

> Well have I experienced his friendship, sincere, unselfish, generous, as true in the darkest days of life as in the brightest; above the wealth of worlds I prize it; and for this latest proof of it he has thanks too deep for words.[167]

At the dinner that followed the Mass the cardinal stated that the elevation of Keane had lengthened his own life, and then alluding to the archbishop's lifelong zeal for total abstinence, he remarked of his appointment as he lifted a glass of water:

> It has cheered my heart, has brought sunshine to me, and to me has been the happiest incident of my life in the last ten or fifteen years, and I propose the health of the Archbishop of Dubuque, in his most cherished beverage.[168]

Eight years later there came a serious break in Keane's health, and when Gibbons learned the news he expressed his sorrow to Archbishop Ireland that so luminous a mind was clouded and that a prelate hardly surpassed for eloquence, zeal, and piety was no longer able to exercise his ministry. "He was," said the cardinal, "one of the most beautiful & disinterested souls I have ever encountered."[169] Unfortunately, Keane never regained his health and early in 1911 he decided to resign his see and to ask Gibbons' permission to take up his residence in Washington with his old classmate, Monsignor James F. Mackin, pastor of St.

---

[167] John J. Toomey and M. C. Sullivan (Eds.), *Souvenir of the Installation and the Investiture with Pallium of Most Rev. John J. Keane, D.D., as Archbishop of Dubuque* (Dubuque, 1901), p. 67.

[168] *Ibid.*, p. 75.

[169] AASP, Gibbons to Ireland, Baltimore, September 13, 1909, copy.

Paul's Church.[170] The cardinal was more than willing that he should spend his last days within his archdiocese, but he first suggested that Rome would probably assent to the appointment of an auxiliary bishop if it were requested. The ailing archbishop was attracted by the idea and asked Gibbons to recommend the matter to the Holy See.[171] The apostolic delegate was agreeable to the proposal, but Rome was unwilling to make the appointment and instead accepted Keane's resignation three months later.[172] Gibbons had not forgotten the archbishop's earlier wish to retire in Washington, and he hastened to assure him of a warm welcome if he should now decide to come. Keane was deeply touched by the offer of hospitality and stated there were no spots nearer and dearer to him than Baltimore and Washington and, he added, "no one in all the world so near to me as your own dear self." But he had now about decided to take quarters at Mercy Hospital in Dubuque and there, as he said, to await the summons home.[173] The summons came seven years later on June 22, 1918, but by that time the cardinal was eighty-four and unable to make the long journey to bury his friend, a final tribute which he would wish to have paid to the memory of one whom he esteemed and loved as he did few other men.

Three months later the cardinal lost another friend with whom he had been on intimate terms for nearly thirty years. Ever since the late 1880's when they had worked and planned together for the university at Washington, Gibbons had retained a warm feeling toward John Farley of New York. At the time that Farley was made a bishop in 1895, he revealed the part that Gibbons had played in that event when he said, "As it was your wise and paternal advice that determined my acceptance of the tender of the Episcopal office, the prospect of the burthens it imposes is brightened by the hope that I may always rely on the same fatherly counselor."[174] In the years that followed that hope was more than fulfilled by the frequent and important questions on

[170] 107-A, Keane to Gibbons, Dubuque, January 11, 1911.
[171] 107-A, same to same, Dubuque, January 12, 1911, two letters.
[172] 107-C, Falconio to Gibbons, Washington, January 14, 1911; Archives of the Archdiocese of Dubuque, Keane's Diocesan Diary, Falconio to Keane, Washington, April 25, 1911, copy.
[173] 107-G, Keane to Gibbons, Dubuque, May 25 [1911]. Keane came to St. Charles College at Catonsville, in April, 1915, where he remained for several months during which he gave weekly conferences to the students.
[174] 94-D-2, Farley to Gibbons, New York, November 28, 1895.

which they co-operated in complete harmony. At the time of the centennial of the establishment of New York as a diocese, Gibbons delivered the sermon at the Mass in St. Patrick's Cathedral on April 28, 1908, and he then paid public tribute to his friend.[175] He rejoiced at the elevation of Farley to the cardinalate three years later, and when they met in Rome in 1914 after the election of Benedict XV he promptly seconded the desire of Cardinal Farley to have Patrick J. Hayes as his auxiliary bishop by recommending his name to the Consistorial Congregation. After the appointment was made, Hayes stated that he would always remember the exceptionally great service and kindness he had done them in Rome in commending to De Lai the presentation of his name.[176] Through the final illness of Farley the Cardinal of Baltimore displayed an interest and sympathy far beyond the ordinary, and through Bishop Hayes and Monsignor Thomas G. Carroll, Farley's secretary, he kept in almost daily touch with New York.[177] He was cheered to learn of the improvement noted in the last week of August, but it did not last and on September 17 death took New York's second cardinal, and in spite of his advanced age, Gibbons made the trip to New York to assist at the requiem for his departed friend.

One of the striking characteristics of Cardinal Gibbons in his relations to his friends which served to deepen their love for him and to quicken their confidence in his guidance, was the loyalty he displayed in their hours of trial. It is easy enough for a man to be pleasant and agreeable with his associates when all goes well with them; it is quite another matter to stand by them when adversity has struck and they have become the victims of attack. Yet this was the unvarying conduct which the cardinal followed when he believed a friend to be the prey of unfairness and misrepresentation of any kind. We have already seen the steadfastness with which he supported Archbishop Keane when the shadows had gathered about him. It was the same with others. After the dismissal of Monsignor O'Connell from the rectorship of the American College in 1895, he grew extremely sensitive and fancied that the cardinal's affection for him had cooled. How

---

[175] New York *Freeman's Journal*, June 20, 1908.

[176] 110-G, Hayes to Gibbons, New York, October 12, 1914.

[177] 118-N, Carroll to Gibbons, Mamaroneck, New York, August 25, 1918. Cf. the writer's article, "Cardinal Gibbons and New York," *Historical Records and Studies*, XXXIX–XL (1952), 5–32.

deeply hurt Gibbons was at this thought was revealed when he told him:

> God alone knows how much I have suffered on account of your sufferings since I went to Rome. You have not been out of my mind for a single day since then. And the event which occurred then — your retirement from the College — has cast a shade over my whole life. You are often even in my dreams. I wake up after enjoying in fancy the pleasure of meeting you again, & of enjoying your company. Even my trip to Santa Fe, with all its distractions, was clouded by the sorrow I felt in your sorrow. And what has made my depression more heavy is the fact that I could not communicate it to any one but Dr. Magnien. After receiving your former letter I have risen from the table without breaking my fast.
>
> There is no anguish keener than that which one feels who is under the imputation (however innocent) of being disloyal to a friend. You were the only friend I ever had in Rome. I have no correspondence with any one there now, except of a purely official nature. You were always a faithful friend to me, & I relied implicitly on your advice.[178]

It would be difficult to imagine a more touching and sincere expression of constancy to a troubled friend than this, and in the years ahead, as we know, O'Connell was to realize the depth of meaning in the cardinal's words.

Another man who had reason to know the quality of Gibbons' loyalty to friends was the Archbishop of St. Paul. Through all the great controversies of the late nineteenth century they had stood shoulder to shoulder, and when Ireland faced one of the major crises of his career in the struggle over the state and the parochial schools, he found no more valiant defender than the Cardinal of Baltimore. In the year after Rome had given a decision in his favor on the schools, Ireland joined twelve other archbishops, fifty bishops, and the immense throng that gathered in Baltimore to honor Gibbons' silver episcopal jubilee on October 18, 1893. In a memorable sermon on that occasion Ireland paid a glowing tribute to his friend during which he said:

> Often have I thanked God that in this latter quarter of the nineteenth century Cardinal Gibbons has been given to us as primate, as leader. Catholic of Catholics, American of Americans, a bishop of

---

178 94-H-1, Gibbons to O'Connell, Baltimore, February 1, 1896, copy.

his age and of his century, he is to America what Leo is to Christendom.[179]

Nor did the succeeding years dim the ardor of love and esteem which Archbishop Ireland had for the cardinal. During the last years of his life he sent greetings to Gibbons in the holiday season, and each message seemed to grow warmer than its predecessor in reminiscing on the loyalty that the cardinal had shown toward him and the providential leadership which he had given to the Church. Needless to say, these testimonies proved gratifying to the old churchman, and at the new year of 1908 he stated that he had, indeed, been loyal to Ireland and had made his cause his own. In doing so he had been impelled by his sense of the justice of that cause, and still more by his personal admiration for the archbishop. He confessed that he had received many a scar in the conflicts and, perhaps, had felt them more keenly than Ireland because he was more sensitive to the sharp stings of the enemy. "But," said Gibbons, "I never faltered & hesitated because I believed your cause was right."[180]

Four years later Ireland sent a particularly ardent greeting at Christmas, in which he stated that the passing years had deepened his conviction that Gibbons was the special gift of Providence to the American Church during a momentous period. To Ireland it would be a sad day when the hand resting on the helm of the ship must relax its hold; he dared not look toward that day with the wonted wisdom vanished and none other to take its place.[181] The archbishop's letter called forth in Gibbons memories of their common struggles over a quarter of a century, and he remarked that he still cherished the hope that he would not quit

---

[179] Ireland, *The Church and Modern Society,* I, 127. The text of the sermon is carried on pp. 105–131. The jubilee had made a happy impression on many (92-N-12, Ireland to Gibbons, New York, October 24, 1893; AASP, Gibbons to Ireland, Baltimore, October 27, 1893, copy). Secretary of State Walter Q. Gresham was one who was quoted as expressing esteem for Gibbons on this occasion. Ireland told the cardinal, "Heretofore, as far as he had observed, the Catholic Church was busied in piling up stumbling blocks on the road which Americans would have to travel over to reach her. Now, this is changed by the conciliatory language & demeanor of Card. Gibbons, & Americans are willing to look the Church in the face & listen to her" (92-Q-2, Ireland to Gibbons, St. Paul, November 1, 1893).

[180] AASP, Gibbons to Ireland, Baltimore, January 2, 1908, copy.

[181] 108-U, Ireland to Gibbons, St. Paul, December 23, 1912.

the busy scenes of this life before Ireland had received the cardinalate which Americans both within and without the Church
believed he richly deserved. "But no new title," he said, "can
add to the esteem & love in which they hold you."[182] Gibbons'
hope that Ireland would be made a cardinal persisted to the end,
and on his visit to Rome for the election of Benedict XV he
made the archbishop the principal subject of an audience he had
of the new Pontiff. He recounted all that he had done for the
Church and, as he said, he took the bull by the horns in expressing the wish that some great recognition would be made of his
eminent services to religion.[183] Ireland was deeply grateful for
this extraordinary favor, but he was not surprised, for, as he said,
he had known Gibbons too long and too well to be surprised at
any act of affectionate kindness that he might perform in his
behalf.[184]

But the red hat for which the cardinal had spoken more than
once at the Holy See never came to St. Paul, and by the time
that Gibbons was approaching his golden jubilee as a bishop
physical enfeeblement had overtaken the sturdy frame of Archbishop Ireland, and he was unequal to repeating his triumph of
twenty-five years before by accepting Gibbons' invitation to
preach the sermon.[185] On the eve of the cardinal's anniversary
day there reached him a final message from his old friend in the
form of a telegram which read, "Mysterious how under the guidance of Providence years respect your steppings."[186] Six weeks
later John Ireland died on September 25. But at the celebration
in Baltimore he was not forgotten, and when Gibbons rose to
speak at the close of the dinner at St. Mary's Seminary, his
thoughts turned to the Northwest. He dwelt on the fact that he
alone was left of all the bishops who had participated in the
plenary council of 1884, and he then stated:

> The last Prelate who has descended below the horizon of the
> tomb was the Venerable Patriarch of the West, the great Apostle
> of temperance, the sturdy Patriot who had endeared himself to the
> American people, without distinction of race or religion, the man

[182] AASP, Gibbons to Ireland, Baltimore, December 25, 1912, *Private,* copy.
[183] *Ibid.,* same to same, Baltimore, September 30, 1914, copy.
[184] 110-G, Ireland to Gibbons, St. Paul, October 5, 1914.
[185] 117-M, Thomas A. Welch [Ireland's secretary] to Gibbons, St. Paul, May 11, 1918.
[186] 118-J, Ireland to Gibbons, St. Paul, August 15, 1918, telegram.

who had contributed perhaps more than any other to demonstrate the harmony that exists between the Constitution of the Church and the Constitution of the United States. Needless to say, I am speaking of John Ireland, the Lion of the fold of Juda.[187]

The celebration of Gibbons' fifty years in the episcopacy signalized as few other events in his long life the unique position he had won in the minds and hearts of the men of his generation both at home and abroad. The day of the anniversary itself, August 16, he observed in a quiet manner at the home of his friend, Martin Maloney, in Spring Lake, New Jersey, where he was the recipient of numerous messages of congratulation.[188] He was consoled, as he said in thanking Bishop Allen, to think that in the burden of his office he was supported by the affection of so many kind friends, and especially by his colleagues in the hierarchy.[189] The date set for the celebration was October 20, and as the day neared more and more congratulations from the highest officials of both Church and State continued to reach the cardinal. Pope Benedict XV told him that he had won the esteem of all Americans in so illustrious a manner that it was hardly surprising that men of every order should now join in paying him honor.[190] The Pontiff later forwarded an ornamental crucifix as a testimony of his affection for Gibbons.[191] President Wilson headed a large group of distinguished citizens in the government and civil life who sent their good wishes, and Bishop William T. Manning of the Protestant Episcopal Church and Rabbi William Rosenau were among those who bespoke the high regard in which Gibbons was held by American religious leaders of other faiths.[192]

---

[187] 119-F, Gibbons' address at jubilee dinner, Baltimore, October 20, 1918.

[188] One of these was a cablegram from Felix Cardinal von Hartmann, Archbishop of Cologne. Since the United States was still at war with Germany, an acknowledgment would have necessitated a license from the War Trade Board to send a communication to an enemy country. Secretary of State Robert Lansing left it to Gibbons' judgment what to do, but in the end the cardinal decided not to acknowledge the greeting (118-N, Lansing to Sigourney W. Fay, Washington, August 29, 1918; 118-P, Fay to Gibbons, Flat Rock Camp, New York, September 5, 1918; 118-Q, Cornelius F. Thomas to Louis R. Stickney, Washington, September 7, 1918).

[189] Archives of the Diocese of Mobile, Gibbons to Allen, Baltimore, August 20, 1918.

[190] AAB, unclassified, Benedict XV to Gibbons, Rome, September 14, 1918.

[191] *Ibid.*, Gasparri to Gibbons, Rome, September 9, 1918.

[192] 119-G, Wilson to Gibbons, Washington, October 21, 1918. An effort to get Wilson to attend the celebration as Taft had done in 1911 was not successful

In fact, so many messages arrived that it must have taxed the cardinal's strength to acknowledge them all. Many of them paid striking tributes to his greatness, but they were so numerous that it would be tedious to relate their contents. Two examples may suffice to illustrate the warmth of their sentiments. John Hays Hammond, the distinguished engineer, told him, "If it were the practice of our Nation to bestow insignia of distinction upon its deserving citizens, you would have high rank among the recipients of the expression of our Nation's esteem and gratitude."[193] And a few days later Henry Noble MacCracken, President of Vassar College, stated, "Upon the roll which history will set up as those whom she delights to honor because they lived American idealism up to the measure of her opportunity, your name, Sir, will surely stand among the very first."[194]

Not only did the first-ranking citizens of his own country seem to vie for the privilege of honoring him, but those of other lands as well testified to the peerless leadership of the cardinal. The English hierarchy sent a delegation headed by Bishop Frederick W. Keating of Northampton and the bishops of France designated Eugène L. Julien, Bishop of Arras, to represent them along with Monsignor Alfred Baudrillart, Rector of the Catholic Institute of Paris, and three other priests. On October 30 the Irish hierarchy, assembled in a general meeting, sent their greetings in a message signed by Cardinal Logue. The jubilarian's youth in their native land was recalled, and regret was expressed that the political crisis through which Ireland was then passing made it necessary for the Irish bishops to remain with their people in this time of danger, and for that reason no delegation could be

---

(LC, Wilson Papers, Oliver P. Baldwin to Joseph P. Tumulty, Baltimore, October 2, 1918). Baldwin was managing editor of the Baltimore *Sun* and said he spoke as an individual and a Protestant. For other messages cf. 119-C, McAdoo to Gibbons, Washington, October 19, 1918; 119-J, Walter George Smith, President of the American Bar Association, to Gibbons, Torresdale, Pennsylvania, October 23, 1918; 119-E, Manning to Gibbons, Camp Upton, New York, October 20, 1918, telegram. In thanking Rosenau the cardinal said, "In these days of trial and distress, it is most comforting to receive so many assurances of affection, especially from those, who like yourself, rejoice in a friendship which has linked us together for many years past" (American Jewish Archives, Gibbons to Rosenau, Baltimore, October 18, 1918, photostat). The writer is indebted to Professor Jacob R. Marcus for kindly volunteering photostats of the Gibbons letters in the archives of which he is director.

[193] 119-K, Hammond to Gibbons, Gloucester, Massachusetts, October 25, 1918.
[194] 119-L, MacCracken to Gibbons, Washington, October 30, 1918.

sent to Baltimore.[195] Cardinal Begin of Quebec extended the greetings of the Canadian hierarchy, and Alphonse A. DeWachter, Auxiliary Bishop of Malines, speaking from London in the name of Cardinal Mercier and the Belgian hierarchy who were not yet free to communicate on account of war conditions, told Gibbons that the whole Catholic world was in admiration of his long and fruitful career, to which was added, "All eyes are turned with deepest respect towards Baltimore the witness of your apostolic labour."[196] The jubilee was widely publicized in the European press, and the Abbé Félix Klein made it the subject of a leading article in *Le Correspondant*.[197] On October 16 Jules Jusserand, Ambassador of France to the United States, extended the congratulations of the French government in which he said:

> The fame and respect which Your Eminence enjoys in your native country are not restricted to her boundaries. The same are felt for you in France, where your great influence, ever exercised in favor of noble causes, and in these latter years in favor of the noblest of all, that of the reign of justice in this world, have won for you the admiration of everyone.[198]

A month later on November 16 the cardinal received from Jusserand the decoration of a commander of the Legion of Honor which France had bestowed upon him. The Italian government, too, instructed its ambassador at Washington to present to Gibbons its sense of high respect and admiration for what were termed, "Your great religious and civil achievements and for your noble work during the difficult period we have just gone through in behalf of the cause of humanity and civilization."[199] Thus did the stream of laudatory messages continue to pour in for a period extending well into the spring of 1919.

The actual date of the celebration in Baltimore found the city and the nation in the grip of the devastating influenza epidemic, and for that reason the festivities as originally planned had to

---

[195] Logue to Gibbons, n.p., October 30, 1918, *Catholic University Bulletin*, XXIV (December, 1918), 161.

[196] 118-V, DeWachter to Gibbons, London, October 7, 1918.

[197] "Le Cardinal Gibbons a l'occasion de ses noces d'or épiscopales," CCLXXIII (October 10, 1918), 1–28.

[198] Jusserand to Gibbons, Washington, October 16, 1918, *Catholic University Bulletin*, XXIV (December, 1918), 160.

[199] 119-S, Vincenzo Macchi di Cellere to Gibbons, Washington, November 28, 1918.

be confined to a Mass in the cathedral and a luncheon that followed at St. Mary's Seminary. However, a postponement was agreed upon and it enabled the cardinal's friends to honor him with more ceremony at a later date, and on February 20, 1919, the full celebration took place in Washington. Sometime before the Pope informed the cardinal of his intention to send a special envoy to this event in order to render more solemn the honors which he would then be paid. For that purpose he designated, as mentioned previously, Archbishop Cerretti, because of the latter's previous residence in the United States where he had won many friends and, too, because the Pontiff knew that Cerretti was especially close to Gibbons.[200] The envoy arrived some weeks in advance, and at a dinner which Gibbons gave in his honor late in January Cerretti delivered to him the special letter of the Pope. The cardinal expressed his gratitude for the message and said that he was doubly touched because it had been placed in his hands by Cerretti, to which he added, "for of all those whom I love in the Eternal City, next to the Holy Father, there is none so dear to me as you, my own dear Monsignor Cerretti."[201]

A few weeks later in the Franciscan Monastery in Washington, Gibbons offered his pontifical Mass of jubilee surrounded by two cardinals, O'Connell and Begin, twelve archbishops, and fifty-eight bishops as well as a large gathering of the clergy and laity. Archbishop Mundelein preached the sermon, and in his response Gibbons recalled a number of events in his life since the Third Plenary Council over which he had presided as apostolic delegate, the youngest bishop in the council. In memory he thanked the bishops of that distant day for not despising his youth, and he then remarked, "If your predecessors in the episcopate were so patient and forbearing to me in my youthful experience, you have always been kind and considerate to me in my declining years."[202] Their kindness on this occasion was accompanied by a large purse which they presented to him at the dinner that followed at the university. The old cardinal later confessed that he had been so taken by surprise at this generous gesture of his fellow bishops that he had forgotten to thank them publicly. He endeavored to make amends, therefore, by writing

---

[200] AAB, unclassified, Benedict XV to Gibbons, Rome, November 18, 1918.

[201] *Ibid.*, unnamed newspaper clipping marked January 22, 1918.

[202] "The Golden Jubilee of Cardinal Gibbons' Episcopal Consecration," *Catholic University Bulletin*, XXV (April, 1919), 203.

Members of the American hierarchy and guests at the celebration on February 20, 1919, of the cardinal's golden jubilee as a bishop. The picture was taken on the steps of Gibbons Hall at the Catholic University of America. Those seated in the front row are, from left to right, Archbishop Cerretti, special envoy of Pope Benedict XV, Cardinal O'Connell of Boston, Cardinal Gibbons, Cardinal Begin of Quebec, and Archbishop Bonzano, Apostolic Delegate to the United States.

to them his gratitude for the gift, but still more, as he said, for their very warm sentiments of esteem and affection.[203]

Cardinal Gibbons lived over two years beyond his golden jubilee as a bishop, and to the end he actively retained his pre-eminence as the leader of the Catholic Church of the United States. From the outset of his episcopal career he had shown the qualities that inspire confidence in others, and in return he had manifested his trust in those who worked with him by delegating to them a share in his great responsibilities. Thus there was forged a bond which linked the cardinal to his fellow bishops and his priest assistants in a way that was calculated to draw them around him almost in the manner of sons about a father. For a period of nearly forty years Gibbons presided at practically all the important meetings of the hierarchy where the issues were discussed and the decisions taken that shaped the course of American Catholic development. He always regarded these meetings with the seriousness that they merited, and one of the features that made them more inviting for the participants was the kindly and gracious reception which their ideas received at his hands. The cardinal realized how much his colleagues counted on his wisdom and tact, and one of the subjects which was on his mind during his last days on earth was the approaching meeting of the university's trustees. He desired very much to go to Washington for that occasion, and he remarked to one of his household, "If I cannot be present at their meetings, at least I will be in my room near my Brothers, so that they can come and consult with me."[204] They had come to this wise little man to consult for nearly half a century, and they had invariably found it rewarding. It was a remarkable testimony to his greatness that the cardinal's leadership of them should have produced not only a profound respect for his judgment, but also a deep and abiding love for the man.

---

[203] Archives of the Diocese of Mobile, Gibbons to Allen, Baltimore, March 5, 1919.

[204] Smith and Fitzpatrick, *Cardinal Gibbons, Churchman and Citizen*, p. 228.

CHAPTER XXIII

Last Years as Archbishop of Baltimore

BALTIMORE . . . remains in my memory as one of the bright-
est and freshest little vignettes in the American sketch book."[1]
Such was the reaction of a foreign visitor to the see city of Cardinal Gibbons in the spring of 1886. It was a judgment that
would have pleased the cardinal, for as the Baltimore *Star* said
of him a quarter century later, "He is a Baltimorean who loves
his city devotedly and intensely."[2] There was never any doubt
about the love which Gibbons had for the city of his birth, and
although by necessity he was absent from home for long periods
of time, he was always happiest when he returned to Baltimore.
For the first twenty years of his administration of the premier
see he had no auxiliary bishop, and thus through the repeated
confirmation tours which he made to all parts of his jurisdiction
he came to know the priests and people very well. While Gibbons
was always attentive to the duties which frequently called him
to minister to his people in the District of Columbia, nowhere in
Washington did he feel the same contentment that he experienced
in the old Baltimore mansion at 408 North Charles Street. He
delighted in the rich historical traditions of certain sections of
the archdiocese, and in the summer of 1888 while confirming in
Charles and St. Mary's Counties he proudly informed Cardinal
Manning of how the people in these rural areas had preserved
the faith planted by the English Catholics 250 years before, and
how he expected before his return home to confirm about 2,500
souls in these agricultural settlements.[3] His numerous trips abroad
and the extended visits he paid to other parts of the United States
in no way lessened, therefore, the love he had for the city and

[1] E. Catherine Bates, *A Year in the Great Republic* (London, 1887), I, 278.
[2] June 6, 1911.
[3] MP, Gibbons to Manning, St. Thomas Manor, Maryland, June 4, 1888.

438

The cardinal ready to confer the rite of confirmation at St. John's Church, Westminster, Maryland. The priest at the right is the pastor, the Reverend Thomas McGuigan.

(Courtesy of the Reverend W. Kailer Dunn)

the State of Maryland which formed the major portion of the archdiocese over which he presided for forty-four years.

James Gibbons was only forty-three when he came to rule the See of Baltimore and by reason of his vigorous young manhood and the relatively simple character of his administrative problems, he found no difficulty during the early years in carrying out the obligations of his office. The area embraced by the archdiocese was less than 7,000 square miles and in 1881 there were around 210,000 Catholics who were cared for by a total of 268 diocesan and regular priests. These priests attended the 168 churches and chapels, and attached to eighty-five of the parishes there were parochial schools with a total enrollment of 14,000 pupils.[4] It was not an insuperable task, therefore, for a bishop to look after the spiritual needs of a jurisdiction of this size. Yet, as we have seen, the passing years brought a tremendous increase of responsibility to Gibbons in ecclesiastical matters of national and international scope, and the added labors gradually took a toll on his health and on the time he might otherwise have given to diocesan business.

For example, in the early summer of 1891 an illness of several weeks forced the cardinal to follow the advice of his doctor to take a rest at Atlantic City, and in the following year a protracted illness gave cause for concern to his many friends and again necessitated enforced absences from home, first at Norfolk and later in Prince Edward Island.[5] But Gibbons was possessed of a substantially sound constitution and endowed with a good deal of resiliency, and after an extended recuperation of this kind he was able to resume his normal work schedule without great effort. What proved to be a more severe handicap in the execution of his tasks as Archbishop of Baltimore, was the almost ceaseless preoccupation of later years with extradiocesan affairs. The number and complexity of these questions often left him only a limited freedom for local concerns, and there were probably times when his subordinates would have wished that their arch-

---

[4] *Sadlier's Catholic Directory . . . 1881* (New York, 1881), p. 71.

[5] Sarah Lee Collection, Gibbons to Miss Rebecca S. Hayward, Baltimore, June 9, 1891; AAC, Gibbons to Elder, Norfolk, June 8, 1892; Sarah Lee Collection, Gibbons to Miss Rebecca S. Hayward, Charlottetown, Prince Edward Island, June 30, 1892.

bishop was not so deeply involved in problems of a broader import to the Church of the nation and of the world.[6]

Among the varied duties that devolved upon Gibbons as archbishop was that of metropolitan of the Province of Baltimore, wherein he was called upon from time to time to lend assistance to his suffragan bishops when they had need of his services. As metropolitan he had the responsibility of presiding at meetings to fill vacancies in the province and of supplying the Roman Curia with information concerning the candidates proposed. When Bishop Becker of Wilmington was transferred to Savannah early in 1886 the metropolitan called a meeting for May 11 at which the bishops of the province drew up a *terna* for the vacant see, and at the same time they unanimously petitioned the Holy See for the appointment of Abbot Leo Haid, O.S.B., of Belmont Abbey to be Vicar Apostolic of North Carolina.[7] Although the name of John S. Foley, pastor of St. Martin's Church in Baltimore, was first on the list for Wilmington, the Roman officials chose the man in second place, Alfred A. Curtis, a convert who had been Gibbons' secretary ever since the latter's advent to Baltimore in 1877. The cardinal consecrated Curtis on November 14, 1886, and on the following Sunday installed him in St. Peter's Cathedral at Wilmington. Meanwhile an interval of two years elapsed before action was taken on North Carolina, but Haid was then elected and he, too, was consecrated by Gibbons.

The long delay in filling the vicariate had been due to the desire of the Holy See that the resignation of John J. Keane as Bishop of Richmond and administrator of North Carolina should first be formally accepted. The negotiations over the new university at Washington, of which Keane was to be the rector, finally advanced to the stage where the public announcement could be made, and with this point settled matters pertaining to the two posts he had vacated could proceed. The consecration of the

---

[6] One of Gibbons' contemporaries, William J. Walsh, Archbishop of Dublin, who was extremely active in Irish national questions was criticized on this score. Early in 1888 Archbishop Tobias Kirby, Rector of the Irish College in Rome, hinted to Walsh to this effect, and Archbishop Ignazio Persico, recently in Ireland on a papal mission, told Manning the same thing in a letter of February 12, 1888, in which he said that it was his own wish and that of a number of the bishops of Ireland that Walsh might be "more attached to his *pastoral* duties." Patrick J. Walsh, *William J. Walsh, Archbishop of Dublin* (Dublin, 1928), pp. 313–314.

[7] Diary, May 25 and 29, 1886, pp. 204–205, 209.

Benedictine bishop on July 1, 1888, drew the suffragans to Baltimore, and on the same day they selected a *terna* for Richmond which consisted of Augustine Van de Vyver, administrator of the vacant see, in first place with Monsignor Denis O'Connell second, and Father James M. Cleary, pastor of St. Mark's Church in Kenosha, Wisconsin, as the third name.[8] As was to be expected, Gibbons expressed a strong preference for O'Connell, an opinion which was shared by Keane.[9] The monsignor was naturally gratified at this latest evidence of the cardinal's favor, but since he felt some doubt about whether or not this was the opportune time for him to relinquish his post as Rector of the American College, he left the entire matter to be decided by Gibbons as he thought best.[10] The cardinal, however, continued in the same mind and two months later he sent off to Cardinal Simeoni another forceful recommendation of O'Connell's candidacy, to which he added a tribute to Van de Vyver's high moral qualities but stated that his foreign birth and training rendered him unfit to preach with eloquence in a diocese where good preaching was a prime necessity among both Catholics and Protestants.[11]

But Gibbons' pleas for his favorite proved to be in vain, for early in the new year Simeoni sent word that he wished O'Connell to remain at the college and, therefore, a new *terna* should be forwarded for Richmond.[12] The new list again put Van de Vyver in first place with George W. Devine, pastor of St. John's Church, Baltimore, as second, and Ignatius F. Horstmann of the Cathedral of SS. Peter and Paul in Philadelphia as third.[13] In sending the second *terna* the cardinal reiterated his objections to Van de Vyver and stated that while Devine was a good pastor he had not, in Gibbons' judgment, the qualities to rule a diocese. For these reasons his choice was Horstmann.[14] Keane, who in the meantime had gone abroad, was concerned over the prolonged vacancy in Richmond but he was opposed to Horstmann. He told O'Connell that he had no doubt the cardinal would be cut

8 84-R-1, Minutes of the Meeting of the Bishops of the Province of Baltimore, Baltimore, July 1, 1888.

9 84-R-3, Keane to Gibbons, Richmond, July 3, 1888.

10 84-V-2, O'Connell to Gibbons, Grottaferrata, August 9, 1888.

11 85-G-6, Gibbons to Simeoni, Baltimore, October 19, 1888, copy in Latin.

12 Diary, January 17, 1889, p. 231.

13 *Ibid.*, February 27, 1889, p. 232.

14 85-S-11, Gibbons to Simeoni, Baltimore, March 8, 1889, copy in Latin,

by his having refused to endorse Horstmann to the Holy See but, he added, "please God, I shall ever try to say & do what I think is right, conte que conte."[15] Whether or not Keane's veto of Horstmann proved decisive at Rome is not known, but in any case, Van de Vyver was finally chosen and Gibbons, accepting with good grace the appointment of the man he had opposed, consecrated his new suffragan in Richmond on October 20, 1889.

In his choice of candidates for other vacancies in the Province of Baltimore the metropolitan was more successful. Upon the promotion of Bishop Kain of Wheeling to St. Louis in 1893, Gibbons and his suffragans discarded the priests' *terna* entirely and placed Patrick J. Donahue, rector of the cathedral in Baltimore, as first on their list, a choice which Rome ratified and the cardinal consecrated Donahue on April 8, 1894.[16] Two years later the names suggested by the consultors of the Diocese of Wilmington were likewise set aside by the bishops when Curtis resigned that see. The unanimous choice of Gibbons and his suffragans for first place in this instance was John J. Monaghan, assistant pastor of St. Patrick's Church in Charleston, who was accepted by Rome and again the metropolitan was the consecrator for Monaghan on May 9, 1897.[17]

With the death in July, 1899, of Bishop Becker the See of Savannah became vacant, and once again the priests' *terna* was rejected as invalid by the bishops because the consultors' term of office had expired and they had not been canonically reappointed. On this occasion Benjamin J. Keiley, vicar-general of the diocese and rector of St. John the Baptist Cathedral in Savannah, was put in first place while Cornelius F. Thomas, rector of the Baltimore cathedral, was second, and J. F. Regis Canevin, pastor of St. Paul's Cathedral in Pittsburgh, was named third. In dispatching the *terna* for Savannah to the Holy See, the car-

---

[15] ADR, Keane to O'Connell, Liverpool, April 27, 1889.

[16] 92-P-4, Gibbons to Ledochowski, Baltimore, October 27, 1893, copy in Latin. The other two names on the Wheeling *terna* had been John J. Monaghan, assistant pastor of St. Patrick's Church, Charleston, and Daniel J. Riordan, pastor of St. Elizabeth's Church in Chicago. Three years before Donahue's consecration Bishop Foley of Detroit was gratified at his appointment as rector of the cathedral in Baltimore. He told Denis O'Connell, "The Card. has made a wise move in transferring Lee to St. Matthew's and making Donahue pastor of the Cathedral . . ." (ADR, Foley to O'Connell, Detroit, October 1, 1891).

[17] 94-Q-10, Minutes of the Meeting of the Bishops of the Province of Baltimore, Baltimore, September 24, 1896.

dinal reminded the Roman officials of the fact that Thomas, the rector of his cathedral, had been put in second place three years before for Wilmington. All that had been said of him at that time, Gibbons declared, was still true, and in the opinion of the cardinal his greater experience now offered a stronger argument for Thomas' fitness for the episcopal office.[18] But when the Holy See came to make its choice many months later Keiley was the man selected, for whom Gibbons was again the consecrator at Richmond on June 3, 1900.

A number of years passed before another suitable opening offered itself for Cardinal Gibbons to secure his friend, Denis O'Connell, as one of his suffragans. But with the death of Bishop Van de Vyver of Richmond on October 16, 1911, a chance to bring his favorite closer to him appeared to be at hand. The cardinal presided at his own residence over the meeting of the Richmond consultors on November 15, and he rejoiced when O'Connell received five of the six votes for first place. A week later the bishops of the province also chose him as first on their *terna,* and at this result Gibbons jubilantly informed his friend that he now had high hopes of success. He had written to Archbishops Farley and O'Connell in the matter, Falconio, the outgoing delegate, was in favor of the appointment, and Archbishop Riordan had likewise spoken of O'Connell for Richmond. "Every circumstance," he said, "is in your favor."[19] Gibbons hastened a warm letter to Cardinal De Lai on the qualifications of O'Connell for the vacant see, in which he summarized the services he had rendered to the American Church as Rector of the University and as Auxiliary Bishop of San Francisco. In conclusion he stated that it would be a great personal consolation to have O'Connell near him in his last years and to have him ruling a diocese for which Gibbons had a special predilection by reason of having governed it himself for five years.[20]

Meanwhile Riordan expressed his regret at the prospect of losing his auxiliary in whom he had found, as he recalled that Gibbons had predicted, a tower of strength and consolation, particularly since the terrible disaster which had overtaken San Francisco in the earthquake and fire of 1906.[21] In this instance

[18] 97-N-5, Gibbons to Ledochowski, Baltimore, August 30, 1899, copy in Latin.
[19] 107-T, Gibbons to O'Connell, Baltimore, November 22, 1911, copy.
[20] 107-V, Gibbons to De Lai, Baltimore, November 28, 1911, copy in Italian.
[21] 107-V, Riordan to Gibbons, San Francisco, November 29, 1911. Riordan

the final decision of Rome was not long delayed, and on January 19, 1912, the cardinal learned through a wire from the Apostolic Delegation that Cardinal Merry del Val had just cabled that he should be informed of O'Connell's appointment to Richmond.[22] There were probably few ceremonies during his many years as metropolitan of the Province of Baltimore that Gibbons performed with a fuller heart than that of installing Denis O'Connell as seventh Bishop of Richmond in St. Peter's Cathedral on the following March 19. In his sermon on that occasion he stated that it was rare, indeed, for any bishop to be chosen for a diocese with so exceptional an approval and concurrence as O'Connell had enjoyed. Addressing the clergy directly, the cardinal said he was persuaded that if they had the selection of their ordinary they would have named O'Connell as their spiritual ruler. "Like the people assembled in the Church of Milan," he continued, "who suddenly cried out: 'Let Ambrose be our Bishop,' you would have exclaimed: 'Let Denis J. O'Connell be placed over us. . . .' " With equal enthusiasm he reviewed the bishop's career in Rome, Washington, and San Francisco, and he mentioned that the new ordinary had now returned to the scenes of his first missionary labors as a priest. In conclusion Gibbons spoke to O'Connell in a personal note when he said:

> And knowing you as I do, I am sure that you will adorn the altar by your faith and piety, and the pulpit by your solid eloquence. And you will adorn the drawing room and the public hall by your varied accomplishments; so that not only will your children be proud of you, but Virginia herself, this grand old State, the Old Dominion, the Mother of Statesmen and Presidents, who has always set her face against the new-fangled political heresies of the day — Virginia, I say, without distinction of faith, will welcome you not only as an enlightened churchman, but also as a patriotic citizen who will take an active interest in the welfare and prosperity of the Commonwealth.
>
> May your reign be prosperous. Prospere, procede et regna.[23]

If Richmond was happy with its new bishop, there was no one

---

repeated these sentiments after the appointment was made (108-B, Riordan to Gibbons, San Francisco, January 23, 1912).

[22] 108-B, Bonaventura Cerretti to Gibbons, Washington, January 19, 1912, telegram.

[23] AAB, unclassified, copy of Gibbons' sermon at Richmond, March 19, 1912.

whose joy was more apparent than the metropolitan who had installed him.

But the choice of candidates for suffragan sees and the consecration and installation of their bishops were not the only functions which Gibbons performed as metropolitan of the Province of Baltimore. In all that concerned their welfare he took a lively interest and endeavored to be of as much assistance as circumstances would permit. A few days after the devastating earthquake which destroyed a large part of Charleston, South Carolina, on the night of August 31, 1886, the cardinal sent a letter of sympathy to Bishop Northrup and stated that something must be done to enable him to repair his damaged churches. "After you have determined on your plan of raising funds," he said, "you may be assured that myself & the diocess will lend you a helping hand."[24] He was as good as his word, and within a month nearly $7,000 was collected in the Archdiocese of Baltimore for the Charleston sufferers. In acknowledging the latest sum received, Monsignor Daniel J. Quigley, the vicar-general, thanked Gibbons for what he termed a splendid token of substantial aid and sympathy.[25]

A year and a half later the cardinal gave his co-operation to a more far-reaching plan which, it was hoped, would strengthen Catholic life in the southern sections of the province. George S. Scott, President of the Richmond and Danville Railroad Company, suggested to Gibbons' friend, Major John D. Keiley, that he present to the bishops the inviting prospect offered by agricultural lands in the southern states for settling Catholic immigrants.[26] Keiley enlisted the cardinal's support for the project and it was agreed that a meeting should be held at Hot Springs, North Carolina. As a consequence, on April 25, 1888, Gibbons, surrounded by Archbishop Elder and the Bishops of Savannah, Wheeling, and Charleston, met with a group of civil and railroad officials which included the Governors of South Carolina, North Carolina, Georgia, and Virginia and on this occasion there was

---

[24] Archives of the Diocese of Charleston, Gibbons to Northrup, Baltimore, September 6, 1886.

[25] 82-A-3, Northrup to Gibbons, Charleston, October 1, 1886; 82-A-5, same to same, Charleston, October 2, 1886; 82-B-5, Quigley to Gibbons, Charleston, October 8, 1886.

[26] 84-B-1, Keiley to Gibbons, New York, January 27, 1888; 84-B-5, Keiley to the Bishops of the South, New York, January 31, 1888, copy.

formed the Southern Immigration Association. In his speech to the convention, Gibbons stated that his purpose in coming to Hot Springs had been to encourage as far as he could the objectives of their meeting. He had traveled, he said, with open eyes over both hemispheres, and as a result of his observations he could say that the United States gave to immigrants advantages which they could obtain nowhere else. He mentioned the rich resources of the region, and he paid tribute to the South's hospitality, something which, as he said, he could attest from personal knowledge for he had lived here and knew it well. But in spite of the promise held out and the rather impressive inauguration of the Southern Immigration Association, it never succeeded in attracting Catholic immigrants in any numbers into the southern dioceses. The reason was the isolationist spirit of the South that cooled any enthusiasm there might have been for welcoming foreigners to the population and, too, the persistence of an unfriendly attitude toward Catholic foreigners in particular.[27]

A further obligation which Gibbons incurred as metropolitan was that of furnishing the Holy See from time to time with his judgments on various questions relating to the Church in the suffragan dioceses. The petition of Bishop Haid to Rome in 1890 that certain counties of North Carolina be given over permanently to the Benedictines was a case in point, and the Prefect of the Propaganda asked the opinion of the metropolitan about it.[28] In reply Gibbons lauded the missionary work accomplished by the monks in North Carolina, but he was opposed to assigning any territory to them on a permanent basis, lest it should later give rise to difficulties such as had occurred elsewhere between the ordinary and religious. However, if Rome should see fit to give over these counties to the Benedictines for a period of forty or fifty years he thought that might be done without injury to the interests of anyone concerned.[29] Some years later the

---

[27] Richmond *Dispatch,* April 26, 1888. The reasons for the failure of the Southern Immigration Association and similar groups are set forth in Rowland T. Berthoff, "Southern Attitudes toward Immigration, 1865–1914," *Journal of Southern History,* XVII (August, 1951), 328–360.

[28] 88-F-1, Simeoni to Gibbons, Rome, December 20, 1890.

[29] 88-G-5, Gibbons to Simeoni, Baltimore, January 8, 1891, copy in Latin. Twenty years later Gibbons and his suffragans petitioned Pius X to erect the Vicariate Apostolic of North Carolina into a diocese with its see at Wilmington (107-G, Gibbons to Pius X, Baltimore, May 31, 1911, copy in Italian). But the

request of Bishop Becker to transfer his residence from Savannah to Atlanta was likewise referred to Gibbons for a judgment,[30] and while the metropolitan was agreeable to the bishop himself moving to Atlanta, he thought it entirely inopportune to change the title of the see itself from Savannah.[31]

He was also consulted on matters of a nature personal to his suffragans. For example, when Bishop Curtis asked to resign the See of Wilmington due to his feeble health and a growing depression over administrative difficulties, Rome made no move until it had learned the opinion of the metropolitan.[32] The cardinal had no hesitancy in recommending that Curtis' resignation be accepted. He said the bishop had mentioned the matter to him several times and his frail health, fear of responsibilities, and ineptitude for administration made it desirable that he be relieved of the burden. Gibbons testified that Curtis was a man of eminent virtue and zeal with a talent for preaching, but it was necessary, he said, to recognize that his lack of administrative ability had contributed to a certain disaffection among the clergy, and that if he remained on his position would probably become more painful and his ministry less fruitful. He would be glad to assure the bishop an honorable position in Baltimore where he was known and esteemed and he would settle upon him an annual pension of $1,000.[33] Some weeks later Leo XIII acted on this advice and after the arrival of Bishop Monaghan in Wilmington in May, 1897, Curtis departed for Baltimore where he took up his residence with the cardinal and served as auxiliary bishop. Upon the death of Monsignor McColgan two years later Gibbons named him his vicar-general, a post he held until his death on July 11, 1908.[34]

Shortly before Curtis left Wilmington the cardinal was approached by Archbishop Martinelli, the apostolic delegate, about a serious complaint he had received concerning one of Gibbons' suffragans. Martinelli had been informed that Becker

---

petition was not granted at this time, and the Diocese of Raleigh was not erected until December 12, 1924.

[30] 94-C-7, Ledochowski to Gibbons, Rome, November 20, 1895.

[31] 94-E-8, Gibbons to Ledochowski, Baltimore, December 13, 1895, copy in Latin.

[32] 94-K-6, Ledochowski to Gibbons, Rome, March 23, 1896.

[33] 94-L-3, Gibbons to Ledochowski, Baltimore, April 12, 1896, copy in French.

[34] Cf. Sisters of the Visitation, *Life and Characteristics of Right Reverend Alfred A. Curtis, D.D., Second Bishop of Wilmington* (New York, 1913).

of Savannah had not had any students studying for the priesthood during his eleven years in the diocese, that there had been
no retreat for the clergy in eight years, and that the number
of priests had declined from twenty-one to eleven since 1886.
The delegate was plainly worried, and he consequently asked
Gibbons to let him know whether conditions in Savannah were
as bad as they had been pictured and, if so, what remedy he
would suggest for their correction.[35] The metropolitan answered
immediately and confirmed the facts on the decline of priests
and the lack of students in the seminary. A few weeks before,
he said, Becker had visited him and at that time he had spoken
of resigning and had inquired if Gibbons would oppose it, to
which the cardinal replied that he would not but would advise
the Holy See to accept the resignation. In conclusion the metropolitan told Martinelli, "I am of opinion that his resignation
would be the best remedy for existing difficulties."[36] As it turned
out Becker did not resign but continued on at Savannah until his
death two and a half years later on July 29, 1899.

Although his obligations as metropolitan of the province consumed a considerable amount of time and effort on the part of
Cardinal Gibbons, the demands made upon him as ordinary of
the Archdiocese of Baltimore were, of course, far more numerous
and exacting. There were constant calls relating to the parishes,
their pastors and people, and in addition the maintenance of
good relations with the many religious communities of men and
women within the archdiocese took a toll on his energies. As he
never embarked upon a serious undertaking of national import
without first consulting his fellow bishops, so in questions of a
parochial character Gibbons sought the advice of his pastors.
When a certain C. F. Fersting of Catonsville observed that the
completion of the steam railroad to that town in 1884 had
brought many additional families into the community, he asked
that a new parish be opened to accommodate them.[37] Gibbons
requested the opinion of the pastor of St. Agnes Church in
Catonsville on the proposal, and when he learned from Father
Elias B. McKenzie that there were only about 600 Catholics
in the whole community and that it could not support two

---

[35] 95-C-9, Martinelli to Gibbons, Washington, January 21, 1897.

[36] 95-D-2, Gibbons to Martinelli, Baltimore, January 22, 1897, *Confidential,*
copy.

[37] 79-R-14, Fersting to Gibbons, Catonsville, September 15, 1885.

parishes, it was the last that was heard of the matter at this time, although five years later St. Mark's Parish was established at Catonsville and St. Agnes then became a mission church.[38]

But at times even the concurrence of the pastor was not enough to bring about the desires of some parishioners. In the late years of the cardinal's life there was an increasing demand from various parish groups for parochial schools but, unfortunately, in a number of cases the money was not always at hand to provide them. Two officers of the St. Vincent de Paul Society of St. Michael's Church at Ridge, Maryland, made a lengthy and earnest appeal with the approval of their pastor in July, 1916, for a parochial school there.[39] Gibbons replied that he had held the conviction for many years that there was need for Catholic schools in the country districts, but there was no fund available from which he could contribute the $1,000 a year which had been suggested. The best that could be hoped for was that he might be able to divert more money from the Negro and Indian mission collection each year toward schools which might be started in these parishes of southern Maryland for the colored.[40] Four years later Michael J. Hogan, S.J., who was in charge of Sacred Heart Church at Mechanicsville, expressed similar concern for the nearly 300 children of school age in his large parish who were without a parochial school.[41] Gibbons told him that sometime before he had been visited by a committee of laymen from Mechanicsville with this in mind, and he agreed that there should be a school; he could only trust that the people would co-operate in the pastor's plan for such and that within a few years the wisdom of Hogan's action would be proved.[42] The suburban sections of the larger cities, too, were feeling the need for schools as, for example, when Matthew F. Halloran of the staff of the United States Civil Service Commission appealed to the cardinal for financial assistance in building a school for St. Jerome's Parish at Hyattsville,[43] a desire that was fulfilled only six years after Gibbons' death.

---

[38] 79-T-10, McKenzie to Gibbons, Catonsville, October 8, 1885.

[39] 113-R, James H. Carroll and Lawrence P. Williams to Gibbons, St. Inigoes, Maryland, July 10, 1916.

[40] 113-S, Gibbons to Carroll and Williams, Baltimore, July 15, 1916, copy.

[41] 126-J, Hogan to Gibbons, Mechanicsville, April 22, 1920.

[42] 126-L, Gibbons to Hogan, Baltimore, April 27, 1920, copy.

[43] 128-C, Halloran to Gibbons, Washington, July 7, 1920.

These facts suggest a definite remissness on the part of the archbishop in furthering this important aspect of diocesan organization and parish life. Although more could doubtless have been done to provide parochial schools through his initiative and insistence — especially in the last years of his life — the matter had not been altogether neglected. In the forty years from 1881 to his death there had been twelve new parish schools opened in the archdiocese and the enrollment had more than doubled during that time to a total of 31,802 pupils by 1921.[44] But all things considered, the progress made in this respect was not what one might have expected, especially in view of the Baltimore synodal legislation on parochial schools of 1886 of which we shall speak later.

One of the gratifying features in the life of any parish is to have its bishop present on occasions of general rejoicing for the pastor and his people. This duty Gibbons fulfilled whenever his busy schedule would permit. Year after year he traversed the archdiocese attending the anniversaries and dedications of churches or the celebrations of special events in the parochial calendar. It would be tedious to recount these numerous ceremonies in any detail but mention may be made of several. On Thanksgiving Day, November 30, 1893, the cardinal laid the cornerstone of the present St. Matthew's Cathedral in Washington and twenty years later in April, 1913, he joined with the pastor, Monsignor Thomas Sim Lee, and his parishioners on the day that the splendid edifice was dedicated.[45] The inauguration of the Pan American Mass at St. Patrick's Church in the capital on Thanksgiving Day, November 25, 1909, likewise drew the cardinal to Washington to add dignity to a celebration which had been initiated by Father Russell, the pastor. On this occasion Gibbons was pleased to meet President Taft and Richard A. Ballinger, Secretary of the Interior, who headed a distinguished group of government and diplomatic officials at the Mass, and at the luncheon which followed he addressed the guests and

---

[44] *Official Catholic Directory . . . 1921* (New York, 1921), p. 27. Five years after Gibbons' death the number of parochial schools in the Archdiocese of Baltimore had increased from ninety-seven to 118 and by 1931 they numbered a total of 140. On this subject cf. Owen B. Corrigan, *The Catholic Schools of the Archdiocese of Baltimore. A Study in Diocesan History* (Baltimore, 1924).

[45] Helene, Estelle, and Imogene Philibert, *Saint Matthew's of Washington, 1840–1940* (Baltimore, 1940), pp. 59–61, 70–71.

Cathedral of the Assumption of the Blessed Virgin Mary, Baltimore.

praised the spirit of brotherhood which the gathering represented. The cardinal traced briefly the Pan American idea, to which James G. Blaine and Elihu Root had contributed so greatly, a tradition which, as he said, had been continued by Secretary of State Philander C. Knox who was a guest at the luncheon.[46] From that time to the end of his life Gibbons always made it a point to be at St. Patrick's for this event, and his last public appearance in Washington was for the Pan American Mass on November 25, 1920, and that afternoon he solemnly blessed the new St. Aloysius School at North Capitol and K Streets.

But his first love among the parishes of the archdiocese was, as one might expect, that of his own Cathedral of the Assumption in Baltimore. In that church he had been baptized in 1834 and from the time he returned in 1857 as a seminarian to live in the city, he had grown to know and to love the old cathedral more than any other church. It was not surprising, therefore, that he should have made careful preparations long in advance to observe its centennial with fitting ceremonies in the spring of 1906. Early in the year he sent out invitations to the American hierarchy in which he urged them to be present, and the warmth of their response must have cheered his heart.[47] On Sunday, April 29, the day of the celebration, the mother cathedral of the United States saw assembled the apostolic delegate, ten arch-bishops, and about fifty bishops to do honor to its chief pastor, his clergy, and his people. Archbishop Ryan preached at the Mass which was offered by Archbishop Farley and in the afternoon Archbishop Glennon was the preacher at the pontifical vespers which were sung by Archbishop Messmer, the cardinal presiding as the ranking dignitary at both services. At the end of the Mass Gibbons spoke to the great throng in the cathedral, and among other things he said, "What Mecca is to the Mohammedan, what the Temple of Jerusalem is to the Jew, what St. Peter's Basilica in Rome is to the faithful of the Church universal, this cathedral is to the American Catholics."[48]

It was an event of which the entire city was proud, and in an editorial on the following day the Baltimore *Sun* struck the

---

[46] Washington *Post,* November 26, 1909.

[47] 103-A, Sebastian G. Messmer to Gibbons, Milwaukee, January 22, 1906; 103-C, William H. O'Connell to Gibbons, Portland, Maine, March 19, 1906.

[48] Baltimore *Sun,* April 30, 1906.

proper note when it stated that the historic events which had happened within the cathedral's walls could be recounted easily enough, but who, it was asked, "can measure the century of faith, inspiration, blessing and consolation that surround it like a halo!" Most of the principal steps in Gibbons' long and eventful career were associated with the cathedral, and a series of ceremonies which he especially cherished in memory was the priestly ordinations which he had performed in its sanctuary. Each year the number of those who received their priesthood at his hands there mounted until by May 25, 1920, the last time he ordained in the cathedral, the total had reached 1,572. It was a service which he likewise performed yearly for the Jesuits, Redemptorists, and other religious orders in his archdiocese, and when the cardinal reached his final ordination on June 29, 1920, with twenty-nine Jesuits in the Dahlgren Chapel of Georgetown University he had attained a total of 2,471 priests ordained which set a record in the American Church that has not since been surpassed.[49]

The relations of the Archbishop of Baltimore with his priests were on the whole of a very easy and friendly character. He observed no formality about appointments to see him, and whenever he was at home they were free to call and to transact business. We have already seen the share which Gibbons took in the advancement of his priests to the episcopacy in cases where he felt they had the proper qualifications, and men like Keane, O'Sullivan, Curtis, and Donahue owed their promotion largely to their archbishop's recommendations. But there were times when a decision of this kind was not easily arrived at on the cardinal's part, and when opposition developed to one of his pastors in a way that added to his burdens. We have spoken elsewhere of the unhappy state of affairs that arose in New Orleans under Archbishop Leray and what a bothersome matter it proved to Gibbons as Rome's official investigator of the trouble.[50] As a consequence of this situation a remedy was sought

---

[49] Diary, September 19, 1905, pp. 307–308. Gibbons calculated the figures in his own hand at this point down to May 25, 1920, when they totaled 2,442. The Georgetown ordination of June, 1920, brought the final figure to 2,471. The nearest approach to Gibbons' record is probably that of John M. McNamara, Auxiliary Bishop of Washington, who by January, 1951, had ordained approximately 1,600 priests.

[50] Cf. I, 181, 192, 232–234, 272–281.

by way of providing Leray with a coadjutor who would have the right of succession.

In the spring of 1887 there entered the discussion from an unknown source the name of Placide L. Chapelle, who since 1882 had been pastor of St. Matthew's Church in Washington. Archbishop Elder of Cincinnati was not well acquainted with Chapelle, and for that reason he inquired about him from several of his fellow priests in the Archdiocese of Baltimore. Edward McColgan, the vicar-general, and Jacob A. Walter, pastor of St. Patrick's in Washington, were both opposed to Chapelle for New Orleans on the score that he lacked firmness and, as Mc-Colgan intimated, that he had a certain deficiency of prudence and learning.[51] But Chapelle found a forceful advocate in Abbé Magnien who, apologizing for his unsolicited opinion, told Elder that he had heard he was seeking information and he thought he ought to know that Chapelle was a most successful pastor, and that whatever trouble there had been at St. Matthew's had arisen from a few meddling and gossiping women.[52] Gibbons, of course, knew better than anyone else outside the Archdiocese of New Orleans how defective in administration the last two French-born archbishops, Perché and Leray, had been, and with that in mind he made it known to Chapelle, himself a native of France, that another Frenchman would hardly be welcome in the southern see. Chapelle was deeply hurt by the cardinal's remark, and on the day of their conversation he wrote him quite frankly that he shuddered to think of how his future life would be embittered by the conviction that Gibbons had excluded him from the candidates for the episcopacy on account of his nationality.[53] There is no record of any reply from the cardinal to the aggrieved pastor, but insofar as New Orleans was concerned at this time the matter ended there, for in August, 1888, the Dutch-born Bishop Janssens of Natchez who had been educated in part at Louvain, received the appointment.

Later, however, it would seem that the cardinal tried to make amends to Chapelle, for at the time that Archbishop Salpointe of Santa Fe was in Rome in February, 1890, seeking to have

---

[51] AAC, McColgan to Elder, Baltimore, April 1, 1887; Walter to Elder, Washington, April 18, 1887, "Confidential."

[52] *Ibid.*, Magnien to Elder, Baltimore, April 11, 1887.

[53] 83-R-3, Chapelle to Gibbons, Washington, November 11, 1887.

Chapelle named as his coadjutor, he informed the pastor of St. Matthew's that he found him to be in good standing at the Holy See owing, as he said, to the repeated recommendations of Gibbons.[54] When the possibility of Santa Fe arose for Chapelle, the cardinal asked the opinion of his consultors who were unanimously in favor of him for the coadjutorship in the Southwest and, knowing Salpointe's wish to have him, Gibbons, therefore, forwarded a recommendation to Cardinal Simeoni in Chapelle's behalf.[55] But in spite of Gibbons' recommendation and of the continuing efforts of Magnien in Baltimore and of Monsignor O'Connell in Rome, the Holy See failed to act.[56] That opposition had arisen in Rome to Chapelle's appointment there was no doubt, although it is impossible to say exactly on what grounds the opposition was based. To O'Connell it was clear that the chief opponent was Camillo Mazzella, the Jesuit cardinal, and he mentioned in passing to Magnien that Archbishop Salpointe was in the midst of a quarrel with the Jesuits. Insofar as Gibbons was concerned, Mazzella was quoted as expressing his fondness for the Cardinal of Baltimore but as adding that Gibbons was easily influenced.[57]

Some months later O'Connell informed Magnien that he had carried Chapelle's case directly to Leo XIII and, without specifying the source of the remark, he quoted to Magnien the following statement, "Card. Gibbons sometimes allows himself to be imposed upon by others."[58] Whether or not the unnamed Roman source had Magnien in mind is not known but, in any case, the Sulpician superior was not daunted, and it was in all likeli-

---

[54] AANO, Salpointe to Chapelle, Rome, February 11, 1890. Gibbons had in the meantime counseled Chapelle to be patient. He told him that only on condition that Salpointe made it plain in Rome that he wanted him as coadjutor would he [Gibbons] give his whole heart to the appointment (AANO, Gibbons to Chapelle, Baltimore, February 28, 1890, *Personal*.

[55] 87-P-3, Gibbons to Simeoni, Baltimore, June 3, 1890, copy in Latin.

[56] AANO, O'Connell to Salpointe, Rome, August 22, 1890; O'Connell to Chapelle, Rome, August 22, 1890; same to same, Rome, October 1, 1890; Magnien to Chapelle, Baltimore, October 9, 1890, *Strictly confidential*. Magnien stated that Gibbons had learned from a letter of O'Connell of September 25 that the appointment was practically assured; but since the cardinal was not free to communicate the official news before the pontifical audience, Magnien enjoined strict secrecy on Chapelle. Gibbons did not know he was writing and, therefore, Chapelle was not to breathe the matter to anyone.

[57] ASMS, O'Connell to Magnien, Rome, December 31, 1890.

[58] *Ibid.*, same to same, Rome, May 2, 1891, *Private*.

hood due to his influence that some weeks later Gibbons dispatched an elaborate defense of Chapelle to the Holy Father. This was by way of reply to a message from the Pope in which he had told the cardinal that he had not seen fit to ratify the choice of Chapelle as Salpointe's coadjutor, since he was of the opinion that a coadjutor to an archbishop should be chosen from among those who were already bishops. Gibbons declared to Leo XIII that he regarded it as an obligation in justice to one of his priests, for whom he had a high esteem and deep affection, to answer the accusations that had been made against him. He concentrated on the charges of lack of learning and prudence, and by way of refutation he detailed the work Chapelle had done as moderator of the archdiocesan theological conferences, as a special lecturer in the university, and the satisfaction he had given both as vice-president of the Bureau of Catholic Indian Missions and as pastor of St. Matthew's. In conclusion he repeated the compulsion of duty which prompted him to inform the Pontiff of Chapelle's reputation as one of his best priests, for, as he said, if the Pope's decision should become known it would place Chapelle in a very painful position.[59] It was surely an extraordinary action to ask the Holy Father to reverse his judgment in a case of this kind but, nonetheless, Gibbons undertook it and succeeded, for on August 21, 1891, Chapelle was at last named as coadjutor of Santa Fe and on the following November 1 the cardinal consecrated him in the cathedral at Baltimore.[60]

The candidacy of another of Gibbons' pastors likewise gave some trouble. Upon Becker's resignation of the See of Wilmington in 1886 the bishops' choice for first place had been Father Foley, pastor of St. Martin's Church in Baltimore. However, as

---

[59] 88-P-9, Gibbons to Leo XIII, Baltimore, May 28, 1891, copy in French. The Pope's letter to Gibbons was dated Rome, April 12, 1891 (88-M-3). Magnien hurried a letter to O'Connell on the day that Gibbons mailed his message to the Pope, and he urged O'Connell at this time to do all in his power to bring about the appointment. He was annoyed that what he termed "party spirit & narrow views & vindictiveness" should have caused Chapelle to be pictured as if he were an unworthy priest. But he concluded, "Happily the decision of the Holy See was not made known & it may be still reversed" (ASMS, Magnien to O'Connell, Baltimore, June 2, 1891, copy).

[60] Referring to this consecration, Bishop Foley expressed his joy to Denis O'Connell that Chapelle had at length reached his goal (ADR, Foley to O'Connell, Detroit, October 1, 1891).

we have seen, it was Curtis, the second name on the *terna,* who had been chosen. A year later Bishop Borgess of Detroit resigned his diocese and Archbishop Elder, metropolitan of the province to which Detroit then belonged, presided at the meeting of the consultors who chose Foley for first place on their list. Anticipating the voting of the bishops of the Province of Cincinnati, Elder asked for Gibbons' opinion on Foley, and recalled that he had spoken to the cardinal sometime before about a fault which he had heard attributed to Foley. Detroit, he said, was a difficult post due in part to the current trouble with a group of Poles and, therefore, Elder felt the bishop would need to be a man who could combine conciliation and firmness in dealing with the problems of the diocese.[61] What reply Gibbons made is unknown but a few weeks later when he learned that Foley had likewise received first place on the bishops' *terna,* he communicated these facts to the Secretary of the Propaganda. The cardinal stated that he was glad to second Foley's name and glad, too, that a chance had arisen to refute the false accusations made against him in Rome the previous year when he had been proposed for Wilmington. After setting down Foley's qualifications in strong terms, he concluded by stating that the appointment ought to be hastened as affairs in the Diocese of Detroit were in a rather bad way and needed someone to take them in hand.[62]

Regardless of that fact, however, Rome was not to be hurried. Almost a year intervened, and that the doubts concerning Foley had not been cleared up at the Holy See, became apparent in early June, 1888, when Simeoni asked for a restatement of Gibbons' views in the case.[63] In reply the cardinal explained that upon hearing a report of Foley's unfitness he had cabled O'Connell to hold up his previous letter to Archbishop Jacobini until he could ascertain the facts. In the meantime he had spoken

[61] 82-S-3, Elder to Gibbons, Cincinnati, June 7, 1887. Gibbons may have felt a certain delicacy about answering Elder's question in a letter. Moreover, since the latter was to be in Baltimore three weeks later, the cardinal may have waited to discuss the matter with him in person. He informed Elder he would be glad to see him on June 27, the day that the archbishop would be passing through the city on his way to Emmitsburg (AAC, Gibbons to Elder, Baltimore, June 20, 1887). The writer is indebted to Father Thomas G. Pater, archivist of the Archdiocese of Cincinnati, for forwarding to him a copy of this letter on March 14, 1951.

[62] 83-B-7, Gibbons to Jacobini, Baltimore, July 11, 1887, copy in Latin.

[63] 84-O-9, Simeoni to Gibbons, Rome, June 9, 1888.

with Monsignor McColgan, his vicar-general, with whom Foley had lived for eight years as an assistant and whose neighbor he had been since he had assumed the pastorate of St. Martin's. McColgan, he said, was a man well known for his priestly character and the monsignor had assured him that he had no doubts about Foley. On the vicar-general's testimony Gibbons felt certain that the charges of unfitness lodged against Foley were untrue and, therefore, he would advise the Holy See to proceed in naming him to Detroit.[64] With this information in their possession the Roman officials felt satisfied, and six weeks later Simeoni informed Gibbons that the appointment had been made, and on November 4 of that year Foley was consecrated by the cardinal as third Bishop of Detroit.

The candidacies of Chapelle and Foley for the episcopal office reveal something of the character of Cardinal Gibbons in dealing with his subordinates and close associates. The first case showed the reluctance which he always displayed to do anything that would hurt another or give offense, and at the same time it served about as clearly as any instance of which there is record to prove the decisive influence which at times the Abbé Magnien exercised in his counsels. In the case of Foley the vindication by so respected a figure as Monsignor McColgan was naturally a powerful factor in removing any doubts that might have lingered in the cardinal's mind concerning the priest's fitness to be a bishop. But apart from McColgan's testimony, Foley had been for years Gibbons' close friend and that fact, too, probably colored his judgment to some extent. As the two cases turned out, the somewhat erratic careers of Chapelle and Foley in their respective spheres, and the traditions that have endured of the inadequacies of their administrations would suggest that, all things considered, it would have been better had Gibbons not exerted himself in their promotion.[65]

---

[64] 84-Q-12, Gibbons to Simeoni, Baltimore, June 30, 1888, copy in French.

[65] There were probably others besides Archbishop Seton who believed that Gibbons had made a mistake in the case of Foley. In the spring of 1905 Seton confided to his diary his wonderment over Gibbons' friendship for Foley (New York Historical Society, Robert Seton Diary, p. 149). It was true that Foley was a traveling companion of the cardinal on a number of occasions, and in August, 1891, the latter spent a week with him in Detroit (ADR, Foley to O'Connell, Detroit, October 1, 1891). There could be no question, therefore, about Gibbons' affection for him.

Needless to say, the relations of Cardinal Gibbons with his pastors were not confined to matters pertaining to their possible advancement to ecclesiastical honors. With a few of these men he had been on terms of intimate friendship even before his own consecration as a bishop. When Monsignor Bernard J. McManus, pastor of St. John's Church in Baltimore, died the terse entry in Gibbons' diary told its own story, "Mgr. McManus," it read, "the dearest friend I have had among the clergy died this morning. Deus det tibi pacem suam, amice cordis mei!"[66] The death of this good priest severed a precious link that had bound the cardinal to the days of his own priestly ministry in the city a quarter of a century before, and he felt the loss keenly. With others the naturally mild-mannered archbishop occasionally found his patience sorely tried, and there were times when he felt compelled to deal resolutely with them. For example, in the spring of 1888 Gibbons had acceded to the wish of John B. Manley, pastor of St. Peter's Church at Hancock, to be transferred to St. Bernard's in Baltimore. In the meantime Manley had spoken with one of the city pastors who informed him that the prospects at St. Bernard's were not good, and with that in mind he asked for another assignment.[67] At this the cardinal was definitely irked. He reminded Manley of their previous understanding, and he stated that on the basis of the

---

[66] Diary, February 28, 1888, p. 222. Some weeks after the death of McManus, the cardinal was asked to intervene with one of his pastors in western Maryland who had incurred the displeasure of Henry G. Davis, ex-United States Senator from West Virginia and a wealthy railroad magnate. Davis complained that Peter R. Weider, pastor of St. Peter's Church at Westernport, Maryland, had taken the parish funds out of the bank at Piedmont, West Virginia, of which Davis was president, and had deposited them in a rival bank. It was also reported that he had influenced some of his parishioners to do likewise. Davis stated that although he was not a Catholic, he had always been friendly to the Church and had made contributions to it. In his mines and on his railroad there were employed from 500 to 600 men of whom a number were Catholics. Therefore, if in the future the priest worked against his interests, Davis thought it fair to ask if the Church could well expect any friendly acts from him. In reply Gibbons was careful not to commit himself beyond saying that he would write to Weider, and that while he would not wish to dictate to the pastor in a matter of this kind, he should like to see him in friendly relations with Davis' bank (Davis Papers, West Virginia University, Letterbook, July 8, 1886–October 24, 1888, p. 537, Davis to Gibbons, n.p., April 2, 1888; Gibbons to Davis, Baltimore, April 3, 1888, copy). The writer is indebted to Harry J. Sievers, S.J., for copies of these letters.
[67] 85-D-1, Manley to Gibbons, Hancock, September 25, 1888.

agreement he had named Father Theodore D. Meade of St. Augustine's Church at Williamsport as Manley's successor at Hancock. Now he learned to his astonishment that Manley did not wish St. Bernard's. He then told the pastor of Hancock:

> Such a sudden change of mind is very annoying to me after having made other arrangements depending upon your transfer, which was made at your own request. You are hereby instructed to remain where you are in Hancock until such time as I can provide another place for you. There is no vacancy in or around Baltimore. You will also please at once notify Fr. Meade to stay where he is.[68]

Two years later Gibbons had agreed to transfer Father Stephen J. Clarke of St. Gabriel's Church at Barton to Frostburg, Maryland, on condition that Clarke should first make arrangements to hold in abeyance any negotiations over the church debt of Barton until a successor to Clarke could be named. Thus when the cardinal received a letter from a lawyer about the debt, he was again very much annoyed. If Clarke could not settle the matter with the lawyer and the Barton congregation, he said, in such a way that he would not be importuned about the debt, he would be obliged to send him back to Barton. "Please inform me at once what can be done in this matter," Gibbons concluded, "& your answer will determine my action."[69] It was apparent from these instances that on occasion he could assume a stern attitude when he felt the circumstances warranted it.

Yet such was not Gibbons' customary manner of dealing with his priests, nor was it in any way congenial to his nature. On the contrary, he usually went out of his way to meet the desires of those who worked under him and when he felt compelled to rebuke them it was done with real reluctance. In the spring of 1894 he had offered the pastorate of Hyattsville to Father John M. Jones, chaplain of Providence Hospital in Washington, partly, it would seem, in the hope of dissuading him from going abroad. Jones, however, was determined to make the trip and he likewise expressed a preference for the pastorate of Govanstown rather than that of Hyattsville. The cardinal took Jones' decision in good part and said that since he was resolved to travel abroad he would give him a letter before he departed and would welcome

---

[68] 85-D-3, Gibbons to Manley, Baltimore, September 26, 1888, copy.
[69] 87-N-8, Gibbons to Clarke, Baltimore, May 31, 1890, copy.

him back when he was disposed to return. "I have been anxious to give you a good place," he said, "and regret that I had promised Govanstown to another priest before you applied."[70] Even with Father Valentine F. Schmitt, pastor of St. Joseph's Church in Washington, who had caused so much ill feeling by his intemperate outbursts from the pulpit and in his correspondence, Gibbons practiced great forbearance. When a new incident of Schmitt's lack of prudence in correspondence arose in May, 1897, and complaint was made to the cardinal, the latter called to his attention the pain he was inflicting by his letters. According to Gibbons, these letters did not at all reflect Schmitt's real character, for he had found him all that could be desired when they conversed together. He then continued:

> But your letters betray a spirit calculated to alienate from you your brother priests. I pray you to meditate on the life of our Lord before committing your hand to paper. I have been always anxious, as you know, to befriend you, but your letters, I grieve to say, have added to my burden & increased my sorrows.
>
> I pray you to read this letter in the spirit of charity which has dictated it.[71]

A reasonable man could scarcely ask for a more conciliatory tone in offering correction to an erring subject.

Not only was Gibbons generally conciliatory toward his pastors, but he showed a similar spirit whenever that was possible in dealing with the laity about parochial affairs. Upon the death of Father John Gloyd of St. Patrick's in Washington in March, 1901, there poured in upon the cardinal a flood of requests from men highly placed in the government — of whom a number acknowledged themselves as non-Catholics — that he name as pastor Dr. Denis J. Stafford who for about seven years had been stationed at St. Patrick's as an assistant.[72] It was the kind of approach that many bishops would have resented; yet there was no trace of resentment on Gibbons' part, and after Stafford had served as administrator of the parish for six months he received the appointment as pastor in late September of that year. St. Patrick's was a parish of first rank in Gibbons'

---

[70] 93-E-6, Gibbons to Jones, Baltimore, April 26, 1894, copy.

[71] 95-P-7, Gibbons to Schmitt, Baltimore, May 14, 1897, copy.

[72] 98-S-2, Thomas Ryan to Gibbons, Washington, April 2, 1901. Box 98 contains at this point several dozen similar requests from Washington laymen.

jurisdiction and the naming of Stafford was all the more unusual in that he had been a priest of the Diocese of Cleveland for the first six years of his ministry, and only in 1891 had he been incardinated into the Archdiocese of Baltimore at the cardinal's invitation. The fact that Stafford enjoyed an excellent reputation as a preacher and lecturer, as well as for high social graces, doubtless played its part in the appointment, along with the fact that the cardinal saw it as an opportunity to give pleasure to the considerable number of government officials who had interested themselves in his promotion. Among the Washington parishes St. Patrick's always held a special place in Gibbons' affection, and it was there that he made his headquarters when he was in the capital. Thus when Stafford died in January, 1908, the cardinal again showed his regard for St. Patrick's and its pastor when he asked the Holy See to name Stafford's successor, William T. Russell, a domestic prelate and a year later recommended him to Archbishop Riordan as coadjutor of San Francisco.[73]

The essential kindliness of the Archbishop of Baltimore to all who lived within his jurisdiction was, perhaps, the principal factor in winning for him the widespread affection and esteem in which he was held. His kindness and sympathy were particularly marked in times of trouble, and his little attentions on such occasions endeared him to countless numbers of his flock. When, for example, Helen McMaster, daughter of the editor of the New York *Freeman's Journal,* took ill in the Carmelite convent in Baltimore the archbishop paid her a visit and, as she related to her father, he told her that she need not think she was going to win her crown so soon and that she would have to work harder for it.[74] Nearly two years later Sister Teresa of Jesus, as she was known in religion, was ready to receive the Carmelite habit, and the archbishop was asked to confer it on her. He informed her father that although he was very busy at the time his regard for both father and daughter,

[73] 107-A, Gibbons to Merry del Val, Baltimore, January 12, 1911, copy in Latin; Gibbons to Vincenzo Vannutelli, Baltimore, January 12, 1911, copy in Latin; 108-C, Gibbons to Riordan, Baltimore, February 2, 1912, copy. For details of Stafford's career cf. the obituary notice in the *Catholic Mirror* of January 4, 1908.

[74] AUND, McMaster Papers, Sister Teresa of Jesus to McMaster, Baltimore, April 17, 1883.

as well as for the pious community of which she was a member, had determined him to accept the invitation.[75] These were courtesies which McMaster and his family probably never forgot. In March of the same year St. Dominic's Church in Washington was largely destroyed by fire. As soon as the news reached Gibbons he made arrangements to pay the Dominican friars a visit of sympathy. The prior, Edward D. Donnelly, O.P., said he could not find words to express their gratitude for his paternal sympathy. "I am sorry that I was not at home when you came," he wrote, "but we shall never forget your kindness & solicitude."[76] Less than two weeks later fire likewise destroyed two of the buildings at St. Joseph's Convent in Emmitsburg, and four days after the fire the community annals noted, "Visit of sympathy from the Archbishop."[77] These were small matters, to be sure, but they left an indelible impression of sympathetic interest and fatherly feeling that in all likelihood endured long after the busy archbishop had forgotten about them.

In regard to the question of nationality among his people the Cardinal of Baltimore never experienced the acute difficulties that some of his fellow bishops had to meet on this score. A large majority of the Catholics in the archdiocese had always been either native-born Americans or English-speaking immigrants. But although Baltimore had not known the tension to which foreign-born immigrants speaking no English had given rise in larger sees like New York and Chicago, the archdiocese had not been entirely free from problems of this kind. An example of such was afforded late in the 1880's when a number of German Catholics in Washington demanded that a legacy left to St. Mary's Parish by the will of Father Mathias L. Alig, who had been pastor from 1846 to his death in 1882, should be used to build a new church.

For over forty years the structure at 5th and G Streets, N.W., had served the German Catholics in the capital, but some of their number were now intent upon a new building. Father Schmitt of St. Joseph's, who was himself of German blood, was strongly opposed to the idea and he outlined his reasons in detail for Gibbons. According to Schmitt, the German Catholics of

---

[75] *Ibid.*, Gibbons to McMaster, Baltimore, January 10, 1885.
[76] 79-G-4, Donnelly to Gibbons, Washington, March 16, 1885.
[77] Archives of St. Joseph's Central House, Emmitsburg, Annals, March 24, 1885.

Washington were not numerous, they were widely scattered over
the city, and whenever they felt the need for sermons or confessions in German they could readily be served at St. Mary's
and St. Joseph's or by Father George Glaab at Immaculate
Conception Church.[78] But less than a year later Glaab was
named pastor of St. Mary's by Gibbons and this young priest
pushed the plan for a new church with great energy. Father
Jacob A. Walter, pastor of St. Patrick's and a consultor of the
archdiocese, was of the same opinion as Schmitt, and after
hearing a report that Gibbons had given his consent to the construction of a new edifice on the site of old St. Mary's, he did
not mince words in remonstrating with his superior. He told
the cardinal:

> It would seem from this that your Washington priests know nothing
> about matters here but that a young inexperienced priest with a
> half dozen obstinate Germans know everything. I am truly sorry that
> you have so poor an opinion of your Washington priests.

Walter ended by saying that he hoped the story was not true,
for if it was he could take no future interest in affairs outside
of his own parish.[79] But despite the opposition of Schmitt and
Walter, the cardinal approved the undertaking and the new St.
Mary's Church was dedicated by Gibbons on June 28, 1891.

A few years later a far more immediate necessity presented
itself in relation to a national group in Washington. Archbishop
Falconio, the apostolic delegate, brought to the attention of
Gibbons the spiritual plight of a large number of Italian immigrants who were engaged in construction work on the new
Union Station, and in expressing his regret that nothing had been
done to provide religious services for these laborers, he stated,
"unless Your Eminence takes urgent measures, many poor souls
will be lost." The delegate offered the assistance of Monsignor
Francesco Marchetti-Salvaggiani, auditor of the Apostolic Dele-

---

[78] 85-K-11, Schmitt to Gibbons, Washington, December 8, 1888. Schmitt's mind
did not change in the matter, and over a year later he repeated the judgment
(87-D-8, Schmitt to Gibbons, Washington, February 12, 1890).

[79] 87-E-5, Walter to Gibbons, Washington, February 17, 1890. Gibbons was
having difficulties elsewhere at this time. A month after Walter's letter was received he told Bishop Keane, "I have many things to annoy me just now,
especially are the Poles giving me trouble" (ACUA, Keane Papers, Gibbons to
Keane, Baltimore, March 28, 1890). For Gibbons' difficulties with a recalcitrant
group of Poles in Baltimore eight years later cf. I, 384.

gation, and of Father Louis R. Stickney, the secretary, to supplement the efforts of the Jesuits at St. Aloysius Church near to the Union Station, if that should prove satisfactory to the cardinal.[80] Gibbons immediately got in touch with Edward X. Fink, S.J., pastor of St. Aloysius, and when the latter hesitated about assigning a priest for sick calls among the Italian work- men unless he had word from his superior, the cardinal then wrote to Thomas J. Gannon, S.J., Fink's provincial, and begged him to instruct the pastor to undertake the work. Delay would be fatal, he said, as proselytizing by the sects had already begun among the Italians and for that reason the Church must act at once.[81]

By this time the German- and Irish-born immigrants of the archdiocese were no longer thought of as separate nationality groups in the same way that they had been in the nineteenth century. When, therefore, in 1912 the Holy See requested of Gibbons a report on the Catholic immigrants living within his jurisdiction, his reply was confined to the Poles, Bohemians, Lithuanians, and Italians. There were, he said, about 20,000 Poles, 8,000 Bohemians, and some 2,500 Lithuanians in the see city, and for these three nationalities separate parishes, parochial schools, and priests of the respective nationalities had been provided. The Poles had five churches with eight priests, the Bohemians two churches with three priests, and the Lithu- anians had one church with a single priest. All three groups were relatively easy to care for since they lived in compact neighborhoods of Baltimore, and they were described by the cardinal as generous in maintaining their churches and schools and faithful to their religion and to their priests.

But with the Italians it was a different matter. In Baltimore they numbered about 2,000 most of whom had come from around Cefalù in Sicily. They did not live close to each other but were scattered over the city, and thus it was difficult to minister to them, although, as Gibbons said, the Pallotine Fathers at St. Leo's Church had shown great zeal in behalf of these immigrants. In the northwestern part of Maryland there was another group of Italians working in the mines who had an Italian priest with them. As for the approximately 2,000 Italians in Washington

[80] 101-D, Falconio to Gibbons, Washington, March 2, 1904.
[81] 101-D, Gibbons to Gannon, Baltimore, March 4, 1904, copy.

they, too, were spread out and were difficult to care for, but Gibbons had asked the Franciscan provincial to appoint one of his Italian-speaking friars from the Franciscan Monastery to look after these immigrants in Washington. Unfortunately, the cardinal concluded, the Italians were generally found to have been very poorly instructed in their religious faith and to be reluctant to contribute to the support of the Church.[82] Insofar as Washington was concerned, the need was partially met late that same year when a chapel was opened for the Italians which eventually became Holy Rosary Church.

As was to be expected, from time to time proposals were made to Cardinal Gibbons about various works in the arch-diocese with some of which he could agree, while in the case of others he felt obliged to withhold his sanction. When a pious woman proposed through Dr. Heuser, editor of the *American Ecclesiastical Review,* that a national shrine to the Sacred Heart be built in Washington along the lines of the famous church on Montmartre in Paris, the cardinal was not in favor of it. Each diocese, he said, had its own needs and some were of a pressing nature, and it was his belief that very few of the hierarchy or laity would be disposed to contribute to a basilica such as had been suggested.[83] Likewise a plan for the St. Vincent de Paul Society of Baltimore, which reached Gibbons some months before the entry of the United States into World War I, must have appeared to him as too ambitious. Robert Biggs, president of the society, proposed to raise $75,000 immediately and enough additional funds to afford the society a working income of $25,000 a year. He cited the difficulties under which the society operated in Baltimore by reason of lack of money, and he stated that as a consequence many important services to the Catholic poor were greatly handicapped.[84]

There is no evidence to show that the proposed drive for funds was sanctioned, but the St. Vincent de Paul Society did establish a central bureau in the city that autumn through which a collection of old clothes and furniture for the poor was con-ducted, and on December 12 the cardinal presided at a meeting where the reports for the year were given on this and other

---

[82] 109-B, Gibbons to De Lai, Baltimore, February 5, 1913, copy in Italian.
[83] ACHSP, Heuser Papers, Gibbons to Heuser, Baltimore, October 9, 1904.
[84] 113-U, Biggs to Gibbons, Baltimore, September 11, 1916.

of the society's activities.[85] That same month Gibbons sponsored a campaign for St. Mary's Industrial School in his see city, and with a view to helping the cause he secured a letter from President Wilson.[86] With the coming of war in the next year and the organization of the National Catholic War Council, the Archbishop of Baltimore, as we have seen, was among the most energetic leaders in promoting the council's far-flung activities. After the N.C.W.C. had determined that the best results could be obtained by setting up local councils on a diocesan and parish basis, Gibbons responded in his own jurisdiction and appointed a large committee who were instructed to co-operate by having the parishes of the archdiocese render all possible aid in making Catholic resources available for the emergency which then confronted the country.[87]

A subject on which Cardinal Gibbons felt compelled more than once to disappoint certain highly placed friends was his refusal to officiate at mixed marriages. In July, 1893, John Lee Carroll, former Governor of Maryland, interceded for a young man whose family was prominent in Washington society in the hope of winning the cardinal to perform the ceremony, and when the latter declined the ex-governor was greatly disappointed.[88] Later in the same year Stephen B. Elkins, who had recently retired as Secretary of War, was informed by Gibbons that he would gladly officiate at his daughter's wedding at St. Patrick's Cathedral in New York, but he made the condition very clear when he said, "It is absolutely necessary for Miss Elkins to become a Catholic before her marriage if she desires to be married in the Cathedral." Marriages between a Catholic and a non-Catholic, he explained, could not be performed in a church, and he added that he had previously been obliged to refuse a similar request from Mrs. William T. Sherman, wife of the general, who had asked the privilege for her daughter's marriage

---

[85] Baltimore *Catholic Review*, December 23, 1916.

[86] 114-H, Wilson to Gibbons, Washington, December 19, 1916. Gibbons was grateful for the President's letter, particularly, as he said, "at this time when so many and difficult problems thrust themselves upon you" (LC, Gibbons to Wilson, Baltimore, December 21, 1916). Ex-President Theodore Roosevelt also sent a letter of greeting to the boys of St. Mary's at the cardinal's request (114-G, Roosevelt to Gibbons, Oyster Bay, New York, December 16, 1916).

[87] 116-C, Gibbons to Owen B. Corrigan, Baltimore, October 19, 1917, copy.

[88] 91-Q-3, Carroll to Gibbons, Bar Harbor, Maine, July 21, 1893.

to a non-Catholic.[89] It was a policy which Gibbons followed to the end of his life, and the invitation of Archbishop Farley in 1909 to officiate at the marriage of the Earl of Granard to Beatrice Mills, daughter of Ogden B. Mills, was courteously declined on the ground of his resolution not to perform mixed marriages either outside or within his jurisdiction.[90]

Such marriages were a subject to which the cardinal had given considerable thought, and in a book which he published in 1908 he stated that they were frequently the occasion for loss of faith on the part of the Catholic party. True, as a result of his personal observations in the Archdiocese of Baltimore, he believed that the Church had gained at least as many as it had lost by reason of marriages of this kind. But this did not mean that Gibbons favored the marriage of Catholics with non-Catholics, for he frankly stated, "My personal experience, however, has little weight when counterbalanced by the overwhelming testimony of missionaries throughout the length and breadth of the land."[91] There was probably more leniency shown toward dispensations for mixed marriages in the Archdiocese of Baltimore under Gibbons than was true in neighboring dioceses. But the cardinal realized in his practical way the inevitability of such marriages and that all the canonical law of the Church could not prevent them. In this, as in so many other occasions of his life, Gibbons was eminent for the good order with which he captained the rear-guard action rather than imposing hierarchical authority on society.

We have already spoken of the relations of Gibbons to the Negro Catholics of his jurisdiction and to the Mill Hill Fathers who had originally come to Baltimore in 1871 from England to work among the American colored population.[92] Ultimately the connection with the English superiors of this society was found

---

[89] Elkins Papers, West Virginia University, Gibbons to Elkins, Baltimore, October 28, 1893. The writer is indebted to Harry J. Sievers, S.J., for copies of the Gibbons letters in this collection.

[90] AANY, Gibbons to Farley, Baltimore, January 2, 1909.

[91] *Discourses and Sermons for Every Sunday and the Principal Festivals of the Year* (Baltimore, 1908), p. 86. A tradition has persisted that Gibbons favored mixed marriages. An example of it can be found in the brief article of Thomas A. Fox, C.S.P., "Some Reflections on the Leakage," *American Ecclesiastical Review,* C (March, 1939), 243, where the statement is made, *"Pace* the departed spirit of Cardinal Gibbons, mixed marriages are a very hemmorhage of leakage."

[92] Cf. I, 247; II, 396–404.

unsatisfactory by some of the American members of the congregation, and they, therefore, expressed the desire to establish a separate group in the United States. When Herbert Vaughan, then Bishop of Salford and superior-general of Mill Hill, learned of this he outlined to Gibbons the procedure that should be followed if the change was to be effected. Insofar as the Archbishop of Baltimore was concerned, it amounted to an expression of his willingness to sponsor the American group and to supervise the establishment of the society under his auspices.[93] Gibbons discussed the question with those who were interested in the separation, and he then told Vaughan that after serious reflection he was willing to accept these priests with the explicit understanding that they should confine themselves as heretofore to the evangelization of the Negroes.[94] As a consequence in May, 1893, he witnessed the fulfillment of the conditions laid down by the English superior and the formal establishment of an independent American branch of the Society of St. Joseph in his see city with John R. Slattery and four other priests composing the first band.[95] Having known the missionary labors of these men for the Negro Catholics over a period of more than two decades, Gibbons was glad to have their headquarters within his jurisdiction and to act as their canonical superior from this time until his death twenty-eight years later.

With the other religious orders and congregations in the Archdiocese of Baltimore the cardinal likewise maintained the friendliest relations. In the autumn of 1883 Robert Fulton, S.J., provincial of the Jesuits' Maryland-New York province, made what he called "the exceedingly bold request" of Gibbons that he be permitted to give the retreat for the archdiocesan clergy.[96] The archbishop was agreeable to the proposal, and in the last week of August, 1884, Fulton preached the retreat at St. Mary's

---

[93] 88-L-5, Vaughan to Gibbons, Manchester, March 24, 1891.

[94] 89-L-6, Vaughan to the Mill Hill Fathers in the United States, Mill Hill, England, January 28, 1892, printed circular; 89-T-13, Gibbons to Vaughan, Baltimore, April 14, 1892, copy.

[95] *Society of Saint Joseph of the Sacred Heart, 1893–1943* (Baltimore, 1943), p. 12. On December 8, 1893, Gibbons solemnly blessed the new St. Joseph's Seminary in Baltimore. From the date of their separation from England to January 1, 1943, the Josephites received 32,703 Negro converts into the Church in their various parishes and missions in the United States and baptized a total of 72,992 souls among the colored. *Op. cit.,* p. 31.

[96] 77-K-10, Fulton to Gibbons, New York, October 27, 1883.

Seminary for Gibbons and his priests. The Archbishop of Baltimore was proud to have the Jesuit scholasticate at Woodstock
College located in his jurisdiction, and he took pride, too, in
the learned publications of its faculty. When Aloysius Sabetti,
S.J., published his *Compendium theologiae moralis* and sent him
a copy, he complimented the author and spoke of it as a fitting
companion to the works of Sabetti's colleagues, Camillo Mazzella
and Emilio de Augustinis, and he hoped it would reflect an
honor equal to the works of these professors upon Woodstock
College.[97] It was a distinct advantage to Gibbons to have these
theologians close at hand for consultation, and between the
Jesuits at Woodstock and the Sulpicians at St. Mary's he was
more than ordinarily well served in this regard. When, for
example, he received an inquiry from a doctor in Georgia concerning the morality of a craniotomy operation, the cardinal
turned in full confidence to Sabetti and asked him to compose a
reply in his name and then to send him the letter and he
would sign it and forward it to the doctor.[98]

That Cardinal Gibbons set a high value on the work which
the Jesuits were doing in the archdiocese and was willing to
go far toward expressing that conviction, was made clear by
an incident which happened in 1888. In the previous year St.
Joseph's Parish in Washington had been relinquished by the
Jesuits who had been in charge since its opening in 1871. The
pastorate was then assumed by the rather eccentric Valentine
F. Schmitt, of whom mention has already been made. Schmitt
maintained that he had found evidence of maladministration on
the part of his predecessor, and he spoke so openly about the
matter that offense was naturally taken by the Jesuits. Fulton,
the provincial, complained to the cardinal and the latter reprimanded Schmitt, obliged him to write a letter expressing his
regret for his unjust and uncharitable remarks, and to promise
not to repeat the offense.[99] While the provincial was gratified at
this action, he further sought a written statement from Gibbons
which, as he said, could be used if occasion should arise to
silence the detractors of the Society of Jesus.[100] Gibbons accom-

---

[97] AWC, Gibbons to Sabetti, Baltimore, October 25, 1884.
[98] *Ibid.*, same to same, Baltimore, September 14, 1886.
[99] *Ibid.*, Gibbons to Fulton, Baltimore, April 20, 1888.
[100] 84-K-5, Fulton to Gibbons, Baltimore, May 8, 1888.

modated with a statement testifying to the satisfaction which he had always experienced with the financial integrity and personal zeal and piety of John P. M. Schleuter, S.J., Schmitt's immediate predecessor as pastor of St. Joseph's, and he closed by saying, "My only object in recording this judgment is to offer some vicarious atonement for injurious and uncharitable words which, I am told, have been spoken against this most worthy priest and which have caused me much pain."[101] He had done all that he could to quiet the storm between Schmitt and the Jesuits but his efforts were not rewarded with complete success, for three years later the cardinal was again found apologizing to the provincial for Schmitt's renewed disparagement of the Jesuit administration at St. Joseph's.[102]

The two most important Jesuit institutions in the Archdiocese of Baltimore were Georgetown University and Woodstock College. At the time that Georgetown, the oldest Catholic college in the United States, celebrated its centennial in February, 1889, the cardinal was present and celebrated the pontifical Mass on February 20 and two days later he shared the place of honor with President Cleveland at the academic convocation where he made an address. Tribute was paid by Gibbons to the founding fathers of the Republic and to their contemporary, Archbishop John Carroll, who had founded Georgetown, and he likened the Jesuit teachers at the college to soldiers of the Cross who were enlarging the bounds of the great republic of letters and religion. In conclusion he remarked, "May those who, in the long years to come, will gather together to celebrate the next Centennial be able to record a success as consoling as that which we commemorate to-day."[103] The place that Georgetown's sister institution at Woodstock held in the cardinal's regard was brought out in 1907 when he learned from Joseph F. Hanselman, S.J., the provincial, that the general of the Jesuits had ordered the scholasticate removed to New York. Hanselman assured Gibbons that his friendship of years for the society made them all the more loath to separate themselves from the congenial atmosphere

---

[101] 84-K-9, Gibbons to Fulton, Baltimore, May 12, 1888, copy.

[102] AWC, Gibbons to Thomas J. Campbell, S.J., Baltimore, October 16, 1891.

[103] John Gilmary Shea, *Memorial of the First Centenary of Georgetown College, D.C., comprising a History of Georgetown University* (Washington, 1891), p. 421. The text of Gibbons' address may be found on pp. 418–421.

of Maryland, and he added that this had been made known in Rome; yet the general had insisted upon the change.[104]

The cardinal was distressed at this news and he determined upon an effort to prevent the move. With an appeal to history, he recalled for Franz X. Wernz, S.J., the general, that from the beginning of Maryland as a colony the Jesuits had been there, that their name was intimately linked up with the Church in this region, and that the society had given the first two archbishops to the See of Baltimore. But of late years, he said, the name of the province had been changed from Maryland to New York-Maryland, the novitiate had been taken from Frederick to New York, and now it was proposed to remove the scholasticate. Woodstock had a suitable climate, good land, and a quiet atmosphere, he contended, while New York held all the dangers of a great city. He did not presume to dictate to the Jesuits, but he would have the general know that in begging him to reconsider his decision he spoke from the deep love he had always felt for the Society of Jesus and, too, as the successor of that great son of St. Ignatius, John Carroll.[105] Wernz replied the following month with elaborate reasons why he could not comply with Gibbons' request,[106] and property was actually purchased in Yonkers, New York, for the scholasticate. But in the end it was not found suitable for the purpose and to the cardinal's joy Woodstock College remained in the location where it had been founded in 1869.

Of all the religious communities in the archdiocese, however, the Sulpicians were nearest to the cardinal's heart. It was quite natural that this should be so, for it was under their direction that he had pursued his priestly studies for six years, and from 1877 to his death it was the Sulpicians who were Gibbons' confessors and among his most intimate advisers. The celebration of the centennial of St. Mary's Seminary on October 28, 1891, gave him an opportunity to declare his esteem for the

[104] 104-K, Hanselman to Gibbons, New York, August 27, 1907.

[105] 104-Q, Gibbons to Wernz, Baltimore, December 8, 1907, copy in Italian. The cardinal likewise asked Monsignor O'Connell, Rector of the Catholic University of America, to write the Jesuit general (ADR, Gibbons to O'Connell, Baltimore, December 19, 1907).

[106] 104-Q, Wernz to Gibbons, Rome, January 14, 1908. In a letter of March 11, 1951, to the writer Edward A. Ryan, S.J., of Woodstock College kindly supplied additional data on the projected move from Woodstock.

Society of St. Sulpice, and on the day of jubilee he presided at the pontifical Mass which was offered in the cathedral by Bishop Patrick T. O'Reilly of Springfield where a distinguished gathering of the alumni heard their former teachers extolled in the sermon of John J. Kain, Bishop of Wheeling. At the dinner which followed in the seminary the cardinal spoke, and among other things he said:

> I have been acquainted with the Sulpician fathers for nearly forty years. I have observed them closely, I have studied their character and spirit, and I solemnly declare that the more I have seen them the more I have admired and loved them.[107]

It was a sentiment which he had expressed more than once both publicly and privately, and the following summer when one of his clerical students, Francis W. Kunkel who had just graduated from St. Charles College, asked the cardinal's permission to become a Sulpician the sentiment was repeated. Gibbons stated that although he had hoped to see young Kunkel as a priest on the missions, he felt that he would be doing more important work in educating students for the ministry. Kunkel's request to join the Sulpicians had come, he said, as a surprise, but it had also brought a satisfaction, for as the cardinal remarked, "I love those men to whom the Church of America and especially the diocese of Baltimore is so much indebted."[108]

Everyone who knew Gibbons realized that he loved the Sulpicians, but it was known, too, that even among them there was a special place in his affections reserved for Alphonse L. Magnien. In 1878, the year after Gibbons had returned to Baltimore as archbishop, Magnien had been named as the sixth Sulpician superior in the United States, a post which he was to occupy for nearly a quarter of a century. In the next year Magnien was made a member of the archbishop's council, and as time passed Gibbons came to rely more and more upon this wise French priest for counsel and advice. The place that Magnien occupied in the life of the Archbishop of Baltimore was recognized by others, and there were times when recourse was had to the Sulpician superior to elicit favorable action from

---

[107] *Church News* (Washington), November 1, 1891.

[108] Gibbons to Kunkel, Baltimore, July 2, 1892, copy. The copy of this letter was kindly furnished to the writer by the late Francis W. Kunkel, S.S., of St. Mary's Seminary, Roland Park, Baltimore.

the cardinal. For example, Father Cornelius F. Thomas, pastor of Sacred Heart Church at Mount Washington, was one who sought the services of Magnien in a minor matter which he wished to have brought to the attention of his ordinary. It happened that Gibbons had sent a certain layman to reside temporarily in the parish house at Mount Washington, and he had stated at the time that he would compensate the pastor for the man's board and room. Three months passed and up to that time no compensation had been received. Although Thomas did not wish it known that he had written, yet he wanted to have the situation clarified, for, as he told Magnien, "the Cardinal forgets and if not reminded, Mr. W. might be here for a century, & I would have to stand all expenses."[109] It was an amusing instance of the confidence which others had in Magnien's ability to get things done.

Any untoward event in Magnien's life was certain to upset Gibbons and when the abbé became critically ill while giving a retreat in St. Louis in the summer of 1897, the cardinal anticipated news of his dear friend with real anxiety, and he was delighted to learn that an operation had been deemed unnecessary.[110] Magnien's condition improved to the extent that he was able to make a trip to France that autumn in the hope of regaining his health. He remained abroad until the following spring, and in announcing a reception in honor of his return the Baltimore *Sun* of May 25, 1898, spoke of him as one of the best known clergymen in the country, and it did not fail to note that he was a close friend of Cardinal Gibbons. Despite the sojourn in France, however, there was never a complete recovery from the illness which had overtaken Abbé Magnien in 1897 and at length in the summer of 1902 Father Jules Lebas, S.S., the superior-general, informed the cardinal that Magnien's protracted illness had become a source of worry to the society, and for that reason it had been decided that for

---

[109] ASMS, Thomas to Magnien, Mount Washington, June 2, 1890. The confidential position which Magnien held with Gibbons was illustrated, too, by such things as the former writing out the appointment of John Gloyd as pastor of St. Patrick's Church in Washington in his own hand, and Gibbons affixing his signature to the copy (93-G-1, Gibbons to Gloyd, Baltimore, May 1, 1894, copy).

[110] ASMS, Gibbons to Edward R. Dyer, S.S., Brooklyn, July 5, 1897. On Magnien cf. Charles G. Herbermann, *The Sulpicians in the United States* (New York, 1916), pp. 312–337.

the good of all concerned he should be replaced in office by Edward R. Dyer, S.S., superior of St. Joseph's Seminary in New York.[111] It was a decision which Gibbons doubtless received with a sad heart; yet all were agreed that something had to be done and Magnien's confrère, the distinguished theologian, Adolphe A. Tanquerey, S.S., who had been teaching at St. Mary's since 1887, told the cardinal from Paris that he had likewise advised the superior-general to make the change.[112]

The heart disease from which Magnien was suffering gradually grew worse and on December 21, 1902, death took the abbé at the age of sixty-five. The cardinal insisted upon celebrating the requiem in the cathedral two days later and giving the absolution for his departed friend. Early in the new year a volume in memory of Magnien was published, and to it Gibbons contributed a preface in which he described all that the abbé had meant to him. He said that their association over twenty-five years had given him the highest esteem for Magnien's learning and upright character. Through the years the Sulpician superior had been in the habit of furnishing to Gibbons estimates of the intellectual and moral qualities of his newly ordained priests, and the cardinal had found that the subsequent lives of these men had verified the abbé's forecasts. He acknowledged that he had frequently employed him in correspondence of a confidential nature, and he spoke of the marked facility, precision, and elegance with which Magnien could write letters in Latin, French, and English. The cardinal also alluded to the abbé's genial disposition, and he recalled how often he had been lifted in spirits as he heard his cheering voice enter his room where he always gave his counsel with great candor and frankness. There were three conspicuous sentiments which Gibbons had observed in Magnien, namely, his love for the Sulpicians, his love of France, and his loyalty to the United States; for, as the cardinal remarked, in all the time that he had served as superior he had never allowed nationalism to show itself in the seminary over which he ruled. Gibbons then concluded:

---

[111] 99-W-3, Lebas to Gibbons, Issy près Paris, August 16, 1902.

[112] 99-W-4, Tanquerey to Gibbons, Issy près Paris, August 17, 1902. Tanquerey expressed regret at leaving the United States where he had spent fifteen happy years, but he stated that he wished to remain in France to finish his book on moral theology on which he was then engaged.

I had been so much accustomed to consult the Venerable Abbé on important questions, and to lean upon him in every emergency, that his death is a rude shock to me, and I feel as if I had lost a right arm. He was indeed *dimidium animae meae*. . . . My chief consolation in my bereavement is found in the consciousness that his brethren inherit his virtues, and will perpetuate the good work which he had prosecuted for the glory of God, the service of his church, and the welfare of our beloved country.[113]

There could be no doubt about the loss which Gibbons suffered in Magnien's death. A few years later there occurred an incident in which the cardinal's mind must have turned back to Magnien, for it was the kind of case wherein he would have instinctively sought his counsel. During the excitement attendant upon the modernist movement a question was raised temporarily about the doctrinal soundness of a number of men who upon investigation were found to be perfectly orthodox. For example, in March, 1910, Cardinal Merry del Val informed the Apostolic Delegate to the United States that both the *Civiltà Cattolica* and the *Osservatore Romano* had recently criticized severely the errors contained in the French translation of Henry N. Oxenham's book, *The Catholic Doctrine of the Atonement*. The volume had originally appeared in 1865 and had gone through several English editions, and it had been translated into French by Joseph Bruneau, S.S., one of the professors of theology in St. Mary's Seminary in Baltimore. The papal Secretary of State directed that Gibbons should be informed of the matter, and that the latter should make inquiries about the manner of Bruneau's teaching and writing.[114] In reply the cardinal confessed that he had not known of the book's existence until Falconio's letter had called it to his attention, but he had instructed Bruneau to prepare a statement on the matter which Gibbons would transmit to the Holy See.[115]

Within a few days Father Bruneau submitted a detailed account of the circumstances of his translation of the Oxenham volume which, he said, had appeared in 1908 with the *imprimatur* of the Archbishop of Paris. He explained that Oxenham was a convert and he admitted that, perhaps, too much stress had

---

[113] *Very Rev. A. L. Magnien. A Memorial* (Baltimore, 1903), p. 8.
[114] 106-C, Falconio to Gibbons, Washington, March 8, 1910.
[115] 106-C, Gibbons to Falconio, Baltimore, March 9, 1910, copy.

been laid by the author on the Franciscan theory about the final motive of the Incarnation. However, Catholic reviewers in both French and English journals were quoted in praise of the work, and Bruneau believed that the translation had been worth while. Oxenham had stated that if anything in his book should lessen reverence for Christ or His atoning love, he would wish that it had been blotted out ere it were written. Bruneau now made Oxenham's words his own, and he concluded by saying that he submitted himself unreservedly to the judgment of the Holy Father and by expressing his regret if there had been anything which had displeased the Pope in his endeavor.[116] In forwarding the statement of Bruneau to Merry del Val, the cardinal remarked that the incident had proved very painful to him and to the Sulpicians who since their advent to Baltimore at the end of the eighteenth century had always been conspicuous for piety, orthodoxy, and devotion to the Holy See.[117]

At the time of Gibbons' golden jubilee as a bishop eight years later the Sulpicians held a reception in his honor at St. Mary's Seminary. Among those who delivered addresses of congratulation to the cardinal at that ceremony was the same Father Bruneau who had meanwhile been entirely cleared in the misunderstanding of 1910, and who now spoke in the role of his responsible office as superior of the seminary's department of philosophy. Wendell S. Reilly, S.S., professor of Scripture, also made an address in which he told Gibbons that unconsciously, he believed, the cardinal had wielded an influence over the institution in the sense that the seminarians had been given to understand that he — who best corresponded to their ideal of a priest — believed in the Sulpician system, made their superior his trusted adviser, and was a personal friend to every professor in the house.[118] The guest of honor was touched by these tributes, and when he rose to reply he stated:

> I solemnly declare with the true sense of the responsibility of my word that Almighty God in His power, mercy and guidance has never conferred a greater blessing on the Church in America than when He inspired Bishop Carroll to invite the Sulpicians of France

---

[116] 106-C, Bruneau to Gibbons, Baltimore, March 13, 1910.

[117] 106-C, Gibbons to Merry del Val, Baltimore, March 15, 1910, copy.

[118] "Reception to Cardinal Gibbons at St. Mary's Seminary, Baltimore," *Catholic University Bulletin,* XXIV (December, 1918), 147.

to come to America. . . . The coming of these men has been a singular benediction to the country. . . . When I look back to the days I spent in the seminary under their guidance and influence, though I may have forgotten much they taught me, I shall never forget what is imprinted on my heart and memory and deepest affection, the lives they led.[119]

No one who heard Cardinal Gibbons on this occasion would have attributed his words to anything but the outpouring of a grateful heart for what the Society of St. Sulpice had meant to him through the more than sixty years since he had first made the acquaintance of the Sulpician Fathers at old St. Charles in 1855.

We have already noted the cordial relations which obtained between the Archbishop of Baltimore and Mount Saint Mary's College at Emmitsburg during the early years of his administration.[120] The regard which Gibbons had for this institution was testified by the fact that when his brother and sister in New Orleans were ready to send their sons away to school, they were directed to the old college in Emmitsburg. The cardinal took a close interest in the boys' progress and at the approach of Christmas in 1885 he instructed Father Edward P. Allen, the president, to see that they were sent to Baltimore for the holidays.[121] In the final year of James G. Swarbrick, the son of the cardinal's sister Bridget, Gibbons requested Allen to give him a private room for the second semester since, as he said, he now had more serious duties to perform and he would thus be enabled to prepare his studies with more attention.[122] When he learned that Charles Semmes, another New Orleans youth at Emmitsburg in whom he took an interest, had contracted a habit of smoking cigarettes, he exacted a promise of young Semmes to give them up. But since the cardinal believed it would be dangerous for him to stop smoking all at once, he told Father Allen, "I would therefore request you to allow him the use of some ordinary cigars till the habit is broken."[123] The cardinal's brother, John T. Gibbons, appreciated the concern which his

---

[119] *Ibid.*, p. 150.
[120] Cf. I, 166, 178, 182–184, 247.
[121] AMSMC, Gibbons to Allen, Baltimore, December 16, 1885.
[122] *Ibid.*, same to same, Baltimore, February 1, 1889.
[123] *Ibid.*, same to same, Baltimore, February 26, 1891.

distinguished relative showed for these young men so far from home, and when his own son James took ill at Mount Saint Mary's he instructed the president that if it should prove necessary, the lad was to be sent to his uncle in Baltimore where he was assured he would have the services of a first-class physician.[124] Young Gibbons recovered from his illness at this time, but four years after his graduation from the college in Emmitsburg he met an accidental death. The cardinal, with whom his nephew had frequently spent holidays while at school, was deeply grieved, and in thanking Archbishop Corrigan for his words of condolence, he stated that they would afford balm to a heart weighed down with sorrow and with sympathy for the loved ones in New Orleans who were crushed by the blow. "He was a youth," said Gibbons, "loved & even revered by his professors & those that knew him."[125]

To the end of his life the cardinal continued to be a strong support to the administrators of Mount Saint Mary's. His assistance was especially appreciated in the dark days after the financial crisis of 1881, and when Allen was able to submit a much more encouraging report of the finances early in 1888 Gibbons told the president that it had proved a great satisfaction to him. This gratifying situation was attributed to God's help and to Allen's wise administration, and as an earnest of his abiding interest in the college he promised to make every endeavor to be present again for the commencement at the end of the year.[126] Allen, to be sure, was not unmindful of what the cardinal's support had meant to the institution during the time of its great trial. For that reason when Gibbons appealed to him as a special favor to make a place on the faculty for Giuseppe Ferrata, an Italian musician who had been recommended by his friend, Eduardo Soderini, former Roman correspondent of the *Catholic Mirror*, the presi-

[124] *Ibid.*, John T. Gibbons to Allen, New Orleans, September 21, 1892. The cardinal had some students preparing for the priesthood at Mount Saint Mary's, and when Allen warned him about one candidate who was not thought worthy to continue Gibbons was grateful. He said, "I commend your vigilance in this matter. If the conduct of aspirants for the ministry had been more closely observed in time, the Church would have been spared many scandals" (*ibid.*, Gibbons to Allen, Baltimore, March 10, 1893).

[125] AANY, Gibbons to Corrigan, Baltimore, January 4, 1901. A brief item on the death of young Gibbons was carried by the New York *Tribune*, January 3, 1901.

[126] AMSMC, Gibbons to Allen, Baltimore, February 9, 1888.

dent stretched a point to do so.[127] It was a courtesy which was deeply appreciated by the young man's uncle, Archbishop Domenico Ferrata, Secretary of the Congregation for Extraordinary Ecclesiastical Affairs;[128] and upon the appointment of Ferrata by Leo XIII as nuncio to France in the following summer, the cardinal reminded Allen that if ever he or any of his professors were to visit Paris they would find a valuable friend in the nuncio.[129]

At the time that President Allen was named fifth Bishop of Mobile early in 1897 the cardinal wrote to congratulate him. In reply the bishop-elect stated that through the nearly thirteen years since he had left his native Massachusetts to work in the Archdiocese of Baltimore, the unfailing kindness and good will of Gibbons had sustained and encouraged him to persevere in his difficult task. "It was only when you spoke and told me not to refuse the burden," said Allen, "that I could bring myself to accept the Presidency of the College." Meanwhile Gibbons had shown him so many marks of esteem and had done so much to make his administration successful that, as he said, wherever he was he would always be grateful to him.[130] On the following May 16 the cardinal consecrated the thirteenth president of Mount Saint Mary's College in his cathedral, and through the years ahead the two men continued their cordial friendship. Gibbons was equally thoughtful of Allen's successors at Emmitsburg and in 1910 it was at his request that Pope Pius X made President Denis J. Flynn a domestic prelate.[131]

Four months before he died the cardinal performed one of his final acts of kindness for the college when he lent the prestige of his name to an appeal for funds which was to be conducted in New York. The request had been made by Monsignor Bernard J. Bradley, president at the time, and by William D. Guthrie who had been appointed to head the drive.[132] In his response Gibbons adduced his official connection as president of the coun-

---

[127] *Ibid.,* Gibbons to Allen, Baltimore, November 12, 1890.

[128] 88-E-12, Ferrata to Gibbons, Rome, December 19, 1890.

[129] AMSMC, Gibbons to Allen, Baltimore, July 28, 1891. Ferrata taught music at the college from November, 1890, to June, 1893, and married the daughter of Ernest Lagarde, professor of English literature. Cf. Meline and McSweeny, *The Story of the Mountain,* II, 234, 243.

[130] 95-D-1, Allen to Gibbons, Emmitsburg, January 22, 1897.

[131] Diary, October 6, 1910, p. 320.

[132] 130-L, Bradley to Gibbons, Emmitsburg, November 15, 1920.

cil of the college as one reason why the institution was particularly dear to him. But, indeed, he added, it should be dear to every American Catholic who was familiar with its splendid history of more than a century. In his opinion it had been well named the "Mother of Bishops," a designation which must seem peculiarly appropriate to New Yorkers, to whom the college had given that fine succession of prelates — John Dubois, John Hughes, John McCloskey, Michael Corrigan, and John Loughlin, first Bishop of Brooklyn. A century before Mount Saint Mary's was sending its graduates to all parts of the United States to help in spreading the gospel of Christ and, said Gibbons, as the second oldest Catholic college in the land with the second oldest theological seminary, it had not only been the mother of bishops but, through its sons, the mother of Catholic colleges as well. The cardinal was happy, therefore, to bespeak the needs of Mount Saint Mary's in the hope that its friends would be generous.[133] The contribution of Gibbons to the institution was summarized by the historians of the college ten years before his death when they wrote:

> We have seen in these pages how he exerted himself to help us in distress, but when the College was once more in smooth waters he showed his appreciation of its system and its Faculty by sending us his three nephews one after the other, by visiting us frequently both officially and otherwise, and showing professors as well as boys by words and acts how much he enjoyed a visit to the Mountain.[134]

Among the decrees passed by the plenary council over which Gibbons presided in 1884, were certain ones which specified in more detail the regulations that should govern the diocesan curia. After the council's legislation had received the formal approval of the Holy See in the fall of 1885, the Archbishop of Baltimore decided upon holding a synod in order to bring local practice into conformity with the conciliar enactments. It was his intention to schedule the synod for the same week as the annual retreat. Having a high respect for both the preaching ability and the legal knowledge of Bishop Gilmour of Cleveland, he invited him to preach the retreat, anticipating, perhaps, that at the same time he might avail himself of Gilmour's advice for the synod. He

---

[133] 130-L, Gibbons to Guthrie, Baltimore, November 15, 1920, copy.
[134] Meline-McSweeny, *op. cit.*, II, 221.

had learned, he said, of the success which had attended the retreats preached elsewhere by Gilmour, and he thus hoped that he would consent to render the same service for the priests of his archdiocese.[135] Gilmour accepted the assignment and at the close of the retreat the cardinal recorded in his diary the satisfaction he felt with the manner in which it had been conducted.[136] A month before the date of these events Gibbons turned, as he so often did on questions of canon law, to Archbishop Corrigan for some counsel. He was inclined, he said, to make his vicar-general a consultor, but before taking action he wanted to have Corrigan's opinion about the propriety of doing so.[137] Corrigan conceded that there was reason for numbering the vicar-general among the consultors, but he added that the bishops of New York had not done so pending a reply to an inquiry on the point which had been made of the Holy See. The matter was settled as far as Gibbons was concerned when the archbishop sent word a week or so later that Monsignor O'Connell had cabled to the effect that vicars-general were not to be named as consultors, although members of religious orders might be appointed if the ordinary so desired.[138] With this authoritative answer at hand, the name of Monsignor McColgan was omitted from those who were named in the synod to compose the board of consultors.

The ninth synod of the Archdiocese of Baltimore was held at St. Mary's Seminary on September 24, 1886, with 115 priests in attendance. The decrees of the plenary council were formally promulgated and regulations were outlined covering the functions of the various diocesan officials, the rights and duties of the parochial clergy, the administration of the sacraments, infractions of discipline, and instructions for the proper celebration of divine services in the churches. Under the heading of parish schools, it was stated that since the welfare of both the Church and State was dependent upon the religious instruction of youth, it was prescribed that every church that did not have a parish school attached to it should erect one without delay unless for grave reasons a postponement should be allowed.[139] As a conse-

---

135 ADC, Gibbons to Gilmour, Baltimore, February 10, 1886.

136 Diary, September 20, 1886, p. 209.

137 AANY, Gibbons to Corrigan, Baltimore, August 22, 1886.

138 81-S-10, Corrigan to Gibbons, Troy, New York, August 28, 1886; 81-U-8, Corrigan to Gibbons, New York, September 9, 1886.

139 *Synodus diocesana Baltimorensis nona* . . . (Baltimore, 1905), pp. 37-38.

quence of the synod, the council of the archbishop was replaced by a board of seven consultors, and for the first time examiners were appointed for the clergy and for teachers, with ten examiners named for the English-speaking schools and three examiners for the German parochial schools.[140] Regulations were likewise laid down for securing titles to ecclesiastical property according to the rules of both canon and civil law.[141] However, these regulations were not sufficiently enforced to prevent a complaint four years later from Martin F. Morris, prominent Catholic lawyer in Washington, concerning the defective titles in church properties with which he was acquainted and which he felt should be remedied.[142] That the role played by the consultors in diocesan affairs was watched in Rome, was clear from the fact that after Gibbons had established St. Benedict's Parish in Baltimore in 1893 with the Benedictines in charge, he was asked by Cardinal Ledochowski if he had first sought the opinion of his consultors. The cardinal was able to assure the Prefect of Propaganda that the question of giving the parish to religious had first been submitted to the consultors for their opinion before arrangements with the Benedictines were completed.[143]

During the years that Bishop Curtis was a member of the cardinal's household he was able to lend assistance in performing various episcopal functions, but after Curtis' death in July, 1908, Gibbons felt the need of help in filling the many calls of this kind that were made upon him. With this in mind, he asked the Holy See for an auxiliary bishop, a request which was readily granted, and on January 10, 1909, he consecrated Owen B. Corrigan, pastor of St. Gregory's Church in Baltimore, who for the remainder of the cardinal's life relieved him of a portion of his burden. But an auxiliary bishop had no rights of succession to the see, and as Gibbons grew older it was entirely natural that speculation should arise from time to time regarding the succession to Baltimore when the cardinal should die. The very close friendship of Gibbons with Denis O'Connell prompted many to believe that the latter might be chosen as coadjutor with the right of succession, and the New York *Tribune* as early as July 12,

[140] *Ibid.*, pp. 14–19; *Hoffmann's Catholic Directory . . . 1887* (Milwaukee, 1887), p. 36.

[141] *Ibid.*, pp. 69–70.

[142] 87-H-2, Morris to Gibbons, Washington, April 4, 1890.

[143] Diary, July 26, 1893, p. 267.

1905, had spoken of O'Connell as having at least "a fighting chance" of obtaining the coadjutorship. With the announcement in December, 1907, of O'Connell's having been made a titular bishop the rumor revived and several of his friends expressed the hope that it might prove true.[144]

But these rumors had no basis in fact, and a year later O'Connell completed his term as rector of the university and departed for San Francisco where he became Archbishop Riordan's auxiliary. Riordan, as we have seen, had begun about this time to think in terms of a coadjutor with the right of succession, but he revealed nothing of his plans for the future to O'Connell. The latter was hopeful that he might be considered for the office, and he had been led to believe that others, too, thought that he should be named. As time passed and nothing was said to him by Riordan, he grew perplexed about whether or not he should mention the subject directly to him. With this in mind, he turned to Gibbons for advice. The cardinal's reply left no room for doubt about his own plans for the succession at Baltimore. He strongly advised O'Connell not to press Riordan for an answer since, as he said, he felt sure that the archbishop intended to ask for him, that the public expected it, and that he believed he enjoyed the confidence of the clergy of San Francisco and of the bishops of the province. When the time came Gibbons would exert all his influence in that direction and he looked forward, he said, to the fulfillment of O'Connell's reasonable desires with as much assurance as he did to the next House of Representatives being controlled by a Democratic speaker. For all these reasons, the bishop should be patient and wait. The cardinal then declared his mind on the succession to the premier see. He said:

> As for my own domestic arrangements, I have made up my mind for a considerable time to be contented with my auxiliary and to have no coadjutor. Things move peacefully and satisfactorily, and my few remaining years I place in the hands of a loving Providence.[145]

If O'Connell had been encouraged by the rumors and the wishful thinking of some of his friends to entertain hopes of succeeding

---

[144] Barry, *The Catholic University of America. The Rectorship of Denis J. O'Connell,* pp. 241–242.

[145] 99-H-6, Gibbons to O'Connell, Baltimore, December 17, 1911, copy. The copy is incorrectly dated "1901."

the cardinal as Archbishop of Baltimore, they were now effectively dissipated upon the receipt of this declaration.

Yet Gibbons could hardly have been unaware of the talk about his successor. By the spring of 1912 he was nearing his seventy-eighth birthday, and that serious concern was felt about the matter was made obvious to him when his auxiliary bishop and nine of his consultors and irremovable rectors presented him with a formal request that he take steps to insure a successor of his own choice by asking for a coadjutor. The petitioners stated that they had so long enjoyed the happiness and peace of his fatherly administration that, in view of what had taken place in other American dioceses, they could not regard the future without serious apprehension. While they prayed and had every reason to expect that the cardinal would be with them for many years, yet he could not but realize that the archdiocese must some day suffer its greatest loss, a loss which would be aggravated a hundredfold if they were totally unprepared for it. For that reason they humbly begged Gibbons to mitigate the sorrow of the future by preserving them from the evils of a vacant see, by taking action now while he was in perfect health and in a position to have his wishes favorably considered by Rome. The cardinal was reminded of the fact that the evils incident to a vacancy in any diocese would be greatly increased in the case of the premier see, because of its proximity to the seat of government, to the Apostolic Delegation, and to the Catholic University of America. A position such as that of Archbishop of Baltimore, it was said, would be considered a point of vantage by anyone whose ambition showed little regard for propriety, for therein he could locate an incumbent who would be subservient to his wishes and further his schemes. "Though we can scarcely bring ourselves to believe," they continued, "that this would be attempted in your lifetime, still it is not inconceivable that such might be the case." Therefore, it was proposed that Gibbons should select three names to be presented to the Holy See and they, the consultors and irremovable rectors, would pledge themselves to vote officially for the three persons whom he would propose to them. In an effort to assure the cardinal of the spirit which motivated their suggestion, the petitioners stated:

We should be pained beyond expression if our action should give rise in your mind to a doubt of our affectionate loyalty to Your Eminence. Our action is prompted by no disaffection towards your benevolent administration either in the past or in the present. We desire no change. Should you in your wisdom and generosity accede to our wishes, we beg that all jurisdiction and authority be retained absolutely by Your Eminence, and that the Coadjutor be given a vacant parish or provided with a residence at the Seminary.[146]

In view of the statement which Gibbons had made to O'Connell five months before on the same subject, it was not surprising that this petition should have met with no success.

As Archbishop of Baltimore the cardinal had the duty of promoting collections for special causes which were ordered by the Holy See, of contributing his share to the Peter's Pence, and of reporting at regular intervals to Rome on the spiritual and temporal conditions in his jurisdiction. In the fall of 1885, for example, he made an appeal to his people in behalf of the missions of the Near East in response to Leo XIII's request, and as a result he was able some months later to forward approximately $4,000 to the Pope for this worthy cause.[147] The amounts of the archdiocesan collections for Peter's Pence varied from year to year with $8,000 in 1893, around $3,000 for 1896, and $2,500 two years later.[148] After a more concerted effort for this collection was urged by the apostolic delegate throughout the American dioceses, the premier see made a better showing and in 1913 the sum amounted to $10,000.[149] The reports which Gibbons submitted on the state of religion in the archdiocese covered all phases of the Church's work, and in setting forth the progress which had been made the cardinal gave generous credit to his priests for what had been accomplished, a fact which more than once drew favorable comment from the officials of the Propaganda.[150]

---

[146] ASMS, Corrigan, et al. to Gibbons, Baltimore, April 20, 1912, copy.

[147] Diary, November 12, 1885, p. 192; March 29, 1886, p. 198. The sum sent was in terms of 20,550 French francs.

[148] Diary, March 7, 1893, p. 265; November 19, 1896, p. 280 (15,000 francs); July 15, 1898, p. 287.

[149] 109-E, Bonzano to Gibbons, Washington, May 31, 1913.

[150] 80-L-9, Simeoni to Gibbons, Rome, February 17, 1886; 94-H-6, Ledochowski to Gibbons, Rome, February 12, 1896.

If the Cardinal of Baltimore declined to be moved by the rumors and the appeal for a coadjutor to succeed him, there were rumors of another kind concerning the disposition of his archdiocese which disturbed him profoundly. He was a man who ordinarily discounted rumors, but by the winter of 1913–1914 the reports had grown so persistent that the Holy See intended to divide the Archdiocese of Baltimore and erect a new see at Washington that the old cardinal determined upon strong measures to prevent the realization of such a possibility. Showing the seriousness with which he viewed these stories, he decided upon a trip to Rome to lay directly before the Holy Father his protest against an eventuality of this kind. Late in February, therefore, he informed Cardinal Merry del Val of his intention to sail from New York on the following May 5, and without disclosing the purpose of his visit, he confined himself to saying that in consideration of his advanced age it might be the last time he would have the privilege of paying his respects to the Pontiff to whom he felt bound by so many ties of duty and affection.[151]

During the spring of 1914 the cardinal consulted with several of his intimate advisers, and before his departure there had been prepared a lengthy statement of the case against the separation of Washington from Baltimore which was embodied in a letter to Pope Pius X, with an even more detailed account for Cardinal De Lai, Secretary of the Consistorial Congregation. The Holy Father was informed that for the previous six years rumors had been reaching Gibbons from various members of the hierarchy and others that a separation was contemplated, and that out of their love and veneration for the See of Baltimore many bishops looked upon this proposal with disfavor and had urged him to make known to the Pontiff certain grave reasons why it should not be carried out. Insofar as Washington was concerned, the Catholics there numbered only about 60,000 and were divided between twenty-one parishes in the city proper and three other parishes in the suburban areas. They had neither the numbers nor the resources to support a bishop, and by reason of the heavy debts on some of these parishes they were compelled to have

---

[151] 109-Q, Gibbons to Merry del Val, Baltimore, February 28, 1914, copy. In an interview of July 16, 1947, with Monsignor Louis R. Stickney who accompanied Gibbons to Rome on this occasion, the writer was told that the trip was made expressly with a view of preventing the reported separation of Washington from Baltimore.

recourse to Baltimore to meet their obligations. Moreover, it would be difficult to recruit a proper clergy for so small a territory, and as it was, Gibbons did not find it easy to supply enough priests in spite of his well-established seminary. As for Baltimore, such a separation would lessen the prestige of the premier see which, in comparison to other American dioceses like New York, Chicago, Boston, and Philadelphia, was very small. A further consideration was the fact that the Archbishop of Baltimore was by appointment of the Holy See *ex officio* Chancellor of the Catholic University of America and many inconveniences would arise were the University to be separated from the chancellor's ecclesiastical jurisdiction. The faithful of the Archdiocese of Baltimore had, it was said, contributed more in proportion to their numbers than any other diocese in the country to the university's financial support, and if the proposed action were to take place it would be only natural that the clergy and laity of Baltimore would take less interest in the university, and would feel aggrieved that they had been separated from an institution which they had supported so loyally. "In the interest of truth," said Gibbons, "I must say that when the University went through its most critical period, were it not for myself and the Clergy of Baltimore, it would have ceased to exist."

At this point the cardinal remarked that while reports of the separation had been current for some time, only recently had it been mentioned that the Apostolic Delegate to the United States had been suggested as the ordinary of the proposed see. Besides the reasons already adduced against the separation, there were, in Gibbons' mind, even more cogent reasons why the delegate should not be named bishop of the national capital. Non-Catholic Americans already regarded the residence of the delegate in Washington with suspicion and distrust, and such an appointment would be certain to heighten their suspicions, and to afford them an opportunity for further emphasizing the traditional theme that American Catholics were ruled by a foreign power. The delegate would receive no more honor in Washington as ordinary than he received in his present capacity, and in addition to this, a succession of ordinaries in the national capital of a different nationality would arouse a bitter prejudice even among the better and well-intentioned non-Catholics. Not only would the delegate thus become the target for anti-Catholic hatred, but it was feared that he would soon be isolated in several ways to the detriment of his higher office as the representative of the Holy See. The cardinal was persuaded of the truth and force of the foregoing considerations, and for that reason he felt the matter should be brought to the knowledge of the Holy Father and a request be made of His Holiness that some step be taken which would put an end to the disturbing rumors. As for himself, Gibbons remarked that his life was now far advanced and he prayed, therefore, that his declining years might not be clouded by the humiliation of a dismemberment of his archdiocese. "The Holy See could not in a more acceptable manner crown my earthly career," he said, "than by sparing me this tribulation which would bring me with sorrow to my grave." With assurances of his steadfast loyalty to the Holy See and his veneration for the person of Pius X, the cardinal closed his appeal with the prayer that the Pontiff might live on for years for the glory of God and the welfare of the Church.[152]

The document addressed to De Lai followed the same general lines as the one to the Pope, although in the letter to De Lai there was a more confident tone that the rumored separation would be unthinkable in Gibbons' lifetime, and thus he was speaking for the future of his archdiocese and for the future of religion in the United States. Even were he to remain silent, he said, the merits of the case would be made known by others, and the wise judgment of the Holy See would prevent it taking place after his death. "But the mere possibility of such an action," he declared, "gives me no rest until I deliver my soul, before I die, of the thoughts that are pressing upon it." To De Lai it was stated that the one argument advanced for making Washington a see which had any weight with judicious men was that of honoring the national capital. The cardinal agreed that there was an element of truth in the idea that the capital of the country should not be under the jurisdiction of another city. But the proper solution to that problem was, as he said, the one suggested to him by Archbishop Bonzano, the apostolic delegate, namely, that the name of Washington be joined to that of Baltimore in the title of the see. This Gibbons thought would be

---

[152] AAB, unclassified, Gibbons to Pius X, Baltimore, May 1, 1914, copies in both Italian and English. In June, 1943, the writer spoke of this document to John F. Fenlon, S.S., provincial of the Sulpicians in the United States, and he replied, "I wrote every word of it."

Cardinal Gibbons ready to land at New York on July 13, 1914, after a trip to Europe. Surrounding the cardinal, from left to right, are Father Louis R. Stickney, his chancellor, Bishop Shahan, Rector of the Catholic University of America, the captain of the *Berlin*, Bishop O'Connell of Richmond, and Father Philip J. O'Donnell, pastor of St. James Church, Boston.

peculiarly fitting as it would link the most venerable name in American Catholic history with one of the proudest names in the history of the nation. In fact, such a union of the two names would be a source of pride to the Catholics of both cities. In closing Gibbons reiterated his belief that the proposed separation would not take place in his lifetime, but indicating that he still entertained some doubt, he added, "If I thought there was any real danger of its accomplishment, I would protest against it with all the earnestness and energy of my soul until my last breath." The cardinal hoped that De Lai would agree with his views, that he might depart from Rome with the consoling assurance that Baltimore and Washington would remain as they were, and finally that the Holy Father would seal their union by joining their names together in the title of the venerable see over which he had presided for thirty-seven years.[153] Gibbons' protest against the dismemberment of his see proved effective at this time and, in fact, a quarter of a century elapsed before the names of the two cities were joined in a dual jurisdiction under a single ordinary on July 22, 1939, and not until November 27, 1947, was a complete separation effected when the two archdioceses were given their own archbishops.

During his years as Archbishop of Baltimore the principal concern of the cardinal was, of course, for the progress of religion in his see, yet he took a lively interest in the affairs of both the State of Maryland and of his home city in the sense that he was always an alert citizen. This fact was appreciated by those in authority, and on the occasion of Gibbons' silver jubilee as a bishop Governor Frank Brown made known that he would be present for the celebration not only, as he said, for the purpose of witnessing the ceremonies, but also to show by his presence the high esteem in which he held the cardinal in common with all the people of Maryland.[154] Some years later another Governor of Maryland, John Walter Smith, told Gibbons he was glad to act upon his recommendation in appointing one of the police commissioners of Baltimore, since it was his desire to give him some substantial evidence of his kindly feelings.[155] We have noted

---

[153] 109-W, Gibbons to De Lai, Baltimore, May 1, 1914, copy.

[154] 92-B-5, Brown to Gibbons, Annapolis, October 13, 1893.

[155] 98-D-2, Smith to Gibbons, Annapolis, April 2, 1900. Gibbons' requests for appointments of this kind were not, however, always successful. Two weeks before Smith declined to appoint a certain Eugene Grannan as police justice

many examples of the care which the Archbishop of Baltimore took to lend his support to worthy civic enterprises and to associate his name and that of the Church with any cause which he felt would serve the public interest. But his spirit of co-operation in these matters did not permit him to approve what he believed to be a falsification of Maryland's history.

When it was proposed, therefore, in 1910 to erect a monument to commemorate Maryland's act of religious toleration of 1649, the Cardinal of Baltimore insisted first upon putting straight the facts of colonial Maryland's religious history. In a plan submitted for his judgment he detected that the act of 1649 and the establishment of religious liberty in America were viewed as co-incidental, and that they were represented as standing for toleration of the same kind and degree. "On the contrary," said Gibbons, ". . . nothing could be further from being historically true." Liberty of conscience, according to the cardinal, had been established in Maryland in 1634 with the foundation of the colony, and the toleration before the period of Puritan rule was in marked contrast to what obtained while the Puritans were in power. He reviewed the penal legislation of the late seventeenth and eighteenth centuries against the Catholics, and from this he drew the conclusion that to erect a monument that would show a Jesuit, a Puritan, and an Anglican as figures representing religious liberty would not only be altogether incorrect, but would even border on a caricature. A memorial to the establishment of religious liberty in Maryland, if it was to be true to history, should not commemorate the act of 1649 but rather the colony's foundation, and for this purpose it should be surmounted by a statue of Cecilius Calvert, the second Lord Baltimore. "I should be heartily in favor of such a monument," he concluded, "which, indeed, the State owes to the memory of Maryland's founders."[156]

---

on the recommendation of the cardinal, since he maintained that Grannan had worked against the party and had given rise to antagonism, facts, as the governor remarked, "of which I presume you are not aware" (98-C-2, Smith to Gibbons, Annapolis, March 14, 1900).

[156] 106-C, Gibbons to J. Wirt Randall, Baltimore, March 17, 1910, copy. Since no copy of Randall's letter could be found, it was not possible to determine where he intended the monument to be placed. Two years before on November 21, 1908, a statue of Cecilius Calvert as the founder of Maryland had been erected in front of the courthouse in Baltimore under the auspices of the Maryland branch of the Society of Colonial Wars. An inscription spoke of Calvert as having established in the colony freedom of religious worship for all Christians and separation of Church and State.

In matters of proposed legislation in Maryland the cardinal had no hesitancy in making his views known if he believed that the measures might affect the morals of his people. When a committee from Charles County sought his endorsement of their campaign for local option on the sale of intoxicating liquors and wished to use his name, Gibbons gave an immediate answer. He had always been very much in favor of local option in the counties, and he believed their moral and material welfare depended upon it. Everyone well knew, he said, that liquor had been the curse of the counties, and he sincerely hoped that in the coming election the efforts made to have local option would be successful. "You are at liberty," he remarked, "to make such use of this letter as you may desire."[157] Some years later, the cardinal made known his opposition to Governor Albert T. Ritchie against Sunday movies. What concerned him most of all, he said, was the rising generation, and he could see nothing but moral and physical injury resulting to the children from moving pictures shown on the only day of the week that made for thought and reflection. The opening of the movie houses on Sunday would, according to Gibbons, destroy whatever religious feeling there was in the children, for it was not to be supposed that the Sunday sermon would have any effect upon minds filled with the anticipated pleasure of seeing sights which, if not immoral, were at least light and frivolous. For that reason he would be highly gratified if Ritchie could see his way clear to vetoing the bill. The governor regretted that he could not agree with Gibbons since, as he said, the bill was to allow the people of Baltimore to vote on Sunday movies, not to permit them outright; thus he very politely declined to veto the measure.[158]

Everything in and pertaining to Baltimore was of interest to Cardinal Gibbons, and to say that he was one of the most familiar and beloved figures in the community would be to state the obvious. His daily walks through the city's streets in the late afternoons were something with which almost everyone was

---

[157] 109-V, R. L. Mitchell, *et al.*, to Gibbons, LaPlata, Maryland, April 27, 1914; *ibid.*, Gibbons to Mitchell, Baltimore, April 27, 1914, copy.

[158] 126-E, Gibbons to Ritchie, Baltimore, April 12, 1920, copy; 126-F, Ritchie to Gibbons, Annapolis, April 15, 1920. John T. Stone, President of the Maryland Casualty Company, wrote Gibbons his warm appreciation for the stand he had taken against Sunday movies (125-P, Stone to Gibbons, Baltimore, March 17, 1920).

acquainted, and the demeanor of the cardinal during these periods of recreation won for him a host of admirers and friends. One who wrote his memories of the Baltimore of these years alluded to these walks of Gibbons and mentioned how the strong yet gentle face of the churchman was lighted with a charming smile and a gleam of interest in the eye when he caught sight of one of his many friends as he strolled along.[159] In the autumn of 1885 a guest in Gibbons' household was invited to walk with him in the early twilight, and he afterward commented, "Every second person he saw knew him, so his hat was hardly two consecutive minutes on his head."[160] As the years passed the citizens of Baltimore came more and more to appreciate his worth, and the Baltimore *Sun* of October 19, 1893, was not exaggerating in its editorial for his silver jubilee when it said, "To Baltimoreans the Cardinal's broad and loyal Americanism is a matter of especial pride."

The principal associations of Baltimore's archbishop were, to be sure, with his own priests and people, yet he was always on terms of easy friendship with many in the city who were not, members of his Church. For example, shortly before he left for Rome to receive the red hat in the winter of 1887, Gibbons remarked to a friend that on the previous evening he had dined with Judge George W. Brown, William Paret, Protestant Episcopal Bishop of Maryland, and Dr. James S. B. Hodges, Rector of St. Paul's Episcopal Church, and he added, "You see we are socially on friendly terms."[161] At the time of his silver jubilee another of Baltimore's distinguished citizens, Daniel C. Gilman, President of the Johns Hopkins University, told Gibbons that since there would be so many who had claim upon his attention during the celebration, he would not venture to call in person. But Gilman did not wish to appear indifferent on a day when so many tributes of respect and affection were being addressed to him. Therefore, he wished to express in writing his congratulations that amid the arduous duties of Gibbons' high station, his health and strength had been preserved and that he had been

---

[159] Meredith Janvier, *Baltimore Yesterdays* (Baltimore, 1937), pp. 87–88.

[160] John J. Donovan (Ed.), *A Papal Chamberlain, The Personal Chronicle of Francis Augustus MacNutt* (New York, 1936), p. 106.

[161] Sarah Lee Collection, Gibbons to Miss Rebecca S. Hayward, Baltimore, January 7, 1887.

able, beyond the bounds of his own communion, to exert, as it was said, "so strong an influence in the promotion of Christian charity and in defense of the political institutions of this land."[162] The cardinal was fond of the famous Hopkins president, and when Gilman and his family went abroad some years later he sent word to Monsignor O'Connell that he wished he would try to find him out in Rome and show him some attention.[163]

But Gibbons' friendships at the Johns Hopkins were not confined to its president. Through his membership in the University Club of Baltimore and in other ways, he had come to know Basil L. Gildersleeve, the internationally known professor of Greek. Gildersleeve was president of the University Club, and upon hearing from Gilman that the cardinal was working on his reminiscences of the Vatican Council, he asked if he would not give a lecture to the members of the club on his impressions of the council. He hoped Gibbons would be able to spare them an hour on one of their field nights, for, as he said, "No lecturer, no subject could be more welcome to us. . . ." Gibbons accepted the invitation and some time later addressed the University Club on the Vatican Council. Gildersleeve's report at the annual meeting in October, 1894, summarized the club's field night programs during the previous year, and in alluding to a lecture by a former military man which had preceded the cardinal's, he spoke of the talk by the prince of the Church who, he said, had permitted the members "to witness the gathering of a great Ecumenical Council itself an army and like an army not foreign to the human

---

[162] 92-J-5, Gilman to Gibbons, Baltimore, October 18, 1893.

[163] ADR, Gibbons to O'Connell, Baltimore, April 10, 1900. The following year Gilman reached the age of seventy and decided to retire from the presidency which he had held for a quarter of a century. At that time Gibbons told him he would make it a duty to be present at a reception in his honor since, as he said, "I desire thus to express my esteem for the retiring President & my regret that the University is soon to lose one who was its ornament & mainstay" (Gilman Papers, The Johns Hopkins University, Gibbons to Gilman, Baltimore, February 11, 1901, copy). Gilman died on October 13, 1908, and two months later there was published a series of excerpts from letters of sympathy to his successor, President Ira Remsen. Gibbons lauded Gilman's citizenship and then said, "But above and beyond all other works which have stamped the name of Dr. Gilman upon the affectionate memory of the citizens of Baltimore, which have merited their gratitude, and which we can point to with especial pride, stands pre-eminent the great university which he established and over which he presided so admirably and so long." "In Memoriam, Daniel Coit Gilman, 1831-1908," *The Johns Hopkins University Circular*, N.S., No. 10 (December, 1908), p. 38.

side of smiles and laughter. . . ."[164] The cardinal's friendly relations with the Hopkins officials extended over many years, and in 1915 in sending his regrets that he would not be able to attend the inauguration of Frank J. Goodnow as the University's third president, he expressed his congratulations and best wishes for the future welfare of the institution, for which the president-elect was grateful.[165]

The unusually close relations of the cardinal with the Baltimore *Sun,* the city's leading newspaper, have already been mentioned. At the time of the death of George W. Abell, the publisher, in 1894, Gibbons preached the funeral sermon in the cathedral, and it gave him an opportunity to speak publicly in praise of the paper which he had read for so many years. He paid tribute to the high moral qualities of the deceased publisher and in doing so he emphasized especially Abell's charities, mentioning the fact that sometime before his death he had given the cardinal a large sum of money for charity on condition that the benefactor should remain unknown. The *Sun,* he said, was Abell's most enduring monument, an enterprise in which he had faithfully maintained the upright principles of his father who had founded the paper. Not long before President Cleveland had told Gibbons of his admiration for Mr. Abell and the *Sun,* and the cardinal knew no herald or vehicle of thought that had done more to make Baltimore known and appreciated by the commercial world than this newspaper. "I can say without fear of contradiction," he continued, "that it is a clean newspaper, a journal which the most delicate Christian maiden may peruse from beginning to end without causing the blush of shame to mantle her cheek."[166] The eulogy was deeply appreciated by the family and three days after the funeral Edwin F. Abell, brother of the publisher, thanked Gibbons from his heart for the noble and touching tribute to his brother. He was likewise grateful for his compliment to the *Sun.* "Such praise from you," he said, "is highly prized, & will greatly strengthen the determination to have

---

[164] 92-V-1, Gildersleeve to Gibbons, Baltimore, December 9, 1893. A copy of the minutes of the annual meeting of the University Club on October 26, 1894, containing a summary of Gildersleeve's remarks was kindly made for the writer by Eldrige Hood Young, secretary of the club, and forwarded in a letter of March 23, 1951.

[165] 111-U, Goodnow to Gibbons, Baltimore, May 5, 1915.

[166] Baltimore *Sun,* May 5, 1894.

it in the future, what it has been in the past."[167] The attachment which the cardinal had for Baltimore's leading daily precluded any doubt about the sincerity of the sentiments which he voiced at the publisher's funeral, and to the end of his life there was only one paper which held first place in Gibbons' mind, and that was the *Sun*.

Yet the *Sun* was not the only Baltimore paper that took pride in the city's most distinguished citizen. The Baltimore *American* was likewise generous in its space and comment on Gibbons' activities, and upon his return from Europe in August, 1895, it carried a full story about his home-coming and the immense crowd that had met him at Camden Station. The warmth of the reception was described but, as it was stated, the words of the cardinal's speech that won more admiration than any others were, "I can say in all candor that my journey homeward gave me more joy than my journey Romewards."[168] Six years later Gibbons returned to Baltimore from a similar journey, and the *American* was in this instance even more generous in its space and tone in the feature entitled, "Royal Welcome to the Cardinal." That Baltimore had by 1901 taken its archbishop to its heart in earnest, was evidenced by the crowd estimated at between 30,000 and 40,000 who gathered to greet him. To the *American's* reporter it was one of the most remarkable demonstrations in the history of the city and never before, it was thought, had a Baltimorean received such an ovation on his return after an absence of a few months. The cardinal rose to the occasion, and to the delight of the crowd he declared that there was no place like home and no home like a home in Baltimore. His attachment to the city was not, he said, to buildings and brick and mortar, but to the living monuments of all that was good and upright among his fellow citizens of whatever nationality or religion. He concluded his remarks in the cathedral

---

[167] 93-G-2, Abell to Gibbons, Woodbourne, May 7, 1894. The *Sun* building was burned in the great Baltimore fire of 1904. A new building was constructed and opened to the public for inspection at a reception on January 17, 1907. The cardinal attended, and he walked down Charles Street in a snowstorm to congratulate his friends, the Abells. Glancing through the window at the snow in the street and contrasting the sight with the joyful gathering within, Gibbons remarked, "Now is the winter of our discontent made glorious summer by this *Sun* of Abell." Gerald W. Johnson, *et al., The Sun Papers of Baltimore* (New York, 1937), pp. 276–277.

[168] Baltimore *American,* August 25, 1895.

by saying that he had always enjoyed the most friendly relations with all his fellow citizens without distinction of race or
creed because he firmly believed in the words, "Behold how good
and joyful a thing it is for brethren to dwell together in unity."[169]

It is not difficult to understand how statements such as these
would endear Gibbons to all Baltimoreans, but in uttering them
he was giving voice to no mere empty sentiment, for he maintained to a marked degree the most amiable intercourse with
those of other faiths. He was always on terms of friendship, for
example, with Bishop Paret of the Protestant Episcopal Church,
and when the latter contemplated a trip to Rome in the spring
of 1910 he asked the cardinal for letters of introduction and for
any personal advice he should think proper to give.[170] Gibbons
was glad to furnish him with an introduction to Monsignor Kennedy of the American College but, unfortunately, the bishop
missed his audience with Pius X, due to the fact that he was in
Rome in Holy Week and the Pope's busy schedule forced a curtailment of the number of audiences. Paret had to leave Rome
before the date which Kennedy had scheduled for an audience,
and meanwhile a false report was published in the Baltimore *Sun*
that he had been unable to secure an audience. The bishop took
the trouble to deny the report and to explain to Gibbons the
circumstances, and he concluded by saying, "I was disappointed
but I feel it was largely my own fault, in making my request at
a time so unfavorable."[171] The cardinal was equally friendly with
Paret's successor, Bishop John G. Murray, and after the publication of Cardinal Mercier's war memoir Gibbons sent the bishop
a copy, which prompted Murray, in thanking him for the book,
to say that while reading it he would think not only of the author,
but also of the donor and with sincere admiration for both.[172]

The other ministers of religion in Baltimore, too, felt the same
kindly feeling for the cardinal as did the Protestant Episcopal
bishops. The Reverend Lincoln A. Ferris, minister of the Mount
Vernon Methodist Church, for one was gratified that Gibbons
should consent to allow him to call with a violinist friend who
wished to play for him on his Stradivarius, and in concluding

---

[169] *Ibid.*, August 27, 1901.
[170] 105-S, Paret to Gibbons, Baltimore, October 6, 1909.
[171] 106-I, same to same, Florence, May 12, 1910.
[172] 126-J, Murray to Gibbons, Baltimore, April 23, 1920.

his note Ferris remarked, "I constantly give thanks to God for your presence in this city and invoke his favor and power to continually rest upon you in your work in our Master's name."[173] A year later the Reverend Oliver Huckel of the Associate Congregational Church was assigned to a new post, and the cardinal wrote to wish him Godspeed and success in his new field of endeavor. In reply Huckel stated that it had been a great happiness to have labored in Baltimore for the previous nineteen years and, he added, "to have been within the circle of your courtesy and gracious influence."[174] It was a sentiment that was shared as well by the Jewish rabbis of the city, and on the occasion of Gibbons' golden jubilee William Rosenau of the Eutaw Place Temple said he considered himself fortunate to have been privileged to work as a rabbi in Baltimore through twenty-six years of Gibbons' tenure of office. In a warm letter filled with the highest praise for the cardinal's qualities and for his friendship for the Jewish people, Rosenau concluded, "Everyone who has ever come in contact with you has instinctively felt that you are 'holy unto the Lord.' "[175]

Gibbons was on especially close terms with Rabbi Rosenau and when Cardinal Mercier visited Baltimore in September, 1919, the rabbi was one of the limited number who received an invitation to the dinner which the cardinal gave in honor of the great Belgian churchman.[176] Another rabbi, Charles A. Rubenstein of the Har Sinai Temple, shared the opinion of his colleague on what Gibbons meant to Baltimore, and to Rubenstein the general outpouring of reverence and respect during the days of jubilee was proof to all that one could rightly esteem a great citizen and properly revere a true man of God in spite of differences in creed.[177] And yet Cardinal Gibbons never compromised the essential dogmas of his Church by his charitable and kindly association with ministers of other faiths. When the Reverend Peter Ainslie, minister of the Christian Temple, stated that in order to have his congregation hear the ministers of all religions he had scheduled a service to be conducted by three rabbis, and asked

---

[173] 111-M, Ferris to Gibbons, Baltimore, March 5, 1915.

[174] 113-V, Huckel to Gibbons, Baltimore, September 28, 1916.

[175] 119-A, Rosenau to Gibbons, Baltimore, October 16, 1918.

[176] American Jewish Archives, Cincinnati, Gibbons to Rosenau, Baltimore, September 9, 1919, photostat.

[177] 119-C, Rubenstein to Gibbons, Baltimore, October 19, 1918.

if he might have the names of several Catholic priests for a similar service, the request was not granted. Gibbons explained that his very high regard for Ainslie would prompt him to accede to his desire but, he said, "there is no prescription that would permit my sending any of my clergy to the service such as you outline in your esteemed letter of March 27th."[178]

All who knew Gibbons well understood how much he loved Baltimore and how deeply moved he was at any untoward event in its life. That was probably in the mind of Archbishop Williams when he extended his sympathy to the cardinal a few days after the disastrous fire of 1904. On February 7–8 of that year there took place the third greatest conflagration in American history, when most of the central business district of Baltimore was destroyed with damages estimated as high as $100,000,000. In thanking the archbishop for his words of sympathy, the cardinal confessed that it had been a terrible calamity but, as he said, "Our citizens are not dismayed. They hope in time to make the city more beautiful & regular than it was before."[179] Actually the fire led to an improved design for the streets and to better fire protection, and in the development of these plans Gibbons took a close interest. A new sewerage system was projected and for all these improvements large loans had to be floated. When the cardinal was invited to attend a meeting concerning these matters he regretted that a pressing engagement would keep him away, but he did not let the occasion pass without offering some salutary advice. He had no hesitancy in recommending the sewerage system and the loans, but he wished, he said, to invite attention to the sacred trust which loans of this kind imposed and how scrupulously exact and honest the men should be who had charge of the disbursement of the funds. They should be actuated solely by the highest civic virtues and by pride in the improvement and adornment of their city; consequently they should rise above all political influence and personal interest. "Indeed," said Gibbons in conclusion, "to recognize any influence other than the city's good & benefit, would be to betray their trust, as well as the confidence of their fellow citizens."[180]

---

[178] 125-U, Ainslie to Gibbons, Baltimore, March 27, 1920; 125-W, Gibbons to Ainslie, Baltimore, March 29, 1920, copy.

[179] AABo, Gibbons to Williams, Baltimore, February 20, 1904.

[180] 102-J, Gibbons to Louis K. Gutman, Baltimore, April 25, 1905, copy.

Of all the thoroughfares of the old city which Gibbons had grown to love so much he was especially fond of Charles Street, on which for nearly half a century he had maintained his residence and up and down whose expanse he had enjoyed his daily walks. He had always taken a particular pride in the homes and shops along this street, and for that reason when the Charles Street Association of merchants held a dinner meeting at the Hotel Rennert on March 10, 1921, it was natural that they should wish to hear from him. The old churchman was by this time within two weeks of his death, and he was much too feeble to do more than to send a verbal message by his secretary, Father Albert E. Smith. One of the members who heard Smith was quite moved by what had been said, and the following day he wrote the cardinal that his message had been an inspiration to all and he knew everyone present felt a deeper love for Charles Street as a result of it. He wondered whether Gibbons would not sometime put on paper the sentiments he had expressed through Father Smith, or if it would be possible for him to grant the writer an interview on the subject of Charles Street and his love for it.[181] There would probably have been few things, aside from his religious duties, which the aged cardinal would have performed with more real joy than to have recorded his reminiscences of the street on which he had lived so happily since 1877. But by the time this letter reached him Gibbons' strength had seriously ebbed, and aside from several fleeting glimpses of him caught as he was carried in or out from an automobile ride about the city during the next ten days, the residents and shopkeepers of Charles Street next saw James Gibbons in the silence of death which came to him at number 408 on March 24.

---

[181] 133-M, Arthur E. Hungerford to Gibbons, Baltimore, March 11, 1921.

CHAPTER XXIV

American Citizen

I have no excuse to make for offering some reflections on the political outlook of the nation; for my rights as a citizen were not abdicated or abridged on becoming a Christian prelate, and the sacred character which I profess, far from lessening, rather increased, my obligations to my country.

Thus did Cardinal Gibbons introduce his article on "Patriotism and Politics" to the readers of the *North American Review* in April, 1892.[1] He stated that it was his purpose, in view of the approaching presidential election, to discuss the ethical aspects of politics, and to outline the principles by which political life should be governed in order that the integrity of the democratic system might be preserved from corruption and decay. There was, indeed, no need for the cardinal to offer an apology for speaking on this subject to the American people. We have already noted the numerous instances in which he proved the deep love which he had for his country and the high value which he always attached to the duties of citizenship. Gibbons not only counseled a patriotic support of the government upon the part of all who would heed his words, but in his own life he practiced that civic virtue to a marked degree. Whether in national emergencies of war, or in projects for social reform in time of peace, officials of the federal, state, and city governments knew that they could count on his enlightened leadership to support them whenever they chose to ask for it. It was this lifelong service to the finest ideals of citizenship that earned for him in his eighty-second year the striking tribute of former President Theodore Roosevelt when he said, "taking your life as a whole, I think you now occupy the position of being the most respected, and venerated, and useful citizen of our country."[2]

---

[1] CLIV, 385.

[2] 114-P, Roosevelt to Gibbons, Oyster Bay, New York, January 5, 1917.

Cardinal Gibbons in Dayton, Ohio, on May 14, 1903, where he visited the National Cash Register Company. Left to right, the Reverend Martin Neville, pastor of Holy Angels Church, Mr. John H. Patterson, President of the N.C.R., the cardinal, and an unidentified priest.

Praise such as this is not won without signal accomplishment and, one might add, without personal knowledge that comes of long association and admiration. It was ever the cardinal's conviction that his role as a citizen and his high position as a churchman could be made to serve the best interests of both Church and State by a ready response on his part to invitations to associate himself with men in public life. Some of these calls, to be sure, came to him merely by reason of the ecclesiastical office which he held, but a great many others sprang from the esteem and affection which men of prominence conceived for him once they had made his acquaintance. The attractive personality of the cardinal, the enlightened interest which he took in public questions, the exquisite tact of which he was a master, and the delicate courtesies which from time to time he extended to public officials prompted them to turn in increasing numbers to him as one in whose judgment they could place their confidence, and in whose company they could find an easy and pleasant relationship.

From his earliest years as Archbishop of Baltimore Gibbons made frequent trips to Washington to be the guest of government officials or to confer with them about problems in which they had a mutual interest. For example, in 1879 Alexander H. Stephens, the former Vice-President of the Confederacy who was then serving in the House of Representatives from his native Georgia, stated that he was anxious to make the archbishop's acquaintance, but in consequence of his physical infirmities he had not been able to call upon him. Gibbons accepted Stephens' invitation to dine and on this occasion met a number of other congressmen, among them Charles J. Faulkner, former American minister to France and at the time a representative from West Virginia.[3] In the same fashion some years later the historian, George Bancroft, who had retired in Washington, gave a dinner in Gibbons' honor to which Chief Justice Morrison R. Waite and Secretary of State Thomas F. Bayard were invited to meet the cardinal.[4] As the years went on Gibbons' presence at social gatherings in the capital became a feature of many of these affairs, and when Joseph G. Cannon, Speaker of the House of Repre-

---

[3] 74-I-7, Stephens to Gibbons, Washington, February 5, 1879; 74-J-7, Faulkner to Gibbons, Martinsburg, West Virginia, February 20, 1879.
[4] 82-K-5, Bancroft to Gibbons, Washington, January 4, 1887.

sentatives, was making arrangements for the annual Gridiron Dinner in 1906, he told the cardinal he was very desirous of having him as a guest. Cannon realized that the date would come during Lent but since the dinner was to be held on St. Patrick's Day, which he had observed was very generally celebrated by Catholics, he trusted that he would not find it objectionable. Gibbons accepted the invitation and enjoyed the company of his friend, President Roosevelt, and the many other distinguished figures who filled the large dining room at the Hotel Willard on that evening.[5] Thus was the circle of his acquaintance among the principal men in the national government broadened, and Gibbons' gracious manner won him friends with whom he remained on cordial terms to the end of their lives.

The attention of one's friends is never more appreciated than in a time of sorrow. All his life Gibbons showed a quick sympathy for anyone — in high or low station — upon whom there had fallen the burden of bereavement, and this sympathy was often extended to men in public life. For example, when Secretary Bayard suffered the double affliction of losing his wife and daughter within a short space of time, Gibbons offered his condolences and stated that he would pray God who alone could heal the troubled heart, that He might give to Bayard and his family the peace and resignation to bear the burden which Providence had sent to them. The statesman was touched by what he termed "your kind and Christian letter of sympathy and friendship" in his hour of grief, and he wished Gibbons to know his grateful appreciation.[6] The Archbishop of Baltimore was likewise attentive in the domestic trials of another Secretary of State, James G. Blaine. On March 4, 1885, the day that Grover Cleveland, Blaine's victorious rival, was inaugurated as President, the sister of the Republican leader, Mrs. Robert C. Walker, was buried from the cathedral in Baltimore with Blaine present for the funeral. Gibbons presided in the sanctuary at the requiem Mass which was sung by his secretary, Father Alfred A. Curtis, who also preached the eulogy.[7] Five years later when he had become Secretary of State, Blaine lost his son Walker after an illness of

[5] 103-B, Cannon to Gibbons, Washington, February 14, 1906; Washington *Post*, March 18, 1906.

[6] Letterbook, Gibbons to Bayard, Baltimore, February 6, 1886, p. 173; 80-E-7, Bayard to Gibbons, Washington, February 7, 1886.

[7] Diary, March 4, 1885, p. 181.

only a few days, a young man before whom a promising political career seemed about to open, and in less than three weeks his daughter Alice died. The cardinal waited for some time due, as he said, to his reluctance to obtrude upon the sacred privacy of Blaine's grief until it had been somewhat mellowed by time and assuaged by Christian resignation. But he now wished to convey to him the assurance of the deep sympathy which he had felt in his bereavement in common with so many of Blaine's fellow countrymen. "May the Lord," he concluded, "heal the wounds which He has been pleased to inflict on you."[8] Two and a half years later the former secretary who had left office in June, 1892, entered upon his last illness, and through Mrs. Blaine word reached the cardinal that he was desirous of speaking with him. After Blaine's death on January 27, 1893, his widow thanked Gibbons for the kind and friendly promptness with which he had responded to her husband's wish to see him.[9]

Likewise at the time that General Philip H. Sheridan died in August, 1888, the cardinal was about to depart for Toledo, but he postponed his trip in order to preach at the funeral which was held at St. Matthew's Church in Washington. In the sermon he stated that the Civil War, unlike other wars, had sealed the unity of the nation, and it was his belief that Sheridan would be mourned in the South as well as in the North since he felt satisfied that the charges made against the general of unnecessary cruelty to his enemies during the war had been unjust. After eulogizing Sheridan as a soldier and a citizen, Gibbons concluded by speaking of him as a Christian who had firmly believed in the immortality of the soul, a consideration which, he said, would now be a source of consolation to the general's bereaved family. President Cleveland attended the funeral which was held with

---

[8] 87-L-1, Gibbons to Blaine, Baltimore, May 1, 1890, copy.

[9] 90-U-3, Harriet S. Blaine to Gibbons, Washington, December 8, 1892; 91-E-8, same to same, Washington, February 14, 1893. In her first letter Mrs. Blaine stated her husband wished to see the cardinal on "a little matter of pecuniary business. . . ." After his death her thanks were extended also for what she called — with a meaning that is not clear — "the patience with which you waited for his request — a request alas! which never came." The remark would seem to suggest that Gibbons was hopeful that Blaine might express a wish to die in the Church of his mother. Blaine's father was a Presbyterian, but his mother was a devout Catholic; the statesman himself became a member of the Congregational Church in his early years. Whether or not the allusion in the widow's letter was to matters relating to Blaine's religious views at the time of his death, however, it is impossible to say.

an impressive display of military pageantry, and the universal commendation with which his sermon was received by the press of the country naturally proved gratifying to the preacher.[10]

But courtesies of this kind from Cardinal Gibbons were not confined to the occasions of sorrow in the family circle of men of prominence. The appointment of Edward Douglas White as a senator from Louisiana in 1888 won his hearty congratulations, and in expressing his gratitude White remarked, "For so many years & in so many ways has your kindness been shown me that I know not how to adequately thank you for it. . . ." The friendship between Gibbons and White endured through the years, and nearly a quarter of a century later the cardinal renewed his congratulations when his old friend was named Chief Justice of the Supreme Court.[11] In a similar manner Stephen B. Elkins was pleased at Gibbons' recognition of his appointment as Secretary of War by President Harrison, and in acknowledgment Elkins expressed the wish that many more years might be added to an already illustrious and useful life which, he said, "has not only blessed and made better our own people but those of other countries."[12] The cardinal never lost a chance of com-

---

[10] Washington *Post,* August 12, 1888; ADR, Gibbons to O'Connell, Baltimore, September 20, 1888. For the text of the sermon cf. *A Retrospect of Fifty Years,* II, 234–242. Three years later upon the death of General William T. Sherman, who had been baptized a Catholic in his youth but had not been brought up in the faith, Gibbons counseled Archbishop Corrigan to permit the general's son, Father Thomas E. Sherman, S.J., to read the Catholic burial service and to be present himself at the funeral. Sherman's wife had been a devout Catholic and their children had been raised in that faith. He expressed no dissent when his daughter repeated the acts of faith and contrition shortly before his death and after he had lapsed into unconsciousness the general was given the last rites of the Church (AANY, Gibbons to Corrigan, Baltimore, February 18, 1891). At the time of the death of the general's wife three years before Father Sherman had informed the cardinal of the inconsolable grief of his father and had begged Gibbons to write him a note of sympathy. "Pardon a son's freedom," he said, "justified by your delicate attention to her whom God has kindly taken home" (85-K-8, Sherman to Gibbons, New York, December 7, 1888). The cardinal responded at once to the request, which brought the old soldier's gratitude, in which he said Gibbons' sympathy had been the source of great consolation to him and, as he added, "will always remain with my children to confirm them in their knowledge that their Mother commanded the respect of the High as well as the love of the humble" (85-L-8, Sherman to Gibbons, New York, December 16, 1888).
[11] 84-Q-6, White to Gibbons, New Orleans, June 25, 1888; 106-T, same to same, Washington, December 22, 1910.
[12] 89-K-5, Elkins to Gibbons, Washington, January 20, 1892.

mending one of his friends in public life when he performed an action which he felt would redound to the welfare of the country and the advancement of morals. When Secretary of State William Jennings Bryan sent him a copy of a lecture which he had given on "The Making of a Man," wherein the author had defended the doctrines of the Trinity and the existence of miracles, Gibbons congratulated him on his effort and his success in warming the hearts of others toward these fundamental beliefs of the Christian faith. He found it all the more praiseworthy, he said, "when so many who bear the title of clergymen are doing their utmost to undermine and shatter the faith of the people in these same important truths."[13]

The regard in which Cardinal Gibbons was held in the public mind was illustrated repeatedly by the marked attentions which were paid to him wherever he went. Shortly before he traveled to Boston in January, 1908, to confer the pallium on Archbishop O'Connell, the Governor of Massachusetts, Curtis Guild, Jr., sent a pressing invitation for him to accept his hospitality since, as he said, he did not wish his visit to pass without offering him some personal attention either in a public or a private capacity as he might think best.[14] In the latter years of Gibbons' life there was held on the second Sunday of the new year at St. Patrick's Church in Washington a reception which was called "Cardinal's Day" when many of the capital's outstanding residents turned out to greet him. At the gathering in 1917 Senator Oscar W. Underwood of Alabama was one of the speakers, and he recalled the fact that he was from the South where the cardinal had begun his episcopal career. Underwood stated that the real milestones that marked the beginning and the end of eras were not so much great events as great men and great names. To the speaker Gibbons' name marked such a milestone, and in conclusion he said:

And as the decades roll on and others will come to fill the places that we occupy today, men will recognize that there is no one who

---

[13] LC, Bryan Papers, Gibbons to Bryan, Baltimore, April 27, 1914.

[14] 104-S, Guild to Gibbons, Boston, January 25, 1908. Some years before Charles F. Mayer, President of the Baltimore and Ohio Railroad, urged Gibbons to avail himself of his offer of a private car for a trip to Mexico where, he told him, "You will find hosts of friends in Mexico, for you are widely known of there and universally admired and respected" (93-Q-10, Mayer to Gibbons, Baltimore, January 29, 1895). Gibbons, however, did not make the trip.

has lived in our day and generation, that has been a more truly loyal citizen of this great republic, who has stood with more faith, more firmness for the ideals of American liberty and American freedom, than His Eminence, whom we are delighted to be with today.[15]

One of the most singular things about the cardinal's career as a citizen was the close relations he maintained over so many years with the occupants of the White House. Late in life he recalled that as a child in Baltimore he had been held in his mother's arms to see President Andrew Jackson pass in a parade.[16] Moreover, he had seen every president since Abraham Lincoln and had known a number of them very well. The first chief executive with whom the cardinal was on terms of real friendship, however, was Grover Cleveland. On more than one occasion during Cleveland's first term Gibbons shared the honors with the President at public functions, and as a consequence of these meetings they became fast friends. It was in these years, as we have seen, that the two men conferred on the Knights of Labor and were featured in the closing exercises of the centennial celebration of the Constitution at Philadelphia. It was President Cleveland, too, who sought the mediation of Gibbons to transmit his gift and congratulations to Leo XIII on the latter's golden jubilee as a priest.[17] Toward the close of Cleveland's first administration he sent the cardinal a copy of one of his final messages to Congress, and in acknowledging it Gibbons took occasion to offer his thanks for the many courtesies which the President had extended to him during the previous four years. "Rest assured," he said, "that

---

[15] *The Patrician,* XII (February 4, 1917), 8–9. The reception that year was held on Sunday, January 14. The "Cardinal's Day" celebration at St. Patrick's in 1911 was described as "International and interdenominational in its scope, an unprecendented tribute of loyalty, devotion, and respect. . . . Diplomats, jurists, members of Congress, prominent business men of the city, Catholic and non-Catholic alike, joined with their humbler brethren in the signal honor to the prince of the Roman Catholic Church in America. Washington has seldom witnessed so significant a manifestation of good will to any man. . . ." (Washington *Herald,* January 9, 1911). Another non-Catholic southerner who spoke in the highest terms of Gibbons was Wilson's Secretary of the Navy, Josephus Daniels. Cf. his *The Wilson Era. Years of War and After, 1917–1923* (Chapel Hill, 1948), pp. 583–584, where he describes being present in the Baltimore cathedral on April 11, 1920, when Gibbons bestowed the insignia of knighthood in the Order of St. Gregory on Admiral William S. Benson, Chief of Naval Operations.

[16] 128-F, Samuel G. Heiskell to Gibbons, Knoxville, Tennessee, July 19, 1920. Heiskell was the author of a book entitled *Andrew Jackson and Early Tennessee History* (Nashville, 1918).

[17] Cf. *supra,* I, 198, note, 322–325, 571; II, 79.

in returning to private life you will bear with you undiminished the high esteem & regard I entertained for you in your public career."[18] When Cleveland ran for the presidency a second time in 1892 the A.P.A. was enjoying one of its periods of greatest strength, and in the course of the campaign Cleveland was made to suffer because of his friendship with Gibbons. The A.P.A. circulated a number of wild stories about his favoritism for Catholics, and among them were the absurd charges that during his first administration the President had installed in the White House a wire to Gibbons' residence and had placed a Catholic at the head of every division of the departments of government. The presidential candidate confessed that he was ashamed to take cognizance of falsehoods of this kind, but since news of them had reached him from several sources he thought it best to end the matter, insofar as it was possible to do so, by branding them as unqualifiedly false in every detail. He then stated:

> I know Cardinal Gibbons and know him to be a good citizen and first-rate American, and that his kindness of heart and toleration are in striking contrast to the fierce intolerance and vicious malignity which disgrace some who claim to be Protestants. I know a number of members of the Catholic Church who were employed in the public service during my administration, and I suppose there were many so employed.
> I should be ashamed of my Presbyterianism if these declarations gave ground for offense.[19]

Despite the criticism of the A.P.A., however, Cleveland was elected on November 1 of that year, and three weeks later he expressed his gratitude for the congratulations of Gibbons, a sentiment which, he said, was shared by his whole household.[20] The following year marked the golden jubilee of Pope Leo XIII as a bishop and the President again turned to Gibbons to transmit his congratulations to the Pontiff. The pleasure attending Cleveland's expression of felicitations was enhanced, he said, by the remembrance that His Holiness had always manifested a lively

---

[18] LC, Cleveland Papers, Gibbons to Cleveland, Baltimore, December 15, 1888.

[19] Cleveland to William Black, Buzzard's Bay, Massachusetts, July 11, 1892, quoted in Will, op. cit., I, 537.

[20] 90-R-5, Cleveland to Gibbons, New York, November 22, 1892. Cleveland added, "I cannot rid myself of a certain feeling of responsibility and a fear that I shall fall short of doing my full duty to the people who have trusted me."

interest in the prosperity of the United States and a great admiration for its political institutions. "I am glad to believe," he remarked, "that these sentiments are the natural outgrowth of the Holy Father's solicitude for the welfare and happiness of the masses of humanity, and his especial sympathy for every effort made to dignify simple manhood and to promote the moral and social elevation of those who toil." The gratification that Leo XIII had shown in receiving a gift copy of the Constitution which Cleveland had sent to him six years before, now led the President to suggest that if it were thought acceptable he would be pleased to forward a volume containing the official papers and documents written by him during his previous term of office.[21] Cardinal Rampolla promptly made it known to Gibbons that the Pope was extremely pleased at Cleveland's thought of him and would be very happy to receive the book.[22]

When it came time to prepare the inscription which the gift should bear, the President asked for Gibbons' advice as to how it should be worded, and having in mind no doubt his unpleasant experiences of the campaign year, he hoped the cardinal would not misinterpret his motive if he suggested that the matter be kept from the newspapers. "They behave so badly," he said, "I am not willing to gratify them."[23] At the time Gibbons was in Chicago attending the Parliament of Religions and the annual meeting of the archbishops. He offered a text for the inscription, and told the President that he had learned both by cable and letter from Rome of the special delight which Cleveland's message had given to the Pope. Two weeks later he acknowledged receipt of the gift for Leo XIII and stated that he had forwarded it to the Holy See. And in regard to the question of publicity, Gibbons remarked, "I shall do all I can to shelter your kind message from newspaper notoriety which is so distasteful to refined feelings."[24]

---

[21] 91-M-2, Cleveland to Gibbons, Washington, June 9, 1893, copy.

[22] 91-P-1/1, Rampolla to Gibbons, Rome, July 1, 1893.

[23] 91-U-2, Cleveland to Gibbons, Washington, September 10, 1893. Cf. also 91-U-1, same to same, Washington, September 1, 1893.

[24] LC, Cleveland Papers, Gibbons to Cleveland, Chicago, September 5, 1893; *ibid.*, same to same, Baltimore, September 20, 1893, *Personal*. The cardinal congratulated the President and Mrs. Cleveland on the birth of their daughter, "the first child, I am told, ever born to a President during his incumbency of the Presidential office. May this young queen be a source of unalloyed gladness & consolation to her parents."

Cardinal Gibbons offering the closing prayer on October 3, 1899, at the ceremonies in Washington which witnessed the presentation of a sword to Admiral George Dewey, which had been voted to him by Congress. At the cardinal's right is President McKinley and the admiral is at his left.

A few days after the inauguration of William McKinley as Cleveland's successor in March, 1897, James A. Gary, the Postmaster General, said he had learned that Gibbons would be pleased to meet the new President. McKinley had instructed Gary to tell the cardinal that he would be delighted to see him on any day that he found it convenient to call.[25] Thus early in the administration Gibbons made the acquaintance of the man, who in the following year sent for him to learn his opinion about the advisability of the United States retaining the Philippines after the war with Spain.[26] The cardinal had occasion to confer with McKinley a number of times in these months on matters pertaining to the war and, too, to participate with the President at various public functions such as that of October 3, 1899, when McKinley presented to Admiral George Dewey the sword voted to him by Congress, with Gibbons pronouncing the benediction at the ceremony.[27] Enough has already been said to illustrate how close the cardinal was to Theodore Roosevelt who succeeded to the presidency on the death of McKinley in September, 1901. Roosevelt's election in 1904 brought into greater prominence another friend of Gibbons' when Charles W. Fairbanks, senator from Indiana, was elected as vice-president. The cardinal's congratulations pleased Fairbanks who told him, "No word has come to me which is more gratifying than yours."[28] During the Roosevelt administration he continued to be friendly with Vice-President and Mrs. Fairbanks, and it was through the invitation of the latter as President General of the Daughters of the American Revolution, that he was asked to give the benediction at the dedication of Continental Hall in Washington, an invitation which he was not able to accept because of a previous engagement.[29]

But the friendship of Gibbons with Roosevelt and Fairbanks proved to be the occasion of some embarrassment to him in the spring of 1910 after the two men had retired from office. In the course of a tour around the world Mr. and Mrs. Fairbanks visited Rome where, as Fairbanks later explained to Gibbons, they had been prompted by the urging of Catholic friends and by their

---

[25] 95-K-11, Gary to Gibbons, Washington, March 16, 1897.

[26] Cf. II, 98.

[27] Will, *op. cit.,* II, 791.

[28] 101-R, Fairbanks to Gibbons, Washington, December 10, 1904.

[29] 102-G, Cornelia C. Fairbanks to Gibbons, Washington, March 27, 1905.

own desires to seek an audience of Pius X. On the day previous to the date fixed for the audience, however, Fairbanks had scheduled a talk before the Methodist Association at their church in Rome. For some time resentment had been growing in Vatican circles against the proselytizing methods of this group in the Eternal City, and when the Fairbanks engagement was announced word reached the former vice-president through Monsignor Kennedy of the American College that the audience would have to be canceled if he carried through his appearance before the Methodists. Fairbanks could see nothing incongruous apparently about the Methodists trying to win converts among the Catholic population of the Italian capital, and for that reason he declined the audience with the Pope, although he attended a luncheon and reception in his honor at the American College before leaving Rome. A few days later he gave a detailed explanation of what had happened to Gibbons not knowing, as he said, what accounts of the incident had appeared in the American papers. Fairbanks recounted his conversations with Monsignor Kennedy, and he then told the cardinal:

> I replied that it would be absolutely impossible for me to break my engagement to speak; I had made a rule never to do so; that I had always held myself free to address Catholics and Protestants of all denominations whenever they desired and whenever it was possible; that I had treated all absolutely alike in this regard; that I had traveled many miles and delivered many addresses to Catholic bodies, and that one of the two occasions when I was absent from the Senate I went to Chicago to aid in the dedication of a great Parochial School and I said that some of the best friends I had, amongst whom I mentioned your good self, understood all of this perfectly. I said that while I regretted that the question had arisen the alternative left me no course but to forego the pleasure of the audience and keep my engagement in the afternoon.[30]

The press, to be sure, had played up the matter and there were some who used the episode to air their dislike for the Church, and what they termed the bigotry and intolerance of Catholics. In an effort to set before the American public the reasons behind the Vatican's stand, Archbishop Ireland stepped into the breach with a forceful interview to the press at Chicago which was

---

[30] 106-B, Fairbanks to Gibbons, Berlin, February 15, 1910.

published in the New York *Times* of February 9 and in all the leading papers of the country. Ireland made it clear that the Fairbanks address to the Methodist Association was the real cause of the audience being refused, not the Methodist Church in general. He instanced the offensive methods employed by the group in giving prominence in their bookstore in Rome to books that were slanderous of Catholics generally, and insulting to the Pope in particular. Fairbanks' address before this group naturally led Catholics in Rome to infer a certain approval of the Methodists' procedure, and under the circumstances a papal audience the following day would have given rise to still greater confusion concerning the Vatican's position. The archbishop was at pains to make it clear that his remarks were not intended to include the Protestant churches in Rome in the same category as this special Methodist group, but about the latter he left no doubt where he stood. The interview closed by Ireland saying he was departing for New York where he would be glad to answer any further inquiries. "I am not too old," he said, "to enter a fight when the occasion requires it."

Cardinal Gibbons was visiting in New Orleans when he read the interview, and he hastened to express his delight with his friend's action. He told the archbishop, "You have taken the sting out of the wound inflicted on the Vice President by making known to the American people the pernicious activity of the Roman Methodists."[31] A month later the cardinal sought to smooth over the ruffled feelings at the Holy See by sending Cardinal Merry del Val a copy of Fairbanks' letter and assuring him that the former vice-president had always been very friendly to Gibbons, and that during his tenure of office he had ever shown sympathy and courtesy to Catholics. If the incident had occurred thirty or forty years before, said the cardinal, the Church in the United States would have suffered a great deal more than it actually had in this instance, owing to the growth and influence of the American Catholic body. He thought the affair would have one good result in opening the eyes of Catholics and fair-minded non-Catholics to the reprehensible methods employed by the Methodists and, too, in preventing Americans in the future from holding up the United States as a formally Protestant country and, therefore, in sympathy with the anti-

---

[31] AASP, Gibbons to Ireland, New Orleans, February 9, 1910, copy.

Catholic and antipapal proselytism of the Methodists in Rome. When Fairbanks returned home Gibbons said he hoped to have an opportunity of telling him that the Holy Father was always most courteous in granting audiences to Protestants and Jews, and that in declining to receive him he must now be convinced that the Pontiff had been actuated by a high sense of unpleasant duty.[32]

Hardly had the Fairbanks incident begun to fade from the public mind, when a similar one took place which caused even more excitement. Theodore Roosevelt arrived in Rome the first week in April on his return from a hunting trip in Africa, and once more the visit provoked a public storm when Roosevelt grew angry at the Vatican's request that he cancel an engagement with the Methodists and, in turn, lost his temper with the Protestant group when one of their number made an insulting reference to Pius X. In the end Roosevelt left Rome without visiting either the Vatican or the Methodists.[33] The affair caused a great deal of commotion on both sides of the Atlantic, and there was concern in political circles as to the effect that it might have on the American electorate. Gibbons visited President Taft at the White House soon after the news broke, and as he

---

[32] 106-C, Gibbons to Merry del Val, Baltimore, March 11, 1910, copy. The *New Century,* a Catholic weekly paper published in Washington and edited by Humphrey J. Desmond, carried an editorial on February 12, 1910, on the Fairbanks incident in which criticism of the Vatican was expressed for its failure to reciprocate the courtesies which the United States had extended to the Holy See a few years previous in the Philippines. "We ourselves," said the *New Century,* "would welcome the day when all the diplomats shall be sent out of the Vatican and sentenced to teach catechism to the neglected Italians; but we suppose that while they are there, they must earn their wages; and incidentally make a blunder now and again. This particular affair may be the achievement of some major domo of the Vatican. The pious peasant Pope may have known nothing of it." When this editorial came to the notice of Gibbons he wrote Desmond a letter — a copy of which could not be found — in which he took the editor to task for his disrespectful tone toward the Holy See. Desmond replied that knowing the kindness and consideration which the cardinal had always shown for the Catholic press, he was ready to admit that the *New Century* must certainly have been at fault in the matters adjudged in Gibbons' letter. He assured him that there would be no recurrence of any ground for a similar complaint in the future. "We desire to make The New Century," he said, "in all respects safely Catholic, inculcating at all times loyalty to the Church, respect for the Holy See and zeal for the spread of religion" (AAB, unclassified, Desmond to Gibbons, Washington, March 3, 1910, printed).

[33] Henry F. Pringle, *Theodore Roosevelt. A Biography* (New York, 1931), pp. 513–515.

was leaving he remarked, "The President and I both regret this incident." Later that day Frederick W. Carpenter, Taft's secretary, heard that the Associated Press were going to carry a story that the President had expressed regret over Roosevelt's conduct in Rome. He hurriedly got in touch with Gibbons and was told that in view of the possible implications the cardinal would state that he had arranged his call at the White House before the trouble in Rome, that his visit had no bearing on what had happened there, and that the President had taken no part in the matter and had expressed no opinion about it. With this information Carpenter assured his chief that he believed Taft's attitude would be entirely clear, and that the news agencies would indicate that he had made no comment on Roosevelt's Roman visit.[34]

Actually, however, the news story from Washington as carried in the New York *Times* of April 7 and in many other papers revealed something of the hurried efforts to explain away the cardinal's remark when it quoted the statement of Gibbons given above as he was leaving the White House, added that conflicting versions began to circulate that very afternoon as to what had been said between Taft and Gibbons, and in conclusion stated, "It was explained that the Cardinal meant simply that he and the President regretted that any unpleasantness whatever had occurred — not that they regretted the attitude taken by the ex-President." A month later Robert J. Collier, editor of *Collier's Weekly,* who was a Catholic, a stanch Republican, and a warm admirer of Roosevelt's endeavored to use his good offices to restore harmony between the ex-President and the Catholics. He proposed to Gibbons that he should give a private dinner to which he would invite Roosevelt, the cardinal, and a few other prominent men since, as he said, he felt sure Gibbons shared his desire that the sooner the Roman incident was forgotten the better it would be. The cardinal assured Collier that he cherished the warmest regard for Roosevelt and valued his friendship highly. He confessed, too, that Catholics owed him a great debt of gratitude for the many and singular evidences of good will toward the Church which he had shown during his administration. However, Gibbons was not satisfied

---

[34] LC, Taft Papers, memorandum of Carpenter to Taft, Washington, April 6, 1910.

that his presence at the proposed dinner would be correctly interpreted, and for that reason he politely declined lest his action should give rise to further misunderstanding and mis-representation.[35]

Yet in spite of the tension over the unfortunate incident in Rome in the spring of 1910, it did not cause a break in the friendship of Gibbons and Roosevelt, for in the following year, as we shall see, the former President came to Baltimore for the civic celebration of the cardinal's jubilee where he publicly lauded him in the highest terms. During the Bull Moose cam-paign of 1912 a fanatic in Milwaukee tried to assassinate Roosevelt on October 14. Gibbons promptly wired his joy at the reported prospect of a speedy recovery for the former President and said he prayed God to preserve his valuable life, to which Roosevelt responded with a telegram saying how deeply touched he was by the cardinal's sympathy.[36] Four years later the political picture was complicated by the refusal of the Progressive Party to return to the Republican fold, and by their persistence in nominating Roosevelt on a separate ticket. Following the Chicago convention in early June, the former President declined the Progressives' nomination and urged his followers to re-enter the Republican ranks and to support Charles Evans Hughes. Later in the summer Gibbons told Roosevelt that he need not say how much he regretted that he had not received the Republican nomination for President. He then continued:

But there are compensating advantages. Never were you more honored and never was your influence greater than today. . . . Your political, military and economic views are eagerly accepted and *ap-propriated* by both political parties.[37]

Whatever the exaggeration involved concerning the extent of Roosevelt's influence at the time, it doubtless proved comforting

[35] AAB, unclassified, Collier to Gibbons, New York, May 7, 1910; Gibbons to Collier, Baltimore, May 10, 1910, copy. The year that Roosevelt died Callan O'Laughlin, a Washington newspaperman and a Catholic who had acted as Roosevelt's secretary on the trip in 1910 and as the intermediary between the ex-President and the Vatican, came to see the cardinal when the Roman incident was probably rehearsed (ANCWC, William T. Russell to Gibbons, n.p., December 12, 1919, copy).
[36] 108-M, Gibbons to Roosevelt, Baltimore, October 15, 1912, telegram in copy; Roosevelt to Gibbons, Chicago, October 17, 1912, two telegrams of the same date.
[37] 113-T, Gibbons to Roosevelt, Southampton, New York, August 19, 1916, copy.

Cardinal Gibbons and former President Theodore Roosevelt at the opening of the victory loan drive, Oriole Park, Baltimore, September 29, 1918. The hand and hat in the left corner are those of Bishop John G. Murray of the Protestant Episcopal Diocese of Maryland.

(C. C. Knobeloch, Baltimore)

balm for the old campaigner. The two men who had been friends for many years continued so to the end, and two years before Roosevelt's death he acknowledged receipt of the cardinal's latest book, and it was at this time that he paid the striking tribute to Gibbons' citizenship which we noted above.[38] On January 6, 1919, Theodore Roosevelt died peacefully in his sleep at Oyster Bay, and thus there was broken the closest personal tie which Gibbons ever enjoyed with a President of the United States.

We have already seen a good deal of the cordiality which obtained between William Howard Taft and Cardinal Gibbons, a friendship which was made manifest to all the world in June, 1911, when the President traveled to Baltimore to do honor to the cardinal at the latter's golden jubilee celebration. But with Woodrow Wilson, Taft's successor, there was never the warmth that marked Gibbons' dealings with Cleveland, Roosevelt, and Taft. In the month following Wilson's inauguration the cardinal was formally presented to the President by Frederic C. Penfield, who some weeks later was named American ambassador to Vienna where he served with credit through most of World War I. Gibbons had given the opening prayer at the national convention of the Democrats in Baltimore on the previous June 25 when, as Penfield recalled, he had been acclaimed by practically all the delegates of the gathering that had nominated Wilson for the presidency.[39] Yet the outbreak of the Mexican

---

[38] Cf. II, 500.

[39] LC, Wilson Papers, Penfield to Joseph P. Tumulty, New York, April 4, 1913. President Wilson was the last chief executive to accept an invitation to attend the annual Pan American Mass at St. Patrick's Church in Washington. He was present on November 27, 1913, for that event with his wife and daughters. The cardinal presided at the Mass and the sermon was preached by Charles W. Currier, Bishop of Matanzas, Cuba. In view of the strained relations at that time between the United States and Mexico, Currier's disagreement with the view of those who urged war as a necessary evil, was regarded as significant. "War is the natural enemy of order," said the preacher, "and, therefore, of that which is good, beautiful, and true" (New York *Times,* November 28, 1913). Wilson's acceptance of the invitation had been protested in advance by the Brooklyn Christian Endeavor Union. Moreover, in a Thanksgiving Day sermon before representatives of five Protestant denominations at the Washington Heights Baptist Church of New York the Reverend John R. Mackay, pastor of the North Presbyterian Church of that city, assailed the President. Mackay maintained that he meant no criticism of the Catholic Church when he stated that Wilson had his own church and pew in which to worship and, therefore, his presence at St. Patrick's was termed "an outrage when done by a Protestant Christian."

persecution of the Church soon after Wilson took office found the two men at variance in their views on this and other questions. However, in the conduct of the negotiations concerning the Mexican Church, as we have seen, there was never any open unpleasantness between them, even if the friendly spirit of the days of Roosevelt and Taft was no longer present.[40]

Not long after Penfield's introduction of Gibbons to the President there began to be heard in various quarters a rumor that Wilson on this occasion had failed to give the cardinal his title, but had referred to him as "Mr. Gibbons." It proved impossible to trace the origins of this story but, at any rate, it continued to spread and to cause chagrin in Catholic circles. Monsignor Russell, who had been present at the interview, finally decided to do what he could to kill the report, and on March 6, 1915, the *Catholic Review* carried Russell's explanation of the circumstances, and in it he said:

> We called at the White House because the Cardinal desired to pay his respects to the President. I was present at the whole interview. I can say if the President addressed the Cardinal as Mr., I did not hear him; and furthermore, I am convinced that he did not do so, as I was not more than two feet from the President during the whole interview, and I heard all the conversation that took place. I do not believe the President would consciously do anything that might be considered as a lack of courtesy or consideration for any Catholic priest or prelate.[41]

The New York *Times* published an editorial on November 29, 1913, entitled "Misdirected Criticism" in which it disagreed with Mackay and stated that Wilson's action had manifested the spirit of true Christianity. The *Times* alluded to the prevalence of the Catholic faith in South America, as well as among many citizens of the United States, and the editorial concluded, "The attendance of the President at St. Patrick's Church on Thanksgiving was but a proper expression of sympathy with the sentiment of the occasion."

[40] This fact was stated a few years later by the cardinal's secretary, Father Eugene J. Connelly, to a woman who was seeking to use Gibbons' influence to have her husband appointed to a federal office. Connelly quoted the cardinal as saying that the cordial relations that had existed with the former five occupants of the White House no longer prevailed, nor had there been any tendency that way. Connelly continued, "He [Gibbons] and the president are at variance over the great national questions, which has not helped any in making for friendlier feelings" (113-F, Connelly to Mrs. John J. Boylan, Baltimore, February 17, 1916, copy).

[41] Russell sent a copy of his remarks in the *Catholic Review* to Wilson's secretary and said he had made them in justice to the President. If Tumulty saw no reason for not doing so, he would be pleased if he would show them to

But in spite of Russell's denial, there were a number who remained skeptical, and he and Gibbons continued to receive inquiries about the truth of the charge.[42] A certain uneasiness was felt in the White House over the persistence of the reported discourtesy to Gibbons on his first visit to Wilson, and it was probably with that in mind that in the autumn of that year the President sent him an autographed engraving of himself for which the cardinal thanked him and, in turn, wished him many years of happiness in his future life with Mrs. Edith Bolling Galt to whom the President had recently become engaged.[43] Gibbons' brief and simple note brought a prompt response, in which Wilson said, "May I not express to your Eminence my very deep and sincere appreciation of your generous message of October ninth? It gave me the deepest pleasure and gratification."[44]

In Wilson's campaign for re-election in 1916 the story about the interview of 1913 figured rather prominently and caused grave anxiety on the part of some of the Democratic leaders. The western headquarters of the Democratic National Committee asked the President's secretary, Joseph P. Tumulty who was himself a Catholic, for data by which they might authoritatively deny the falsehood then circulating through the Middle West. Tumulty supplied copies of Russell's remarks in the *Catholic Review,* a statement from Gibbons, and the dates of the cardinal's calls at the White House in 1913.[45] But Redmond F. Kernan, a prominent Catholic Democrat, was not content with

---

Wilson (LC, Wilson Papers, Russell to Tumulty, Washington, March 8, 1915).

[42] Bishop Keiley of Savannah for one was not entirely convinced by Russell's denial and asked Gibbons to set him right about what had really happened (111-N, Keiley to Gibbons, Savannah, March 15, 1915). The cardinal kept no copy of his reply and simply wrote across the top of the letter "Ans'd." An effort to secure Gibbons' answer in the archives of the Diocese of Savannah-Atlanta was unavailing. Bishop Francis E. Hyland stated to the writer in a letter of July 24, 1950: "I beg to say, after a thorough search of our files, that there is no record here of any correspondence between Cardinal Gibbons and Bishop Keiley in regard to President Wilson's attitude toward the Cardinal." Cf. also 113-N, John D. Crimmins to Gibbons, New York, May 29, 1916.

[43] LC, Wilson Papers, Gibbons to Wilson, Baltimore, October 9, 1915.

[44] 112-M, Wilson to Gibbons, Washington, October 14, 1915.

[45] LC, Wilson Papers, William J. Cochran to Tumulty, Chicago, August 19, 1916. Cf. John M. Blum, *Joe Tumulty and the Wilson Era* (Boston, 1951), for the chapter, "The Klan and the Hyphen," pp. 88–109, for the leading role Tumulty played in relation to Wilson and issues that touched the Catholic Church in these years.

this evidence, and in mid-October he went to Baltimore where he received a further denial from Gibbons that the President had ever shown any discourtesy toward him. Kernan was told that only the day previous Wilson had granted an important request of the cardinal's, and it was added that Gibbons was growing weary of denying all this foolish gossip.[46] From Baltimore Kernan went on to New York where he met Frank I. Cobb, editor of the New York *World,* who told him that he had spoken to the President about the report of his use of "Mr." to Gibbons, and that Wilson had pronounced it "preposterous." Wilson was quoted as saying that at the interview in question he had not offered the cardinal a chair since diplomatic usage decreed that an ambassador be received by the President standing to imply their equality, and Wilson had treated Gibbons as one having that rank.[47] At the same time a reporter of the New York *World* called on Gibbons and told him of the reported opposition of the Catholic Church to Wilson in such places as Indiana, to which the cardinal replied that he knew nothing about the Catholics in Indiana opposing the President until that moment. He then stated:

> I do not believe there is any truth in it. For myself, I am not in politics and I never have authorized any one to quote me as favoring either candidate for the Presidency. Every Catholic voter has an inherent right to vote according to his own individual conscience, and I am sure that the Roman Catholic hierarchy of the United States would never interfere with that right.[48]

The excitement over the supposed slight to the cardinal continued to draw fire to the very end of the campaign, and on election day the New York *Times* of November 7 carried one of the final notices of the matter in the form of a denial from Tumulty at Asbury Park, New Jersey, who once again quoted the Russell statement of the previous year. This last effort of the President's secretary had been issued to help scotch what

---

[46] *Ibid.,* Kernan to Tumulty, Baltimore, October 17, 1916. Kernan attributed the rumors to Thomas Fortune Ryan and others whom he termed "Republican traitors to their country within the Democratic Party," who were attempting to make the public believe that the Catholic Church was opposed to or could be used against Wilson.

[47] *Ibid.,* Kernan to Gibbons, Bloomfield, New Jersey, October 18, 1916, copy; same to same, Bloomfield, October 20, 1916, telegram in copy.

[48] New York *World,* October 20, 1916.

This picture was taken beside the cathedral in Baltimore on April 11, 1920, following the ceremony in which Gibbons invested Admiral William S. Benson, Chief of Naval Operations, with the insignia of knighthood in the Order of St. Gregory the Great. At the cardinal's right is Josephus Daniels, Secretary of the Navy, and at his left is Admiral Benson.

Democratic leaders of the Bronx maintained were the Republicans' efforts to inject the religious issue into the closing hours of the campaign. How much effect the whole affair had in drawing Catholic votes away from Wilson on November 7 it is impossible to say, but that for months it had been the cause of embarrassment and discomfort to the two principals, there was no doubt. In any case, there was no interruption of the periodic and polite communications between the President and the cardinal, and soon after Wilson suffered his stroke in Colorado in September, 1919, Gibbons hastened an expression of sympathy, a courtesy which three months later was returned when the old churchman was confined to his bed by illness.[49]

By the time the country prepared for another election campaign to choose a successor to Wilson the Cardinal of Baltimore was nearing his eighty-sixth birthday. By coincidence he was scheduled to be in Chicago the second week of June, 1920, for the silver jubilee of Archbishop Mundelein, the same week in which the Republicans gathered for their nominating convention. Gibbons was invited by the convention committee to offer the opening prayer on June 10, and he accepted the invitation. The nomination of Warren Harding which followed soon thereafter drew the cardinal's congratulations to the candidate, to which was added the remark that whatever the outcome of the election might be, as he said, "I feel the honor that has come to you is well deserved, and I shall always cherish the pleasure of your acquaintance."[50] In the autumn of that year the cardinal's brother, John T. Gibbons, read a statement of Bourke Cockran complaining of the fact that Harding was reported to have said that if elected he would have nothing to do with bringing the question of Irish freedom to the attention of Great Britain. It was apparent that the cardinal had privately communicated his preference for Harding to his brother, since Mr. Gibbons remarked that he intended to vote for the Republican nominee but, he added, "I would be very glad to read some kind of a reasonable contradiction from the candidate whom you admire so much & at an early date."[51]

---

[49] 123-K, Tumulty to Gibbons, Washington, October 4, 1919, telegram; LC, Wilson Papers, Gibbons to Wilson, Baltimore, January 1, 1920.
[50] 127-U, Gibbons to Harding, Baltimore, June 22, 1920, copy.
[51] 129-T, Gibbons to Gibbons, New Orleans, October 16, 1920.

What answer the cardinal made is not known but, in any case, his preference of candidates was carefully concealed two days before the election when he preached in the cathedral. He alluded to some despondent prophets who were in the habit around election time of predicting the overthrow of the government and of other dire consequences that would ensue. "I have been listening," he said, "to these forebodings for the last sixty years." In every instance, he continued, the people had awakened the day after election to find the government transacting its business as quietly as if no election had taken place. From the inauguration of Lincoln to the present hour the cardinal had been the personal witness of tremendous social and political upheavals which had threatened to rend the nation asunder. He had no uneasiness, therefore, about the future of the United States, for he rested his hopes on the enlightenment and patriotism of its citizens, foreign-born as well as native, on the wisdom of its statesmen, and on the valor of its soldiers. In conclusion he referred to the voting which would take place in two days, but far from making any pronouncement concerning the candidates, he merely stated:

> Pray earnestly this morning that over-ruling Providence may select for us a Chief Executive endowed with equity and justice; and that his administration may redound to the temporal and spiritual welfare of our beloved country, and to the preservation of our political and social institutions.[52]

During the course of the campaign of 1920 Cardinal Gibbons gave an interview in favor of the League of Nations which was carried by the Baltimore *Sun* of October 21 and by many other papers. The statement upset some of the Republican leaders who were opposed to the league, and after the election of Harding one of his principal supporters, Colonel George Harvey, editor of the *North American Review,* referred to the matter in a letter to his friend, Monsignor John W. Norris, pastor of St. Peter's Church in New Brunswick, New Jersey. He said he had spoken of the interview to Harding, and the latter had assured him that he had not attached any importance to Gibbons'

---

[52] 130-E, copy of Gibbons' sermon preached in the Baltimore cathedral on Sunday, October 31, 1920. This was the cardinal's last sermon in the cathedral and it was published in the Baltimore *Sun* of March 25, 1921, the day after his death.

remarks and had not for a moment questioned his friendliness or sincerity. Harding had authorized Harvey to extend to His Eminence his warmest greetings, and to express the hope that among the first whom it would be his privilege to receive in the White House would be the cardinal whom, along with all good citizens, he held in the deepest reverence.[53] By the time this news was conveyed to Baltimore the aged prelate had entered upon his last illness, and it was left to the discretion of his secretary whether or not it should be presented to him.[54] There was no doubt of the sincerity of the message of the President-elect, but by the day of Harding's inauguration on March 4, 1921, the cardinal was less than three weeks removed from death, and he was thus denied the pleasure of seeing his candidate as the occupant of the executive mansion.

No man who had attained the prestige of Cardinal Gibbons with the leaders in national life could hope to escape from requests that he use his influence in behalf of those who were not so highly favored. From his early years as Archbishop of Baltimore up to a short time before his death, Gibbons was the recipient of an almost constant stream of appeals that he intervene to secure favors of one kind or another, either for friends or the acquaintances of friends. Many of these requests, it is true, represented persons who had a real need, although in the case of others, it was often merely personal advancement that was sought through the medium of the cardinal's influence. With all, regardless of their motive, he displayed a never-failing politeness, but in a number of instances he did not see his way clear to intervene directly. A case in point was that of a woman for whom Archbishop Elder stood sponsor in the hope that Gibbons would try to secure her a position in the government. The cardinal's answer illustrated both the predicament in which he found himself at the time and how he often handled such matters. He told Elder:

> With every disposition to serve any one you recommend, I fear I can do nothing for the lady. Since the election of Mr. Cleveland appeals for patronage have poured in on me so fast from different parts of the country, until my letters become a drug in the administration market. However I will endorse any letter you may send in

[53] 131-S, Harvey to Norris, Santa Barbara, December 29, 1920.
[54] 132-H, Norris to Albert E. Smith, New Brunswick, January 7, 1921.

her behalf, but tell her not to come as Washington is filled with applicants.[55]

Doubtless there were other times in the years ahead when Gibbons felt fully as overwhelmed by petitions of this kind as he indicated to the Archbishop of Cincinnati in the early summer of 1885. The question of the appointment of Catholic chaplains, however, was a matter which fell more properly within his province, and at intervals he made recommendations of certain priests to the White House, occasionally at the suggestion of the President himself.[56] In 1895 Archbishop Corrigan informed Gibbons that Father John P. Chidwick of St. Stephen's Church in New York desired to enter the naval service and he asked, therefore, that the cardinal speak to Cleveland about it. Gibbons did so and thus there took place the appointment of the man who three years later gained fame as the chaplain of the ill-fated *Maine*.[57]

Requests for the cardinal's favor ranged over a wide variety of types of which a considerable number had to do with appointments to the diplomatic service. For example, upon the announcement of the retirement of James B. Eustis as ambassador to France in 1896 that post was sought by Bellamy Storer, a former congressman from Ohio and a recent convert to the Catholic Church. Storer outlined for Gibbons the reasons why he desired to go to Paris and asked for his intervention with President McKinley, a favor with which the cardinal promptly complied. Although Storer did not receive the Paris ambassadorship, his support of McKinley was rewarded in the following spring by his being named American minister to Belgium, whereupon he expressed his thanks to Gibbons for the kindly interest which the latter had taken in the matter.[58] Occasionally pressure

[55] 79-M-9, Elder to Gibbons, Cincinnati, June 10, 1885; AAC, Gibbons to Elder Baltimore, June 12, 1885.

[56] For example, on one occasion President Roosevelt told the cardinal, "I think there will shortly be a vacancy in the chaplains in the army to which I should like to appoint a priest. Can you recommend one?" (99-C-3, Roosevelt to Gibbons, Washington, October 5, 1901; LC, Roosevelt Papers, Gibbons to Roosevelt, Baltimore, October 7, 1901.)

[57] 93-Q-6, Corrigan to Gibbons, New York, January 28, 1895; AANY, Gibbons to Corrigan, Baltimore, January 31, 1895; 93-R-3, Gibbons to Cleveland, Baltimore, February 4, 1895, copy.

[58] 94-U-8, Storer to Gibbons, Cincinnati, December 14, 1896; 94-W-10, McKinley to Gibbons, Canton, Ohio, December 31, 1896; 95-N-8, Storer to Gibbons,

was put on the cardinal to give the endorsement of his name wherein he sensed the inappropriateness of his intervention, and in cases such as these he wisely sought the counsel of friends who could properly guide him. When Thomas Fortune Ryan of New York attempted to gain Gibbons' support for the election of Senator Underwood as leader of the senate, it was not forthcoming. Ryan asked Bishop O'Connell of Richmond to have the cardinal approach Senator Henry F. Ashurst of Arizona with a request that he vote for Underwood. Gibbons, however, submitted the matter to Senator David I. Walsh of Massachusetts who was thoroughly familiar with the situation and who strongly advised him to have nothing to do with it since, as he said, in the first place it was not an issue which involved any principle which would justify interference from one in Gibbons' position and, second, it would do no good as the senator from Arizona had already committed his vote.[59]

The fact that the Cardinal of Baltimore managed to remain on friendly terms with both Republicans and Democrats, plus the fact that he always maintained a discreet silence about his personal political affiliations, probably accounted for the more or less uninterrupted flow of calls for his aid, regardless of what party was in power. That Gibbons followed political movements with the keenest interest we know, but not even to members of his own household was it ever divulged to which party he gave his vote when he went to the polls.[60] Following the election of 1900, wherein there were loud outcries of imperialism by the Democrats against McKinley and his administration, the cardinal expressed his satisfaction to Archbishop Ireland that the election had passed off so quietly and that the nation had

---

Cincinnati, April 27, 1897. Some years later the cardinal was similarly approached by Archbishop Ireland in behalf of the St. Louis railroad magnate, Richard C. Kerens, whom Taft appointed soon thereafter as ambassador to Vienna (AAB, unclassified, Ireland to Gibbons, St. Paul, June 16, 1909, enclosing Ireland to Kerens, St. Paul, June 16, 1909, copy; Kerens to Gibbons, St. Louis, March 14, 1910).

[59] 124-G, Ryan to O'Connell, New York, *Confidential*. There was no date on the letter, but the incident took place sometime in December, 1919; *ibid.,* Walsh to Gibbons, Washington, n.d., *Confidential*.

[60] Monsignor Louis R. Stickney informed the writer in an interview of May 6, 1951, that he often accompanied Gibbons to the polls, but in all the years he lived with him he could not recall a suggestion of any kind from the cardinal which might have indicated his party affiliation.

acquiesced so readily in McKinley's victory over Bryan. But in his opinion many of the American Catholic papers had cut a sorry figure during the campaign, and he was plainly irked at their conduct. "They were hysterical in their abuse of the dominant party," he said, "& foretold that the country would go to perdition if their views were not upheld at the polls. They lack a judicial spirit in their utterances."[61]

One might imply from these remarks that Gibbons' sympathies were with the Republicans, but even to so close a friend as Ireland it was not stated specifically. Four years later a friend of the cardinal's, Henry G. Davis, former senator from West Virginia, received the nomination for vice-president by the Democratic Party at its convention in St. Louis. The candidate approached Gibbons some weeks later, and in a bid for his support he said, "The very warm regard I have always entertained for you, and which you have so graciously permitted me to show, leads me to express the thought that you will aid us as far as you can consistently do so." The cardinal's reply made it clear that he had too high a regard for his character as a churchman to engage actively in the field of politics. He told Davis:

> My first impulse, on reading of your nomination to the Vice-Presidency was to congratulate you on the honor conferred on you by your fellow-citizens. But I hesitated to write, fearing my letter might be construed in a partisan sense, and that I might be considered as espousing publicly a political party.
>
> The delicate position I fill has always debarred me from giving public expression to my political views.
>
> Whatever may be the outcome of the campaign, your friends, among whom I claim to be one, will rejoice in the well-merited distinction conferred on you.[62]

Although the candidate was doubtless disappointed at his failure to enlist the support of Gibbons, the tactfulness of the latter's response to his request left no just grounds for complaint.

A few days in advance of a bitterly fought municipal election in Philadelphia a year later, the Secretary of the Navy, Charles J. Bonaparte, grew alarmed at the danger to the Church which

---

[61] AASP, Gibbons to Ireland, Baltimore, November 20, 1900, copy.

[62] 101-K, Davis to Gibbons, Elkins, West Virginia, August 25, 1904; Gibbons to Davis, Baltimore, August 31, 1904, *Personal,* copy.

he sensed from a report that Archbishop Ryan had accepted an invitation that might publicly commit him if he were to accept. The campaign had been characterized by revelations of serious corruption and scandals in both camps, and Bonaparte thus urged the cardinal to warn Ryan. Gibbons assured his friend that he was no stranger to what he termed "the seething political cauldron in Philadelphia." But he felt quite certain that the archbishop would not in any way interfere with the election issues by a public utterance, although he confessed an apprehension that some churchmen in Philadelphia might suffer from the imputation of partisanship cast upon them. He stated that the gospel for the following Sunday contained the words, "Pay what thou owest," which would afford him an opportunity to preach in his own cathedral on the evil of political graft. "But of course," he concluded, "my remarks will be impersonal."[63]

Some years later the presidential campaign of 1912 witnessed a serious recrudescence of anti-Catholic bigotry with the *Menace,* founded in the previous year, leading the way. The familiar accusations of the existence of a Catholic political machine were heard, and it was stated that by its intrigues the foundation of American institutions and liberties was threatened. The charges were the grossest calumnies, for as a non-Catholic historian of the movement stated, "So far as the Catholic Church was concerned there was not the least evidence of any such organized body."[64] As groundless as these charges were, they proved a source of distress to the cardinal who, as we have seen, had always been at pains to prevent even the suggestion of a Catholic political party. He told Archbishop Ireland how of late he had been watching the growth of the movement against the Church which he judged to have begun about the time of the announcement of the two new American cardinals, Farley and O'Connell, in the autumn of 1911. But so far, he said, all was peaceful in Baltimore and he informed his friend that he had recently been invited to open the Democratic

---

[63] LC, Bonaparte Papers, Gibbons to Bonaparte, Baltimore, November 1, 1905. The sermon for the twenty-first Sunday after Pentecost was later published in Gibbons' *Discourses and Sermons,* pp. 487–496, where the preacher dwelt on the virtue of justice and the various kinds of dishonesty by which it was violated. He stated, too, that it was a subject which ought to be treated more frequently from the pulpit.

[64] Myers, *History of Bigotry in the United States,* p. 267.

National Convention the following month in his see city with prayer.[65] Ireland thoroughly agreed that anti-Catholic sentiment was on the rise and the archbishop — a pronounced Republican — concluded by saying, "Be on your guard while invoking blessings upon the Democratic Convention. Pray hard for the country, not so much for the party. I still hope that Mr. Taft will be nominated & elected."[66]

Needless to say, Gibbons' appearance before the Democrats on June 25 was carried off with a fine impartiality for the political issues at stake in that hotly contested nominating body, and the same could be said for his final participation in a national convention eight years later at Chicago. We have already mentioned the coincidence of his presence in Chicago for the Mundelein jubilee during the week of the convention. When the Republican leaders learned that the cardinal would be in the city, they quickly got in touch with the Archbishop of Chicago and asked him to prevail on Gibbons to open one of the days of their proceedings with prayer.[67] The cardinal accepted and on June 10 he came before the convention where he received a great ovation. He used a paraphrase of Archbishop Carroll's prayer for the nation, added several paragraphs on the general religious sentiments of the American people, and closed with the following words which were carried by the Baltimore *Sun* and other leading papers on June 11:

> I have been, O Lord, in my day a personal and living witness of the many tremendous upheavals which threatened to rend the nation asunder, from the inauguration of Thy servant, Abraham Lincoln, even unto this day. But Thou hast saved us in the past by Thy almighty power and I have an abiding confidence that Thou wilt be graciously with us in every future emergency.

Gibbons had prayed over the Democrats at Baltimore in 1912

---

[65] AASP, Gibbons to Ireland, Baltimore, May 25, 1912, copy.

[66] 108-H, Ireland to Gibbons, St. Paul, June 8, 1912. Archbishop Riordan, too, was a Taft man. He acknowledged that Roosevelt had given the Catholics many marks of favor but, as he told the cardinal, "Mr. Taft is superior, and the needs of the country will be in safer and more conservative hands should Mr. Taft be elected" (108-H, Riordan to Gibbons, San Francisco, June 10, 1912).

[67] 127-E, Mundelein to Gibbons, Chicago, May 21, 1920; 127-F, Gibbons to Mundelein, Baltimore, May 22, 1920, telegram in copy; 127-G, Fred W. Upham to Gibbons, Chicago, May 24, 1920, telegram; *ibid.,* Gibbons to Upham, Baltimore, May 24, 1920, telegram in copy.

and over the Republicans at Chicago in 1920, but to neither party did he make any public commitment, and those who might have been curious about the cardinal's political faith could only indulge their imaginations concerning the camp to which he owed his allegiance.

Two days before the national election on November 5, 1912, which closed a colorful three-cornered contest between Taft, Wilson, and Roosevelt the Cardinal of Baltimore preached in his cathedral on the subject, "Will the American Republic Endure?" It was a sermon that reflected the keen and intelligent interest which he had always manifested in public affairs, and in urging his audience to take seriously their duties as citizens, he stated that it was his profound conviction that if ever the Republic were to disappear its downfall would be due, not to a hostile invasion, but to what he termed "the indifference, lethargy and political apostacy of her own sons." And the preacher then added:

> There are three conspicuous citizens who are now candidates for the Presidency. Whatever may be my private and personal preference and predilection, it is not for me in this sacred pulpit or anywhere else publicly to dictate or even suggest to you the candidate of my choice.[68]

The exhortation to civic virtue which was the main theme of the closing portion of Gibbons' sermon, lost nothing by the emphasis he gave to such a concept of his office as a churchman. He never seemed to grow weary of speaking on the subject of the need for alert citizenship, and on the harmony which existed between the Catholic Church and the American Republic. For example, in his book, *Our Christian Heritage,* which appeared in 1889 he included a chapter entitled, "The Religious Element in Our American Civilization," and seven years later his volume addressed to priests, *The Ambassador of Christ,* contained a chapter on "The Study of Men and the Times" in which he explained the importance of public issues to the Church and the necessity, therefore, for priests to inform themselves on these questions. The minister of Christ, he contended, was pre-eminently the friend and father of the people, and for that reason he could not remain indifferent to the social, political,

---

[68] *A Retrospect of Fifty Years,* II, 214.

and economic problems affecting the interest and happiness of the nation. And yet every pronouncement of this kind that came from the cardinal was fittingly blended with his role as a teacher of morals. In a sermon which he called "Obedience to All Lawful Authority" he deplored a lack of reverence for those in authority as one of the greatest social diseases of the age. Gibbons would not have citizens uncritical of their government, but he pleaded for a calm and dispassionate judgment on the acts of those in authority, rather than a reckless and partisan carping which served no good purpose. Neither had he any illusions about the evil of corruption in politics but, as he said on this occasion, the moral condition of the state is what the citizens make it. The state was the creation of the citizens and, as he put it, "The destiny of the commonwealth, under God, is in our own hands."[69]

Certainly there was no citizen of the United States in his time who did more to keep high the moral tone of the nation than the Archbishop of Baltimore. Every measure that would improve the state of public morality received his support. When, for example, the Reverend Wilbur F. Crafts, a Protestant minister of New York, asked for his endorsement of a petition to Congress that a law be passed against Sunday work in the government's mail and military services and in interstate commerce, it received a prompt compliance. Gibbons lauded those who were contending against the violation of the Christian Sabbath by unnecessary labor, and in reminding the minister of the pronouncement of the Third Plenary Council of Baltimore on this subject, the cardinal said he was most happy to add his name to that of the numerous petitioners.[70] About three years later he won wide acclaim when he denounced the Louisiana lottery in a letter to General George D. Johnston who headed an antilottery committee. Since the evils of the lottery had spread over the land and into Maryland and the District of Columbia, he maintained that he felt free to speak about them. The New Orleans *Daily Picayune* of January 16, 1892, carried the cardinal's strong letter to Johnston, in which he said that a

---

[69] *Discourses and Sermons,* p. 500. Cf. *Our Christian Heritage,* pp. 472–483; *The Ambassador of Christ,* pp. 249–266.

[70] 85-K-1, Crafts to Gibbons, New York, December 1, 1888; 85-K-5, Gibbons to Crafts, Baltimore, December 4, 1888, copy.

business whose manifest and inevitable result and influence on the people was such as that of the lottery, ought to be killed. It was an enemy to the honesty and peace of the community, to the happiness and comfort of the home, and to individual thrift and enterprise and, he concluded, "it is the duty of every upright citizen and earnest Christian to aid in its dethronement or suppression."

Gibbons' statement was widely publicized in the press of the country and won much favorable comment from both the newspapers and private individuals. Among those who wrote him was his brother John who said the cardinal's letter to Johnston had put his name on the lips of everybody in New Orleans. "It was a splendid document," he said, "it covered the case exactly & while it carried dismay into the Lottery camp it afforded great consolation to both Catholics & Protestants who were conscientiously fighting the infamy."[71] The pressure of public opinion against the lottery proved to be so effective that on February 4 the New York *Times* announced that the effort to renew its charter in Louisiana had been abandoned. When the cardinal received a plea two years later to speak out against the rebirth of its activities at Tampa, Florida, he had no hesitancy in reiterating his objection to the lottery on principle, and of adding that he would even be glad to see a law forbidding the transmission of tickets or prizes through the mails and express companies of the country.[72]

Another question of public morals which drew repeated condemnations from Cardinal Gibbons was that of divorce. As a bishop of the Catholic Church it was to be expected that he should have opposed divorce as contrary to the doctrine of his

---

[71] 89-Q-7, Gibbons to Gibbons, New Orleans, March 5, 1892. Senator Edward Douglas White of Louisiana told him, "I was gratified beyond measure. Its tone and temper could not be excelled, and it will do a world of good. It puts the Church, speaking through you, on the highest possible plane. Every Louisianian will feel grateful to you for it" (AAB, unclassified White to Gibbons, Washington, January 19, 1892). The Baltimore *Sun* of January 18, 1892, carried the favorable reactions to Gibbons' lottery letter from a number of other papers. The cardinal himself congratulated Archbishop Janssens of New Orleans on the prospective abolition of the lottery, and with delicate tact attributed its disappearance as "due in no small measure to your unpurchasable rectitude & to the words you spoke in season" (AANO, Gibbons to Janssens, Baltimore, February 16, 1892).

[72] 93-A-9, S.H. Woodbridge to Gibbons, Boston, January 16, 1894; 93-B-4, Gibbons to Woodbridge, Baltimore, January 17, 1894, copy.

Church. But he never failed to associate his doctrinal objection with a picture of the grave social evils which resulted to the nation as a consequence of homes broken in the divorce court. In fact, in an essay he published in 1916 under the title "The Claims of the Catholic Church in the Making of the Republic," the cardinal advanced the Church's struggle against divorce as a genuine contribution to the welfare of American society.[73] Again and again he cited the figures for the growth of divorce in the United States, and warned of the peril to family life that would ensue if it were not checked. "How can we call ourselves a Christian people," he asked, "if we violate a fundamental law of Christianity? And if the sanctity and indissolubility of marriage does [sic] not constitute a cardinal principle of the Christian religion, I am at a loss to know what does."[74] On his eighty-sixth birthday a reporter of the New Orleans *Times-Picayune* interviewed the old churchman at the home of his friend Robert T. Shriver at Union Mills, Maryland. In his account of the interview which was published in his paper on July 23, 1920, the reporter stated that at the very outset Gibbons had brought up the subject of divorce, a matter which he was quoted as considering "the greatest social and domestic danger of the present day." Asked what he would recommend to offset the evil, the cardinal stated that the remedy was twofold: first, moral, to keep the home undefiled and united through a religious motive; and, second, legal, to pass the recently pro-

---

[73] *A Retrospect of Fifty Years*, I, 259–261.

[74] Gibbons, *The Catholic Church and the Marriage Tie* (Buffalo, 1899), p. 12. This brochure was No. 6 in the pamphlet series of the Catholic Truth Society. Gibbons spoke and wrote frequently on the evils of divorce. For example, he joined with Henry C. Potter, Protestant Episcopal Bishop of New York, and Colonel Robert G. Ingersoll in a symposium entitled "Is Divorce Wrong?" which appeared in the *North American Review*, CXLIX (November, 1889), 513–538. Samuel W. Dike, corresponding secretary of the National Divorce Reform League, thanked the cardinal for his contribution, and remarked, "This will be especially useful to us as showing that the Church recognizes the importance of those minor reforms in legislation which are only steps towards her own position and to the ideal of State or National Law" (87-E-8, Dike to Gibbons, Auburndale, Massachusetts, February 21, 1890). Nine years later an article of Gibbons' on divorce was read in England by the Reverend Frederick George Lee, vicar of All Saints Church, Lambeth, who was so pleased with it that he said he had ordered forty copies to be sent to all the Anglican bishops whom, he hoped, would read it with the deepest interest. Lee stated that Cardinal Newman was "a near connection of mine" (97-J-3, Lee to Gibbons, Lambeth, June 12, 1899).

posed Jones Bill which favored a constitutional amendment empowering Congress to make uniform divorce laws for all states.

A further problem in the realm of public morals which frequently elicited the attention of Gibbons was that of religious intolerance. It was a question that was certain to arouse his interest, which was not surprising in view of his naturally benevolent disposition toward others and, too, of the fact that he belonged to a Church that had often felt the lash of intolerance. In the history of American Catholicism no man succeeded better than the cardinal in preserving the finest traditions of tolerance toward those of other religious faiths, while at the same time never compromising his position as a bishop of the Church of Rome. His broad spirit of charity was, of course, well known throughout the country, and at the time of the persecution of the Jews by Russia in 1890 it was given public expression. Gibbons was appealed to by one of the editors of the *Jewish Exponent* to voice his condemnation of the treatment of the Russian Jews, and he gave an immediate response. In a statement that reviewed the debt which Christians owed to the Jewish religion, he stated, "I am disposed to speak very strongly in this matter as I feel it at heart." He mentioned the reputation enjoyed by Jews as husbands and fathers of their families, and he remarked that if there were individuals of the Hebrew race who had committed offenses against the law in Russia, they should be dealt with according to the code governing all civilized governments. Such would be sufficient to insure justice, and likewise to protect the Jewish people from so drastic a remedy as the policy of extermination. "I express the ardent hope," he concluded, "that all nations, through their governments, will become more and more tolerant in matters of religion as we are in this country; that they will take these United States as their guide, where all men, standing equal in the sight of God, are equal before the law."[75]

But in spite of the protests from the United States and other countries, the Russian Jews continued to suffer severely and in

---

[75] 88-E-6, B. H. Hartogensis to Gibbons, Baltimore, December 13, 1890. Gibbons' reply of December 15, 1890, to Hartogensis and his statement to a reporter of the *Jewish Exponent* four days later were published in that paper on December 19, 1890, and reprinted in other Jewish journals such as the *Menorah,* X (January, 1891), 46–47.

November, 1905, a committee of prominent citizens of Baltimore was formed to assist in the problem of their relief. Gibbons attended a meeting in the mayor's office, and as the Cincinnati *American Israelite* of November 30 reported, he made a moving speech on what the world owed to the Hebrew race, and how all men of good will should now respond to the call for pity and charity that had reached them from the stricken Jews. Repeatedly in after years he spoke out in behalf of the persecuted Hebrew race, for example, in November, 1919, when he exhorted his priests and people to lend assistance to the Jewish War Relief Committee that was gathering funds for the aid of their suffering coreligionists of central Europe. Some years after the cardinal's death Rabbi William Rosenau, who had known him intimately for nearly thirty years, wrote an article in which he stated that Gibbons had proved, both by the performance of deeds and the exercise of his influence, that he had always stood ready to help whenever Gentile co-operation and assistance were needed for the Jewish people.[76]

The Salvation Army likewise was the beneficiary of Gibbons' kindliness to his fellow citizens of other faiths. A few months following the close of World War I, a drive was launched for funds to continue its benefactions to the men in the armed services. The cardinal was asked for an endorsement of the drive and the New York *Times* of April 18, 1919, carried his answer to the chairman of the national committee, in which he stated that along with his fellow citizens he had rejoiced in the splendid work that the Salvation Army had done for the fighting men, and he had been impressed by the fact that the returning troops were high in its praise. He was also more than happy to commend the organization because it was free from sectarian bias, for, as he said, the man in need of help was the object of its effort, and never was there a question of his creed or color. Naturally Gibbons' response gave great satisfaction at

---

[76] "Cardinal Gibbons and His Attitude toward Jewish Problems," *Publications of the American Jewish Historical Society,* No. 31 (1928), 219–224. This article reprinted a number of letters exchanged between Gibbons and Rosenau on Jewish questions. For other evidences of Gibbons' efforts for the Jews cf. the Chicago *American,* October 27, 1913, and the Cincinnati *Enquirer,* November 24, 1919. The writer is indebted for photostatic copies of the items in Notes 75 and 76 to Professor Jacob R. Marcus, director of the American Jewish Archives, Cincinnati 20, Ohio.

the Salvation Army headquarters, and in thanking him for his letter the national chairman of the drive commented:

> Expressing, as it does, that spirit of broad tolerance and democracy which has made you beloved and venerated by all Americans, irrespective of race and creed, it will be a great help to Commander Booth and those associated with her in the effort to raise the funds so essential to the efficiency of their labors for humanity.[77]

All through the years Cardinal Gibbons followed the deliberations of Congress very closely, and from time to time he used his prerogative as a citizen to speak his mind on measures before the national legislature. As the ranking dignitary of a Church that was made up so largely of immigrants, and as one who was himself of immigrant parentage, he naturally felt a particular interest in legislation affecting the immigrant. In the closing days of his second administration in 1897 Grover Cleveland had vetoed a bill that would have restricted immigration by a literacy test. However, the advocates of the idea were not discouraged and they later returned to the attack. At a time when some believed that a similar bill would be enacted by Congress in 1906, the cardinal informed President Roosevelt that he regarded restrictions of this kind on immigration as unwise. He recalled the forceful veto message of Cleveland nine years before, and he stated that in his opinion the country should never forget the debt it owed to the immigrant. He hoped, therefore, that the President would see his way to prevent the passage of the bill if it came to him for his signature.[78]

The bill failed to pass in 1906 but six years later a new effort was made. In reply to an inquiry from Rabbi Rosenau concerning his judgment on restricting immigration by means of a literacy test, Gibbons made it clear that he was still strongly

[77] 121-F, Charles Whitman to Gibbons, New York, April 17, 1919. Gibbons' reputation as an enemy of religious intolerance endured long after his death. As recently as February, 1950, in the first of the lenten conferences in the Cathedral of Notre Dame of Paris which were preached by Father Michel Riquet, S.J., a former prisoner of the Nazis, he quoted the cardinal as having said, "With all my heart I pray that religious intolerance may never take root in our beloved country; that the only king ever to rule over our consciences be the King of Kings; that the only prison ever built among us to punish the sin of unbelief or false belief be the prison of troubled conscience; that the only motive for our adherence to the truth be not fear of man but the love of the true and the good." *Catholic News* (New York), March 24, 1950.
[78] LC, Roosevelt Papers, Gibbons to Roosevelt, Baltimore, June 7, 1906.

opposed to such a policy. He felt it would do great harm for, as he said, if the immigrant were industrious and thrifty he would make a useful citizen whether or not he were literate. "The educated schemer," said the cardinal, "is in more ways than one more dangerous than the honest workman, even though he be illiterate."[79] President Taft vetoed the bill in 1912, and the reappearance of the proposed legislation in the Wilson administration found Gibbons again in the camp of the opposition. In a letter which he wrote in response to a request for an expression of his views, he outlined his reasons and stated that such a bill would bar the entrance of great numbers of desirable citizens to the United States who, although they might not be able to read or write, possessed health, virtue, good sense, business ability, and a desire to succeed with high honor. He cited the example of Charlemagne as one who had been illiterate, as also some of those who had entered the new world on the *Mayflower* and the *Ark* and the *Dove* in the early seventeenth century to lay the foundations of the colonies of Massachusetts and Maryland. What would the United States have amounted to as a nation, he asked, if after the Revolution its founders had closed its portals to honest but illiterate immigrants? Many of the nation's greatest men had been either immigrants or the sons of immigrants, and Gibbons stated that he still cherished the hope that his country might remain the refuge of honest and virtuous men and women who conscientiously believed their native lands did not afford them the rights and advantages that good men craved. In conclusion he expressed the wish that President Wilson might veto the most recent immigration restriction bill and that the United States would continue to welcome good men and women to help it grow greater and stronger, while at the same time they secured for themselves the blessings of comfort, happiness, and peace.[80] Although Wilson vetoed the bill embodying a literacy test, the proponents of the measure continued their efforts and finally in 1917 it was enacted into law over the President's head. The cardinal and his friends had

---

[79] American Jewish Archives, Gibbons to Rosenau, Baltimore, May 5, 1912, photostat.

[80] 111-C, Gibbons to Jacob Epstein, Baltimore, January 21, 1915, copy. The letter to Epstein was published in the New York *Herald* of January 25, 1915, where it was stated that a protest meeting against the bill held that day in the Victoria Theater featured the reading of the Gibbons message.

lost in their struggle to keep open the United States to the honest but unlettered immigrant. It was not the first contest of this kind that he had lost, nor would it be the last.

Another defeat for Gibbons' position on a public question involved the ratification in January, 1919, of the eighteenth amendment to the Constitution. From his earliest years he had been a strong advocate of a temperate use of intoxicating liquors. In February, 1871, he had delivered a lecture on that subject at the invitation of a non-Catholic group at Wilmington, North Carolina, wherein he described the evils of intemperance, and the lecture was so successful that several days later he was asked to repeat it in Raleigh.[81] Gibbons continued his encouragement to the temperance movement, and in 1891 he cut short his summer holiday in order to be in Washington for the twenty-first general convention of the Catholic Total Abstinence Union of America. He presided at the Mass in St. Patrick's Church and afterward addressed the delegates in Lincoln Hall, where he stated that he would have felt recreant to his duty were he to have absented himself and failed to welcome them to the archdiocese. He made it clear that he was not a teetotaler when he alluded to the fact that, unlike Bishop Keane who was present, he was a temperate man but not a temperance man. But in conclusion he said that the more the principles of the C.T.A.U.A. were embodied in the hearts of the American people, the stronger and more stable would the nation's political and social fabric become.[82] There could be no reasonable doubt, therefore, about the attitude that the cardinal took on the question of the abuses that intemperance entailed, even though he personally indulged in a moderate way and on occasion took liquor for social and medicinal purposes.

---

[81] 72-D-5, Theodore N. Ramsay to Gibbons, Raleigh, February 23, 1871; 72-D-6, James W. King to Gibbons, Wilmington, February 25, 1871.

[82] *Proceedings of the Twenty-First General Convention of the Catholic Total Abstinence Union of America, held in the City of Washington, D. C., August 5th and 6th, 1891* (Philadelphia, 1891), pp. 43–44. Fourteen years later Gibbons was present with President Roosevelt in Wilkes-Barre at the thirty-fifth general convention of the C.T.A.U.A. on August 10, 1905. But at that time the tension between the coal operators and the miners overshadowed the temperance issue, and in his speech the cardinal spoke on the relations of capital and labor and did not mention temperance at all. New York *Herald,* August 11, 1905. On this movement cf. Sister Joan Bland, *Hibernian Crusade. The Story of the Catholic Total Abstinence Union of America* (Washington, 1951).

As the temperance agitation gained momentum in the last years of the century Carry Nation's vigorous and dramatic campaign to rid Kansas of the liquor traffic attracted national attention. When the cardinal was asked for his opinion about the happenings in Kansas, he replied, "I have never been able to convince myself that what we call total abstinence is essential to morality." He cited the examples of France and Italy where people daily drank wine with no ill effects to their morality or their health, and he mentioned that even at the Vatican the papal doctors had prescribed wine for the use of Leo XIII. One of the features of the program which he especially deplored was the impossibility of enforcing total abstinence upon large communities which, according to Gibbons, led, in turn, either to hypocrisy or to illegality, and he named the State of Maine as an example of what he meant. The cardinal's remedy was a high license system by which the license to sell liquor would be very costly. Moreover, licenses should be given only to reputable citizens, the number of saloons should be strictly limited in each community, and severe fines should be imposed for infractions of the law with a revocation of the license in the case of a repeated offense. This, said Gibbons, had been done in Maryland with good results, and in his own state he had even suggested that the license fee be fixed as high as $1,000.[83]

But in spite of the forces arrayed against the movement toward national prohibition of intoxicating liquors, it gained ground steadily and by 1915 it had become formidable. When Gibbons was asked for his opinion on the proposed federal law he had his secretary reply that his reasons for opposing prohibition were many. Added to the familiar ones which he had previously made known, was the spirit of fanaticism that in many places had recently taken hold of the promoters of the

---

[83] "Cardinal Gibbons on the Saloon," an editorial in *The Review* (St. Louis), VII (February 14, 1901), 371. There were others besides Gibbons who reprobated the excesses of some of the temperance campaigners at this time. Daniel Hudson, C.S.C., spoke out against the fanaticism of some Catholic temperance advocates, and he said, "The Catholic Church is not a mere temperance society, and a total abstinence pledge is not necessarily a passport to Paradise, as not a few would seem to suppose" (*Ave Maria*, XXXIX [August 11, 1894], 160). Bishop Spalding of Peoria was pleased with Hudson's remarks and in sending his congratulations, he stated, "These people if they had power would make us a sect of Methodists" (AUND, Hudson Papers, Spalding to Hudson, Peoria, August 13, 1894).

movement and had gone so far as to lend encouragement in some states to a prohibition against the importation of wine for the celebration of Mass. This the cardinal regarded as an interference with the rights of conscience. To cure the evil of excessive drinking he advanced the policy of local option as one that was much more likely to succeed, and he said that when it became evident in a community that the sale of intoxicating liquor was being abused, he believed that the voters of that locality should have the right to say by their ballots whether the abuse should continue or cease.[84] At the time the United States entered World War I two years later the prohibitionists redoubled their efforts and put the campaign on the basis of a war measure. The New York *Times* of April 29, 1917, carried a feature article on the question, in which it quoted Gibbons as saying, "I would regard the passage of a Federal prohibition law as a national catastrophe, little short of a crime against the spiritual and physical well-being of the American people." After advancing his standard arguments against the measure, he concluded by saying that he believed the country could attain national temperance, but he remained firm in the conviction that any enactment of a widespread prohibition law was a long step backward.

Gibbons did not falter as the campaign progressed, and as the prospect of a constitutional amendment drew closer he stepped up his opposition. On February 6, 1918, the New York *Times* published a statement from the cardinal in which he said that the state legislatures should not bow to the fanaticism which seemed to be ruling the country in respect to this issue. He predicted that if prohibition became a law illicit stills would spring up all over the land which would make low-grade whiskey that would do more harm than good. It had been stated, he said, that liquor was injurious to health, but he instanced the sale of many articles in the average drugstore which were far more injurious, some of which would be deadly if taken

---

[84] 111-P, Eugene J. Connelly to D. H. Campbell, Baltimore, March 23, 1915, copy. In the same week Connelly replied in Gibbons' name to an inquirer in Chicago concerning the cardinal's views on vivisection. He stated that Gibbons had expressed himself sometime before against vivisection but his views were those of a layman, not a surgeon. He then added, "He is always open to conviction and in this matter will be guided by the conclusions of the medical fraternity" (111-P, Connelly to S. G. Brabrook, Baltimore, March 25, 1915, copy).

internally. Yet no one would think of closing the drugstores because they sold such products. Once more he characterized the enactment of such a law as a calamity, and gave it as his view that such would be a step toward the abridgment of American liberties. "Those favoring it," he said, "won't be satisfied and will try to impose other obnoxious laws until our liberty will be worth little." Henry S. Pritchett, President of the Carnegie Foundation for the Advancement of Teaching, among others was delighted with Gibbons' outspoken views, and it cheered him to know that there was a leader of the Church with the courage and the foresight to make such a statement. He was sure it would have great weight with thinking men in all parts of the country for, as he added, "such men have long admired and respected, not only your religious guidance, but also your patriotic devotion as an American."[85]

Obviously the cardinal could not withstand a movement of this kind without incurring criticism. When he gave out another statement to the Associated Press in January, 1919, that received wide distribution, he was bitterly attacked by William H. Anderson, Superintendent of the New York Anti-Saloon League. Anderson said that the cardinal's remark that prohibition would interfere with securing wine for sacramental purposes was false, and he further charged him with supporting resistance to the law because the distillers and saloonkeepers of Maryland belonged and contributed to the Catholic Church. The New York *Tribune* on January 27 wired Gibbons the text of Anderson's remarks and advised him that its columns were open to any telegraphed reply he might care to make at their expense.[86]

But it proved unnecessary for Gibbons to answer Anderson. The following day the New York *World* of January 28 carried a lengthy defense of the cardinal from Lemuel Ely Quigg, a former congressman and prominent New York newspaperman who was the son of a Methodist minister. Quigg said he had supposed that there was one American who was immune from what he termed the "insolent, slurring attacks of the Prohibitionist lobby," and that was the Cardinal of Baltimore. "If there is any one in our country," he continued, "who enjoys its universal

[85] 116-V, Pritchett to Gibbons, New York, February 6, 1918.
[86] AAB, unclassified, New York *Tribune* to Gibbons, New York, January 27, 1919, telegram.

love and respect, certainly he is that dear old man." Quigg maintained that in his fifty years of public life the cardinal had come to be the leader of all Americans and that he had won a place that gave him universal attention, and at the same time what he termed "the tribute of uncovered heads." He summarized Gibbons' position on the disputed question in a manner that delighted his many admirers, among whom was Thomas F. Gailor, Protestant Episcopal Bishop of Tennessee, who congratulated the cardinal on the bold stand which he had taken and called it that of a Christian statesman. To Bishop Gailor the prohibition law represented a triumph for religious intolerance, and he wanted Gibbons to know his gratitude for the declaration he had made in behalf of religious freedom.[87] The cardinal had thus done his best to prevent the folly of the eighteenth amendment but the forces aligned against him and those who shared his views were too strong, and it took the unhappy experiment of fifteen years to convince a majority that the road to national temperance did not lie along the route of federal legislation.

A second constitutional amendment that had much in common with the one that had brought national prohibition, and which was ratified a year and a half later, was that of woman suffrage. In the struggle that preceded their enactment both amendments drew support from many of the same elements of American society and were often opposed by the same groups. In the case of woman suffrage, Cardinal Gibbons was in the camp of the opposition as he had been with prohibition. In the spring of 1913 he was invited by Mrs. Robert Garrett, a prominent Baltimore woman who was a leading figure in the local fight against the movement, to attend an antisuffragist meeting. He excused himself from the meeting on the grounds that he did not go out at night except in extraordinary circumstances, but he assured her of his sympathy with the aims of the meeting, and he availed himself of the opportunity to set forth in detail the reasons for his opposition to woman suffrage, arguments which he repeated many times in the next few years.

Equal rights, said the cardinal, did not imply that both sexes should engage promiscuously in the same pursuits, but rather that each sex should discharge those duties which were adapted

---

[87] 120-H, Gailor to Gibbons, Memphis, February 12, 1919. Cf. also 120-E, Laurence J. Kelly, S.J., to Gibbons, Yonkers, New York, January 31, 1919.

to its physical constitution and were sanctioned by the canons of society. To debar woman from certain pursuits was not to degrade her. To restrict her field of action to the gentler avocations of life was not to fetter her aspirations after higher things. On the contrary, to secure to woman not so-called equal rights, but those supereminent rights which could not fail to endow her with a sacred influence in her own proper sphere was to enhance her dignity, for as soon as woman trenched on the domain of man she must not be surprised to find that the reverence once accorded to her would be in part withdrawn, and she would be destined to be soiled by the dust of the political arena. Gibbons instanced the rowdy scenes which were then almost a daily phenomenon in England as a result of the suffragist movement there, and he feared they foreshadowed what might take place in the United States. The insistence on woman's participation in politics was calculated, in the cardinal's mind, to rob her of all that was amiable and gentle and to give her nothing in return but masculine boldness and effrontery. Moreover, this insistence habitually emphasized woman's rights without a word about her duties and responsibilities. The result was that women were distracted from their true vocation which was the home and the cultivation of the domestic virtues of love for their husbands and children.

In deprecating woman suffrage Gibbons insisted that he was pleading for woman's dignity, that he was contending for her honor and striving to perpetuate the peerless prerogatives inherent in her sex, the charms and graces, as he said, which had exalted womankind and made her the ornament and coveted companion of man. He reminded his correspondent that because women did not vote, it did not follow that they were deprived of the right of suffrage by proxy. So powerful was the influence of a sensible matron over her husband and sons, he maintained, that they would often follow her counsel. He gave as an example the case of the son of Themistocles, the Grecian general of the fifth century B.C., who once asked his father for a favor. Themistocles had replied, "My son, I cannot grant you that favor; you must have recourse to your mother. For I rule Athens, Athens rules Greece, Greece rules the world, but your mother rules me." Woman was queen, indeed, said the cardinal, but her empire was the domestic kingdom. Though she was debarred from voting, it was she who brought into the world the nation's future citizens; it was she who reared and molded the characters of its future statesmen and rulers. In conclusion he cited the familiar story of Cornelia, the mother of the Gracchi, famous Roman tribunes of the second century B.C., who was once asked why she wore no jewels. Cornelia pointed to her two little sons and replied that they were her jewels which she would one day bequeath to the Roman Republic. "If Cornelia," said Gibbons, "instead of shaping the minds and hearts of her sons to deeds of virtue and patriotism at home, had wasted her time in the Roman Forum, history would never have recorded the noble exploits of the Gracchi."[88]

Many times during the course of the campaign for the nineteenth amendment Cardinal Gibbons repeated these sentiments. In his eightieth birthday interview, for example, which appeared in the Baltimore *American* of July 24, 1914, he signaled out three current movements for denunciation: the tyranny of Carranza and Villa in Mexico, the excesses of the Industrial Workers of the World, and the violent agitation of the suffragists in England. Both by public statements and by private advice to inquirers, he continued his efforts to prevent the fulfillment of the program of the advocates of woman suffrage.[89] Nor did he fight alone, for there were many Americans who felt as he did, and on the occasion of the first antisuffragist convention in Washington in December, 1916, his strong message to the meeting won him a laudatory editorial in the New York *Times* of December 10 in which it was stated:

> Most observers agree with him that in the States where women vote their vote has not altered results or improved the tone of public life. . . . A great dignitary of the Catholic Church, a great citizen, venerable by character, experience, wisdom, as well as years, cannot be thrown to the lionesses or lightly laughed down. It was time to speak bluntly. There are many millions in his church, in other churches, who hold permanently these views.

---

[88] 109-E, Gibbons to Mrs. Garrett, Baltimore, April 22, 1913, copy.

[89] 111-P, Eugene J. Connelly to Miss Catherine Hagerty, Baltimore, March 20, 1915, copy. Five years later when Louisiana was reported as favoring the nineteenth amendment, Gibbons had his secretary express his regret to his brother John in New Orleans, and to say, "He can see nothing but a trail of evil following in the passage of female suffrage. . . ." (126-U, Secretary to John T. Gibbons, Baltimore, May 24, 1920, copy).

But the views of Gibbons and the opposition failed to gain the ascendancy and on August 26, 1920, the nineteenth amendment to the Constitution granting the vote to women was declared ratified. With a national election only a few weeks distant, it was not strange that many should have wondered what the cardinal's opinion would be about the action women should now take. Knowing the profound respect which he had always shown toward the observance of the country's laws, it was not difficult to anticipate his attitude. On September 20 he gave an extended statement to the News Service of the National Catholic Welfare Council which was published in the *Record* of Louisville on September 30 and in most of the other Catholic papers of the country. At the outset he remarked:

> While I have always been opposed to Woman's Suffrage because I felt that political activities would tend to withdraw women from the more delicate and sacred pursuits of home life, now however, that the vote is theirs, I strongly urge upon all of them the exercise of suffrage, not only as a right but as a strict social duty.

He then emphasized the emancipating influence which the Catholic Church had exercised in behalf of women through Christian history as in contrast to her role in antiquity. He added that although women's ethical influence and spiritual power might now be lessened by the demoralizing effects of active participation in the political arena, yet it behooved Catholic women to take their new social duty seriously in the hope that they could minimize the evil forces that might menace the family and the home, the most essential factors in Christian civilization, by the extension of the suffrage. As an example of what he meant, he cited the proclamation of some of the more militant suffragists that they would aim to secure a national divorce law similar to that prevailing in Soviet Russia and Sweden, where divorce was permitted whenever a husband or wife desired it for any so-called cause or no cause at all. This, said Gibbons, was the sort of thing that Catholic women could help to combat by their use of the ballot. "It therefore becomes the duty of Catholic women to register and vote," he concluded, "and especially in the coming presidential election." In carrying out this duty he gave them a final reminder that they had an obligation to bring to bear upon politics their predilection for righteousness in choosing their candidate, as well as their desire and determination that American civilization should always conform to the enduring principles of Christianity.

We have had a number of occasions to speak of the interest which Gibbons took in the problems of education, an interest which was in no way diminished as he passed into old age. In 1915 there was introduced into the legislature of Ohio a bill to compel the reading of the Bible in the public schools. Some months before the cardinal had given an endorsement to the Reverend Wilbur F. Crafts, a Protestant minister, for the general reading of a book containing stories from the Bible. However, this statement was construed by some to mean that Gibbons approved the reading of the Bible in the public schools, and Louis P. Link, a state senator in Ohio, wrote to inquire if this was a correct interpretation of what he had said. The cardinal explained the circumstances of his previous statement to Crafts and he made it clear that no mention had been made, nor had anything been said, to give the impression that he had intended it as an endorsement for reading the Bible in the schools. "As things stand," he told Link, "I am opposed to this as it gives a teacher the opportunity to make such selections and comments as may offend the religious beliefs of the scholars. It is an entering wedge that might lead to great abuse."[90]

Four years later a more comprehensive legislative proposal on education became the center of widespread discussion with the Smith and Baer Bills in Congress which would create a federal department of education and grant federal aid to public schools. Archbishop Moeller of Cincinnati was inclined to oppose this legislation, and in his perplexity about the matter he sought the cardinal's counsel. Gibbons, in turn, submitted the question to Monsignor Edward A. Pace, Vice-Rector of the Catholic University of America, and asked him to give an opinion on the proposed bills. In response Pace outlined the various features of the Smith and Baer Bills, in which he said that neither measure explicitly deprived the states of control over their schools but left each state free to accept or reject federal aid. The only reference to the nonpublic schools, he remarked, was the provision in the

---

[90] 111-Q, Link to Gibbons, Columbus, March 25, 1915; Gibbons to Link, Baltimore, March 26, 1915, copy. The cardinal likewise denied to Rabbi Rosenau the interpretation put on his endorsement of the book (American Jewish Archives, Gibbons to Rosenau, Baltimore, March 27, 1915, photostat).

Smith Bill that no part of the appropriations should be used for the support of any religious or privately endowed or owned school. To Pace's mind this stipulation would strengthen the public schools at the expense of the private institutions, and for this reason he thought the American hierarchy should give the question their close attention. He foresaw a certain amount of good in federal control in the sense that it would thus be easier to remedy discrimination and, too, that it might prove helpful if the federal government should establish standards that had to be met in order to earn its aid. In this case the Catholic schools might qualify for federal aid on their merits. On the other hand, the movement toward federal control might go to extremes, as had recently happened in Michigan where an attempt had been made to force all children to attend the public schools. With all this in mind Pace urged strongly that there should be a committee in Washington who could speak authoritatively for the hierarchy on these questions, and thus forestall any measure that threatened the welfare of the Catholic schools. The opinions of the university professor were accepted in their entirety by Gibbons in his answer to the Archbishop of Cincinnati, and among the other points which he made his own was Pace's suggestion for a competent committee in Washington. As he said, "Such a Committee became a necessity for war purposes; it is more necessary for the protection of our rights in the matter of education."[91]

Meanwhile the archbishops acted and appointed a committee to investigate the proposed federal education bills with the understanding that the committee would report back at the meeting of the hierarchy the following September.[92] By the summer of that year the legislation had appeared in Congress under the form of the Smith-Towner Bill, and Senator Ransdell of Louisiana informed Gibbons that he had heard it said that the measure now met all objections of the Church. However, he was not so sure that it did, and for that reason he would like to have the cardinal's opinion. It was apparent from Gibbons' reply that he had not altogether made up his mind on the matter. He confessed

---

[91] 120-C, Moeller to Gibbons, Norwood, Ohio, January 20, 1919; ACUA, Pace Papers, Pace to Gibbons, Washington, January 27, 1919, copy; AAC, Gibbons to Moeller, Baltimore, January 28, 1919.

[92] 120-L, Minutes of the Meeting of the Archbishops, Washington, February 21, 1919.

that he had given it considerable thought but he had not arrived at any clear-cut views. He intended to submit the question to the general meeting of the hierarchy in September, and after that he would be in a better position to give advice. His uncertainty at that time was revealed when he told Ransdell:

> At the present time, I fear, that if this bill is passed it will put an entering wedge involving the rights of Catholics in the matter of education. A good feature about it however, is to me the placing of education under federal control. If I thought this bill would supercede certain state bills I would have less objection to it, for the reason that it would be more satisfactory to deal with a few intelligent men in Washington than is the case now where we have to deal with so many petty, narrow officials of each state.[93]

At their meeting in September, 1919, the bishops decided that the bill before Congress would militate against the interests of Catholic schools, and it was thus a relief to them when the platforms of the two major parties omitted any endorsement of the Smith-Towner Bill at their conventions in the summer of 1920.[94] By the time that it had again become an issue Cardinal Gibbons was dead.

The unique position which Gibbons had attained as a citizen was never more apparent than at the time of his various jubilees and the prominence accorded to him at important public functions. The festivities that marked his twenty-five years as a bishop in 1893 called forth tributes from all over the land. The Baltimore *Sun* of October 19 hailed him editorially as one who belonged to the class of men who had made the world of their day richer morally, intellectually, and industrially by their lives, and in the opinion of the *Sun* the cardinal's broad and loyal Americanism was a matter of special pride to Baltimoreans. A dinner in Gibbons' honor for civic officials was given on October 19 at the Carrollton Hotel under the auspices of the Catholic Club of the city, and there Vice-President Adlai E. Stevenson led the distinguished audience in tributes to the guest of honor. A feature

---

[93] 121-W, Ransdell to Gibbons, Washington, June 11, 1919, *Personal;* 121-XYZ, Gibbons to Ransdell, Baltimore, June 12, 1919, copy.

[94] Archbishop Austin Dowling of St. Paul used the case of the Smith-Towner Bill to emphasize to the hierarchy the need for a strong Department of Education in the N.C.W.C. to watch over such matters (128-G, Dowling to Gibbons, St. Paul, July 21, 1920, a circular letter to the American hierarchy).

of the evening was the reading of a letter from President Cleveland, who expressed regret that the pressure of public business prevented him from joining with those who testified to their respect and esteem for the cardinal.[95]

The *Jewish Exponent* of Philadelphia in its editorial of October 20 likewise extended the congratulations of the Jewish community to Gibbons, and they rejoiced that the Catholic Church in the United States had patterned itself after him, one of its best exemplars, a fact for which they thought all Americans should be grateful. The New York *Tribune* on October 22 paid tribute to the liberal views of the cardinal, but as a liberal, it was stated, his influence had never been shown by any exhibition of offense to those of the hierarchy who held to old ideas and ways. "Between the extremes of both parties," said the *Tribune,* "he stands as a harmonizer, a peacemaker." For all his splendid qualities the editorial writer felt that Gibbons might well be considered as a fit candidate for the Papacy at the next conclave. The New York *Times* of the same day took as the theme of its editorial Gibbons' oft-repeated views on Church and State in the United States which it highly approved. But in a less gracious manner it read the American Catholics a lesson about the only way in which the *Times* could conceive those harmonious relations might be endangered, namely, if Catholics should bid for government aid to their schools. There were numerous other expressions of affection and esteem for Gibbons on this occasion from many parts of the country, but it would be tedious to record them here.

Insofar as public functions were concerned, Cardinal Gibbons made every sacrifice to join the leaders of the nation at such celebrations when an invitation was extended to him. At times, however, his crowded schedule made it impossible to attend events of this kind. For example, on the day the Statue of Liberty was unveiled in New York harbor, October 28, 1886, he was kept away by a meeting of the archbishops over which he had to preside at his residence. Nonetheless, he sent a message to William M. Evarts, former Attorney General of the United States who was in charge of the arrangements, in which he expressed his desire to join with his fellow citizens throughout the land in rejoicing at the erection of this noble monument which, as he

---

[95] Baltimore *Sun,* October 20, 1893.

remarked, "will be another reminder of the ties which bind us to France, our faithful friend when friends were few."[96] Some years later he was invited to open the dedicatory ceremonies of the Louisiana Purchase Exposition at St. 'Louis with prayer. On April 30, 1903, Gibbons shared the platform at St. Louis with President Roosevelt and ex-President Cleveland where his prayer was again borrowed in part from that of Archbishop Carroll, to which he added the plea that, "As this new domain was added to our possessions without sanguinary strife, so may its soil never be stained by bloodshed in any foreign or domestic warfare."[97] In the spring of 1908 John Barrett, Director of the International Bureau of the American Republics, and Senator Elihu Root asked the cardinal if he would give the invocation at the laying of the cornerstone of the Pan American Union building on May 11. He was glad to join with President Roosevelt on that occasion, and two years later he repeated the same service when President Taft on April 26, 1910, headed the large assembly that witnessed the formal dedication of the marble edifice at 17th and B Streets, N.W.[98]

The ceremonies surrounding Cardinal Gibbons' silver jubilee as a bishop in 1893 and his golden episcopal jubilee of 1918 — splendid as they were — were far overshadowed by the magnitude and splendor by which the nation did him honor in 1911 as he reached the fiftieth anniversary of his priesthood and the twenty-fifth year of his cardinalate. By that time his position in national life had been firmly established, his name was a household word throughout the land, and the occupant of the White House, William Howard Taft, numbered him among his intimate friends. The date of his ordination fell on June 30, but long before that plans began to be formulated for a celebration that would go into history as the most remarkable demonstration of universal love and esteem for a private citizen which the United States had ever witnessed. The origin of the idea came from

---

[96] *Colorado Catholic* (Denver), November 20, 1886.

[97] 100-F-5, Thomas H. Carter, President of the National Commissioners of the Louisiana Purchase Exposition to Gibbons, Helena, Montana, January 7, 1903. St. Louis *Globe-Democrat,* May 1, 1903.

[98] 104-W, Barrett to Gibbons, Washington, April 15, 1908; Root to Gibbons, Washington, April 17, 1908; Barrett to Gibbons, Washington, May 5, 1908, *Personal;* 106-F, same to same, Washington, April 11, 1910. Washington *Post,* May 12, 1908, and April 27, 1910.

Oliver P. Baldwin, editor of the Baltimore *Sun*, who was impressed by the brilliant reception held in New York in the cardinal's honor on the evening of May 10 which had drawn nearly 2,000 of the city's elite from all walks of life.[99]

On May 19, therefore, the *Sun* announced the resolutions passed by the Baltimore city council giving its warm approval to the idea of a civic celebration for their foremost citizen who was described as "a pattern for Americans, an illustrious example to all men, without distinction of creed or party. . . ." During the next few weeks the state-wide committee appointed by Governor Austin L. Crothers of Maryland, and representing men of all classes and religious faiths, was preoccupied with the details of extending the invitations to persons of prominence and making preparations for the celebration. Among the earliest to signify that he would be there was Theodore Roosevelt who told Father John L. Belford, pastor of Nativity Church in Brooklyn, "The Cardinal is a trump; and I earnestly desire to do him honor."[100] Two days before the demonstration the New York *Herald* published a lengthy interview which Gibbons had given to L. Frank O'Brien the week before. The article in the *Herald* of June 4 was proof of the fact that, although the cardinal had an extraordinary love for his country, he was not blind to its faults, for virtually the entire interview was given over to a discussion of what he believed to be the greatest defects in American life. The evils which the old churchman arraigned were Mormonism and divorce, the imperfect and secularized system of public education, the desecration of the Christian Sabbath, the unreasonable delays in carrying into effect decisions of the criminal courts which permitted criminals to evade the law, and finally the corruption and frauds which often attended elections. Coming as they did from one who had earned the right by his peerless citizenship to speak frankly about the moral delinquencies of the Republic, these strictures pronounced two days before the nation's leaders gathered to pay him such signal honor, were received with the earnestness and spirit in which they had been delivered.

[99] New York *Herald*, May 11, 1911. *History of the Great National Demonstration held in Baltimore, June the sixth, 1911 in Honor of Cardinal Gibbons to Commemorate the Fiftieth Anniversary of his Priesthood and the Twenty-fifth of his Elevation to the Cardinalate* (Baltimore, 1911), p. 17.

[100] 107-G, Roosevelt to Belford, New York, May 19, 1911.

On the afternoon of June 6 there gathered in the Fifth Regiment Armory in Baltimore an estimated crowd of 20,000 persons for the civic celebration of the cardinal's jubilee. President Taft arrived from Washington shortly before on a special train that carried Vice-President James S. Sherman, Champ Clark, Speaker of the House of Representatives, members of the cabinet and the Supreme Court, and large delegations from both houses of Congress. In fact, as the Washington *Post* reported the next day, "The business of the United States government, superficially at least, was at a standstill for four hours yesterday owing to the exodus of public men to attend the anniversary ceremonies. . . . Assistant secretaries held down the lid in most of the government departments, most of the cabinet officers going to Baltimore on the President's special train." Chief Justice White made a special trip from New Orleans for the event, and practically every important man in the governments of the United States and of Maryland was in evidence on the huge platform. Ten speeches were made during the course of the afternoon with Governor Crothers leading off with a word of welcome from Maryland to the distinguished assemblage. He was followed in turn by the President, Sherman, Roosevelt, Senator Elihu Root, Ambassador James Bryce of Great Britain, Clark, Joseph G. Cannon, former Speaker of the House of Representatives, Mayor James H. Preston of Baltimore, and finally the cardinal. All the speeches were brief but during the talks the encomia heaped upon the guest of honor for his striking attainments as a citizen and his example of what all Americans should be, were of a kind rarely accorded to any man at any time in history.

After hearing Governor Crothers testify to the services rendered by Gibbons to the State of Maryland, the great audience rose in greeting to the President of the United States. At the outset Taft ventured to say that the present assembly could find few counterparts in history. They had gathered, he said, not as members of any religious denomination nor in any official capacity, but rather to recognize and to honor in Cardinal Gibbons his high virtues as a member of the political community and one who in his long and useful life had, as he expressed it, "spared no effort in the cause of good citizenship and the uplifting of his fellowmen." The President lauded the services which Gibbons had given to the nation by his inculcation of respect for constituted authority, for religious tolerance, and for the wholehearted interest which he had always shown toward the moral and material welfare of all elements of the population. "But what we are especially delighted to see confirmed in him and his life," said Taft, "is the entire consistency which he has demonstrated between earnest and single-minded patriotism and love of country on the one hand, and sincere devotion to his church and God upon the other." That the cardinal might long continue to occupy the high position he had always had in the secular movements of the Republic was, said the President in conclusion, "the fervent prayer of Catholic and Protestant, of Jew and Christian."[101]

Taft's address was then followed by those of Sherman, Roosevelt, and the others during which it seemed that each speaker vied with his predecessors in his attempt to extol the old churchman. Root struck a note that was especially pleasing to Gibbons, when he stressed the harmony that had obtained in the United States under a system of separation of Church and State but which, he was at pains to emphasize, did not mean separation of the commonwealth from religious faith. He said:

> It means that our American doctrine of separation of Church and State does not involve the separation of the people of America from religious belief. It means that our American doctrine of religious toleration does not mean indifference to religious faiths. It means that with all our commercialism, with all our wonderful progress in the power to produce wealth, with all our differences between ourselves as to the possession and distribution of wealth, the people of America believe in ideals and feel the guidance of faith in things higher than their material position.[102]

In his turn Ambassador Bryce found it significant that men of all religious faiths, or none, could assemble to honor a man whose life illustrated so well the fundamental principles of Christianity. "There are diversities of Governments," he said, "but the same spirit, and in His Eminence, and in his life, there is drawn out a beautiful model and example of those virtues which belong to our common Christianity and which we can all honor alike."[103]

---

[101] *History of the Great National Demonstration* . . . , pp. 45–47, contain Taft's speech. This volume carries the texts of all the speeches delivered, as well as numerous messages of congratulation to Gibbons from all parts of the country.
[102] *Ibid.*, p. 51.
[103] *Ibid.*, p. 53.

Thus the tributes flowed on through the remarks of Clark, Cannon, and Preston until it reached the moment when the cardinal rose to reply. He first assured the vast audience of his profound gratitude for all that had been said, and stated that he was overwhelmed with confusion by the praise of himself that he had heard. He felt satisfied that the speakers had portrayed their subject, not as he was in reality, but as he ought to be. "But I have become so enamoured of your portrait," he continued, "that it shall be the endeavor of my life to imitate and resemble that portrait more and more during the few years that remain to me in this world." Gibbons claimed one merit, and that was an earnest and ardent love of his native country and its political institutions. He was persuaded that the government of the United States was one of the most precious heirlooms ever transmitted to posterity, and he thought that both churchmen and laymen ought ever to lend it assistance by the observance of its laws and by the integrity of their private lives. He recalled the bequest of Benjamin Franklin in the constitutional convention of 1787 that they open each day's proceedings with prayer for divine guidance, and he mentioned that from Washington to Taft the chief executives of the Republic had almost invariably invoked the aid of God in their inaugural addresses. The daily prayers in both houses of Congress, the recognition of the Christian Sabbath, and the annual proclamations by the President of a day of national thanksgiving to God were all, according to Gibbons, further manifestations of the religious spirit that animated the American government.

The guest of honor then spoke with approval of the sentiments of Root on the true meaning of separation of Church and State in the United States, and as a final thought he dwelt upon the depth of gratitude which citizens of the country owed to it for the extraordinary blessings it had conferred upon them. It thus behooved every citizen, said the cardinal, to unite in lifting up the hands of the President and the other public servants even as Aaron and Hur had once held aloft the hands of Moses. He would have all Americans impress upon their minds the divine truths that the President and his colleagues were divinely appointed ministers of the law, that they were the representatives of God, and that they represented Him by whom kings reigned and lawmakers decreed just things. He concluded by saying,

"And, therefore, it should be the duty and the delight of every citizen to co-operate with our Chief Magistrate and his aides, and to bless them as they are steering along the destinies of our beloved and our glorious republic."[104]

June 6, 1911, would ever remain as one of the most memorable days in a long life that had been filled with events of an unusual character. And yet Gibbons took the demonstration in the same unruffled manner that he had met most of the striking circumstances of his colorful career. In fact, it was later said of him, "There was not in all the thousands a more unassuming man than he who was the central figure of the demonstration."[105] In this Cardinal Gibbons revealed the true greatness of which he was made. At the close of the big day he attended a dinner in his honor at the home of Mayor Preston where Vice-President Sherman headed a company that included twenty-four United States senators, four foreign diplomats, two Protestant bishops, and many other prominent men.[106] The entire affair of June 6 had been without precedent, and the Washington *Post* of the following day was not exaggerating when it remarked, "Such a demonstration was never before seen on this hemisphere. Probably the world never witnessed a more generous outburst of enthusiasm for one with whose theological principles many of the participants are at variance." Once more the press of the nation rang with Gibbons' praises, and with reflections which the great demonstration had stirred in the hearts and minds of the American people. It afforded an opportunity to many editorial writers to give expression to their views regarding not only the cardinal, but also the Church that he represented. For example, the New Orleans *Picayune* of June 9 felt the celebration in Baltimore had been an entirely fitting and deserved tribute to its subject. But to the *Picayune* it had likewise been a recognition of the great and

---

[104] *Ibid.*, pp. 58–61.

[105] *Ibid.*, p. 63.

[106] *Ibid.*, pp. 65–68. That day there was delivered to Gibbons' residence a large bouquet from the Reverend Arthur B. Kinsolving, Rector of St. Paul's Protestant Episcopal Church, which enclosed a note that read, "Will His Eminence, the Cardinal, be pleased to accept a few flowers from his neighbors in this rectory, with their warm congratulations on his attainment of today's unique and sacred anniversary. May his gracious and helpful presence bless for many years to come the community in which he is so genuinely beloved, and upon which his illustrious life and achievements have conferred high distinction" (107-H, Kinsolving to Gibbons, Baltimore, June 6, 1911).

useful work that the Catholic Church had done in the United States, by what it called "strict devotion to its tenets and the avoidance of seductive suggestions to undertake an extension of its power and influence by intermeddling with affairs of state."

Naturally so stirring an event was not allowed to pass without the cardinal furnishing to the Holy See a detailed description of its character, and as the news spread in Rome he received the congratulations of a number of old friends and acquaintances, among whom was Cardinal Rampolla, the former Secretary of State.[107] Nor were friends at home less gratified. "It was truly magnificent," wrote Archbishop Ireland, "something that Catholics everywhere are proud of." In reply Gibbons told him he appreciated his letter more than any he had received and, he added, "their name is legion." No description, he said, could adequately paint the scene; the celebration was a spontaneous outburst of good will on the part of the citizens irrespective of race or religion, and the speeches had all been in the best of taste and had flowed from the heart. "After the President's, which I think was the best," he told Ireland, "I liked Senator Root's most, because he happily accentuated the idea (so much needed abroad) that separation of Church & State implied no antagonism."[108] Later Theodore Roosevelt acknowledged the cardinal's thanks for his attendance at the celebration by saying that few things had given him greater pleasure; and several months later when he had received the commemorative volume of the demonstration he spoke in even more enthusiastic tones. The former President was glad to have had a part in the jubilee event, for it was a good thing to have been concerned in honoring an American citizen who, he said, "has so signally honored America, and who by his life, by his works, and by his words, has taught us just what America stands most in need of learning."[109]

---

[107] 107-J, Gibbons to Merry del Val, Baltimore, June 10, 1911, copy; Rampolla to Gibbons, Rome, June 23, 1911; J. Palica, secretary of the chapter of Santa Maria in Trastevere to Gibbons, Rome, June 27, 1911.

[108] 107-J, Ireland to Gibbons, St. Paul, June 16, 1911; AASP, Gibbons to Ireland, Baltimore, June 19, 1911, copy. The cardinal added a postscript which read, "Yesterday I lunched en famille with the President. I was the only guest outside his immediate family, & brothers with their families who have come to celebrate the Silver Jubilee of his marriage."

[109] 107-M, Gibbons to Roosevelt, n.p., September 12, 1911, copy; Roosevelt to Gibbons, Sagamore Hill, September 17, 1911; 107-T, Roosevelt to Gibbons, New York, November 21, 1911.

The golden jubilee of Gibbons' priesthood was climaxed in October of 1911 by a three-day celebration which was largely ecclesiastical in character. Two weeks before the opening of the final phase of his anniversary festivities, the cardinal preached in the cathedral on Sunday, October 1, in which he reviewed the progress of both Church and State since 1861. He stated that all the priests with whom he had been ordained that year were now dead and all the bishops who had begun their episcopal careers with him in 1868 were gone except Bishop John J. Hogan of Kansas City. Moreover, he was one of the nine survivors of the seventy-two bishops who had attended the plenary council in 1884. The bishops, priests, and laity, he said, constituted a triple alliance in the Church far more formidable and enduring than alliances of kings and potentates, since it was an alliance cemented by divine charity. He urged loyalty to both the Church and State on the part of the faithful, and he then turned to the United States government.

Three issues, said the cardinal, were now before the American people and he was opposed to all of them. They were the election of United States senators by popular vote, the making of the acts of state legislatures subject to the suffrage of the people, and the recall or removal of unpopular judges before the expiration of their terms of office. "No one questions the ability, the sincerity and patriotism of the advocates of these changes in our organic laws," he said. But he hoped he would not be regarded as presumptuous in saying that in his opinion the wisdom of the proposed changes should be seriously questioned. Gibbons was unimpressed by the argument that legislatures were subject to corruption and, therefore, should not elect the senators, for if that was the way one reasoned so, too, would be the people from whom the legislators sprang. Subjecting acts of the state legislatures to mass vote, was to his mind substituting mob law for established rule, and to recall a judge for decisions that were unpopular was an insult to the dignity, the independence, and the self-respect of the judiciary. Far less menacing to the Republic was an occasional corrupt or incompetent judge than one who would be the habitual slave of a capricious multitude, and who would be constantly adjusting his decisions in compliance with the popular whims of the day.[110] Thus did the old cardinal

---

[110] 107-N, copy of Gibbons' sermon of October 1, 1911.

air his views on the proposed amendments to the Constitution which at that time were under discussion.

As the time drew near for the events that had been scheduled for the third week in October he received a letter from his old friend Michael Jenkins who told him that in commemoration of the jubilee his family had struck off a series of gold, silver, and bronze medals. Jenkins had been very generous to various charities of the Archdiocese of Baltimore over the years, and the cardinal was deeply touched at this latest manifestation of his friendship and loyalty. "If I had the selection of the name which would be so closely associated with the jubilee celebration," he told him, "I would have chosen you in preference to any other citizen of Baltimore."[111] At the time of the civic demonstration in June it had been decided to present Gibbons with a gift that would be a fitting memorial of that event. Therefore, on October 7 there took place in the reception room of the city hall the presentation by Mayor Preston of a silver service set of over 250 pieces which bore the cardinal's coat of arms. He assured the assembly of his gratitude, and he remarked that it would be preserved in the archiepiscopal household for generations to come as a souvenir of the close ties of friendship that had bound him to his fellow citizens of Baltimore and of Maryland. In thanking the mayor and the city council, he hoped it would not be invidious if he mentioned several to whom he felt especially grateful, namely, Bishop John G. Murray of the Protestant Episcopal Diocese of Maryland, Oliver P. Baldwin, editor of the Baltimore *Sun*, and Messrs. James R. Wheeler and Frank A. Furst.[112]

On Sunday, October 15, the solemn pontifical Mass was celebrated in the cathedral by the cardinal in the presence of Archbishop Falconio, the apostolic delegate, nine archbishops, and forty-six bishops. The sermon at the Mass was preached by Archbishop Glennon of St. Louis, who stated that Gibbons' career had been unique not only in the American Church but in the history of the Church in general. Speaking of the cardinals of an earlier day, he said:

> We may not deny their greatness, their learning, their consecration; but, unlike any one member of either group, our Cardinal

[111] 107-N, Gibbons to Jenkins, Baltimore, October 4, 1911, copy.
[112] *History of the Great National Demonstration* . . . , pp. 85–88.

stands with the same devotion to his country as Richelieu had for France, cultivating a citizenship as unstained as Newman, and while reaching out to a broader democracy than even Cardinal Manning, he still remains pre-eminent in his unquestioned devotion to Holy Church.[113]

At the dinner which followed Bishop Maes of Covington was the bearer of an honorary degree of doctor of sacred theology which had been conferred on the cardinal by the University of Louvain.[114] On Monday, October 16, a parade up Cathedral Street of parochial school children and of parish societies was viewed from the steps of the cathedral by Gibbons and his guests. For two hours the marchers filed past with over 30,000 in line and with nearly 100,000 lining the streets as they went by. The cardinal sat or stood at the head of the cathedral steps, constantly acknowledging the salutes of the thousands who filed past him and, as the Baltimore *Sun* reported the next day, "while fatigued by the strain of the two hours of constant watching, he remained to the end." On Wednesday, October 19, the jubilarian received 6,000 parochial school children in the cathedral as the closing episode of the celebration. News of the festivities in Baltimore was carried back to various parts of the country by the participants, and Gibbons' old friend, Archbishop Keane, rejoiced at the description given to him by his successor in the See of Dubuque of how well everything had gone.[115] Once more full details of the event were forwarded to the Holy Father, and Cardinal Merry del Val assured Gibbons of the satisfaction which Pius X had experienced in hearing of the honors that had been paid to him.

---

[113] Baltimore *Sun*, October 16, 1911.

[114] 108-N, Gibbons to Paul Ladeuze, Rector of the University of Louvain, Baltimore, October 29, 1911, copy in French. In thanking Ladeuze for the degree, Gibbons referred to the assistance which Louvain had given to the young American Church for so many years through the American College there.

[115] 107-P, Keane to Gibbons, Dubuque, October 17, 1911. There were some, however, who were not so pleased. Abbot Charles H. Mohr, O.S.B., of St. Leo Abbey in Florida told Arthur Preuss, editor of the *Review* in St. Louis, that he thought all these "rallies" were but hollow show. "Like Leo XIII Gibbons has smothered trouble but he has not cured it," he said. Mohr had gone to the jubilee because Bishop William J. Kenny of St. Augustine had desired it, not because he admired the cardinal. "Glennon's sermon," he remarked, "was a disappointment to me — too much glorification of the man & not of the priest. Maybe he felt he was advocating a 'lost cause' for not once did he become enthusiastic" (Archives of the Central Bureau, St. Louis, Mohr to Preuss, St. Leo, Florida, October 30, 1911, copy through the kindness of Colman J. Barry, O.S.B.).

The various functions had revealed, he said, the appreciation felt for his outstanding services as a citizen and as a pastor of souls, and in conclusion Merry del Val remarked:

> The manner in which gentlemen holding the highest offices of the State, many of them non-Catholics, availed of the occasion of your Jubilee to publicly testify their admiration for Your Eminence redounds to the honor of Holy Church, and Catholics in every clime have rejoiced in the honor shown her distinguished son.[116]

Time and again during his life the Cardinal of Baltimore had publicly voiced his profound veneration for the American Constitution as an instrument of government. It was that sentiment which in part inspired his sermon of October, 1911, in which he deprecated the suggested amendments relating to the election of United States senators and the recall and referendum. In the months after World War I there was renewed agitation for simplifying the amending procedure of the Constitution, but it was a movement with which Gibbons had no sympathy. With this in mind he joined the National Association for Constitutional Government and gave to that organization all the encouragement which his advanced age and duties would allow. The Washington *Post* was likewise opposed to rendering the Constitution easier of amendment, and saw behind the movement a group of fanatical radicals and self-seeking demagogues. It was immensely pleased, therefore, when Gibbons' membership in the association was announced, and in a brief editorial of November 19, 1919, in compliment of his action, it was stated, "There are few men to whom in times of stress and peril the country instinctively turns for counsel and guidance. Conspicuous among them is his eminence Cardinal Gibbons. . . ."

The last article which the cardinal wrote some weeks before his death pertained to the Constitution and was published in the *Catholic Review* of Baltimore on February 19, 1921. "As the years go by," he said, "I am more than ever convinced that the Constitution of the United States is the greatest instrument of government that ever issued from the hand of man." He emphasized the personal liberties which had found protection in the document, and he instanced especially that of religious freedom.

---

[116] 107-R, Gibbons to Merry del Val, Baltimore, October 26, 1911, copy; 107-V, Merry del Val to Gibbons, Rome, November 24, 1911.

Other features of the Constitution that earned his praise were the autonomy enjoyed by the several states and the sacred privilege of the ballot. In reviewing the crises of American history through which the Constitution had carried the nation, the aged cardinal believed in retrospect that the Civil War had been a blessing in disguise, since it had made the true position of the states clear and had more firmly united them than ever before. However, he regarded the disputed Hayes-Tilden election of 1876 as a blow struck at the very foundation of the national life, because the declaration of Hayes' election ran counter to the prevailing opinion that Tilden had won. "Happily," he said, "this crisis which filled me with more fear for the safety of the Republic than did the four years of civil war, passed without the privilege of voting losing any of its sacred and solemn character."

Speaking of the role played by the Supreme Court in protecting the constitutional liberties of the citizens, the cardinal remarked that he, perhaps, was the only American who had known all the chief justices from the time of John Marshall. "I knew Chief Justice Taney, the successor of Mr. Marshall," he stated, "and admired him for his true Christian faith no less than for his legal acumen. He was a frequent attendant here at the high Mass in the Cathedral." The article on the Constitution was taken up by the secular press and published in full by the New York *World,* the Philadelphia *Public Ledger,* and the St. Louis *Globe-Democrat,* as well as being given in generous excerpts in many other newspapers. It was appropriate that the last article from Gibbons' pen should have been devoted to a subject which he had repeatedly championed over nearly sixty years since his ordination as a priest. He had spoken many times of the sacred character of the Constitution, but probably none was more eloquent and effective than this final summary of his appreciation for its contribution to the welfare of the land which he so dearly loved.

In the lives of most men there occurs a noticeable slackening of interest in the events of the outer world as they reach old age. Such, however, was not the case with Cardinal Gibbons. About two weeks after his eighty-sixth birthday he was interviewed at the home of his friend Martin Maloney in Spring Lake, New Jersey, and the reporter stated in the Baltimore *Sun* of August 9, 1920, that despite his years the cardinal continued to follow public affairs as keenly as before, and that his grasp was as firm and the mental processes by which he reached his opinions as sure and active as they had ever been. Moreover, the thorny problems which then beset his own country and the entire world induced no spirit of pessimism in the aged churchman. Asked if he did not think his age was worse than preceding periods of history and that crime was now more rampant, Gibbons quickly replied in the negative. The blame for the widespread impression that human affairs were growing worse, he said, was to be laid in good measure at the door of the newspapers. He charged the press with publishing all the great crimes simply because the people read them with avidity. If there were 100 families residing in a town and a sensational and disedifying incident occurred in one of them, he maintained, that one incident was published in all its salacious details, while the tranquil lives of the other ninety-nine families remained unnoticed.

After Cardinal Gibbons had entered upon the illness from which he never fully recovered, he gave the final interview of his life in the closing days of 1920 to Bruce Barton, then a reporter for the *American Magazine*. A member of Gibbons' household had previously told Barton not to mention death, for the cardinal, he said, was still the youngest man in the house in spirit and he added, "I think he would like to go on living for another hundred years."[117] Gibbons had the more readily agreed to the interview when he learned that his remarks would be read by a million or more young men. He told Barton that he liked young men, and when the reporter commented on the youthful appearance of the priests of his household, Gibbons replied, "Until you are forty, seek the companionship of men who are older. After that, keep a vital contact with those who are younger." He said that until his recent illness he used to walk every afternoon from five to six o'clock with one or more of the students from St. Mary's Seminary. In this way he met young men from every section of the United States who told him of their hopes, their ambitions, and their plans. "And do you want to know what I say to them?" he asked. "I say, 'Young man, *expect* great things! Of God, your fellow men, yourself, and America.' "

When asked if he thought the world was growing better, the cardinal replied that it was, and by way of proof he reminisced

---

[117] Bruce Barton, "Young Man, *Expect* Great Things! An Interview with Cardinal Gibbons," *American Magazine*, XCI (March, 1921), 5.

about the days of slavery in the South which he had witnessed as a boy, and how that iniquitous institution had disappeared from American life. He saw advance, too, in the rise of the rate of literacy among the population, in the higher standards of business practice, and in the growth of religious tolerance. On the subject of tolerance Gibbons cited the bitter days of Know-Nothingism through which he had lived as a young man, and he recalled the notorious "blood tubs" that were used at the polling booths for spattering a voter who had not cast his ballot to please the Know-Nothings. This was evidence of a growth in toleration, and for the rising generation he thought there were few things of more value than to cultivate the habit of looking at questions from the other man's point of view. "Say to your young men for me," he told Barton, " 'Be tolerant. Forget the prejudices that separate you from other men, and remember the great common ties that bind us all together as children of God, traveling the same road of life together.' "[118]

The reporter then inquired what program of life the cardinal would recommend for success. In his answer he emphasized work, patience, and thrift. Theodore Roosevelt was, to his mind, an example of a man who owed much of his success to his tireless labor, and in Lincoln he found a prototype for patience as a quality that contributed greatly to his achievements. "I looked upon his features only once," he said, "and that at his funeral. But the impression that his tremendous patience made upon me as a young man has never been forgotten."[119] Gibbons would have the young men who heeded his counsel count upon contradiction and disappointment as necessary accompaniments of their lives, for these were the stuff of which character and manhood were made. As for thrift, he confessed that to urge it might sound trite. It was trite, but he had no apology to make in offering it as a necessary quality for success in life. The evils of the Louisiana lottery, he said, had been caused by an abuse of that virtue, and many business depressions could have been avoided had greed and overreaching been tempered by the spirit of thrift. "The law of God is the law of thrift," he remarked, "and no man transgresses that law, either in his personal or business affairs, without incurring a penalty."[120]

---

[118] *Ibid.*, p. 6.   [119] *Ibid.*   [120] *Ibid.*, p. 7.

The cardinal then passed to the value that was to be found in the companionship of good books. As a young man, he told Barton, he had read widely in the masters of English literature when the works of Addison, Johnson, Goldsmith, and the like had held his attention through many days. To the reading of these masterpieces of English prose, he attributed the cultivation of an easy and effective style of writing which had proved valuable to him throughout his life. In later years his reading had turned more to history, and especially to American history, and within the past few months, he said, he had read the recently published four volumes of Albert J. Beveridge's *Life of John Marshall,* as well as new biographies of Jefferson and Jackson. He had known every President since Lincoln, he remarked, and it prompted him to ask if Barton had ever considered what a splendid testimony it was to the soundness of democracy that the United States had never had what he called a "bad or mean or really incompetent man as president." In Gibbons' mind, evil could not reach and permanently hold high position either in politics or in business in the United States. "That is one reason why I say," he commented, " 'Young man, *expect* great things of America!' "[121]

The cardinal's sympathy with the young men of the nation just at that time was real. He knew the conditions in the business world which made it so difficult to find employment and to get oneself established in life. But by way of keeping their spirits high, he recalled the trying days that followed the Civil War, the Black Friday of September, 1869, when Gould and Fish tried to corner the ready gold supply of the country, and the panic of 1873. Yet the United States had come back after all of these harassing experiences, and it would do so again. He then quoted the biblical verse, "Whom the Lord loveth He chasteneth," and he confessed that it was a very hard verse, indeed, for American youth to learn. But those who were old like himself knew its meaning, for the chastening of adversity was an act of God's love, not of His punishment, since human nature was not fitted to stand the strain of unremitting prosperity. What the world needed most, according to Gibbons, were men of character and ideals. It needed young men like the hero of *Tom Brown's School Days* who knelt down and offered up his prayers in the dormitory

---

[121] *Ibid.*

at Rugby in spite of all taunts; it needed men who had the courage to stick to virtue, the truth, and high thinking through adversity and prosperity alike. Such men were not made by easy times alone; they came only through the molding and hardening of trial, disappointment, and difficulty.

Barton had told Gibbons that the interview would appear around the time of Easter, and he asked, therefore, if he had any message for his readers in keeping with that feast. In reply the cardinal referred again to the reporter's remark that men were then depressed and discouraged, and that led him to a brief review of our Lord's exaltation on Palm Sunday and the dreadful fate which He suffered on Good Friday. The thought prompted the old man to say:

> This is the message of Easter — the message of eternal Faith. At the darkest hour the stone of discouragement is rolled away; despair is lost in glory. And only those whose hope has died, a martyr to their doubts, fail to share in the splendor of the resurrection.

In conclusion he returned to the theme with which he had begun, for of all the elements he had mentioned as necessary for success in life, said Gibbons, faith was the greatest of all. "Those who throw up their hands in discouragement when the first snow falls, fail to profit when the sunshine of spring returns. And no great thing comes to any man unless he has courage, even in the dark days, to expect *great* things; to expect them of himself, of his fellow men, of America, and of God."[122]

The Barton interview was an unusually buoyant message from an enfeebled old man in his eighty-sixth year who was then only about three months removed from death. It clearly illustrated the keenness of interest and the soundness of judgment of which Gibbons was still capable, as well as his readiness to respond to a request for counsel to American youth in a period of uncertainty. Among the many young men who doubtless read the article, a student in the Graduate School of Business Administration at Harvard University wrote his congratulations to the cardinal, and told him, "I think it is one of the most helpful and inspiring pieces I have ever read in my life." The student was conscious of his lack of ability to write well, and for that reason he said he would appreciate it if Gibbons would send him the

---

[122] *Ibid.*, p. 92.

names of the books which had helped him to develop his style of writing.[123] But the letter was written three days before the death of Cardinal Gibbons and the request, therefore, had come too late to receive a reply. It was fitting that the final interview of the Cardinal of Baltimore addressed to the American people should have embodied so many of the ideals for which he had fought in the cause of good citizenship, for long before this time the soundly balanced judgments which he had so often enunciated had become a guide to many of the great, voiceless multitude of his fellow countrymen. Viewing the peerless citizenship which the cardinal had displayed over the lengthy span of his years, and the extraordinary hold that he had taken on the hearts and minds of Americans of all religious faiths, it was hardly an exaggeration to say, in the words of an admirer some weeks after his death, "He was, more than any other man, in and out of official life, the mentor of the nation."[124]

---

[123] AAB, unclassified, A. B. Wight to Gibbons, Cambridge, March 21, 1921.

[124] Allen Sinclair Will, "Cardinal Gibbons in His Public Relations," *Catholic World,* CXIII (May, 1921), 191.

CHAPTER XXV

Preacher and Writer

THE earliest extant copy of a sermon of Cardinal Gibbons bore the title "Good Use of Time" and was dated January 1, 1861, six months before he was ordained to the priesthood.[1] In view of his many remarkable achievements over the next sixty years, it is evident that the exhortations to the proper use of time which as a seminarian he had incorporated into his text, found practical application in the youthful preacher's later scheme of life. From the outset of his priestly ministry Gibbons made it clear that he had a very high ideal of the preaching office. The thought of using the pulpit for any other purpose than the inculcation of moral values and the instruction in religious truths, was abhorrent to him. As the pastor of St. Bridget's Church in Baltimore he had preached on the first Sunday of the new year 1863, and at that time he reviewed for his people the suffering and sorrow that had come upon the nation during the previous year by reason of the Civil War. Amid the conflict, he said, they had heard nothing from the Catholic pulpit to excite their passions or to give them a thirst for blood; rather the American Catholics had heard in their churches only of God's glory and man's need for peace, of Christ and Him crucified. Gibbons then made reference to certain unnamed preachers who, he said, had abused their sacred calling by invoking the God of battle instead of the God of peace in a manner that had inflamed the worst passions of their auditors. "A fearful responsibility," he continued, "awaits those who have sounded the new blast from their church desks, & fanned the flame of civil hatred and dissension. These will have their judgment, let us attend to ourselves."[2]

---

[1] 71-D-1, handwritten copy of sermon on "Good Use of Time," January 1, 1861.
[2] 71-F-1, handwritten copy of sermon on "Time," January 4, 1863, and later dates.

The study of the cardinal. The picture above the desk is that of St. Philip Neri.

It was an idea which Gibbons never abandoned, and a generation later he gave it a more forceful expression. Revealing the importance which he attached to the priest in the capacity which he characterized as "the herald of the gospel," he devoted two chapters to the subject in his book, *The Ambassador of Christ.* After speaking of the sublime theme of God and His relations to men which should ever engage the attention of a preacher, the cardinal reprobated abuses such as the delivery of tiresome and perfunctory sermons, the substitution of thundering and aggressive tones for the lack of ideas, the indulgence in vituperation and outbursts of anger, and the use of the time allotted for the sermon in speaking only of dollars and cents without any allusion to the gospel. Showing how strongly he felt about the matter he continued:

> I can hardly conceive a spectacle more cowardly and contemptible than that of an anointed minister taking unwarrantable advantage of the immunity which his sacred office bestows on him, protected by the armor of his priestly robes, sheltering himself behind the breastworks of the pulpit, and pouring forth volleys of offensive language that he would not dare to utter to a gentleman in the streets. Such license must arouse in every honest breast sentiments of righteous indignation. The people came for bread, and they received a stone. They came for peace and consolation, and their hearts were filled with sadness and irritation.[3]

It was a complaint which was never uttered by those who listened to the sermons of James Gibbons. All the evidence, both written and oral, is agreed that he was a most pleasing, interesting, and effective preacher. After he had spent many years in the ministry, Gibbons formulated four simple rules for good sermons which he lists as follows: have a definite object in view, borrow as freely as possible in both thought and expression from the Bible and especially from the New Testament, commit to memory at least the leading facts in logical order, and be intensely earnest in the delivery of the sermon. Two other suggestions which he maintained were of importance were simplicity of language and, except on extraordinary occasions, brevity in length.[4]

---

[3] *The Ambassador of Christ,* p. 274.

[4] *Ibid.,* pp. 282–283. Gibbons' point of simplicity of language was in accord with one of the rules of Cardinal Newman who once wrote, "He who is ambitious will never write well, but he who tries to say simply what he feels, what religion

The style which Gibbons himself employed was, indeed, always simple and, in fact, often commonplace. But in regard to the final criterion by which any sermon must be judged, namely, its effectiveness — insofar as one is able to assess so intangible a matter — there would seem to have been no doubt in Gibbons' case. The large crowds that gathered to listen to him from the earliest days of his ministry in Baltimore and his missionary career in North Carolina and Virginia, and which continued through his more mature years as Archbishop of Baltimore, bore striking testimony to that fact. Certainly the crowds were not drawn by Gibbons' eloquence in the common meaning of that term, as once they had been drawn to a Lacordaire; and just as certainly it was not the majesty and beauty of his diction which accounted in part for the elite audiences who came to hear Newman. All who heard Gibbons, however, were agreed that he had an unusually engaging tone of voice, and that there was a fine clarity and crispness of enunciation that added to the attractiveness of his discourses. But aside from these physical qualities, it is difficult to explain the popularity he enjoyed as a preacher on any other ground than that of the practical themes simply expressed which struck a personal note in the minds of his hearers, and the winning personality and obvious earnestness with which Gibbons drove home the moral lessons which he set before his audiences.

The subjects upon which the cardinal chose to speak were generally of a kind which would have a real interest for the majority of devout churchgoers. In 1908 he published a volume containing over fifty such sermons, the subjects of which, as he stated in the preface, had been the fruit of nearly fifty years of meditation, and which had been to him personally a source of joy and comfort, of strength and fortitude, during half a century.[5] They dealt with such themes as the general judgment, Christ our Friend, the mission of Christian parents, the road of suffering as the path to eternal glory, Christian marriage, the uses of adversity, why the Church honored the Mother of God,

---

demands, what faith teaches, what the Gospel promises, will be eloquent without intending it, and will write better English than if he made a study of English Literature." Daniel M. O'Connell, S.J. (Ed.), *Favorite Newman Sermons,* 2 ed. (New York, 1940), p. 414.

[5] *Discourses and Sermons for Every Sunday and the Principal Festivals of the Year,* p. v.

the sanctification of one's ordinary actions, and the obedience owed to all lawful authority. As was customary, the topic of the sermon was often suggested by the gospel of the Mass as, for example, an explanation of the role of the Holy Spirit in the life of the Church on Pentecost Sunday, or the conditions for attaining eternal happiness on the feast of our Lord's ascension into heaven. But whatever the subject might be, Gibbons treated it in a clear and unadorned way, and he often introduced helpful illustrations from real life to clarify his point. For example, in a sermon which he entitled "The Race for an Unfading Crown," the cardinal instanced the rivalry with which candidates contended for the American presidency as a temporary and earthly honor, as well as recalling his personal observation of how reluctant Cardinal Sarto was to accept the crown of the Papacy in 1903.[6] In this manner he rendered more vivid his point of the fading character of earthly honors, and thus concluded the sermon with more effect by emphasizing the unending joys of a heavenly crown won through leading a good life.

The reputation of Gibbons as a preacher was enhanced after he entered the episcopacy in 1868, and as a consequence the passing years brought an increasing number of invitations to speak from every part of the country. Some of these were no doubt prompted by the international fame which by the late 1880's attached to his name, and by the ties of personal affection which in a number of cases bound him to those who had extended the invitations. But whatever the motive that lay behind the requests, they were not infrequently more numerous than he could fulfill. Even as Bishop of Richmond he often traveled outside his jurisdiction to preach as, for example, at the dedication of the Cathedral of St. John the Baptist in Savannah in November, 1873, where about 6,000 persons, his largest audience to date, heard him speak; at the consecration of the Cathedral of the Assumption in Baltimore in May, 1876, and at the dedication of St. Mary's Church in Hoboken, New Jersey, in November, 1878.[7] During the years from 1886 to 1911 Gibbons was the only cardinal in the United States, and in that quarter

[6] *Ibid.*, pp. 117–119.

[7] Smith and Fitzpatrick, *Cardinal Gibbons, Churchman and Citizen*, p. 85. Gibbons published the texts of two of these sermons along with nineteen others in Volume II of his *A Retrospect of Fifty Years.*

of a century he was the preacher at many of the most important national Catholic events. Reference has already been made to a number of these occasions, such as the conferring of the pallium on Archbishop Katzer of Milwaukee in 1891, the centennial of the Archdiocese of New York in 1908, and the silver jubilee of the Catholic University of America which was celebrated in April, 1915.[8]

Deeply devoted as he always was to his friends, the cardinal found a special joy in responding to their invitations to speak on the memorable occasions in their lives. On May 17, 1895, he preached in the Cathedral of the Holy Cross in Boston on the second day of the celebration of the golden sacerdotal jubilee of Archbishop Williams. He devoted most of his sermon to remarks on the priesthood, and to a review of the progress of the Church in Boston and New England since the early years of the century. Near the end he alluded to Williams' distaste for public praise, but he stated that there were times and circumstances when private feelings should be sacrificed to the imperative demands of public recognition. Those who knew something of the cordiality that had marked the relationship of the two men for nearly twenty years, realized the sincerity of the cardinal when he then added:

> We have learned to admire and love you for your sterling honesty of purpose, for your candor and straightforwardness of character, and for all those qualities of mind and heart that make the man. There is no Prelate of the American Church in whose judgment we have placed more implicit reliance than in yours. Even when you were younger in years, we looked up to you as a judicious counsellor. But now we can claim you as our Nestor in years, as well as in wisdom.[9]

A year later Gibbons performed a similar service for another close friend when he preached in the Cathedral of St. Peter in Chains at Cincinnati on June 10, 1896, for the golden jubilee of Archbishop Elder's priesthood. Once more a brief discourse on the grandeur of the priestly office was followed by a review of the jubilarian's eventful life. In this instance the cardinal was on familiar ground for, as he said, the Elder family had settled in Maryland around 1730, and theirs was an old and honored

---

[8] *Ibid.*, II, 30–46, 148–155, 190–205.
[9] *Ibid.*, II, 123–124.

name in Maryland history. With an obvious reference to the agitation of the American Protective Association against Catholics and foreigners which was just then so prominently in the minds of everyone, he remarked, "If any man has the right to claim the privileges of an American citizen, that man is William Henry Elder." He then described the incident from the *Acts of the Apostles* wherein St. Paul had invoked his rights as a Roman citizen when he was threatened with being scourged at Jerusalem, and he stated that of late there were some in the United States who were themselves scarcely naturalized as citizens who desired to inflict, if they could, civil and religious disabilities on men like Elder, who were to the manner born and whose fathers before them had been citizens of the Republic. "But against all such aggressors," said Gibbons, "we will protest, and say what Naboth said to the king of Syria [*sic*]: 'God forbid that I could surrender the heritage of my fathers.' "[10] He congratulated the archbishop in the name of the Cincinnati clergy, laity, and the citizens of the city generally, and he concluded by congratulating Elder in his own name, for as he said:

> There are many common ties that bind us together. We were both born in the same city of Baltimore; we were baptized within the limits of the same Cathedral parish; we were educated in the same old State of Maryland, the land of the sanctuary, and the cradle of civil and religious liberty; the same Pontiff that elevated Your Grace to the Episcopal dignity, imposed the hands of the priesthood on me; and we exercised the sacred ministry in the same diocese.
> May it be my privilege to walk in your footsteps, though at a distance, and to imitate your beautiful and bright example.[11]

Even on formal occasions of this kind the sermons of Gibbons rarely lacked evidence of one of his most striking characteristics as a preacher, namely, the fidelity with which he observed his own rule of borrowing freely in thought and expression from the Sacred Scriptures. The quotations from the *Acts of the Apostles* and *3 Kings* in the sermon at Elder's jubilee, illustrated the dependence with which he relied on the Bible to give point and tone to his discourses. Six years before he had preached on June 30, 1890, at the consecration of the Cathedral of SS. Peter

---

[10] *Ibid.*, II, 107. The incident of Naboth, in 3 Kings 21:1 ff., involved the King of Samaria, not Syria.
[11] *Ibid.*, II, 114–115.

and Paul in Philadelphia, where he drew a parallel between the prelates of that see and the kings of Israel in their respective labors for the newly consecrated cathedral and the ancient temple of Jerusalem. Kenrick who had laid the foundation of the cathedral was, according to Gibbons, like David, a man after God's own heart; Wood, who had completed its construction, possessed no small share of Solomon's wisdom and foresight; and Ryan, who had seen the work to completion, was likened to King Joas who had adorned the temple in the Holy City.[12] Sermons delivered at events such as these, did not lend themselves with the same ease to the profusion of scriptural references which one finds in the ordinary discourses spoken before the cathedral congregation in Baltimore. But in general Gibbons' use of the Bible showed an uncommon knowledge of the sacred books and a familiarity with their history and personnel that were quite extraordinary even for his day.

Another feature of the sermons of Cardinal Gibbons was the cognizance which he took of current events and the moral lessons that might be drawn from them. For example, in 1894 there was a widespread interest in both England and the United States on the subject of the reunion of Christendom. It had arisen in part from the conversations which had begun between Lord Charles Halifax and Abbé Fernand Portal sometime before, and which eventually involved Cardinal Vaughan and a number of high ecclesiastics in Rome. In fact, it was said that the hopes of the Roman Curia that large numbers of the English were about to return to the Catholic Church "never ran higher than in the closing weeks of 1894."[13]

Gibbons was aware of this fact and on Sunday, November 4, 1894, he made it the theme of his sermon. He centered his treatment of the subject around the life and times of St. Charles Borromeo, whose feast day it was, and at the beginning he frankly admitted the lamentable abuses that had crept into the lives of many prominent churchmen in the days of St. Charles. But no member of the teaching Church, he said, was exempt from the liability of falling from grace. True, the Church claimed to be infallible when defining doctrine, but this had nothing to do with the personal peccability of its teaching body. This thought drew

Gibbons on to describe how Borromeo had helped to reform the Church from within, and to deplore the attempts of Charles' contemporaries, Luther and Calvin, to reform it from without. The cardinal then spoke of the current interest in reunion, and it was his belief that the conditions for such were easier than was generally imagined. He made it clear that while there could be no compromise on the doctrines and moral code that Christ had bequeathed to His Church, yet the Church could modify its discipline to suit the circumstances of the times. Gibbons remarked that he had received several letters from influential Protestant divines expressing the hope for reunion and inquiring as to the probable basis for such a reconciliation, and he then stated:

> This reunion is the great desire of my heart. I have longed & prayed & worked for it to the best of my poor ability during the three & thirty years of my ministry. I have prayed that as we are bound to our separated brethren by social & family, & by natural & commercial ties, so may we unite to them in this bond of a common faith. Separation is estrangement; union is love. Gladly would I give my life for this devout consummation.[14]

Too much has been said concerning the alertness of the Cardinal of Baltimore to all the great events, both of joy and sorrow, in the life of his country to warrant further statement here. But some repetition may, perhaps, be justified to show how the cardinal employed the pulpit to discharge his high concept of citizenship. Immediately following the death of President McKinley from an assassin's bullet on September 14, 1901, Gibbons

---

[14] 93-M-13, handwritten copy of sermon at the cathedral of Baltimore, November 4, 1894. On June 20, 1894, Leo XIII had issued his encyclical, *Praeclara gratulationis publicae,* on the subject of the reunion of Christendom. The English text was carried in the *American Catholic Quarterly Review* for October of that year, for which Gibbons contributed a brief article entitled "Introductory Remarks to the Pope's Encyclical" (XIX, 721–777). The cardinal welcomed the idea of reunion, but he stated, "One cannot be with Christ unless he be with His true Church. And in His Church He set up in Peter and his successors an authority which should be at once the rule of faith and the bond of union. All in opposition to that divine ordinance, all who separate themselves from it, cannot expect to have part with Christ; they will be against Christ" (p. 776). In an editorial note of November 1, 1894, the *Independent* of New York took exception to Gibbons' statement when they said, "We give the Cardinal credit for more charity than these words indicate. He certainly believes that a great many people are 'with Christ' who are not in the Roman Catholic Church. He does not believe that we Protestants are all 'against Christ.' "

issued a circular to his clergy with instructions that a memorial service should be held for the late President in all the churches of the Archdiocese of Baltimore on September 19, the day of the funeral at Canton, Ohio. He personally presided in the cathedral on that occasion and preached the sermon. He found it difficult, he said, to think of a murder more atrocious, wanton, and meaningless than the assassination of McKinley, for no court in Europe or in the civilized world was more conspicuous for moral rectitude and purity, or freer from the breath of scandal than the official home of the late President. "He would have adorned," said the cardinal, "any court in Christendom by his civic virtues." The suggestion had been made in the press since McKinley's death that the President should give up public receptions for his personal safety; but it was a suggestion with which Gibbons did not agree. He said:

> No, let the President continue to move among his people and take them by the hand. The strongest shield of our chief magistrate is the love and devotion of his fellow-citizens. The most effective way to stop such crimes is to inspire the rising generation with greater reverence for the constituted authorities, and a greater horror for any insult or injury to their persons.

The American people, Gibbons continued, had prayed for the President's life; it had not pleased God to grant their petition. But, said the cardinal, no one should infer from this that the prayers were in vain, for if God had not saved the life of McKinley, he had preserved the life of the nation which was of more importance than that of an individual. McKinley had passed away, honored and mourned by the nation, and Theodore Roosevelt had succeeded at once to the title, honors, and responsibilities of the presidential office. "What a striking illustration," said Gibbons, "of the strength of our Government!" He urged that the American people should now rally around Roosevelt to uphold and to sustain him in bearing the formidable burdens so suddenly thrust upon him. Only a moment, he remarked, intervened between the death of the President and the existence of his successor in the plenitude of the presidential power. In other countries the assassination of the ruler meant revolution, and revolution meant death. "How futile then is the murder of the President," the cardinal concluded, "since provision is made for an endless chain of succession, & what a striking evidence is here of the stability of our Government!"[15] The sermon of the cardinal at the McKinley memorial service, as was the case with so many that he preached, was given very wide circulation through the American press and elicited much favorable comment.[16]

Favorable reaction to sermons of the cardinal were of frequent occurrence, but only rarely was it given to Gibbons — as to any preacher — to hear that a sermon of his had been the cause of resolving a crisis in the life of one of his hearers. A case that came to the cardinal's knowledge in 1916 was of that nature. Dr. William Dandridge Turner, a non-Catholic physician of Virginia, informed him that twenty-seven years before he had suspected that he had contracted leprosy. His concern brought him to Baltimore for consultation with several eminent doctors with whom he conferred early one Sunday morning. They concurred with his opinion that the disease was leprosy, and their judgment confirmed Turner in his determination to commit suicide as the easiest way out of his difficulty. From this point the story is best related in the doctor's own words. He told Gibbons:

> I left my friends, still planning the best means of ending my life so that my death should seem natural. It was a beautiful Spring morning and there was a quietness and a peacefulness of approaching oblivion. Just as I got opposite the Cathedral, the doors and the windows being open, something seemed to invite me in, not that I believed, for I did not. But it seemed to me that I was tired and maybe would rest. I tried to whisper to the usher that I did not care to go too far, but he walked me until I was within three or four seats of the front. You preached that morning and what I do not know, I can never tell, but you preached to *me;* you looked in my face so many times; and Your Eminence, you used these very words, "Those whom the Lord loveth, He chasteneth." "You may

---

[15] 99-A-10, handwritten copy of sermon at the cathedral of Baltimore, September 19, 1901. Another example of a sermon dealing with a public event was that entitled "Will the American Republic Endure?" which the cardinal preached in his cathedral on Sunday, November 3, 1912, two days preceding the bitterly contested national election of that year. It may be read in *A Retrospect of Fifty Years,* II, 206–215.

[16] For example, Father Felix Ward, C.P., of Louisville, Kentucky, told him that the papers there had carried it in full and, he remarked, "nothing that has been said on the assassination of the President has so impressed the people." The city assessor of Louisville had informed Ward that the employees of the city hall, both Catholic and non-Catholic, had discussed Gibbons' remarks and that all had declared there was nothing like it in delicacy, patriotism, and statesmanship (99-B-3, Ward to Gibbons, Louisville, September 20, 1901).

have a fair body, one beautiful to look upon, and yet it may be covered with sores and disfigured!" You finished your sermon and sent me away with your blessing, to fight; and with a tiny ray of sunshine of belief entering my soul. All thoughts of suicide were gone, and the sequel is that I returned home, and in less than six weeks my body was as perfect as it ever was and as it is today. So many times I have thought I would write and tell you this and just as many times I would think it presumption, and not do so. The little seed of hope which you planted in my heart that Sunday, began to grow, and in the course of time I made a public profession of my allegiance to God. . . .

This letter is longer than I wish it to be, but if I told you all of the part that you have played in my life, it would be much longer.[17]

It is rare, indeed, for any preacher to receive such evidence as this of the effectiveness of words uttered from the pulpit, and Gibbons must have humbly thanked God that he had been made the channel of grace to a soul in distress. That his ministry in the pulpit was of assistance to many we know, and two men who had listened to the cardinal preach on numerous occasions said of him after his death, "His sermons were sermons of helpfulness. He spoke to the hearts of people, for he knew the hearts of men." There could be no doubt of the accuracy of their judgment, and these same close witnesses stated that through most of his years in Baltimore during which he preached in the cathedral on the first Sunday of each month the crowds that gathered to hear him were very large. Several years before he died Gibbons gave up this practice and appeared in the cathedral pulpit only a few times each year. But he continued to preach at the conferring of confirmation and at similar ceremonies in other parishes throughout the archdiocese, and he rarely declined an invitation to preside at the various exercises of the colleges and schools within his jurisdiction where, it was said, "his classic and genial addresses were always welcomed and appreciated."[18]

It was evident, both from the volumes of sermons which he published and from the numerous handwritten copies which he left after him, that the Cardinal of Baltimore gave a great deal of time and care to their preparation. In their composition, as in the many and varied forms which his writing took, he was well

[17] 113-F, Turner to Gibbons, Ocean View, Virginia, March 8, 1916.
[18] Smith-Fitzpatrick, *op. cit.*, p. 85.

served by the classics of English literature which he had read
as a younger man, for as he told Bruce Barton some months
before he died, this early reading proved valuable in helping him
to cultivate an easy and effective style.[19] One of the earliest published writings of Gibbons was in the form of a pastoral letter
on the temporal power of the Papacy which he addressed in 1871
to the clergy and laity of North Carolina.[20] It was a medium of
instruction for his people which he employed at intervals in
later years when subjects such as Christian education and the
progress of American Catholicism engaged his attention. As he
came into greater prominence the cardinal was asked from time
to time to write the introduction or foreword to new books.
Among these were Charles Warren Currier's *Carmel in America*
(Baltimore, 1890), Augustin Largent's *Life of Father Charles
Perraud* (New York, 1896), *Life and Characteristics of Right
Reverend Alfred A. Curtis* (New York, 1913) by the Sisters of
the Visitation, Hilaire Belloc's edition and completion of John
Lingard's *History of England* (New York, 1912), and Claude G.
Bowers' *The Irish Orators* (Indianapolis, 1916). In most cases
Gibbons confined himself to a few brief paragraphs in which he set
down some general observations about the subject of the book as,
for example, in the Lingard-Belloc work, where he paid tribute to
the original research of Lingard in writing history based on facts,
and not, as he said, on the "ex-parte nostrums and positive lies" with
which many historians had so long inflicted the English people.[21]

But there was one introduction to a book in which the cardinal
extended himself in a way that he later had reason to regret. In
1891 James Jeffrey Roche published the *Life of John Boyle
O'Reilly* which carried a rather lengthy introduction by Gibbons.
He expressed unqualified admiration for O'Reilly's career as an
Irish patriot and writer and for his later activities as a journalist
and poet in the United States where, it was said, as a member
of the staff of the Boston *Pilot,* he had risen from the status of
a penniless and unknown fugitive from an Australian prison to
a position where at his death the best and noblest men in the

---

[19] Bruce Barton, "Young Man, *Expect* Great Things! An Interview with Cardinal
Gibbons," *American Magazine,* XCI (March, 1921), 7.
[20] *A Circular Letter on the Temporal Power of the Popes Addressed to the
Clergy and Laity of the Vicariate Apostolic of North Carolina* (Baltimore, 1871).
[21] John Lingard and Hilaire Belloc, *The History of England* (New York, 1912),
I, iii.

United States vied in doing honor to his name.[22] It was the last that was heard or thought about the introduction to Roche's book until eight years later when William E. H. Lecky, the noted author of the *History of European Morals* and of the histories of England and Ireland, published a volume which he called *The Map of Life. Conduct and Character.* Therein Lecky cited the fact that in his early life O'Reilly had been a member of the Fenian Brotherhood in Ireland, and that he had joined a regiment of hussars for the express purpose of seducing his fellow soldiers and of betraying his trust. To Lecky the adulation of O'Reilly by the cardinal revealed a "perversion of morals" which would see the violation of military duty as worthy of praise, and the historian was shocked that Gibbons had not included a single word that would imply that O'Reilly had done anything for which he should have been ashamed.[23] The comments of Lecky were taken up by one signing himself "British Catholic" in a letter to the *Times* of London of November 2, 1899, where it was stated that the writer had been prepared to welcome the American cardinal as the preacher at the opening of the new cathedral of Westminster until he had read Lecky; now he thought Gibbons would have to give a satisfactory explanation of his introduction to the biography of O'Reilly if he were to be received in London with the warmth that Cardinal Vaughan anticipated. The New York *World* of November 5 made matters sound much worse than they really were by publishing a news item which carried the sensational headline, "English Slurs at Cardinal Gibbons. Catholics in London Threaten to Make His Visit There Next Year Very Unpleasant. Weak Pretext for Hatred of Irish." And to add to the woeful picture, the *World* showed its own anti-British bias over the Boer War then in progress by dragging in the sympathy of the Irish for the Boers.

It was an unpleasant situation which the Cardinal of Baltimore felt he could not ignore. He decided, therefore, to write a letter of explanation to Cardinal Vaughan. He told him that

---

[22] James Jeffrey Roche, *Life of John Boyle O'Reilly* (New York, 1891), pp. v–viii. After O'Reilly's widow had read the introduction, she wrote to express her appreciation and to thank him, as she said, "in the name of my dear dead husband, who would have considered his life most fitly rounded, could he have foreseen the magnanimous words of your kindly sanction" (88-A-5, Mary O'Reilly to Gibbons, Charlestown, Massachusetts, October 15, 1890).

[23] Lecky, *op. cit.* (London, 1899), pp. 105–107.

Lecky had reasonably assumed that he was acquainted with the fact that O'Reilly had been a Fenian, had entered the hussars, assumed the uniform of the queen, and had taken an oath of allegiance for the express purpose of betraying his trust and of seducing the soldiers of his regiment. "I feel it due to myself & to the interest of truth to declare," said Gibbons, "that till I read Mr. Lecky's criticism I did not know that Mr. O'R. had ever been a Fenian, a British soldier, or that he had tried to seduce other soldiers from their sworn allegiance." In fact, he confessed, he had never read a line of Roche's biography for which he had written the introduction, and the only acquaintance he had with O'Reilly's early history was the vague information that for some political offense, the nature of which he had not learned, he had been exiled to the penal colony from which he had afterward escaped. Gibbons maintained that he had known O'Reilly only as a quiet and unobtrusive gentleman of conservative views who was a devoted Christian and a model husband and father, and whose literary merit had brought him the esteem of the most cultivated citizens of New England, including such writers as Holmes, Lowell, and Whittier. The cardinal acknowledged that it might seem strange to some that anyone should undertake to write an introduction to a work, the merits of which he had not previously ascertained by personal examination. Without pretending to justify such an action — or still less to hold it up as an example to others — he confessed that this was not the first time that he had written an introduction for a book that he had not read, having relied in all cases on the integrity and judgment of the author. An introduction to a biography, he said, may enunciate sound principles without committing its writer to the views of the biographer, since it was the province of the latter and not of the former to have a thorough knowledge of the subject and to pronounce judgment on his public and private life. Gibbons then concluded:

> I am the more desirous of sending these words of explanation because I have regarded Mr. Lecky as a man of a sober & dispassionate mind, as well as of distinguished ability. While sometimes obliged to differ from his conclusions, I must bear testimony to his deep historical research, & I cheerfully confess that I am indebted to him for many profitable & entertaining hours.[24]

---

[24] 97-T-10, Gibbons to Vaughan, Baltimore, November, 1899, copy. Father

Cardinal Vaughan at first attempted to have the London *Times* publish Gibbons' letter, but when they declined to take it he sent it to the *Tablet* where it appeared on December 2. After its publication Lecky wrote to Vaughan to say that he would revise his remarks in the next edition of the *Map of Life,* and the Cardinal of Westminster concluded by stating to Gibbons that those who sent such letters as that of "British Catholic" to the *Times* were practical apostates or bad Catholics and no attention should be paid to them. Gibbons should reassure himself, therefore, that he would be received with the utmost respect and enthusiasm when he comes for the opening of the cathedral of Westminster.[25] The incident did not pass unnoticed in St. Paul, and Archbishop Ireland counseled Gibbons not to write any more introductions to books that he had not read. The cardinal acknowledged that he had given him good advice, but he said, "I fear I am incurable in this respect." He alluded to the fact that Ireland himself had failed at one time in this particular, for he stated that in self-vindication he could say to him, " 'Tu quoque,' & 'Medice, cura teipsum,' " to which he added, "You see I am in excellent company." He told the archbishop that he had been prompted to send the explanation of his action to Vaughan by reason of an exaggerated notion of the importance of the letter of "British Catholic" in the London *Times,* having been misled by the New York *World's* account to believe that "British Catholic" was the mouthpiece of the English Catholics.[26]

We have had many occasions to refer to another form which the cardinal's writings often assumed, namely, articles in the leading American Catholic and secular periodicals and there is no need, therefore, to speak of them again in any detail. His earliest effort in this respect was a series of eight unsigned articles which he wrote jointly with Bishop Lynch of Charleston on various aspects of the Vatican Council which they were then

---

John R. Slattery, S.S.J., sent Gibbons copies of several letters he had written in defense of the cardinal's action to Lady Herbert of Lea, Vaughan, and Monsignor Denis O'Connell, all of which were dated November 10, 1899 (97-T-1, 2, 3).

[25] 97-U-4, Vaughan to Gibbons, Westminster, December 7, 1899.

[26] AASP, Gibbons to Ireland, Baltimore, January 5, 1900, copy. Gibbons was likely referring here to Ireland's introduction to *The Life of Father Hecker* by Walter Elliott, C.S.P. (New York, 1891), which raised such a storm during the Americanism controversy.

attending and which appeared between February and September, 1870, in the *Catholic World*.[27] Among the Catholic journals, Gibbons' most frequent contributions were directed to the *American Catholic Quarterly Review* where, for example, during the five years between 1883 and 1888 he wrote on subjects such as "The Law of Prayer," "Relative Influence of Paganism and Christianity upon Morals," "Christianity and Modern Science," and "The Relative Influence of Paganism and Christianity on Human Slavery."[28] Occasionally, too, foreign periodicals carried articles by Gibbons, such as his essay on "Irish Immigration to the United States" in the *Irish Ecclesiastical Record* of February, 1897, and his brief memoir entitled "My Memories" which appeared in the *Dublin Review* in the spring of 1917 and was reprinted several months later by the *Living Age*.[29]

With less frequency Cardinal Gibbons made contributions to the secular journals of the United States as, for example, his brief article on the "Life of a Sister of Charity" in the *Ladies' Home Journal* of April, 1893.[30] Two years before he had participated with two prominent doctors, of whom one was William Osler, and three women in a symposium which was carried by the *Century Magazine* of February, 1891, under the heading, "On the Opening of the Johns Hopkins Medical School to Women." The cardinal was strongly in favor of their admittance to the famous medical school in his see city, and he quoted precedents from history to support his view that women should be educated in medical science.[31] In January, 1907, his name again appeared in the *Century Magazine* over an article entitled "The Moral Aspects of Suicide,"[32] concerning which the cardinal had especially requested that his quotations from the Bible should be left in the language of the Douai version, a request with which

---

[27] These articles, after certain minor revisions, were published nearly a half century later by Gibbons in *A Retrospect of Fifty Years*, I, 30–185.

[28] VIII (October, 1883), 577–596; X (October, 1885), 696–710; XIII (January, 1888), 1–11; XIII (October, 1888), 577–588. These articles were later used as chapters in Gibbons' *Our Christian Heritage*.

[29] *Irish Ecclesiastical Record*, 4th Series I (February, 1897), 97–109; *Dublin Review*, CLX (April, 1917), 163–172, which was reprinted in *Living Age*, 8th Series VI (June 23, 1917), 718–724.

[30] X (April, 1893), 4.

[31] Cf. XLI (February, 1891), 632–633, for Gibbons' statement.

[32] LXXIII (January, 1907), 401–407.

the associate editor complied without question when he forwarded to Gibbons an honorarium of $200 for the article.[33] But his favorite medium of publication among the secular journals was the *North American Review*. Reference has already been made to the views of Gibbons expressed in the most important of these articles which included his contribution to the symposium entitled "Is Divorce Wrong?" in November, 1889, and an essay called "Wealth and Its Obligations" in the issue of April, 1891.[34] When he decided in 1916 upon editing some of the articles and sermons he had previously published or delivered for *A Retrospect of Fifty Years,* he selected three that had appeared in the *North American Review,* namely, "Patriotism and Politics" of April, 1892, "Personal Reminiscences of the Vatican Council" of April, 1894, and "The Church and the Republic" from the issue of March, 1909. His request for permission to reprint was readily granted by Colonel George Harvey, the editor, and in communicating it to the cardinal he remarked, "But I am filled with sorrow that I have not now more articles from your pen for publication in the Review."[35] By that time, however, Gibbons had ceased to do much writing, and for the remaining years of his

---

[33] 103-P, R. U. Johnson to Gibbons, New York, October 25, 1906.

[34] CXLIX (November, 1889), 513–538. Gibbons' statement on divorce is contained on pp. 517–524; CLII (April, 1891), 385–394.

[35] 113-V, Harvey to Gibbons, New York, September 21, 1916. Cf. CLIV (April, 1892), 385–400; CLVIII (April, 1894), 385–400. The article, "The Church and the Republic," CLXXXIX (March, 1909), 321–336, appeared at a time when the anti-Catholic campaign of Thomas E. Watson of Georgia was beginning to gather momentum. The cardinal doubtless had this in mind when he took note of the synods of two Protestant churches that, he said, had recently deemed it just and wise to proclaim to the American people that Catholics could not be trusted in political office because of their allegiance to the Pope (pp. 323–324). Later he spoke of the removal of civil disabilities in early American history, and he then remarked, "The removal of these civil disabilities has always, I believe, been considered a triumph of the American spirit; and the Lutheran and Baptist synods will find it difficult to persuade the public to write their synodal concept of religious liberty and civil equality upon our statute books. . . ." (p. 326). The article called forth a reply. Henry C. Vedder, professor of church history in the Crozer Theological Seminary at Chester, Pennsylvania, objected that Gibbons had done a grave injustice to the Baptists and their views on religious liberty, as well as having stated many falsehoods on the doctrines and practices of the Catholic Church. Vedder was unsuccessful in his efforts to have his reply appear in the *North American Review,* so he published it in the form of a thirty-paged pamphlet which he called *Baptist "Bigotry and Intolerance." A Reply to Cardinal Gibbons* (Chester, 1909).

life his name appeared very rarely as a contributor to periodical literature.

Mention of Gibbons' article on wealth in the *North American Review* of April, 1891, raises the question as to just how much he employed the talents of others in his publications. In this instance, as we have previously noted, he stated in his diary that the chief credit for the article belonged to Father Patrick J. Donahue, his chancellor at the time, to whom he had given, as he expressed it, "some leading thoughts & hints." We have seen, too, that he publicly credited Ireland and Keane with help in drawing up the memorial on the Knights of Labor at Rome in 1887. Moreover, we know that he submitted the manuscript of *The Faith of Our Fathers* to Camillo Mazzella, S.J., a professor of theology at Woodstock College in 1876, for a critical reading, and thirteen years later that Salvatore M. Brandi, S.J., of the same institution performed a similar service for *Our Christian Heritage*. But beyond collaboration of this kind and in these few instances, it is impossible to say to what extent others had a hand in what the cardinal wrote. It was altogether understandable that a busy public figure like Gibbons should on occasion seek the help of others in writing, or in critically reading his manuscripts. But it would be quite unwarranted to deduce from these few known cases that he was accustomed to publish material which had been written by others. That he sought the expert knowledge of theologians, in treating matters of doctrine and morals, was entirely commendable and such reliance bore testimony to his wisdom and good sense in not going into print before his writing had been examined by specialists. There may, indeed, have been other instances where his assistants wrote articles in his name as in the case of Donahue, but no evidence of such was discovered beyond what has been stated. To be sure, from time to time rumors and gossip circulated to the effect that the cardinal employed someone to do his writing for him, but these remarks never emerged from the shadowy realm of suggestion and supposition, and the absence of any substantial evidence to the contrary constitutes a cogent argument for the fact that with a few exceptions the Cardinal of Baltimore was himself the true author of his published works.

The most important contribution which Cardinal Gibbons made as a writer was, of course, by his books. Between 1876 and 1916 he published five books, although the last two, *Discourses and Sermons* in 1908 and *A Retrospect of Fifty Years* which appeared eight years later, consisted almost entirely of sermons preached on various occasions in former years or reprints of articles which had originally appeared in the Catholic and secular journals. The most famous of Gibbons' books was undoubtedly *The Faith of Our Fathers* which the firm of John Murphy and Company of Baltimore put on the market in the closing weeks of 1876. We have previously spoken at length concerning the origins of this work and the reception accorded to it in the first year of its publication.[36] But the unusual fame which *The Faith of Our Fathers* attained, and the fact that at the present time, seventy-five years after its publication, it is an active item in religious book stores in the 110th edition with an estimated two million copies distributed, offers further evidence of the extraordinary effect which this volume had upon the lives of many of its readers. About a year after it came out Henry F. Parke, vicar-general of the Diocese of Wheeling and pastor of St. Francis Xavier Church at Parkersburg, West Virginia, told the author that only those who had devoted long years to the work of the missions in mixed populations like that of West Virginia could fitly appreciate it. Parke thought it emphatically the book for the millions, and that this was its highest eulogy. "It has already taken root in this quarter," he said, "& will please God, be a fixture in every household that I can influence."[37] Before the end of that year Gibbons had word from the grandnephew of Chief Justice Marshall that a reading of the book had induced him to become a Catholic and to study for the priesthood.[38]

Through the succeeding years a steady stream of letters continued to reach the cardinal which attributed to his book either the removal of prejudice against the Church or conversion to its faith. A Florida Presbyterian, who remained true to his own denomination, thought it would be well for all Protestants in the land to read *The Faith of Our Fathers* and have their preju-

---

[36] Cf. I, 86, 145–152.

[37] 73-G-3, Parke to Gibbons, Parkersburg, October 23, 1877.

[38] 73-J-11, John A. Marshall to Gibbons, Orleans, Virginia, December 17, 1877. About a year later W. M. Nelson, a student at the Seabury Divinity School in Faribault, Minnesota, said he was likewise prompted to become a Catholic and to study for the priesthood as a result of reading the book (74-G-6, Nelson to Gibbons, Faribault, January 12, 1879).

dice against Catholicism removed; while two women of Nokesville, Virginia, said it had been the instrument of settling their
doubts and of confirming their belief in Catholicism.[39] Near the
end of his introduction to the volume Gibbons had stated,
"Should the perusal of this book bring one soul to the knowledge
of the Church, my labor will be amply rewarded."[40] Certainly
his reward proved more than merely ample, for again and again
through the years this sentence was quoted to him by those who
wished him to know that they had found their way into the
Catholic fold through a reading of *The Faith of Our Fathers*.
Especially did this seem to be true in the early years of its circulation of persons who lived in the South. A widow in Burke
County, Georgia, for example, received a copy of it from an
old Irish well digger who had edified her by his holy life, and
by the happy mood in which he bore his poverty and humble
station. It was her desire that Gibbons should know that the
latter's labor on the book had been repaid, for some months
before she had been baptized a Catholic.[41] And yet the conversions that resulted from a reading of Gibbons' work were by no
means confined to the South. From far-off Montana Territory
he heard from a man who had been a Presbyterian, but who had
become a Catholic through reading *The Faith of Our Fathers*.
He had taken refuge from the subsequent bitterness of his
family by settling down at an Indian mission where he was
living with the Jesuits and hoped some day to enter their order.[42]

Nor were the conversions to Catholicism which were accounted
for by the book of Cardinal Gibbons restricted to those in a
lowly station of life. Dr. George A. Sterling told him that as the
attending physician of a convent a copy of the volume had come
into his hands as he sat at the bedside of a dying sister. He had
always been a member of the Protestant Episcopal Church and
was, in fact, a senior warden of the church of that denomination
in Sag Harbor, Long Island. The reading of Gibbons' book had

[39] 73-N-6, J. Dabney Palmer to Gibbons, Monticello, Florida, January 28, 1878;
73-R-9, Mrs. James M. Beckham and Emma Beckham, Nokesville, April 29, 1878.
[40] *Op. cit.*, p. xvii.
[41] 74-U-5, A. Virginia Palmer to Gibbons, Green's Cut, Georgia, December 13,
1879. Another correspondent who quoted Gibbons' statement and said he owed
his conversion to the book was N. D. Weber of Red Wing, Minnesota (77-I-6,
Weber to Gibbons, Red Wing, July 21, 1883).
[42] 78-Y-6, David H. B. Evans to Gibbons, St. Ignatius Mission, Montana
Territory, December 29, 1884.

convinced him that the Catholic Church was the true one. He
had likewise been influenced, he said, by the fact that in his
medical practice he had noted the contrast by which the dying
Catholic and Protestant were ushered into eternity and, too, by
the fact that never in all his years as a physician had he been
approached by a Catholic woman seeking the destruction of the
unborn life within her womb, or asking him to help usher into
existence an illegitimate child.[43] In another case a Methodist
minister, his mother, wife, and three children had entered the
Church as a consequence of the minister reading the cardinal's
book. The ex-minister told of his financial difficulties as a result
of losing his source of income, and a few days thereafter he
gratefully acknowledged a sum of money which Gibbons had sent
to him and he assured the cardinal that he should not worry too
much about them, for, as he said, "we have been far happier
since our conversion, despite our poverty!"[44] Some years later a
similar message was received from a former minister of the
Protestant Episcopal Church who had been converted through
the book, and who was then on the eve of his departure for Rome
to study for the priesthood.[45]

Even from abroad the author learned of the good which his
book had accomplished. A doctor who had been educated in the
universities of Scotland and France, and who was at present a
member of the faculty of medicine of the University of Paris,
stated that on one of his numerous visits to Lourdes he had recited the Our Father for the gift of faith and had then sought
something to read on the Church. He secured a copy of *The Faith
of Our Fathers* and there were two features of the work which
had especially impressed him, namely, the accuracy of its facts
and quotations and, second, the great truth which before had
never struck him, namely, the necessity for a supreme authority
in the Church. He wished the cardinal to know, therefore, what
deep learning he felt lay behind the popular style of the volume,

[43] 80-H-8, Sterling to Gibbons, Sag Harbor, New York, February 11, 1886;
80-Q-14, same to same, Sag Harbor, March, 1886. Another doctor by the name
of Latimer became a Catholic through reading *The Faith of Our Fathers,* and
his conversion was said by the pastor of St. Mary's Church, Bryantown, Maryland,
to have caused something of a sensation in the community (84-S-5, Edward M.
Southgate to "Rev. dear Father," Bryantown, July 12, 1888).

[44] 82-V-7, G. Seth Williams to Gibbons, Terre Haute, Indiana, June 25, 1887;
82-W-7, same to same, Terre Haute, June 29, 1887.

[45] 92-W-3, John D. Benson to Gibbons, Brooklyn, December 23, 1893.

and also the absolute fairness and accuracy with which the quotations had been used. To the doctor it was the very book to convince and convert educated and cultured persons who labored under a religious prejudice.[46]

That *The Faith of Our Fathers* played a part in the conversion of a number of highly educated people, there was no doubt. George Parsons Lathrop, who served for some years as associate editor of the *Atlantic Monthly* and later as editor of the Boston *Sunday Courier,* was a case in point. Lathrop had married Rose Hawthorne, the younger daughter of Nathaniel Hawthorne, and they were both received into the Catholic Church in March, 1891, by Father Alfred Young, C.S.P. Some months later Lathrop asked his pastor, Father Thomas Joynt of St. Mary's Star of the Sea Church in New London, Connecticut, if he should inform the author about the conversion of himself and his wife, and the pastor had urged him to do so. Lathrop wanted the cardinal to know, therefore, that here were two souls who, as he put it, "were largely converted by your cogent, simple, sincere & winning presentation of the truth."[47] After the writer's death in 1898 his widow interested herself in the victims of incurable cancer, and with a view to consecrating her life to their welfare, she founded the religious sisterhood known as the Servants for Relief of Incurable Cancer. Many years later Mother Alphonsa, as she was known in religion, told the cardinal that upon reading his book she had been at once relieved of her difficulties about becoming a Catholic. It had made her respect and devotion to Gibbons constant and deeper with the passing of time and, as she said, "kept me observant of the beautiful influence of your holy power during many years."[48]

---

[46] 98-B-2, J. Gowling Middleton to Gibbons, Paris, January 12, 1900.

[47] 88-N-5, Parsons to Gibbons, New London, May 8, 1891. About three weeks previous the cardinal was informed by Paul Ajas that after a period of defection from the Church he had been brought in contact with Father John H. Fox, pastor of Holy Cross Church at Sea Bright, New Jersey, who, said Ajas, "saw after a few moments of conversation that argument or persuasion would hardly have any effect upon me." Fox, therefore, gave him a copy of *The Faith of Our Fathers* which he spent the whole night "devouring" in an effort to find a loophole, but instead it ended, according to Ajas, "by my being thoroughly humbled and conquered by your kind, loving and forcible exposition of our Faith." He wanted the cardinal to know, therefore, of his gratitude for the help he had been given to return to the Church (88-M-4, Ajas to Gibbons, Sea Bright, April 13, 1891).

[48] 103-H, Mother Alphonsa Lathrop, O.S.D., to Gibbons, Hawthorne, New

Another distinguished convert in whose life *The Faith of Our Fathers* played a part was Frederick J. Kinsman, Protestant Episcopal Bishop of Delaware. Kinsman had visited Gibbons many years before his conversion in the company of Dr. William T. Manning, then rector of Trinity Church, New York, and later Protestant Episcopal Bishop of New York, in the interests of a proposed conference on faith and order. Kinsman stated that the kindness which they had experienced on that occasion encouraged him to address himself to the cardinal again. He had shared, he said, for many years of his life the impression of many Americans that to be a Roman Catholic one could not be sympathetically American. "To Your Eminence," he remarked, "I owe the banishing of this superstition." About twelve years before he had been much struck by an address of Gibbons which he had read in the papers, and he had ever since followed as closely as he could the cardinal's utterances and actions, and through them, he commented, "I have come to see that the Roman Catholic Church is the best guarantee for preserving the Christian ideals of American life." He had now become convinced that Catholicism was the true faith and he wished, therefore, to ask Gibbons' advice about what he should do after leaving the Protestant Episcopal Church. On that day many years before when Kinsman and Manning had visited the cardinal Kinsman had seen Gibbons standing in the oriel window over the entrance to his residence ready to welcome and bless them. He had often thought of this as representing an attitude of fatherly benediction, of the Church's willingness to welcome wandering sons and thus, as he said, "in my own perplexity and distress, I have ventured to make this personal request. If it is presumptuous intrusion, I humbly apologize."[49]

Needless to say, Kinsman's inquiry was viewed as no act of presumption and the cardinal hastened to reply from his summer holiday at Spring Lake, New Jersey, and to say that for some time he had been following the bishop's fortunes with lively in-

---

York, June 16, 1906. Several years before William T. Doyle, who had been a student at St. Charles College when *The Faith of Our Fathers* was published, remarked to Henry F. Brownson, "I was astonished to hear that the Jesuits claim that one of their number wrote 'Faith of our Fathers.' . . . Can you inform me how this originated?" (AUND, Henry Brownson Papers, Doyle to Brownson, Milwaukee, May 20, 1902.)

[49] 122-V, Kinsman to Gibbons, Bryant Pond, Maine, August 4, 1919, *Personal.*

terest and earnest prayer that God would direct his footsteps to the Church. He was not surprised to learn that Kinsman should have imbibed the prejudiced view that Catholicism and Americanism were incompatible; but all, he said, is harmony in God's way, and in His mind religious liberty and the United States were no doubt linked together for His own divine purposes. "Only from Christianity," said Gibbons, "can America draw the blood that will give her life for the future and that strong nourishment will come to her from Christ through the Church." He felt he understood the kind of companionship which Kinsman then needed in spiritual and intellectual matters, and after having given the case considerable thought he had decided that nowhere would he be more at home, more free, and in more congenial surroundings than at the Catholic University of America in Washington. As Chancellor of the University he invited Kinsman to take up his residence there as his guest, where he could avail himself of the library and enjoy a wide choice of companionship. The cardinal closed by saying that he would be happy to see or to hear from Kinsman at all times, and he added, "should you think a guide would be of any use in the new country you expect to penetrate I am happy to offer my services."[50]

Due to the serious illness of his father and to other circumstances in the bishop's family, he was unable to avail himself of Gibbons' hospitality in Washington, although later that year the cardinal offered him a position on the faculty of the university and volunteered to give him substantial financial assistance until he could see his way through his domestic problems and become adjusted as a Catholic. At Gibbons' direction Kinsman came to Baltimore in late November, 1919, where the cardinal received him into the Church and gave him a warm letter of introduction to Bishop Louis S. Walsh of Portland, Maine, in whose diocese he was then living.[51] Some months after Kinsman's reception as a Catholic the cardinal had a set of his books forwarded to him, and in thanking him the new convert remarked that he owed

---

[50] 122-W, Gibbons to Kinsman, Spring Lake, August 8, 1919, copy.

[51] 123-A, Kinsman to Gibbons, Bryant Pond, August 13, 1919; 123-U, Gibbons to Kinsman, Baltimore, November 22, 1919, copy; 123-V, Gibbons to Walsh, Baltimore, November 24, 1919, copy; 123-W, Kinsman to Gibbons, Portland, Maine, November 27, 1919. In this last letter Kinsman thanked the cardinal for the latter's gift of $500 given with the thought that he might need it after having lost his former income.

very much to *The Faith of Our Fathers,* which had settled various points for him and had thrown light on many questions in his mind. He had read the volume at a time when he was working over some matters pertaining to the development of what he called "the papal principle." His investigation had involved a number of technical points of dogmatic theology and he had sought the answers in many directions. "But I can not remember," he concluded, "that I found anywhere a clearer statement of the essential facts than in Your Eminence's books, although I was long blind to the full significance of the Petrine texts."[52]

Still another couple who owed their conversion in good measure to *The Faith of Our Fathers* was the famous lecturer and writer, John L. Stoddard and his wife. Mrs. Stoddard was the first to inform the cardinal of how much they felt indebted to him for their new faith. "Your *Faith of Our Fathers,*" she said, "was of incalculable help to us." She was not a Catholic from birth by reason of her father having fallen away from the Church, and she had been raised an Episcopalian, she said, and had been confirmed by Gibbons' friend, Bishop Paret of Maryland. Several months later her husband gave a lengthy description to Gibbons of his search for spiritual peace, and he stated that during the time he was making his study of the Church it was through the direction of Father Heinrich Bruders, S.J., of the University of Innsbruck that he had been given a copy of the cardinal's work.[53]

Thus to the end of his life Cardinal Gibbons continued to receive numerous and touching testimonies of the extraordinary effect which his book had had upon souls in every walk of life. On his eighty-fifth birthday he was greeted by a Negro then living in Boston, who said that he had lately seen the cardinal's picture in the Boston papers and it had carried him back in memory to the years when as a representative of the Maryland Sunday School Union he had — without knowing who he was —

[52] 127-R, Kinsman to Gibbons, Bryant Pond, June 12, 1920. In Kinsman's spiritual autobiography, *Salve Mater* (New York, 1920), he mentioned Gibbons briefly (p. 196) and he dedicated his volume, *Americanism and Catholicism* (New York, 1924), to the cardinal's memory and referred to him a number of times *passim.*

[53] 123-P, Ida M. O'Connell Stoddard to Gibbons, Meran, Tirol, October 25, 1919. Mrs. Stoddard stated that Father Bruders was then going over the manuscript of her husband's story of his conversion. It was later published under the title *Rebuilding A Lost Faith* (New York, 1921).

frequently met Gibbons in the streets of Baltimore where, as he expressed it, "I always received your kindly smile." It was while viewing a procession of the prelates into the cathedral during the Third Plenary Council that he had found out the identity of the man who had smiled at him in the streets, and he then bought his book which led to his conversion to Catholicism which, he said, "is truly the Faith of every person of African lineage."[54] A year later the cardinal received congratulations for his last birthday on earth from a reporter of the New Orleans *Times Picayune*, who had interviewed him for his paper on the occasion of Gibbons' final visit to that city in the previous March. He reminded him now of what he had said at that time concerning the part which *The Faith of Our Fathers* had played in his conversion, and he begged the cardinal for an autographed photo which he would always cherish as a memento of an eminent and noble friend, "friend, indeed," he said, "for it was Your Eminence that touched the chord that brought the Divine notes of our Holy Faith to my ears."[55]

It was to be expected that a work which had enjoyed such a phenomenal sale among English readers should attract those who for one reason or another were interested in having it appear in other languages. A year and a half after its publication the Swiss house of Benziger Brothers brought out a translation in German, and the New York branch of the same firm agreed to pay Gibbons five cents per copy on all copies of the German translation sold in the United States.[56] The cardinal learned sometime thereafter of a French translation that was in progress,[57] and eventually the book was translated into all the principal European languages, including Swedish and Bohemian, and in 1896 it was put into Braille for the use of the blind, an edition to which Gibbons contributed a special introduction.[58] Late in 1892 word reached the cardinal from a missionary in Japan that he proposed to translate it into Japanese, and he asked, therefore,

[54] 122-T, Robert Leo Ruffin to Gibbons, Boston, July 27, 1919.

[55] 128-G, Frank S. Berlin to Gibbons, New Orleans, July 21, 1920.

[56] 73-T-5, Benziger Brothers to Gibbons, New York, June 10, 1878; 74-G-5, same to same, New York, January 7, 1879; 74-H-6, contract between Benziger and Gibbons, New York, January 27, 1879.

[57] 77-J-1, Ella B. Edes to Gibbons, Rome, August 8, 1883.

[58] 94-G-11, F. D. Morrison, Superintendent of the Maryland School for the Blind, to Gibbons, Baltimore, January 16, 1896.

for permission to make certain changes in the text in order to render it more suitable for Japanese readers. In reply Gibbons stated, "I freely consent that you should make slight changes and thus accommodate it to the habits and customs, the genius and temperament of the country." He told the missionary that up to that time the circulation of the English edition had exceeded 200,000 copies, not to mention the editions in foreign tongues, and he hoped that the Japanese translation would prove as fruitful of conversions as the original edition had in the United States.[59]

Gibbons' reply to the missionary made no claim to any financial return from the sale of his book in Japan, and it was evident that he expected none. The various transactions of these years over *The Faith of Our Fathers* took place before the international copyright law of March, 1891, had won general recognition and enforcement. For example, when Lawrence Kehoe, manager of the Catholic Publication Society in New York and American representative of Burns and Oates of London, sought the cardinal's permission for a reprint of the book in England, he stated that the English firm would not wish to go ahead without his consent, although he frankly stated, "there is no law requiring them to ask your permission."[60] But regardless of the question of copyright, it was clear that Gibbons was not interested in profits but in the use to which his book might be put for the good of souls. The cardinal did not bother himself, therefore, on this score, and as far as one can see, whenever he was approached on the subject he contented himself with any reasonable arrangement which prospective distributors might propose and let it go at that.

Insofar as his original publisher was concerned, at the time that the book first appeared it had been agreed that cloth-bound copies should sell for $1.00 and paper-bound copies for fifty cents, with the author receiving five cents per copy on the former and two and a half cents per copy on the latter until 10,000 copies had been sold. Thereafter the publisher stated that this per-

---

[59] 90-U-4, Gibbons to E. Raguet, Baltimore, December 9, 1892, copy.

[60] 77-P-5, Kehoe to Gibbons, New York, March 20, 1883. Kehoe said that Burns and Oates did not wish to imitate the John Murphy Company of Baltimore who had taken up Cardinal Manning's *Eternal Priesthood* without asking his leave, "knowing as they did (or ought to know)," he added, "that I was the Cardinal's American Publisher."

centage should cease and he would assume all risks as to changes in price of the book.[61] Periodically Murphy furnished Gibbons with statements of the progress of sales as, for example, when he told him that *The Faith of Our Fathers* had gone into its thirty-third edition in September, 1888, with a reprint of 8,000 copies which raised the total in circulation to date to 167,000.[62] If Gibbons had been seriously interested in financial returns it would seem that he could surely have struck a better bargain with Murphy than he did. Three statements that he received from his publisher in the later period of his life made it evident how relatively little profit he had earned from the sales of his famous book. In these years the cardinal was paid a penny for each copy sold, and the following figures, each for a period of six months, afford a good index to the number of sales and to the amount of return which reached the author.

July 31, 1912–January 31, 1913
55,548 copies sold — $555.48 paid to the author
January 31, 1916–July 31, 1916
37,195 copies sold — $371.95 paid to the author
January 31, 1920–July 31, 1920
22,170 copies sold — $221.70 paid to the author[63]

But regardless of the financial aspects of *The Faith of Our Fathers,* the purpose which the author had in mind in writing the book, namely, to set forth the truths of the Catholic religion in a simple way that would appeal to the great masses of the American public, was fulfilled far beyond his most sanguine expectations. That the work should have sold over 22,000 copies in a six-month period a year before Gibbons' death, bore eloquent testimony to the aged cardinal of how genuinely the reading public appreciated the book he had written as a young missionary bishop over forty years before. *The Faith of Our Fathers* was by all odds the most popular work in apologetics ever published by an American Catholic and, in fact, by reason of its tremendous circulation and the enlightenment it has brought to so many readers on the teachings of the Catholic

---

[61] ADR, Murphy to Gibbons, Baltimore, September 18, 1876.
[62] 85-P-16, John Murphy Company to Gibbons, Baltimore, January 31, 1889.
[63] 109-A, statement of John Murphy Company to Gibbons, Baltimore, January 31, 1913; 113-S, same to same, July 31, 1916; 128-P, same to same, July 31, 1920.

Church, it deserves to rank among the most effective apologetic works in Christian history.[64]

Thirteen years intervened between the publication of Cardinal Gibbons' best known work and the appearance of his second book, *Our Christian Heritage,* in November, 1889. In the introduction to the new volume he made it clear that its contents were not intended as a polemic against Protestants. It had nothing to say against any Christian denomination that retained faith in at least the divine mission of Christ, and far from despising or rejecting the support of Protestants who held that belief, he stated, "I would gladly hold out to them the right hand of fellowship, so long as they unite with us in striking the common foe." Nor was the cardinal addressing professional freethinkers, agnostics, and atheists. Rather he had in mind those who, he feared, were increasing in number, namely, persons who through association, the absence of Christian training, a distorted education, and pernicious reading had become estranged, not only from the teachings of the gospel, but even from the truths of natural religion that underlay Christianity.[65] He admitted that by reason of constant interruptions and pressure of his ministerial duties, he had misgivings that some of the questions discussed in the book might not have been treated with the fullness which their importance demanded, and in his aim to be brief he likewise feared that at times he might have been wanting in clearness and precision. But he consoled himself with the hope that the reader's appetite might be whetted by a reading of the volume, and that it might lure him on to satisfy his hunger for truth and righteousness in larger and more learned works.[66]

In thirty-five chapters running to over 500 pages the author discussed in his customary simple language, but with the familiar richness of biblical quotations and with a wealth of reference to works in theology, philosophy, history, and science that did credit to the breadth of his reading, the subjects which he felt

---

[64] Mention has already been made of the work of Edward J. Stearns, *The Faith of Our Forefathers* (New York, 1879) which was written in refutation of Gibbons' book. As recently as 1947 another volume entitled, *The Catholic Religion and the Protestant Faith* by J. E. L. Winecoff (Boston, 1947) was published with a view to contrasting the teaching of the Bible with that of the Papacy. It was presented in the form of a dialogue between Gibbons and a Protestant opponent.

[65] *Op. cit.,* pp. 1–4.

[66] *Ibid.,* pp. v–vi.

would be most useful to the class of readers for whom he was writing. These chapters included such fundamental topics as the existence of God and His attributes, the dignity and efficacy of prayer, man's free will, the divinity of Christ, the relations of the Church to science, a comparison of moral and social conditions in Christian history and pagan antiquity, and an essay on the rights and duties of the laboring classes. The concluding three chapters were devoted to religion as the essential basis of civil society, the religious element in American civilization, and the dangers which to the mind of Gibbons then threatened American civilization.

Our Christian Heritage was not long in circulation before its author began to receive reactions from various readers. John Gilmary Shea, the church historian and editor of the *Catholic News* of New York, characterized it as a book that was preeminently needed and one that contained weapons against infidelity that would rouse many to serious thought.[67] Bishop Maes of Covington found the volume a kindly yet forceful appeal to the religious instincts ever in the hearts of Americans. The expression of these instincts, according to Maes, was fast becoming a reason for reproach, but he hoped that with Gibbons' book it would again be in honor.[68] A number of Protestant readers took the trouble to write to the cardinal after they had read *Our Christian Heritage,* among them John H. Keatley, a federal judge in Alaska. Through reading agnostic literature and the philosophy of the skeptics, Keatley had for some years experienced painful doubts regarding the divine origin of the Christian religion. But he now stated:

> I desire to say to you, if I may be permitted, that "Our Christian Heritage" is a complete and satisfactory answer to atheism and agnosticism in all their degrees, and I humbly believe that no such service has been rendered Christianity by any single individual, during this century, as you have rendered in this instance.[69]

[67] 86-U-2, Shea to Gibbons, Elizabeth, New Jersey, November 17, 1889.

[68] 87-C-2, Maes to Gibbons, Covington, January 20, 1890. A month later a correspondent inquired concerning a report that had been circulated in southern Maryland that *Our Christian Heritage* had not been written by Gibbons but by "your *coadjutors,* whoever they may be" (87-E-3, J. Francis Coad to Gibbons, Charlotte Hall, St. Mary's County, Maryland, February 17, 1890). No reply to Coad's inquiry could be found.

[69] 87-B-4, Keatley to Gibbons, Kansas City, Missouri, January 17, 1890. Two

Although Gibbons' modesty would have discounted the extravagant claim made by Judge Keatley for his book, he was doubtless gratified to learn that it had produced so favorable an impression. A year later a member of the Protestant Episcopal Church gave it as his opinion that if *Our Christian Heritage* could be placed on the tables of every family in the land it would be the medium of doing great good in making all Americans better Christians and citizens.[70] Likewise Thomas F. Wilkinson, Justice of the City Court of Albany, New York, found the volume an inspiration. "It has sensibly affected me for good," he said, "& I shall commend it to others with the hope that they may in like manner be benefited."[71] Such were a few of the many messages which Gibbons received in the first years after its publication.

Shortly before the book appeared the cardinal notified a number of editors that he was having the publisher send copies of *Our Christian Heritage* to them for review. He explained to Martin I. J. Griffin, editor of the *Irish Catholic Benevolent Union Journal,* that it had been designed to refute the arguments of infidels and to demonstrate the superiority of Christian over pagan civilization, while to another editor he stated that although the volume was small in compass its preparation had cost him some years of anxious thought.[72] As a matter of fact, the work was widely reviewed in both Catholic and Protestant journals, as well as in the secular press, and in the main it was well received although it did not escape criticism. The *Catholic Union and Times* of Buffalo on November 14, 1889, editorialized it as good from cover to cover and said it ought to reach an edition of five million copies! But they took the publisher to task for its make-up which they thought repellent to good taste, and they were especially incensed at the flaming picture of Gibbons which they considered libel on one whom they called "the most modest

---

years later Keatley was still enthusiastic about *Our Christian Heritage* and he said that time and again he had pointed it out to acquaintances as an effective exposition of the feelings that should animate and inspire all who had, as he put it, "an earnest and unselfish desire to see our common country and native land prosper in all that constitutes true greatness" (89-N-4, Keatley to Gibbons, Sioux City, Iowa, February 17, 1892).

[70] 88-G-10, Andrew J. French to Gibbons, Oneida, New York, January 16, 1891.
[71] 89-D-3, Wilkinson to Gibbons, Albany, November 24, 1891.
[72] ACHSP, Griffin Papers, Gibbons to Griffin, Baltimore, October 12, 1889, *Personal,* copy; LC, Miscellaneous Papers, Gibbons to S. H. Kauffmann, Baltimore, October 12, 1889, photostat. The name of this last journal was not given.

and unassuming of ecclesiastics." The Boston *Herald* of November 19 anticipated that it would be attacked, and stated that it would be rather amusing to watch the devices to which those condemned by the book would resort in order to prejudice the reading world against it. The Chattanooga *Sunday Times* of November 24 regretted that Gibbons' zeal for his Church had perverted his mental vision, so that he saw in every advance of civilization the working of his own religion, while the Chicago *Tribune* on December 7 felt it was not necessary to endorse all the positions taken by the cardinal in saying that *Our Christian Heritage* was adapted to be useful to a high degree among the American people at that time. The *Saturday Review* of New York on November 16 used the book to moralize on the evil of citizens not voting, and they felt Gibbons was right in deploring the fact that many of the better class of citizens stood aloof from practical politics.

The *Independent* of November 28, the leading New York Protestant weekly, liked the work for its defense of Christian principles, but they regretted that, in their opinion, Gibbons had sometimes been unfair to the Protestant churches as, for example, in repeating charges against Luther which on the broad ground of charitable construction they thought could not be maintained. The *Independent* considered the cardinal's tone "high, bold and sound" on the questions of temperance, Mormonism, the relations of capital and labor, and the need for social and industrial reform. But on the school question they were entirely opposed to his position, nor did they share in what they called "his rather depressing and discouraging view of the subject." Nonetheless, they were glad to find the school question discussed in the frank way that the author had handled it, although to the *Independent* he had shown too little recognition of the prime duty of a people to educate its youth on a national basis, in the national spirit, and in a national way. Among other Protestant periodicals the *Presbyterian and Reformed Review* devoted a fairly lengthy review to the book two months after its publication. It was written by Charles W. Shields of Princeton University who thought, as he said, that its appearance so soon after the holding of the Catholic Congress at Baltimore in November, 1889, "may be taken as another sign of the growth of an American spirit in the Roman Church." Shields particularly commended the cardinal's friendly attitude toward Protestants and his emphasis on natural and revealed religion rather than on dogmas; and all this had been stated in a clear, popular style, and with what Shields considered remarkable force and acuteness. The chapter on the rights and duties of the laboring classes was, according to the reviewer, especially timely and conservative in tone, and to Shields the whole book breathed a patriotic spirit. "It is an excellent Roman Catholic manual," he said, "of the evidence of our common Christianity."[73]

But the most extended and critical review of *Our Christian Heritage* came from an unexpected source. Three months after the book appeared the *Lyceum* of Dublin carried a review entitled "A Popular Philosophy of Theism," which was unsigned but which it was later learned had been written by one of the Jesuits of the Irish province. The reviewer approached his task as a professional theologian, and as such he found the book seriously wanting. Since, he said, the object of the work was to bring home the claims of theism and Christianity to minds that were estranged, he was very doubtful how that could be accomplished. If the reader had the wish to believe, he was of the opinion that *Our Christian Heritage* would prove helpful, but if a reader were unwilling to believe or even coldly critical the arguments advanced, he thought, would have little weight and, worse still, they might prove injurious. The cardinal's arguments were not to be understood, it was said, as generally inconclusive; yet as contained in his pages they often seemed inconclusive. Gibbons was excused in part by the fact that space had prevented him from giving a clear, detailed exposition and a close and developed reasoning to his thought. The reviewer believed that a good deal would have to be assumed which unfriendly readers would not grant, and steps in the various arguments had to be omitted which ordinary readers would not supply.

The *Lyceum* writer was particularly censorious of the fact that the metaphysical proof for the existence of God, which he said was almost universally admitted to be the strongest, had not even been mentioned. Again few, even among Catholic thinkers, would accept Gibbons' statement that the beauty, harmony, and order displayed in the world must be the work of a supremely intelligent being. In the argument for God's existence from conscience

---

[73] I (January, 1890), 152–153.

as used here, the Dublin writer saw abundant evidence of Newman's *Grammar of Assent*. But, he said, "he fails to bring out
what Cardinal Newman develops so patiently and forcibly; that
conscience, because it is *emotional*, speaks to us of a personal
lawgiver, distinct from, and superior to ourselves." In similar
fashion the reviewer was critical of Gibbons' treatment of God's
omnipresence and providence, as well as aspects of his handling
of the problems of prayer and the immortality of the soul. The
review was not entirely negative, however, and there were words
of commendation for the style, the choice and use of illustrations,
and for the arguments adapted to the popular intelligence. In
fact, the chapter on the divinity of Christ as attested by our
Lord and His disciples was pronounced excellent. It was believed
that the book would be of service to those who felt unhappy in
their deprivation of the Christian heritage, as also to those who
had come into the heritage and who would now understand and
prize it more after reading the cardinal's volume. "But it does
not seem well suited," the reviewer concluded, "and it is not
perhaps intended, to change sceptical or hostile readers into
believing Christians."[74]

The answer to the unfriendly review of *Our Christian Heritage*
in the Dublin journal is, perhaps, best given in the author's own
words. As soon as the attention of Father Anthony M. Anderledy,
General of the Society of Jesus, had been called to it, he sent
an apology to the cardinal in which he expressed his deep sorrow that a member of his society should have written in such a
spirit. "The review is not only bitter in tone," he said, "but it is unjust, inasmuch as it does not take sufficient account of the express
scope of the work and of the class of readers for whom it was
intended." Anderledy assured Gibbons that such a thing would
not happen again, and he inquired if there was any reparation
which the society could offer to him.[75] The cardinal said that he
was profoundly touched by the evidence of Anderledy's sensitive
regard for his literary reputation, and he remarked that a copy
of the *Lyceum* containing the review had been sent to him by
some unknown hand. Gibbons confessed that he considered the

---

[74] *Lyceum*, III (February, 1890), 140–142.

[75] 87-G-5, Anderledy to Gibbons, Fiesole, March 27, 1890. A month later Alfred
Murphy, S.J., vice-provincial of the Irish province, likewise sent his apologies for
the review (87-J-8, Murphy to Gibbons, Dublin, April 25, 1890).

criticism in some particulars unfair and captious, inasmuch as the reviewer had not borne in mind the aim of the work as indicated in the introduction, nor the class of readers for whom it had chiefly been written. On the point of having omitted the metaphysical argument for the existence of God, the cardinal said he had passed it over because he thought the average American reader would find it too abstruse and would hardly grasp it. But despite the fact that he regarded the criticism as too exacting, he wished to assure the Jesuit general that it had left no painful impression on his mind, and he had considered it as a fitting offset to the too partial and favorable notices which the book had received from the Catholic, Protestant, and secular press of both the United States and Europe. Nor had the review affected in the slightest the esteem he entertained for the Society of Jesus. He stated that so great was his confidence in the ability and discretion of the Jesuit Fathers at Woodstock College that he had requested Father Brandi, one of the professors there, to read the manuscript of a large portion of *Our Christian Heritage* before he had ventured to publish it. In a postscript the cardinal stated, "I hope your Reverence will deal lightly with the writer. I would be sorry to see him suffer on my account."[76]

The spirit in which Cardinal Gibbons met one of the inevitable hazards of authorship was typical of the magnanimity which characterized his reactions to personal criticism. But the severity of the Irish Jesuit did not discourage him from further writing, and in November, 1896, there appeared his third volume, *The Ambassador of Christ*. It was dedicated to the bishops and priests of the United States, and in the preface the author stated that the motive that had impelled him to undertake the work was his sincere affection for his devoted fellow laborers among the clergy, and his desire to see the kingdom of God extend its spiritual empire far and wide

---

[76] 87-H-7, Gibbons to Anderledy, Baltimore, April 8, 1890, copy. Since the records of the publisher of Gibbons' books are no longer extant it is not possible to give the total sales on any of them. But in the three six-month periods previously cited for *The Faith of Our Fathers,* there were 326 copies of *Our Christian Heritage* sold which would represent a fairly active sale in the years 1912, 1916, and 1920 for a volume that had been published in 1889. Gibbons received twenty-five cents per copy for each copy of this item that was sold. Cf. 109-A, John Murphy Company to Gibbons, Baltimore, January 31, 1913; 113-S, same to same, July 31, 1916; 128-P, same to same, July 31, 1920.

throughout the country.[77] Gibbons did not think that any age or country had ever presented a more inviting field for missionary labor than that which the United States exhibited at that time. The American people, he said, were fundamentally a religious people. To his mind they possessed in a marked degree the natural virtues that were the indispensable bases for the supernatural life, and their deep sense of justice and fair play, their bravery and generosity, their frank, manly, and ingenuous manner, and their industrious and temperate habits were all conducive to the spread of religious truth.[78] Appearing as it did in one of the worst years of A.P.A. bigotry, the new book did not ignore that unpleasant factor of American life. But these "periodical whirlwinds," as the author called them, swept over the land like upheavals of nature but soon subsided after spending their force. To Gibbons' mind, they were not an unmixed evil, for they served the useful purpose of purifying the moral atmosphere, of clearing the spiritual skies, and of giving observant men a better insight into the uncreated world. He likened them to winnowing winds that separated the wheat from the chaff, and the cardinal believed that the periodic outbursts of bigotry rendered the members of the Church more loyal to their religion and awakened in serious and honest minds outside the fold salutary reflections that often resulted in their conversion.[79]

The Ambassador of Christ was, of course, addressed principally to the clergy as its title indicated. In a text of less than 400 pages running over thirty-one chapters the cardinal covered virtually every aspect of the priesthood from its divine origin and excellence through the virtues that should especially characterize the priest in his relations to God, to himself, and to the fellow men whom he served through his ministry. Gibbons revealed the paramount importance he attached to the priest as a man of books by giving seven chapters to the need for constant study. Here the Sacred Scriptures, the writings of the fathers of the Church, dogmatic and moral theology, canon law, the Greek and Latin classics, and the values of English literature each received separate treatment. His own taste and

---

[77] *Op. cit.*, pp. x–xi.
[78] *Ibid.*, pp. vii–viii.
[79] *Ibid.*, pp. v–vi.

reading habits received particular emphasis in the chapter called "The Study of Men and the Times," in which he stated that after the Bible the study of mankind was the most important and instructive pursuit for the priest. To Gibbons history and biography offered the best corrective for the faults into which young priests sometimes fell by attaching undue weight to matters of minor significance, or by treating lightly subjects of grave importance. He felt, too, that these subjects helped to develop moderation in one's judgment, since a study of the past showed that few men were either altogether perfect or, on the other hand, totally depraved.

He made here a strong plea for the writing of honest history based on the sources, and he was glad to observe that of late years the writing of biography had shown great improvement in this respect. In the opinion of the cardinal, the best models of biography were the inspired penmen of the Bible for, as he said, "David's sin, Peter's denial, Paul's persecution of the early Church, the worldly ambition of the sons of Zebedee, the incredulity of Thomas, are fearlessly recorded without any attempt at extenuation or palliation."[80] And to drive home his point, he quoted the remark that had been made some years before by Pope Leo XIII to Cardinal Manning when he said: " 'It has been too much the fashion in writing history, to omit what is unpleasant. If the historians of the last century had written the Gospels, for example, we might never have heard of the fall of Peter, or of the treachery of Judas.' "[81] But in his preoccupation with the things of the mind, the author of *The Ambassador of Christ* did not forget the practical works of the ministry and there were chapters on the priest as a preacher, catechist, instructor of converts, as well as chapters on his ministerial relations to the parochial school, the parish choir, the sick, and the dead. The volume closed with a chapter which was called "Consolations and Rewards of the Priest."

Copies of the new book were sent to the American hierarchy and their acknowledgments of the work contained the highest praise for its contents. It would be tiresome to record all their

---

[80] *Ibid.*, p. 253.

[81] *Ibid.*, p. 252. This remark of Leo XIII was repeated by Manning to Dom Aidan Gasquet, the English historian and future cardinal, and Gibbons read it in the London *Tablet* for July 6, 1895.

judgments, but several are worthy of some notice. Archbishop Chapelle of Santa Fe thought the cardinal's future biographer would have to study seriously what he called "this finished portrait of your soul, if he desires to convey to his readers a true idea of what you were like."[82] Bishop Denis M. Bradley of Manchester congratulated the hierarchy of the United States that one of their number had been found worthy and capable of doing so much to promote God's glory among the men of his own time, and of perpetuating that same glory for future generations.[83] Another New England bishop, Thomas D. Beaven of Springfield, found the work so tessellated with biblical quotations aptly intertwined with kindred thoughts, that he felt he had in hand a highly interesting commentary on the Bible.[84] John M. Farley, Auxiliary Bishop of New York, remarked that all knew how Gibbons' time was taken up, for no priest in the country, he believed, had so many calls and distractions, and yet, he added, "amidst all this you find time to write such eminently useful books."[85] Cardinal Vaughan was particularly pleased with the chapters on catechetics and congregational singing, and he said the book would be of the greatest assistance in the education of the English clergy and he intended to propose to his fellow bishops that it be used in their central seminary, St. Mary's College, Oscott.[86] Archbishop Kain of St. Louis had asked Gibbons to autograph a copy for Daniel S. Tuttle, Protestant Episcopal Bishop of Missouri. After Tuttle had read a portion of the book he wrote to say that he felt it had a ring of manly tribute to American characteristics, and its kindly estimate of the differences that beset the ministers of various creeds, together with the loving suggestions of how to work for unity, had gone to his heart.[87]

The Ambassador of Christ was a book which obviously had a special appeal for directors of seminaries and their charges, and soon after its publication the cardinal learned that it was being used for spiritual reading in the seminaries of the Archdioceses of Baltimore, New York, Boston, St. Paul, and St.

---

[82] 94-V-1, Chapelle to Gibbons, Santa Fe, December 21, 1896.
[83] 94-W-2, Bradley to Gibbons, Manchester, December 28, 1896.
[84] 94-G-1, Beaven to Gibbons, Springfield, January 21, 1896.
[85] 94-G-7, Farley to Gibbons, New York, January 13, 1897.
[86] 95-F-4, Vaughan to Gibbons, Westminster, February 4, 1897.
[87] 95-B-3, Tuttle to Gibbons, St. Louis, January 12, 1897.

Louis.[88] Maurice Francis Egan, professor of English in the Catholic University of America, judged it as the best of the cardinal's books and, as was to be expected, he was especially delighted with the encouragement that had been given to a study of English literature. Egan had fancied, he said, that Cardinal Manning's *Eternal Priesthood,* which had come out in 1883, had almost exhausted the subject of the vocation to the priesthood but, he added, "I am of a very different opinion now."[89] Father Brandi, who meanwhile had exchanged his professorship at Woodstock for a post on the editorial board of the *Civiltà Cattolica* in Rome, considered the work as admirably done and he said he would soon review it in the Jesuit journal and hoped to see it translated into Italian.[90]

The nature of the cardinal's new book precluded extended reviews in the secular press but brief notices of it appeared in a number of newspapers, and it was noteworthy that many of them carried similar comments to that of the Brooklyn *Eagle* of March 12, 1897, where is was stated, "Its teachings are applicable to the ministers of every Christian creed, and there is scarce a page in the volume wherein the holder of a sacred commission from any source cannot find profitable suggestion and wise counsel."[91] The *Canadian Church* of Toronto, an organ of the Protestant Episcopal Church, said in its issue of February 4, "There are a good many books which may be recommended to the parish priest. We hardly know a better than this one of Cardinal Gibbons." The *Herald* of Syracuse, New York, paid high praise to *The Ambassador of Christ* on February 14, and concluded, "For so high a dignitary of a church supposed to be intolerant of what it regards as error in every form this is, to say the least, very remarkable. 'It behooves us to profit by the example of our adversaries,' says the Cardinal."

[88] 95-A-2, Edward R. Dyer, S.S., to Gibbons, Yonkers, New York, January 2, 1897; 95-A-5, John B. Hogan, S.S., to Gibbons, Brighton, Massachusetts, January 6, 1897; 95-C-2, Patrick R. Heffron to Gibbons, St. Paul, January 16, 1897; 95-D-7, P. V. Byrne, C.M., to Gibbons, St. Louis, January 25, 1897.

[89] 94-G-10, Egan to Gibbons, Washington, January 14, 1896.

[90] 95-C-6, Brandi to Gibbons, Rome, January 20, 1897.

[91] Papers carrying similar comments were the following: St. Paul *Dispatch,* March 13, 1897; Providence *Journal,* January 31, 1897; Brooklyn *Citizen,* January 31, 1897; Milwaukee *Journal,* January 25, 1897; Burlington (Vermont) *Free Press,* January 25, 1897.

Abroad, a reviewer in the London *Tablet* of March 13 was at times reminded by Gibbons' book of the spiritual writings of Rodriquez or Scaramelli. "Many of our English clergy," he wrote, "will welcome this emphatic witness of the American Cardinal to the paramount duty of working for conversions, and to the need of new methods to meet new wants." Favorable notices likewise appeared in France where, among others, the *Univers* of July 6, and in the spring of 1898 the *Semaine religieuse d'Avignon* of March 19 and *La Croix* of Avignon on April 3, all spoke highly of the volume. Yet, as in the case of Gibbons' previous volumes, there were not lacking critical voices as, for example, the *Union* of Manchester, New Hampshire, which on January 27, 1897, took issue with the cardinal for expressing what they said was his wish that American children be indoctrinated with "the heritage of his faith" at public expense. But what was probably the most severe attack on *The Ambassador of Christ* came some months later from the fiery convert editor, William Henry Thorne, who called Gibbons' praise of Americans "senseless taffy" in view of their crimes against the Indians and their bigotry against Catholicism. To Thorne the cardinal was not a man of deep and comprehensive thought, nor was he capable of making clear and sharp distinctions as to the exact moral and comparative values of ancient and modern literary and political characters. For these reasons Thorne thought he should stick to his trade as a churchman and a teacher of souls in the peculiar and exclusive line of his vocation.[92]

Mention has already been made of the fact that the last two works published by Cardinal Gibbons were for the most part reprints of articles or the edition of sermons which he had preached on various occasions. *Discourses and Sermons,* which he dedicated to the professors of St. Mary's Seminary in Baltimore, came out in 1908 and eight years later he dedicated his two-volume work, *A Retrospect of Fifty Years,* to the rector and professors of the Catholic University of America.

---

[92] "Cardinal Gibbons' New Book," *Globe,* VII (June, 1897), 136–144. During the three six-month periods mentioned for Gibbons' other books *The Ambassador of Christ* sold a total of 303 copies, for which he was paid twenty-five cents per copy by his publisher. Cf. 109-A, John Murphy Company to Gibbons, Baltimore, January 31, 1913; 113-S, same to same, July 31, 1916; 128-P, same to same, July 31, 1920.

Bishop Dennis J. Dougherty of Buffalo expressed appreciation of the latter, but he said he had found the *Discourses and Sermons* the most useful book of its kind that he had in his library. He had availed himself of it frequently for sermons, and he concluded, "I hope Your Eminence will forgive me for so appropriating your own arms."[93] In thanking Gibbons for the two-volume work, Archbishop Mundelein remarked that *The Faith of Our Fathers* had been one of the first books he had been given to read as a boy and since then he had passed on many a copy of it to persons both inside and outside the Church.[94] But regardless of the popularity enjoyed by Gibbons' earlier works, Archbishop Prendergast thought *A Retrospect of Fifty Years* would far surpass them all in attractiveness for the general public.[95]

The devotion of the Cardinal of Baltimore to intellectual pursuits was shown in more ways than in the publication of books, for he always displayed the most friendly and sympathetic interest in any project that would advance scholarship. Being the keen student of history that he was, he fully sensed the value to the American Church of the rich archives of the premier see over which he ruled. When, therefore, Martin I. J. Griffin of the American Catholic Historical Society of Philadelphia in 1886 sought his permission to make copies of some of the documents, he experienced not only a gracious reception at Baltimore but he found Gibbons, as he said, "even solicitous that these manuscripts might be made available for historical students." A good deal of work was done in arranging and indexing the documents during the succeeding years with the active encouragement of the cardinal, and in his desire to assure

---

[93] 114-K, Dougherty to Gibbons, Buffalo, December 22, 1916. Whether or not there was any serious plagiarism in print of Gibbons' books is not known but, in any case, when he arrived in New Orleans for his annual visit in 1911 he was asked by a reporter if he was writing a new book, and the cardinal was quoted as having replied, "No, I am not, but some persons are writing new publications from my books." New Orleans *Daily Picayune*, February 28, 1911.

[94] 114-N, Mundelein to Gibbons, Chicago, January 2, 1917.

[95] 114-N, Prendergast to Gibbons, Philadelphia, January 4, 1917. In the three six-month statements previously cited, the *Discourses and Sermons* sold a total of 302 copies for which Gibbons received twenty-five cents a copy. In the single period, January 31–July 31, 1920, *A Retrospect of Fifty Years* sold forty copies on which the cardinal received thirty cents each. Cf. 109-A, John Murphy Company to Gibbons, Baltimore, January 31, 1913; 113-S, same to same, July 31, 1916; 128-P, same to same, July 31, 1920.

their preservation he had a special vault constructed to house the papers.[96]

Not long after the Catholic historical society had been established in Philadelphia, he congratulated its officers and stated that an organization such as theirs would do much to excite greater reverence for the pioneers of religion in the United States and to preserve the records of their good deeds.[97] Moreover, he accepted an invitation to address the society and on March 31, 1891, in the Academy of Music at Philadelphia he pointed out the value for future generations to know as fully as possible the lives of the great men of both Church and State, and once more he exhorted the society to gather all the documents it could acquire for, as he remarked, "it may be most important to preserve a single letter. That letter may be an important link in a chain of historical evidence."[98] Gibbons was similarly encouraging to the United States Catholic Historical Society of New York. Although he was not able to comply with the request of its secretary in the spring of 1888 that he should read a paper before the society, he did prepare a paper three years later on his missionary experiences in North Carolina which was read for him at the meeting of May 25, 1891.[99] A quarter of a century later he rejoiced when Bishop Shahan and five of the historians of the Catholic University of America launched the *Catholic Historical Review,* and he wrote a letter for the first issue of April, 1915, in which he foresaw the new journal as a means of making the scholarly work of the university better known. He stated that through the medium of the *Review* the treasures of history would be at the command of the public, for the average man and woman had not the time to delve into the hidden stores of knowledge which history guards.

[96] "The Archives at Baltimore," *Records of the American Catholic Historical Society of Philadelphia,* XXI (1910), 85–86. Cf. also Henry J. Browne, "The American Catholic Archival Tradition," *American Archivist,* XIV (April, 1951), 134–137, for the Baltimore archives.

[97] ACHSP, Gibbons to Thomas C. Middleton, O.S.A., Baltimore, March 13, 1885, copy.

[98] "Public Meeting in the Academy of Music, Philadelphia," *Records of the American Catholic Historical Society of Philadelphia,* III (1888–1891), 53. Cf. the writer's "Cardinal Gibbons and Philadelphia," *ibid.,* LVIII (March, 1947), 87–102.

[99] 84-K-7, Marc F. Vallette to Gibbons, New York, May 9, 1888. The paper was entitled "Reminiscences of North Carolina," *United States Catholic Historical Magazine,* III (1889–1890), 337–352.

"Nor have they the training," he said, "which would enable them to garner the lessons, and select the truths, that are of greatest need or afford the best intellectual enjoyment."[100]

Besides lending encouragement to scholarly projects, Cardinal Gibbons was from time to time of real assistance to individual scholars. From his advent to Baltimore as archbishop up to the death of John Gilmary Shea in February, 1892, he gave constant aid and support to the church historian in problems pertaining to his writing and his use of the Baltimore archives.[101] When a committee was organized early in 1885 to give financial assistance to Shea for his major work, the *History of the Catholic Church in the United States,* Gibbons' generous response won the gratitude of the historian who considered his obligation to the cardinal extreme since, as he said, "your name comes with all the historic weight of our most ancient See."[102] Shea's request for permission to begin his research was granted at once, and he was informed that whenever he came to Baltimore he would have free access to the archives, to which Gibbons added, "You will please also be our guest during your stay."[103] As the centennial of the American hierarchy neared in 1889, Shea suggested that a volume of documents containing the pastoral letters, synodal statutes, etc., of the Archdiocese of Baltimore be published to commemorate the anniversary along the lines of one recently issued for the Archdiocese of Quebec. The cardinal assured him he would not mind the expense involved if Shea could personally undertake the work, and he invited him to come to Baltimore when he had recovered from his illness so that they might talk over the matter.[104] Gibbons

---

[100] *Catholic Historical Review,* I (April, 1915), foreword.

[101] Cf. 73-R-6, Shea to Gibbons, Elizabeth, New Jersey, April 26, 1878, on the papers of Charles I. White; 78-D-3, same to same, Elizabeth, May 22, 1884, wherein Shea advised the cardinal against allowing J. Thomas Scharf, author of *The Chronicles of Baltimore* (Baltimore, 1874), an unrestricted use of the White Papers.

[102] 79-D-1, Arthur J. Donnelly to Gibbons, New York, February 1, 1885; 79-K-1, Shea to Gibbons, Elizabeth, May 1, 1885.

[103] 79-N-4, Shea to Gibbons, Elizabeth, June 20, 1885; ACHSP, Shea Papers, Gibbons to Shea, Baltimore, June 23, 1885.

[104] 85-O-8, Shea to Gibbons, Elizabeth, January 12, 1889; ACHSP, Shea Papers, Gibbons to Shea, Baltimore, January 14, 1889. The projected volume of documents never materialized. Occasionally Gibbons made a personal investigation in the archives as, for example, in an effort to locate the papal brief erecting the See of Louisiana and the Two Floridas in 1793. He failed in his search, but told Arch-

followed the progress of Shea's major work with the closest interest, and when the third volume appeared he sent a further sum of money for the project, said he had already read a good portion of the new volume, and remarked, "I admire the freedom & the tact with which you have written of the evil consequences of sending Bishops to this country without the concurrence of the American Episcopate."[105]

The cardinal likewise used his influence to further literary and scholarly pursuits when that was called for. For example, the editor of the *American Catholic Quarterly Review* had been disappointed at receiving a refusal from Cardinal Manning to contribute an article for his journal and he, therefore, entered a plea with Gibbons to intervene in his behalf. The Cardinal of Baltimore agreed to do so, and in making his request he sent along to Manning a clipping from a Chicago newspaper giving prominence to some recent remarks of the English cardinal. It helped to give point to Gibbons' compliment when he said, "Your Eminence's name is a household word among us, & any subject from your pen is eagerly read."[106] The effort was successful and Manning forwarded an article on "The Law of Nature Divine and Supreme" with the remark, "I have done your bidding 'obturare ora leonum!' "[107] Gibbons thanked him for the contribution and he added the comment, "It is a marvel to me how you have time to write so much. This will be a strong plea for your canonization after you are called to your reward."[108] Sometime later a letter of recommendation from the

---

bishop Janssens of New Orleans that he would have Shea make a more thorough investigation on his next visit to Baltimore (AUND, New Orleans Papers, Gibbons to Janssens, Baltimore, December 30, 1890).

[105] ACHSP, Shea Papers, Gibbons to Shea, Baltimore, February 12, 1891. Most of the Gibbons-Shea correspondence was published in Peter Guilday, *John Gilmary Shea* (New York, 1926), pp. 81–111.

[106] MP, Gibbons to Manning, Baltimore, January 25, 1888.

[107] 84-C-6, Manning to Gibbons, Westminster, February 13, 1888. The article appeared in the *American Catholic Quarterly Review*, XIII (April, 1888), 193–198.

[108] MP, Gibbons to Manning, Baltimore, February 25, 1888. A year or so before Cardinal Newman told Gibbons that when he had been approached by Philip Schaff, author of the seven-volume *History of the Christian Church* (New York, 1858–1910), asking for his endorsement of a translation of the fathers of the Church, he had given Schaff a letter in the belief that he was a Catholic. After learning his mistake he now sought the historian's address from Gibbons so that he might write him accordingly (81-V-10, Newman to Gibbons, Birmingham, September 23, 1886). A few years after the *American Ecclesiastical Review* was founded Gibbons told Herman J. Heuser, the editor, that observation convinced

Cardinal of Baltimore to Father Peter de Roo who was doing research in Rome on the pontificate of Alexander VI was said to have opened to him the secrets of the Vatican Archives, and to have insured him the active co-operation of the prefect, Joseph Cardinal Hergenröther.[109] When Shane Leslie was beginning the research for his biography of Cardinal Manning he approached Gibbons through Cardinal Farley for permission to use Gibbons' letters to the English cardinal, to which there was the immediate reply that Leslie was at liberty to publish his correspondence with Manning on labor and social questions. He added, "You might also inform him that I have some other data & correspondence with the Cardinal which I would place at the disposal of Mr. Leslie if he desires to have them."[110]

Having the interest in history that he did, it was not surprising to learn that when Gibbons heard from Cardinal Bourne in May, 1919, that Ludwig von Pastor, the famous historian of the Papacy, was in grave need he should have responded very generously. Not only did he send money personally, but he appealed to other members of the American hierarchy for Pastor and interested the National Catholic Welfare Council in his behalf. Naturally the historian was grateful and when he thanked the cardinal the latter told him that he was happy to help for, as he stated, "Your work is of such an international character, that any effort to aid in its completion, might well be esteemed a privilege."[111] About a year before his death Gibbons instructed his secretary to have the N.C.W.C. send an additional $560, and it was remarked at that time that the cardinal had already contributed around $2,000 to Pastor.[112] One of the final benefactions of this kind to Catholic scholar-

---

him that Heuser had been tenacious of the high purpose he had conceived for the journal while, he said, "your success in enlisting in the cause both intelligence and scholarship is deserving of praise and encouragement" (ACHSP, Heuser Papers, Gibbons to Heuser, Baltimore, October 23, 1897).

[109] 87-R-1, De Roo to Gibbons, Baerle-Drongen, Belgium, July 20, 1890. De Roo's work, *Material for a History of Pope Alexander VI* (New York, 1924) came out in five small volumes.

[110] 109-F, Farley to Gibbons, New York, May 19, 1913; AANY, Gibbons to Farley, Baltimore, May 21, 1913.

[111] 123-V, Gibbons to Pastor, Baltimore, November 24, 1919, copy.

[112] ANCWC, Albert E. Smith to John J. Burke, C.S.P., Baltimore, February 20, 1920. The correspondence covering this case was published by the writer in "Cardinal Gibbons' Assistance to Pastor's *History of the Popes,*" *Catholic Historical Review,* XXXIV (October, 1948), 306–318.

ship which Gibbons performed was his gift of $1,000 to help defray the expenses of the *Catholic Encyclopedia*.[113]

Although the main concern of Cardinal Gibbons in these matters was for projects under Catholic auspices, he by no means restricted his patronage and help to exclusively Catholic interests. When, for example, Ferdinand Brunetière, one of the editors of the *Revue des deux mondes,* lectured at the Johns Hopkins University in March, 1897, at the invitation of President Gilman, he noted that present in the first row was Cardinal Gibbons and the French ambassador to Washington.[114] Later that same year the cardinal complied with the request of Stanford University for a sample of the catalogue of the Vatican Library and was able to secure it through the good offices of Cardinal Rampolla.[115] Even at a time when as Chancellor of the Catholic University of America he was gravely worried over its financial future because of the failure of its treasurer, he consented to serve as a member of the advisory council in favor of an endowment fund for the University of Virginia, providing that he would not have to assume any financial obligation or promise attendance at meetings.[116] Four years later Wilbur L. Cross, professor of English in the Sheffield Scientific School at Yale University, wanted to introduce selected narratives of the Old Testament for study. The chairman of the National Conference on Uniform Entrance Requirements in English, however, told him a similar attempt had been made and had failed, because in certain states reading the Bible in the schools had been prohibited by law. But since it was to be only an elective, Cross was permitted to go ahead with his plan and he, therefore, wrote to various Protestant, Catholic, and Jewish ministers for advice. He later described the result in his memoirs when he wrote:

> The man who gave me the wisest counsel was Cardinal Gibbons who expressed deep interest in the endeavor to promote the study of the Old Testament as literature. In order to keep my literary aim clear, he advised me to include in any book of selections parts

113 128-Q, John J. Wynne, S.J., to Gibbons, New York, August 2, 1920.
114 Ferdinand Brunetière, "Dans l'est américain," *Revue des deux mondes,* CXLIV (November 1, 1897), 100.
115 95-Q-1, Rampolla to Gibbons, Rome, June 7, 1897; 95-Q-11, Gibbons to Rampolla, Baltimore, June 28, 1897, copy.
116 Duke University Library, Gibbons to Thomas Nelson Page, Baltimore, June 25, 1904; same to same, Baltimore, August 16, 1904.

of the Apocrypha, which was once liberally drawn upon by English writers when every man sat in peace "under his vine and his fig tree, and there was none to fray them." He himself when a young man had carefully read Webster's "Speech in Reply to Hayne" to determine the influence of the Bible upon the orator's style, and at my request he had some of the notes he took on this famous speech copied for me. Nothing better could be said in favor of the Bible as literature than what the Cardinal wrote me: "Apart from its inspirational character, the Bible still remains the one means of culture." I read one of his letters to the Conference in 1909 and the Bible immediately went on the reading list for boys and girls. It has not yet been removed.[117]

Another non-Catholic scholar to whom the cardinal was of great assistance was Dr. J. Franklin Jameson, director of the Division of Historical Research of the Carnegie Institution of Washington. When Jameson was going abroad in the spring of 1906 to make preliminary arrangements for a series of guides to the materials for American history in foreign archives, Gibbons furnished him with a letter of introduction to Cardinal Merry del Val, papal Secretary of State.[118] After the work got under way he likewise wrote letters of introduction to Prospero Alarcon, Archbishop of Mexico, for Professor Herbert E. Bolton of the University of California and later to Cardinal Gotti, Prefect of the Congregation of the Propaganda, for Professor Carl Russell Fish of the University of Wisconsin who were to prepare the respective guides on the Mexican and Italian archives.[119] In requesting the letter for the latter, Jameson stated that Bolton had derived great benefit from the cardinal's introduction at Mexico City where the archbishop had shown him much favor and had put himself to considerable trouble in providing the California historian with recommendations to other Mexican bishops.[120] Upon the appearance of Fish's *Guide to the Materials for American History in Roman and other*

---

[117] Wilbur L. Cross, *Connecticut Yankee. An Autobiography* (New Haven, 1943), pp. 133–134.

[118] Carnegie Institution of Washington, Jameson Papers, Jameson to Gibbons, Washington, February 24, 1906, copy.

[119] *Ibid.*, Jameson to Gibbons, Washington, August 26, 1907, copy; Gibbons to Jameson, Baltimore, September 16, 1907.

[120] *Ibid.*, Jameson to Gibbons, Washington, January 16, 1908, copy. Cf. also same to same, Washington, March 31, 1908, copy; Gibbons to Jameson, Baltimore, April 1, 1908.

Archives in 1911 Jameson sent Gibbons a complimentary copy in appreciation for his assistance, and for what he termed, "the high privileges at Rome which it brought us."[121]

Some weeks in advance of the second annual meeting of the American hierarchy Jameson suggested that the bishops of the United States might be persuaded to help finance the completion of Conrad Eubel's *Hierarchia Catholica* which he pronounced "a work of most remarkable scholarship." But the cardinal replied that the agenda for the forthcoming meeting was already so crowded and the demands upon their funds so numerous that he did not think it would be practical to raise the question.[122] Soon thereafter, however, he was able to give a favorable response to an appeal from Jameson for a letter to Gustav Cardinal Piffl, Archbishop of Vienna, to allow Dr. Oskar Mitis, director of the Vienna Staatsarchiv, and his staff to have access to the archdiocesan archives. The case had arisen from the desire of the Michigan Historical Commission to have copies of certain documents made from the records of the Leopoldinenstiftung, the Austrian missionary society that had given so much aid to the Church of the United States during the nineteenth century. Gibbons stated that since Jameson was so thoroughly familiar with the subject he would suggest that he draw up a letter, which the cardinal would then make his own and transmit to Piffl on his official stationery.[123]

Long before the death of Cardinal Gibbons his highly eventful life and the esteem in which he was held by so many Americans had suggested to a number of persons the idea of a biography of the famous Archbishop of Baltimore and the desirability of

---

[121] *Ibid.*, Jameson to Gibbons, Washington, March 30, 1911, copy. Four years later Percy T. Fenn, Protestant Episcopal rector of St. John's Church, Wichita, Kansas, who said he had many Catholic friends and associations, asked the cardinal if he would write a letter of recommendation for his son who hoped to win a fellowship at Harvard to do graduate work in history. He enclosed a form to be used in addressing Charles Homer Haskins, dean of the Graduate School at Harvard and professor of medieval history. Gibbons' compliance with this request of a stranger brought prompt gratitude in which Fenn said, "I owe you a debt I can never repay" (111-B, Fenn to Gibbons, Wichita, January 14, 1915; 111-D, same to same, Wichita, January 27, 1915).

[122] *Ibid.*, Jameson to Gibbons, North Edgecomb, Maine, August 9, 1920, copy; Gibbons to Jameson, Spring Lake, New Jersey, August 12, 1920. Gibbons cited his recent aid to Pastor as an example of these demands.

[123] *Ibid.*, Jameson to Gibbons, North Edgecomb, Maine, August 31, 1920; Gibbons to Jameson, Baltimore, September 3, 1920.

612   JAMES CARDINAL GIBBONS

having him write his memoirs. Monsignor Russell, who had been closely associated with the cardinal both in Baltimore and as pastor of St. Patrick's Church in Washington, thought at first of writing the biography. But when he learned that Gibbons had given access to the archives to Allen Sinclair Will, city editor of the Baltimore *Sun,* for this purpose he determined to abandon the idea and to leave the field entirely to Will. Meanwhile the latter, a non-Catholic, who had the advantage of almost daily chats with the cardinal, continued his work and in 1911, the year of Gibbons' golden jubilee as a priest, he published a popular biography in one volume.[124]

The appearance of the cardinal's two volumes, *A Retrospect of Fifty Years,* late in 1916 furthered interest in the subject of his memoirs, for in spite of the title, these volumes were, as has been said, merely reprints of articles and sermons. In any case, the Century Company which published *Century Magazine* made an attractive financial offer to Gibbons for a manuscript that would embody his memoirs. It was proposed that it would be used both serially in the magazine and later in book form. But the cardinal instructed his secretary to reply that in view of his recently published work he had not the material to call upon, nor the leisure to devote to further writing at that time.[125] But Century was not to be put off, and in expressing their disappointment at the decision, they emphasized the need for a real autobiography of Gibbons by quoting a review of *A Retrospect of Fifty Years* that had appeared in the New York *Sun* on January 28, 1917, where it had been said:

> Important as this record is, the few explanatory pages in which the author allows his personality to appear are so interesting that the regret is unavoidable that the venerable Archbishop of Baltimore has not chosen to relate his own experiences instead.

It was a true judgment on the book but, nonetheless, the second request from the Century Company received a negative answer.[126]

---

[124] 106-M, Russell to Gibbons, Washington, August 11, 1910. John Murphy Company of Baltimore was the publisher of Will's *Life of James Cardinal Gibbons* in 1911.

[125] 114-L, C. Le Barstow to Gibbons, New York, December 27, 1916; *ibid.,* Eugene J. Connelly to Le Barstow, Baltimore, December 29, 1916.

[126] 114-U, Le Barstow to Connelly, New York, January 31, 1917. Written across the letter was "Negatively."

There were more than the reviewer in the New York *Sun* who were prompted by Gibbons' latest volumes to ask for a real autobiography from the old churchman. Archbishop Keane hoped that he would write one more book which he should call "The Moral of My Retrospect." If Gibbons answered that his previous works conveyed their moral clearly enough, Keane would venture to reply in the negative. "No one knows better than yourself," he said, "the shallow superficiality of even 'clever minds,' as the world says." The reading public would have only a hazy and general impression from these books, and they needed to have the conclusions clearly drawn and persuasively enforced. "Do please, beloved friend," he pleaded, "do this for the coming generation, — for they will need it."[127] The following spring the cardinal published a brief article in the *Dublin Review* which he called "My Memories," which was a true memoir on a few selected topics such as his experiences during the Civil War and his impressions of men like Cardinal Newman, President Cleveland, and General Sheridan.[128] It was exactly the type of thing for which his friends and admirers had been calling, and John J. Wynne, S.J., one of the editors of the *Catholic Encyclopedia,* told him, "It is etching to perfection, impossible to efface. What an impression it will make in England and a desire for more."[129] The next year the *World's Work* of Doubleday, Page and Company made a similar offer to publish the memoirs in both serial and book form. They won a promise from Gibbons to dictate his reminiscences on certain subjects to his secretary, Father Albert E. Smith, who would assist in their preparation for publication. But the negotiations dragged on for over a year without anything substantial being done, and in the end that effort, too, failed to bring out a full autobiography of the cardinal.[130]

[127] 114-L, Keane to Gibbons, Dubuque, December 28, 1916.

[128] CLX (January–April, 1917), 162–173.

[129] 115-N, Wynne to Gibbons, New York, May 21, 1917.

[130] 119-Q, French Strother to Smith, Garden City, New York, November 18, 1918; 123-M, Strother to Gibbons, Garden City, October 14, 1919; 123-N, Strother to Smith, Garden City, October 20, 1919; 123-R, same to same, Garden City, November 6, 1919. In this letter Strother suggested as subjects for Gibbons' reminiscences: Americanism and the Church, labor leaders he had known, liquor and the law, leaders of the old and new South, the best expression of the American ideal, and personal impressions of Leo XIII. Cf. also 126-C, same to same, Garden City, April 7, 1920.

Meanwhile Allen Sinclair Will, Gibbons' first biographer, had joined the faculty of the Pulitzer School of Journalism at Columbia University and for some weeks before the cardinal died Will was in correspondence with Father Smith on the subject of a full biography to be published after Gibbons' death. The enfeebled old man, who had by this time entered upon his last illness, at first signed a document giving Will permission to undertake the work. But he later grew disturbed about the matter and as a result a request was made of Will to return the document and it was destroyed. Smith explained that the cardinal was reluctant to exclude from the field any other person who might wish to take up the task, and he thought that might be the case if the document was allowed to stand. It was made clear, however, that Will had the cardinal's full consent to bring out an enlarged and revised edition of the previous biography after his death, and it was in this form that the two-volume work appeared in 1922.[131]

"I do not hesitate to say that the priest who aims at being thoroughly equipped for the ministry, must be a habitual student from the period of his ordination."[132] There could be no doubt that this dictum of Cardinal Gibbons, offered to the American clergy after more than thirty-five years in the priesthood, was one which he faithfully practiced all his life. For one whose days were filled with constant interruptions and a schedule of work and engagements that would fatigue a far more robust man, the amount of time which the cardinal managed to devote to reading and to study was truly remarkable. His sermons, almost entirely lacking in the oratorical flourishes that characterized those of his friends Archbishops Ireland and Keane, were yet filled with effective quotations from the Old and New Testaments and with apt illustrations chosen from history and the classics of literature. No one but a man who had given long hours of study to the Bible, to the Greek and Roman

---

[131] 132-E, Will to Smith, New York, January 4, 1921; 133-D, Smith to Will, Baltimore, February 18, 1921, copy. Will had received an offer for publication of a two-volume biography from the Century Company and he was anxious that they should either be shown written evidence that he was the authorized biographer, or have that information conveyed verbally by Father Smith to a Century representative (133-E, Will to "My dear Cullen," New York, February 21, 1921). Will's two-volumes were published by E. P. Dutton & Company of New York.

[132] *The Ambassador of Christ*, p. 173.

classics, and to the history of the Church, of the United States, and of Great Britain could possibly enrich the content of his sermons and the narratives of his books and articles in the way Gibbons did.

Prescinding from the personality and fame of the Cardinal of Baltimore, it was the learning, presented in so simple a way that a child could understand, that accounted in good measure for his popularity as a preacher and a writer. Nothing he ever said from the pulpit or composed for the printed page gave evidence of careless preparation. Of majestic eloquence and elegance of diction there was little, but what was lacking in these qualities was more than compensated by the soundness of judgment, the clarity and simplicity of language, the richness of illustration, and the unmistakable tone of earnestness and sincerity that pervaded every subject on which he preached or wrote. It was not difficult to picture him seated before his roll-top desk or in the armchair of his small study on the second floor of the old mansion on North Charles Street surrounded by his many books. It was in that modest room that Cardinal Gibbons, shut away from the busy stir of life below, took counsel with the spiritual and intellectual masters, and enriched his agile mind with the learning that showed to such great advantage when he mounted the pulpit of the cathedral or presented his ideas to the public through a new article or book. It was there, too, that he experienced the reality of his own saying, "Silence, solitude, and study are the three great prerequisites for knowledge."[133]

---

[133] *Ibid*, p. 172.

CHAPTER XXVI

The End

IN SPITE of the fact that Cardinal Gibbons lived to within four months of his eighty-seventh birthday, his health had never been robust. Of a slender build and a little less than average height, his physical resources were not great and he, therefore, quickly felt any severe strain. In the early days of his priesthood when he was still in his late twenties he had charge of two churches which were a mile or more apart on opposite sides of the Patapsco River, and the necessity of rowing back and forth across the river, to fulfill his obligation of saying Mass at both churches each Sunday often compelled him to fast as late as one o'clock. These prolonged fasts had a detrimental effect upon his digestion, and as a result all his life Gibbons suffered from a sensitive stomach and consequent periods of nervous exhaustion. It was this trouble which the cardinal had in mind when as an old man he was asked the formula to attain great age, to which he had replied in a way that was long remembered, "Acquire an incurable ailment in your youth."[1] As a result of this condition he was always very abstemious at table, and besides eating relatively little he confined his diet to the simplest dishes. Stewed chicken, corncakes, and smearcase or cottage cheese were among his favorites, and he liked a little straight whisky before his meals and often enjoyed a drink called bonny clabber which was chilled milk that had begun to ferment. Even when dining out Gibbons adhered strictly to his simple diet, and on one occasion his hostess had gone to considerable trouble to secure fresh crabs for a Friday dinner only to have the cardinal inquire what they were and then request a boiled egg![2] By such caution he was

---

[1] New York *Times,* September 24 and October 8, 1950.

[2] Interview with Mrs. Mark Shriver, Baltimore, March 7, 1947.

616

usually able to guard his delicate stomach against the ravages of excessive or rich foods, and thus hold to a minimum the unpleasant consequences of his poor digestion.

Another means which Gibbons employed to preserve his health was regularity of life. He rose at six o'clock each morning, took about a half hour or so for his toilet and some setting-up exercises, and then devoted about fifteen minutes to prayers at the *prie-dieu* in his room in preparation for his daily Mass which he always said punctually at seven o'clock. Following Mass he made a thanksgiving of fifteen or twenty minutes at his kneeler in the cathedral sanctuary and then took a light breakfast at eight, read the Baltimore *Sun* and a part of his breviary, and from nine to about noon of each day he either received callers or attended to his correspondence and other business. Around noon the cardinal changed from his house cassock to civilian attire and with cane in hand he then took a brisk walk through the streets of the neighborhood. Dinner about one o'clock was his principal meal, which was taken in a leisurely manner with Gibbons leading the conversation on topics of the day or on some book which he happened to be reading. He was always intent that the conversation at table should remain free from business matters, and for that reason he did not suffer the injection of discussions of this kind at meals.

Following dinner the cardinal smoked a cigar and took a siesta of a half hour, an invariable rule from which he never departed and which, he claimed, enabled him to rise refreshed for renewed work. After further reading in his breviary he was then ready for more business and about four-thirty or five o'clock each afternoon he stepped forth into Charles Street for his second and longer walk of the day. On these twilight walks, which for so many years were a familiar feature of Baltimore life, he was often accompanied by a guest, a priest of his household, or in later years by one of the seminarians from St. Mary's. Weather permitting, he never omitted his walks, and it was during these periods of exercise that he found relaxation in greeting his many friends and acquaintances along the city streets. He returned to his residence about five-thirty and then recited his rosary walking up and down the corridor. A modest supper about six-thirty was followed by another cigar during recreation,[3] and after that the recitation of matins and lauds from the breviary which he always anticipated for the following day. By nine o'clock each evening, unless he had gone out for dinner, the cardinal was usually ready to retire to his room where he read and studied before his night prayers which were recited in time for him to be in bed at ten o'clock. It was an exceedingly simple regime, but it was carried out with such constant regularity that all knew when and where to expect the cardinal at any hour of the day.

As Gibbons observed a strict routine at home, so he likewise had his schedule for the holidays which he took at regular intervals away from Baltimore. Almost every year he spent several weeks around the beginning of Lent with his family in New Orleans where he delighted in the company of his brother John and family and his sisters Mary and Bridget and the latter's children. There was a record of longevity in the family on the side of Mrs. Gibbons who had died at eighty in May, 1883, and when the cardinal departed for his final visit to New Orleans in February, 1920,[4] at the age of eighty-five his sister Mary was ninety-three and his brother John was nearing eighty-three. Moreover, each summer Gibbons took a holiday of several weeks at the seashore, in the earlier years as Archbishop of Baltimore at Cape May, New Jersey, or Southampton, Long Island, and in his last years at Ballingarry, the summer home of Martin Maloney at Spring Lake, New Jersey.

But the favorite refuge of the cardinal for a period of rest was always with his dearest friends among the laity, the Shrivers of Union Mills, Maryland, a rural settlement about seven miles

---

[3] On Gibbons' visits to Ballinrobe in Ireland he was frequently the guest of the parish priest. In the years 1875 to 1903 the pastor was James Canon Ronayne who was known to have an aversion to tobacco. It was said that at times Gibbons smoked in his bedroom to avoid inconvenience to his host, and that on one occasion a parishioner called to see the cardinal, and meeting Ronayne at the door, he inquired if His Eminence was within; whereupon the pastor was said to have replied, "Yes, don't you smell him?" (Letter of James Canon Fergus to the writer, Ballinrobe, January 21, 1946.) The facts on the cardinal's daily routine were taken in the main from Smith-Fitzpatrick, *Cardinal Gibbons. Churchman and Citizen,* pp. 192–213, and from interviews with the Right Reverend Louis R. Stickney.

[4] 124-W, Gibbons to Frederick J. Kinsman, Baltimore, February 12, 1920, copy.

The cardinal at recreation, pitching horseshoes and quoits at the home of the Shrivers at Union Mills, Maryland.

(Courtesy of Miss M. Madeline Shriver)

from Westminster. He used to call the home of T. Herbert Shriver the "Lower House or House of Commons" to distinguish it from that of the latter's brother, Frank Shriver, which was located on a little hill nearby and which was termed by Gibbons the "Upper House or House of Lords." In the simple and dignified atmosphere of this Catholic family Cardinal Gibbons felt thoroughly at home. He frequently remarked that they were a constant source of edification to him and that he knew of no finer Catholic family than the Shrivers.[5] Here he relaxed from the cares of his office and here, too, he found the quiet and peace to think through some of the serious problems which at times confronted him. At Union Mills, as in the city, a definite program was followed throughout Gibbons' stay with time apportioned for his Mass and prayers, reading the papers and answering his mail, walks through the countryside or an occasional game of pitching horseshoes or quoits. His meals, too, were taken with the same punctuality that he observed in town. The principal feature of the evenings spent by Gibbons in this secluded spot was the euchre games of which he was exceedingly fond. He did not care to play auction bridge since he disliked sitting out at times as the dummy, and the zest with which he would win a hand of euchre was emphasized by the cardinal rapping his ring in glee on the top of the table as he clinched the game with a trump.

He entered with entire sympathy into the lives of the Shriver family, and he was a special favorite there as elsewhere with the children. On one winter day when the children were sliding downhill on their sleds the cardinal watched from a distance with great interest, and he became so taken up by the sight that he was asked if he would like to try it; he replied that he would, and forthwith one of the Shriver boys accompanied the Prince of the Church on a sled ride down the hill! But the euchre games, the long walks, and the sociable chats at Union Mills were never allowed to displace any of his customary devotions, and each evening after supper Gibbons led the Shriver family in reciting the rosary as he walked up and down

---

[5] Smith-Fitzpatrick, *op. cit.*, p. 217. It was in early May of 1869 that Gibbons had the pleasure of receiving old William Shriver into the Church, for which his family had long been praying, and of giving the old man his first Communion (*Catholic Mirror,* May 8, 1869).

the porch in the summer and strode through the long parlor in the winter evenings. This family, to whom he was so endeared, knew the cardinal's likes and dislikes in detail, and as a result the Shriver girls understood how to serve him as temporary secretaries in answering his correspondence and to prepare the dishes which he relished, while their brothers drove him back and forth to the city, discussed with him current baseball or horse racing news in which he was very interested, and sometimes accompanied him on his walks or afforded him opposition at quoits or horseshoes.

It was a simple life, that at Union Mills, but everything about Cardinal Gibbons was simple, and that is one reason why it appealed to him so strongly. Normally he did not wish other members of the clergy with him at the Shrivers, although at times he would bring along close friends like Bishop O'Connell of Richmond or Bishop Shahan from the university in Washington.[6] In the home of T. Herbert Shriver a small oratory had been arranged where the cardinal said his Mass each morning surrounded by the family, and it was in that little chapel that he said the last Mass of his life on December 9, 1920, after having been brought to Union Mills from Emmitsburg where he had suffered a relapse of his illness four days before.[7]

It was not until late in the year 1920 that there appeared the symptoms of a break in the cardinal's normal health. He had spent the early days of March, as we have said, in New Orleans with his family, and upon his return he continued to work with his accustomed vigor through the spring and summer. He passed his eighty-sixth birthday at Union Mills with the Shrivers where he received a wire of congratulations from his brother John who chided him that he was still far in the rear of their sister Mary who, he said, now had her feet firmly fixed on the ladder toward ninety-five and never missed her

---

[6] The above facts were gathered from interviews with Miss M. Madeline Shriver at Union Mills, July 9, 1945; Mrs. Mark Shriver at Baltimore, March 7, 1947, and through the kindness of the writer's friend, the Reverend W. Kailer Dunn, with Mrs. Hilda Shriver in New York, February 26, 1950.

[7] Smith-Fitzpatrick, *op. cit.,* p. 218. There was also a private oratory at Ballingarry in Spring Lake. Mrs. Maloney wrote Gibbons in the late summer of 1919, "I cannot tell how we all miss you, and the great privilege of Holy Mass each morning" (123-D, Margaret A. Maloney to Gibbons, Spring Lake, August 27, 1919).

Cardinal Gibbons in 1918 seated in the company of Bishop O'Connell of Richmond on the porch of the residence of B. Frank Shriver at Union Mills, Maryland.

three meals each day over and above a few lunches.[8] The following month he spent several weeks with the Maloneys at Spring Lake and left there for Baltimore on August 23 in good health and feeling refreshed after his stay at the seaside.[9]

Once more Gibbons resumed his ordinary work schedule, and on October 11 he left for Asheville, North Carolina, where at the invitation of Father Patrick F. Marion, the pastor, he presided two days later over the consecration of St. Lawrence Church in the company of Bishops Haid, O'Connell, Russell, and Philip R. McDevitt of Harrisburg. Three weeks after his return from North Carolina the cardinal had an engagement for Sunday, November 7, to administer confirmation at St. Patrick's Church in Havre de Grace, Maryland. Early that morning he complained to his secretary, Father Smith, that he had spent a restless night and that the condition of his throat made him fearful that he could not preach. But when he saw the large crowd gathered in the church he changed his mind, and after the gospel of the Mass the cardinal rose to address the congregation. In the course of his sermon Gibbons suddenly and without warning faltered, and had it not been that several who were close by sprang to his side he would have fallen. Yet after a few moments he seemed to steady himself and he finished the sermon from a chair with his accustomed earnestness. He later confirmed a class of over 100 children and adults, and before the day was out held two receptions for groups who wished to meet him.

Upon the cardinal's return to Baltimore there seemed to be no ill effects from the brief attack at Havre de Grace and through the remainder of the month he went about his business as usual and presided on November 25 at the annual Pan American Mass in Washington and that afternoon dedicated the new school of St. Aloysius Parish in the capital. The first reports of the cardinal's illness brought many inquiries about his condition, and among them that of Governor Albert C. Ritchie of Maryland immediately expressed relief at learning that the indisposition had only been a passing one, while Gibbons' brother in New Orleans showed his uneasiness by

---

[8] 128-K, John T. Gibbons to Gibbons, New Orleans, July 23, 1920, telegram.

[9] AAB, unclassified, Gibbons to Albert E. Smith, Spring Lake, August 15 and 16, 1920.

scolding the cardinal that he should follow closely the directions
of his doctor and take more rest.[10] While there seemingly had
been a quick comeback after Havre de Grace, the old churchman continued during November to suffer periodic recurrences
of labored breathing, difficulty in ascending the stairs, and
momentary losses of consciousness. But the general appearance
of the cardinal offered reassurance to his close associates, and
for that reason they were free from alarm and even believed
that in time he would be himself again.

On December 3 Gibbons welcomed Archbishops Dougherty
and Hayes, Monsignor William H. Ketcham, and Father Edward
R. Dyer, S.S., to the annual meeting of the board of directors
of the Commission for Catholic Missions among the Colored
People and the Indians, and he presided at their sessions in
his residence without any apparent difficulty. Two days later
he endeavored to fulfill a promise to pontificate on Sunday,
December 5, at St. Joseph College, Emmitsburg, at a Mass in
honor of the recent beatification of Louise de Marillac, foundress
with St. Vincent de Paul of the Daughters of Charity. But
he was too weak to say the Mass as he had planned, although
he presided from the throne, and that afternoon he was driven
by automobile to Union Mills where in the home of Miss Mary
O. Shriver he spent the next four weeks in the hope of recovering
his health. Gibbons' condition at this time was described by
his physician, Dr. Charles O'Donovan, for the cardinal's brother.
O'Donovan stated that there was no organic trouble of any
kind, but for the previous three weeks his patient had been
much weaker than usual and he could not walk even about
the house without tottering and feeling faint. "While he sits
in his chair," said the doctor, "he is as well as ever and can
attend to any matter that comes before him with complete
satisfaction." Gibbons had complained of no pain and his
appetite was about as it always had been and, said O'Donovan,
after the eighteen-mile drive from Emmitsburg to Union Mills
he had played eleven games of euchre before going to bed.

---

[10] 130-J, Ritchie to Gibbons, Annapolis, November 8, 1920; 130-P, Gibbons
to Gibbons, New Orleans, November 19, 1920. Although John had remarked at
this time that all were well in New Orleans, two weeks later he wired the cardinal,
"Our sister Mary died early this morning. Will be buried Friday morning" (131-A,
Gibbons to Gibbons, New Orleans, December 2, 1920, telegram).

In summary the doctor could attribute the condition of the cardinal to nothing except the increasing physical weakness of one of advanced age.[11]

This general debilitation continued at Union Mills and on December 9 Gibbons said Mass for the last time in the Shriver oratory, but he was now so weak that he could not descend the steps to give the family Communion, and they came through the little sanctuary to the foot of the altar where they received the sacred Host from his hands with Bishop O'Connell standing at the side of the enfeebled cardinal. Although he soon was unable to leave his bed unaided, he insisted upon being carried downstairs to preside at a little ceremony in the family parlor on the evening of December 16 where he presented to Miss Mary Shriver the splendid portrait of himself which had been painted by Miss Marie deFord Keller.[12] But the exertion had apparently been too much for him, and after a sinking spell

[11] 131-F, O'Donovan to John T. Gibbons, Baltimore, December 7, 1920, copy.

[12] For the details of Gibbons' last days cf. Smith-Fitzpatrick, *op. cit.*, pp. 214–236, and Will, *Life of Cardinal Gibbons*, II, 1024–1068. The writer also had the benefit of two lengthy interviews on these matters on July 26, 1945, and July 16, 1947, with Monsignor Stickney who was rector of the cathedral at the time of the cardinal's death. The portrait which was presented to Miss Shriver on December 16, 1920, and which is generally considered the best of the four portraits of Gibbons painted by Miss Keller, is at present on loan from Robert Shriver to St. Mary's Seminary, Roland Park, Baltimore. A second Keller portrait belongs to Miss Madeline Shriver and hangs in her home at Union Mills; a third was purchased for the city of Baltimore by a number of subscribers and hangs in the Knights of Columbus Club. The fourth and final Keller portrait, finished only within recent years, was presented to St. Charles College, Catonsville, as part of the centennial celebration of Gibbons' alma mater on November 16, 1948, largely through the efforts of the Reverend W. Kailer Dunn. Cf. the appreciative article of Gerald W. Johnson, "The Cardinal's Portrait," Baltimore *Evening Sun,* May 22, 1930, which was written after he had viewed the work in Miss Keller's studio. Gibbons was likewise painted in 1888 by the celebrated artist, George P. A. Healy, and this picture hangs in the residence at 408 N. Charles Street, Baltimore (cf. 84-F-10, Healy to Gibbons, Paris, March 26, 1888; 84-U-6, same to same, Portland, Oregon, August 6, 1888; 85-A-9, same to same, New York, September 7, 1888; 86-G-6, same to same, Veules, Seine Inférieure, France, August 4, 1889). In 1892 Gibbons sat for Adolfo Muller Ury and this picture is now in the parlors of Caldwell Hall at the Catholic University of America. In 1898 the cardinal was painted by Eduardo Gordigiani whose picture was later presented by several of Gibbons' admirers to the university and now hangs in the main reading room of the Mullen Library. One of the last portraits of Gibbons was that done by Dario Gobbi in 1915 which today hangs in the lobby of Curley Hall at the university. A bronze bust of the cardinal executed in 1911 for his golden sacerdotal jubilee by Joseph Maxwell Miller of Baltimore is placed in the foyer of Gibbons Hall at the university.

the cardinal was anointed at two o'clock on the following morning. Once more he rallied, however, and he was able to assist at the Christmas midnight Mass which was said by Father Smith in his bedroom with the Shriver family and the two Bon Secours Sisters who were his nurses in attendance. It was the first Christmas in fifty-two years that James Gibbons had not celebrated a pontifical Mass. The scene was far removed from the pomp and ceremony with which the old cardinal had formerly been surrounded on this feast, but the simplicity of the bedroom chapel was relieved by a large bouquet of roses sent to him for Christmas from New Orleans and by the singing of the familiar Christmas hymns which were dear to his heart by a quartet from St. John's Church in Westminster. Christmas greetings poured in by wire and letter from numerous friends who wished to remember the stricken churchman, and Cardinal Gasparri cabled a message from Pope Benedict XV which read:

> His Holiness begs of the Lord every grace and comfort to Your Eminence, who in your laborious life has rendered such service to the Church. He sends to you with paternal affection his special Apostolic Benediction.[13]

During the days of his illness at Union Mills there were visits from many who were near to Gibbons such as his vicar-general, Bishop Corrigan, Archbishop Bonzano, the apostolic delegate, Bishops Shahan and Russell, and members of the faculties of the Catholic University of America and of St. Mary's Seminary. His time was spent in chatting with these friends and the Shrivers, with a good portion of each day given over to prayer and meditation from the *Imitation of Christ*. Moreover, on days when he felt fairly well his secretary or some other person read to him sections from the seven-volume *Constitutional and Political History of the United States* by Herman E. von Holst, and the cardinal would often interrupt to make comments on what had been read. He understood, however, the gravity of his illness, and for that reason as the year 1920 drew to a close he begged to be allowed to return to Baltimore where, as he told his secretary, he wished to die in his own home. A further reason which he gave was his

---

[13] Smith-Fitzpatrick, *op. cit.*, p. 222.

desire to see the cathedral again, every stone of which was dear to him, for no bishop ever loved his cathedral more than the Cardinal of Baltimore. After the doctors had given their consent arrangements were made, therefore, to convey the invalid to Baltimore, and on January 3 he left Union Mills, the scene of so many happy days, for the last time in an automobile driven by Robert T. Shriver. As they passed through Westminster Dr. O'Donovan called his patient's attention to two of his priests, Fathers Thomas McGuigan of Westminster and Thomas Wheeler, pastor of Our Lady of Mount Carmel Church in Thurmont, who were standing along the curb. The cardinal lifted his head, smiled, and gave the two pastors his blessing, and from that point on he seemed to brighten and improve as they neared Baltimore. By the time they reached the Mulberry Street entrance to his residence the clergy of the household were assembled to receive him, and when one of them jokingly asked if he was now ready to sing his *Nunc dimittis*, there was a momentary flash of the old spirit as the cardinal smilingly replied, "Not yet, I hope."[14]

Meanwhile the messages of good will and the inquiries about Gibbons' health multiplied to such an extent that it must have proved something of a burden to answer them. The day after his return to Baltimore the Secretary of State, Bainbridge Colby, cabled from Montevideo, "Please cable through Navy Washington to the U.S.S. Florida news of Cardinal. Alarmed by published reports his illness."[15] It was only one of scores of such messages which poured into the cardinal's office during these anxious days. Back again in the beloved environment of the old mansion where he had lived for over forty-three years, Gibbons' strength picked up somewhat, and although he was no longer equal to his customary walks, he was well enough through the next two and a half months to take frequent automobile rides through the city. On these rides he stopped occasionally at various Catholic institutions for brief visits as, for example, when the Baltimore *American* of March 11 reported him as having visited Bon Secours Hospital the previous day to see the ailing Monsignor George W. Devine, pastor of St. John's Church. The

---

[14] *Ibid.*, pp. 223–226.

[15] 132-E, Colby to Secretary of Gibbons, Montevideo, January 4, 1921, cablegram.

last of such visits came on the feast of St. Joseph, March 19, when five days before his death, Gibbons, in the company of his secretary and three of the priests of St. John's Church, called at the Little Sisters of the Poor where he appeared in excellent spirits as he passed through the lines of sisters and their aged charges who knelt for his blessing. Through these days he referred again and again to his desire to deliver his Easter message to his people in the cathedral on March 27, and to be present for the semiannual meeting of the Board of Trustees of the Catholic University of America in Washington on April 1.

But his wish in this regard was not to be granted, for after his customary ride on Sunday, March 20, with Father Edwin L. Leonard of the cathedral staff, the Bon Secours Sister who was nursing the cardinal noticed a sudden change early that evening and summoned the priests. He had suffered a lapse of memory and had asked to be taken home. One of the priests placed him in his chair and wheeled him through the corridor several times while pointing out to him familiar objects. He then returned him to his room and the nurse asked if he recognized it. His face brightened as he pointed to the pictures of his old friends, Fathers McManus and Gaitley, on the wall and with this the temporary loss of memory had passed. The cardinal had expressed, too, a desire to see Archbishop Bonzano and on Monday, March 21, the apostolic delegate paid him a visit and spoke briefly with him. The following morning he received holy Communion for the last time, having previously been anointed and made the profession of faith prescribed for a dying bishop. The priests of the household gathered about him as he sat in his chair after dinner on March 22, and after he had chatted with them in his usual manner for a time, he suddenly paused and said:

> Gentlemen, you do not know how I suffer. . . . Faith must ever be the consolation of all men. Without Faith we can accomplish little. Faith bears us up in our trials. I find that this is true more and more every day.[16]

On Tuesday, March 22, Bishop Corrigan consulted Dr. O'Donovan on the advisability of issuing a bulletin which would in-

---

[16] Smith-Fitzpatrick, *op. cit.*, p. 233.

form the public of the fact that Cardinal Gibbons' illness had taken a decided turn for the worse, and that his doctors held out no hope for his recovery. It was felt that this should be done since the outside world was not aware of the steady decline that had set in the previous Sunday evening. Meanwhile the cardinal became unconscious on Tuesday evening and remained in that condition through most of the next day. Near midnight of Wednesday he woke and told Father Stickney, rector of the cathedral, that he would die on the morrow. In the absence of his regular confessor he requested Stickney to hear his confession, and soon thereafter he lapsed again into unconsciousness until death took him on the morning of Holy Thursday, March 24, at 11:30 o'clock. Gathered about the cardinal's bedside as he breathed his last, were Father Stickney, who read the prayers for the dying, the other priests of the household, Arsenius Boyer, S.S., the cardinal's confessor, his nurses, the Sisters of Bon Secours, and the Sisters of Divine Providence who for many years had been in charge of the domestic department of his residence. At that moment Bishop Corrigan was in the cathedral blessing the holy oils and the edifice was filled with worshipers.[17]

Hardly had the news of the cardinal's death been flashed to the country and the world than there began arriving at the residence a stream of cables, telegrams, and letters from men and women in every walk of life which attested the extraordinary place he had won in their hearts. Cardinal Gasparri cabled in the name of Pope Benedict XV, "The august Pontiff has learned with profound sorrow of the death of His Eminence Cardinal Gibbons. He offered up prayers for the soul of the worthy prelate and sends heartfelt condolences to Your Lordship, to the clergy

---

[17] *Ibid.*, pp. 234–235. The famous English writer and lecturer, Gilbert K. Chesterton, came to Baltimore to deliver a lecture late in March, 1921. When he arrived at his hotel two priests were waiting to greet him with a message of welcome from one whom he characterized as "a great American whose name I had known from childhood and whose career was drawing to its close. . . ." During his stay in the city Chesterton, of course, learned of the critical condition of the cardinal. Writing later of his visit, he said that on one occasion he had sat down on a stone seat near the Washington Monument and spoken with two children, and he continued, "in front of me soared up into the sky on wings of stone the column of all those high hopes of humanity a hundred years ago; and beyond there were lighted candles in the chapels and prayers in the ante-chambers, where perhaps already a Prince of the Church was dying." G. K. Chesterton, *What I Saw in America* (New York, 1922), pp. 71–72.

and to the faithful of the Archdiocese."[18] Within a few hours after the cardinal's death President Warren G. Harding sent the following telegram:

> In common with all our people I mourn the death of Cardinal Gibbons. His long and most notable service to country and to church makes us all his debtors. He was ever ready to lend his encouragement to any movement for the betterment of his fellowmen. He was the very finest type of citizen and churchman. It was my good fortune to know him personally and I held him in the highest esteem and veneration. His death is a distinct loss to the country, but it brings to fuller appreciation a great and admirable life.[19]

Through March 24 and the succeeding days messages of condolence continued to reach Baltimore from numerous members of the American hierarchy, the apostolic delegate, Vice-President Calvin Coolidge, Chief Justice Edward D. White, Secretary of State Charles Evans Hughes, President John Grier Hibben of Princeton University, Governor Edward I. Edwards of New Jersey, Ambassador Jules Jusserand of France, Generals John J. Pershing and Leonard Wood, and the Protestant Episcopal Bishops of New York and Maryland, William T. Manning and John G. Murray. Not only individuals, but groups and societies of various kinds hastened to voice their sense of loss and their appreciation for what Gibbons had meant to the cause they served. Numbered among these were the American Committee for Relief in Ireland, for which the cardinal had issued an appeal to the American people as one of the final acts of his life, the New York Board of Jewish Ministers, the National Association for the Advancement of Colored People, the Salvation Army, the Retail Merchants Bureau of Baltimore, the French High Commission, and the Building Trades Councils of New Orleans and Baltimore. The mere enumeration of their names indicated the breadth of the late cardinal's appeal and the affectionate regard in which they had held him. From abroad cables came from Cardinals Bourne of Westminster, Logue of Armagh, and Begin of Quebec, and from one as far removed as Archbishop Francis M. Redwood of Wellington, New Zealand.[20]

---

[18] 134-Q, Gasparri to Corrigan, Rome, March 25, 1921, cablegram.

[19] 134-F, Harding to Corrigan, Washington, March 24, 1921, telegram.

[20] These messages, along with many others, are contained in AAB, Boxes 133–135, and run from March 24 to April 1, 1921. During the cardinal's last illness

On the day following the death of the cardinal, the Baltimore *Sun,* his favorite newspaper, featured a lengthy editorial in which it endeavored to assess his career and what it had meant to the world, to the country, and to Baltimore. His high attainments in the affairs of both Church and State were given ample praise, but it was stated that it was now not the great churchman or religious diplomatist that was so fondly recalled, as it was the person of the man and the rare beauty of his character. It was his loving heart, his kindly personality, his charity, sympathy, and simplicity which were uppermost in memory and the *Sun* thus concluded, "whatever our religious creed may be, we feel that he belongs to all of us alike and that humanity today is better and purer and nobler for the life that has just come to its earthly close."[21] Practically all the leading secular papers from the Atlantic to the Pacific gave generous space to full accounts of Gibbons' history and expressed their appreciation of the significance of his life to the Church and the nation in glowing editorials. For example, the New York *Times* on March 25 said that for many years his name had been one that "had the majesty of ecclesiastical, moral and intellectual authority, the

President Wilson had sent him a message of sympathy which in all likelihood had been prompted by Wilson's secretary, Joseph P. Tumulty. At the time of Gibbons' death Wilson had been out of office for three weeks. By this time his former secretary had fallen from favor with the ex-President, and although Wilson's Secretary of State, Bainbridge Colby, J. Fred Essary of the Baltimore *Sun,* and Tumulty joined in urging Wilson to pay a public tribute to the late cardinal in the hope of improving his public relations, as a recent writer has put it, "their letter was ignored." John M. Blum, *Joe Tumulty and the Wilson Era* (Boston, 1951), p. 262.

[21] Father Albert E. Smith, the late cardinal's secretary, took serious exception to two points in the editorial of the *Sun,* namely, to what he considered the belittling remarks concerning the temporal power exercised by the Papacy in Italy for centuries and, second, to the comparison of Gibbons and Luther as reformers of the Church who worked in different ways (135-J, Smith to John H. Adams, editor-in-chief, Baltimore *Sun,* Baltimore, March 29, 1921, copy). The *Sun* likewise carried on March 25 a cartoon which showed Gibbons soaring aloft into the heavens over Baltimore while he glanced back upon the cathedral and the city he had loved with his hand extended in benediction. The editorial was later issued in pamphlet form and the cartoon was carried as a cover and given the title "Vale," with a second cartoon, bearing the caption "At Tulip Time," which represented two figures, a man bowed in grief and a woman kneeling before the doorway of 408 N. Charles Street with the flower beds showing at the right. It was a touching reference to the interest taken each springtime by Gibbons and many Baltimoreans in the crocuses and tulips which bloomed alongside the cardinal's residence, and which Folger McKinsey, the Benztown bard, referred to on more than one occasion in his poems which appeared in the Baltimore *Sun.*

dignity, influence and power of a great nature and mind." To the *Times*, "He was one of the wisest men in the world." The New York *Herald* of the same day declared:

> The death of Cardinal Gibbons is more than the passing of an old man and honored churchman. It is the ending of the life of a great American, a fine figure in the national scene.
>
> In the sense that Francis of Assisi is everybody's saint, James Gibbons was everybody's Cardinal. No matter what their religious beliefs, Americans who knew him held him in the highest respect and esteem.

Thus did a sorrowing nation pay tribute in a manner that has never been equaled before or since on the death of an American churchman. As one writer said some weeks later, "Cardinal Gibbons must have been close to the realities that underlie the structure of the world in order to have gained these tributes."[22] In fact, the death of few churchmen in modern times had called forth so spontaneous and widespread a manifestation of loving esteem, for one would have to go back to that January day of 1892 when the tremendous throng followed the mortal remains of Cardinal Manning from the Brompton Oratory to its resting place in Kensal Green, to find a parallel to the universal grief shown on the death of Cardinal Gibbons.

By reason of the fact that the cardinal's death had occurred in Holy Week his remains were not brought to the cathedral until Monday, March 28, when there was held the first of a series of requiem Masses for the repose of his soul with one day assigned to the children, another to the religious, and a third to the laity of the archdiocese. From his death on Thursday until the following Monday morning the body lay in the little bedroom of his residence which he had always occupied, clothed in purple vestments and with a white miter on the head. There his close friends viewed the remains, and it was only on Monday when the body lay in state before the high altar of the cathedral with the red hat resting against the foot of the casket and the numerous decorations which Gibbons had received from foreign governments and civic organizations displayed nearby, that there began to gather the immense crowds which filed past the cata-

---

22 William J. Kerby, "James Cardinal Gibbons. An Interpretation," *Catholic World*, CXIII (May, 1921), 148.

falque. It was estimated that over 200,000 people were admitted to the cathedral during those three days and nights as the long lines that formed a block away on Mulberry Street slowly moved forward to view for the last time the face of one whom they had learned to love in life. It was not until Thursday morning that the cathedral was closed to the public a few hours before the funeral which was announced for ten o'clock. Meanwhile Governor Ritchie of Maryland had issued a proclamation requesting that all persons throughout the state refrain from work and activity of every kind for one minute to offer a prayer of gratitude for the cardinal at the moment that the funeral was scheduled to begin, a proclamation that was seconded by one from the Mayor of Baltimore and from the president of the city's leading trade organization.[23]

By the morning of March 31 there had arrived in Baltimore two of Gibbons' fellow members of the College of Cardinals, William O'Connell of Boston and Louis Begin of Quebec, along with Archbishop Bonzano, who as Apostolic Delegate to the United States was to be the celebrant of the pontifical requiem, nine other archbishops, and forty-three bishops.[24] The President of the United States was represented at the funeral by Postmaster General Will H. Hays. Among the mourners were Chief Justice White, the Governors of Maryland and Ohio, members from the two houses of Congress, the envoys of a dozen foreign nations, and a score of Protestant and Jewish clergymen, together with a vast throng of minor prelates and priests from Baltimore and other cities, who filled the cathedral to its capacity.

The funeral sermon was preached by Archbishop Glennon of St. Louis who emphasized at the outset the universal sorrow which the cardinal's death had evoked as an evidence of the love which men had for him. After sketching the high points of Gibbons' career, the preacher spoke of the materialist philosophy which had done such grave harm to society during the previous half

---

[23] Will, *op. cit.*, II, 1058–1060.

[24] A pontifical requiem was also celebrated for Gibbons in his titular church of Santa Maria in Trastevere at Rome by Archbishop Cerretti which was attended by eight cardinals, and on April 4 another requiem was sung in St. Joseph's Church in Paris where Louis Cardinal Dubois, Archbishop of Paris, eulogized Gibbons in the name of the Catholics of France. This latter Mass was attended by Dennis Cardinal Dougherty, Archbishop of Philadelphia, who was on his way home from Rome where he had received the red hat in the consistory of March 7 (Baltimore *Catholic Review,* April 16, 1921).

century. To meet this challenge, said Glennon, divine Providence had raised up three men who had boldly proclaimed the supernatural and divine truths for their generation and these three were Leo XIII, Manning of Westminster, and Gibbons of Baltimore. Gibbons' role had been performed through such means as *The Faith of Our Fathers,* which Glennon pronounced the best apologia for the Catholic faith in the English language, his leadership of the Third Plenary Council, his championing of the Knights of Labor, and his fatherly guidance of the Catholic University of America. Stating that he was drawing a parallel from the dying request of a national hero of other days, the preacher said, "the Cardinal were he to speak, would, I believe, leave as a heritage, his body to Baltimore, his heart to the University and his soul to God." He recalled the vigor with which the aged churchman had led the American Church during World War I and had resisted the attempt of a foreign government as late as September, 1920, to interfere with the composition of the American hierarchy. As an illustration of how the cardinal's buoyant spirit and the profound love he had for his country had remained with him to the end, he quoted from Gibbons' final Christmas message in which he had said, "I face our future not only without apprehension, but with unshaken faith in our American institutions, because these are based upon the message of Christianity." As he neared the end of his sermon the Archbishop of St. Louis made a plea for a remembrance of the cardinal in the prayers of all his friends, and he then concluded:

> So also let us hope that in the white light of that Resurrection we are still commemorating, the Saviour triumphant, meeting His servant in the garden there, may greet him with the words of eternal life: "I am the resurrection and the life, he that believeth in me, though he be dead, shall live," and crown him with blissful immortality.[25]

At the end of the funeral Mass there were performed the customary absolutions which were said by four of the late cardinal's suffragans, namely, Bishops Haid of North Carolina, Donahue of Wheeling, Monaghan of Wilmington, and O'Connell of Richmond. With that the long ceremony came to a close and the distinguished assemblage dispersed. Later in the day the body

---

[25] The text of the sermon may be read in Smith-Fitzpatrick, *op. cit.,* pp. 251–262.

of the cardinal was carried from the cathedral by the priests of his household assisted by several laymen, who made their way to the crypt amid the tolling of the bells of the city's Catholic churches. There beneath the cathedral he had loved so dearly the mortal remains of James Gibbons were laid away beside the tombs of six of his predecessors in the See of Baltimore as Bishop Corrigan gave the final absolution and the assembled clergy chanted the solemn tones of the *De profundis*.[26]

It is a relatively easy matter to record the deeds of a man's life; it is quite another matter to analyze the personality of one who has been dead for a generation and whom the writer neither knew nor saw in life. So much has been said about the public career of Cardinal Gibbons that there is no need to rehearse it here. The secret wellsprings of his greatness, which the leading figures of Church and State proclaimed in so unprecedented a way, lay hidden deep in those subtle and intangible qualities which men call character. It is impossible to evoke a perfect portrayal of the man, and yet the character of Gibbons was not a complex one such as that with which the biographers of Cardinal Newman have had to contend. In fact, one might say that the dominant characteristic of the cardinal was his simplicity. Not only was that note emphasized by previous biographers of the Archbishop of Baltimore, but all the living witnesses of his career are agreed that the simplicity of his manner, tastes, habits, entertainments, and style of writing and preaching was a distinguishing feature which everyone observed, and which accounted in no small measure for the ease of approach and the attraction which he had for others. In spite of the fact that for thirty-five years Gibbons was the ranking dignitary of the Catholic Church in the United States, he never gave evidence of the slightest tendency to the aloofness and arrogance that sometimes accompany high office. Honored and extolled as, perhaps, no churchman in modern times has ever been, his natural and graceful simplicity never deserted him, and the gentle dignity and quiet self-respect with which he bore his exalted rank as a Prince of the Church rested serenely upon the conscious certainty that his high office neither needed nor suffered any self-assertion.

The simplicity of the man was conveyed in a hundred different ways. For example, in the days before the automobile he never

---

[26] Will, *op. cit.*, II, 1065.

kept a horse and carriage, and although after the advent of the automobile he thoroughly enjoyed motor rides, he would never accept one as a gift.[27] He always walked whenever that was possible and even in Rome where tradition dictated that cardinals should move about the city in carriages, he continued the practice. As one of his Roman students remarked at the turn of the century, "Cardinal Gibbons when he was here created quite a sensation by walking alone down the Corso, the most crowded street of Rome. . . ."[28] Habits such as there were bound to arouse interest among the masses of men in a famous churchman who preferred to forego the formalities of state and to walk among them. The same held true for the entertainments which amused the cardinal during his hours of relaxation. Any man who could pass an entire evening playing euchre with his friends, while away an hour at horseshoes or quoits, or show a fondness for old and familiar music, where his favorite was "Lead Kindly Light," had, indeed, a great deal of the common touch about him. It made those around him feel that, in spite of the great distance that separated them in social rank, they had in Gibbons one who understood and appreciated the world in which they moved. Moreover, men especially felt at ease with the great churchman when he would light up a cigar after dinner and sit down among them for a friendly chat about subjects which held their attention. Gibbons liked baseball and he followed the game closely enough to discuss it intelligently, and horse racing was also a sport in which he showed a keen interest. Now and then he would place a modest bet on a horse through one of the Shriver boys, and on one occasion in New Orleans the cardinal attended the races.[29] Another form of entertainment in which Gibbons took delight and where his simplicity of taste showed up was in dining out with friends. "I dine out," he once said, "because Christ dined out."[30] But here, too, he preferred a simple style. Shortly after the marriage of one of the Shriver girls she invited the cardinal

---

[27] *Ibid.*, II, 986.

[28] ACUA, Cooper Papers, John M. Cooper to Mr. and Mrs. James J. Cooper, Rome, January 16, 1900.

[29] Interview of the writer's friend, the Reverend Edward V. Cardinal, C.S.V., with Gibbons' nieces, Mrs. Mary Swarbrick Stanton and Mrs. Margaret Gibbons Start, and a grandnephew, Gibbons Burke, New Orleans, May 24, 1946. To Father Cardinal the writer expresses his thanks for this interview as well as for the inquiries regarding Gibbons material he was generous enough to make in Paris.

[30] Smith-Fitzpatrick, *op. cit.*, p. 209.

to dinner, and with all the enthusiasm of a new bride she decorated the table with her finest gifts. After a brief effort at trying to peer around the decorations in order to see the faces of the other guests with whom he wished to converse, Gibbons acknowledged to his hostess that she had some lovely wedding presents, but they had now seen them and he would suggest, therefore, that she remove them from the table.[31]

But this simplicity of manner and taste sprang in part from the cardinal's intense interest in people. In other words, it was their persons that interested him, not their station in life nor the wealth or prestige that attached to their names. He had a truly remarkable memory for names and faces which, of course, proved exceedingly flattering to those whom he met, and more than once he was able to surprise a man or woman whom he had not seen in a long time by calling their name as they came forward in the receiving line at one of his new year receptions in Baltimore or Washington.[32] Everyone seemed to hold some kind of interest for Gibbons, and he once remarked that he had never met anyone from whom he had not learned something.[33] This personal concern created, in turn, a deep impression on others, and one who had known the cardinal well over a long period of time gave it as her opinion that his outstanding quality was his faculty for entering into other people's interests.[34] On his visits to Rome, for example, he never failed to see his students from the Archdiocese of Baltimore, and one of them stated after a visit of this kind, "He seems to take lots of interest in his men — encouraged us all and told us not to work too hard."[35] His priests were at liberty to call to see him without appointment at any time, and even children felt free to ring the doorbell at 408 N. Charles Street and to ask for His Eminence.

On one occasion a visit of this kind brought out not only his

---

[31] Interview of the Reverend W. Kailer Dunn with Mrs. Hilda Shriver, New York, February 26, 1950. When Gibbons went for a sitting for his portrait he would normally drop in casually from one of his walks and inquire by telephone from the desk downstairs at the St. James Hotel if Miss Keller was free to take him at that particular time. Interview of the writer with Miss Marie deFord Keller, Baltimore, July 9, 1945.

[32] Smith-Fitzpatrick, *op. cit.*, pp. 199–201.

[33] Interview with Miss Madeline Shriver, Union Mills, July 9, 1945.

[34] Interview with Mrs. Mark Shriver, Baltimore, March 7, 1947.

[35] ACUA, Cooper Papers, John M. Cooper to James J. Cooper, Rome, June 18, 1901.

love for children but, too, his high sense of obligation to even the lowliest members of his flock. There happened to be a current fad in Baltimore at the time for collecting autographs and the youngsters were calling with great frequency in a desire to secure the signature of the cardinal. One day Father Stickney answered the door and found several little boys who asked for Gibbons' autograph. He sent them along their way with the word that the cardinal was too busy to be interrupted. Later he informed Gibbons that he had saved him a trip downstairs; whereupon the cardinal inquired who had called, and when he was told who it was and the purpose which had brought them, he delivered a rather sharp rebuke to the rector of the cathedral by commanding him never to do such a thing again since he was the archbishop of these little children every bit as much as he was of anybody else.[36] Even during formal ceremonies Gibbons was sensible of the presence of others and Oliveira Lima, Ambassador of Brazil to the United States, once remarked after attending a Mass in the cathedral, "On his archiepiscopal throne, instead of keeping his eyes lowered, the image of Christian humility, he sits with his head erect, glancing at those present, distinguishing one from the other, recognizing them."[37]

His reputation for friendliness and approachability occasionally involved Gibbons in situations which afforded opportunity for the exercise of his well-known tact. The cardinal once met a woman at a social gathering whose curiosity was greater than her discretion, and she made bold to ask him how far he thought the infallibility of the Pope extended. With the faintest smile he replied, "Madame, that is not an easy question. All I can say is that a few months ago in Rome His Holiness called me 'Jibbons.' " As one who overheard the exchange later wrote, "The subtlety of this reply was probably lost on the inquirer."[38] The tact and delicacy with which Gibbons invariably governed his personal relations was partly motivated by the dread he always entertained of hurting the feelings of another person. It was this

---

[36] Interview with Monsignor Stickney, Baltimore, July 26, 1945.

[37] Oliveira Lima, *Nos Estados Unidos impressões politicas e sociaes* (Leipzig, 1899), p. 298. The writer is indebted to Manoel Cardozo, associate professor of Latin American history in the Catholic University of America, for the translation of a lengthy passage relating to Gibbons from the work of Lima.

[38] Nicholas Murray Butler, *Across the Busy Years. Recollections and Reflections* (New York, 1940), II, 331.

sentiment together with the quickness of his perception that saved more than one situation. One afternoon some children called on Gibbons in the company of a gentleman to present the cardinal with a few trifling mementos of their handiwork. Their chaperon addressed the prelate in their name, and in doing so he deprecated the value of the gifts but emphasized the motive which the children had in offering to him these simple testimonials of their affection. Immediately the children's faces revealed their hurt at the remarks made about the value of their gifts. Gibbons sensed their feelings at once, rose from his chair, went to the table, and picked up the trinkets, and as he looked them over carefully he exclaimed several times, as if to himself, "Aren't they wonderful!" He then turned and passed them around to the priests and others in the parlor, and by that time the faces of the children were again wreathed in smiles as they listened with delight while His Eminence delivered to them a little speech of thanks for their thoughtfulness.[39]

This exquisite tact was displayed at numerous times in his life and in the most widely varied circumstances. When he was a young missionary bishop in North Carolina he was compelled to travel around the state in any conveyance he could find and in all kinds of weather. Notices of his appearance were sometimes tacked to trees and the local inhabitants were thus made aware of his approach. On one such occasion Gibbons arrived in a torrential rain at the crude little shack where he was to speak to find a single man waiting to hear him. The bishop's concern for the soul of the man, together with his reluctance to hurt or disappoint him, caused him to put on his robes and to preach the sermon to the congregation of one. Years later the same man, long since a convert to the Church, told how he went up to the preacher after the talk and said, "Mr. Gibbons, I want to join your religion."[40]

This supreme consideration for the feelings of others not only endeared them to his person, but it gave them a much kindlier feeling toward the Catholic Church, if it did not always bring about their conversion. The Reverend Joseph Fort Newton, at one time pastor of the Church of the Divine Paternity in New

---

[39] Smith-Fitzpatrick, *op. cit.*, pp. 195–196.

[40] Letter of Edward F. Coyle, S.S., to the writer, Baltimore, November 26, 1950. Father Coyle met the man to whom the incident happened many years later in North Carolina.

York, told how as a small boy he had heard his minister criticize the Catholic Church Sunday after Sunday. Having read in a local paper that Cardinal Gibbons lived in Baltimore, he wrote to him and related the stories he had heard of Catholicism and asked if they were true. In time there came a letter in the cardinal's own hand in which he commended the lad for not believing ill of the Church or of any man without first knowing the facts. In order to help enlighten him, he sent young Newton a copy of *The Faith of Our Fathers* which the latter read and long retained. In summarizing the episode many years later Newton stated that when Cardinal Gibbons died a Mass was sung for him in St. Patrick's Cathedral in New York and he attended the services because, as he said, "a great man had taken time out of his busy life to answer with his own hand the scrawled letter of a boy in Texas."[41] Consideration of this kind for remote and unimportant strangers was a common thing in the life of Gibbons, and it was a matter of no surprise, therefore, that an awareness of his kindly spirit in time spread all over the land.

Another outstanding characteristic of the man was his sympathy and generosity to those in distress. Hardly a month passed that there was not some new manifestation of the cardinal fulfilling the priestly role of healing and consoling, of comforting and providing for the unfortunate insofar as his means allowed. Disasters like the yellow fever epidemic in the South in 1878 and the periodic famines in Ireland aroused his immediate sympathies, and there were few calls made upon his purse that went unheeded. In fact, to the very end of his life, even when conditions in Ireland were normal, the relatives and old friends in County Mayo were the recipients of his bounty and generosity.[42] He was deeply moved, for example, at the plight of certain Protestant ministers who had entered the Catholic Church and who had thus lost the source of their income, and at one time he suggested the creation of a fund for their support and a petition to the Holy See to admit them to minor orders so that these men might serve as catechists and preachers and thus have legitimate

[41] Joseph Fort Newton, *River of Years: An Autobiography* (Philadelphia, 1946), pp. 33–34.
[42] Interview with Thomas Canon O'Malley and Mrs. Catherine Casey, a cousin of Gibbons, Partry, County Mayo, Ireland, June 14, 1950.

claims to a salary.[43] Another class who excited his charity were priests who had fallen on evil ways, and when Bishop Messmer of Green Bay asked if he would take a priest as a chaplain in Baltimore who had compromised his usefulness in Green Bay by intemperance, the cardinal replied that although he had no vacant chaplaincies at the moment, he had given instructions to the sisters at St. Agnes Hospital to provide a room for the priest at his own expense where he would support him for a year.[44]

The consideration which Gibbons showed for all persons, and the generosity he displayed toward those who were in trouble, were more than matched, as we have seen repeatedly, by his love and fidelity for close friends. Prelates like Archbishops Elder, Ryan, Keane, and Ireland, Bishops O'Connell and Shahan, and priests like Fathers McManus, Magnien, and Stickney were witnesses in their lifetime to the reality of the words which the cardinal once spoke in a sermon on Christ as our Friend. There he had declared that among the blessings and enjoyments of this life, there were few that could be compared in value to the possession of a faithful friend who, as he said:

> will defend you when you are unjustly assailed by the tongue of calumny, who will not forsake you when you have fallen into disgrace, who will counsel you in your doubts and perplexities, who will open his purse to aid you without expecting any return of his favors, who will rejoice at your prosperity and grieve at your adversity, who will bear half of your burden, — who will add to your joys and diminish your sorrows by sharing in both.[45]

All these things he had done again and again for his friends. Ireland, for example, acknowledged more than once what it had meant to have the cardinal's defense when he had been unjustly assailed; Denis O'Connell was a notable instance of Gibbons' fidelity when a friend had fallen into disfavor; John Keane's doubts and perplexities in moments of trial were calmed in no small measure by his sympathetic counsel; and William Elder at both Natchez and Cincinnati testified to the purse that had been

[43] 97-A-5, Elder to Gibbons, Cincinnati, January 11, 1899; AAC, Gibbons to Elder, Baltimore, January 13, 1899.
[44] 99-E-6, Messmer to Gibbons, Green Bay, November 2, 1901; *ibid.*, Gibbons to Messmer, Baltimore, November 5, 1901, copy.
[45] *Discourses and Sermons,* pp. 32–33.

opened at Baltimore when disasters overtook his dioceses. Bishop Shahan was a special favorite in the last years of Gibbons' life, and Shahan was not only supported in his administration of the university but sustained as well in some of his more ambitious projects like that of the National Shrine of the Immaculate Conception, for, as Gibbons would say, the bishop was a dreamer, but the Church needed dreamers.[46] Moreover, his deep personal attachments were not confined to the clergy. We have already seen the love he had for the Shriver family, and Michael Jenkins, the Baltimore financier, offered another example among the laity. When Jenkins died in September, 1915, the cardinal made no effort to conceal his grief, and at the funeral in the cathedral he stated that his personal loss was of a kind that could not be fathomed. "His departure has left a void in my heart," he said, "which time cannot fill. It is only the vital and consoling influence of religion that can reconcile me to my bereavement."[47]

But whatever may be said of the winning characteristics of the Cardinal of Baltimore, it was the priestly quality of his daily life which most attracted those who came into frequent contact with him, and who found spiritual comfort and encouragement by the religious and otherworldly temper of his mind. It was that quality that gave purpose and meaning to his charity and kindness toward others. Priestly he was in every word and action of his life; yet there was nothing particularly striking about the cardinal's piety. Unlike Newman and Manning and other churchmen, Gibbons left no intimate journals or diaries through which his biographer might gain a picture of his inner spiritual life. He was not given to speculation, and there was little of the ascetic or mystic about him. The cardinal was rather a man of action with an intensely practical turn of mind. Yet the more than average fidelity with which he observed all the religious exercises and devotions of his priestly office gave a tone to his daily living and established him in the minds of others as a true man of God.

Without, therefore, much apparent soul-searching James Gibbons went serenely on his way, but this same priestly bearing was always with him at the altar, in the pulpit, and in his con-

[46] Interview with Monsignor Stickney, Baltimore, July 26, 1945.

[47] A Retrospect of Fifty Years, II, 247. The remarks of Gibbons at the Jenkins funeral, September 11, 1915, may be read on pp. 243–248.

fessional near the sanctuary railing where in his more vigorous years he heard confessions on Saturday afternoons and after his morning Mass whenever a request was made of him. He had a keen sense of the ecclesiastical proprieties and his outward deportment was thus never the subject of unfavorable comment.[48] It was no mere accident that St. Francis de Sales was Gibbons' favorite saint, for there was a sweetness and kindliness of manner about the Cardinal of Baltimore that suggested the great Bishop of Geneva.[49] His was a spiritual greatness that rested upon a foundation of natural benignity, which precluded the possibility of harshness of treatment or meanness of expression about anyone. As such this happy combination produced a result that is exceedingly difficult to attain even in the best of lives, for Monsignor Stickney who was the cardinal's house companion for thirteen years and Bishop Shahan who had known him well from 1891 to his death, both stated that they had never heard him utter an uncharitable word about any man.[50]

The motto on the coat of arms of Cardinal Gibbons was "Emitte Spiritum Tuum,"[51] and rarely did a churchman carry out with more consistency his role as an agent for sending forth the divine spirit among men. Any movement that would advance the cause of religion received his strong support.[52] But it was not alone by his books, sermons, and help to organized movements that Gibbons exercised his zeal for the spread of God's word; it was in his daily contact with men, in his bearing, in the cast

---

[48] Archbishop Seton stated in his memoirs that he once talked to Archbishop Riordan about the evils of clerical ambition and he added, "Cardinal Gibbons also spoke with me once about a notorious case of episcopal jobbery, in strong reprobation of ambition among the clergy." Robert Seton, *Memories of Many Years* (*1839–1922*) (London, 1923), pp. 163–164.

[49] Smith-Fitzpatrick, *op. cit.*, pp. 195, 207.

[50] Interview with Monsignor Stickney, Baltimore, July 26, 1945; copy of an informal talk given by Shahan to the students of the Sulpician Seminary, Washington, April 12, 1921, on the subject of Gibbons and kindly loaned to the writer by the Reverend Walter J. Schmitz, S.S.

[51] Pierre de Chaignon la Rose, "The Arms of His Eminence Cardinal Gibbons," *American Ecclesiastical Review*, XLV (July, 1911), 2–11. Gibbons changed his coat of arms in 1911 because of the faulty heraldry in the original; the Gibbons family, Baron Baltimore, the Blessed Mother, and the cardinal's patron, St. James, were all worked into the symbolism of the coat of arms.

[52] For example, Gibbons' zeal prompted him to try to hasten the beatifications of Louise de Marillac (89-N-5, Gibbons to Leo XIII, Baltimore, February 17, 1892, copy in French) and of Mother Elizabeth Seton (126-C, Gibbons to Antonio Cardinal Vico, Baltimore, April 8, 1920, copy in Latin).

of his thoughts, and even in the choice of the words he used in ordinary conversation. It was a characteristic of Gibbons that struck many people, among them the prominent English non-Catholic writer, J. E. C. Bodley, who visited him in Baltimore in March, 1889, and who said of the cardinal, "in sentiment he is the most evangelical person I have ever met with."[53] Ambassador Lima likewise noted his alertness to inject a spiritual note into mundane matters but, as he said, "it is exercised in such a benign, dispassionate, evangelical manner that it never shocks the different religious sentiment or the agnostic indifference of his interlocutor. He is always a missionary who speaks to convince educated people and not to intimidate uncultivated people."[54] The comments of the two foreign visitors caught the spirit with which Gibbons executed so brilliantly his apostolate among both Catholics and non-Catholics, as well as his unfailing realization of the priestly office and its obligation to advance the spiritual and moral order in all that he did.

But regardless of how many virtues and noble qualities one may have no man is perfect, and in this Cardinal Gibbons was no exception to the universal law of human frailty. There was about him a certain vanity which, although it escaped entirely the deeper and more unpleasant features of strong pride, was, nonetheless, observable. It manifested itself in small and quite inoffensive ways such as his desire to win at cards, his love for the pomp and splendor of ecclesiastical processions wherein he was arrayed in his scarlet robes, and in the skillful way he had of drawing to himself a table conversation that showed signs of straying into other channels. When one recalls that for so many years he was the first Catholic churchman of the Republic and was thus paid the most unusual honors and adulation, it is remarkable that this tendency confined itself within the narrow range of such trivial expressions as have been mentioned. Surely if ever a man were given opportunities for free rein to his vanity, that man was James Gibbons. And yet his vain little foibles, guileless and transparent as they were, were never allowed to develop into an exhibition of pride and arrogance that gave

---

[53] Shane Leslie, *Memoir of John Edward Courtenay Bodley* (London, 1930), p. 217.

[54] Lima, *op. cit.*, p. 298.

serious offense to his equals and repelled those of lower rank than himself.[55]

More serious, perhaps, was the tendency which the cardinal showed at times to dodge or to shift his ground in unpleasant situations. There were occasions in his life when his failure to face up strongly to a problem was the cause of embarrassment to his associates as, for example, in 1886 when he wavered in his support before the Holy See of a national university and called forth a rebuke from Bishop Keane. There was the reluctance he showed to assume responsibility for sending Bishop Gilmour to Rome in 1885 to defend the conciliar legislation of Baltimore, and there was his failure in 1898 to speak out in an energetic manner against the injustices that were being practiced against the Catholic missionaries among the Indians, a defect which Gibbons himself partly acknowledged later in a communication to his fellow bishops. These and a number of lesser instances in Gibbons' life made apparent the deep aversion he had to giving offense to anyone; but as Keane had reminded him, there were times when his effort to please everyone jeopardized the prospect of his pleasing anyone.

But to magnify these relatively few cases of temporizing and momentary weakness to the point of implying cowardice, would not be to take the true measure of his moral courage. No man who staked his reputation before the highest tribunals in the Church as Gibbons did in the case of the Knights of Labor, or in his masterful speech at Rome in March, 1887, on the relations of Church and State in the United States, could be said to lack courage. Neither was it the conduct of a weak man to defend with all the power he could summon the policies of Archbishop Ireland in regard to the schools, and the American Church itself against the charges of those who spoke of a heretical Americanism. Nor was it weakness that prompted Gibbons to persist to the end against placing Henry George's *Progress and Poverty* on the *Index of Forbidden Books,* when in doing so he experienced the pain of alienation from Archbishop Corrigan who for years had

---

[55] Interviews with Monsignor Stickney, Baltimore, July 26, 1945; Monsignor Louis O'Donovan, Baltimore, July 9, 1945, who was Gibbons' secretary from 1909 to 1919; Miss Madeline Shriver, Union Mills, July 9, 1945; Reverend W. Kailer Dunn with Mrs. Hilda Shriver, New York, February 26, 1950.

been a close friend and counselor. A morally weak man cannot be depended upon in any circumstances that require a display of fortitude, and that could never be said of Cardinal Gibbons. True, it was not his way to be audacious; on the contrary, he was gentle and peaceful by nature. But when he had taken time to consider every aspect of a grave problem, to consult with advisers, and to make a final judgment nothing swerved him from his purpose, as was evidenced at Milwaukee in August, 1891, in his bold sermon against the evils of excessive nationalism within the Church. In the process of arriving at a final decision, it is true, he revealed more than once how disagreeable he found it to do anything that would offend another, and for this reason he resorted on occasion to stratagems that bolder spirits like Ireland and McQuaid would have scorned. And who will say that his conciliatory way of meeting trouble was not at times the better way as, for instance, when he refused to yield to the urging of the Archbishop of St. Paul in 1891 to assemble the metropolitans for a head-on conflict with the German nationalists? If there were times when Gibbons' mildness restrained him when he might better have gone forward, there were also times when that peaceful spirit guided his steps into the path of true wisdom and redounded to the advantage of the Church.

Allied to this tendency to avoid unpleasant issues, there was also the desire to put the best construction on disagreeable events. Here again Gibbons' peaceful nature asserted itself in an effort to heal the wounds of conflict, but in so doing the true circumstances were sometimes overshadowed by his too favorable picture and misunderstanding was the result. One instance of this in his life was the letter that he wrote to Pope Leo XIII in January, 1893, after the latter had established the Apostolic Delegation in Washington. The cardinal had been opposed to its erection, as had most of the American bishops; yet when he was faced with a *fait accompli* in the delegation he spoke of the joy and satisfaction with which the American Catholics had greeted the event. His kindly and generous heart likewise betrayed him into judgments in regard to his close friends which at times would better not have been made, and it would be difficult, for example, to maintain that the heart did not overrule the head in such cases as his support of men like Chapelle and Foley for the episcopacy.

But when the long career of Cardinal Gibbons is examined at close range there is little else that can be found that would indicate real defects in moral character. The very absence of any serious evidence against him on the part of his enemies — for like every other man of prominence he was not free from enemies — is in itself significant. Steeped as he often was in bitter controversies that rocked the American Church, if there could have been discovered any moral delinquencies that would have served the enemy's cause they would have been used. To be sure, Bishop McQuaid more than once made reference to the vanity of the Cardinal of Baltimore, Archbishop Ireland, who, nonetheless, was not an enemy, was once or twice found alluding to his lack of fortitude, some of the Catholic editors of extreme nationalist views mentioned now and then the dangerous liberalism which Gibbons was fostering in the American Church, and Protestant critics from time to time charged him with a less than honest portrayal of the teachings of Catholicism. But when these things had been said, there was little of a substantial nature left to adduce against the cardinal.

Apart entirely from the minor moral delinquencies that revealed themselves in the character of Gibbons, there were deficiencies of another nature which were not related to character in the strict sense. He was, for example, quite unoriginal. There was no great project which owed its origins to his personal initiative and which he brought to completion. The Third Plenary Council of 1884 arose as a result of the suggestion of bishops of the Middle West, the university was largely the idea of Bishop Spalding, and the defense of the Knights of Labor probably owed as much in origin to Keane and Ireland as it did to Gibbons. But once these movements had been launched, there was no single factor that contributed more to their ultimate success than the manner in which the cardinal stepped forward with the great prestige of his office and name to lead them, and here his management was well-nigh perfect. The same lack of originality showed itself in his sermons and writings, for one would look in vain in what he preached and wrote for evidence of the gifted researcher, orator, and prose writer. Yet there has never been a more effective exponent before the American public of the truths of the Catholic faith. If one turned to the field of administration there, too, there was little of striking accomplishment to record for Gibbons' long tenure of the See of Baltimore. True, through the early and mid years of his time as archbishop, there was nothing exceptional by way of either progress or retrogression. But as he grew older defects in administration appeared in his failure to initiate new parishes and to further the advancement of parochial schools. A remedy for these deficiencies might well have been provided by the appointment of a young and vigorous coadjutor to relieve the old churchman of many of the duties of ecclesiastical administration. But he was decidedly cool to the suggestion of a coadjutor when it was made in the spring of 1912, and the possibility of an improved administration of the arch-diocese through this medium was passed over, with what was probably a mixture of attachment to old ways and the reluctance to have close at hand an archbishop with whom he would have to share his authority.[56]

When one considers the life of the cardinal in its entirety and the accomplishments which he attained, one is more and more impressed by the lack of anything extraordinary in his make-up to account for his success. But the failure to find brilliance of mind, depth of learning, mastery of administrative detail, re-sourceful and fighting qualities of leadership, powerful oratory, and majestic diction should not deceive one into believing that Cardinal Gibbons was not a singularly gifted man. His gifts of prudence, discretion, and delicacy of perception were of an altogether uncommon order, and they were employed to the ut-most advantage in his dealings with others. These gifts, resting upon a noble character and implemented by a quick and agile mind, did more than many others could have done who were far more richly endowed than James Gibbons. Men are not easily led unless leadership is strengthened by love and high respect, and the love which the cardinal engendered for his person was so profound and genuine that it enabled him to accomplish wonders where more gifted men would have failed. As one who knew him well said after he was gone, "Cardinal Gibbons was powerful because he was simple, and his simplicity invited love. It never demanded service."[57]

---

[56] In the writer's interview of July 16, 1947, with Monsignor Stickney he was told that in his last days Gibbons was worried over the possibility that the Holy See would ask for his resignation, but Stickney assured him that Rome did not request cardinals to resign their sees because of illness and old age.

[57] Kerby, *op. cit.*, p. 152.

It was, indeed, in good measure the secret of his greatness, yet simplicity standing alone without high moral principle and intelligence would fail utterly to attain the results which Gibbons gathered in abundance. As one of his closest friends remarked, beyond simplicity the cardinal possessed to a marked degree what St. Thomas Aquinas considered the chief virtue of those who governed, namely, the *discretio rationis,* or the sense of reasonable proportion in all his judgments.[58] It was that quality that raised the execution of policies by the cardinal to the lofty level of statesmanship. These were the traits that permitted him to exercise so profound an influence the while he remained so simple and unpretentious. They were the faculties of mind that imprinted themselves upon the memories of everyone who knew him, for as Canon William Barry, who was the cardinal's guest in the summer of 1893, so aptly stated after close observation, "He reigned in Baltimore like a king, but he met every man like a comrade."[59] No man of ordinary gifts could possibly have had the influence on others that Cardinal Gibbons did. There was here some precious and intangible quality which prompted numerous persons, many of whom were not of his religious faith, to give expression to what he had meant to them, and it was not at all uncommon for the cardinal to receive evidences of this kind from non-Catholic strangers.[60] And once an impression of this kind was made it endured. At the time of his golden jubilee in 1918 Gibbons was reminded of the effect that his presence on board ship going to Europe had created in the spring of 1901. It came from the Reverend George Clarke Houghton, Protestant Episcopal rector of the Church of the Transfiguration in New York, and the words of the minister conveyed an insight into how the cardinal's bearing and speech had appeared to his fellow passengers. Houghton stated:

> Daily meeting you on the Steamer, outward bound for Italy, seventeen years ago, and observing the charm of your manner towards that very large and widely differing number of people of

[58] Thomas J. Shahan, "James Cardinal Gibbons. In Memoriam," *American Ecclesiastical Review,* LXIV (May, 1921), 452.

[59] William Barry, *Memories and Opinions* (London, 1926), p. 203.

[60] For example, a certain Frank Lee wanted Gibbons to know that his life had been what he called, "a blessing and a benediction to me, and countless thousands of others, not of your faith" (128-Q, Lee to Gibbons, New York, August 1, 1920).

many nationalities and beliefs, and their daily growing respect and admiration, and their attentive listening to your instructive addresses on those two Sundays, one could not fail to understand the source of your great success and influence in life and work.[61]

The memories of the Episcopalian rector after an interval of seventeen years bore eloquent testimony to the enduring quality of the impression made by the cardinal upon the strangers with whom he traveled, and it gave evidence as well of how this charm and gracious manner were turned to advantage in exerting an influence for good among those who watched and listened to him.

Eleven years after the death of Cardinal Gibbons the Knights of Columbus erected a handsome bronze statue of the great prelate in a prominent spot facing down 16th Street in Washington. On Sunday, August 14, 1932, President Herbert Hoover accepted the statue in the name of the United States as a gift from the knights. Hoover spoke of having known the cardinal well during the days of World War I, and of the high regard that he had shared with all Americans for the radiant sweetness of his spirit and the kindliness of his wisdom. His life, he said, had been a remarkable demonstration of the power of a quietly noble personality to spread its influence to those who lived far beyond the range of his physical presence. And in seeking to express the spirit and the depth of the love and influence which Cardinal Gibbons had exerted on his fellow men, the President came close to the secret of his greatness when he said:

> He loved God, and to a degree that is seldom equaled he succeeded in carrying into the minds of other people the feeling that the truths of religion are really their primary aids in solving the perplexities of every day living.[62]

It is now more than thirty years since this great soul was called to his eternal reward and the understanding and significance of his life have inevitably dimmed in human memory. Yet Cardinal Gibbons has enjoyed in death a longer remembrance

---

[61] 119-J, Houghton to Gibbons, New York, October 23, 1918.

[62] "President Hoover on Cardinal Gibbons," *The Recorder. Bulletin of the American Irish Historical Society*, V (October 15, 1932), 2. On March 23, 1930, Oliver P. Baldwin published an article in the Baltimore *Sun* entitled "Baltimore's Missing Monument," in which he called attention to the fact that nine years after his death there was still no monument in Baltimore to one whom he characterized as "the greatest man ever born" in that city.

than that accorded to most men, and as we take a parting glance at this remarkable person there rises to our lips the prayer that the Church and the Republic he loved and served so well may, in God's good time, know the mutual peace and harmony for which his life was spent, and that the radiance of his spirit may live on to enliven both with the saving grace of his profound wisdom.

An Essay on the Sources

I N ALL likelihood the general reader will not be very much interested in the sources that were used in writing the biography of Cardinal Gibbons. But for the benefit of professional students, of both American Catholic history and of American history generally, it may prove of value to indicate the main sources employed and to add some explanatory notes concerning them. Since the bibliographical details for the secondary works and periodical literature that were used as background material were supplied in the footnotes, there would seem to be little purpose in listing them again here. Instead it has been thought wise to group the sources into general categories and then to furnish such comment on the principal items in each category as may prove helpful to those who may wish to pursue further the subjects of their interest.

Manuscript Sources: The principal body of historical data for this study was contained in the unpublished correspondence of Cardinal Gibbons and his contemporaries which was found in the various diocesan and institutional archives and manuscript depositories, and which was exploited as fully as possible. Obviously the most important single manuscript collection was the Gibbons Papers which are housed in the archives of the Archdiocese of Baltimore at 408 N. Charles Street. Since the indexing and calendaring of the cardinal's papers have not yet been completed, it is impossible to say exactly how many file boxes they will ultimately fill, but before the work on the papers dating from January, 1904, to Gibbons' death in 1921 was begun, there were ninety-two file boxes and twelve bound volumes with materials of one kind or another pertaining to his life. All the correspondence from January, 1861, to January, 1904, is indexed on cards, and for the correspondence from 1877, the year in which Gibbons became Archbishop of Baltimore, to 1904 there are entries on the finding aids which amount to a calendar of the papers. Meanwhile the calendaring of the papers from 1904 to 1921 is progressing as rapidly as time will permit. The Gibbons Papers comprise all the letters of both an official and a personal character which he saved through a period of over sixty years, as well as hundreds of copies of outgoing letters after October, 1886.

The most important item among the bound volumes was the cardinal's diary which he began in September, 1868, and continued to April, 1917. In good measure it is a chronicle of his official activities and contains few items of a personal nature, but it proved invaluable in checking the accuracy of data drawn from other and less reliable sources. Among the bound volumes, too, was Gibbons' letterbook of the press-copy type in which he placed copies of out-going correspondence down to October, 1886, after which date he preserved copies of his letters in unbound form and these were integrated in chronological order with the in-coming correspondence. The cardinal was very careful about keeping copies of the letters he sent out and in the earlier years he often wrote these out in his own hand, but in his later life they were either hand-copied or typed by a secretary. Although the copies of a number of important items were missing, in general a systematic procedure was followed in this respect and the task of the present writer was, therefore, greatly simplified when he sought the letters of Gibbons elsewhere. The bound volumes also include numerous newspaper clippings of important events in the cardinal's life, bank books, memoranda on financial matters, and a copy of *The Faith of Our Fathers* with marginal notations in the author's own hand. For a general description of these archives the student may consult the writer's article, "A Guide to the Baltimore Cathedral Archives," in the *Catholic Historical Review*, XXXII (October, 1946), 341–360.

Among the other metropolitan sees of the country the archives of New York, Cincinnati, New Orleans, Boston, and St. Paul were of the greatest importance. At St. Joseph's Seminary in New York, where the archives of the archdiocese are housed, the McCloskey Papers, Corrigan Papers, Farley Papers, and Hayes Papers were all investigated and used to advantage, although the material of the greatest value in these archives was found in the extensive correspondence relating to the administrations of Archbishop Corrigan and Cardinal Farley. In Cincinnati the large body of Elder Papers in the records of the archbishop of that see at Mount Saint Mary Seminary of the West was of genuine worth, due to the close association of Gibbons and Elder over many years, and here likewise a few letters from the Moeller Papers proved useful. The fact that Gibbons' family lived in New Orleans, and that he visited that city almost annually, brought him into closer contact than would otherwise have been the case with the archbishops of that see. Consequently, in New Orleans the fairly full Janssens Papers, Chapelle Papers, and Blenk Papers at the chancery office were valuable for the Gibbons biography, and among the correspondence relating to Archbishops Perché, Leray, and Shaw some letters were found that were also of worth. In Boston the somewhat scanty Williams Papers housed in the chancery office were of principal value, although an item or two from the William O'Connell Papers was copied, and in these archives, too, there were found several Roman documents which were not available elsewhere.

The writer did not personally investigate the materials in St. Paul, but through the kindness of the Right Reverend James H. Moynihan, who was in possession of the Ireland Papers while he was writing his biography of the archbishop, and of the Reverend Patrick H. Ahern of St. Paul Seminary, he was given copies of the pertinent correspondence which was of first-rate importance due to the close friendship and collaboration of Gibbons and Ireland. The Gibbons correspondence in St. Paul was of added importance since, strangely enough, the cardinal failed to keep copies of the many letters which he addressed to the Archbishop of St. Paul. A number of other archdiocesan archives in their respective chancery offices yielded a few letters such as the Borgess Papers in Detroit, the Wigger Papers in Newark, the Riordan Papers in San Francisco, and the Bruchesi Papers in Montreal. The writer is indebted in the case of the last two named archives to the Reverend Timothy J. Casey of Serra High School, San Mateo, and the Very Reverend Robert Canon Mitchell for copies of the letters from San Francisco and Montreal respectively.

Apart from the archives of the metropolitan sees those of a number of dioceses proved very rich in their holdings, and among these the first in importance were those of the Diocese of Richmond. Not only did Richmond have numerous letters on Gibbons' time there as bishop from 1872 to 1877, but there was considerable correspondence between him and the successive Richmond ordinaries between the latter year and the time of the cardinal's death. In these archives, however, the collection of the greatest historical significance was the correspondence of Denis J. O'Connell during the years he served as the agent in Rome for a number of American bishops. It was of the highest value in throwing light on practically all aspects of the major problems of the Church in the United States between the years 1885 and 1903. Next in importance to Richmond were the archives of the Diocese of Cleveland where the Gilmour Papers were full and informative and where, too, the Horstmann Papers yielded a few letters.

At St. Bernard's Seminary in Rochester the McQuaid Papers were examined and further insight was gained into the attitudes and policies of the Bishop of Rochester toward Baltimore, especially in McQuaid's correspondence with Archbishop Corrigan and Bishop Gilmour, although there were very few letters in these archives from Gibbons and his close friends. The archives of the Diocese of Charleston proved helpful with about a dozen letters and those of the Dioceses of Covington,

Mobile, Natchez, and St. Augustine each had several items of interest. The archives of the Diocese of Rockford contained the voluminous diaries of Bishop Peter J. Muldoon which were enlightening on matters relating to the National Catholic War Council and its successor, the National Catholic Welfare Conference. In all cases except Rochester the diocesan archives mentioned above were housed in their respective chancery offices. Beyond these the writer learned either through personal visits of himself and friends, or through correspondence, that there was no Gibbons material in the archives of the Archdioceses of Chicago, Dubuque, Louisville, Milwaukee, and Philadelphia nor in those of the Dioceses of Columbus, Burlington, Peoria, Portland, Raleigh, Wheeling, and Wilmington.

Among the institutional depositories visited by the writer those of the Catholic University of America and the University of Notre Dame were the most rewarding. The main sources of information in the archives of the former were naturally found among the records of the administrations of the first three rectors, data which were especially worth while for the chapters on Gibbons' tenure of the office of Chancellor of the University. From the correspondence of former professors like Thomas Bouquillon, William J. Kerby, John M. Cooper, and Peter Guilday a considerable number of items of worth were also copied. Apart from the papers of the administrative officials and professors of the institution, in the manuscript collections which form part of the university's Department of Archives and Manuscripts, there were letters of particular pertinence on Gibbons and the Knights of Labor among the papers of Terence V. Powderly. The papers of the university's fourth rector, Thomas J. Shahan, were consulted at Holy Angels Rectory, Philadelphia, where they are at present in the possession of the Right Reverend Bernard A. McKenna who in August, 1947, was kind enough to permit the writer to examine them and to offer him his hospitality.

At Notre Dame a variety of collections was examined such as the early papers of the Archdioceses of Cincinnati and New Orleans, from which a number of letters of Gibbons to the ordinaries of those sees were copied. Here likewise the papers of leading Catholic laymen like James A. McMaster, Henry F. Brownson, and James F. Edwards all contained a few items of interest on Gibbons' career. The system of index cards for the manuscript materials at Notre Dame facilitated their use and directed the writer to stray letters of worth in other collections such as the numerous papers of Daniel E. Hudson, C.S.C., editor for many years of *Ave Maria*. Many helpful letters were also found in the collections of the American Catholic Historical Society of Philadelphia at St. Charles Borromeo Seminary where the papers of prominent priests and laymen such as Herman J. Heuser, John Gilmary Shea, and Martin I. J. Griffin included Gibbons material. In the archives of Mount Saint Mary's College, Emmitsburg, there were a good many letters pertaining to Gibbons' relations with that institution, and in a similar manner those of Woodstock College yielded a dozen or more letters which helped to illustrate the cardinal's relations with the Jesuit professors there.

One of the most important of the institutional archives for this study were those of St. Mary's Seminary at Roland Park, Baltimore. Here were found the school records of Gibbons at St. Mary's, letters and diaries of some of the Sulpicians of the 1850's which threw light on his student days there and at St. Charles College, and the papers of Joseph P. Dubruel, S.S., and Alphonse L. Magnien, S.S. The Magnien Papers were especially valuable since he was one of the cardinal's closest advisers and the Sulpician superior in the United States for a quarter of a century. In the archives of the Paulist Fathers at the Church of St. Paul the Apostle, New York, there were a good number of letters which were of great value for the chapter on Americanism in the correspondence of Fathers Augustine F. Hewit, Walter Elliott, and George Deshon. Likewise the archives of the National Catholic Welfare Conference at 1312 Massachusetts Avenue, N.W., Washington, contained valuable items from the papers of John J. Burke, C.S.P., and others which made much clearer the role of Cardinal Gibbons in the founding of the National Catholic War Council and its successor. Photostats of a half-dozen or so items from the American Jewish Archives at Cincinnati were also kindly supplied to the writer by the director, Professor Jacob R. Marcus. In the spring and summer of 1950 the writer visited Europe where he was able to secure copies of seven or eight documents relating to Gibbons in the archives of the Congregation of Propaganda Fide, and one important letter of the cardinal to Leo XIII from the Vatican Archives. Copies of thirty-one letters from Gibbons and other American prelates to Cardinal Manning were obtained from the Manning Papers at the Church of St. Mary of the Angels, Bayswater, London, as well as four or five letters of the cardinal in the general archives of the Society of St. Sulpice in Paris.

Insofar as the contacts of Cardinal Gibbons with the government of the United States were concerned, the various collections in the Division of Manuscripts of the Library of Congress were of the first importance. Here the writer found an abundance of material which supplemented the correspondence in the Baltimore archives on Gibbons' relations with the personnel of the federal government during the administrations of Presidents Benjamin Harrison, Grover Cleveland,

William McKinley, Theodore Roosevelt, William Howard Taft, and Woodrow Wilson. While the papers of the first three chief executives yielded a considerable number of worth-while letters on questions such as immigration, Indian affairs, and the Spanish American War, those of Roosevelt, Taft, and Wilson were even more rewarding on matters relating to the Philippines, World War I, and the Paris peace conference. In addition to these, the papers of Charles J. Bonaparte and William Jennings Bryan each contained pertinent material, and on diplomatic questions the writer found a number of letters in the archives of the Department of State at the National Archives which supplemented those used at the Library of Congress.

Printed Sources: Apart from the published works of the cardinal, there were certain other sources of a primary character in print which were of special value for his biography. For example, the *Acta et decreta concilii plenarii Baltimorensis tertii* (Baltimore, 1884) which was the private edition of the sessions of that council, and which embodied the discussions that took place on the major points of legislation and gave the opinions of the individual bishops, was of the utmost importance in the chapter on Gibbons and the council. In like manner the volume *Concilii plenarii Baltimorensis II . . . Acta et decreta* (Baltimore, 1868) served a similar purpose for the council of 1866 in which, of course, he played a much less important role. Moreover, the *Capita praecipua quae emi cardinales S.C. de Propaganda Fide censuerunt a rmis archiepiscopis et episcopis Foederatorum Statuum A.S. Romae congregatis praeparanda esse pro futuro concilio* (Rome, 1883), and the series of Latin documents that followed it before the opening of the council in November, 1884, were also of importance in revealing the position taken by Gibbons and his fellow bishops on specific legislative proposals. In this connection the official decrees as approved by the Holy See and contained in the *Acta et decreta concilii plenarii Baltimorensis tertii* (Baltimore, 1886), with the corresponding volume for the council of 1866, were also used. On the only synod held under Gibbons the decrees printed in *Synodus diocesana Baltimorensis nona* (Baltimore, 1905) were helpful. For the pertinent papal encyclicals and other statements of the Popes, the writer found that the volume edited by John J. Wynne, S.J., *The Great Encyclical Letters of Pope Leo XIII* (New York, 1903), and the more recent *Principles for Peace* (Washington, 1943) edited by Harry C. Koenig, were adequate for his purpose.

Two volumes of speeches and sermons by contemporaries of Gibbons were helpful for the texts of important pronouncements that had influence on the policies of the Church, especially in its relation to the State. They were John Ireland's two-volume work, *The Church and Modern Society* (St. Paul, 1905), and *Loyalty to Church and State*

(Baltimore, 1895) by Francesco Satolli, the first Apostolic Delegate to the United States. Maria Longworth Storer's edition of the correspondence of herself and her husband with President Roosevelt and Archbishop Ireland, entitled *In Memoriam. Bellamy Storer* (Boston, 1923), was also of use for the period after the Spanish American War. For problems relating to the Spanish American War, Volume II of the *Correspondence Relating to the War with Spain* (Washington, 1902) and for those of World War I, the pertinent volumes of *Papers Relating to the Foreign Relations of the United States,* furnished documentary evidence that supplemented the manuscript sources on Gibbons' activities during those two wars. Likewise the four volumes of *The Intimate Papers of Colonel House* arranged as a narrative by Charles Seymour (Boston, 1926–1928) were used. The following memoirs of churchmen supplied additional data on such questions as Americanism and the conflict of the Church and State in Mexico: the fourth volume of Félix Klein's *Souvenirs,* entitled *Une hérésie fantôme. l'Américanisme* (Paris, 1949), and Francis Clement Kelley's *The Bishop Jots It Down* (New York, 1939). Of lesser value in the very scarce memoir literature on the American Church were *Recollections of Seventy Years* (Boston, 1934) by William Cardinal O'Connell and Robert Seton's *Memories of Many Years (1839–1922)* (New York, 1923).

Finally, the writer made good use of a number of documents and pamphlets for various aspects of the more important questions in which Gibbons played a part, and in this category that of Denis J. O'Connell, *A New Idea in the Life of Father Hecker* (Freiburg im Breisgau, 1897) was of real value for the controversy over Americanism, and for the conflict over the public vs. parochial schools *The Two Sides of the School Question* (Boston, 1890), containing the statements of Gibbons, Bishop Keane, Edwin D. Mead, and John Jay at the Nashville convention of the National Education Association in July, 1889, proved serviceable. On the controversy over the rights of the state in education which took place within Catholic ranks in the 1890's, Thomas Bouquillon's *Education: To Whom Does It Belong?* (Baltimore, 1891), the reply of René I. Holaind, S.J., *The Parent First* (New York, 1891), and the extensive answer to Bouquillon published in the *Civiltà Cattolica* of January 2, 1892, and reprinted in an English translation under the title, *Education: To Whom Does It Belong? A Review* (New York, 1892) by Salvatore M. Brandi, S.J., were of importance as key documents in a controversy in which Cardinal Gibbons took an active part.

Works by Gibbons: Much information about Cardinal Gibbons was acquired, to be sure, from his own writings. Sufficient has previously been said about his books and articles to give the reader an understanding of the chief characteristics of Gibbons' written works. His five books were all published by the John Murphy Company of Baltimore and two of them, *The Faith of Our Fathers* (1876) and *The Ambassador of Christ* (1896), were of special value in revealing the man's mentality in the approach he used to win converts to the Church and the ideals he conceived for the American priesthood. *Our Christian Heritage* (1889) showed among other things Gibbons' breadth of reading in profane history and the sacred sciences, and in this volume he reprinted several articles which he had previously published in the *American Catholic Quarterly Review* as concluding chapters to the book. His other two works, *Discourses and Sermons* (1908) and *A Retrospect of Fifty Years* (1916) — the latter in two volumes — embodied either sermons which he had preached many times over the years, or articles which he had published sometime before in journals like the *Irish Ecclesiastical Record*, the *Catholic World*, and the *North American Review*. Here, too, something of the cardinal was shown to the biographer in the selection of subjects which he chose, and in the ideas that he thought worthy of emphasis. Among the fairly numerous articles which he published in different periodicals over a long span of years only a few were autobiographical in character. In this respect the following proved enlightening on certain aspects of his career: "Reminiscences of North Carolina," in the *United States Catholic Historical Magazine*, III (1889–1890), 337–352; "Personal Reminiscences of the Vatican Council," in the *North American Review*, CLVIII (April, 1894), 385–400; and "My Memories," in the *Dublin Review*, CLX (April, 1917), 163–172.

Works About Gibbons: In 1890 there began to appear at irregular intervals down to 1905 a series of very large and unwieldy volumes edited by John T. Reily, a small-town journalist and self-made historian, who had a great admiration for Gibbons. These volumes — now very rare — numbered ten in all and bore various titles of which the most frequent was *Collections in the Life and Times of Cardinal Gibbons*. They contained thousands of pages of privately printed and loosely edited speeches, sermons, reprints from the press, and personal accounts of outstanding episodes in Gibbons' life. The works of Reily were valuable for supplementing other sources and for yielding stray items which could not be found elsewhere. If the editing of these volumes betrayed a lack of professional skill, the thoroughness with which Reily chronicled everything he could find on the cardinal was a tribute to his industry and to his personal devotion to Gibbons and his associates. The principal facts on the life of this private publicist can be found in the brief essay of Raymond J. Teller, "The Conewago Historian: John T. Reily (1856-1924)," in the *Records of the Ameri-*

can Catholic Historical Society of Philadelphia, LXII (June, 1951), 124–132.

During the lifetime of the Cardinal of Baltimore there was published only one biography properly so called, namely, *The Life of James Cardinal Gibbons* by Allen Sinclair Will, which was brought out in 1911 by the John Murphy Company in commemoration of the cardinal's golden jubilee as a priest and his silver jubilee as a cardinal. At the time Mr. Will was city editor of the Baltimore *Sun* and he had the advantage of frequent and lengthy chats with Gibbons, so that the details of the latter's early days which were chronicled by Will enjoyed a special authenticity. The book was popular and eulogistic in tone and made no pretensions to scholarship. Will had a very deep and sincere admiration for the cardinal, and in the final days of the latter's life he secured his permission to expand the work of 1911 into a more pretentious biography. He worked steadily at the task and in November, 1922, there appeared from the press of E. P. Dutton & Company the two large volumes which he called *Life of Cardinal Gibbons, Archbishop of Baltimore.* The author had meanwhile transferred to New York where he had joined the faculty of the Pulitzer School of Journalism at Columbia University, and where he likewise wrote for the New York *Times.* Mr. Will was not a Catholic, but he carefully guarded himself against any slips which might arise from his lack of acquaintance with the Church, by submitting his manuscript to Bishop Shahan, Rector of the Catholic University of America, who had known the cardinal intimately in his later years. Immediately after Gibbons' death Will prepared articles on him for the New York *Times* and the *North American Review,* and in sending on the first of these for Shahan's scrutiny he told him that he was acting in conformity with his intention to submit to the bishop, as he said, "from this time forth, everything I write for publication about our beloved friend Cardinal Gibbons. . . ."[1] Shahan, therefore, served Will in the role of a critical reader, and the late Monsignor Peter Guilday told the present writer that he had been commissioned as one familiar with the archives in Baltimore to select documents for Will's use. The latter produced an able popular biography of Gibbons which, considering the facts that he was a professional journalist and not a trained historian, that he was not of the Catholic faith, and that the work was published less than two years after Gibbons' death, was an achievement of a high order. The Will work in two volumes laid strong emphasis on the public career of the cardinal with proportionately more space devoted to his role as an American citizen than as a Catholic churchman, al-

---

[1] Shahan Papers, Will to Shahan, New York, March 28, 1921; *ibid.,* same to same, New York, April 12, 1921.

though the latter was by no means neglected. Since the author did not have access to all the documents in the archives of the Archdiocese of Baltimore and did not use materials from other archives, the biography could not, of course, be called definitive. But apart from the question of sources, the year 1922 was much too early to expect a work of this kind from any writer, and all things considered Mr. Will executed his task with a high degree of competence with the result that during the past thirty years his biography admirably served both popular readers and serious students who wished to learn something about the Cardinal of Baltimore.

Between the time of the first and second biographies by Will a popular and illustrated work was edited by Monsignor Cornelius F. Thomas, editor of the Baltimore *Catholic Review,* entitled *The Life Story of His Eminence James Cardinal Gibbons together with an Historical Sketch of the Province of Baltimore* (Baltimore, 1917). This work of eighty-nine large pages was purely popular in character and added nothing new on Gibbons to the Will biography of 1911, although some of the data on the archdiocese and its suffragan sees were not assembled in any other book.

Less than five months after Gibbons died his secretary, Father Albert E. Smith, and Mr. Vincent dePaul Fitzpatrick of the staff of the Baltimore *Catholic Review,* completed a small volume which they entitled *Cardinal Gibbons, Churchman and Citizen.* In the foreword to the book, signed on August 15, 1921, the authors disclaimed any idea of writing a complete biography, but they rightly judged that what they had written would be of value to those who were interested in the late cardinal. The special contribution made by the Smith-Fitzpatrick work was the incorporation of numerous and intimate details about Gibbons' personal life, the relating of many anecdotes which illustrated his varied characteristics, and the authenticated data which the authors furnished for the use of future biographers through their long and close acquaintance with the subject. Despite the simplicity and lack of pretension of this book, no student of the life of Cardinal Gibbons can afford to overlook the intimate pen pictures of the man which it contains. Seven years ago there appeared a small and fictionalized work entitled *Larger Than the Sky. A Story of James Cardinal Gibbons* (New York, 1945) by Covelle Newcomb. Although it contained a number of factual errors and introduced imaginary conversations into the narrative, the book of Miss Newcomb was successful in catching the spirit of Gibbons and she told his story in an interesting way. Beyond these no attempts at a biography of the cardinal were made, although special events in his life occasioned several brochures and pamphlets such as the *History of the Great National Demonstration Held in Balti-*

more June the sixth, 1911 in Honor of Cardinal Gibbons (Baltimore, 1911), and these were of assistance in describing particular episodes.

Interviews: At the outset of his efforts to gather information on Cardinal Gibbons in July, 1945, the writer availed himself of the opportunity to talk with as many persons as he could contact who had known the cardinal well. Among them the most enlightening was the Right Reverend Louis R. Stickney, pastor of the Shrine of the Sacred Heart, Baltimore, who from 1908 to 1921 lived with Gibbons and served him as secretary, chancellor, and finally as rector of the cathedral. In two or three lengthy interviews Monsignor Stickney shed a great deal of light on aspects of the cardinal's career which the writer could learn from no other source. While he had the deepest admiration and affection for Gibbons, he showed an objective and realistic approach on various questions that was of immense benefit to the writer. The Right Reverend Louis O'Donovan, late pastor of St. Martin's Church, Baltimore, who was one of Gibbons' secretaries from 1909 to 1919, also furnished a few details which were not previously known. In this connection the writer is likewise indebted to the Most Reverend John M. McNamara, Auxiliary Bishop of Washington, who served as a priest of the archdiocese for nineteen years of Gibbons' administration, and who met him frequently on the cardinal's many visits to St. Patrick's Church in Washington. Bishop McNamara was extremely interested in all that pertained to the biography, and the writer obtained from him a deeper and clearer knowledge of certain characteristics of the cardinal which were conveyed in many conversations about him. Among the laity the writer interviewed six or seven members of the Shriver family with whom Gibbons was so friendly and among whom he spent many of his holidays. From the Shrivers, as well as from his portrait artist, Miss Marie deFord Keller of Baltimore, many sidelights on Gibbons' personal life were gleaned. The same can be said for the interviews which the writer had in January, 1948, in New Orleans with the cardinal's two nieces, Mrs. Mary Swarbrick Stanton and Mrs. Margaret Gibbons Start. Besides those mentioned, he received a number of helpful impressions from other members of the clergy and laity who had known Gibbons and who were kind enough to vouchsafe anecdotes and stories that helped to illumine his character.

The Press: Despite the abundance of manuscript materials and the richness of printed data in books, periodicals, and pamphlets on or by Cardinal Gibbons, there was often no source that would yield certain facts except the secular and Catholic newspapers. Among the secular papers for Gibbons' residence in North Carolina the Wilmington *Journal* was found most useful, while the files of the Richmond *Daily Dispatch* served a similar purpose for his five years as Bishop of Richmond.

After Gibbons' promotion to Baltimore in 1877, the best newspaper coverage on his activities was that of the Baltimore *Sun,* a paper to which he became deeply attached and with which he enjoyed the most cordial relations. On the cardinal's national and international activities the New York *Herald* was probably the best outside his see city, with the New York *Times, Sun,* and *World* offering good supplementary material on occasion. Whenever important missions took Gibbons into distant cities the local press was examined, and in this respect papers like the New Orleans *Times-Picayune* and later *Daily Picayune,* the Philadelphia *Public Ledger,* and the Chicago *Tribune* were of assistance. Virtually all the secular papers used in the biography were consulted in the files of the Newspaper Reference Room of the Library of Congress.

The main source of information in the Catholic press was naturally the *Catholic Mirror* of Baltimore which began publication in 1850 and lasted down to 1908, and for the period from 1913 to 1921 the Baltimore *Catholic Review* served a like purpose. In these two weekly papers the writer found numerous items which were not available elsewhere, and to a lesser degree the *Church News* and later the *New Century,* Catholic weeklies published in Washington, were examined with profit. Outside the Archdiocese of Baltimore many helpful news articles and editorials were copied from other Catholic weeklies, among which the New York *Freeman's Journal* was the most important with the Boston *Pilot* probably ranking second. Full or partial files of the weeklies published within the Archdiocese of Baltimore were used in the archives at 408 N. Charles Street and in the libraries of the Catholic University of America and of St. Mary's Seminary, Roland Park. For issues of Catholic newspapers not available in Baltimore or Washington, the writer employed the extensive newspaper collection of the American Catholic Historical Society of Philadelphia at St. Charles Borromeo Seminary. For foreign press items on Gibbons the *Tablet* of London, a Catholic weekly, was the most useful paper, and for American Protestant opinion the *Independent* of New York was found to be the best.

Secondary Works: For the period of Gibbons' boyhood in Ireland the writer found William Forbes Adams, *Ireland and Irish Emigration to the New World from 1815 to the Famine* (New Haven, 1932) of worth for the political, social, and economic conditions of the country at that time, while Bernard O'Reilly's two-volume biography, *John MacHale, Archbishop of Tuam* (New York, 1890), and Edward A. D'Alton's booklet, *A Short History of Ballinrobe Parish* (Dublin, 1931), were adequate for a description of ecclesiastical affairs in County Mayo during Gibbons' residence there. For the history of the Church in Louisiana after the Gibbons family removed to New Orleans in 1853 and through the rest of the cardinal's lifetime, the volume by Roger Baudier, *The Catholic Church in Louisiana* (New Orleans, 1939), provided a handy compendium of factual data if it was somewhat weak on interpretation. But aside from Gibbons' own works, there was little on the Church in North Carolina and Virginia to serve as general background for the years 1868 to 1877 which he spent in those states. The only items available for North Carolina were the very old and not too reliable volume of Jeremiah J. O'Connell, O.S.B., *Catholicity in the Carolinas and Georgia, 1820–1878* (New York, 1879), and the popular souvenir booklet, *St. Thomas the Apostle Catholic Church, 1847–1947, Wilmington, N. C.* (Wilmington, 1947). For Virginia Catholicism in Gibbons' time there was nothing of any value.

In the absence of a history of the Archdiocese of Baltimore, the writer was compelled to rely on a number of special studies, of which some were of only slight value by reason of the fact that they were purely popular in nature and, in some cases, not always accurate. In this category there might be listed Michael J. Riordan's *Cathedral Records from the Beginning of Catholicism in Baltimore to the Present Time* (Baltimore, 1906); the two-volume work of Thomas J. Stanton, *A Century of Growth. The History of the Church in Western Maryland* (Baltimore, 1900); Owen B. Corrigan's *The Catholic Schools of the Archdiocese of Baltimore. A Study in Diocesan History* (Baltimore, 1924); and Mary M. Meline and Edward F. X. McSweeny's two volumes on Mount Saint Mary's College called *The Story of the Mountain* (Emmitsburg, 1911). The old but generally reliable commemorative works, *Memorial Volume of the Centenary of St. Mary's Seminary of St. Sulpice* (Baltimore, 1891) and John Gilmary Shea's *Memorial of the First Centenary of Georgetown College, D. C., Comprising a History of Georgetown University* (Washington, 1891), were also of use. Among the parish histories that of Helene, Estelle, and Imogene Philibert, *Saint Matthew's of Washington, 1840–1940* (Baltimore, 1940), was easily the best and reference was likewise made to the *Souvenir Book. Sesquicentennial. Saint Patrick's Parish* (Baltimore, 1942) for Gibbons' brief stay there as a priest. For the religious communities in the archdiocese and the cardinal's relations to them, the following were found of value: Charles G. Herbermann, *The Sulpicians in the United States* (New York, 1916); James M. Hayes, *The Bon Secours Sisters in the United States* (Washington, 1931); John F. Byrne, C.Ss.R., *The Redemptorist Centenaries* (Philadelphia, 1932); and *The College of Notre Dame of Maryland, 1895–1945* (New York, 1947) by Sister Mary David Cameron, S.S.N.D. One of the few monographs of any scientific value for the Church in this region was Leo J. McCormick's *Church-State Relationships in Education in Maryland* (Washington, 1942).

For the history of the Catholic Church of the United States generally during the period of Gibbons' life there was no extensive work available, since the narrative of the old four-volume *History of the Catholic Church in the United States* by John Gilmary Shea (New York, 1886–1892) ended with 1866. Information, therefore, had to be sought out in various diocesan histories, ecclesiastical biographies, and monographs. Among the diocesan histories, besides the volume of Baudier cited above, three were of real value, namely, John H. Lamott, *History of the Archdiocese of Cincinnati, 1821–1921* (New York, 1921); John Rothensteiner's two-volume *History of the Archdiocese of St. Louis* (St. Louis, 1928); and the best history of any American diocese, namely, the three large and scholarly volumes of Robert H. Lord, John E. Sexton, and Edward T. Harrington entitled *History of the Archdiocese of Boston* (New York, 1944). Among the biographies of Gibbons' contemporaries the most notable were the informative three-volume work of Frederick J. Zwierlein, *Life and Letters of Bishop McQuaid* (Rochester, 1925–1927) and Sister M. Hildegarde Yeager, C.S.C., *Life of James Roosevelt Bayley, First Bishop of Newark and Eighth Archbishop of Baltimore, 1814–1877* (Washington, 1947). To a lesser extent the following proved useful: John L. Spalding's biography of his uncle, *The Life of the Most Rev. M. J. Spalding* (New York, 1873); John Cardinal Farley, *Life of John Cardinal McCloskey* (New York, 1918); Walter Elliott, C.S.P., *Life of Father Hecker* (New York, 1891); and Stephen Bell's popular *Rebel, Priest and Prophet, A Biography of Dr. Edward McGlynn* (New York, 1937). Among the foreign churchmen whose lives touched that of Gibbons the following biographies were used to advantage for his European connections: Edmund S. Purcell, *Life of Cardinal Manning, Archbishop of Westminster* (New York, 1896), two volumes; Shane Leslie, *Henry Edward Manning, His Life and Labours* (London, 1921); J. G. Snead-Cox, *The Life of Cardinal Vaughan* (London, 1910), two volumes; Ernest Oldmeadow, *Francis Cardinal Bourne* (London, 1940); and to a lesser extent the two volumes of Wilfrid Ward, *The Life of John Henry Cardinal Newman* (New York, 1912); and Patrick J. Walsh's *William J. Walsh, Archbishop of Dublin* (Dublin, 1928). Likewise helpful for the Church in Europe in the late nineteenth century were the two volumes of Eduardo Soderini translated from the Italian and entitled *The Pontificate of Leo XIII* (London, 1934) and *Leo XIII, Italy and France* (London, 1935).

More important than the diocesan histories and ecclesiastical biographies, however, were the scientific monographs and serious histories of particular movements or events. In this category the following were especially helpful: Henry J. Browne, *The Catholic Church and the Knights of Labor* (Washington, 1949); Fergus Macdonald, C.P., *The Catholic Church and the Secret Societies in the United States* (New York, 1946); and Daniel F. Reilly, O.P., *The School Controversy (1891–1893)* (Washington, 1943). For the university over which Gibbons presided as chancellor from 1889 to 1921 the writer's work, *The Formative Years of the Catholic University of America* (Washington, 1946) was used, as well as the three successive volumes in the series, namely, Patrick H. Ahern, *The Catholic University of America. The Rectorship of John J. Keane, 1887–1896* (Washington, 1948); Peter E. Hogan, S.S.J., *The Catholic University of America. The Rectorship of Thomas J. Conaty, 1896–1903* (Washington, 1949); and Colman J. Barry, O.S.B., *The Catholic University of America. The Rectorship of Denis J. O'Connell, 1903–1909* (Washington, 1950). On the subject of the anti-Catholic movements during Gibbons' mature life, Gustavus Myers, *History of Bigotry in the United States* (New York, 1943) was helpful for the A.P.A., and for the earlier manifestations of this kind W. Darrell Overdyke, *The Know-Nothing Party in the South* (Baton Rouge, 1950); Lawrence F. Schmeckebier, *History of the Know Nothing Party in Maryland* (Baltimore, 1899); and Sister Mary St. Patrick McConville, *Political Nativism in the State of Maryland* (Washington, 1928) were useful. For the background to the conciliar legislation of the American Church the volume of Peter Guilday, *A History of the Councils of Baltimore, 1791–1884* (New York, 1932), was of real assistance and the two volumes of Cuthbert Butler, O.S.B., *The Vatican Council* (New York, 1930) served in a similar way for the ecumenical council that Gibbons attended at Rome in 1869–1870. On problems related to immigration and Catholic population growth the best work is still that of Gerald Shaughnessy, S.M., *Has the Immigrant Kept the Faith?* (New York, 1925). In the absence of a definitive history of the National Catholic Welfare Conference and its forerunner, the popular book of Michael Williams, *American Catholics in the War* (New York, 1921), served a useful purpose in giving the main outlines of the organization of the National Catholic War Council and its activities. For Gibbons' relations to the institutions of the American Church abroad, reference was made to J. Van der Heyden, *The Louvain American College, 1857–1907* (Louvain, 1909) and Harry A. Brann's *History of the American College . . . Rome* (New York, 1910), neither of which, however was a work of a scholarly character. For purposes of identification of ecclesiastical personnel and similar facts, the writer had constant reference to the successive volumes of the

Catholic Directory for the United States and to the *Annuario Pontificio* for the Universal Church.

Since there were no recent scholarly histories of the States of Louisiana, North Carolina, Virginia, and Maryland, nor of the cities of New Orleans, Wilmington, North Carolina, Richmond, and Baltimore wherein the cardinal lived at various periods of his life following his return from Ireland in 1853, the writer was compelled to rely on such information as he could find in the older and more popular volumes on these places, the respective city directories, several scholarly monographs, and the publications of the state historical societies. For New Orleans and Louisiana in the 1850's, aside from the works of Baudier and Overdyke mentioned previously, several articles in the *Louisiana Historical Quarterly* supplied useful information on Louisiana politics during the 1850's, and here, too, the observations of foreign visitors helped to supplement the data on social conditions in New Orleans in those days. For the years 1868–1872 that Gibbons spent in North Carolina the writer's needs were excellently served by the definitive monograph of J. G. de Roulhac Hamilton, *Reconstruction in North Carolina* (New York, 1914). The five-volume work of Archibald Henderson, *North Carolina. The Old State and the New* (Chicago, 1941), likewise provided some facts, and one or two articles in the *North Carolina Historical Review* were of further use. Insofar as Virginia and Richmond were concerned for the five years, 1872–1877, that Gibbons served there as a bishop, the writer relied mainly on Richard L. Morton's *Virginia Since 1861* (Chicago, 1924), Matthew Page Andrews' *Virginia. The Old Dominion* (New York, 1937), and W. Asbury Christian's *Richmond. Her Past and Present* (Richmond, 1912).

In the case of Maryland and Baltimore, the scene of most of Gibbons' active life, again the lack of any scholarly and up-to-date histories of the state and city was felt. However, on the state William Starr Myers, *The Self-Reconstruction of Maryland, 1864–1867* (Baltimore, 1909) was helpful for the period of the cardinal's early priesthood, and for the city the old volume of J. Thomas Scharf, *The Chronicles of Baltimore* (Baltimore, 1874), afforded a handy reference for tracking down particular facts. The three volumes edited by Clayton Colman Hall and entitled *Baltimore. Its History and Its People* (New York, 1912) and the more recent and popular *Baltimore on the Chesapeake* by Hamilton Owens (Garden City, 1941) here and there supplied additional sidelights on the history of the city. But the best work in this respect was the scholarly monograph of Charles Hirschfeld, *Baltimore, 1870–1900: Studies in Social History* (Baltimore, 1941), which was excellent on subjects such as social reform and labor conditions in the city; and for data on population growth and other aspects of social conditions, the writer found William Travis Howard, Jr.'s volume, *Public Health Administration and the Natural History of Disease in Baltimore, Maryland, 1797–1920* (Washington, 1924) useful. On Maryland and Baltimore, particularly in the 1850's and through the era of the Civil War and Reconstruction, the *Maryland Historical Magazine* carried seven or eight articles that were read with real profit.

For the general social history of the United States during the lifetime of the cardinal the writer frequently consulted the pertinent volumes of the History of American Life series and here Allan Nevins' *The Emergence of Modern America, 1865–1878* (New York, 1927) and Arthur M. Schlesinger's *The Rise of the City, 1878–1898* (New York, 1933) were especially valuable. On the intellectual trends during Gibbons' earlier life, Ralph Henry Gabriel's *The Course of American Democratic Thought. An Intellectual History Since 1815* (New York, 1940) served a purpose that was fulfilled for the cardinal's later years by Henry Steele Commager's *The American Mind. An Interpretation of American Thought and Character Since the 1880's* (New Haven, 1950). For the lives of statesmen with whom Gibbons had fairly frequent contacts, reference was made to biographies such as Eric F. Goldman's *Charles J. Bonaparte. Patrician Reformer. His Earlier Career* (Baltimore, 1943) which was especially helpful, and to Allan Nevins, *Grover Cleveland. A Study in Courage* (New York, 1932) and the two works of Henry F. Pringle, *Theodore Roosevelt. A Biography* (New York, 1931) and *The Life and Times of William Howard Taft* (New York, 1939), the latter in two volumes. Pertinent material was also found in the eight-volume work of Ray Stannard Baker, *Woodrow Wilson. Life and Letters* (Garden City, 1927–1939). As background for the diplomatic questions in which Gibbons was involved Thomas A. Bailey, *A Diplomatic History of the American People,* second edition (New York, 1942), answered the purpose, and occasionally special studies in diplomacy were consulted such as Charles Callan Tansill's *The Foreign Policy of Thomas F. Bayard, 1885–1897* (New York, 1940). On the general history of immigration into the United States, the volume *We Who Built America. The Saga of the Immigrant* (New York, 1939) by Carl Wittke was very good, and for developments in the American press Frank Luther Mott's *American Journalism. A History of Newspapers in the United States through 250 Years, 1690 to 1940* (New York, 1941) was enlightening on the secular press, but contained practically nothing on the Catholic press. In this connection the slender volume of Apollinaris W. Baumgartner, *Catholic Journalism. A Study of Its Development in the United States, 1789–*

1930 (New York, 1931), is not an adequate history of the American Catholic press and the subject still awaits a definitive treatment.

A final source of information among published narratives which yielded some interesting insights into contemporary religious, social, and economic conditions were the accounts of foreign visitors. In this category the writer sought out the views of a number of the better known travelers through the United States, insofar as they related to Baltimore, New Orleans, Richmond, and the South generally. Here he found material in James Stuart's two volumes, *Three Years in North America* (Edinburgh, 1833); Edward S. Aby's three volumes called *Journal of a Residence and Tour in the United States of America* (London, 1835); Charles Dickens, *American Notes* (London, 1842); Alexander Mackay's three volumes, *The Western World* (London, 1850); Thomas Colley Grattan, *Civilized America* (London, 1859) in two volumes; William H. Russell, *My Diary North and South* (Boston, 1863); Anthony Trollope, *North America* (London, 1868); George Augustus Sala, *America Revisited* (London, 1882) in two volumes; and for Gibbons' last days *What I Saw in America* (New York, 1922) by G. K. Chesterton.

Periodical Literature: The writer has already mentioned the use that was made of the state historical journals of Louisiana, North Carolina, and Maryland. Among the Catholic journals the *American Ecclesiastical Review* (Philadelphia) carried a number of articles that were very useful for the theological questions and movements that arose during the cardinal's lifetime, and in this regard the *Catholic World* (New York) was also of prime importance. The *American Catholic Quarterly Review* of Philadelphia was used frequently, although ordinarily this journal did not give as much free rein to its contributors on controversial issues as the two mentioned above. In the early years after its inauguration in 1895 the *Catholic University Bulletin* was a scholarly journal which was primarily important in that period for reflecting the intellectual trends and tastes of the faculty over which Gibbons presided as chancellor. But later it became more popular, and in these years its chronicle of events in university life was useful for data on the cardinal's participation in the activities of the institution. Another periodical from which several articles were drawn was the *Records of the American Catholic Historical Society of Philadelphia*. Here such items as "The Organization of the Catholic Total Abstinence Union of America, 1866–1884," by James J. Green (LXI [June, 1950], 71–97) and the writer's article, "Cardinal Gibbons and Philadelphia" (LVIII [March, 1947], 87–102) were of assistance. The annual volumes of the *Historical Records and Studies* of the United States Catholic Historical Society of New York contained an article or two of worth for the Gibbons biography, and there the principal one was "The 'Italian Problem' in the Catholic Church of the United States, 1880–1900," by Henry J. Browne (XXXV [1946], 46–72). Likewise the *Review of Politics* of recent years has featured a number of articles on American Catholic history that were found of value on the Church in Gibbons' time, and in this sense the following by Thomas T. McAvoy, C.S.C., are worthy of mention: "The Catholic Church in the United States between Two Wars" (IV [October, 1942], 409–431); "Americanism and Frontier Catholicism" (V [July, 1943], 275–301); "The Formation of the Catholic Minority in the United States, 1820–1860" (X [January, 1948], 13–34); and "Bishop John Lancaster Spalding and the Catholic Minority, 1877–1908" (XII [January, 1950], 3–19). Likewise in the *Review of Politics* the article of Aaron I. Abell, entitled "The Reception of Leo XIII's Labor Encyclical in America, 1891–1919" (VII [October, 1945], 464–495), presented some interesting views, as also a few interpretations with which the present writer would not altogether agree.

Among the Catholic journals devoted to history in whole or in part, however, the most important contributions for the biography of Gibbons were found in the *Catholic Historical Review,* where of recent years there has appeared an increasing number of scholarly articles on phases of American Catholicism since the 1880's that were of the greatest assistance. For example, the two articles in the issue of July, 1945, by Thomas T. McAvoy, C.S.C., "Americanism, Fact and Fiction" (XXXI, 133–153), and Vincent F. Holden, C.S.P., "A Myth in 'l'Américanisme'" (XXXI, 154–170), were excellent for the chapter dealing with the cardinal's part in that movement. Similarly the two articles of John J. Meng entitled "Cahenslyism: The First Stage, 1883–1891" (XXXI [January, 1946], 389–413) and "Cahenslyism: The Second Chapter, 1891–1910" (XXXII [October, 1946], 302–340) represented the first effort made in many years to deal in a dispassionate manner with that once heated conflict. Again, the articles of John T. Farrell on "Archbishop Ireland and Manifest Destiny" (XXXIII [October, 1947], 269–301); "Background of the 1902 Taft Mission to Rome" (XXXVI [April, 1950], 1–32) and a second installment of the same title (XXXVII [April, 1951], 1–22) were of aid in setting out the background to the Church's participation in the diplomacy of the period of the Spanish American War. Two other articles from this journal that merit mention were Francis P. Cassidy, "Catholic Education in the Third Plenary Council of Baltimore" (XXXIV [October, 1948], 257–305; [January, 1949], 414–436) and "Peter E. Dietz Pioneer Planner of Catholic Social Action" by Henry J. Browne (XXXIII [January, 1948], 448–456).

Index*

---

* The names of churches, schools, institutions, newspapers, etc., are entered under the place name rather than the proper name, with cross reference from proper name.

Priesthood and Episcopacy
Relationships with Vatican
School Controversy (Faribault-Still-
water Case)
Secret Societies
Third Plenary Council
World War, National Catholic War
Council, and Post War Problems
Apostolic Delegation
Apostolic delegation for U. S., I:
600–602, 610, 614–615, 630–635,
650–651; on apostolic delegate to
Mexico, II: 217; conferred red
biretta on Satolli, I: 650; effort at
reconciliation between Corrigan and
Satolli, I: 642–645
Bishop of Richmond
Appointed administrator of See of
Richmond, I: 110–111; appointed
Bishop of Richmond, I: 115, 117,
120; farewell dinner in Richmond,
I: 161; receives pallium, I: 173–
174
Cardinalate
Addresses at red hat ceremony, I:
302; false report on cardinalate, I:
297–299; felicitations on cardinalate from Catholic sovereigns, I:
294–296, 304; notification letter and
red zucchetto presented, I: 301–
304; possibility of cardinalate seen,
I: 291–293; Rome trip for cardinal's hat, I: 305, 314–315, 505;
separation of Washington from
Archdiocese of Baltimore, II:
486–489
Catholic University of America
Annual collection, II: 145, 155;
appeal to hierarchy for more students, II: 185; chairman, university
committee, I: 393; cornerstone
blessing, I: 410; donations, 1919,
II: 201, 202; financial support, II:
158; on intercollegiate athletics for,
II: 164–165; Keane's dismissal, II:
40–42; Knights of Columbus gift,
II: 147–148, 157, 165; lay students,
II: 163–164; letter to Leo XIII
on, I: 405; O'Connell in controversy at, II: 182–183, 186–190; reaction to university's financial crisis,
II: 152–153; request for priests
at, I: 411; Schroeder case, II: 54;
Shahan as rector, II: 191, 192;
silver jubilee Mass for, II: 196;
support of university urged by
Leo XIII, I: 474; Third Plenary
Council schema, I: 401; university
chancellor, I: 395, 422–438; university letter, 1918, II: 199

Childhood and Early Life
Baptism sponsors, I: 3; birth, I:
3, 11; early schooling, I: 14, 16–17;
employment as clerk, I: 26–27;
enjoyment of athletics, I: 35; first
rank in class, I: 41; honor awards
in college, I: 36–37; interest in
religion, I: 26, 28; love for serious
reading, I: 38–39; love of sports,
I: 15; love of study, I: 15; parents, I: 3; record in seminary, I:
41–42; see also Personality and
Physical Characteristics
Civic and Political Interests
Constitution
Centennial celebration of U. S.
Constitution, I: 317–318, 573;
Maryland constitution amendment,
II: 400; on prohibition, II: 535–
539; on woman suffrage, II:
539–543
Dedicatory Exercises and Exhibits
As citizen, II: 500–563; benediction
given at Chicago fair, 1893, II:
17; Castle Garden fair, I: 586;
civic celebration for golden jubilee,
1911, II: 547–553; Columbian
Exposition buildings, dedication
prayer, II: 16; Constitutional Cen-
tennial, I: 317–322; dedication of
Continental Hall, II: 509; interest
in civic enterprises, II: 489–492;
Maryland religious toleration monument, II: 490; on Confederacy
and Union, I: 46; patriotism, II:
82; prayer for public authorities,
II: 5; Vatican exhibit at Columbian
Exposition, I: 621–622; visits White
House, I: 285–286; World's Con-
gress Auxiliary, II: 13; World's
Parliament of Religions, II: 17,
18, 20–21
Miscellaneous
On educational problems, II: 543–
545; Keiley for diplomatic assign-
ment, I: 286; on Louisiana lottery,
II: 528–529; political affiliations,
II: 523–524; Salvation Army, bene-
ficiary of, 532–533; Union Pacific
insurance system, I: 538
Internationalism
Africa
Congo Free State case, II: 315–319
Armenia
Aid offered to Armenians, II: 313
Europe
On Belgian proposal regarding Ar-
ticle 15, II: 276; interview with
Reading regarding Treaty of Lon-
don, II: 270–271; member, Inter-

Miller, Joseph Maxwell, bust of Gibbons executed, II: 195n, 623n

Mill Hill Fathers, established in Baltimore, I: 143; settlement in Richmond, I: 144; work with Negroes, I: 178, 566; II: 467–468; see also Josephites

Mill Hill Fathers Seminary, see England. Mill Hill Fathers Seminary

Mill Hill Sisters, settlement in Richmond, I: 144

Mills, Beatrice, Gibbons' attitude on mixed marriages, II: 467

Milner, John, End of Controversy, I: 85

Milwaukee Catholic Citizen, Ireland's summons to Rome, I: 661; Testem benevolentiae, II: 70

Milwaukee Columbia, attack on Ireland, I: 663

Milwaukee Daily Journal, story on Milwaukee sermon by Gibbons, I: 376–377

Milwaukee. St. John's Cathedral, pallium conferred on Katzer, I: 375; St. Francis Seminary, silver jubilee sermon, noted, I: 391; terna for Milwaukee, I: 338n

Milwaukee Sentinel, Heiss interview, cited, I: 361

Mirror, see Baltimore Mirror

Missionaries, in the Congo, II: 317

Missions, see Society for the Propagation of the Faith

Missions, Indian, see Bureau of Catholic Indian Missions

Missions, Negro, interest of Gibbons' London visit, 1887, I: 566

Mitis, Dr. Oskar, Gibbons' aid for access to Vienna archives, II: 611

Modernism, climax reached, II: 169–170; origin, II: 170

Modern Woodmen of America, archbishops disapprove condemnation, I: 479–480; decision on membership sought, I: 478; denunciation by Holy See, I: 479, 481; favorable judgment of archbishops, I: 480

Moeller, Henry, Archbishop, Catholic University of America fund, II: 156; federal aid to public schools, II: 543; Mexican constitution, protest, II: 219; on New York terna list, I: 264

Moes, Rev. Nicholas A., theologian for Third Plenary Council, I: 223

Mohr, Charles H., O.S.B., Gibbons' ecclesiastical jubilee celebration, II: 556n

Molly Maguires, riots in coal regions,

I: 487–488; suspected as secret society, I: 441

Monaco, Raffaele, Cardinal, secret societies, I: 465, 474

Monaghan, John J., Bishop, consecrated by Gibbons, 1897, II: 442; funeral Mass of Gibbons, II: 632; on Wheeling terna, II: 442n

Monasticism and religious orders, Philippine feeling against, II: 101

Moniteur de Rome, aid to American hierarchy regarding Roman Curia, I: 580; Bouquillon articles, I: 703; George articles suppressed by O'Connell, I: 590; Gibbons' pastoral on loss of Propaganda's properties, I: 270 Gibbons' trip to Portland, report, I: 329; Knights of Labor memorial, I: 515–516

Monitor, see San Francisco Monitor

Monk, John C., M.D., converted, I: 107–108; death, I: 109

Monroe Doctrine, interpretation by U. S. and Great Britain, II: 83

Montgomery, George T., Bishop, appointed coadjutor of San Francisco, II: 188n

Monticone, Giuseppe, Monsignor, archivist of Propaganda, I: 280n

Montreal. St. James Cathedral, pontifical Mass of Congress, II: 323

Monumental City, see Baltimore, Monumental City

Mooney, Joseph F., Monsignor, Catholic University of America terna, I: 430; cited regarding war-camp activities, II: 256

Moore, John, Bishop, Abbelen case, I: 350; American College burses, I: 189; Bishop of St. Augustine, I: 145, 156, 160; discord with Dwenger on work of plenary council, I: 261; Dwenger visit to Washington, 1886, I: 609; German question, I: 344–345; McGlynn case, I: 568, 573; recommendations of Foley to Rome, I: 364; Roman proposal on delegate explained, I: 605; secret societies, I: 460–461; Third Plenary Council, I: 252, 260

Moore, Patrick, student at St. Charles College, I: 125

Mora, Michele de la, Bishop, Carranza attack, II: 218; persecution of Church reported, II: 210

Moran, Patrick, Cardinal, Australian socialistic trend, I: 535–536; Catholic University of America, I: 420; McKinley death, II: 110; Third Plenary Council, I: 263

Council, I: 224

O'Gorman, Thomas, Bishop; assisted with papal letter on Americanism, II: 27; audience with Leo XIII, noted, II: 23; consecrated Bishop of Sioux Falls, II: 34, 38; delegation to greet Satolli, 1892, I: 624n; McGlynn statements, judgment on, I: 590; "Memorandum," 1902, II: 118n; paper on Pope's independence, II: 342, 343; Philippine affairs, II: 115; Rome mission for friars' case, II: 112, 114; Rome visit, 1869, I: 92n; Taft mission to Rome approved, II: 118

O'Grady, Rev. John, National Catholic War Council statement, I: 540

O'Hara, William, Bishop, Gibbons' consecration, I: 70; Third Plenary Council, I: 234

O'Hern, Charles A., Monsignor, Vatican's treasure requested moved, 1919, II: 283n

O'Hern, Lewis J., C.S.P., war chaplains, II: 234, 242, 294

O'Keefe, Rev. Matthew, editor, Catholic Mirror, II: 386; Gibbons' choice for Wheeling terna, I: 135; terna for North Carolina, I: 62

Olympic (vessel), noted, II: 193

O'Mahoney, Daniel J., O.S.A., sent as teacher to Philippines, II: 120

Onahan, William J., American Catholic Congress, secretary, II: 14; Irish Catholic Colonization Association, secretary, I: 194; noted regarding paper by O'Gorman, II: 342

Onthank, Joseph, classmate of Gibbons, I: 40; death, I: 41

Oregonian, see Portland Oregonian

O'Reilly, Bernard, Monsignor, biographer of Leo XIII, I: 329

O'Reilly, Charles J., Bishop, Catholic Church Extension Society, II: 405

O'Reilly, Rev. Michael, pastor, St. Bridget's Church, Canton, I: 48

O'Reilly, Patrick T., Bishop, Sulpician centennial, II: 472

O'Reilly, Thomas, Knights of Labor, I: 520; praised Gibbons' memorial, I: 518

Order of the American Union, anti-Catholic organization, I: 444–445

Order of the Legion of Honor, decoration to Gibbons, II: 259

Order of Leopold II, grand cordon conferred on Gibbons, II: 259

Oreglia, Luigi, Cardinal, at election of Pius X, II: 354

Orlando, Vittorio, government resigned,

II: 280; Roman Question, II: 280

Orozco, Francisco, Archbishop, Carranza attack, II: 218

Orphans, see Baltimore. St. Mary's Industrial School; see Sisters of St. Francis

Osservatore Cattolico, Satolli's visit, I: 628

Osservatore Romano, article in defense of Irish by Ella Edes, I: 345n; Gibbons' pastoral letter on American College property case, I: 270; noted for article on Gibbons as cardinal, I: 303; source of Baltimore news questioned, II: 383–384; Testem benevolentiae, II: 70

O'Sullivan, Jeremiah, Bishop, Bishop of Mobile, I: 290; consecrated by Gibbons, I: 290; name submitted to Rome for episcopacy, I: 190

Otis, Elwell S., release of prisoners in Philippines, II: 94–95

Our Lady of Good Counsel Church, see Baltimore. Our Lady of Good Counsel Church

Our Lady of Perpetual Help Church, see Washington. Our Lady of Perpetual Help Church

Our Lady of Victory Church, see St. Louis. Our Lady of Victory Church

Oxenham, Henry N., The Catholic Doctrine of the Atonement, errors in, II: 475–476

"P's," secret society, 1916, I: 483

Pace, Edward A., Monsignor, accompanied Satolli to U. S., 1892, I: 624; McGlynn statements, judgment given, I: 590; opinion on education bills asked by Gibbons, II: 543–544; pastoral letter, 1920, II: 307; protonotary apostolic, II: 169; refused title of monsignor, II: 169; terna for Catholic University of America rectorship, II: 197

Pacelli, Eugenio, Cardinal, see Pius XII, Pope

Page, Thomas Nelson, cited regarding Italian-Vatican relations, II: 267; tribute by Gibbons, II: 221; U. S. protection for American College, II: 229

Palestine, holy places, Gibbons' request for aid, II: 282n

Pallen, Condé B., press leak regarding U. S. delegation, I: 637; Satolli criticism, I: 628

Pallotine Fathers, Italian immigrants, II: 464

on Savannah *terna*, II: 442; with
Gibbons on trip to Rome, 1895, I:
473
Thorne, William Henry, critical of *The
Ambassador of Christ*, II: 603; Gib-
bons' action regarding Americanism
and Leo XIII, critical of, II: 73;
secret societies, I: 469
Thornton, Amasa, appeal for Cuban
aid, II: 129
Tierney, Richard H., S.J., Church in
Mexico, II: 211
Tighe, Robert, assistance for nephew
sought from Gibbons, II: 312; Gib-
bons' schoolmate, I: 14, 14*n*
Tighe, Thomas, Gibbons' schoolmate,
I: 14, 17
Times, see London *Times; New York
Times*
Times Magazine, see New York *Times
Magazine*
Times-Picayune, see New Orleans
Times-Picayune
Timon, John, Bishop, cited regarding
Third Plenary Council, I: 61
Tittoni, Tommaso, Italian foreign min-
ister, II: 280–281
Toledo *Index*, edited by Abbot, I: 654
Toledo. St. Vincent's Orphan Asylum,
property case, II: 325–331
Toleration, religious, Gibbons' views on,
II: 531–533
Tolton, Rev. Augustus, Gibbons' kind-
ness to Negroes noted, II: 398
Toronto *Canadian Church, The Ambas-
sador of Christ*, review, II: 602
Touraine (vessel), referred to, I: 473
Tracy, Benjamin F., suggested Hend-
rick as Archbishop of Manila, II: 119
Trade unions, attitude of Chatard
toward, I: 491–492; attitude of
Feehan toward, I: 492; attitude of
Gibbons toward, I: 492; attitude of
Seghers toward, I: 491–492; begin-
ning, I: 486; discussed in Third
Plenary Council legislation, I: 487
Trades-Unionist, address to wage earners
in Maryland, I: 542
Transylvania, aid requested by Gibbons,
II: 282*n*
Trastevere. Basilica of Santa Maria,
titular church of Gibbons, I: 307;
O'Connell appointed vicar, II: 33
Trave (vessel), cited, II: 107
Traynor, W. H. J., president, A.P.A.,
noted, II: 35
Treaty of Ghent, *see* Ghent, Treaty of
Treaty of London, *see* London, Treaty
of
Treaty of Paris, *see* Paris, Treaty of
Treaty of Versailles, *see* Versailles,

Treaty of
Tribune, see Chicago *Tribune;* New
York *Tribune*
Trinity College, *see* Washington. Trin-
ity College
Truth, edited by Price, II: 409
Tumulty, Joseph P., cited regarding
League of Nations, II: 285; Wilson's
reported discourtesy to Gibbons, II:
Turinaz, Charles F., Bishop, campaign
517
against Americanism noted, II: 58
Turner, William Dandridge, M.D., in-
fluenced by Gibbons' sermon, II:
573–574
"Tusculum," I: 9
Tuttle, Daniel S., Bishop, on *The Am-
bassador of Christ*, II: 601
Tyler, Robert O., cited regarding press
censorship, I: 45

Ukrainian Catholics, *see* Greek Ukrain-
ian Catholics
Umbria (vessel), I: 314, 567
Uncles, Rev. Charles R., first Negro
priest ordained in U. S., I: 398
Underwood, Oscar W., quoted as
speaker, "Cardinal's Day," 1917, II:
505–506
Union, see Manchester *Union*
Union League, activities noted, I: 76
Union League Club, Chicago, speech by
Ireland, II: 30
Union Pacific Railroad, insurance sys-
tem for employees, I: 538
Unions, Trade, *see* Trade unions
Unitarians, attitude toward Spanish
American War, II: 90
United Brotherhood of Clan-na-gael,
Irish revolutionary society, I: 456
United States, Catholic population, 1890,
I: 331; mediator, Great Britain and
Venezuela, II: 85; Protestantism,
1885, I: 607
United States Catholic Historical So-
ciety, Gibbons' paper, 1891, II: 605;
meeting, 1891, I: 83*n*; secretary
noted regarding Gibbons and laboring
classes, I: 528
United States Civil War, end of, I: 56
United States Congress. Senate, Ca-
hensly memorials, I: 374*n*
United States Constitution, Gibbons on,
II: 557–558; fourteenth amendment,
see Civil rights; eighteenth amendment, *see* Prohibition; nineteenth
amendment, *see* Woman suffrage
United States Constitution Centennial,
I: 316–317; 319–320; 573; Gibbons
invited to participate, I: 317–322
United States Food Administration,

conservation of food for export, 1918, II: 261

United States, foreign relations with Great Britain, arbitration treaty, 1911, II: 204

United States Insurance Company, payment suspended, I: 11

United States Office of Indian Affairs, Indian case, II: 389–390

United States Supreme Court, Gibbons on, II: 558

United States War of 1898, peace negotiations opened, 1898, II: 95; treaty, 1898, II: 81; war declared, II: 57

Univers, on *The Ambassador of Christ,* II: 603; Gibbons' endorsement of Hecker, II: 56

Universal military training, see Military service, compulsory

University of Laval, *see* Quebec. Université Laval

University of North Carolina, *see* North Carolina. University of

University of Notre Dame, *see* Notre Dame. University of

University of Virginia, *see* Virginia. University of

Urban College, *see* Rome. Urban College

Ury, Adolfo Müller, portrait of Gibbons painted, II: 623*n*

Vallette, Marc F., Gibbons' efforts for labor, pleased with, I: 528

Van Buren, Martin, President, inauguration, I: 11–12

Van de Vyver, Augustine, Bishop, accompanied Gibbons to Rome, 1880, I: 197; acknowledged gift of Mass stipends from Gibbons, I: 188; consecrated by Gibbons, 1889, II: 442; death, 1911, II: 443; on Richmond *terna,* II: 441

Vannutelli, Serafino, Cardinal, aid requested by Gibbons for O'Connell, II: 44; favored Ireland's school plan, I: 677; Zahm's book, II: 65

Vannutelli, Vincenzo, Cardinal, approved O'Connell's Fribourg address, II: 54; Eucharistic Congress Mass, London, 1908, II: 321

Vatican, concern for immigrants, I: 339; erects new jurisdiction for Gibbons, I: 72; on Gibbons' participation in constitutional centennial, I: 322; on representative for U. S., I: 595–596; pro-German propaganda against, II: 278*n*; requested treasure moved for safekeeping, 1919, II: 283*n*; school controversy, I: 673; Secret Treaty of London, II: 267–268, 272;

sinking of *Arabic,* II: 231; war action criticized, II: 250–252

Vatican Council, I: 93–100; controversy on papal infallibility, noted, I: 88, 136

Vaughan, Herbert, Cardinal, American hierarchy centennial, I: 417; arbitration tribunal, appeal for, II: 84; brought missionaries to U. S., I: 144; Corrigan pastoral on private property, noted, I: 564; death, noted, II: 320; interest in school plan, I: 701; Mill Hill Fathers, superior, I: 143; opposition to *Edinburgh Review* on Catholic Church, II: 8; quoted on schools, I: 181; reunion of Christendom, II: 570; Roche book, II: 576–578; on *The Ambassador of Christ,* II: 601; tour of U. S., 1872, I: 143; visited by Gibbons, I: 314

Vaughan, Rev. Kenelm, approved Catholic part in World's Parliament of Religions, II: 20

Vedder, Henry C., Baptist *"Bigotry and Intolerance." A Reply to Cardinal Gibbons,* II: 580*n*

Vélez, Carlos Garcia, Pan American Union dedication delegate, II: 130

Venezuela, boundary dispute with Great Britain, II: 83–85; law of 1824, noted, II: 348–349

Venissat, Ferdinand, student at St. Charles with Gibbons, I: 38*n*

Ventura (vessel), II: 290

La Vérité Française, attack on Dufresne, II: 57; published Maignen's essays, II: 58

Vérot, Augustin, Bishop, against defining papal infallibility, I: 99; arrangement with school board, I: 653–654

Versailles, Treaty of, signed, 1919, II: 285

Veuillot, Louis, editor of *Univers,* II: 56

Villa, Francisco, regime denounced by Gibbons, II: 207

Villa-Zapata faction in Washington, II: 216

Villeneuve, Rev. Alphonse, paper at European Catholic Congress, I: 367

Virginia (State), Conservatives, popularity of, 1873, I: 122; devastated by armies, I: 122; increase in religion, 1872–1877, I: 161–162; number of converts confirmed by Gibbons, I: 132; population, 1870, I: 122; public school system established, I: 123; readmitted to Union, I: 122; University of, Gibbons on advisory council, II: 609

734

Errata

Volume II

Page

2, Note 1	'fantôme,' instead of 'fantome,' for the accent
33, Note 89, l. 4	'Francesco di Paolo', not 'de Paula'
42, l. 12	'impossibile', not 'impossible'
51, Note 138, l. 1	'Américanisme', not 'Américanism'
94, l. 4	'Nueva,' not 'Neuva'
121, l. 6 after the quotation	'Nueva,' not 'Neuva'
142, l. 4	'anxious' in place of 'intent'
179, l. 15	a comma after 'June,'
201, Note 177	September '24', not '20'
204, Note 1, l. 9	'manufacturers,' not ',amufactures'
263, l. 6 from bottom	'Antoine,' not 'Adolphe'
293, Note 75, l. 7	'stricken,' not 'striken'
300, l. 10	Remove 'City'
316, Note 16, l. 1	'Girolamo,' not 'Gerolamo'
324, l. 8	'created', not 'raised'
341, l. 17	Insert 'should' before 'remonstrate'
354, Note 132, l. 7	'Feier' — capital for 'F'
383, l. 9	'The' for 'That' at beginning of sentence remove the 'pp'
407, l. 21	'1913,' not '1914'
413, l. 4 after indented quotation	'forward', not 'forth'
439, last l.	'could,' not 'would'
442, l. 3	French accent for 'coñte que coñte'
444, l. 2 from bottom	Remove the comma after 'Prospere'

541, l. 16	'singled,' not 'signaled'
654, l. 7 from the bottom	'As far as', not 'Insofar'
681, l. 10 of 2nd col.	'Giacomo,' not 'Giacoma'
685, l. 7 of 2nd col.	'Díaz' for Diaz - accent over the 'i'
686, l. 19 of 1st col.	'Dubreul' not 'Dubruel'
687, l. 31 of 1st col.	'Tomás' for 'Thomás'
688, l. 15 from bottom of 1st col.	'coadjutorship,' not 'suffraganship'
696, l. 3 of 2nd col.	'Gómez' — for accent over the 'o'
699, l. 18 from bottom of 2nd col.	Insert after 'bishops' the following: 'I:'
708, l. 13, 1st col.	Insert after 'Marillac, Louise de the following: 'Marists, I: 223.'
713, l. 3 of 2nd col.	'cardinalate,' instead of 'consecration'
716, l. 11 of 2nd col.	Remove 'D.S.B.' after 'O'Connell, Jeremiah J.'
730, l. 25 of 2nd col.	Insert ''II:' in place of 'I'.